Buy the Truth
and do not sell it —
Proverbs 23:23

Charles Key

Final Report

Final Report on the Bombing of the Alfred P. Murrah Building

April 19, 1995

The Oklahoma Bombing Investigation Committee

Library of Congress Catalogue Number: 2001117318

Copyright 2001 by The Oklahoma Bombing Investigation Committee

Published by: The Oklahoma Bombing Investigation Committee

All rights reserved.

Printed in the United States of America

No part of this book may be reproduced in any manner whatsoever without written permission except in the case of brief quotations embodied in critical articles and reviews. For information, address The Oklahoma Bombing Investigation Committee, P.O. Box 75697, Oklahoma City, Oklahoma 73147.

The Oklahoma Bombing Investigation Committee
    Final Report on the Bombing of the Alfred P. Murrah Building
    April 19, 1995

p. cm.

Includes bibliographical references and index.

ISBN: 0-9710513-0-5 (pb)
ISBN: 0-9710513-1-3 (hc)

    1. Oklahoma City Federal Building Bombing, Oklahoma City, Okla.,1995. 2. Bombing investigation—Oklahoma—Oklahoma City. 3. McVeigh, Timothy—Trials, litigation, etc. 4. Nichols, Terry, 1955—Trials, litigation, etc. 5. Terrorism—Oklahoma—Oklahoma City.
        I.   Title

HV6432.045 2001   364.16'4'0976638
                                      QBI01 –200445

First Edition

DEDICATION

This Publication is dedicated to the individuals who died on April 19, 1995.

---

1. Lucio Aleman
2. Teresa Alexander
3. Richard Allen
4. Ted Allen
5. Baylee Almon
6. Diane Althouse
7. Rebecca Anderson - rescuer
8. Pamela Argo
9. Sandy Avery
10. Peter Avillanoza
11. Danielle Nicole Bell
12. Oleta Biddy
13. Shelly Turner Bland
14. Olen Bloomer
15. James Boles
16. Mark Boltc
17. Cassandra Booker
18. Carol Bowers
19. Peachlyn Bradley
20. Woody Brady
21. Cynthia Brown
22. Paul Broxterman
23. Gabreon Bruce
24. Kimberly Burgess
25. David Burkett
26. Donald Burns, Sr.
27. Karen Gist Carr
28. Michael Joe Carrillo
29. Rona Linn Chafey
30. Zachary Chavez
31. Robert Chipman
32. Kimberly Clark
33. Anthony Christopher Cooper, II
34. Antonio Ansara Cooper, Jr.
35. Dana Cooper
36. Harley Cottingham
37. Kim Cousins
38. Aaron Coverdale
39. Elijah Coverdale
40. Jaci Rae Coyne
41. Kathy Cregan
42. Richard Cummins
43. Steven Curry
44. Sgt. Benjamin Davis
45. Diana Day
46. Peter DeMaster
47. Castine Deveroux
48. Sheila Driver
49. Tylor Eaves
50. Ashley Megan Eckles
51. Susan Jane Ferrell
52. Chip Fields
53. Katherine Ann Finley
54. Judy Fisher
55. Linda Florence
56. Donald Fritzler
57. Mary Ann Fritzler
58. Tevin Garrett
59. Laura Garrison
60. Jamie Lee Genzer
61. Margaret Goodson
62. Kevin "Lee" Gottshall, II
63. Ethel Griffin
64. Capt. Randy Guzman
65. Cheryl Gradley Hammons
66. Ronald Harding
67. Thomas Hawthorne, Sr.
68. Adele Higginbottom
69. Anita Hightower
70. Gene Hodges, Jr.
71. Peggy Holland
72. Linda Colleen Housley
73. George Howard
74. Wanda Lee Howell
75. Robbin Huff
76. Dr. Charles Hurlburt
77. Jean Hurlburt
78. Paul Ice
79. Christi Jenkins
80. Norma Jean Johnson
81. Raymond Johnson
82. Larry Jones

83.	Alvin Justes	125.	Lanny Scroggins
84.	Blake Ryan Kennedy	126.	Kathy Lynn Seidl
85.	Carole Sue Khalil	127.	Leora Lee Sells
86.	Valerie Jo Koelsch	128.	Karan Shepherd
87.	Carolyn Kreymborg	129.	Chase Smith
88.	Teresa Lea Lauderdale	130.	Colton Smith
89.	Kathy Leinen	131.	Victoria Sohn, Master Sgt.
90.	Carrie Ann Lenz 6 mo. Pregnant with son, Michael James, III	132.	John Thomas Stewart
91.	Donald Leonard	133.	Dolores Stratton
92.	Lakesha Levy, Airman First Class	134.	Emilio Trapia
93.	Dominique London	135.	Victoria Texter
94.	Rheta Long	136.	Charlotte Thomas
95.	Michael Loudenslager	137.	Michael Thompson
96.	Donna Luster	138.	Virginia Thompson
97.	Robert Lee Luster	139.	Kayla Marie Titsworth
98.	Mickey Maroney	140.	Rick Tomlin
99.	Brenda Daniels Marsh	141.	LaRue Treanor
100.	J.K. Martin	142.	Luther Treanor
101.	Rev. Gilberto Marintez	143.	Larry Turner
102.	James McCarthy	144.	Jules Valdez
103.	Kenneth McCullough	145.	John Karl VanEss, III
104.	Betsy McConnell	146.	Johnny Wade
105.	Linda McKinney	147.	Bob Walker, Jr.
106.	Cartney Jean McRaven, Airman First Class	148.	David Walker
107.	Claude Medearis	149.	Wanda Watkins
108.	Claudette Meek	150.	Michael Weaver
109.	Frankie Ann Merrell	151.	Julie Marie Welch
110.	Derwin Miller	152.	Robert Westberry
111.	Leigh Mitchell	153.	Alan Whicher
112.	John Clayton Moss, III	154.	JoAnn Whittenburg
113.	Trish Nix	155.	Frances Williams
114.	Jerry Lee Parker	156.	Scott Williams
115.	Jill Randolph	157.	W. Stephen Williams
116.	Michelle Ann Reeder	158.	Clarence Wilson
117.	Terry Smith Rees	159.	Sharon Wood-Chestnut
118.	Mary Rentie	160.	Ronota Woodbridge
119.	Antonio Reyes	161.	Tresia Jo Worton
120.	Kathryn Ridley	162.	Buddy Youngblood
121.	Trudy Rigney	163.	Calvin Battle
122.	Claudie Ritter	164.	Peola Y. Battle
123.	Christy Ross	165.	Andrea Blanton
124.	Sonja Sanders	166.	Lola Bolden
		167.	Peggy Clark
		168.	Juretta Guiles

ACKNOWLEDGMENTS

An endeavor like this cannot be accomplished without the help of many people. It truly is an undertaking that one must experience to understand its many difficulties and requirements. This *Final Report* could not possibly have been completed without the tremendous help and support of certain people.

First and foremost, I want to thank my wife Janice. She never complained or protested since the beginning when I chose to go down this path. She not only supported and stood with me, but also provided many, many hours in the production of this report. My children, Kyan, Josh, Jacob and Chelsea, have been a blessing throughout this experience. I can never thank them enough for their unwavering understanding and support in this long, and oftentimes difficult, project.

I extend warm thanks to the members of the Oklahoma Bombing Investigation Committee: V. Z. Lawton, Dale Phillips and George Wallace. They provided me with guidance and sage counsel that was invaluable. This endeavor also would have been impossible without their support, guidance, encouragement and friendship. I also must thank Ken Blood for his long-standing support and his extremely important role as the Chairman of the petition drive to impanel the Oklahoma County Grand Jury. I must also thank the wives of each of these men for supporting their husbands and this important work.

Great appreciation is given to the hundreds of people who supported completion of this project with generous donations, words of encouragement and prayers. They are too numerous to list, but the benefits of their perseverance with us in this project cannot be calculated.

Sharlene Davis' role in bringing this monumental task together cannot be overstated. Her writing and editing proficiency and analytical support were incalculable. Without her contribution, this report could not have been completed.

Several members of the scientific and engineering community lent their expertise to this report in analyzing the bombing effects on the Murrah Building: Robert G. Breene Jr., Ernest B. Paxson, Dr. Frederick C. Hansen, Roger Raubach, Sam Cohen, and Robert Frias. A special thanks to all of you, and particularly to Air Force Brigadier General (retired) Benton K. Partin and Robert D. Vernon.

I am grateful, also, to investigators Jim Grace and Larry Curts who followed up and documented the many leads that came our way, and who spent many hours away from their families in pursuing those leads. Also Roger Charles, Bill Jasper, and Craig Roberts provided research, analysis and counsel that was very valuable. Susan Hart lent her considerable writing and editing skills and contributed in numerous other ways. Cate McCauley, Greg Chalk and Michael Grace provided important research assistance.

I would also like to thank all the witnesses who had the courage to tell their stories and had the determination to do their part to see that justice was served. Our hope is that your honesty will motivate others to tell the truths they know that are still hidden from the public.

To all those friends, acquaintances, and even complete strangers who have offered their encouragement over the years, thank you. Your faith and heartening words have made a tremendous difference, much more than you realize.

Many people who contributed to this report asked not to be identified because of the positions they hold in media, law-enforcement or government. They cannot be named because of concerns that, because of their positions, they may be subjected to unfair scrutiny or intimidation by the media or government. To them I say thank you for your help in sending us down the right path and for your insight on certain points.

I owe a special debt of gratitude to the late Glenn Wilburn (and to his wife Kathy) for sharing his thoughts, research and ultimate wish for resolution of this case with me. His love for Chase and Colton, his two grandsons, and for Kathy and Edye are shown by his determination to expose the truth of the Oklahoma City Bombing, how it came about and its aftermath.

Diana Day was a friend and fellow church member. When I was first elected to the Oklahoma House of Representatives in 1986, she became my first secretary. She later took a job with HUD in the Murrah Building, and died in the Oklahoma City Bombing. She was a wonderful person and a joy to be around. Her parents, Bill Sr. and Frankie, also fellow church members, have always been supportive, as have Bill Jr. and sister Dayna. Thanks you all.

Loving thanks are given to my parents Bill and Catherine for always believing in me even though they were deeply concerned for my well-being. Also, my father- and mother-in-law, Lloyd and Dorene, supported and encouraged Janice and me every step of the way. Both of our parents were always there when we needed them. Also, my brothers Paul and Tim, their wives and many other family members were always supportive.

Finally, I thank God for always giving me and us the strength to keep going and always providing what we needed. Many times we were faced with an obstacle that we thought we couldn't overcome. Many times we were close to giving up. Many times we thought that few people cared anymore. Each time He provided a way to carry on.

Charles Key

TABLE OF CONTENTS

DEDICATION v

ACKNOWLEDGEMENTS vii

PREFACE xvii

BOARD OF DIRECTORS xix

I. OVERVIEW 1

II. PRELIMINARY HEARING

A.	Overview	3
B.	Black's Law Dictionary	3
C.	Introduction	4
D.	Testimony of FBI Agent Jon Hersley	4
E.	Testimony of Charles J. Hanger	8
F.	Final Arguments and Conclusions	10

III. THE FEDERAL TRIALS OF TIMOTHY MCVEIGH AND TERRY NICHOLS

A.	Overview	13
B.	Background	15
C.	Motive	16
D.	Forensic Evidence	23
E.	The Mercury Marquis	47
F.	McVeigh's Clothes	55
G.	The Bomb Components	65
H.	Roger Moore Robbery	86
I.	Rock Quarry Robbery	95
J.	Barrels	102
K.	The Ryder Truck	104
L.	Final Summations	137
M.	The Verdicts and Sentences	141

IV. THE EYEWITNESSES

A.	Overview	147
B.	Prior to April 1995	147
C.	Prior to Friday, 14 April 1995	149
D.	Friday, 14 April 1995	152
E.	Saturday, 15 April 1995	154
F.	Sunday, 16 April 1995 (Easter Sunday)	156
G.	Monday, 17 April 1995	158
H.	Tuesday, 18 April 1995	161
I.	Wednesday, 19 April 1995 (Before the Bombing)	163
J.	Wednesday, 19 April 1995 (Following the Bombing)	168
K.	Conclusions	170

V. DAMAGE TO THE ALFRED P. MURRAH FEDERAL BUILDING

A.	Overview	171
B.	Witnesses to the Explosion	171
C.	The Official Story	175
D.	Reports of Other Bombs	175
E.	Seismographic Evidence	179
F.	Independent Government-Sanctioned Reports And Expert Opinions	182
G.	Evaluation of Published Explanations Concerning the Structural Collapse of the Alfred P. Murrah Federal Building	194
	Photos	257

VI. PRIOR KNOWLEDGE

A.	Overview	263
B.	Prior Warnings Provided to Government	264
C.	General Warnings by Government Before Bombing	266
D.	Oklahoma City Police Department Receives Tip	268
E.	Conversations Show Prior Knowledge	268
F.	Bomb Squad Sightings Indicate Prior Knowledge	276
G.	S.W.A.T Sighting Suggests Prior Knowledge	278
H.	Trigen	279
I.	Conclusions	279

VII. THE SEARCH FOR JOHN DOES AND OTHERS UNKNOWN

A.	Overview	281
B.	The Middle-Eastern Connection	281

C.	The White-Supremacist Connection	284
D.	Original APB on 19 April 1995	289
E.	The Search for Middle-Eastern Conspirators	290
F.	The Search for White Supremist Conspirators	295
G.	Conclusions	311

VIII. THE OKLAHOMA COUNTY GRAND JURY

A.	Background	313
B.	Oklahoma Bombing Investigation Committee Formed	314
C.	Efforts to Intimidate OKBIC	315
D.	Law Applicable to Conduct of Grand Jurors	316
E.	The Grand Jury Proceeding	316
F.	One Indictment Issued by Grand Jury	317
G.	Grand Jury Final Reportr Issued 30 December 1998	318
H.	Aftermath	323
I.	Improprieties by Judge William Burkett	325
J.	Conclusions	326

IX. GOVERNMENT IMPROPRIETIES

A.	FBI Puts Victims' Rescue on Hold While They Rescue Documents	327
B.	FBI Quashes Reports of Other Explosive Devices Found in Building	327
C.	ATF Unlawfully Stores Munitions in a Federal Office Building	328
D.	FBI fails to Record or Videotape Interrogations and Interviews	330
E.	FBI Refuses to Release Surveillance Tapes and Satellite Photos of Oklahoma and Kansas Confiscated after Bombing	331
F.	FBI Holds Nichols' Family in Custody Without Legal Representation and Without a Warrant	331
G.	Courts Do Not Hold Those Who Perjured Themselves Accountable for their Testimony	332
H.	FBI Fails to Follow-up on Leads to John Does	334
I.	OKC Command Post Orders Leads on John Doe #2 Held in Abeyance	335
J.	FBI Fails to Investigate 1034 Fingerprints	335
K.	Government Fails to Pursue Leads on Elhoim City Residents	336
L.	FBI Lies to Court	337
M.	FBI Denies Nichols Legal Representation During Interrogation	337
N.	Judge Dismisses Grand Juror for "Trying to Do his Job"	338
O.	Government Ignores Warnings from Government Informants	339
P.	Government Intimidates Informants and Witnesses	339
Q.	ATF Tells Agents To Not Come In	342
R.	FBI Falsifies Results and Slants Testimony to Favor the Prosecution	342
S.	FBI Decides Type of Bomb Without Proper Scientific Evidence	345

T.	FBI Fails to Take Residue Samples from Bomb Scene for Comparison as Evidence	348
U.	Government Fails to Secure Building After Warnings	348
V.	FBI Cancels APB on Middle-Eastern suspects	349
W.	Government Ignores Witnesses to Suspects in Building Before Blast	349
X.	U.S. Army Takes Action Against Members Assisting with Rescue	350
Y.	Judge Matsch Chooses to Ignore Remark Showing Juror was Biased	350
Z.	FBI 302 Reports Reflect Erroneous Witness Statements	351
AA.	Government Ignores Contradictory Sightings of Ryder Trucks and Other Vehicles	351
BB.	FBI Keeps FEMA Investigators 200 Feet From Building	352
CC.	Government Destroys Crime Scene Before Proper Investigation of Blast Damage	352
DD.	Government Determines Revenge for Waco Was Motive within Minutes of the Blast	353
EE.	Prosecutors Deliberately Try to Mislead Jurors	353
FF.	Oklahoma County District Attorneys Office Belittles Grand Jury	354
GG.	Court Places Trial Documents Under Seal	354
HH.	FBI Refuses to Accept Evidence from Television Reporter	355
II.	FBI Fails to Properly Secure Evidence (Q507)	355
JJ.	Government Ignores Scientific Analyses of Blast Damage	355
KK.	Prosecution Withholds Discovery Evidence from Defense	355
LL.	Prosecutors Defy Judge's Order Regarding Interrogation of Defense Witnesses	356
MM.	Government Fails to Continue JD #2 Investigation	356
NN.	FBI Fails To Follow-up Leads To Female Accomplices	356
OO.	Government Ignores Another Lead	357
PP.	Federal Judge Makes Ruling Without Reading Evidence	358

X. RECOMMENDATIONS 359

XI. EPILOGUE 363

APPENDIX

Map of Downtown Oklahoma City	371
ATF Agent in Front of Building, 9:30 a.m.	372
OHP Radio Logs	373
Eglin AFB: Explosive Test Structure	374
Firehouse Magazine Cover; Inside Article Verifies Multiple Explosives Found	376
Gen. Benton Partin's Report	378
Traffic ticket Issued to McVeigh Near Elohim City	397
Murrah Columns Identified by Partin	398
FEMA Report on Bombing, 30 August 1996	399
McVeigh Phone Call to Elohim City	405

ATF News: Free-Falling Elevator	406
DoD Atlantic Command	408
FEMA Situation Report	409
Cary Gagan Letter of Immunity	410
Jacksonville Times Union: Papers vs. Survivors	411
Stan Hammon Affidavit	412
Kochendorfer Affidavit	413
Kochendorfer Complaint	414
INS Document Canceling APB on Strassmeir, 7 Feb 96	415
Jane Graham Statement	416
Nazi-Middle East Connection; Two Articles	419
Portland Oregonian article on Judge Wayne Alley's Prior Warning	420
Ray Brown fax to Key, Handwritten	422
Ray Brown Fax to Key, 27 June 1995	432
Tiffany Bible Affidavit	435
Trigen Log Showing Police Response to "Bomb Threat"	436
USA Today, article re: Harvey Weathers	437
UNSUB (John Doe #2) Sketch	439
US Forces Command Daily Log	440
ATF Field Documents	441
Carol Howe Trial Documents	443
"A Closer Look," *Media Bypass* on KFOR Video	449
ATF Agent – McVeigh Look-a-Like	450
Mike Johnstone Trip Report	451
Houston Chronicle	463
Wayne Alley: Preliminary Hearing	465
Grand Jury Petition Statement	467
Grand Jury Petition Statement. Signature Form	468
Grand Jury Petition Supreme Court Ruling	469
Grand Jury Petition Appeals Court Win	470
Henry Gibbons'	472
(VFW) Iraqi Soldier Resettlement	475
Washington Times article on Iraqi resettlement	476
Lawsuit: Hussain vs. KFOR-TV and Jayna Davis	478
JD Reed, *Working Interest* Article	485
Writ of Mandamus	486
Hussain DUI citation	495
FOI: Explosive Device Sketch	496
FOI: Two Suspects, Reward	497
FOI: French Interpol	498
FOI: U.S. Interpol Update on JD #2, 5-5-95	499
FOI: FBI Memo of Vehicle & 2 JD Suspects	500
Rick Sinnett OK Grand Jury Complaint	501
Chevie Kehoe AP Story	502
Linguistic Support	504

Twilley/Khalil Police Report	506
Robert G. Breene Correspondence	510
Al Norberg	514
C. Frederick Hansen Letter	515
Roger Raubach Letter	520
Strassmeir Driver's License	522
John Doe #2 Justice Dept. Release	523
Joe Harp Statement	524
Partin to Pat Morgan Letter	525
Ernest B. Paxson Letter	530
Virgil Steele Affidavit	532
Arlene Blanchard Statement	534
Transcript of Conversation Regarding Sting Operation	535
Sam Cohen Statement	541
Melvin Beall	543
Bob Blackburn	548

INDEX 549

Preface

In the years following the bombing of the Alfred P. Murrah Building in downtown Oklahoma City on April 19, 1995, the Oklahoma Bombing Investigation Committee has compiled volumes of evidence, eyewitness interviews, court transcripts, and reports of scientific experts to result in the Final Report of this Committee. Additionally, we have utilized evidence presented to us by private detectives hired by the Committee.

I was serving in the Oklahoma Legislature as a State Representative at the time of the bombing. Almost immediately, survivors and relatives of victims of the bombing began contacting me to express concerns they had about the manner in which the Federal Government was conducting the investigation. Within two months of the bombing, several explosives experts had come forward to present evidence that the destruction to the building could not possibly have been caused by one ammonium nitrate-fuel oil (ANFO) bomb.

On the very day of the bombing, survivors were interviewed by the media who stated that they had felt the building shaking, similar to experiencing an earthquake, just prior to the explosion. Some of them even stated that the shaking sensation allowed them enough time to seek shelter underneath their desks, which they credit with saving their lives. This certainly supports the evidence that more than one bomb caused the destruction to the Murrah Building.

Within hours of the bombing, sightings of suspicious characters seen in downtown Oklahoma City early that morning were reported, and all point bulletins (APBs) were immediately circulated by law enforcement. Curiously, the APBs were withdrawn once Timothy McVeigh was apprehended slightly over an hour after the bombing.

All of these facts came to my attention within days of the bombing. So many broken-hearted families affected directly by the bombing had unanswered questions and implored me, in my capacity as an elected official, to pursue further investigation into the case. This resulted in the formation of the Oklahoma Bombing Investigation Committee by private citizens, which was funded solely through the private sector.

We have sufficient proof to support our original contention that the Federal Government indeed had prior knowledge of the bombing. Our findings bear out the fact that Timothy McVeigh did not act alone; at the very least, he had the physical assistance of Terry Nichols. Evidence we have amassed establishes that multiple John Does were involved.

This Report analyzes court proceedings, beginning with McVeigh's preliminary hearing in El Reno, Oklahoma, going through the Oklahoma County Grand Jury, and concluding with the federal trials of McVeigh and Nichols. We show where crucial eyewitnesses were not called to testify in the federal trials if their testimony showed McVeigh in the company of others. Dozens of eyewitnesses were led to believe that they would be called

to testify in the federal trials, but when they were not, they were dismayed and insulted to learn that not only was their testimony going to be ignored, but federal prosecutors were labeling them as "not credible."

We have presented information as we have discovered it and there are questions that may never be answered. Our one common goal has been, from the beginning, to arrive at the truth. Our journey has taken us down many paths. We have endeavored to present all possible evidence, rather then culling out what may support only one theory.

Our Committee is realistic enough to know that all legal avenues have been exhausted. By the time this Report is published, Timothy McVeigh will have been executed. For some, that will provide the closure they need. However, the scope of the "worst terrorist attack in American history" demands answers to questions that remain. It is our hope that our Final Report will generate a public outcry for justice, and the only way this could be realized would be if Congressional hearings into the actions of certain federal agencies were held.

Over the past six years since the bombing, much of the evidence we have accumulated has been ignored or derided by the mainstream media. We are not the enemy. We are not anti-government. It is because we love our country that we demand and have the right to expect the best possible government.

It is our belief that the bombing in Oklahoma City will not be the last terrorist attack on U.S. soil. Since all of the perpetrators have not been caught, they are still free to continue their work. This will happen again.

We serve no political agenda. We did not do this for personal gain or glory. We did this in order to preserve our country and to make our world safer for future generations.

THE OKLAHOMA BOMBING INVESTIGATION COMMITTEE

V.Z. LAWTON

V. Z. Lawton is native to Oklahoma. He was Born in Newkirk, Oklahoma in 1931. In 1934, he moved to Oklahoma City and has lived there since. V.Z. attended Classen High School, then received a bachelor's degree in business administration from the University of Oklahoma. V. Z. has been a real estate broker, a homebuilder and a stockbroker. Beginning in 1987, he worked with HUD, first as a building inspector, then in the Native American authority. V. Z. was at his desk in the Murrah Building when the bomb exploded in 1995. He retired in 1997. V. Z. has been active in sports since 1967, having served as State Chairman for the Oklahoma Racketball Association (RBA) 1973-76, Regional Commissioner for the International RBA1975-6, and as National Commissioner and member of the Board of Directors for the International RBA 1976-79. He plays handball and has been an active golfer since 1966, currently playing at the Lincoln Park Golf Course.

DALE L. PHILLIPS

Dale Phillips is a native Oklahoman, born in Enid, Oklahoma in 1942. He graduated from Midwest City High School and attended Cental State College in Edmond, Oklahoma. His military service includes both active duty and reserves. Dale has organized and managed more than one hundred little league teams, and served as president of the Del City Junior Sports Association in 1973. He held various offices with the Del City, Ok Jaycees in the 1960's, and worked with pro-family organizations in the 60's and 70's. Dale has worked in the insurance industry since 1963, and, in 1979, formed Enterprise Investments, Inc. and Enterprise National Life Insurance Company. In 1985, he purchased Old Surety Life Insurance Company and merged the insurance businesses. He serves as president of these companies. Dale is a singer and songwriter who has recorded and performed, mostly for the benefit of civic organizations, since 1987.

GEORGE B. WALLACE

George Wallace, United States Air Force career officer and fighter pilot, flew assignments in the United States, North Africa, Europe and Southeast Asia. He served a tour in the VietNam conflict flying F-105's. George came to Oklahoma in 1972 as the Air Force advisor to the Air Force Reserve F-105 Fighter Group. He retired in 1978 at the rank of Lieutenant Colonel. In 1982, George founded Sunbelt Recycling and still owns the company. George attended the University of Wisconsin and is a graduate of Oklahoma City University. He has been active in Boy Scouts of America, and served two terms on the School Board of Bishop McGuinnes High School.

CHARLES KEY

Charles Key was on Oklahoma state representative for twelve years (1986-1998) during which time he served on the Banking and Finance, Criminal Justice, Revenue and Taxation, and Education committees. He served as Republican Whip during part of his tenure. Charles was born in Lubbock, Texas in 1954, then moved to Oklahoma City in 1959 and has lived there since. He is married and is an active member of the Church of Christ. He attended Oklahoma City Community College and Oklahoma City University, and has been an independent insurance and securities representative and an active member of the Lion's Club and The American Businessman's Club (AMBUC). For recreation, Charles and his three children participate in Tae-Kwon-Do classes.

Chapter I.

OVERVIEW

On 19 April, 1995, at 9:04 a. m., the blast from an explosion or explosions ripped through the Alfred P Murrah Federal Building in downtown Oklahoma City, Oklahoma. The blast destroyed the federal building and caused severe damage to several other buildings in the downtown area. As a result, 169 persons, including 19 children, were killed, and hundreds of others were maimed or injured. Federal authorities called it the single largest terrorist attack in United States history.

The Murrah Federal Building housed several federal offices, including those of the Social Security Administration (SSA), Alcohol, Tobacco, and Firearms (ATF), Housing and Urban Development (HUD), a U.S. Army recruiting office, and the chambers of several federal judges, as well as a federal credit union and a daycare center. The structure was a nine-story building made of steel and reinforced concrete, and it was reduced to rubble in a matter of seconds.

At about 10:30 that morning, approximately 60 miles east of Oklahoma City in Perry, Oklahoma, a highway patrolman took note of a rickety 1977 yellow Mercury without a license plate speeding down the highway. He pulled the vehicle over and cited the driver for driving without a license plate. Then the patrolman noticed a bulge under the driver's jacket. When asked, the driver advised the officer that it was a gun. He was promptly arrested for carrying a concealed weapon and was taken to the Noble County Courthouse to await arraignment. He was booked under the name of Timothy James McVeigh.

As rescue workers began the horrendous task of helping the injured and locating the bodies of the dead, law enforcement officers began searching for evidence and witnesses for any clues to help identify the perpetrators of this crime. Within a matter of hours, the FBI had located a piece of axle and a license plate thought to have been part of the truck used in the bombing. Through a check of the vehicle identification number (VIN), they were able to trace the vehicle, a 20-foot 1993 Ford truck, to a Ryder truck rental agency located at Elliott's Body Shop in Junction City, Kansas. Employees of the body shop told investigators that, on 17 April, they had rented the truck to a Bob Kling from Decker, Michigan, who was accompanied by a second individual. They provided descriptions of both men to an FBI sketch artist. These sketches, known as John Doe #1 and John Doe #2, were immediately released to the news media for publication and television airing.

As federal agents continued their investigation, they visited the Decker, Michigan address that Bob Kling had provided to the Ryder rental agency. This was the home of James Douglas Nichols and his brother Terry Lynn Nichols, although Terry was currently residing in Herrington, Kansas. A check with the Michigan Department of Motor Vehicles also revealed that a Timothy McVeigh had a driver's license listed at the same address.

Through interviews with family and neighbors, it was learned that McVeigh and the Nichols brothers had been experimenting with small explosives and that McVeigh had a large stash of possible bomb-making materials. With this information, federal agents obtained a search warrant and found fuel oil, 28 bags of fertilizer, blasting caps and safety fuses. They arrested James Nichols and issued a warrant for the arrest of his brother. Terry Nichols presented himself at the Herrington, Kansas, police station on April 22nd and submitted to arrest.

Meanwhile, on 21 April, the FBI received a phone call identifying John Doe #1 as being Timothy McViegh. The tip came from a former co-worker of McVeigh who had seen the sketch on TV. He also said that McViegh held very militant, anti-Government views and was extremely angry over the deaths of the Branch Dividians in Waco, Texas two years previously on 19 April. The FBI ran a check on McVeigh through the National Crime Information Center and found that he was already in custody in the Logan County, Oklahoma jail. They took him into federal custody and transported him to the El Reno Federal Penitentiary in El Reno, Oklahoma , about 30 miles west of downtown Oklahoma City. A preliminary hearing to determine probable cause was held at the penitentiary. The indictment charged Timothy McVeigh and "Others Unknown" with the bombing of the Murrah Building.

Then, abruptly, the FBI announced that they were no longer looking for John Doe #2, that they no longer believed there was a John Doe #2. They issued statements calling into doubt the accounts of numerous eye witnesses; they ignored scientific and engineering experts' information; they threatened witnesses who wouldn't be quieted with obstruction-of-justice charges; they discontinued the quest to determine if the "Others Unknown" were involved in a conspiracy and, if so, how; they developed a new theory and chose to ignore everything that didn't fit their new theory; they destroyed or ignored physical evidence. They chose not to call a single bombing victim as a witness in the trials of McVeigh and Nichols in Denver Colorado.

The victims who survived the Oklahoma City bombing and the families of those who died still have questions. They want the truth about all who were really involved and for all the guilty to be punished. They are not satisfied to settle for the easy answer as provided by the Government. The truth is the only thing that will allow them to completely heal. Many do not feel that they have yet heard the whole truth or that everyone involved has been brought to justice. Their reasoning on this is justified, given all the evidence on a Middle-Eastern connection and numerous independent sightings of Timothy McVeigh with a dark, Arabic-looking individual in the days before and the day of the bombing.

There is also the nagging question of whether the ATF and FBI had prior warning of the bombing—in light of the fact that the ATF agents did not report to work that morning. Numerous witnesses overheard or were directly told that the ATF had been pre-warned.

So what is the truth? What evidence is there that a larger conspiracy existed and that those guilty have gone unpunished? This report will present that evidence. After reading it, you decide.

Chapter II.

THE PRELIMINARY HEARING

The information included in this chapter is taken directly from the Preliminary Hearing Transcript. Because of overlapping questions and answers and interjections by counsel and the court, some of the testimony will appear to be confusing and contradictory.

A. OVERVIEW

This chapter discusses witnesses who stated they had seen Timothy McVeigh (or John Doe #1) with one or more other individuals prior to, or after, the Murrah Federal Building bombing. The majority of these witnesses were interviewed by the FBI. Because many of them were brought to Denver, Colorado to testify for the Government in the trials of Timothy McVeigh and Terry Nichols, they had a reasonable expectation of testifying. However, this was not the case. Many of their stories have not been widely heard before.

The Federal Government filed an affidavit to show probable cause naming not only Timothy McVeigh and Terry Nichols, but also "Others Unknown." In a preliminary hearing eight days after the bombing, the Government presented its case against McVeigh to show probable cause.

B. *BLACK'S LAW DICTIONARY*, 4TH Edition, Revised

The following definitions from *Black's Law Dictionary* are significant because there have been prosecutors and other public officials who have attempted to discredit or dismiss some of the witnesses in this case. Yet, federal prosecutors used the testimony of many of them in order to bring charges against McVeigh.

> *Credible Person: One who is trustworthy and entitled to be believed.*
>
> *Credible Witness: One who is competent to give evidence; also, one who is worthy of belief.*
>
> *Probable Cause: [a] "A reasonable ground for belief in the existence of facts warranting the proceedings complained" [Owens vs. Braetzel]; [b] "An apparent state of facts found to exist upon reasonable inquiry [that is, such inquiry as the given case renders convenient and proper] which would imbue a reasonably intelligent and prudent man to believe, in a criminal case, that the accused person had committed the crime charged, or, in a civil case that a cause of action existed." [Brand vs. Hinchman]*

C. INTRODUCTION

Timothy McVeigh's Preliminary Hearing to hear evidence of probable cause was held on 27 April 1995, just eight days after the bombing of the Murrah Federal Building. McVeigh was being temporarily housed in the El Reno Federal Correctional Institute where the hearing was held. (Nichols' Preliminary Hearing was held 18 May 1995, also in El Reno, before U.S. Magistrate Ronald L. Howland.) (For an Affidavit showing probable cause, see pgs. 472-474.)

The Court's appointment of counsel is made under statutory provisions that provide for two attorneys to be appointed for anyone charged with a potential death-penalty offense. Two days after the bombing, on 21 April, John Coyle and Susan Otto were appointed as McVeigh's public defenders. Private defense counsel were Paul Looney and J. Brent Liedtke; Kevin McNally was attorney for the Death Penalty Resource Counsel Center, which is under the auspices of the United States courts. Representing the Federal Government were Merrick Garland, Associate Deputy Attorney General, and Arlene Joplin.

On 24 April, the Monday following their appointment, Coyle and Otto filed a motion to withdraw as McVeigh's counsel. Otto presented their arguments very movingly to presiding Judge Howland as she told of the many friends and acquaintances she had lost in the bombing. Although sympathetic, Howland overruled the motion and the proceedings commenced.

Howland set forth the purpose of the preliminary hearing when he said, "We are not going to determine whether the Defendant is guilty or innocent; simply probable cause and reasonable basis."

D. TESTIMONY OF FBI AGENT JON HERSLEY

The accounts of eyewitnesses to events prior to and after the bombing were recited by Agent Jon Hersley, a 20-year veteran with the FBI. He did not identify the witnesses by name, but rather by number. The actual witnesses did not appear, with the exception of an Oklahoma Highway Patrol trooper. When defense attorney Coyle asked Hersley about his involvement in the case,

FBI Agent Jon Hersley

Hersley responded that he had not reviewed any documents or papers in connection with the case to prepare for his testimony in this hearing. However, he admitted discussing documents, exhibits and information with U.S. attorneys, but denied discussing the case with them.

Hersley confirmed that the testimony he was giving was primarily furnished to him by Rick Hahn (FBI explosives expert). He testified that he also received information from Bill Jockney (FBI explosives expert), Jim Norman (bombing explosives expert), an employee in the Medical Examiner's Office, other agents and a "bomb tech."

In describing his job duties in connection with this case, he testified that his role was to "...identify some of the other subjects that were involved in the bombing." He further explained that he had made telephone calls and kept copies of evidence, but not the originals. Additionally, he coordinated the efforts of other FBI offices in an effort to identify additional suspects and to prevent any further death or injury.

Hersley's testimony revealed that some of the witnesses were shown a composite drawing of a suspect. The drawing was compiled from information provided by employees of Elliott's Body Shop in Junction City, Kansas. Other witnesses were shown a still photo spread, while others participated in a live lineup held at the Oklahoma County Jail in downtown Oklahoma City.

Though names of witnesses were not used in the preliminary hearing, based on Hersley's testimony, we have been able to determine the identity of several of them, and those names appear in parentheses. Some of these witnesses may be duplicated in another chapter in this report.

1. Witnesses at Elliott's Body Shop

Hersley provided the following information: The Ryder truck used in the Oklahoma City bombing was traced to the Ryder rental facility at Elliott's Body Shop in Junction City, Kansas. The truck was rented on 17 April 1995 to an individual using the name "Kling." The FBI interviewed three employees at Elliott's, one female and two were males.

    a. One of the two male employees (Tom Kessinger) was sitting in the area where the rental took place and observed the rental, but did not participate in it. He did not have any conversation with the two people renting the truck, but overheard their discussion with the female rental agent during the transaction. He heard one of the customers give his name as "Bob Kling." (This employee provided descriptions for the composite drawings of John Doe #1 and #2.)

    b. The female employee (Vicki Beemer) completed the paperwork for the rental. When shown the composite drawing of John Doe #1, Hersley testified that she said it resembled the person who had rented the truck. She was not shown a photo spread and did not participate in the live lineup.

    c. The second male was Eldon Elliott, owner of Elliott's Body Shop. Agent Hersley testified that Elliott was present as the rental was taking place. The individual renting the truck asked Elliott if he could use the telephone, which Elliott allowed him to do. Elliott was not shown a photo spread and did not participate in the live lineup.

OKBIC Note: Although Hersley testified in the Preliminary Hearing that the Elliott employees participated in creating the composite, his conclusions were later refuted by the Elliott employees in the federal trials. In fact, at Fort Riley, Tom Kessinger assisted the sketch artist in creating the composite. When the composite was subsequently presented to Beemer, she stated that she could not add or take away from the drawing and could not identify the likeness as being the person to whom she had rented the truck. She testified for the defense in both federal trials. Eldon Elliott testified for the prosecution in both trials, stating that Timothy McVeigh was the person who had rented the truck.

2. Witnesses at the Dreamland Motel

The FBI canvassed hotels and motels in Junction City, Kansas and discovered that an individual resembling the composite of John Doe #1 had stayed at the Dreamland Motel from 14 to 18 April 1995. Employees there verified that he had occupied Room #25.

    a. Dreamland Witness #1: The owner-manager (Lea McGown) was shown a photo spread and identified McVeigh as the guest occupying Room #25 on 14-18 April. She was at the front desk and rented the room to him on 14 April. On 17 April, she witnessed McVeigh arrive at the motel in the Ryder truck. At 4:00 a.m. on 18 April, she looked out her window and saw McVeigh sitting in the cab of the truck with the cab light on. He appeared to be reading what could possibly have been a map. When she looked out her window an hour later, the truck was gone.

    b. Dreamland Witness #2: This witness (Hilda Sostre) was employed at the motel as a maid. She was shown only the composite drawing and confirmed that it bore a strong resemblance to the occupant in Room #25. Agent Hersley said she further stated that, on one occasion, she went to Room #25 to clean it. Assuming that McVeigh had left, she started to open the door when he opened it instead.

    c. Dreamland Witness #3: Hersley testified that he did not know the sex or identity of Witness #3. It was later determined that Eric McGown, the manager's son, was this witness. He was shown the composite drawing and agreed that it resembled the occupant of Room #25.

3. Witnesses in Oklahoma City Who Saw John Doe #1

Hersley testified that three witnesses in Oklahoma City had identified the composite sketch of John Doe #1. They had seen him in the vicinity of Murrah Building between 8:40 a.m. and 8:55 a.m. on the morning of 19 April 1995. They did not, however, participate in the live lineup, nor were they shown a photo spread because they had seen Timothy McVeigh on television and had called FBI Agent Hibbard in response to these broadcasts. They could not confirm that the person they had seen was Timothy McVeigh.

OKBIC Note: Hersley later contradicted this testimony when he testified about the witnesses individually, as follows:

    a. Witness #1: Female. She identified the composite as strongly resembling McVeigh and reported having seen him at the Murrah Building one week prior to the bombing, and possibly again on 17 or 18 April. Additionally, she positively identified McVeigh in the live lineup as the person she had seen prior to the bombing.

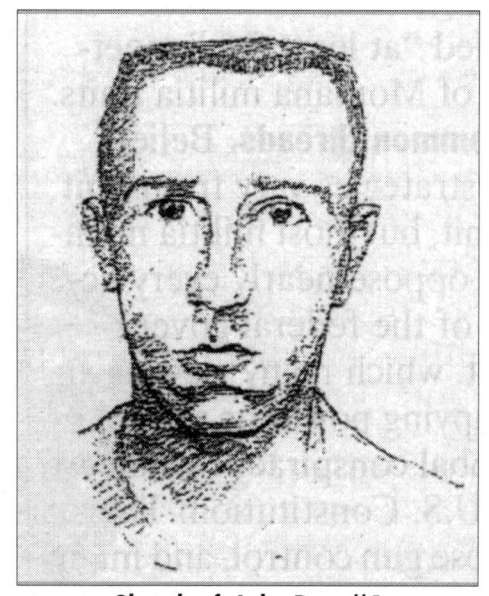

Sketch of John Doe #1

b. Witness #2 (Gary Lewis): Male. This witness observed McVeigh and a John Doe in a Mercury Marquis between 8:30 and 8:45 a.m. on the morning of the bombing. This observation was made from the Journal Record Building, directly across the street from the north side of the Murrah Building. The witness saw the Mercury in a parking lot south of the Journal Record Building, and across the street north of the Murrah Building. He identified McVeigh from the composite, rather than from a photo lineup.

c. Witness #3: Female. Hersley described her as a meter maid; therefore, she was an employee of the Oklahoma City Police Department. She was in the vicinity of Robinson Avenue and Park Avenue when she saw a Ryder truck going south on Robinson at approximately 8:40 a.m. on 19 April. The truck approached her at a very show rate of speed; she thought the driver was going to stop to ask questions. As the car neared, it turned west on Park Avenue, which placed the witness behind the truck. She did not obtain the license tag of the truck. Hersley could not state whether or not the witness confirmed another person in the truck other than the driver.

4. Live Lineup Witnesses

Under questioning by Coyle, Hersley testified that the following witnesses participated in a live lineup:

a. Witness #1 (This witness is also named as Witness #1 above): She positively identified McVeigh in the lineup as being the individual she saw at the Murrah Building a week before the bombing and possibly again on the 17th or 18th of April.

b. Witness #2: Selected two possible suspects in the lineup, including McVeigh.

c. Witness #3: This witness could not identify McVeigh in the lineup, but later told an agent that he had, indeed, recognized him, but had not wanted to identify him because McVeigh had looked directly at him. Witness had seen McVeigh at the Murrah Building.

d. Witness #4: This witness was unable to identify McVeigh in the lineup, but stated that she had seen an individual resembling McVeigh at the Murrah Building. Hersley testified that he did not know the date or time when this witness made her observation.

Timothy McVeigh

5. Oklahoma City Witnesses to the Ryder Truck

a. Videotape: Agent Hersley testified that a videotape was retrieved from the Regency Tower apartment building on Northwest Fifth Street between Hudson and Harvey Avenue. A Ryder truck was seen heading east toward the Murrah Building, a block away. Hersley further stated that the videotape does not show McVeigh in or about the Murrah Building.

b. **Witness at bombsite:** Hersley stated that there had been a witness who saw the Ryder truck directly in front of the Murrah Building where it exploded. The witness was not shown a photo spread, nor did he participate in the live lineup. However, he was shown a composite drawing; but it cannot be determined from Hersley's testimony if the composite depicted John Doe #1 or John Doe #2.

6. Witness to Occupant of Room #25

Hersley testified that, on 15 April 1995, a Chinese restaurant in Junction City received a telephone order for a delivery. The caller gave the telephone number of the Dreamland Motel, his room as #25, and his name as "Kling." The deliveryman (John Jeffrey Davis) was subsequently shown a photo spread but could not identify McVeigh as the customer to whom he had made the delivery.

OKBIC Note: According to Davis, the FBI tried to coerce him into changing his testimony, but he never did. In *Portraits of Guilt*, Jeanne Boylan reported that Davis told her that when he made the delivery, another man answered the door and he saw McVeigh sitting on the bed. Davis vehemently denied this in the federal trials. (Source: *Portraits of Guilt,* Jeanne Boylan, Pocket Books, 2000, pg. 261)

Sketch of John Doe #2

7. Apprehension and Arrest of Timothy McVeigh

Hersley testified that, when McVeigh was detained by the Oklahoma highway patrolman near Perry, Oklahoma, he was driving a yellow Mercury and was armed with a Glock 45 weapon. The first bullet in the chamber was one commonly known among law enforcement officers as a "cop killer." McVeigh gave only his name, address and date of birth to the officer.

According to Hersley's information, residue of penta erythrite tetral nitrate (PETN) was found on McVeigh's shirt. PETN is an explosive commonly used in detonating cord. Hersley did not know if there is any other use for the explosive.

E. TESTIMONY OF CHARLES J. HANGER

Charles J. Hanger is a state trooper with the Oklahoma Highway Patrol, having worked there since September 1976. He received a *subpoena duces tecum* to bring certain items with him to this Preliminary Hearing, including the probable cause affidavit, confiscated property report, jail booking information and the videotape from the video camera that was mounted on his car. The videotape does not show the arrest of Timothy McVeigh; he brought the tape because it was listed on the sheet of evidence. The tape does, however, show the events preceding the arrest: it captures the Mercury and shows Hanger walking around it.

Hanger testified that he first came in contact with McVeigh shortly before 10:30 a.m. on 19 April 1995. He was northbound in the left lane, slightly over a mile south of State Highway 15 at the Billings exit on Interstate-35. He spotted McVeigh in the right lane driving a 1977 Mercury Marquis that had a primer spot on the left rear quarter panel. He stopped McVeigh, and, as he approached the car, noticed that McVeigh was sitting in it with the car door open. He informed McVeigh that he had stopped him because his car was not tagged. McVeigh explained that he had recently purchased the car, which was the reason he did not have a tag. Hanger asked him to produce a bill of sale for the vehicle, and McVeigh replied that the person from whom he had bought the car had not yet filled out the bill of sale form.

Oklahoma Highway Patrolman Charlie Hanger

Hanger then asked McVeigh to produce his driver's license, and noted that it was in the name of "Timothy James McVeigh." At that time, Hanger noticed a bulge in McVeigh's jacket on the left side and up under the left edge of his arm. After looking at the driver's license, Hanger asked McVeigh to slowly move his jacket back so he could look underneath it. He then retrieved the gun and ordered McVeigh to hold up his hands as they walked to the rear of McVeigh's car. At that point, Hanger drew his gun. The trooper asked him why he was carrying a gun, and McVeigh stated that he had the right to carry it for his own protection. Hanger cautioned McVeigh about carrying the gun because it could result in a police officer mistakenly shooting him. McVeigh agreed that such a scenario was possible. Hanger noted that McVeigh had numerous opportunities to draw his gun, but had not done so.

McVeigh volunteered that he also had a knife in his possession, which he surrendered to Hanger. As they stood at the rear of the car, McVeigh told the trooper that he also had a pouch containing an extra clip for his gun, which he surrendered. Hanger then placed McVeigh in his patrol car and belted him in.

McVeigh explained that he had bought the car from a Firestone dealer in Junction City, Kansas and that the salesman's name was Tom. Further, he said that the car he had traded in had a tag on it, but he did not transfer it to the new car because it "…did not belong there." He also volunteered that he was in the process of moving to Arkansas and had already delivered a load of his belongings there and was returning to retrieve more. Hangar does not keep a tape recorder in his patrol car; therefore, he was unable to record the conversations he had with McVeigh.

Hanger used his cellular phone to make inquiries about McVeigh. He told the dispatcher that he thought the car might be registered in Missouri because of a sticker he had seen on the window. McVeigh interrupted and told him that the sticker was an Arkansas sticker. Hanger then directed the dispatcher to check Arkansas records, and the subsequent report showed that the car belonged to an individual there but that the registration had expired.

In the patrol car on the way to jail, McVeigh was polite and did not appear to be afraid. The ride from where he was stopped to the Noble County Jail was approximately 18 to 20 miles, and the trip took 15 to 20 minutes. According to Hanger, McVeigh was cooperative and polite, never threatening or aggressive. Hanger said that, at the time of the arrest, he was aware that the Murrah Building had been bombed, but he did not link McVeigh to the crime.

F. FINAL ARGUMENTS AND CONCLUSIONS

Merrick Garland, associate deputy attorney general, argued that McVeigh should be detained because he posed a flight risk due to the fact that he did not have a permanent address and because he had a history of living in multiple states over a short period of time. Garland further emphasized that, since McVeigh was possibly facing a death sentence, this would be incentive for him to flee.

Further, Garland stated that there was probable cause to believe that McVeigh had violated 18 U.S.C. 924 and the court was bound by 18 U.S.C. Section 3142E that "…requires the court to order detention if it finds no conditions would reasonably assure the appearance of a person as required…and [if] the safety of any other person in the community" were at risk. With regard to "safety of the community," Garland said, "…look at the crime itself. He's [McVeigh] shown willingness to kill innocent children, law enforcement officers and ordinary people…."

Following the above presentation, Judge Howland noted that McVeigh was charged with Section 844, Title 18, specifically paragraph f: "malicious damage by an explosive to federal property." Howland concluded that all elements of the statute were satisfied by probable cause evidence. He continued, "The Court also finds…an indelible…trail of evidence that starts in Junction City and ends up at the front door of the Murrah Building." He also commented that McVeigh had been identified in Junction City and in Oklahoma City, and that the Ryder truck and Mercury had been identified as well at both sites. Judge Howland therefore ordered that McVeigh be detained due to risk of flight and endangerment to the community.

Susan Otto, McVeigh's court-appointed attorney, pointed out that John Coyle had been contacted the previous Saturday night regarding the lineup. Otto stated that she and Coyle were both "present during the composition of the lineup although we were not allowed to participate in it." They were also present when the witnesses were brought in. She expressed concerns that eyewitness testimony might be tainted because of extensive media coverage and requested the Court to issue an order whereby the government would be allowed to conduct only live lineups at which she and Coyle would be present, or that the lineups be videotaped. Otto further requested that, if the Court denied the above request, the defense be allowed to be present at any and all FBI photo spreads. She stressed that it was critical for the defense to be allowed to see and hear from witnesses in person regarding identifications. The Court ordered defense counsel to submit a motion and a brief making that request.

Attorney Garland objected to the defense's request to hold lineups in abeyance until their motion and brief were submitted, and to their request that lineups be videotaped. He noted that further investigation would be impeded if photo spreads were not allowed.

Otto stated that if the Government was concerned about delaying the investigation, the defense would be agreeable to allowing conversations between the Government and eyewitnesses to be recorded during a photo spread. At this juncture, the Court ordered Otto to make a motion to record testimony of eyewitnesses during a photo spread. She agreed to submit the motion the following day. Otto then expressed the hope that the Government would record conversations with witnesses in the meantime. Garland refused to honor that request, and the Preliminary Hearing was concluded.

OKBIC Note: It is important to note that Timothy McVeigh was indicted because of evidence provided by eyewitness accounts of his actions while in the company of other persons in the days up to, and on the day of, the bombing. However, in the federal trials, prosecutors selectively culled out eyewitnesses to "Others Unknown" and did not call any witness who testified to seeing McVeigh in the company of others.

Chapter VIII.

FEDERAL TRIALS OF MCVEIGH AND NICHOLS

A. OVERVIEW

The trials of Timothy McVeigh and Terry Nichols were originally scheduled to be tried in Lawton, Oklahoma with U.S. District Judge Wayne Alley presiding. However, Judge Alley's office and staff had received injury during the bombing (see pgs. 465-466); and, upon defense motions, a change of venue to Denver, Colorado was ordered by the 10th Circuit Court of Appeals, and Judge Alley was replaced with District Judge Richard Matsch. The defendants were charged with

Count 1--Conspiracy to use a truck bomb to destroy the Alfred P. Murrah Federal Building in Oklahoma City and to kill and injure the persons in it;

Count 2--The use of a truck bomb as a weapon of mass destruction against the persons in the building (168 persons were killed as a result of the bombing: Those killed within the Murrah Building itself were 115 federal employees, 19 children in the childcare facility and 29 visitors to the building. Those killed outside the building were one person in the Athenian Restaurant, two people in the Water Resources building and one person in the parking lot. Additionally, one rescue worker was killed during the rescue effort;

Count 3--The use of a truck bomb against the building (because it was owned and used by agencies of the government of the United States); and,

Counts 4-11--First degree murder of federal law enforcement officers, including:

- 4 agents of the U.S. Secret Service
- 2 agents of the U.S. Customs Service
- 1 agent of the Drug Enforcement Agency
- 1 agent of Housing and Urban Development

The premise of the Government case is that McVeigh and Nichols, alone and in concert with one another, planned and executed the bombing of the Alfred P. Murrah Federal Building in Oklahoma City, Oklahoma, on Wednesday, 19 April 1995; that this was accomplished by a series of well-thought out and deliberate steps; and that the actions taken to accomplish their end were as follows:

1. The use, under an alias, of a debit phone card to keep in touch and to locate bomb-making materials, with the intention that their calls could not be traced;

2. The purchase of ammonium nitrate by Nichols from a co-op in McPherson, Kansas;

3. The purchase of nitromethane by McVeigh from a racetrack in Ennis, Texas;

4. The purchase of barrels in which to mix and transport the bomb;

5. The robbery, by Nichols, of Roger Moore (a gun dealer and friend of McVeigh) at Moore's home in Arkansas in order to finance the bombing;

6. The theft of blasting caps and other bomb-making components from a rock quarry in Marion, Kansas, by McVeigh and Nichols;

7. The rental of a Ryder truck by McVeigh to transport the bomb to Oklahoma City;

9. The stashing of the get-away car in Oklahoma City by McVeigh the Sunday before the bombing, and his being picked up and returned to Kansas by Nichols; and,

8. The mixing of the bomb components in the Ryder truck at Geary State Park Lake just south of Junction City, Kansas, by McVeigh and Nichols;

10. McVeigh driving the Ryder truck with the bomb to Oklahoma City and parking it in front of the Murrah Building where he detonated it.

McVeigh was arrested less than an hour and a half later by an Oklahoma Highway patrol officer who stopped him for not having a license tag on his car and held him for carrying a concealed weapon. Two days later authorities had connected McVeigh to the bombing and found that he was already incarcerated in the Logan County Jail in Oklahoma.

McVeigh and Nichols were tried in separate trials. The McVeigh trial began in Denver on 24 April 1997. Defense lead counsel was Stephen Jones (court-appointed attorney from Enid, Oklahoma). He was assisted by Chris Tritico, Jerri Merritt, Rob Nigh, Cheryl Ramsey, Mandy Welch, Richard Burr, Bob Wyatt, Randy Coyne and Mike Roberts. The federal prosecutors were Joe Hartzler (lead), Beth Wilkinson, Larry Mackey, Jamie Orenstein, Scott Mendeloff, Vicki Behenna, Aitan Goelman, Patrick Ryan (U.S. attorney from the Western District of Oklahoma) and FBI special agents Jon Hersley and Larry Tongate. Nichols trial began 03 November 1997. His court-appointed lead attorney was Michael Tigar, who was assisted by Ron Woods, Adam Thurschwell, Reid Neureiter, and Jane Tigar. Lead prosecutor was Larry Mackey with assistance from attorneys Sean Connelly, Beth Wilkinson, Geoffrey Mearns, Jamie Orenstein and Aitan Goelman and U.S. attorneys from the Western District of Oklahoma, Patrick Ryan and Randal Sengel.

During opening comments, prosecutors outlined the evidence and witnesses they would present during the trial. At Nichols' trial, prosecutors said that Nichols helped McVeigh with every phase of the bombing from the planning to acquiring the bomb ingredients, to dropping off the get-away car, to actually mixing the bomb. They claim that Nichols was in Herrington, Kansas, on the day of the bombing because he planned it just that way.

Defense attorneys outlined the exceptions they would take with the Government evidence. Attorneys for Nichols reminded the jury that to convict Terry Nichols, they must be convinced that he knew of McVeigh's final goal and intentionally contributed toward achieving that goal. Also, they advised that McVeigh was not alone in the Ryder truck at the Murrah Building, yet no witnesses had identified the other occupant in the truck as being Nichols.

Michael Fortier, who says McVeigh told him he and Nichols planned to bomb the Murrah Building and who, supposedly, was aware of all actions taken toward that goal, was not charged as a conspirator in the bombing. He agreed to testify for the prosecution and pled guilty instead to charges of (1) lying to the FBI; (2) concealing knowledge of the bombing; and, (3) transporting guns. According to the Government, he was not an active participant, but did have prior knowledge. He was subject to a prison term of 23 years, which could have been mitigated to as little as two years based on the prosecutioir's recommendation. (Source: *New York Times,* May 98)

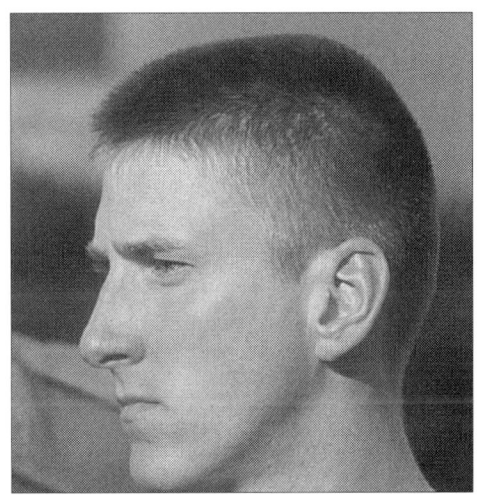

Timothy McVeigh

The case against McVeigh and Nichols was built primarily upon evidence gathered at Nichols' home. When the Ryder truck rental was traced to McVeigh, he had given the address of Nichols' brother in Decker, Michigan, as his home address. Through this address, the FBI began to look at Terry Nichols' involvement. The subsequent search of Nichols' home found a debit calling card in the name of Daryl Bridges. This card was paid for via money orders from Nichols and McVeigh. By analyzing the calls made on the card, the FBI was able to track the alleged movements of McVeigh and Nichols to show that they were in the area when certain key events took place. The FBI was also able to trace calls to various businesses that sell components needed to build the bomb.

In this chapter we will give the key evidence and witnesses presented at the trials by the prosecution, points made by the defense in their cross-examinations and the witnesses that testified during the defense presentation. OKBIC comments and pieces of evidence not presented at trial will also be included. There will be very little testimony related to John Doe #2 (or #3 or #4) because he was not on trial and, apparently, was a figment of someone's imagination or has ceased to exist.

B. BACKGROUND

Timothy McVeigh, Terry Nichols and Michael Fortier met in the U.S. Army during basic training at Fort Benning, Georgia. They had all entered the army on 24 May 1988. Upon completion of basic training, their entire company was transferred to Fort Riley, Kansas. McVeigh began a close association with both Nichols and Fortier, though it does not appear that Nichols and Fortier were particularly close friends with one another. Nichols, who was Fortier's Platoon Guide, left the army in May 1989 and moved back to the family farm in Decker, Michigan. Fortier was honorably discharged in May 1991. He returned home to Kingman, Arizona and began attending a community college there. McVeigh was honorably discharged 31 December 1991 after a tour of duty in Desert Storm where he was highly decorated. He had applied for a position with Special Forces and was accepted, according to the Defense's opening statement, but "had lost a considerable amount of weight and frankly physically wasn't up to it; so he...dropped out the second day...." He moved back home to Pendelton, New York for awhile. In the spring of 1993, he visited Fortier in Arizona. He was working the gun show circuit by then.

Terry Nichols

C. MOTIVE

According to the Government, the reason McVeigh and Nichols blew up the federal building in Oklahoma City was because they had developed a distrust of the Government and thought that it had become too powerful and was overstepping its authority. The incidents at Ruby Ridge and Waco were acts that incensed McVeigh and Nichols and fueled their hatred of the Government and convinced them that some kind of offensive action was necessary. The Government needed a "wake-up call" that American citizens would no longer tolerate its abuses.

The Prosecution

As with any murder trial, prosecutors tried to prove motive or intent. However, in his instructions to the jurors, Judge Matsch told them that, in this case, "Proof of motive is not essential." Nonetheless, prosecutors spent considerable time showing what they believed McVeigh's motive to be:

> *Everyone in this great nation has a right to think and believe, speak whatever they want. We are not prosecuting McVeigh because we don't like his thoughts or his beliefs or even his speech; we're prosecuting him because his hatred boiled into violence, and his violence took the lives of innocent men and women and children. And the reason we'll introduce evidence of his thoughts, as disclosed by those writings and others, is because they reveal this premeditation and his intent, and intent is an element of the crime that we must prove.*

> *Over time McVeigh's anger and hatred of the Government kept growing; and in the late summer of 1994 -- and this is nine months before the bombing -- he decided that he had had enough. He told friends that he was done distributing antigovernment propaganda and talking about the coming revolution. He said it was time to take action, and the action he wanted to take was something dramatic, something that would shake up America, he said, and would cause ordinary citizens, he thought, to engage*

in a violent revolution against their democratically elected government, just like **The Turner Diaries**; *and of course, just like the main character in the book, he would become the hero.*

The action he selected was the bombing, and the building he selected was the federal building in Oklahoma City. We'll provide you with testimony on this. And he offered two reasons for bombing—or for selecting that particular building; first he thought that the ATF agents, whom he blamed for the Waco tragedy, had their offices in that building. As it turns out, he was wrong; but that's what he thought. That was one of his motivations; and second, he described that building as, quote, "an easy target." It was conveniently located just south of Kansas and it had easy access. It was just a matter of blocks off of an interstate highway, Interstate 35, through Oklahoma City travelling north; and the building is designed—is such that you can drive a truck up. There is an indentation at the sidewalk in front of the building. You can drive a truck right up and park a truck right there in front of the building, right there in front of the plate glass windows...in front of the daycare center.

The day that he selected for the bombing also has significance. He selected April 19th. Of course, first, that was the anniversary of Waco, and he wanted to, as he said, avenge death that occurred at Waco; and second, April 19th a couple of centuries ago, in 1775, that's the day that the American Revolution is reported to have begun. That's the day that the opening shot was fired in Concord/Lexington. The day is known as Liberty Day.

So as indicated by the materials that McVeigh carried with him -- you'll see the stuff that he got from his car -- he envisioned that by bombing the building in Oklahoma City he would bring what he thought would be liberty to this nation....(On that morning), the T-shirt he was wearing virtually broadcast his intention. On its front was the image of Abraham Lincoln; and beneath the image was a phrase about tyrants, which is a phrase that John Wilkes Booth shouted in Ford's Theater to the audience when he murdered President Lincoln. And on the back of T-shirt that McVeigh was wearing on that morning, the morning of bombing, the morning that he was arrested, was this phrase: It said, "The tree of liberty must be refreshed from time to time with the blood of patriots and tyrants." And above those words was the image of a tree. You'll see that T-shirt; you'll see the tree; you'll see the words beneath the tree, and you'll notice that instead of fruit, the T-shirt --the tree on the T-shirt bears a depiction of droplets of scarlet-red blood.

...Inside McVeigh's car, law enforcement agents later found a large sealed envelope. It contained writings and magazines from...photocopies from magazines and from newspapers. You'll see all those documents in evidence, and they will give you a window into McVeigh's mind. And they'll enable you to see his intention, to know his pre-meditation, and to understand the twisted motive behind this deadly offense. To give you just two examples of the material you will see, enclosed in that envelope were slips of paper bearing statements that McVeigh had clipped from books and newspapers.

*And one of them was a quotation that--from a book that McVeigh had copied. And it was a book that he had read and believed in like the Bible. The book is entitled **The Turner Diaries**. It's a fictional account of an attack on the federal government which is carried out with a truck bomb blowing up a federal building and killing hundreds of people. And the clipping that McVeigh had with him on this day of the bombing talks about the value of killing innocent people for a cause. It reads -- and he highlighted this -- "The real value of our attacks today lies in the psychological impact, not in the immediate casualties."*

Another slip of paper that he had in that envelope in his car bears a quotation from one of our founding fathers, one of the founding fathers who fought the British to establish democracy in America. The printed portion on that piece of paper reads, in part, "When the government fears the people, there is liberty...."And hand-printed beneath those printed words, in McVeigh's handwriting, are the words -- it's printed above, and he had it like a bumper sticker, almost. He had printed beneath, "Maybe now there will be liberty." These documents are virtually a manifesto declaring McVeigh's intention.

The Prosecution called several witnesses to testify about the defendants' ideology and about the literature McVeigh and Nichols possessed, e.g., G. William Nellis, FBI agent, found the videotape, *Waco, the Big Lie,* in the search of Nichols' home.

Michael Fortier was questioned at length about McVeigh's activities and conversations. He provided the following testimony:

Q. While you were at Fort Riley, did Mr. McVeigh ever share any literature with you?

A. Yes, sir, he did.

Q. Tell us about that, please.

A. Mr. McVeigh brought to me a book called **The Turner Diaries**. He urged me to read it, which I did.

Q. Did you have any conversation with him about it?

A. None that I can recall....

Q. Did you notice any change in McVeigh's attitude during this period when he was in Kingman during the middle section of 1994?

A. He became--he started to become more defensive, keeping weapons behind his doors in his house. He was collecting wood from TruValue to burn in his wood-burning stove in his home. In the meantime, he was stacking it in his backyard. He explained to me why he was stacking it *where he was, that he didn't want--or he wanted to use as some type of berm to block bullets in case there was ever any type of Waco-style raid on his home. He just became defensive.*

Q. Did he ever talk to you about being at war or declaration of war during that period of time?

A. I remember one statement he made to me driving in his car. He was driving me back to Kingman to my house and he said that he thought the U.S. Government had declared war on the American public and that they were actively taking our rights away.

Q. Do you recall any plans you had for the 4th of July that year?

A. Yes. Tim had made a flyer of his thoughts and ideas and collections of quotes from our Founding Fathers. He condensed it all into -- onto one piece of paper; and I had photocopied a bunch of them at work, and we were going to pass them out on the 4th of July. We never did, though, because Tim got called away. He went to Buffalo. Something was the matter with his grandfather; and I didn't have no interest in doing that by myself, so it never came to be.

McVeigh's cousin, Kyle Klaus, testified. He said their families grew up attending family occasions together. While he was in his senior year of highschool and McVeigh was in the service, in the fall of 1991, Klaus received a package from McVeigh. Inside were a letter and a copy of *The Turner Diaries* which he read. When McVeigh came home at Christmas time, they discussed it from a Brady Bill standpoint. McVeigh told him that if the Government continued infringing on people's rights, "it might come to this" —a civil war like described in the book. In the spring of 1992, Klaus again received a package from McVeigh. Inside was another book, *The Hunter*, by the same author. Klaus said he does not believe in gun control, but McVeigh's books were too extreme for him. Then, Klaus told about watching the news on 19 April 1995 regarding the Oklahoma City bombing. He said that "as soon as they had realized how they believe that the bombing occurred, I said it was right in line with *The Turner Diaries*." The following day, Klaus contacted the FBI and told them about the books.

A friend of McVeigh from Michigan, Kevin Nicholas, was called to testify. He said that he met McVeigh in 1992 while working on the Nichols' farm run by Terry Nichols' brother, James, and owned by the Nicholses' mother. He said he had seen McVeigh with a copy of *The Turner Diaries*. He also said they talked about Waco, but never about taking any action.

Nicholas said he had received "three dozen or so" letters from McVeigh and recognized the handwriting. He identified a letter McVeigh had sent to Nicholas' aunt dated 08 February 1995 and which Nicholas had read. The letter began, "Kevin hurt his back, eh?" and continued as follows:

As far as the main context of your letter, I really don't know what to tell you, except write your representatives in Congress. They represent the people and they listen to them. (Yea, right!) No, really, let me try to explain: I was in the educational/literature dissemination (desert wind is wreaking havoc on my already scratchy writing) field for quite some time. I was preaching and, "passing out" before anyone had ever heard the words "patriot" and "militia." (Just got out of the wind.) "Onward and upward." I passed on that legacy about a 1/2 year ago. I believe "new blood" needs to start somewhere; and I have certain other "militant" talents that are short in supply and greatly demanded. So I gave all my informational paperwork to the "new guys" and no longer have any to give. What I can send you, is my own personal copies; ones that are just "getting dust -- or gathering dust," and a newsletter I recently received. If you are willing to write letters, I could pass your name on to someone; but let there be no doubt, with the letters I have in mind, the literature that would be forwarded to you for copying; etc., you would probably make a list. (Currently, there are over 300,000 names on the Cray Supercomputer in Brussels, Belgium; of "possible and suspected subversives and terrorists" in the U.S., all ranked in order of threat,) Letters would be of an "on notice" nature, like the ones many people, "myself included," wrote to Lon Horiuchi (The FBI sniper who blew Vicki Weaver's head off) saying, in effect: "What goes around comes around"...."Hey, that's just the truth, and if we're scared away from writing the truth because we're afraid of winding up on a list, then we've lost already. "To sin by silence when they should protest makes Cowards of men." (Abe L.) If the founding fathers had been scared of a "list," we'd still be under the tyrannical rule of the crown. They knew, with out a doubt, that by signing the Declaration of Independence, they would be sentenced to death, for high treason against the crown. But they realized something was more important than their soul or collective lives--the cause of liberty. Hell, you only live once, and I KNOW you know it's better to burn out, than ...... rot away in some nursing home. My philosophy is the same--in only a short 1-2 years, my body will slowly start giving away--first maybe knee pains, or back pains, or whatever, but I won't be "peaked" anymore. Might as well do some good while I can be 100% effective! Sorry I can't be of more help, but most of the people sent my way these days are of the direct-action type, and my whole mindset has shifted, from intellectual to ...."animal," (Rip the bastards heads off and shit down their necks!, and I'll show you how with a simple pocket knife...etc.) So take your time, read all the enclosed paper work, and maybe pass it on to other interested parties. If you want to go on a propaganda mailing list, let me know. See ya, The Desert Rat

The enclosure to the letter had both McVeigh's and Nichols' fingerprints on it.

The Defense

In McVeigh's trial, in the opening remarks, the Defense tried to eliminate any similarities between the Oklahoma City bombing and *The Turner Diaries*. The following comments were made:

> *The proof however that we will offer is that the narrator--that is, the first-person account in **The Turner Diaries**--never indicated that the bombing of the FBI headquarters was done to, quote, "wake up America," close quote, or, quote, "to send a message to the government," close quote, or for that matter to the American people.*
>
> ***The Turner Diaries** will be in evidence, and the proof will show that the expressly stated purpose for the fictional bombing to destroy the FBI headquarters and the subbasement*

Stephen Jones

was that it had a bank of computers which were to be used for implementing what the author described as an Orwellian Big Brother style of an internal passport system which would enable the FBI to keep a record of whereabouts of the citizens at all times, a fictional account clearly distinguishable from the Government's proof.

*Well, the evidence will show the FBI isn't even in the Murrah Building in Oklahoma City. Its headquarters were at 50 Penn Place, some four or five miles away. The proof is that in **The Turner Diaries**, the motive for bombing of the FBI headquarters was not the motive of the Government's proof ascribed to Mr. McVeigh. It was the need to destroy a specific military target in an ongoing war that was already in place between the Government and the revolutionary organization. In short, it's a work of fiction.*

In the Terry Nichols trial, the Defense called numerous witnesses who spoke of McVeigh's apparent obsession with the Government. The purpose seemed to be to call attention to the fact that these witnesses all heard McVeigh make anti-Government statements, but none of them ever heard Nichols make similar statements or heard McVeigh refer to Nichols as holding the same views. The following is a summary of those witness statements:

The Prosecution
Dale Steven Hodge went to school with McVeigh (McVeigh was one year older) and lived across the street from him between his fifth and twelfth grade years. After that, McVeigh moved to a new house with his father about two miles away. While McVeigh was in the service, Hodge received 66 letters from him. He saw McVeigh after he left the army and thought him to be more withdrawn and more political. McVeigh gave Hodge a copy of *The Turner Diaries* before he left in 1993. McVeigh continued to correspond and eventually gave him an address in Flint, Michigan where he could write back. Hodge said McVeigh's letters became more and more anti-Government with nothing personal in them. In one letter read in court, McVeigh told him,

> *Those who betray or subvert the Constitution are guilty of sedition and/or treason, are domestic enemies and should and will be punished....I have sworn to uphold and defend the Constitution against all enemies, foreign and domestic, and I will....And I will because not only did I swear to, but I believe in what it stands for in every bit of my heart, soul and being....Blood will flow in the streets, Steve. Good vs. evil. Free men vs. socialist wannabe slaves. I have come to peace with myself, my God, and my cause. And I feel that I do not have to justify myself to anyone, to defend my position....The struggle now is not one of insecurity—am I insane—but one of how people—how can people not see what I do as the obvious truth.*

Mr. Hodge said that he received a letter from McVeigh in July 1994 ending their friendship because of "ideological differences."

The Defense

During the Nichols' trial, the Defense pointed out that the letters always said "I" and not "we." When asked if McVeigh ever mentioned the name Terry Nichols, Hodge said no. The Defense put on several people as witnesses who told about McVeigh's viewpoint and literature, but nobody who heard that Nichols held these same views.

The Prosecution

Anthony Palmer, an NCO in the Army with McVeigh, said that he and McVeigh corresponded after McVeigh left the service. He said McVeigh often included neo-Nazi literature for him to read.

Norma Chloe Koalska, a teacher's assistant in Kingman and Lori Fortier's maid of honor, said she met McVeigh on 09 July 1994 at her daughter's birthday party which he attended with the Fortiers. Later he came by her house and gave her and her husband some anti-Government literature

In the spring or early summer of 1993, when McVeigh was living in Kingman, Arizona, he worked part-time for State Security Services. Larry Clinton Chapman, the chief of security, testified that, when McVeigh picked up his last paycheck, he gave Chapman some xeroxed copies of anti-Government literature with a six page article on "U.S. Government Initiates Open Warfare Against American People" and a three page packet with articles on "What do You Know about the Waco Inferno?", "Why the Armed Citizens in America?", and "Waco Shootout Evokes Memory of Warsaw '43." Another employee of State Security Services, Gary Wayne Steinberger, relieved McVeigh on his shift. McVeigh had brought up a television and VCR to work one night. When Steinberger arrived, McVeigh put in a video tape negative toward the Government and their actions against the Branch Davidians in Waco, Texas, which they watched. Steinberger said the tape showed federal agents using flame throwers and a tank to enter the Davidian building. The tape lasted about 20 minutes, then McVeigh gave him some literature from a three-ring binder: a pamphlet titled "United States Government, or Nazi Germany?". He said that, though McVeigh gave him this literature, he did not push his ideas on him.

Joseph Hartzler

Daryl McCraw also worked for State Security Services. He worked the shift before McVeigh, and McVeigh was his relief. They went target shooting and tactical shooting together through their work, and McCraw commented that McVeigh was an expert shot. In April 1993, they went to a gun show together. McVeigh started talking explosives and invited McCraw to attend a survival camp with him, but McCraw could not go.

Lauren Merville Alainger and a girlfriend from college went on spring break to Mount Carmel, just south of Waco, Texas. Lauren was taking a photography class and her friend was a communications major hoping to be a reporter. They decided to go to the Branch Davidian stand-off and see if they could find any interview or photographic opportunities. McVeigh was there, and they spoke with him and took his picture. He was selling bumper stickers which had anti-Government sayings on them, such as "A man With a Gun is a Citizen. A Man Without a Gun is a Subject" and "Politicians Love Gun Control" and "Fear the Government that Fears Your Gun."

D. FORENSIC EVIDENCE

The Prosecution

A massive team was assembled in Oklahoma City on the days following the bombing to search for and gather evidence of the crime. FBI Agent Patrick Daly headed the evidence response team (ERT) at the Oklahoma City bomb-site. He testified that, several days after the bombing, he found some mangled truck parts near the bombsite. ATF Agent Lowell Sprague and FBI agents Donald Sachtleben, David Opperaun and Anthony McCallum identified various truck parts found at the bomb scene. FBI Agent Alton Wilson identified a particular part (Q507) found in the parking lot across the street from the Murrah Building.

Edward Paddock, an engineer with Ford Motor Company, explained what all the different truck pieces were and concluded that the pieces were from a single truck; therefore, the bomb was carried in one truck which had been made by Ford.

1. The Ryder Truck Axle

The Prosecution

The axle to the Ryder truck was a key piece of evidence in locating the Ryder rental agency where the truck was rented. It was found by Richard Nichols, a maintenance worker for the Regency Tower Apartments, outside his building, about a block west of the Murrah Building on 5th Street. (For a map of downtown Oklahoma City, see Appendix p. 371.) He had been at work the morning of the bombing, and his wife was coming to pick him up so he could accompany her when she took their nephew, who was staying with them, to the doctor. He was still inside when she arrived at 9:00, so she went into the building to get him. He described the following events:

> *Well, as I walked out the door, I greeted my wife in a small foyer, which is two glass doors before you enter out to the street. And we laughed because she heard my keys jingling, and she always made a joke that she could always hear me coming. As we stepped out into the street, we took approximately two steps when there was a horrific explosion. Glass covered us. And my wife got real nervous, and she kind of spun around, and she asked what was going on. And I told her that the boilers in our building had blowed up....*

So we made the lunge to get to the car because we was getting showered with glass and rocks, and we opened up the door. I had a hold of the door of the car. My wife bent down to get my nephew out, when I heard a whirling noise like a boomerang coming from my left side, which would have been from the direction of the Murrah Federal Building. As I looked up, I seen a big chunk of something coming at us. I didn't know what it was at the time. I remember telling my wife to get down.... I don't remember if I pushed her on down into the car. She was setting [sic] down kind of like on the doorjamb trying to get him [the nephew] out of his seat belt. And I can't remember if I pushed her on down into the car, but this object hit the car, right about the windshield and the passenger side of the car. At the time it jerked up the back of the car. Then the car shot backwards out of my hands. I went back to the car. I grabbed my wife. I grabbed my nephew. I pulled them both out of the car and tried as best as I could to kind of like mother hen them underneath me and take them across the road. I was still under the assumption that my building was coming down behind us, and I wanted to make as much room as I could between us and that building. I looked up the street, and behind the Water Resources I could see black smoke. I looked back at my car. That's when I first noticed that it was an axle that was laying by my car. I told my wife, "No," I said, "it was a car bomb. Somebody tried to blow up the Water Resources." And I still hadn't known it was the Murrah Federal Building because of the smoke and the debris still coming down.

Mr. Nichols looked at some time-lapse film from the Regency Towers showing the street in front of the building. His car was visible with his wife in the car, but also could be seen a Ryder truck going down the street. At 8:57:15 the truck was moving in front of the Regency Towers. It then moved up slightly and stopped. At 8:57:18, the truck had moved forward again and only the very rear of the truck was visible. At 8:59:58 his wife had entered the building. (He was coming down on the elevator.) The last frame on the film is a shot of the elevator at 09:00:21. After that, "everything stopped. All the electric went out, cameras quit, everything. The bomb had just blown up."

FBI Agent James Elliott was on-scene in Oklahoma City after the bombing and was given a partial vehicle identification number (VIN) from the axle housing to check on. The number provided was 6.4PVA26077. He explained that the vehicle identification number is a 17-digit number which is displayed on all vehicles on the dashboard and, on most vehicles, also on the driver's side post. It is unique to each car or truck manufactured in the United States. The last five numbers are sequential as the vehicle comes off the manufacturer's assembly line.

Agent Elliott recognized the eight digits of the number starting with the "PV to be a confidential vehicle number (CVIN). He said,

It's a number which is stamped at various places on hard parts of a vehicle as it's being manufactured and is essentially hidden from public view, so that, should the vehicle be stolen and the public vehicle identification number changed, the vehicle can be traced.

He said he called the National Crime Insurance Bureau in Dallas, which maintains records of automobiles manufactured and sold within the United States, and gave them the eight digit number so that it could be traced.

Agent Elliott said he did not recognize the beginning of the number, so he went to the Regency Towers and examined the rear-axle housing that the CVIN was on and saw the number on the housing. He then telephoned the National Crime Insurance Bureau again. They provided him with the entire 17-digit VIN and told him that the truck was registered to Ryder Rental, Incorporated in Miami, Florida and was a current rental. He then provided the information to the duty agent at the command post who, in his presence, called the information into the FBI headquarters. The FBI then used this information to contact Ryder and Ford Motor Company.

Edward Paddock with Ford Motor Company checked the VIN for the FBI, and found that the vehicle was a 1993 F-series-type truck. It was manufactured by Ford from 15 February to 25 March 1993 and sold approximately 01 March 1993 to Ryder Truck Rental. Ryder purchased 400 trucks on the same purchase order.

Around 25 April 1995, Mr. Paddock was asked by the FBI to help identify some of the debris from the bomb scene. He described his assistance:

> *I met the agents that were in charge at the time and was introduced to other agents that had started going through some of the parts being extracted from the scene. And they asked if I could work with them for the next several days, which turned out to be about a week or so. I went through all of the debris that had been recovered, some that had been recovered before I got there. We went through all of that, and then we went through all of the barrels that were being brought in on a day-to-day basis; and we went through each and every piece that was brought in.*

Mr. Paddock said that, using the VIN, they were able to identify the truck in question. Ford went to Ryder and bought back the next vehicle off the assembly line, which also would have been built to Ryder specifications. Ford then disassembled the truck to make it into exhibits for the courtroom to better explain some of the parts that would be discussed in court, and laid the parts out in the order in which they would be arranged on a vehicle. They mounted the parts on wheels and frames to make it easier to move around the courtroom. Mr. Paddock then pointed to various items on the frame and explained to the jury what they were. He identified the items that were like-items to the ones found in Oklahoma City (the axle, springs, mount, etc.) He noted that the demonstration axle had a VIN that was one number higher than the axle recovered at the bomb scene.

2. The Ryder Truck License Plate

The Prosecution
Agent Elliott received an assignment later that day to work in the Evidence Control Center (ECC) which was located in a warehouse on 4th Street between Classen and Western, a few blocks from the Murrah Building. On his way there, he saw two Oklahoma County auxiliary sheriffs at the corner of the Athenian Building looking at a piece of twisted metal. He stopped and examined it and saw

that it was a piece of bumper with what appeared to be a Florida license tag contained within it with the number 26R visible. He seized it as evidence and took it to the ECC. When the license plate was removed from the bumper, he found the full license plate number to be NEE26R. This was the tag from the Ryder truck.

3. Ryder Truck Part Q507

The cargo box on the Ryder truck was made of fiberglass on the outside and wood on the inside. A piece of this box was found in Oklahoma City. It was placed in a bag with other pieces of evidence, taken to the Evidence Control Center and later shipped to the FBI lab. Several numbers are associated with this item. They are listed below for clarity's sake in the ensuing discussions:

CT-4/21-06   A bag and all its contents including the piece (Called 06 at trial) of the Ryder truck. The number was assigned at the bombsite and correlates to a map marked to show where the FBI claimed to have found it.

664   (Government exhibit). A piece of the Ryder truck box with wood on one side and fiberglass, painted red and yellow, on the other side. Part of CT-4/21-06.

Q507   Number assigned to 664 by the FBI lab.

665   (Government exhibit). A photo of 664.

J4784   (Defense exhibit). A book of FBI photos from the bombsite with the FBI photo log in the front of the book.

J4784A   (Defense exhibit). FBI photo showing a yellow object. (The photo log says this photo is Q507, but it is not.

Frame 4   Frame number of photo in J4784A, the yellow object, misidentified as Q507.

Q507 was considered a key piece of evidence. Much court time was taken up with testimony about this piece. A summary of that testimony follows:

The Prosecution
FBI Agent Ronald Kelly identified Exhibits 664 and 665. He said he found the piece of paneling in the parking lot across the street from the Murrah Building. He noticed it because it was the red and yellow colors of the Ryder truck. He said it was "definitely situated with the red and yellow side up; and it was situated mostly flat, maybe a little bit elevated…. There was a photograph taken of the item in place."

The Defense

Agent Kelly was put through a grueling cross-examination. He was evasive during much of the testimony, but the Defense hammered at the witness until they received a direct answer to their questions. The Defense's contention was that Q507 was not found at the bomb scene and that the events as depicted in the photographs support this conclusion. There is the problem that the photo log, the frame number assigned, and the photo of the item do not match, indicating that the number assigned at the scene was intended for another item. In the photograph taken at the scene, the piece of evidence in the center of the photograph is a metal piece. The yellow and red Ryder truck piece is off to the side, indicating that the photographer intended to take a picture of the metal piece, and the truck part just happened to be in the picture also. Testimony went as follows:

Q. Look at the book that you have there that's marked J478 and see if you can find Frame Number 4....

A. This is the one labelled Frame No. 4 on the the photograph...

Q. Now, what I'm showing you has been marked as J478A; is that correct? Can you read the...

A. Yes, I can, that's correct.

Q. Is this the photograph that you identified as being marked as Frame Number 4 on the log sheet identifying CT-4/21-06?...This is not a picture of what you have—what we now call Q507, is it?

A. No, it is not.

Q. And this is not a picture of CT-4/21-06; is that correct?

A. No, it is not.

Q. But what we do know by looking at this photograph is—centered in the frame is whatever this yellow item is; right?

A. There is a yellow object in the center, yes, sir.

Q. And by looking at it, you can tell clearly that it's a picture of that item; right? That was what was intended to be photographed in that picture, right? You agree?

A. I would say that the photo accurately represents what it was photographing, yes.

Q. The photograph that you have introduced on Thursday wherein Q507 is shown does not center what we now call Q507 in the center of the frame, does it?

A. The photograph Q507 is not the same frame as what's indicated on the log; that's correct.

Q. Perhaps my question was not artful. I apologize. that's in evidence—already in evidence as Government Exhibit 665, you see that?

A. Yes, I do....

Q. Now, this is what you have claimed is Q507—right what I'm pointing at. Can you see that?

A. Yes, I can.

Q. Is that what you are saying is Q507 today?

A. Yes, I am.

Q. Now, that is not centered in the frame, is it?

A. No, it isn't, it's off left of center.

Q. This—what's more prominent in the picture is this metal piece right here; is that correct?

A. That is correct.

Q. As a matter of fact, there was another picture taken of—a close-up of this same piece of evidence. Is that right?

A. That is right.

Q. Do you know what this evidence was marked?

A. No, I don't recall at this time.

Q. There is not a picture of Q507 with it centered in the frame. Is that right?

A. No, there is not.

Q. There's not a close-up taken of Q507. Is that right?

A. No, there is not.

Q. And the reason for that is that you received Q507 from a citizen and you didn't find it in the parking lot, yourself. Isn't that right?

A. That is absolutely incorrect.

Q. What really happened is you happened to find Government Exhibit 665 that had what appeared to be Q507 in it later. Right?

A. No, sir. That particular photograph, which I thought was photographed in place, when I checked with him at the time of the recovery, was determined to not have been photographed in place. After recovering the item, I placed it as closely back to the original location and photographed it after the recovery, though, sir. So it accurately depicts where it was found, but that's not the photograph of it in place before recovery.

Q. If I understand what you're telling me, this photograph is a—the item was removed without being photographed, and you took it back and put it back and took a photograph?

A. It was recovered and bagged, after what I thought was photographed in place. Upon checking with Agent Wilson, found out that he had not photographed it, that's correct. So to at least document where it was found, we took this photograph after it had already been recovered.

Q. So you picked it up, moved it, and then put it back where you thought you found it; right?

A. We were still in that location as I was recovering it, and I checked with him; but, yes, that accurately depicts what I did.

Q. How many times did that happen?

A. As I recall, just this one instant.

Q. Do you have a note, record, memo, memoranda, anything detailing that at least this item of evidence was moved, placed back, and then photographed?

A. Again, not a formal note, unless it appears on the evidence log or his notes. I'd have to review those notes that he took.

Q. Well, you reviewed the evidence log, didn't you?

A. Yes. On this particular item, I do recall again—I had checked with him to see if it was photographed in place, and it had not. And we again just documented its location.

Q. Perhaps my question was inartful, and I apologize. Did you review the evidence log?

A. I have reviewed it on several occasions.

Q. Nowhere on the evidence log does it detail that this item of evidence was removed and placed back where you thought you found it and photographed. Right?

A. No, sir, there was not; and likewise, we did not make a note that we recovered it as we did. That's correct.

Q. And you have no note, record, memo, memoranda, anything detailing the time that you found—that you claim you found Q507. Right?

A. Again, that was SA Wilson who was in charge of recording the administrative details of my recovery.

Q. And would he have been required to note the time and the location somewhere?

A. That would be a general rule of what we do, yes, sir.

Q. Is this a written rule?

A. No, it's just a guideline that we follow.

Q. Is the guideline written?

A. We have some written guidelines, yes, sir.

Q. My question to you, sir, is this rule written, this guideline written?

A. Noting the time that a item of evidence was recovered?

Q. And the place.

A. Yes, sir.

Q. Where would I find that?

A. Again, you'll find that on—should be located on the evidence log and photo log that SA Wilson was recording.

Q. I'm sorry, my question was inartful. Where would I find the written guideline?

A. Again, the written guidelines for evidence and recovery are in different locations. The evidence recovery teams have their guidelines, we have our guidelines located in the laboratory, so you'd have to determine which guidelines you're talking about.

Q. Where would I find the written guideline which says you shall note the time and place of a item of evidence, where it's found?

A. Again, our administrative manual, the general administrative manual for the FBI contains that. The ERT manual for collection of evidence also contains those type of items.

Q. Do you still have Defendant's Exhibit J478 there in front of you?

A. Yes, I do...Again, there appears to be several items that were bagged before they were recovered—I'm sorry—they were bagged and recovered before they were photographed, which may have indicated Mr. Wilson wasn't present at the time of recovering.

OKIC Note: On page 29, his testimony says Q507 was the only item not photographed in place.

Q. Oh, so he wasn't always there when you found the item?

A. Not all the items. Again, he was in the vicinity; and I may have been bagging items before they were photographed. He was, again, in the area, though.

Earlier testimony during this cross-examination would seem to contradict the above last answer:

Q. And how long after you found it did you call Special Agent Wilson over to make the photograph?

A. Again, I probably recognized it on the initial survey of the area, and then it may have been one of first half a dozen or so items I picked up; but, again, once I started recovering evidence, Mr. Wilson—Agent Wilson was with me at that time. And at the moment I recovered it and bagged it, he was with me at that time.

Q. My question to you, sir—and I apologize if it was inartful—how long after you found it did you call him over to photograph it?

A. He was standing next to me in the general area photographing it prior to me recovering it, I believe.

Dr. Frederick Whitehurst was a supervisor in the FBI lab at the time of the bombing. He provided testimony which refuted the above statements:

Q: (In September 1995) did Special Agent David Williams make to you any statement or comment regarding the origin of how Q507 was found?

A: Yes

Q: What did he say?

A: That the piece of evidence that had the ammonium nitrate and the paint on it had been provided to us by--to the FBI by a civilian. It raised an issue with identifying that piece as actually coming from the Ryder truck; and he said, Well, it's a moot point because a civilian *brought it in. And he said, you know, we've got a problem with the chain of custody, so we're not going to use it.*

The Prosecution
Later testimony by Agent Steven Burmeister, an explosives expert in the FBI lab, however, said that Q507 never went to the paint lab. Another piece did that was recovered by a civilian. Whitehurst probably confused these two pieces.

OKBIC Note
However, if one looks at Dr. Whitehurst's statement above, he did not say that the item went to the paint lab, but that it was the item with paint on it--presumably a reference to the Ryder truck paint that was on the reverse side of Q507.

The Prosecution
Agent Burmeister explained some of the terms related to explosives:

> 1. **Inorganic explosive**: "Typically one that is water-soluble.... An inorganic explosive would typically be those that are in the nature of a nitrate or a perchlorate or chlorate-based....An inorganic material has a variety of shapes; but typically it's in a crystalline form." It would include ammonium nitrate.
>
> 2. **Organic explosive**: "One which is typically soluble in an organic solvent,... such as methanol, ethanol or acetone."
>
> 3. **Oxidizer**: "A material which essentially provides oxygen for any type of a reaction to take place.... Not the explosive itself, but components within these explosives are considered oxidizers....Ammonium nitrate is considered an oxidizer...."

When the pieces of the Ryder truck arrived at the lab, Agent Burmeister conducted the explosives residue testing on them. He said he found no explosives residue on any of the pieces except Q507. For his examination he cleaned the microscope area with bleach and an organic solvent. He had put on a new lab coat that day and wore double gloves. A piece of paper was placed over the microscope stage. He said he found some amazing results. Testimony is given below:

Q. Now, turning to the unpainted side, what did you find when you examined that side of Government's Exhibit 664 under the microscope?

A. There was a portion of this object that had a covering of a white crystalline or clear crystaline material.

Q. What did it look like under the microscope?

A. Under the microscope, it looked like little particles of table salt.

Q. Were they all over Government's Exhibit 664?

A. No. It was isolated to a particular region within the range of the microscope screen. Some of the particles were actually embedded up in the wood-type surface, up underneath it; and some were yet—actually had to pull back the fiberglass materials to some of these crystals that were embedded up underneath. And that was—that's what was observed....

Q. What did you do when you saw those crystals?...

A. Well, like in the past when I have seen objects like that for testing, I will take and remove one of those crystals and perform a color spot test on that crystal to check for a possible oxidizer.

Q. What did you determine?

A. That it gave a strong positive for diphenylamine.

Q. Which means what?

A. Well, a strong positive with diphenylamine indicates to me that it's a possibility of a strong oxidizer present, and a strong oxidizer being something like ammonium nitrate or a chlorate-type salt.

Agent Burmeister said he then took a series of photographs of the "crystals in place." One of these photos was shown to the jury. He was asked,

Q. What was the significance of the fact that some of these crystals were actually embedded into this material?...

A. Well, it would have been embedded by some sort of force; and I would believe from the blast that it would have been forced into the surface....

Q. And did you conduct a series of tests to determine what that—what those crystals were that were on Government's Exhibit 664?

A. Yes.

He said that he performed a chemical spot test which showed the crystals to be "inorganic." He then tested with a polarized light microscope, with a Fourier Transform Infrared Spectroscope which focuses down to single little particles, and an X-ray diffraction test that looks at the crystal itself. He said that

A. ...with the use of the Gandolfi camera attachment, we can take an individual crystal—that is, plucking off of the surface a single crystal, inserting it into this instrument, and developing an array of X-ray beams that are diffracted off of that sample. We can get a known crystalline pattern.... You can then compare it to known samples that have been run and see similarities. It's very much like a fingerprint-type match.

Q. And these three tests that you've just described: Did they all indicate the presence of ammonium nitrate crystals?

A. Yes. Each one was consistent with ammonium nitrate....

OKBIC Note
"Indicating the presence of" and "consistent with" do not mean the same thing. The first means that the test "showed it to be" and the second means that "it did not rule it out."

The Prosecution
Agent Burmeister said he conducted other tests. The ion chromatography test looks at the negative portion of the material, and they "identified the presence of the nitrate ions." Two other test results "found ammonium ions." The Prosecution continued:

Q. Based on all those results,... did you make an identification of the crystals that were found on Q507?

A. The culmination of all of those techniques identified the crystals as ammonium nitrate.

Q. And did you have any doubt after conducting all those tests that those were ammonium nitrate crystals embedded in Q507?

A. No doubt whatsoever.

Michael Tigar

The Defense
During cross-examination, the Defense asked about a street sign taken from the parking lot across the street from the Murray Building, the same location where the FBI said that Q507 was found. When it was examined in the lab, Agent Burmeister said he found ammonium ions and nitrate ions on the object, but he "couldn't attribute it to any significance"...because the ions happen naturally. Then the Defense called into question the crystals that Agent Burmeister said he found on Q507 in an implied comparison with the ammonium and nitrates found on the street sign:

Q. As a matter of fact, when you have like nitrate ions on a surface...nitrate ions can attract ammonium ions and they can attach together before you test it. Right? That can happen?

A. The—you really don't know that—you don't know that the nitrate ions are attached to some other metal. It could be sodium, potassium. You don't know.

Q. Sure. But my point is ions, ammonium ions and nitrate ions, can attract together naturally. Isn't that right?

A. Given the right conditions, it could....

Q. Is it true that ammonium ions and nitrate ions can crystallize on their own?

A. They can certainly do that, yes.

Q. And when you find crystals, you don't know under what circumstances they crystallized, do you? In other words, you don't know if they started from a prill of ammonium nitrate or if they joined together naturally and formed crystals, do you?

A. Well, that's part of the analysis and the size of the crystal and the shape. There are certain conditions that come into play that you have to analyze those to make that determination.

Q. But you don't necessarily know, do you?

A. The—When you look at the surface, I've seen a lot of material when it's recrystallised. I spent some time doing microcrystal work, and there is under—When the material recrystallizes and precipitates out, there's a different appearance that's formed when it's doing it.

Q. Did you have any discussions with other experts in the field back in 1995 regarding the crystallization of ammonium and nitrate ions?

A. I don't believe I've had specific conversations in that area. I know from my background in microcrystal work that what I've seen before and what tests I've run at that time.

Q. Did you have a discussion with Dr. Fred Whitehurst about ammonium ions and nitrate ions on May the 4th, 1995—May the 3rd, 1995?

A. I don't have a specific recollection. Dr. Whitehurst and I, especially during my training period, routinely would discuss ions and how they interact within the environment; and certainly that—It would be consistent with a conversation I may have. I don't recall that particular conversation you're talking about.

Q. Were you still in training on May the 3d, 1995?

A. No.

Q. You were just working together with Dr. Whitehurst in the same lab?

A. Yes.

Q. And you did work together from time to time?

A. Yes....

Q. Now, when you—Did you find, through your research and discussions with other people in your lab, that nitrates are ubiquitous in the environment?

A. That's correct, they are.

Q. What does that mean?

A. It means that unfortunately with our environment, with the pollution that occurs, there are nitrates present as rainwater comes down. And they are present not only from the rainwater, but there are other sources of nitrates in the environment. So detecting nitrates on surfaces doesn't necessarily mean anything at the time. You need to have some sort of history of that material. You also need to have some sort of control samples; that is, a—what is the normal background of that area. So those are the things that you have to take into consideration before understanding what a nitrate reading means....

Q. Did you take soil samples from the area around which Q507 was found?

A. No, I did not.

Q. Now, you took no soil samples from around the area from which Q507 was found. Right?

A. I'm not sure that it was actually on soil that the Q507 was recovered.

Q. How about anything around the area where Q507— Did you take any samples?

A. No other evidence was collected in that vicinity, no....

Q. Without taking the samples from around the ground area from where something is found, in discovering the amount of nitrates in the area, you don't know if the nitrates from the ground attached themselves to the subject object, do you?

A. Well, I have no reason to believe that the ground itself had nitrates on them.

Q. But you didn't check, did you?

A. It's typically not a procedure that I would actually take only --

The Court: Just answer the questions, please.

The Witness: Sorry.

Q. Did you check?

A. I did not check the soil or the surface around that object....

Q. You have information in the FBI laboratory or have you received information from others that an explosive could detonate, deposit nitrate only, and before analysis have ammonium ions form?...

A. If you do a water extract of a material and you take that extract and you let it sit for some period of time and you only detect nitrate ions in that solution, there is a possibility that that nitrate can convert over to ammonium ions, and then those ammonium ions can convert back over to the nitrate ions. The concentration is low, but there is a back-and-forth if you let the solution sit. I recall an instance with Dr. Whitehurst in which that event took place, and I believe he presented that to me at the time.

Q. He wrote you a memo about that, didn't he?

A. Boy, I'm not sure if he wrote me a memo. I remember discussing that feature with him....

Q. Is this a memo that you received from Dr. Whitehurst on May the 4th, 1995?

A. I recall receiving the memo itself. I'm not—I think I've seen the attachments. I'm not sure if the attachments came at the same time as the memo. But I do recall seeing the attachments.

Q. This memo was the result of a...conversation that you and Roger Martz had with Agent Whitehurst regarding this case. Is that right?

A. I don't recall that. I don't recall that I had a conversation and that precipitated this memo. I don't recall that.

Q. Did you look at this memo? You read the memo after you got it. Right?

A. Yes.

Q. The memo discusses searching for ammonium nitrate?

A. Yes.

Q. It discusses the things we were talking about regarding the ubiquitous nature of nitrates?

A. Yes.

Q. *It discusses things relevant to your investigation in this case, does it not?*

A. Well, the material that's presented here was all review to me, and at the time none of it was new information that I was receiving from Dr. Whitehurst. I remember receiving it and reading over it; and there wasn't anything in the memo that struck me as being something I should have taken note of. I already knew what was in the memo.

Q. *And did you utilize it in any form or fashion in your investigation in this case?*

A. No. Not really. Because there wasn't anything new brought up in this memo. I had already had my ideas set forward. The ideas coincided with what was presented in the memo.

Q. *What ideas?*

A. About the nature of ammonium nitrate, the presence of ammonium and nitrate ions at a scene, the significance of those ions. Those are things which I had already known prior to even coming to that crime scene.

OKBIC Note
During cross-examination, Agent Burmeister also admitted that ammonium nitrate could be found in "dozens" of different explosives, so there is no concrete proof that ammonium nitrate fertilizer was used in this bomb. Additionally, the Defense pointed out that no other explosive materials such as blasting caps, detonator cord, or nitro-methane fuel were found at the bomb scene.

The Prosecution
Next Agent Burmeister said he performed two tests to determine if there were any high explosives present in the sample, and found none. These tests, the scanning electron microscope with the energy dispersive X-ray analysis (SEM/EDXA) looks at the elements that are present in the crystal itself. He did find the presence of aluminium, silicon and sulphur—elements not found in ammonium nitrate. He did not find oxygen or nitrogen or hydrogen, other components of ammonium nitrate. He said this was because, on the periodic element chart, those three elements are below the Element Number 11, and the machine will not test anything under Element Number 11 (which is sodium). The following exchange took place:

Q. *So that doesn't mean ammonium nitrate wasn't here; it just means this machine couldn't detect those elements; is that right?*

A. That's correct. But the fact that we're not seeing anything higher than sodium helps support the **fact** (emphasis added) *that there is actually nitrogen, hydrogen, and oxygen present because they're below the sodium.*

Agent Burmeister said he then conducted further analysis "to determine the significance of the aluminium, the silicon and the sulphur. He took samples of some prills and some ground, or crystalline, ammonium nitrate to ICI in Canada to conduct tests with their chemists. He showed a bottle of ammonium nitrate prills seized in the search of Nichols' home. He said he had already analysed these prills before going to Canada and had determined that they were ammonium nitrate prills. In Canada, he learned the ICI formula for their low-density prills produced in Joplin, Missouri in 1994. He made a comparison of the ICI prills and the prills found at Nichols' home:

Q. What were the results?

A. The prills that were from Mr. Nichols' residence closely related to the prills that were from the Joplin plant—ICI Joplin plant—and the results were consistent with one another....

Q. Did Mr. Nichols—the prills seized from Mr. Nichols' residence have the same elements in the additive that were in the known ICI prills?

A. Yes.

Q. Did they have the same elements that were in the known ICI prills in the coating?

A. Yes.

Q. And after you conducted that analysis, did you go back to your laboratory and review the elemental analysis that you had done on Q507?

A. Yes. When I reviewed it, it struck me.... I was seeing the same elemental profile in the ICI prills that we were examining as the ones that I saw on the Q507 (meaning the aluminium, silicon and sulphur).

Q. Now, did you see every single element that you had seen on the ICI prill?

A. When the ICI prills were examined for the interior portion, I was seeing the same elemental profile, yes.

Q. How about for the coating?

A. Not for the coating, no.

Q. So what were you able to determine about the crystals on Q507?

A. The crystals were consistent with originating from a prill, a commercial prill.

Q. Why is that significant that these crystals came from a prill?

A. Because they're—Having these elements present, they did not come from a crystalline form—pure crystalline form of ammonium nitrate.

Agent Burmeister said that this was significant because, in explosives such as dynamites, emulsions and water-gel explosives, "Generally speaking, it's the crystalline form of the ammonium nitrate that's present in these products." So, "based on this elemental profile, it was consistent with originating from a prilled form of ammonium nitrate" (and not from a dynamite or a gel or an emulsion type explosive).

The Defense
On cross-examination, Agent Burmeister acknowledged that, at some point after testing was completed on the wood paneling piece, the ammonium nitrate crystals disappeared. He said that this could have occurred as a result of testing or possibly because of the wood getting too much handling. The Defense pointed out that this "disappearance" had made it impossible for them to conduct their own scientific tests and questioned whether the crystals ever really existed, or if the wood had become contaminated with ammonium nitrate due to improper handling procedures.

The Defense addressed this also with another of their witnesses. Dr. John Lloyd, a charter chemist and fellow with the Royal Society of Chemistry in England and an officer in the Order of the British Empire (an honor bestowed by the queen for contributions in forensic science) . Formerly, he was the senior principal scientific officer on a special merit personal promotion to the United Kingdom's Government Home Office of Forensic Science Service. He suggested that the wood panel (Q507) should have been put into a desiccator to preserve the crystals.

The Prosecution
Prosecutors called witness Linda Jones to testify. Ms. Jones was the Principal Forensic Investigator with "the Forensic Explosives Laboratory, which is part of the Defense Evaluation and Research Agency, which is part of the Ministry of Defense in England." She is also an Officer of the British Empire. She said her lab is responsible to "examine devices suspected of being explosive devices that have been made safe; finds of materials and equipment, for example, suspected bomb factories; post-explosion scenes, and debris and the residue analysis." She said she conducts "some of the most serious investigations that occur on the mainland of Great Britain."

In March 1996, Ms. Jones was asked by the U.S. Government to act as a forensic explosives consultant and provide a second opinion on the crime scene. She said she has "reviewed Steven Burmeister's finding with respect to Q507 and some other of the trace evidence." To make her bomb assessment, she "reviewed video footage, photographs, charts and plans;" she "examined some items from the crime scene;" and she "was briefed by case agents as to the crime-scene management." She said she was given no reports about the blast damage or the type of blast. She did "review plans and drawings of the building that were done prior to the bombing." A portion of her testimony follows which deals with piece Q507:

Q. Now, were you surprised when you learned that Agent Burmeister had recovered ammonium nitrate crystals from Q507?

A. I don't know if I was surprised. I was pleased for him. I—I haven't found crystals, but as Mr. Burmeister explained, anything is possible; that it was a—It was good. Yes, we --

Q. In your work, have you found ammonium ions and nitrate ions when you've studied bombing crime scenes?

A. Yes.

Q. Is that less significant than finding ammonium nitrate crystals?

A. Yes.

Q. What's the difference?

A. Again, the ions -- we can't necessarily say the ammonium and the nitrate come from the same crystal. If we find ammonium and nitrate together in one crystal, we know it's together....

Q. As part of your analysis in this case, did you review Agent Burmeister's work on Q507 and all of his laboratory notes and chromatograms and all those charts that he made?

A. I don't know if it was all, but I examined a lot of them. I examined all his instrumental printouts and some notes that he made, yes.

Q. And have you come to a conclusion about his analysis?

A. Yes.... I concluded that what Mr. Burmeister analyzed were ammonium nitrate crystals....

Q. What causes pitting and cratering on a metal surface?

A. When a...high explosive detonates, bits—very small particles of the unconsumed explosive—but again away from the center of the charge, are going to be flung out traveling at sometimes miles a second, but also fragments of the container that the explosive was in and the surroundings. Now, a lot of these particles and fragments will be very, very small. I mean they'll be fractions of an inch. And this damage is caused by their impacting on the metal surface.

Q. Are they impacting at a very high rate of speed?

A. Yes. They'll be traveling at miles a second.

Q. Is this also consistent with your analysis and Mr. Burmeister's analysis of Q507 of the crystals being pushed out and impelled into that piece of the box?

A. Yes, it is.

"Based on her review of Mr. Burmeister's analysis of Q507," she said that she had "concluded that the bomb most probably contained, or certainly included, an ammonium-nitrate-based explosive."

She also stated that, "provided they had a basic knowledge of explosives and access to the materials, it would be fairly simple" to build the bomb.

The Defense
Dr. John Lloyd, in testifying about Q507, stated that there was scorching evident on the piece and that scorching occurs at about 250 degrees centigrade. Ammonium nitrate vaporizes at about 200 degrees centigrade. (The inference was evident: Since there was scorching on the wood panel, how could ammonium nitrate still be present? In his testimony, Dr. Whitehurst said that, with the prevailing weather conditions after the bombing, it should have been impossible for any ammonium nitrate crystals to have survived. His testimony about this follows:

> *Ammonium nitrate is very hydroscopic--means it picks up water very quickly. I find it an enigma what I'm looking at: that the ammonium nitrate crystal survived in 100 percent humidity, didn't pick up water in that hundred percent humidity situation. (If) there is any humidity at all, they would absorb water, and pretty soon you'd have a little spot of water. You wouldn't have a crystal. (In the lab) when we try to analyze it with the X-ray powder diffractometer, very often it picks up water, with a solution instead of a crystal, and our lab is a very controlled environment.*

4. Unidentified Leg

The Defense
The McVeigh defense team called Dr. Thomas Marshall, retired chief state pathologist in Northern Ireland, to testify. His credentials are significant. He was made a commander of the Order of the British Empire, CBE (one step below a knight), and is a fellow of the British Association in Forensic Medicine, past president of the International Association of Forensic Sciences (the premier English-speaking organization of forensic doctors and scientists), past president of the British Association in Forensic Medicine (the premier organization in the United Kingdom of those people practicing forensic pathology), and past president of the Northern Ireland Medical/Legal Society. He has published over 50 articles or book chapters in forensic pathology, and estimates that approximately 15 percent of the articles were in the area of explosive injuries. Several of the articles have been in the area of injuries caused by bomb devices.

Marshall testified that he has studied injuries and deaths where a terrorist bomb prematurely detonated. He commented, "These bombs are homemade, and they do go off prematurely at times." He said that included ANFO bombs. In examining the files of the Oklahoma City Medical Examiner's Office, he is familiar with a leg that the medical examiner had been unable to identify to any of the victims. He stated,

> *This is an extra left leg.... This must be an extra victim.... 169th victim.... It falls into the category of finding a portion of the body and nothing else is identifiable.... It's a maxim in this work that you always have the minimum number of bodies. You really can't state the maximum number because some can be completely disintegrated...*

Explosions can do funny things. You can have two people side-by-side and one can be disintegrated and killed and the other person only injured.... With the bombs that we have had most in Northern Ireland, the pattern of injury, the distribution of injury on the body can often tell you the relative position of the victim to the seat of the explosion.

He concluded that the left leg must be the 169th victim, and must have been close to the truck bomb. He described a case where a person carrying a bomb was disintegrated except for his penis. The Defense drew the conclusion that the extra leg may have belonged to one of the bombers.

5. The Ryder Truck Key (Q2323)

The Prosecution
The Prosecution called Dawn Hester to the stand. She was a photographer assigned to the Houston, Texas office of the FBI who was sent to Oklahoma City to photograph evidence for the Evidence Response Team. She identified photographs she had taken on 22 April 1995 of a key the FBI said had been found in the alley behind the YMCA building. She said it was "on the side of the alley, near a dirt area with a lot of grass." This key was given an identification number of Q2323.

OKBIC Note:
The OKBIC finds it strange that, in both trials, the Prosecution chose to put the photographer on the stand rather than Mark Young, the agent who, according to Ms. Hester, actually found the key.

The Defense
The Defense asked her the following:

Q. *Do you know how long that alley had been roped off as part of the crime scene?*

A. *No, I don't.*

Q. *Do you know how many civilians had been up and down that alley prior to the time it got roped off?*

A. *No.*

The Prosecution
Ford Motor Company was able to provide the FBI with the key code based on the assembly specifications for the particular VIN. Edward Paddock explained that the lock sets come from Hurd Lock Corporation in boxes. At the time of installation, the lock set is picked out of the box, and the key code is recorded on the specifications.

He said a particular key code could be repeated in ten percent of the lock sets in a particular box; and these boxes would go to the Kentucky plant, which only manufactures F-series heavy trucks, so these lock codes would not be found on any other type vehicles.

The Defense

Mr. Paddock was asked about the key sets on cross-examination. His answers seemed to contradict the testimony he gave above:

Q. *Do you know if Hurd Lock Corporation sold key sets and lock sets to automotive plants for Ford?*

A. *Yes, they did.*

Q. *Do you know if they used some of the same key codes that were provided to the truck plant?*

A. *I don't know one way or the other.*

Q. *So there could certainly be a lot more keys and locks coded the same in that order of 400 that was made to build this exemplar in what you've determined to be the truck at the crime scene?*

A. *I would certainly say that there could be. "A lot more?"—I'm not sure I'd agree with that....*

Q. *You did some research into keys in connection with your work for the FBI, did you not?*

A. *That's correct....*

Q. *And did you determine that the standard key for a fleet truck such as this one would have an H stamped into the head of the key?*

A. *I believe that's correct, yes.*

Q. *Have you had a chance to look at Government's Exhibit 700, a key?*

A. *I've probably seen it, yes.*

Q. *Did it have an H stamped in the head?*

A. *I don't recall.*

Charles Edwards with the Hurd Lock Corporation said that, in the summer of 1996, he was contacted by the FBI and asked to make a lock set for a 1993 F700 truck using Key Code 108B529. He then went to the code charts and wrote down the series of cuts associated with that code and had two keys cut to that code. He explained that the key is built first, and the lock is built around the key. The ignition and door locks use the same key, and the "first six cuts from the tip of the key operate the ignition lock. The last six cuts from the tip of the key operate the door locks. The cuts in the fifth and sixth position operate both the ignition and the door locks...." He was then shown Q2323 which he identified as the same type of Ford 10-bit key that was manufactured in 1993. He testified that, prior to coming to court, he had tried Q2323 in the locks that he had built for the FBI, and it had turned the lock.

The Defense
The Defense tried to cast doubt on the veracity of the FBI by asking pointed questions Mr. Edwards would have no way of knowing, but, presumedly, designed to make the jurors wonder about the same questions:

Q. Do you know where—were you told where Government 699 (Q2323) came from?

A. No, sir.

Q. You don't know how it came into the possession of the FBI at all?

A. No, sir, I don't.

Q. Do you know why it took until 1996 for them to ask you to do this?

A. No, sir, I don't.

Q. Do you know if the key was tested for fingerprints before you were asked to perform your work?

A. No, sir.

Q. Or explosives residue, whether those kinds of tests were performed on it?

A. No, sir, I don't

Q. Did the key that was provided to you appear to have any damage to it, either from abrasives or --

A. None that I could see.

Q. Were you provided with anything associated with the key, such as a Ryder tag or a key chain or anything of that nature?

A. No, sir.

OKBIC Note
During the Nichols' trial, Vickie Beemer (the desk clerk at Elliott's Ryder truck rental agency in Herington, Kansas) testified for the Defense. She said that the Ryder key has a "yellow tag that's got 'Ryder' written on the key chain."

Mr. Edward's testimony continues:

Q. In connection with the work that you did with the FBI, you noticed, I suppose, yesterday that the key that was marked as Government's Exhibit 699 had a Q number on it, Q2323, I believe?

A. Yes, sir.

Q. In connection with your work with the FBI, did you conduct an examination of an automobile-style lock assembly which would be consistent with the ones made by Hurd Corporation for Ford which the FBI identified as Q118?

A. No, sir, I don't believe I ever saw that.

Q. To see if the key would fit that lock?

A. No, sir.

Q. Did you ever examine a door-lock assembly identified by the FBI as Q1183 which appeared to be a Ford-style double-sided lock set to see if the key would fit that set?

A. No, sir, I don't recall doing that, either.

Q. Did you examine a lock assembly identified by the FBI as Q2134, a damaged lock set, to determine whether the key would fit that lock?

A. I don't recall that, sir. Let me say one thing. It seems during my first visit to Denver, they showed me pieces of another lock set, but it wasn't a Ford lock set....

Q. Well, let me ask you this, if I may, Mr. Edwards. Did you ever examine a lock set taken from the scene of the Murrah Building to determine if that key would fit the lock set?

A. No, sir, I didn't....

Q. The work that you performed began in 1996, the summer?

A. Yes, sir.

Q. Do you know when it was that the FBI discovered what the VIN number was?

A. No, sir, I don't know.

E. THE MERCURY MARQUIS

Trooper Charles Hanger with the Oklahoma Highway Patrol was on duty in eastern Oklahoma on the morning of 19 April 1995. At about 10:20 that morning, he was northbound on Interstate-35 in the left-hand lane just north of Perry, Oklahoma where he started to pass a vehicle and noticed that "it was not displaying a tag." He described the vehicle as "a yellow 1977 Mercury Marquis, four-door, with a primer spot on the left rear quarter panel." He pulled in behind the vehicle and turned on his lights to signal the driver to pull over. The driver pulled over to the right shoulder and stopped. The trooper pulled in behind him. He got out and stood behind his door. The driver of the Marquis also got out of his vehicle and started walking toward the trooper. Trooper Hanger said he was able to see both his hands. He told the driver why he had stopped him, and the driver said he had just purchased the vehicle and did not have a tag. Trooper Hanger asked to see his driver's license, and the driver pulled a camouflage billfold out of his rear pocket. As he did so, the trooper noticed a bulge under his left arm, beneath his windbreaker-type jacket. Trooper Hanger told him to slowly pull back his jacket. Direct testimony follows:

Q.. Okay. Physically, what did he do?

A. His jacket was zipped just a little bit. He unzipped it and began pulling it back.... He said, "I have a gun."

Q. What did you do at that point?

A. At that point, I reached for the bulge in the jacket...and instructed him, "Get your hands up and turn around."... I pulled my weapon, and I stuck it to the back of his head.... I said, "Walk to the back of your car."

Q. When you got to the back of his car, what did you do?

A. I instructed him to put his hands on the trunk, to spread his legs, and he did so.... Then I removed the weapon from the underneath side of the jacket...(and) threw it on the side of the roadway.

Q. At this point in time in the encounter, did Defendant McVeigh make any statement to you?

A. Yes.... He told me that he had a clip also on his belt with the—a pouch that contained an ammunition clip.... I removed that clip, also tossed it on the shoulder of the road.... He said, "I also have a knife.". ...I again pulled the jacket back, removed the knife, threw it on the shoulder of the roadway, also.... I asked him why he would be carrying a loaded firearm.

Q. What did he say?

A. He felt like he had the right to carry it for his protection.

Trooper Hanger then placed the man under arrest and placed the clip from the gun, the extra clip and the knife in the trunk of his patrol vehicle. He said he checked the chamber of the gun and removed a .45 caliber Black Talon round from the firing chamber. He described a Black Talon as "a destructive round that when fired into a person, it expands with tentacles and does more severe damage than a normal round to the inner part of the body." He said the other bullets in the two clips contained just "round ball ammunition." He took the man's gun into the patrol car with him.

The driver's license identified the man as Timothy McVeigh. Trooper Hanger then called his dispatcher and asked that a check be done on McVeigh to determine if he had a criminal record or any outstanding warrants. While waiting on this check, Trooper Hanger looked for the serial number on McVeigh's gun. McVeigh quoted the number to him, saying, "VM769." Trooper Hanger told him, "Well, you're close. It's VW769." Trooper Hanger provided the serial number to the dispatcher for a check. He was informed that Mr. McVeigh "was not wanted; that he had no criminal history, and the gun was not reported stolen." He also had the dispatcher check the vehicle identification number (VIN) from the car and the safety sticker. He was told the car was not stolen. The testimony continued:

Q. At this point in the encounter, did you seek Defendant McVeigh's permission with regard to anything in relation to his car?

A. Yes.... I asked him if I could search his car.

Q. What did he say?

A. He said yes.... And then I entered the front seat area of the car—the door was still standing open—looked around the front seat area and also in the glove box, and then I glanced into the back seat and wasn't in there very long.

Q. While you were in the car doing this cursory search, did you notice anything on the front seat?

A. Yes.... There was a blue ball cap, there was a piece of lined writing paper with some writing on it, and an envelope, legal-sized envelope about a quarter- to a half-inch thick.

Q. Did you notice what writing was on the piece of paper?

A. No.

Q. Did you pick up and examine the legal-sized envelope a quarter- to a half-inch thick?

A. Yes.

Q. And was it sealed, or open?

A. It was sealed.

Q. What did you do with the envelope?

A. I left it on the seat.

Trooper Hanger asked McVeigh what he wanted to do with his car and its contents. He was told to just leave it there.

Trooper Hanger then testified that the patrol vehicle he drove had been assigned to him for about 10 months; he had received it new; it had never been assigned to anyone else; he had never transported high explosives or anyone charged with an offense related to high explosives or anyone that he later learned had used high explosives. Testimony then concerned a business card found in the patrol car after McVeigh had been in it. The Prosecution first asked questions to establish that the card could not have belonged to anyone but McVeigh.

Q. When you begin a shift in your squad car, do you follow any routine practice?

A. Yes.... I look around on the floor, front floor, rear floor area to make sure there is nothing laying around that could be used as a weapon against me that may have been left in the car.

Q. Does your review of the inside of the squad car vary at all depending on how you used the car the last time you had it?

A. If you've transported a prisoner, a little more thorough.

Larry Mackey

Q. When you entered your squad car on the morning—or on Saturday, April 22, 1995, to go to work that day, (having been off on Thursday and Friday), did you follow this normal practice?

A. Yes....I looked in the front floorboards and the rear floorboards, the seats, all the area I could see around from where I was sitting in the driver's seat.

Q. Completing your review of the inside of the car, do you discover anything?

A. Yes.... I discovered a crumpled business card in the right rear floorboard of my unit.

Q. All right. And where was that located?

A. Directly behind the front passenger's seat.

Trooper Hanger then said that no one had been in his vehicle since McVeigh's arrest except himself and his wife when he had taken her to lunch on 19 April after booking McVeigh. He said that his wife was not a customer of the business whose name was printed on the card and the handwriting on the back of the card was not hers. Questions regarding the card continued:

Q. All right. And would you read the card into the record, please, the reverse of the card.

A. It says, "Dave," then in parenthesis, "TNT at $5 a stick, need more." Below that is a telephone number, "708-288-0128." Below that, it says, "Call after 1 May, see if I can get some more."

Q. Now, you testified that you found this card on the right rear floorboard behind the passenger's seat. Where was Defendant McVeigh sitting on April 19?

A. Directly in front of where the card was found there in the passenger's seat.

Q. Have you examined the structure of the passenger's seat where Defendant McVeigh was seated?

A. Yes.

Q. If someone is sitting in the front passenger's seat, placed an article from their pocket in the area between the seat back and the seat cushion, what could happen -- would that article be able to pass through to the back?...

A. After looking at the seat, yes, it's possible. It's an open area. You could stick your hand all the way through it.

Q. All right. After you found this business card with the TNT reference written on the reverse side in your car, what did you do with the card?

A. I placed it inside a Noble County court clerk's envelope.... I then took that envelope containing the card to the command post in Oklahoma City and advised what I had and asked that it be turned over to the FBI.

OKBIC Note
This business card was from Paulsen's Military Surplus Company. (It is discussed in testimony on page 90) When Jennifer McVeigh (Timothy's sister) testified, she identified the handwriting on the back of this card as belonging to her brother.

The Prosecution
The Prosecution then changed direction and began a series of questions to show that McVeigh could have driven the distance from the Murrah Building to the location of his arrest within the timeframe that had passed between the bombing and his detainment:

Q. Now, at the beginning of your testimony, you testified that you arrested Tim McVeigh driving north on I-35 between Mile Markers 202 and 203 on the morning of April 19....And I believe you testified that this was 1 mile south from the Billings exit on I-35.

A. Yes.

Q. In anticipation of your testimony here today, did you perform any measurements between the point at which you arrested Defendant McVeigh on April 19 and the place where the Murrah Building once stood in downtown Oklahoma City?

A. Yes.

Q. What did you do?

A. I measured the distance from that location, from the location of the Murrah Building to the point of arrest between 202 and 203, and also timed the amount of time it took to drive from that location to the arrest point.

Q. At what speed?

A. At the posted speed limit that was posted on April 19, 1995.

Q. How far was the point of Defendant McVeigh's arrest from the site of the Murrah Building in downtown Oklahoma City?

A. 77.9 miles.

Q. Driving at the speed limit posted on April 19, 1995, how long did it take you to drive from the Murrah Building location to the place where you arrested Defendant McVeigh?

A. 75 minutes and 15 seconds.

Q. If you leave the site of the Murrah Building at 9:02 a.m. and drove to the post—drove the posted April, 1995 speed limit on interstate highways, where would you be at 10:17?...

A. It would put me at the same spot of the arrest, between Mile Marker 202 and 203 a mile south of the Billings exit.

William Eppright, III works for the FBI lab. He was sent to Oklahoma City on 19 April as part of the Evidence Response Team (ERT) to participate in the search of the bombing area. Then on 21 April, he was assigned to go to the Evidence Control Center, a secured warehouse in Oklahoma City, "to coordinate and receive any possible evidence from a vehicle that was being brought to that location."

The car was brought to the warehouse late afternoon that day on a flatbed trailer. It was Timothy McVeigh's Mercury Marquis. Agent Eppright said it had "a lot of body putty, rust-type material" on the driver's rear quarter panel. He provided the vehicle's VIN (7Z60A613847) from the log he kept of his search that day. Then, he said, "the Mercury was transported to the rear of the warehouse by the operator of the flatbed truck and the tow-truck driver.... And then I secured a perimeter around the vehicle...."

Agent Eppright had photographs taken of the outside of the vehicle. Then, about 6:40 that evening, a group of agents from the Chemical Residue Recovery Team arrived, headed by Agent Steven Burmeister. The car was opened by Agent Burmeister and he was the first person in the vehicle. He had air samples taken and photographs of the car's interior. Then Agent Burmeister removed the items from the car. He handed them to Agent Eppright who labelled and bagged the items. Agent Eppright said he wore cotton gloves and changed them periodically throughout the process. He said he packaged each item individually.

One of the items recovered from the car was an 8½" x 11" white piece of paper that contained handwriting. The court exhibit of the document contained holes that were not on the document when it was recovered. Agent Eppright said the holes were punched in it "in an attempt to conduct a paper examination to possibly—or to match it up with another potential source of paper to compare the two and see if they were the same." He was asked to read the document, which said:

> *Not Abandoned*
> *Please do not tow*
> *Will move by April 23*
> *(Needs battery and cable)*

OKBIC Note
The Government argument is that McVeigh parked his Mercury behind the YMCA on 16 April and placed this note in the car so that it would not be towed away and would be available for his getaway after the bombing on 19 April. Timothy's sister, Jennifer, identified his handwriting on this piece of paper.

The Prosecution
Agent Eppright said that, at 7:00 that evening, he was handed a white envelope from the Mercury and opened it. He first "created a clean work area on the table [by] putting down sheets of 8 ½ x 11" white paper on the table." Inside the envelope he found two stacks of papers with a handwritten notation on the top of one stack. The note said, "Obey the Constitution of the United States and we won't shoot you."

Eppright said that he directed photographs to be taken of the envelope and the papers as he went through the stacks. Excerpts from some of the documents, including pages 61 and 62 of *The Turner Diaries*, are provided below:

> *Staffers, But the real value of our attacks today lies in the psychological impact, not in the immediate casualties.*

For one thing, our efforts against the system gained immeasurably in credibility. More important, though, is what we taught the politicians and the bureaucrats. They learned this afternoon that not one of them is beyond our reach. They can huddle behind barbed wire and tanks in the city or they can hide behind the concrete walls and alarm systems of their country estates, but we can still find them and kill them. All the armed guards and bullet-proof limousines in America cannot guarantee their safety. That is a lesson they will not forget.

Next were presented sheets taken from the envelope that contained clippings that had been cut and pasted to them. The prosecution asked Agent Eppright to read portions into the record. The first was a clipping from "The American Response to Tyranny":

Q. All right. And how does that begin?

A. That begins, "At sunrise, on Wednesday, April 19, 1775 --"

Q. Let me stop you there. You said April 19. What does the printed portion of this document state as the date?

A. The printed portion states April 29.

Q. Has there been a change made?

A. Yes, sir, there has.... The change has been that the 29th has been altered to reflect the 19th.

Q. All right. Go ahead and continue to read, please.

A. "At sunrise, on Wednesday, April 19, 1775, 400 government troops arrived in Lexington, Massachusetts, to disarm the citizens so as to destroy any potential resistance to the growing tyranny of government in that time. About 100 colonists, none of whom had any strictly personal reason for becoming involved in what was about to occur, gathered with their assault rifles on the green just above the bridge. No family members were in jail, neither had they been shot by the British. No economic gain motivated those men to stand against the British forces. No monetary value could have been placed on the risk to life that they faced. They stood, and fought, on principle for their rights and for liberty. And once that historic day-long battle began, farmers and merchants from miles around came to join the fight against the government. How many of us have thought about the brave stand at Lexington—the armed confrontation which started the War For Independence and resulted in the creation of our beloved United States of America? Today, however, most people will not become concerned enough about their freedom to shut off their televisions and look out their doors until something affects them personally and directly. The motto of many American militias was, quote, 'Don't tread on me,' end quote, which was symbolized by a coiled rattlesnake—an animal which when left to exist *peaceably threatens no one but when trodden upon strikes as viciously and with as deadly an "effort" as any creature on earth.*

Another highlighted portion taken from John Locke's *Second Treatise of Government* was read into the record:

I have no reason to suppose that he who would take away my liberty, would not, when he had me in his power, take away everything else; and therefore, it is lawful for me to treat him as one who has put himself into a "state of war" against me; and kill him if I can, for to that hazard does he justly expose himself, whoever introduces a state of war and is aggressor in it.

An excerpt from a more recent article was also read into the record:

The recent 51-day siege and massacre of nearly 100 men, women and children in Waco, Texas, was a crime of the greatest magnitude. It was a cruel, sadistic, brutal crime. It was a crime which violated nearly every article of the Bill of Rights and every civil right of the" rebellious" religious group which lived at that facility. It resembled the burning and obliteration of Christian cities and the annihilation of their inhabitants by Mogul hordes in earlier centuries.

There is no longer any doubt," THE U.S. GOVERNMENT HAS DECLARED OPEN WARFARE ON THE AMERICAN PEOPLE....

However, the enemies of freedom—who are the enemies of America, must be made to know that we will not only resist their evil agenda, their imposed decadence, and their oppression, but we will physically fight! They must know that we will not shrink from spilling their blood. The great Thomas Jefferson, author of the Declaration of Independence and third president of the United States set the example for patriots when he said, quote, "The tree of liberty must be refreshed from time to time with the blood of patriots and tyrants; it is its natural manure."

Other highlighted excerpts read in court follow:

Executions.... They deployed in a military manner against American citizens. They slaughtered 80-plus people, committed acts of treason, murder, and conspiracy . . ."

But no issue has drawn the military into civilian law enforcement like the 'war on drugs.' Under that banner, the government has begun an orgy of seizures that make mockery of the supposed sanctity of private property and constitutional guarantees of reasonable search and seizure, and due process of law. Citizens are given assurances we must surrender a liberty here and a constitutional right there to regain domestic security.

While sifting the foul ashes of Waco, where power gone mad backed Lady Liberty into a corner and shot her in the head, **Soldier of Fortune** *has learned the "drug issue" may be more of a ruse than a reason for this march down the slippery slope toward martial law.*

As the Waco trial slowly unfolded in federal court in San Antonio, testimony by Bureau of Alcohol, Tobacco and Firearm agents, the Gestapo of G-men reluctantly revealed that ATF's raid training was led by Army Special Forces. Reporters ran for the phones, and Army spokesmen confirmed involvement of Green Berets in training some 80 ATF agents, as part of final preparations for the bloody raid on the Branch Davidians' religious compound.

OKBIC Note
Jennifer McVeigh also identified handwriting on the above documents as belonging to her brother.

The Prosecution
Agent Steven Burmeister was the agent in charge of examining the Mercury Marquis at the Evidence Control Center. He and Agent Ronald Kelly actually performed the search. He was asked what the results of the search were, and he answered that "No explosive residues were detected inside the vehicle itself from the swabs that we were taking."

The Defense
The Defense pointed out that, if McVeigh had explosives residue on his hands and clothes, there should have been some residue transferred to the car seats, the door handle and the steering wheel.

F. MCVEIGH'S CLOTHES

The Prosecution
When McVeigh was arrested and taken to the Noble County jail, his clothes and personal effects were held in custody by the sheriff's office. Oklahoma Highway Patrol Trooper Charles Hanger provided the following testimony regarding the process McVeigh's clothes went through at the Noble County Jail.

Q. Once you got to the jail, where did you and Defendant McVeigh go?

A. We went to the booking area of the jail....

Q. Now, during the course of the booking process, did you happen to observe Jailer Moritz holding any items of Defendant McVeigh's property in her hands?

A. Yes.... I saw her holding a pair of earplugs.

Q. When Defendant McVeigh had placed all the items in his pockets on the booking counter, did you see what jailer Moritz did with that property...?

A. She put it in the bank bag....

Q. And at the conclusion of the booking process, did Jailer Moritz ask you to assist her in any way with respect to that process?

A. Yes, she did.... She asked if I would go with him when he changed out his clothing.... I instructed him to remove his clothing and to place them in the bag that he had been given.

Q. Did you see him drop any of that clothing on the floor, or where did the clothing go?

A. It went in the bag.

Q. What happened to the paper bag with Defendant McVeigh's clothing?

A. It was placed on the floor there next to other bags.

Q. What sort of clothing was Defendant McVeigh wearing on his upper body when you arrested him on April 19?

A. He had a lightweight windbreaker-type jacket, was blue in color.... And he had a tan-colored T-shirt with a picture of Lincoln on the front. And on the back, it had a picture of a tree and some writing on it.... He had another light-colored T-shirt that was either dark blue or black, three-quarter-length sleeves.

Q. And the body was white?

A. Yes, light.

Q. Let me show you—Let me ask you—Let me ask you some questions relating to the file room where you left the clothes. What type of security protects the security in the file room where you left Defendant McVeigh's clothing?

A. The same security that protects the whole jail. The jail is a secured area. You can only access it by the elevator which takes a key; and once getting off the elevator, you are confronted with a large steel-barred door which is padlocked. And then also on the stair area—there is a stairwell in the jail, however, that—it also has a large steel door that is locked; and at the top of the stairway is another barred door. However, it does not have a padlock on it.

Q. And where is the file room in relation to these secured locations?

A. It's within the confines of that area that I described.

Q. *Is it in any way accessible to the general public?*

A. *No.*

Q. *Is it in any way accessible to other employees of the court facility other than law enforcement people and jailers?*

A. *No.*

Q. *Now…What was Defendant McVeigh wearing below his waist?*

A. *A pair of faded jeans and some black military-style lace-up boots.*

Q. *Now, what color were the jeans?*

A. *Black*

On 21 April, 1995 shortly after noon, FBI Agent Louis Hupp arrived at the Noble County Jail to fingerprint Timothy McVeigh. He also took McVeigh's belongings into federal custody. Deborah Thompson, with the sheriff's office retrieved his clothes, personal effects, and bedding items and provided them in a cardboard box to Agent Hupp, along with an inventory list that she was asked to type up. Agent Hupp testified that he carried the box with him to the airport and placed it on a seat in the FBI plane that he was flying on. It was the only item in that seat. After this, he had no further contact with the box, which was taken to the FBI lab and examined by Agent Steven Burmeister.

The Defense
When the fingerprints on the fingerprint card and the shavings from underneath McVeigh's nails were analysed, there was no explosives residue found on these items. Defense witness, Dr. Lloyd, found it hard to believe, given the amount of ammonium nitrate McVeigh is supposed to have handled.

The Prosecution
The blue jeans, the windbreaker, both t-shirts and the boots were examined. When Agent Burmeister received them, they were in individual sealed plastic bags. Items found in the pockets (cash, two Bicentennial gold coins, a wallet, a black belt, two lime-green earplugs, a container, a Rolaids packet that was open, and a Casio watch), which had been packaged together, were also examined. He said he cleaned the work area with a solvent and a bleach solution, and put on a clean lab jacket. He put on a pair of gloves, applied a piece of disposable brown paper to the table and took a vacuum swabbing of the area surrounding the work site. The swab was examined and no explosives residue was detected. He discarded the swab, opened his first bag and put on a second pair of gloves. He said he changed his gloves as he handled different testing equipment and clothing items. He first examined the items for any visible particles, then did a solvent extract looking for any organic explosives. No residues were found on the wind-breaker or on the boots.

The Defense
Dr. Lloyd, in his analysis of the test results on the boots, said,

> I find it very surprising that anybody could have handled the quantity of ammonium nitrate that has been alleged and not become contaminated even with a single prill or a single particle. I think that is quite remarkable.

The Prosecution
On the blue jeans, Agent Burmeister concentrated on the pockets because they are "high-traffic areas." He cut the pockets away from the jeans, marked them for left and right, and did a solvent extract.

He said that the solvent extract "is usually a larger volume of the solvent. That large volume needs to be reduced down to a smaller volume, and so it's dried down to a concentrated solution.... That concentrated solution is then examined with the instruments...." Whenever he sees a certain explosive present in one test, in order to confirm it, "we have to go to another test with equal sensitivity."

In the left pocket of the blue jeans, he identified nitroglycerin and a finding of "being consistent for the presence of" PETN. He said there could be three possible reasons for the presence of nitroglycerin: (1) "Nitroglycerin can be found in some heart medications and nitroglycerin patches, (2) "It's present in ammunition which is found in weapons, and anyone who is a shooter or goes out to fire weapons can actually develop nitroglycerin and get it on their clothing" and (3) "Nitroglycerin is present in explosives, and anyone who is exposed to an explosive that would contain nitroglycerin could get it onto their clothing."

In the right pocket of the jeans, he said he found nitroglycerin and also PETN. PETN is not found in nature; it is only found in high explosives. It is "a white, crystalline, powdered explosive in its raw form, very much like table salt or sugar." He explained that "a commercial product that contains PETN in a powder form is considered det [detonation] cord, in which there is a liner down the center of this powdered explosive; and it's wrapped on the outside with some sort of cloth or plastic coating... looks like string—or rope, rather—is about the best way to put it. And if I were to cut that rope, down the center of it, is this powder. And the powder itself is loose. It's not compacted or casted. And so if you cut it, it's going to flake around in a little powdered form; so it's easily transferred into the air." When asked what would occur "if you were working with a cut section, trying to attach it to a blasting cap or detonator, he answered that "the PETN powder will be dispersed onto your hands." He said more PETN was found in the right pocket than in the left pocket, based on "a semi-quantitative analysis.". He speculated that if a person were right-handed (which McVeigh is), "you would have more activity into a right pocket with your hand; so I would consider that that right pocket would have more explosive placed into it.

PETN was also found on the T-shirt with the blue arms, somewhere on the lower half of the shirt. Agent Burmeister said he conducted numerous checks on the shirt. The following testimony occurred:

Q. What is the significance of using that many machines or instruments to identify PETN on Mr. McVeigh's T-shirt? What does it tell you?

A. Well, it tells me that the levels were definitely there in identifiable levels and that each technique cross-checked the other technique, so it was a positive finding.

Q. Now, you said "identifiable levels." Do you do any kind of quantitative analysis in explosive residue examinations?

A. No.

Q. Why not?

A. One, finding it in a particular object—to me, a quantitative level doesn't mean anything in the sense that if I do conduct a quantitative analysis, I would have to conduct that in the known area each time in the same type of conditions....If I go even larger, I've increased the concentration; or we can go conversely and go smaller. The levels are going to change.

The Defense
Dr. Lloyd said that an "analysis should determine or estimate as far as possible how much of the detected substance is present." The following testimony took place:

Q. And what's the purpose of quantifying your results in trace analysis?

A. Oh, quite simply and obviously, the evidential significance of the trace depends on how much there is of it....

Q. Why?

A. Any laboratory which handles explosives is inevitably going to acquire some level of contamination. It may be very small. It may be very high. One can't make assumptions about it. It is something which has to be experimentally determined.

Q. And once you determine what the level of your background contamination is, then what can you do with that information?

A. It will provide with you a guide of what you should consider to be significant in your questioned samples. Given that you have determined the quantities in those....

For example, a person who had been in recent contact with explosives might be contaminated with a substantial amount of explosives. He might be contaminated with a very small amount if the contamination was an event that had occurred sometime ago. Of course one can't be precise, but at least it is of some assistance to an investigator to know these things....

If, for example, one was working in a laboratory where background levels of contamination were of the order of ten nanograms, then if one obtained quantitatively a result of ten nanograms on a specimen, then clearly one could not accept that as a valid result. It is really too near -- or it is on the base-line level. One would expect to see substantially more than ten nanograms on your questioned sample if you are going to say this is a significant result.

The Prosecution

The second T-shirt was the one with the writing on it. Agent Burmeister said he conducted four tests and identified PETN on this shirt also.

The package with the items from McVeigh's pockets were not given a "Q"-number at the lab, but were labelled "also submitted." Agent Burmeister said he got a general reading on these items which was positive and decided to give the earplugs further examination. The earplugs were "foam-rubber-type objects that are designed for placing into the ear, and they're sort of in a cylindric—a tubular-type shape, cylindrical-type shape" that can be "molded to fit inside someone's ear..." He said that the reason he examined these particular items was because

> *they would be a good surface for the handling of an explosive.... High explosives would be absorbed very readily into this material. And obviously, if you're handling it to place it into an ear or something like that and if it's on your fingers, it would be transferred to that particular object....*

Agent Burmeister said he found three residues on the earplugs: nitroglycerin, EGDN and PETN. He explained his conclusions:

> **Nitroglycerin**...*if we look at the nitroglycerin, we're back up to the same level with the nitroglycerin as being possibly from a propellant.*
>
> **EGDN**
> *EGDN is a material which is often added to dynamites for temperature regulation for cold weather use; so EGDN in combination with nitroglycerin now sort of elevates the interest level of nitroglycerin. Those two in combination to me suggest a dynamite.*
>
> **PETN**
> *PETN alone obviously is in the same category as before, something from a det cord, for example.*

Agent Burmeister said that EGDN and PETN are not the kind of substances that you would commonly find in public areas. He was asked what the significance was of finding these three residues on a single item. He answered,

> *I think it indicates that the likelihood of contamination is small....These are diverse items, and they're only found in that one particular specimen....there is really no possibility that contamination could have come into play....*

He said he based this conclusion on several different factors:

(1) *the exposure that people would have had to high explosives,*
(2) *the environment at which it was collected,*
(3) *the vessels at (sic) which it was collected in,*
(4) *the type of explosives that we're actually looking at.*

Agent Burmeister continued:

All of the explosives that we know have what we call a vapor pressure, and the vapor pressure is a phenomenon as to how much vapors are actually emanating or coming off of a particular object. Some materials such as nitroglycerin have high vapor pressures, where vapors are coming off pretty readily. PETN has a very low vapor pressure, so there is very few vapors actually coming off of the surface. So as far as vapors being transferred, it would be unlikely. More so, it would actually be the particle itself being moved around. [Furthermore], it's my opinion that it would not transfer through the paper bag in several days…..The same for the plastic bag.

The Defense
The Defense questioned why, if PETN were found in these bomb components, none was found at the bomb scene.

The Prosecution
Linda Jones (English explosives expert) addressed this question in her direct testimony:

Q. Now, in these post-blast investigations, is it common to find high-explosive residue at a bombing crime scene?

A. With the large explosive devices—for example, the truck bombs that contain thousands of pounds of improvised explosive—then it's fairly rare to find residues that we can specifically say have come from the explosive.

Q. Why is it so rare?

A. A number of factors. One, because there is so much damage that the—the best pieces for residue recovery are going to be—have come from fairly close to the explosive; so if you've got a very big bomb, those big—those best pieces are likely to be shattered into very small pieces, and they may not be recovered or recognized. There is also the complication that there is a lot of contamination of items by dirt and debris at the scene. For example, there will be a lot of dust. In general, a lot of dirt.

Q. And what about if a device functions properly? Would most of the explosive and the explosive components be consumed?

A. Yes, they will….

Q. Are there certain explosives that can be used in an explosive that you would think would be even less likely to be recovered at a bombing crime scene?

A. If we talk about these large truck bombs, yes. There would be the boosters and the initiation system.

Q. If... detonation cord were used as part of the booster or the initiation system, would you think it would be likely to recover PETN residue at a bombing crime scene?

A. I've yet to find it; and I know some of our big bombs almost certainly contained detonating cord.

Q. So were you surprised when you learned that in the Oklahoma City investigation there was no PETN recovered or no EGDN or no RDX or any other high explosive like that?

A. No, I wasn't surprised in the slightest.

The Defense
On cross examination, the Defense pointed out that Agent Burmeister had placed the box of items on the floor, which could have transferred any contaminants from the floor to the box and onto the table. His records did not show that he had subsequently tested the box. Burmeister admitted that there is no written policy for examining the box, and he only makes an annotation if the test shows a positive reading for contamination. The Defense pointed out that, since there is no notation when the test shows negative, there is also no record of whether or not the agent actually tested the box.

English Chemist Dr. Lloyd did not agree with Agent Burmeister's conclusions. His testimony in this regard follows:

Q. Do you agree with the findings of Special Agent Burmeister with respect to the forensic testing of the earplugs?

A. No....I do not accept the presence on the earplugs of PETN. The results that were obtained were a GCECD, which was a negligible response. And GCECD, in the conditions used, is a technique that is of very little value to the detection of explosives. There was a very weak GC/Chem response. The GCMS was negative. The LCMS was negative. It is not reasonable that it could be claimed that this result is consistent with PETN.

Q. What are the earplugs made of?

A. They're made of foam plastic.

Q. Are you familiar with Dr. Robin Hiley's work regarding DNPNT?

A. Yes, I am.... It's used as an additive in foamed plastics, particularly polyurethane, to cause the plastic to foam.

Q. What findings did Mr.—Dr. Hiley make with respect to DNPNT and forensic testing?

A. He found that by GC/Chemiluminescence techniques it was confusable with PETN and RDX.

Q. When you say "confusable," what does that mean?

A. That they would give rise to a response that could be mistaken for these explosives, depending on the conditions.

Q. Have you seen anything performed—any tests performed by the Federal Bureau of Investigation on these earplugs to determine if the PETN they were finding was in fact the result of the earplugs mimicking the PETN?...

A. I haven't—I have seen no tests. It's possible that the GCMS might have picked it up; but if it was present in small amounts, which evidently it was, I think that is perhaps unlikely.

Q. Now, who is Dr. Robin Hiley? We've been talking about him.

A. He is in Linda Jones' laboratory. He's responsible for the research unit there.

The Prosecution
Agent Burmeister was asked about an international conference the FBI conducted in 1993 where explosive residue analysis and protocols were discussed. (Protocols refers to written procedures and parameters.) He gave the following testimony:

Q. During that conference, did you discuss the explosive residue protocol that you and others had created?

A. One of the things that we tried to do with that particular conference and symposium was to try to develop an actual international protocol, one in which we could all agree on as being the best one. It's kind of difficult to do with some international guests in particular, some countries in South America which did not have the type of instrumentation that we had. So it was kind of difficult. But what it allowed us to do is actually present our explosive residue protocol and allowed people in the audience to discuss it, and it was a healthy meeting.

Q. You did that back in 1993?

A. Yes.

Q. Did you make changes to your protocol based on the comments you had received from others?

A. *The modifications were very small. Our protocol was agreed, and it was well received.*

Q. *Do you continue to review your protocol as you're conducting tests through the years?*

A. *Yes. It's a protocol that's evolving as we go along, almost on a day-to-day basis.*

The Defense

Dr. Whitehurst testified that "protocols" the FBI claimed to have had in place from 01 April 1995 to present and dated 19 December 1996 were, in fact, lab notes and a first draft of protocols he tried to help establish but which were never finished. Some of the concerns at that time were that the carpet in the area was vacuumed (which puts particles into the air), but not shampooed; doors into the area were not locked and egress was available; people in the explosives unit sometimes went to the bomb range, then came directly into the lab. Whitehurst said that often they would

> *come back from the bomb range and go into the Explosives Unit with the clothes they've had on at the range. There is a high likelihood that they've brought explosive residues back from the bomb range, and so if you put something on that floor, there is a high likelihood that you're going to pick up some contamination from the floor.*

In May 1995, while working as a supervisor in the FBI lab, Dr. Whitehurst did a study to determine contamination in the lab. His study found residues of PETN and RDX in the evidence handling and storage areas. He wrote a memo to Agent Burmeister with attachments. One of the attachments was a list of organic compounds that may be found in gun powder (bullets), with PETN being one of them.

Dr. Whitehurst told about another study done in 1992 to determine how long EGDN would last on blue jeans. A group from the lab went to the FBI Bomb Range at Quantico and blew up an explosive close to the jeans that were hanging on a clothesline. The blue jeans were placed in plastic bags. Other jeans with no EGDN residue were put into other bags. The bags were put together and stored for about four years. When the contents were removed, all of the jeans had EGDN on them. Therefore, some explosives residue can travel through air and from bag-to-bag or box-to-box. No other residues were found on the blue jeans; however, another residue was found on the box. The following testimony transpired:

Q: *What do you mean?*

A: *We hadn't used it. The box was a brand new box out of a stack of boxes. It didn't make sense. The data was consistent with the presence....of PETN being on the box*

Q: *On the outside of the box?*

A: *Yes, on the outside of the box.*

Q: *Where was it stored?*

A: It was stored on top of some bookshelves up over....close to the ceiling in my office.

Dr. Lloyd, the English chemist, then explained controls that are in place in both Belfast and in Ms. Jones lab: There is total exclusion of anyone with recent explosives contact. They have a weekly monitoring and cleaning program. Upper limits for contamination have been established; and, if those limits are breached, work is stopped.

The Defense then attacked the FBI's credibility. They pointed out that Burmeister's superior, David Williams, had concluded early in the investigation that the bomb was made of ammonium nitrate without any conclusive proof to back the claim. The FBI lab report stated that a bottle of 98% nitromethane had been found at Nichols' house without any reference that it had been found in model airplane fuel sitting next to a box containing model airplane parts.

OKBIC Note
In a report from the U.S. Department of Justice (DOJ) Inspector General (IG), the FBI lab was highly criticized for taking evidence out of context and using it to incriminate a defendant—just as with the model airplane fuel above. As a supervisor in the FBI lab, Frederick Whitehurst first highlighted this problem to upper management; and when no corrective action was taken, he contacted the IG office. He later testified before the U.S. Senate, and was subsequently reprimanded and suspended. (See Chapter 9.) This information was not made known to the jury.

The Prosecution
David Williams, FBI-certified as an examiner of hazardous devices and as a tool mark examiner, was assigned as the principal examiner for the bombing crime scene in Oklahoma City. He prepared the final FBI report of all areas based on dictation by the various agents.

The Defense
The Defense made the point that Agent Williams had prepared reports for areas in which he had no training or expertise, i.e. metallurgy, paint analysis, DNA, finger-printing, and tire tread analysis. He said that, in Oklahoma City, he did not actually search for evidence; he functioned as a coordinator. Each team leader was responsible for collecting and preserving their different areas of the crime scene. Not all team leaders were from the lab. Back at the lab, he gave directions to put his initials on all evidence checked into the lab—rather than the initials of the actual persons who checked the items in. Defense pointed out that this procedure prevents the Defense from knowing who actually performed the work and from being able to question that person.

G. THE BOMB COMPONENTS

According to the Government, the bomb that exploded in Oklahoma City was an ANFO bomb made of ammonium nitrate and fuel oil. However, what prosecutors presented at trial was actually an ANNM bomb made of ammonium nitrate and nitromethane. The Daryl Bridges' phone card (owned by McVeigh and Nichols) shows numerous calls to locations that sell these ingredients: farm supplies, chemical companies, hobby shops, fuel suppliers and race-tracks. Through these calls, the

Government was able to make a case that Nichols and McVeigh bought the products necessary to build the bomb.

The Prosecution
Linda Jones, the English explosives expert, said "from all the aspects I examined, I concluded that the bomb was a very large bomb; and as a rough estimate, it would have been likely to have contained between, very approximately, 3,000 and 6,000 pounds of a mid-velocity-range explosive—high explosive."

The Defense
During cross-examination, Agent Burmeister with the FBI admitted that ammonium nitrate could be found in "dozens" of different explosives, so there is no concrete proof that ammonium nitrate fertilizer was used in this bomb. The Defense also made the point that no other explosive materials such as blasting caps, detonator cord, or nitro-methane fuel were found at the bomb scene.

The Prosecution
The prosecution presented numerous witnesses in their attempt to prove that McVeigh and Nichols obtained the bomb components. Their accounts follow:

1. Ammonium Nitrate

Ammonium nitrate is a fertilizer and is used in bulk on farms; therefore it can be bought at farm supply stores. It can be bought in prill or powder form and can be high-grade or low-grade. When bought, there is no marking on the bags to identify which type it is. Farmers can fill out a tax exempt form for large purchases and do not have to pay tax on the sale.

The Prosecution
The Government attempted to show that McVeigh and Nichols bought two tons of ammonium nitrate and stored it in a storage shed until they were ready to use it. They called witnesses from Mid-Kansas Co-op who testified to selling some large quantities of the fertilizer.

Robert Nattier, president and general manager of Mid-Kansas Co-op in Moundridge, Kansas for the past 20 years, testified. The company carries petroleum products and miscellaneous farm supplies, such as feed, herbicides and fertilizer. The fertilizers are sold as dry products, liquid and anhydrous ammonia. In 1994, Mid-Kansas Co-op sold only low-grade ammonium-nitrate fertilizer. The only markings on the bag read "ammonium nitrate fertilizer, 34-0-0" (which means the bag contained 34 percent nitrate, zero percent phosphate and zero percent potash). The company orders fertilizer and does not know if it is high-grade or low-grade. Nattier did not know the difference between the two types. The bags were marked "explosives" and had a yellow symbol indicating this substance was an oxidizer.

Nattier described their service/sales policies. They accept cash, checks or credit cards. They have a three-ticket receipt system: white copy goes to the main office, yellow stays at the place of sale and pink copy goes to the customer.

He identified two yellow receipts for ammonium nitrate sold to "Mike Havens" from the McPherson, Kansas branch. This is an urban branch and sells to many walk-in customers. The first sale discussed was on 30 September 1994 for forty 50-pound bags (1 ton) at a total cost of $228.74. The salesman was Jerry Showalter. The second receipt was dated 18 October 1994 for the same amount of fertilizer at the same cost. The salesman was Rick Schlender. In both cases, "Havens" was not a member of their co-op and paid cash.

Nattier also explained the process of filing a Kansas tax exemption form in order for a customer to deduct the six percent sales tax from their purchase. Few cash-sale customers ever fill out a tax-exempt form. This customer did not fill one out.

The Prosecution
The first ton of fertilizer was sold to Mike Havens by Gary Showalter who had worked at the Mid-Kansas Co-op in McPherson, Kansas for 18½ years. He said the store had between 75 and 150 customers per day. On the morning of 29 September 1994, he received a call from the Galva, Kansas branch (seven miles east) asking if his store had two tons of ammonium nitrate. He told the other salesman that his store only had 40 bags or one ton. The next afternoon, a man came in to make the purchase. He mentioned having inquired the previous day about the ammonium nitrate. Showalter did not recognize the man and said he knew 85-90 percent of his regular customers. The man identified himself as Mike Havens. Havens told him he was planting wheat at a small farm he had just purchased in Flint Hills, Kansas, which is near Council Grove. Showalter advised Havens that ammonium nitrate might not be a good idea since this type of fertilizer can damage seeds. Havens said he and his father had done it before and it had worked well for them in the past. Showalter said farmers have not used that technique since the mid-to-late '60's. He felt there were better, more economical ways to fertilize a wheat field. Havens made the purchase in cash for forty 50-pound bags and paid the sales tax, even after Showalter told him about tax exemptions. Showalter does not remember loading the fertilizer, but Havens did ask him when he could purchase another ton. The transaction lasted 3-5 minutes.

Showalter described Havens as being "Caucasian, …late 30's, early 40's, …5'9" to 5'10," …average build, … dark brown or black [hair], …relatively short and well-trimmed," He was "clean-shaven" and was wearing "slacks and a sport shirt." Showalter could not remember if Havens wore glasses or not. He said Havens was definitely not Timothy McVeigh.

The Defense
The Defense questioned why Mr. Showalter's memory was better at trial than it had been shortly after the bombing:

> Q. And you told them [the FBI] at that time—this is a week after the bombing—you had no recollection of any large purchases there at the co-op other than the NCRA buying ammonium nitrate. Tell the jury what NCRA is.
>
> A. NCRA is National Co-op Refinery Association. It's an oil refinery in town….

Q. And then three days later on Sunday, Agent Coffey with the FBI—excuse me—with the ATF and Agent Budke, B-U-D-K-E—remember him?

A. I remember the meeting....

Q. Okay. And he—By that time, you all had located the ticket for September 30. Is that correct?

A. That's correct....

Q. And you told him you had no recollection of that transaction?

A. I told him that I made the ticket out, it was a cash sale, not check, and it was for 40 bags of ammonium nitrate.

Q. And you told him you didn't have any idea who Mike Havens was and couldn't give a description?

A. That's correct.

Q. Okay. And you told them that based on these sequence of sales tickets that you were the one who likely loaded this order up because you didn't write up the subsequent sales ticket?...

A. That's possible, yes....

Q. Now, this was May, '95. You're telling the Government you don't have any recollection of the transaction. Is that correct?

A. That's correct....

Q. Okay. And then you started meeting with the FBI agent, Mr. Hersley over here, and Mr. Mendeloff. Is that correct?

A. That's correct.

Q. Okay. Can you give us an estimation of the month and year?...

A. Well, let's see. I believe it was about a year ago last October. That would be '96....

Q. Okay. And was it at that time that you began to recall the event and could describe the person?

A. It was during those meetings, yes....

The Prosecution
Fred Schlender, manager of the Mid-Kansas Co-op in McPherson, Kansas, sold the second ton of ammonium nitrate to "Mike Havens" on 16 October. At the trial, he described Havens as being "a white male, I would say approximately 35, 40 years of age, around 5' 8" to 6-foot tall, slight build. I'd say 165 to 175 pounds.... Hair color would have been a light brown, short hair but not a crew cut, but light brown in color." He also said the customer did not have any facial hair and was dressed in jeans, a shirt and (he believed) a coat.

Mr. Schlender said the customer drove a dark-colored pick-up truck with a light-colored camper shell on the back. The trailer was red and was

> a pickup-style trailer, ...where you cut the—behind the cab between the bed. They cut that off and attach a hitch so the bed of the truck can be used for hauling purposes.... I believe there was a—It was—I would say a 1960's Ford-type trailer, pickup trailer. And it had white-type lettering on the end gate.... The trailer was in good condition.... There was no rust that I can remember. And nothing cut off on the back side.

The Defense
The Defense produced an FBI 302 report which was a record of the original FBI interview with Schlender. They asked Schlender to read the report aloud as part of the court record. The 302 report read as follows:

> Schlender reviewed his daily planner. Schlender had general recollections of the sales transaction reflected in receipt no. 96582. Schlender indicated he could not be a hundred percent sure of his recollection, but he did recall two white males making that purchase. Schlender advised the white males arrived at the co-op driving pickup truck with a camper shell, pulling a trailer. The driver of the truck came into the cooperative and made the purchase. The passenger of the truck remained in the truck up until the truck was brought around and backed up to the warehouse. At that time the passenger exited the truck and watched the loading of the fertilizer into the trailer. Schlender described the individual making the purchase approximately six foot, medium to slight build, light brown hair, mid-30s to 40 years of age. Schlender believes the purchaser may have been wearing a coat, but he could not specifically recall the color of the coat. Schlender spoke briefly with the purchaser who indicated he was going to use fertilizer to plant his wheat. Schlender advised this was somewhat unusual in that it had rained on October 17, 1994, and that farmers generally do not plant immediately after a rain. Schlender also indicated that most of the farmers he deals with use liquid nitrogen fertilizer in planting wheat.
>
> Schlender briefly saw the passenger as he loaded the fertilizer into the trailer. Passenger exited the truck to watch Schlender load the fertilizer. Schlender could recall the passenger being a white male approximately the same age, mid-30s or a little older, with clean-cut hair.

Schlender described the truck as late 1970-style possibly Dodge three-quarter-ton, four-wheel-drive pickup truck. Schlender believes the truck may have had a Kansas license. Schlender could not recall seeing any rust or prominent paint on the truck, indicating that it appeared to be in good condition for a truck of that age.

Schlender described the trailer as a bed portion of a single-axle pickup truck. Schlender believed it was made from a 1960 model, three-quarter-ton Ford pickup. Schlender could recall the trailer was red in color with white Ford lettering on the tailgate. Schlender indicates the trailer was in fairly good condition with a bumper and standard taillights. Schlender could not recall if the taillights were working. Schlender could not recall the trailer having a license tag.

The Defense

The witness had a sketchy or changed memory of the truck and buyer. The driver or Mike Havens was not wearing glasses. (Nichols always wears glasses.) Also the salesman remembered Havens had a Kansas tag on his truck. (Nichols had a Michigan tag at that time, and did not get a Kansas tag until April of 1995.) They continued to cross-examine him about the truck:

Q. When you described the vehicle the first time, you said it was a Dodge; is that correct?

A. Said it possibly a Dodge.

Q. And you said it was a four-wheel-drive?

A. Possibly a four-wheel-drive.

Q. And three-quarter-ton?

A. Possibly three-quarter-ton.

Q. What year Dodge did you estimate it was?

A. Late 70's.

Q. And you described the individual at the first meeting, didn't you?

A. That's correct.

Q. Said he was 6-foot tall?

A. Said he was approximately 6-foot tall.

Q. Now you're changing that today in front of the jury to 5-foot-8 to 6-foot?

A. I'd say approximately 6-foot tall in my mind.

Q. 5' 8" to 6-foot?... Didn't tell them 5' 8" to 6 feet?

A. No, I did not.

Q. What other description did you give of the vehicle that you recall? You've read those memorandum of interview.

A. Yes, I have. It was dark-colored with a light-colored topper.

Q. And what else?

A. As we described earlier, late 70's style Dodge three-quarter-ton, four-wheel-drive.

Q. And the trailer: What did you describe the trailer as at that first meeting?

A. It was a red pickup-bed-style trailer.

Q. Okay. And it was a Ford cut-off trailer?

A. Possibly a Ford.

Q. And it had white lettering?

A. Possibly white lettering on the tailgate....

Q. How did you describe the vehicle in front of the grand jury?

A. Described it as a dark-colored, possibly a dark-blue Dodge four-wheel-drive, three-quarter-ton pickup.

Q. Well, you left out the word "Dodge" when you went to the grand jury, didn't you?

A. Excuse me. I did.

Q. Did the prosecutor suggest to you that was a problem because Mr. Nichols' vehicle was a GMC?

A. No, they did not.

Q. But when you got in front of the grand jury, you only described it as a blue vehicle?

A. I said dark-colored, I believe....

Q. (In regard to the cash sale on the ammonium nitrate) *you told them* (the grand jury) *no, it wasn't unusual, didn't you?*

A. I told them no, it was not unusual for the practice of fertilizing, going with the wheat.

Q. And further, the grand jury asked you if you talked to the person about where he was farming; is that correct?

A. I talked to the customer, yes.

Q. And you told them you had no conversation relating to where he was farming?

A. I did not recall at that time.

Q. Yes. You recalled that later after meeting with the prosecutors?

A. I recalled that later going over the events that occurred many times, in my own mind.

Q. Now, in the original FBI interview, you suggested to them that if they gave you a line-up of pickup trucks, you could pick out the pickup truck.

A. I wanted to be certain of my choice, sir.

Q. And when this agent and the prosecutor met with you, did they show you a line-up of pickup trucks?

A. No, they did not.

Q. Did they show you a series of photos of one pickup truck?

A. Yes, they did.

Q. And whose pickup truck was that?

A. They did not say whose it was.

Q. And it was all the same pickup; is that correct?

A. Yes, it was.

Q. And you made a choice that, yeah, that looks like the pickup?

A. I said I believed that was the pickup....

Q. How—When was the second meeting you had with this agent and the prosecutor after September, '96?

A. It would have been in October of '96.

Q. *Did they bring more photos of the same vehicle to you?*

A. *They did.*

Q. *Were you able to pick out the vehicle at that time?*

A. *First time I looked at the photos, I did not agree with the view. I couldn't see through the back window looking in the side view of the pickup, so I told them I wasn't certain. But they brought other photos at the second time.*

Q. *Now, was this a line-up with different trucks in it, or was this more photos of Mr. Nichols' truck?*

A. *More photos of the same truck....*

Q. *When was the next meeting?*

A. *Next meeting was in January of this year....*

Q. *Did they show you photos of the pickup?*

A. *Did not show me photos of the pickup at that time.*

Q. *Did they show you photos of the Donahue trailers?* [Meaning trailers used at the Donahue ranch where Nichols had worked.]

A. *Did show photos of the Donahue trailers.*

Q. *What else did they discuss?*

A. *At this time, I don't know of any other things we discussed, sir.*

OKBIC Note
In April 1996, Agent Hersley, other agents and prosecutors went to Mid-Kansas Co-op and purchased ninety 50-pound bags of Triple 13 fertilizer and loaded them in the back of a Ryder truck. No explanation was given for why this was done.

OKBIC Note
Anyone buying this amount of fertilizer would not have known if the substance were "high grade" or "low grade" ammonium nitrate, since it is not marked on the bags. Low grade absorbs fuel oil which will cause the ammonium nitrate to be less explosive, if too much is used; high grade is in prill form and needs to be crushed or ground.

The Prosecution
FBI agent Joanne Thomas was called to the stand. She was a back-up photographer for the FBI. She assisted in the search of Nichols house on South Street in Herington, Kansas, and in

photographing evidence found. Her two areas of responsibility in the search were the kitchen and the living room. She testified she had found one of the receipts for the ammonium nitrate in a drawer in Nichols kitchen. It was being used as a wrapper for two $50 gold pieces. She stated she "found some, what looked like coins--some in stacks and some in a plastic bag"--behind some tea towels. Among them were "two Elizabeth $50 gold coins" wrapped in a pink slip of paper with tape, which was discovered to be the "Mike Haven's" ammonium nitrate receipt. The coins appeared to be collector's items.

2. Fuel Oil

A truck bomb requires some kind of fuel to mix with the fertilizer. The Government contends that racing fuel, nitromethane, was used, and that McVeigh and Nichols also checked into the availability of anhydrous hydrazine, a pure form of rocket fuel, to mix with the nitromethane. The Prosecution pointed out that the book, *The Turner Diaries*, told that it could be purchased at racetracks, hobby shops and chemical companies.

The Prosecution
McVeigh had a high school friend named David Darlak. They both graduated in spring, 1986 and maintained their friendship, seeing each other once or twice a week. They would shoot guns, play basketball, ride three-wheelers, and just generally "hang out." Darlak was working for a sign painting shop, Rosewood Signs, in Tonawanda, New York. He lived in Wheatfield, New York with his family, including a brother named Michael who was involved as a mechanic on a friend's modified dirt racing car. McVeigh lived in Pendleton, New York with his father. In 1988 Darlak and McVeigh purchased nine acres of land "with lots of trees" on the side of a mountain in Humphrey, New York, about 50 miles south, for $7,000. Darlak said McVeigh wanted to build a bomb shelter on it. They kept the land until late 1992.

In the summer of 1988, McVeigh joined the army, and Darlak joined later in the year. They were not stationed together, but did correspond. McVeigh was honorably discharged in early 1991. Darlak was dishonorably discharged in April 1992 after serving 10 months in military confinement for an alcohol-related automobile accident. After release from the military, Darlak lived in Wheatfield with his family, and McVeigh lived in Pendleton with his father. They resumed their friendship and saw each other frequently. Darlak was again working at Rosewood Signs, and McVeigh was working for the security company.

Darlak said that shortly after coming home, McVeigh gave him a copy of *The Turner Diaries* to read. Later that summer, McVeigh asked for it back so he could give it to someone else to read. Then, that fall, according to Darlak, McVeigh left without saying goodbye, and he did not hear from him again for two years.

In the fall of 1994, Darlak said he received a call at work from McVeigh. McVeigh told him he was in Kingman, Arizona working at "Value Hardware." He asked Darlak if he knew where he could buy some racing fuel. He said no, and McVeigh asked him to try and find out and purchase some for him. Darlak asked why, and McVeigh told him he had to go—that he was at work, and asked for his home phone number. Darlak was living with his sister then, and gave McVeigh that number. He said that a couple days later, there was a message on the answering machine to "forget about the fuel oil." He said he never saw or spoke to McVeigh again.

OKBIC Note
According to the list of phone calls on the Bridges' calling card there was a call made to Rosewood Signs on 28 September 1994. This call was placed at 1:51 p.m. and lasted nine minutes and 42 seconds. The call to Darlak's sister's home occurred on 01 October at 4:44 p.m. and lasted one minute, 44 seconds. These calls came from Nichols' house in Marion, Kansas—not from Kingman, Arizona.

The Defense
Darlak told the Defense that he had first been contacted by the FBI a couple of days after the bombing and had interviewed with them about 10 times since. The Defense asked why it was that the timeframe of the telephone calls from McVeigh in Arizona had changed from the time Darlak testified before the grand jury. At that time (09 May 1995), Darlak told the grand jury that the call had come "roughly one year before." The Defense implied that his testimony had been influenced by the FBI. They asked him,

Q. Which would have been May of 1994?

A. Correct.

Q. One year prior?

A. Correct.

Q. To the time that you appeared. So you told the federal grand jury that the telephone call from Mr. McVeigh had come in the spring and not the fall.

A. I said roughly a year, and it wasn't roughly a year; it was shorter than that.

Q. Well, it was roughly less than half of that, according to what you're saying today.

A. Yes.

Q. So did you change your mind at some point in time about when the phone call had come?

A. I didn't change my mind. I more clearly remembered exactly when it was.

Q. Your recollection improved over time?

A. Yes, it did. I was pretty—May was just a couple months after the bombing, and I was pretty shaken after that.

Q. Did your recollection improve over time during the course of your meeting with FBI agents?

A. It improved over time thinking about it.

Q. Did the FBI agents urge you that the phone call had been made in the fall --

A. No, they did not.

Q. -- of 1994? Did they talk about that subject with you?

A. Yes, they did.

Q. Were they concerned about the timing of the call?

A. I don't know if "concern" is a word that I would use.

Q. Interested?

A. Interested, yes.

The Prosecution
Linda Juhl was a customer service representative with Mid-America Chemical Company in Oklahoma City, which sold wholesale and retail, mostly to water treatment plants and plating companies, but also did special ordering for people. She testified that she received a phone call in the fall of 1994 from a man looking for anhydrous hydrazine. She told the caller that they did not carry it, but might be able to order it. She offered to have one of the salesmen call him back, but he declined and did not leave a phone number.

OKBIC Note
The Darrell Bridges' calling card shows four calls to Mid-America chemicals in Oklahoma City on 26 September 1994: (1 & 2) from the HRK Resale Shop in Marion, Kansas at 10:43 and 10:45 a.m. Not answered: (3) from the HRK Resale Shop at 10:48 a.m. for one minute and 55 seconds; and (4) from the Kahns Amoco payphone in Lincolnville, Kansas at 3:30 p.m. for one minute and 03 seconds.

The Prosecution
Glynn Tipton was a salesman and warehouse manager with VP Racing Fuels in Manhattan, Kansas. His company sells fuel for high-performance racing vehicles including cars, motorcycles and go-carts. On 01 October 1994, he was at the Sears Craftsman Nationals race just south of Topeka, Kansas selling fuel. A person who called himself "John" visited him, asking about availability of 55-gallon barrels of anhydrous hydrazine, which was not available. John also asked about the cost of nitromethane, which was $1200 per drum. Each drum weighed approximately 500 pounds. John

said he was moving from Junction City to Salina, Kansas and had no phone. Tipton gave him a business card and told him to call back Monday afternoon for information on the anhydrous hydrazine. John left after this conversation. Tipton pointed out McVeigh in the courtroom as being "John." He said he was 90 percent certain of the identification.

At the time, Tipton did not know what anhydrous hydrazine was and had to check with Wade Grey in their company's chemical division. Grey told him that, "...if you mixed nitromethane with anhydrous hydrazine...it would become a bomb or be explosive." Grey thought Tipton should call the ATF about this, which he did.

He said that a week or two after this, he received a call from "John" asking if he had had any luck obtaining the anhydrous hydrazine. He asked John if he was intending to mix nitromethane and the anhydrous hydrazine, and was told no. He told John that his contact was unable to provide any anhydrous hydrazine; but, if he wanted to leave a phone number, he would continue to look. John said he still did not have a phone.

OKBIC Note
The Bridges' phone record shows a call to VP Racing Fuels in Manhattan, Kansas on 07 October 1994 at 4:21 p.m. lasting two minutes and 13 seconds.

The Prosecution
Stuart Doyle with the FBI in Kansas was called to testify in regard to an interview he held with Glynn Tipton on 01 May 1995. The interview was in connection with the above credit card call. Tipton told Doyle about his encounter with "John" on 01 October 1994 at the Sears Craftsman Nationals. Tipton first described John as 5'8" to 5'10", then said about 6'0" when he remembered John and he were not on the same eye-level while talking. Doyle said he had shown Tipton two photos: McVeigh and Nichols. He did not tell Tipton that "John" was shown in that line up nor did he ask Tipton if he had seen any television coverage of the bombing. Doyle related their conversation wherein Tipton told him that John had slender features in the face, that he couldn't be sure that McVeigh was John—but they resembled each other. Tipton said that John had a "very slender build, narrow face, jaw line, two-to-three days growth (of beard), short hair." Tipton could not make positive identification of John from the pictures, he said, because he was shown a photo of McVeigh without facial hair.

OKBIC Note
In her testimony, Lori Fortier (Michael's wife) said that in early October 1994, McVeigh and Terry Nichols showed up in Kingman, Arizona and stopped by their place. She said McVeigh looked different than she had ever seen him before:

Q. *Describe how he was dressed.*

A. *He was dressed like in a Harley shirt, and he had a bandana around his head; and he looked like a biker. His hair was grown out, and he had a scruffy beard.*

OKBIC Note
Lori said that a few days later, Nichols went to Las Vegas. The Bridge's phone record for this period shows that, on 06 October, two calls were made from Fortier's house to Nichols' ex-wife Lana Padilla's house in Las Vegas. Calls were made from Fortier's house to fuel companies on 07 October, and another call to Lana Padilla's was made on 11 October from Fortier's house.

The Defense
The Defense tried to cast doubt on the identification Mr. Tipton made of McVeigh. That testimony follows:

Q. And do you recall telling the agent on May 1, 1995 that the pictures—two pictures you looked at—one of them the person's face was thin like John's but that you could not be positive that McVeigh was the subject known to you as John?

A. That is correct.

Q. Did you see Mr. McVeigh's arrest on television and when he was led out of the Noble County Jail in the orange jumpsuit?

A. I believe at one point in time I might have seen him in the orange jumpsuit.

Q. Now, when you saw him in the orange jumpsuit, did you assume at that time that that was the person you knew as John?

A. No....

Q. Okay. Did you ever see the depictions of John Doe 2 or John Doe 1 prior to May 1, 1995, a composite sketch?

U. S. Attorney Pat Ryan

A. I believe I remember seeing some, yes.

Q. And at any time prior to May 1, 1995, did you call the FBI to tell them that you thought the person that you were viewing on television as Timothy McVeigh might be the person you had encountered in October named John?

A. No, I did not call anybody.

OKBIC Note
Mr. Tipton was called by the Prosecution to testify in the McVeigh trial, but not in the Nichols trial. The Defense, however, did call Mr. Tipton as a witness during the Nichols trial.

The Prosecution

Timothy Chambers from V. P. Racing Fuels attends auto races to sell fuel to the contestants. He drives an 18-wheel tractor-trailer filled with fuel and sets up at the racetrack. He testified that, on 21 October 1995, he was at the Motorplex racetrack in Ennis, Texas, and was approached by a man who wanted to buy three 55-gallon barrels of nitromethane. The man told him that he "and a bunch of buddies get together every year at this particular race and they purchase nitromethane." The man told him "about Harley bikes that they have in Oklahoma City." Mr. Chambers said that the man paid another VP employee, Brad Horton, for the fuel, and was given a service pass to bring his truck into the pit area. About 45 minutes to an hour later he returned in a pickup that was not shiny, and had a faded-white camper shell on it. Mr. Chambers used the electric lift to pick up the barrels, then scooted them onto the pickup truck. He said that this individual also bought a used siphon pump. He was then asked to describe the individual. The following testimony occurred during Nichols' trial:

Q. What did he look like?

A. Probably I'd say about 5' 11" or so. He had a medium build to him, like a blond—sandy blond-colored hair. Cheekbones kind of stuck out a little bit, you know, out this way, you know. They were stuck out; and then his nose wasn't like a real long nose. It was like at an angle—angle nose.

Q. Do you remember anything about his eyes?

A. Kind of close together. I don't know eye color or anything. Just kind of close.

Q. Did this man's face remind you of anything or anyone?

A. I mean to me, being from Texas, I kind of just figured he looked kind of like a possum, so--

Q. Do you remember what this man was wearing?

A. Probably blue jeans, T-shirt top. That was --

Q. Would you take a look at Terry Nichols, the defendant sitting over there?

A. Uh-huh.

Q. Was that the man who purchased three drums of nitromethane from you on October 21?

A. No.

Q. Was the customer older, or younger than Mr. Nichols?

A. Younger. Younger than him.

The Prosecution asked Mr. Chambers if he had ever driven from Pauls Valley, Oklahoma to Ennis, Texas. He replied that he had and that the distance is approximately 170 miles. The Prosecution then produced a phone record of the Bridge's calling card showing a call at 3:21 p.m. on 20 October 1994 from the Amish Inn in Pauls Valley to check on the balance remaining on the card. The Prosecution contended that McVeigh and Nichols, in Nichols' truck, stayed at the Amish Inn in Pauls Valley on the 20th, then drove to the racetrack in Ennis, Texas the following morning and bought the nitromethane.

The Government contends that Nichols rented a storage shed in Herington, Kansas to store the nitromethane. Helen Mitchell with the Mini-Storage was called to testify. She identified a contract made out for storage Unit #2, signed by "Shawn Rivers" with an address of Route 3, Box 83, Marion Kansas (Nichols' Address). The rental agreement was signed on 22 September 1994, and four months' rent was paid at that time. On 04 October 1994, another four months' rent was paid, which paid through 22 May 1995. (At Nichols' trial, The Defense stipulated that the handwriting for Shawn Rivers was that of Timothy McVeigh.)

The Prosecution called FBI Agent Gary Witt to provide testimony about his visit to the storage shed where the nitromethane was allegedly stored. His testimony follows:

Q. At some point, Mr. Witt, were you also asked to go to the storage shed at Industrial Park in Herington, Kansas?

A. I was.

Q. And which storage shed were you asked to look at?

A. Storage Space No. 2 at the Mini Storage Shed Partnership in Herington, Kansas....

Q. And what did you observe on the floor?

A. Observed these three semicircle patterns, rust-colored, that were in direct line with each other across the width of that space....

Q. What did you do with respect to these three semicircles that you saw on the floor of the shed?

A. I measured dimensions of each of them.

Q. And tell us about how you went about measuring these semicircles.

A. Used just a contractor's grade tape, and I came up with dimension of 22 1/2 inches for -- which was identical for each of them. But it was difficult getting a precise measurement because the lines were not precise. They were -- they just were irregular, but that was approximate.

Q. Now, following the measurements at the Herington shed, were you asked to go to VP Racing Fuels?

A. Yes.

Q. What were you asked to do there?

A. At the VP Racing Fuel in Manhattan, I measured a standard barrel that was labelled—blue barrel—nitromethane racing fuel.

Q. Let me show you what's been marked as Exhibit 2097..... How does that compare with what you viewed at VP Racing Fuels?

A. It's exactly the same.

Q. What did you do with respect to this barrel of nitromethane at VP Racing Fuels?

A. I measured the outside and inside dimensions of the barrel to determine the diameter, as well as the height of that barrel from rim top to bottom rim.

Q. And what did your measurements reveal?

A. With respect to the outside measurements, on the diameter, I came up with 23 inches. The inside measurements were 22 3/8 inches, and the height of that barrel was 34 3/8 inches.

The Prosecution

FBI Agent William Bodziak, an examiner of documents, footwear and tire-tread impressions, said he went to the Mini-Storage, Unit #2, in Herington, Kansas on 22 April 1995 to examine tire tracks. He described the tracks:

> The tracks were double tire tracks, meaning that the left side of the vehicle had two tires mounted side-by-side. On the right side, they had two tires mounted side-by-side, so there would be a total of four tracks in the rear of the vehicle. They were very deep. They had—They were perpendicular to Shed No. 2. They terminated before reaching the wall of Shed No. 2, and they were directly centered on Shed No. 2.

He said that these wheel alignments are "common to trucks which are equipped to carry heavier loads." He was not able to recover any tread markings from the tire tracks because it had been raining before he got there and had washed out the tread markings. He said,

> the tracks were deep. The bottoms of the tracks were wet. They were darker in color.... The depth indicates that the weight of the truck that made them was significantly heavy enough in conjunction with the soil condition to leave this deep of a track.... They were much more—much deeper than any other track in the entire area at the Herington Industrial Storage Shed.

Agent Bodziak also examined the distance between the tire tracks. He said that this distance can vary on different types of vehicles. He measured "the distance between the center point of the two tires on the left and the center point of the two tires on the right"...to determine if a vehicle "could be excluded as having made that track or could be considered as one that possibly made that track." He said that,

> *you measure from the center of the tires, the center of the double tires; in this case, the ridge between the two tires. You would find the dead center of that point and measure directly across the vehicle at a 90-degree angle to the center ridge or center point between the right two tires.*
>
> *...Other measurements can be made, and I made two. One is the outside-to-outside.... [This] would be the outer edge of the left tire to the outer edge of the right tire.... The third one was from the inner edge... of the inner tire to the inner edge of the other tire.*

He said he obtained another Ryder truck in Alexandria, Virginia that came from the same purchase order, with the same specifications, as the truck that was rented from Elliott's. Its sequence number was "123 vehicles prior to the one that was rented at Elliott's."

He made measurements of the track width of the Alexandria truck and compared the two truck measurements. The distance between the center-to-center measurement on both vehicles was 73 ½ inches. The outer-to-outer measurements from one side of the truck to the other were 92 inches on the tire treads in Herington, and 92 3/8 inches on the Alexandria truck. The inside-to-inside measurements were 55 inches in Herington and 54 3/8 inches on the Alexandria truck. He said that the center-to-center measurement is the most reliable, and the differences between the other two measurements is not significant because of "the erosion that occurred."

He said he also measured the distance from the tracks to the door of the shed to determine if there was sufficient clearance for a truck to back up and for someone still to be able to walk between the truck and the building, as follows:

> *At the Shed No. 2 in Herington, I measured the distance between the ends of the tracks on the left side as 10' 2" and the ends of the tracks on the right side as 9' 7" between the ends of those tracks and the shed of wall—the wall of Shed No. 2.*

He also measured the distance on the Alexandria truck from the rear wheel to the rearmost portion of the truck. This measurement was 8' 5 ½". His calculations showed that there was sufficient space for a 20-foot Ryder truck "to fit into the space between the ends of the double tire tracks and the wall of the shed"...and that "there was still 20 1/2 inches remaining on the left side as you faced the shed and 17 ½ inches on the right side as you faced the shed."

The Defense
On cross-examination, the Defense concentrated on the fact that the ground was wet and, therefore, the truck would leave deeper tread marks.

Q. ...So the wetter it is, the lighter the vehicle has to be to leave a track that deep and that wide. Right?

A. No, I don't—I don't think you could say that. That's certainly possible, but I don't think you could say that in all instances.

Q. Well, then, it's not your testimony that if it isn't wet—If it's completely dry and the ground is hard, it's not your testimony that that truck, given the—with the same weight, is going to leave a track that deep, are you?

A. No, certainly the wetness would be a part of it.

Q. And you didn't check how long it had been raining or how much it had been raining, did you?

A. Just that there was considerable rain.

Q. I'm sorry. My question was did you check to find out how long it had been raining and how much it had been raining?

A. No, I didn't.

Q. And so you can't say what the weight was of the vehicle that left the track. Right?

A. I couldn't say even if I did know that information.

Q. If it was wet enough, a truck that was empty could leave a track that deep, couldn't it?

A. I couldn't say that.

Q. Didn't check, did you?

A. I don't think there's a basis for determining that.

Q. Did you run your truck over some wet ground to find out?

A. I don't have a truck.

Q. You rented one, didn't you?

A. In Alexandria, Virginia, not in Herington, Kansas.

Q. Did you run it over some wet ground?

A. No. The ground would not be the same as it was in Herington.

Q. Did you go to Herington, Kansas, and rent a Ryder truck and run it over some wet ground?

A. I wouldn't be able to reconstruct the exact conditions.

Q. Sure. Now, when you go out there and you make your measurements and you take your molds and you take your photographs, one thing you don't learn by doing all of that is when that track was put there, do you?

A. That's correct.

Q. You can't tell the ladies and gentlemen of this jury how it got there.

A. No.

Q. Can't tell them who put it there.

A. No.

Q. Can't tell them anything other than the fact that there's some tracks there that fit one of many types of vehicles that may be out on the road.

A. That's correct.

During closing argument, the Defense stressed that Agent Bozniak had never checked with Budget, Penske, or any other truck rental company to see how many trucks on the road had that axle width. They also made the following points:

> Now, Mr. Mackey said a little while ago about the storage sheds and the lack of ammonium nitrate that, if you will recall, the person from the—from the ammonium nitrate sales said they were on a pallet wrapped in plastic and that's why there is no ammonium nitrate prills on the bottom of the bag or poured out of the broken bags in the storage sheds in Kansas. Did William Bodziak tell you, did he testify, about the tracks that most certainly would have been left by the large vehicle that would have had to pick up a 2,000-pound pallet of ammonium nitrate and put it in the back of a Ryder truck? No, he didn't. Now, assuming that somebody picked up that 2,000-pound pallet of ammonium nitrate all by himself and put it in there, in that truck, without breaking open the plastic, I guess that makes sense; but it doesn't make sense, ladies and gentlemen, because there is no Hercules in this case. Something had to pick that pallet up, or somebody had to break that plastic open and move those bags. If they moved the bags, the ammonium nitrate would have fallen off onto the floor and they'd have found it; but they didn't. Now, I guess they can come back in a minute and say these guys are so smart that they swept out the storage units, cleaned it all up, did

some forensic testing to make sure that there was no PETN, EGDN or any other type of explosive residue left before they shut the door and drove off. Logic, ladies and gentlemen. It doesn't make sense. It's not right.

OKBIC Note
Peter McDonald, an ex-Firestone tire engineer who wrote the book on tire track identification used by law enforcement agencies, reviewed the FBI photographs taken at the Herington storage shed and at Geary Lake at the request of McVeigh's lawyers. At the trial, he was seated with McVeigh at counsel's table during the Prosecution's presentation of tire tread analysis testimony, and was available to testify if the FBI agents had overstated their case. He addressed his findings in an article, "Tracks tell more about Okla. bombing," in the Tire Dealers Newspaper, dated 02 March 1998. His conclusions were that,

1. Mr. Nichols' GMC pickup had one tire of a different design from the other three; the position of the odd tire was consistent with the tracks in the FBI photo.

2. One of the vehicle's tires was mounted backwards, with the Department of Transportation code number showing on the outside—a detail also consistent with that seen in the photo.

3. A portion near the shoulder of one of the newer tires had untrimmed rubber protruding from its surface—rubber put there by pin vents used during the mold phase of the manufacturing process.

4. In addition to tracks of the rental truck and Mr. Nichols' pickup, the Harrington [sic] photo shows the imprint of an all-season passenger radial.

5. Tracks of vehicles other than those used by the two convicted conspirators also can be seen in the photo taken at the nearby Geary Lake park.... The FBI's Geary Lake photo suggests the presence of an unidentified second truck as well as unknown passenger cars.

In regard to the FBI investigation, Mr. McDonald said, "I can't say they botched it. But I've never heard they did anything to follow up. And the defense isn't in a position to do that kind of stuff."

OKBIC Note
There were numerous calls the Government says were made in connection with trying to buy the ingredients for the bomb. They pointed out that, after 21 October, no other phone calls were made to chemical companies. (For a list of phone calls, see Appendix, p. .)

OKBIC Note
Since the call to Rosewood Signs and to David Darlak's sister were made from Terry Nichols' house, and since it was McVeigh's voice both times, McVeigh was obviously in Kansas rather than Arizona on 29 September and 01 October 1994, contrary to what Darlak said McVeigh told him.

The Defense
The Defense suggested that someone else may have had access to the Bridges' calling card and used it without permission; however, the Prosecution shot down this theory with witness John Kane, executive vice-president from AMNEX, the company that supplies service for the Spotlight debit calling card which "Daryl Bridges" used. He told the jury that "Daryl Bridges" had never requested a new PIN number as is normally done if a PIN has been compromised.

H. ROGER MOORE ROBBERY

Roger Moore and his girlfriend, Karen Anderson, lived in Royal, Arkansas. His wife, Carol, lived in Florida. Timothy McVeigh met Roger Moore on the gun show circuit and they became friends, with McVeigh staying at Moore's ranch and working there for a period of time. Anderson, was also Moore's partner and travelled with him helping him at the gun shows. In 1994, Moore was no longer attending the gun shows, but Karen Anderson was still working them and was living at Moore's home.

In the early hours of 05 November 1994, Moore claims to have been robbed. He said he had stepped outside his house when he saw a man in a black ski mask, holding a gun. Moore was ordered back inside where he was blindfolded and tied up. He heard the man rummaging through the house and thought that there might have been a second individual with him, but he could not be sure. Moore was untied long enough to help load his possessions into the back of his van, then was retied. The robber left in Moore's van with Moore's gun collection, gold coins, jade Tiki dolls and other miscellaneous items.

The Prosecution
The Government claims that Terry Nichols committed this robbery because neither he nor McVeigh had jobs at the time; they had already spent $2,775 for nitromethane; and they would have more expenses coming up. According to Michael Fortier, McVeigh told him that "Terry did Bob" and used a pistol grip shotgun. ("Bob" was an alias used by Moore.) The Prosecution also submitted that Nichols had no alibi for the time of the robbery. His wife was in the Philippines and wouldn't return until 17 March 1995. He had quit his job at the Donahue ranch in Marion, Kansas on 30 September 1994 to go on the road with McVeigh; therefore, he had no job and he also had no home. He wasn't at any gun shows or buying surplus items at the DRMO. He had opportunity to drive to Royal, Arkansas, rob Roger Moore, and drive back to the Sunset Motel in Junction City, Kansas where he was staying that night. Nichols had stayed at the Sunset Motel several times previously; but, on 05 November, he told motel owner, Mesbah Chowdhury, that he was checking in for a friend. He filled out the registration card for "Joe Kyle" with a Michigan address and took the key—an attempt, says the prosecution, to "cover his tracks."

According to the Prosecution, the Bridges' calling card record shows that Nichols tried to call McVeigh at this father's house in Pendleton, New York the following morning to tell him about the success of the robbery. McVeigh, however, had probably not yet returned from a gun show he was attending in Ohio, because the phone call was quite short. Later that day, records show a call to Lana Padilla's work number; the call was forwarded to her home. Then, from the Tru-Value

Hardware in Manhattan, Kansas, there were two calls to Pendleton, New York again for about a minute each time, then another call to Padilla's house. McVeigh, apparently tried to return the calls. Records show a call from the Convenience Mart in Pendleton, New York to the pay phone at the Tru-Value in Manhattan. The call was not answered. McVeigh tried again on 07 November, but received no answer. (At the McVeigh home in Pendleton, the FBI later found a piece of paper in Jennifer McVeigh's handwriting with Nichols' name and the phone number of the Tru-Value store.)

Nichols then purchased another $100 money order for the Daryl Bridges' phone card. (The money order has his handwriting and fingerprints.) The Prosecution questioned why Nichols would need the phone card since he would be leaving for the Philippines in two weeks, and the card could not be used there. They pointed out that Nichols was obviously still working with McVeigh and the additional money on the calling card was for McVeigh's use while Nichols was gone.

When the FBI searched Nichols' home, Agent Jerry Tucker found a Marion National Bank note pad. In it were payment stub records for the Daryl Bridges' phone card. These records showed all payments were made by money order, as follows:

17 Feb 94	$ 50
22 Aug 94	$ 50
29 Sep 94	$ 30
07 Nov 94	$100
21 Jan 95	$100
14 Feb 95	$100

A few days later, Prosecutors said, Nichols rented another storage shed (Unit #37) at Boot's U-Store-It in Council Grove, Kansas (He had already rented unit #40 at the same facility on 17 October under the name "Joe Kyle.") This time, he used the name "Ted Parker" and gave his address as Decker, Michigan. An employee of Boots U-Store-It, Sharri Furman, testified that she handled the rental for "Ted Parker," and that he had been driving a blue pickup truck with a white camper shell. When she saw Nichols' picture on television in mid-May 1995, she recognized him as being "Ted Parker" and called the FBI. The Prosecution pointed out that there had been no change in Nichols' status since he had rented Unit #40 on 17 October. The only reason he needed another storage shed was to hide the property he had stolen from Roger Moore. (Later, when interviewed by the FBI, Nichols told them that he had used the name "Joe Kyle" as an alias. He did not provide them with the name "Ted Parker" because, according to the Prosecution, Nichols was afraid the FBI might find the storage shed for "Ted Parker" and then find the articles stolen from Roger Moore.)

FBI Agent Joanne Thomas searched the living room closet at Nichols' house and found a notebook labeled "Fat Little Wireless Neatbook." Inside were handwritten notations including "PO box @ Manhattan." Mary Jasnowski, team lead at the search, also identified the book. She was asked to read notes from a page in the book:

Yes. It says, "Joe Kyle," K-Y-L-E, the number sign, "40. Coun," C-O-U-N slash "Gro," G-R-O, slash "Kan." Then there's a number 10-17 over 94, plus sign, 12-17 over 94.

And then on the next line is "37 Ted Parker," P-A-R-K-E-R. 11 dot 17 dot 94 plus 01 dot 31 dot 95. And then "ditto" on the next line.

The Defense stipulated that "Shawn Rivers" was Timothy McVeigh and that "Joe Kyle" was Terry Nichols. However, on cross-examination, the defense established that Nichols had stopped using the storage sheds when he moved into his house about a month before the bombing.

That evening, 07 November, prosecutors say Nichols checked into the Travelers' Motel in Manhattan, Kansas, using the alias "Ted Parker" from Lum, Michigan, with the Michigan license tag of YX1640 (again transposing the six and the four.) He went to the Mini-Mart that evening and, at 5:59, checked his calling card balance. Back at the motel, he called the McVeigh number in Pendleton again. The conversation lasted one minute and 14 seconds. McVeigh went to the Convenience Mart in Pendleton and called the Mini-Mart in Kansas seven times without success. Then finally, at 7:22 that evening, from the motel, Nichols called McVeigh at his father's home and spoke to him for six minutes and nine seconds.

McVeigh had been friends with Roger Moore and was familiar with the house and its contents. According to the prosecution, McVeigh had told Nichols what to expect at Moore's home and had helped him plan the robbery. Much of Moore's property was later recovered at Nichols' house in Herington, Kansas when the FBI searched it on 22 April 1995: The quilt on Nichols' bed was identified as Moore's--further substantiated by Marife Nichols' testimony that she had not bought it; nor had it been on the bed when she left to visit the Philippines in September 1994. Other items belonging to Moore were also found at Nichols' house, including guns, ammunition, four army motion detectors, and two safe-deposit keys.

Kevin Nicholas, McVeigh's friend in Michigan, attended three gun shows with McVeigh in 1994 and 1995. He said McVeigh used the alias "Tim Tuttle" at the gun shows. The last one Nicholas attended was in January 1995 at Grand Rapids, Michigan. At that show, he said McVeigh was selling tracer ammunition which had been sent to Nicholas' house in Nicholas' name through McVeigh. McVeigh told Nicholas that he had obtained the tracer rounds from a gun dealer in Arkansas named "Bob" and that he had "screwed him some way out of some money or something," and that is why he did not have it delivered to himself directly. Nicholas also said McVeigh referred to "Bob" and said, "...he'd be an easy guy to rob because he lived way back in the sticks and, you know, there was woods around his house and stuff." The Defense asked him if the conversation about tracer rounds had occurred in 1992 when Nicholas was married to Jo Lynn rather than in 1994. Nicholas said no.

The Defense
The Defense claimed that the "robbery" at Roger Moore's house was actually an insurance scam. They called Moore's neighbors, his insurance agents, local sheriff officers and private investigators to testify. Much of the testimony shows that Moore told different stories to different people at different times.

Moore's next-door neighbors for five years were Martin Walton "Walt" Powell and his wife Verta (called "Pudge"). Their son, Lance, lived in a trailer house on their property. Walt Powell was a retired firefighter, and Lance was working for a marina in 1994. Walt said he first met Moore with Karen Anderson. He later met Carol Moore who was introduced to him as Roger's sister.

On the morning of 05 November 1994, Moore rang the Powell's door bell. Mrs. Powell answered the door. She said that Moore rushed in past her and said he had been robbed. He had a handgun in his pant's waist in back. He asked to see her husband, but she told him that Mr. Powell was not at home. Moore then asked to use the phone. On the phone he said he didn't know "how many people." He then asked Mrs. Powell to get her husband, so she called her son, Lance, to come stay with Moore. While she was waiting on her son to arrive, she said that Moore made a couple of more calls. He pulled a card out of his pocket to make the calls, but she did not know if the calls were local or long distance. She said she was about four feet away and he talked low, so she could not hear everything he said.

After 10 to 15 minutes, Lance arrived, and Mrs. Powell went to get her husband who was working at the church on a new sanctuary. Lance said Moore again used the phone after his mother left. He heard Moore say that "they got it all."

Mrs. Powell returned with her husband in about 20 minutes. She heard her husband ask if Moore had called the sheriff. Moore said he had not. Lance testified that Moore said it was because they (the sheriff) couldn't get there in time to help him. Moore told them about the robbery, then called the sheriff. Walt and Lance Powell accompanied Moore back to his house to reconnect his cut phone lines. Lance testified that Moore told them the robbery could have been committed by the Government "'cause they do things like that to keep people in check or intact." Walt Powell said that previously Moore had given him an anti-Government videotape and another on Waco. He had also told him about NATO trying to take over the United States.

Mr. Powell testified that, when they arrived at Moore's house, Deputy Ronald Karchefski from the Garland County Sheriff's Office in Hot Springs, Arkansas was sitting in Moore's kitchen. The prosecution asked Powell the following:

> Q: And did you go up to Mr. Moore's house after the deputies arrived, or before they arrived?
>
> A: After
>
> Q: So, if someone said you went up there before, they'd be wrong?
>
> A: That's correct.

However, Deputy Karchefski testified that he arrived at Moore's home about 11:30 that morning. Moore wasn't home, but he found him at the Powell's house between 11:50 a.m. and noon that day. He said Moore got a phone call and talked for a moment, then handed the phone to the deputy. He took the name and phone number of the caller that he later gave to Captain Sanders from the Investigations Division. The Prosecution said that "someone" had been asked to search the file for that piece of paper with the name and phone number, but was told it was not in the file. He asked the deputy the following:

> Q: *And no one's ever seen that piece of paper. Correct?*
>
> A: *To my knowledge, they haven't.*

The deputy also said that Moore told him he had a live-in girlfriend who was currently visiting in Louisiana; but Moore was not able to furnish any details regarding her address or phone number in Louisiana.

Shelby Terry, a criminal investigator with the Garland County Sheriff's Office, testified to receiving a call at home at 11:35 a.m. on 05 November to go to Roger Moore's home. He testified that a patrol deputy was already there when he arrived. Moore told him that he had seen one person, but suspected maybe a second person had been there also. He said he had been tied with flex cuffs (a wire device used by law enforcement as a second set of handcuffs). Moore was eventually able to work his hands free of them. (Terry said that the "flex cuffs" were thinner than those used by police officers and were actually wire ties that are used to tie batches of cable together.)

Sheriff deputies found Moore's van a short distance away in a wooded area behind his property and Terry searched it about two hours after having arrived at Moore's house. Moore told him where to look in the van for the serial numbers of the guns that had been stolen. Instead of the serial numbers, Terry found cash. A further search found a paper under the bunk bed with the following:

> *Federal agent is my name.*
> *Killing women and children is my game.*
> *I'm from the Government.*
> *I'm here to help you.*

Mr. Terry said Moore told him that when he was confronted by the robber, he asked if he was a federal agent from the ATF. Later he told Terry that he thought McVeigh had robbed him. He told Terry that McVeigh was from New York and was out of Fort Riley, Kansas and had served in Desert Storm. He did not, however, tell Terry that McVeigh had an address in Kingman, Arizona.

At the time of the Moore robbery, Terry Nichols was staying at the Sunset Motel in Grandview Plaza, Kansas (about two miles east of Junction City, Kansas). The owner-manager of the motel, Mesbah Chowdhury, identified registration forms and testified. He said that Nichols had stayed at his motel several times registering in his own name. However, on 05 November 1994 (the day of the robbery), Nichols told Chowdhury that he was renting a room for a friend and registered under the name "Joe Kyle." Prosecutors said this was an attempt to hide his movements on the day Moore was robbed. The Defense in Nichols' trial stipulated that the handwriting was Nichols'.

The Prosecution called FBI Agent Gary Witt to testify in regard to distances related to the Moore residence. Through this testimony the Government tried to show that McVeigh was at a gun show in Ohio and could not possibly be the one who robbed Roger Moore; therefore, according to their point of view, it must have been Nichols—who was within driving distance of the Moore residence. A portion of Witt's testimony follows:

Q. Were you asked to go to the residence of Roger Moore?

A. Yes, I was.

Q. Where is that located?

A. Approximately 6, 7 miles west of Hot Springs, Arkansas, on State Highway 270.

Q. And were you also asked to go to a location that was provided to you where his van was reportedly stashed following a reported armed robbery?

A. Yes, I was.

Q. And generally speaking, where was that location in connection to either Mr. Moore's residence or to Royal, Arkansas?

A. It was in a very secluded area off a narrow gravelled roadway. It was a side road. It was tree-choked— brush-lined area.

Q. Now, are you familiar with the Sunset Motel in Junction City, Kansas, or Grandview Plaza?

A. I am.... It's on a road, a frontage road to I—Interstate 70. It's Flint Hills Boulevard. It would be an area of probably two-to-three miles west of Junction City proper in this small township of Grandview Plaza.

Q. Now, let me show you what has been received in evidence as Exhibit 1757.... You see the date of this registration?...What is that?

A. 11-5-94.

Q. And did that date correspond with the date you had been provided for the reported armed robbery of Roger Moore?

A. It does.

Q. And did you have occasion to...determine the distance, both mileage and driving time, between the place in which the Roger Moore's van was reportedly stashed and the Sunset Motel?

A. Yes....

Q. And how long did it take you to drive the -- from this location in Royal, Arkansas, to Grandview Plaza, Sunset Motel?

A. Approximately 9 1/2 hours. 9 hours and 36 minutes to be exact.

Q. And how many stops did you make along the way?

A. Three.

Q. And how much -- what was the mileage between Royal, Arkansas, and the Sunset Motel?

A. 518 miles, approximately.

Q. If a person were to leave Royal, Arkansas, at 11:00 a.m. on [sic] the morning, would they have sufficient time, according to your calculation, to reach the Sunset Motel the same day?

A. Absolutely.

Q. Mr. Witt, what was the mileage, according to the 1997 Rand McNally Road Map from Royal, Arkansas, to Kent, Ohio?

A. Royal, Arkansas, to Kent, Ohio, just over 900 miles, 909, 910. 909 is what I came up with.

[The Prosecution]: Now, your Honor, we would ask at this time that stipulation with respect to, that's dated October 18, 1997, with respect to Mr. McVeigh in a gun show in the nights...

Judge Richard Match

THE COURT: Okay. It's been stipulated, agreed, and therefore we accept that "Timothy J. McVeigh was at the Niles Gun Show outside Akron, Ohio, on Saturday, November 5, 1994. Akron, Ohio, is approximately 235 miles from Lockport, New York. Timothy McVeigh was a registered guest that weekend at the Knight's Inn Motel in Kent, Ohio, a nearby city to Akron." That was agreed.

Larry Hethcox, a helicopter pilot with the Little Rock Police Department, testified that, in the fall of 1994, he put an advertisement in the paper for a gun he wanted to sell. Moore and Karen Anderson came to look at it. Moore used an alias, but Hethcox could not remember the name he used. Moore bought the gun, a 700 ADL, .308 caliber Remington. After the robbery, Moore called and wanted the serial number of the gun, but Hethcox did not have it and instead gave him the name of the place where the gun was purchased. While on the phone, Moore told him about the robbery. Moore said that the robber had fired his gun outside the house. (In her testimony, Mrs. Powell said she had not heard a gunshot that morning although she had heard shots from the direction of Moore's house at other times.) Moore also told Hethcox that the robber had taken weapons, money and paintings valued at over $100,000. Hethcox saw Moore again the next summer (after the bombing), and Moore asked if the FBI or ATF had contacted him. He answered yes, and Moore commented that the media had treated him badly.

Moore had wanted to hire a private investigator, so an elderly neighbor asked an acquaintance, John Brown, to call Mr. Moore. In November 1994, Brown was working for attorneys in a private consulting and investigation business. He contacted Moore by phone. Brown testified that Moore wanted to hire a private investigator because Moore thought the sheriff was not treating him fairly. No one was working on his case. Moore also felt that someone from the Sheriff's Office might be involved in the robbery. (Brown said he did not accept the case because his time was already obligated to ongoing criminal investigations.)

Richard Reyna, also a private investigator, met with Moore on 30 September and 01 October 1995 at the Sands Motel and Casino in Las Vegas. According to Reyna, Moore told him that "he would not hurt Tim McVeigh and he could not hurt Tim McVeigh;" that only his guns were stolen and he was surprised that the other weapons were not touched. Moore reportedly said that, on the day of the bombing in Oklahoma City, he had more weapons in his home than were found at the Davidian compound in Waco, Texas. On cross examination, the Prosecution elicited testimony that Moore had made it clear that McVeigh was not the robber, but that he suspected McVeigh was part of it; that he could not identify the person; and that he only suspected that there was a second person. On redirect testimony, Reyna said Moore told him that he did not have insurance to cover the loss and the robbery ruined or would ruin him. He reiterated that Moore saw only one person and that person was wearing a ski mask.

Rodney Bowers, a reporter for the *Arkansas Democrat Gazette* in Little Rock, Arkansas, interviewed Moore. Moore told him, "Whatever I was doing for the FBI is f----- up because they [the media] blew my cover." Bowers said Moore felt the Sheriff's Office was not interested in investigating his case, and felt that maybe someone in the Sheriff's Office was involved. Moore questioned the fact that they had found his vehicle so soon--20 to 30 minutes--after the robbery; that it was found two to three miles from his house on an abandoned logging road; and that the list of gun serial numbers hidden in the door panel of his van were missing.

Moore had insured his house and contents with the Jan Dies Insurance Agency in Hot Springs, Arkansas on 18 August 1992. Dies testified that the policy was for a new house in his name only. The application showed the "single" block checked for marital status. Dies recalled that when she asked if he had any luxury items (including guns) that he wanted to insure, he told her no. She, therefore, allowed only $1,000 for luxury items. On 05 November 1994, Moore came to the office to make a claim: $8,700 cash, multiple guns, gold, silver, and precious stones.

On 16 November 1994, an insurance claims agent, Richard Spivey, went to Moore's house to interview him. He tape-recorded the conversation and took photographs. At this time, Karen Anderson was also present. She later provided the FBI with a list of serial numbers for the stolen guns. (Several of the guns found at Nichols' house matched the serial numbers on this list. But, strangely, one of the guns on the list matched a confiscated gun that actually belonged to Nichols. The Defense strongly raised issue over this, suggesting that the list Anderson provided was made to match the guns confiscated in the search of Nichols' home.) During the interview with Spivey, Moore added to the list of stolen items, for a total of 77 firearms (rifles, shotguns, pistols), ammunition, jewelry, "stones", cash, gold, silver, four vibrator detectors, and a video camera. These assets were valued at $63,400. The total covered by insurance was $5,913. Spivey commented that he did not think all the guns would fit in the little closet where they were supposedly stored. During the interview, Moore said he asked the robber, "Are you a Fed?" Moore mentioned three possible suspects for the robbery. Two of the were Timothy McVeigh and a Mr. Trickel. On cross-examination, the Prosecution elicited concurrence that Moore was not in a hurry to get his money; the policy had not recently been taken out; and he was in a financial position to have owned the things he claimed had been stolen. On redirect, the Defense found that Moore had a net worth in excess of $1 million. Also, Spivey said Moore had shown him some silver coins from under his bed that the robber had missed.

A couple of weeks later, Moore called Jan Dies' office. Her daughter, Jan Priddy, who also worked there, told Moore that her mother was with a customer, and she refused to put his call through. Priddy said he became very angry and told her he would be down and "smear her all over the counter." Dies returned Moore's call and said he was aggravated because he was not being contacted like he thought he should be. He felt people were not working on his claim. Dies said that during his visit to her office in November, Moore kept repeating, "The Feds did it." He reportedly showed her a badge, "very official looking in a black case, a flip, looked like a billfold-type thing." He told her "Don't tell anyone I showed you this." He said he was researching, trying to find his stolen guns. He also told her he was going to put explosives around his house--that if anyone came on his property, they would be blown up.

The Defense called Barry Lawrence Ostentoski as a witness. Ostentoski is the son of Lana Padilla and was Nichols' stepson for about six years. He accounted for Nichols' whereabouts for most of November 1994. He testified that Nichols had visited twice in November. The first time was for a few days. He camped in the desert that time. When he left, he went to Zion National Park in Utah. The second visit was for a week. He stayed at the Padilla house and went to the Philippines at the end of the stay.

When Nichols left Padilla's house on 22 November 1994 to fly to the Philippines, he left a letter with her to be opened if he did not return by a specified time. Ostentoski said he had read the letter and, following its directions, had found approximately $20,000 hidden in a kitchen drawer. He said he also had gone to the storage unit noted in the letter and where he saw army-issue camping equipment, skis, boxes, a tent and a gas cooking stove. He also found a briefcase with a makeup kit, a wig and pantyhose inside. One of the items still had the price tag on it. He did not find a ski mask. (The FBI claims to have found a black ski mask in the shed. Ostentoski's mother, Lana Padilla, said that, when Nichols returned from the Philippines, he told her he had used the mask and wig to scare his wife Marife on Halloween; however, Marife was in the Philippines at Halloween, and she testified that she had never seen these items.) Ostentoski said he also found a toolbox. Inside were a handgun and a few tools. He found a cigar box containing jade and boxes with silver and gold coins inside. He stated that these did not surprise him because Nichols always had gold bars and gold and silver coins. (Ostentoski had earlier provided to the FBI a jade Tiki doll from the storage shed which matched a Tiki doll in a photograph provided by Moore.) He also said that in the spring of 1995, his mother told him that McVeigh would be picking up the television that was stored in the garage. On cross-examination, the Prosecution asked if he had looked in the blue pickup with the camper shell. He answered yes. He said he did not remember seeing camouflage clothing, but did see a catalog and some cooking utensils.

The Prosecution
On closing argument, the Prosecution highlighted the reasons why the jury should believe Moore's story about the robbery:

(1) Moore told the police where McVeigh would likely be found.

(2) He called the police week-after-week checking on status.

(3) He demanded the insurance company help find the robbers.

(4) He contacted a private investigator because he thought the Sheriff wasn't doing enough to find his stolen possessions.

(5) One of the guns stolen, a Hornet rifle, had belonged to Moore's father. The rifle had been in Moore's possession for the past 30 years. (This was one of the rifles found in the search of Nichols' house.)

(6) Moore did not need the money. He was worth over $1 million.

(7) Moore would not have given away $60,000 worth of items to get back $5,900 from the insurance company.

I. ROCK QUARRY ROBBERY

The Prosecution
The Government claimed that McVeigh was looking for detonation ("det") cord. They called Gregory Pfaff to the stand. He testified that he met McVeigh in early 1992 when Pfaff was working for Lock and Load Distributors, selling their products at gun shows. They sold special application ammunitions, such as explosive-tip ammunition, tracers, incendiary rounds and prefragmented bullets. They did not sell det cord because it was a highly controlled product. He said that, for the past several years, he had owned the Brooklyn Delicatessen in Harrisburg, Virginia.

Pfaff said McVeigh contacted him in the September/October 1994 timeframe to see if he could get some det cord for him. (Det cord is a hollow tube with PETN inside. FBI Agent Burmeister testified the lab found PETN in McVeigh's pants pockets and on his ear plugs.) Pfaff told McVeigh that he would check into it, but said he actually had no intention of doing so. (The Bridges' calling card showed several calls to the Brooklyn Delicatessen in Harrisburg, Virginia from an Amoco Station payphone in Wamego, Kansas: three calls on 24 September for 18 seconds, for a no answer and one for five minutes, 28 seconds. On 01 October, there were two more calls: the first one for two minutes, 26 seconds and the second for one minute, 56 seconds.)

The Prosecution contended that when McVeigh was unable to buy the det cord, he and Nichols broke into a munitions magazine at the Hamm Rock Quarry in Marion, Kansas on 02 October 1994 and stole items needed to detonate the bomb. The Prosecution pointed out that the quarry was just down the road from the Donahue ranch, and Nichols drove by it every other week on his way to the bank.

Timothy Donahue testified that he had hired Nichols the first week in March 1994 and provided a house on his property for the hiredhand. He said Marife joined Nichols about a month after he moved in. Nichols worked there for about six months. His last day was 30 September, and he quit work around noon that day. Donahue quit work around 7:00 p.m. and went by Nichols' residence. He said he saw Nichols' pick-up truck with a camper shell on it for the first time and a silver car. He identified a picture of McVeigh's 1987 Chevrolet Spectrum as the car he saw. He also said he saw a man working on something, possibly the camper shell, at the back of Nichols' pick-up truck. He identified this man as McVeigh. He said he went inside with Nichols to look at a waterbed Nichols was selling. He wrote a check for the bed and gave Nichols his final paycheck. He said that, during the next two days, he drove by the house at least three-to-four times to see if Nichols had vacated the property yet. Finally, about 7:00 p.m. Sunday evening, 02 October, he saw Nichols leaving. When he went inside the house, all Nichols' belongings were gone, and the only thing left was the waterbed.

The Defense
During cross-examination, Donahue said he was first interviewed by the FBI on 21 April 1995, before he had seen any news coverage of the arrest of Timothy McVeigh. The Defense recounted the description he had provided the FBI at that time: "approximately 35 years old,…five-foot-eleven,…a thin build,…dark hair,…mid-ear length,…a scraggly brown beard, did not have eyeglasses,…(and) sloppy in appearance. During McVeigh's trial, the Defense then asked,

> Q. And didn't you also tell the FBI that if you put glasses on the composite sketch of John Doe No. 1 and changed the hair, it looked like Terry Nichols to you?
>
> A. Somewhat, yes.

The rock quarry had been closed down in early October according to Allen "Bud" Radke, an explosives expert at the quarry. The following Monday, when they came back to work, they found the quarry had been robbed. He described some of the explosives they used at the quarry: To blow up the rock, they use an emulsion mix stick and ANFO (or fuel-treated fertilizer), and they charge it with an electrical blasting cap. He said an emulsion mix stick is "two inches in diameter, 16 inches long. It kind of looks like a big sausage stick in a white plastic wrap." They bought it in 55-pound boxes with 25 sticks per box. They also used non-electric blasting caps for specialized work. On these, they usually used the ones with a 60-foot cord and a No. 8 delay and with orange shock tubes. These parts were stored in explosives magazines at the quarry.

Mr. Radke said some of the magazines had been broken into and four to five cases of electric blasting caps (250 caps per case) were missing. Also missing was a partial case of non-electrical blasting caps (called Primadet) which had held about 75 to 80 caps. Seven cases with about 175 emulsion mix sticks (called Tovex) were also missing. The Tovex was stored in a trailer and the lock on the trailer had been drilled out. He was shown a picture of blasting caps and "sausages" seized from Nichols' residence and identified them as being the same kind that were stolen from the quarry. (When the FBI searched Nichols' home on 22 April 1995, they found Tovex, non-electrical Primadet, and 60 feet of eight-second delay blasting caps with orange shock tube.)

Cullen Scott with the FBI testified that he recovered the broken padlock from the local Sheriff's Office who had taken it into evidence. Thomas Brown, also with the FBI, testified that he participated in the search of Nichols' house on 03 May 1995 and found a box in the basement with a cordless Mikita drill, two batteries for the drill and some extra drill bits. Steven Burmeister said that he found some tubing and tested it. He said that the interior components of the tubing (HMX and aluminum powder) were consistent with the type of explosive that is found in Primadet.

James Cadigan with the FBI also testified. He works in the FBI lab in the Firearms and Tool Marks Unit. He did some drilling comparisons on the padlock from the quarry and the drill bits recovered from Nichols' home. The lock cylinder had both a shallow and a deep drill impression in it. Also, striations, or scratches were left by the tip of the bit. Cadigan used a drill bit confiscated from Nichols' basement that showed signs of wear and drilled holes with it. A microscopic examination was conducted. He determined that "this drill bit produced marks that were contained in the padlock." On cross-examination, the Defense made the following points:

Q: Mr. Hartzler (prosecutor) was asking you about some of these differences...in your photos, Government's Exhibit 157. And he specifically said, "Is it fair to say that all of these ridges that I pointed out show up in the same area of the photograph?" Do you recall that?

A. Yes, sir.

Q. But you still don't see any of those in yours, do you?

A. No, sir.

Q. They just don't exist over here, do they?

A. No, sir, they do not.

Q. Now, you were talking about the way these grooves can be made on here; and I -- I think you said something about it's ground on a grinder. That makes an independent print, if you will, for each lock.

A. For each drill bit, yes, sir.

Q. How many drill bits came off that same grinder?

A. Hundreds of thousands.

Q. Or more?

A. Yes, sir.

Q. And let me see if I understand exactly what you're saying here. Is that based on this? You can tell that these lines that are not symmetrical is the same as this one right here. Is that right?

A. I'm sorry. If you could repeat.

Q. The lines on the part you took out of the lock, even though they're not symmetrical, it's your claim that these are the same that match your symmetrical lines; right?

A. No, sir. This is a photograph of some of the marks that I saw as I examined the lock. It's not all of them that I based my identification on. I took this picture to illustrate some of the marks that I saw.

Q. Sure. And you clearly brought the one that you thought was the best?

A. I brought the one that would show what I--some of what I saw, yes, sir.

Q. That you thought was the best. Right?

A. Yes, sir.

Q. And this is the same bit made on the same grinder that you couldn't match on the shallow impression as regards the other quarter-inch mark on the box; right?

A. I could not identify the shallow impression, yes, sir.

Q. Because there was not any significant, separate, identifiable marks to exclude one or the other bit in the same box; right?

A. I don't understand that....

Q. You authored a report, did you not, or took part in a report that came from the FBI lab?

A. Oh, yes, sir.

Q. And your tool-mark examination is included within the report. Right?

A. Yes, sir.

Q. *Now, when you were discussing the shallow part of the lock in your report, --*

A. *Yes, sir.*

Q. *-- did you say as regards the two individual bits, "However, due to a lack of sufficient corresponding individual tool marks of value, no further association could be made"? Do you recall that?*

A. *Yes, sir.*

Q. *And what you were saying there was I can't tell if either one of these bits made the shallow impression because they both appear to be close enough to the same?*

A. *What that says is that they could have made this impression, but I can't identify it to the exclusion of any other tool produced.*

Q. *Even though they were ground on separate grinders.*

A. *On separate grinders?*

Q. *Or the same grinder; right?*

A. *Correct.*

The Defense
The Defense called William A. Tobin with the FBI Lab. He received the box with the Makita drill and bits on 02 June 1995, prior to the items going to Cadigan. He admitted that, when he received the box from the Explosives Unit, there had been an accident and "water was prevalent" in the box. The contents were "moldy and heavily moisture-laden," with the "steel inside corroded." The Defense showed him a photograph of three bits. The one in the center had corrosion on the side. When asked, he did not know which drill Cadigan had tested.

The Prosecution
In his testimony, Michael Fortier claimed to have seen some of these stolen munitions. He said that he received a letter from McVeigh in August 1994 saying that he and Nichols had decided to "take some type of positive offensive action." Fortier wrote back expressing curiosity. About a week later, McVeigh showed up at his door and stayed a few days. McVeigh told Fortier that he and Nichols were going to blow up a building and asked Fortier to help. He declined. That fall, Fortier claimed to have received a call from McVeigh asking him to rent a storage locker, to rent it outside the city, to use an assumed name and to pay cash. Fortier looked for a storage unit but did not find one available. A few days later, McVeigh arrived in town and rented a locker, using his own name to rent this one because, according to the Prosecution, he had to show his driver's license to rent this unit.) He said he was staying in the desert and Nichols was with him. He stayed about a week. One night at 9:00, he again showed up at Fortier's door, asking him to come see something. Fortier accompanied him in his car, following Nichols in his blue truck with the white camper shell, and they

went to McVeigh's storage locker. They went inside, and Fortier saw a box with a yellow or orange diamond shape on the outside that said "explosives." A blanket covered what looked like another dozen boxes. McVeigh, reportedly, spent the night at Fortier's, and told him about robbing the rock quarry and using a Mikita drill to break a padlock and gain entrance to one of the explosives storage areas.

Lori Fortier testified that on 14 December 1994, the day before Michael Fortier's birthday, while McVeigh was in Kingman, they visited him at his room in the Mohave Motel. She said the following events took place:

> *He asked us to bring tape, wrapping paper, a couple boxes, and a stock to a Mini-14. And before we went to the motel, we went to Wal-Mart and got tape and I think wrapping paper, also. And then we went to the motel and we saw Tim.... When we got there, Tim took the two boxes, and he had like a—like a large boxful of blasting caps; and he separated the blasting caps into the two smaller boxes, an then he asked me to wrap the boxes in wrapping paper.... [He said] That he wanted them in Christmas wrapping paper in case he was stopped, like anyone wouldn't think it was conspicuous, because it was the Christmas season.*

Kevin Nicholas, McVeigh's friend in Michigan, also testified about items that could have been stolen from the rock quarry. He said that, shortly before Christmas 1994, he received a phone call from McVeigh from the Speedway Truck Stop about 15 miles from his home. McVeigh had had an accident and wanted Nicholas to pick him up. He found McVeigh parked between two semi-trailers in the back of the station, with all his bags sitting on the ground behind and beside the car. Nicholas started grabbing McVeigh's bags and throwing them into his pickup. McVeigh told him not to handle the "Christmas presents," that he would get them himself. Nicholas asked him what was in them, and was told, "I'll tell you later." Later, McVeigh told him the packages contained blasting caps. He did not say where he had gotten them, but he did say that he got them "dirt cheap."

Fortier testified that, on the 18th of December 1994, he received a call from McVeigh who said he had been rear-ended in Michigan with the blasting caps in the trunk of the car.

OKBIC Note
The Bridges' calling card shows a call to Fortier on 18 December at 7:00 p.m. from the Speedway station in Saginaw, Michigan.

The Prosecution
McVeigh stayed with Nicholas until the middle of January 1995. Nicholas attended a gun show with McVeigh in early December 1994 at Kalamazoo, Michigan. At the show McVeigh introduced him to a man by the name of Dave Paulsen. Following this, according to Nicholas, McVeigh took a couple of trips: On the first one, he went with James Nichols to collect money for some soybeans. On the second trip, he went to the Chicago area to see Dave Paulsen.

OKBIC Note
The Daryl Bridges' calling card also shows numerous unanswered calls were made to Paulsen's house while McVeigh was visiting Nicholas, as follows:

UNANSWERED CALLS TO PAULSEN FROM OTHER LOCATIONS ON THE DARRYL BRIDGES CALLING CARD

DATE	LOCATION CALLS MADE FROM
14 Dec 94	2 calls from the Mohave Motel in Kingman, AZ
15 Dec 94	1 call from the Mohave Motel in Kingman, AZ
17 Dec 94	1 call from the U.S. Grant Motel in Matoon, IL
18 Dec 94	1 call from the U.S. Grant Motel in Matoon, IL
18 Dec 94	1 call from a Laundromat in Gilman, IL
18 Dec 94	1 call from a Laundromat in Melrose Park, IL
18 Dec 94	3 calls from Speedway Service Station in Melrose Park, IL (1 of these to Paulsen's Military Supply was for 48 seconds.)
18 Dec 94	1 call from Welsh Oil in Chesterton, IN
27 Dec 94	1 call from BP America in Maumee, OH
27 Dec 94	1 call from McDonald's in Findlay, OH
27 Dec 94	2 calls from Irv's BP Gas in Yellow Springs, OH
04 Jan 95	1 call from Bay Medical Center in Bay City, MI
07 Jan 95	2 calls from Burger King in Markham, IL
07 Jan 95	3 calls from King's Gas Station in Markham, IL (2 of these were brief conversations to Paulsen's Military Supply)

The Darryl Bridges' calling card also shows numerous calls were made to Paulsen during this timeframe from other locations. None of the calls were answered except calls to his business number, as noted:

UNANSWERED CALLS TO PAULSEN FROM OTHER LOCATIONS ON THE DARRYL BRIDGES CALLING CARD

DATE	LOCATION CALLS MADE FROM
14 Dec 94	2 calls from the Mohave Motel in Kingman, AZ
15 Dec 94	1 call from the Mohave Motel in Kingman, AZ
17 Dec 94	1 call from the U.S. Grant Motel in Matoon, IL
18 Dec 94	1 call from the U.S. Grant Motel in Matoon, IL
18 Dec 94	1 call from a Laundromat in Gilman, IL
18 Dec 94	1 call from a Laundromat in Melrose Park, IL
18 Dec 94	3 calls from Speedway Service Station in Melrose Park, IL (1 of these to Paulsen's Military Supply was for 48 seconds.)
18 Dec 94	1 call from Welsh Oil in Chesterton, IN
27 Dec 94	1 call from BP America in Maumee, OH
27 Dec 94	1 call from McDonald's in Findlay, OH
27 Dec 94	2 calls from Irv's BP Gas in Yellow Springs, OH
04 Jan 95	1 call from Bay Medical Center in Bay City, MI
07 Jan 95	2 calls from Burger King in Markham, IL
07 Jan 95	3 calls from King's Gas Station in Markham, IL (2 of these were brief conversations to Paulsen's Military Supply)

The Prosecution
David Paulsen had met McVeigh at a gun show in Kalamazoo, Michigan the first weekend in December 1994 when they had booths close to each other. Paulsen had seven tables and McVeigh had one. Paulsen worked weekends for his father's military surplus catalog business, selling merchandise at gun shows. He said he was interested in some gun parts McVeigh had and looked at them. He ended up getting two mercury switches which he traded for a magazine pouch for gun clips. He said McVeigh asked him if he would want to buy some blasting caps. Paulsen said he pretended to be interested, but had no intention of buying them because there is no market for them. He gave McVeigh a business card which was later found in Trooper Hanger's patrol car after McVeigh's arrest. Paulsen provided a written deposition which was read in court. Part of the written statement follows:

> *I recognize this…as a copy of my father's business card. The front says "Paulsen's Military Supply," and it's got an address in Antigo, Wisconsin. I gave this card to Timothy McVeigh…. It's my card, and it's got my number on the back where it says "Dave" and then a phone number. I wrote the name and phone number. In other writing it says, "TNT at $5 a stick, need more. Call after 1 May, see if I can get some more.' "I do not know who wrote that. At the time McVeigh was arrested on April 19, I had not provided any dynamite to him. With respect to the call after 1 May, I made that up when I told him I was going to talk to a guy in May. There is no explanation for why I made that up. I gave him the phone number so I could get more gun parts from him if he got them.*

J. BARRELS

The Prosecution
McVeigh and Nichols supposedly obtained plastic barrels in which to mix and transport the bomb. Telephone records for 19 October 1994 show that, on the Bridges' calling card, calls were made from the Denny's Restaurant payphone in Wichita, Kansas to several companies that sell barrels (or "drums", as they are called in the industry.) These calls began at 10:36 in the morning and continued through 11:22 a.m. (The Prosecution was not able to present evidence as to where Nichols and McVeigh got the barrels; but, according to the Prosecution, they did find some because four were found in Nichols' garage.)

FBI Agent Robert Morton said that he found fragments of plastic in the search of downtown Oklahoma City. The testimony went as follows:

> Q. …Could you open that bag and just show the jury what's in that bag and just briefly describe it for them….
>
> A. What this is, it's a white plastic material that I recovered along the edge of the sidewalk and the street. The material is melted and burned.

Q. *There are numerous plastic fragments --*

A. *Yes, there are. So myself and several other people, we basically walked the street back and forth looking in a lot of particular areas for any kind of evidence that we could see.*

Q. *And the items in that bag, did you find all along that street?*

A. *Yes, I did.*

Linda Jones, the explosives expert from England, testified that she examined the plastic fragments that were recovered at the scene, "Some of them were damaged consistent with, for example, them having been close to an explosion."

The chief division counsel for the Omaha division of the Federal Bureau of Investigation, Mary Jasnowski, was called as a witness. She was team lead for the search of Nichols' home. She said she personally searched the garage and found four 55-gallon, white plastic barrels. She described the barrels:

Q. *All right. Tell the jury what they are observing here with the photograph we've marked as Exhibit 191.*

A. *Well, these are the four barrels as we found them. They were stacked on top of each other; and they were, I believe, located -- I can't remember now whether it was the north wall or which direction. I'd have to look at my chart to tell you where it was, which wall.*

Q. *All right. And what are these blue things that are in the -- on this exhibit?*

A. *I'm sorry. These are the rims of the barrels. They are not lids. They are the rims of the barrel.*

FBI Special Agent Jeffrey C. Hayes said that he received an assignment from Agent Mendeloff to track down the barrel manufacturer. He contacted drum manufacturers that produced natural-colored, high-density polyethylene, which was the type recovered from Nichols' garage. A company called Smurfit manufactured two drums and Van Leer manufactured two others.

He then tried to track down the manufacturers who provided the raw ingredients for the barrels. He contacted these suppliers by phone as per a list provided by Mendeloff. Agent Hayes asked for the help of Theodore Udell, Smurfit engineer, in fact-finding whether other drum manufacturers used the same materials in their plastic barrels that Smurfit used. The Defense objected to the testimony of Udell because the products he was checking on would be proprietary and it is highly unlikely that one manufacturer would tell another what ingredients were used to make their barrels. The Judge instructed the jury as follows:

> *Telephone calls made by Mr. Udell of Smurfit and by Agent Hayes was based on hearsay and could not be considered to be reliable information about the chemical*

composition of the competitors' product....In your consideration of the evidence in this case, you must now disregard any information provided to them in the course of the telephone calls which they testified they made.

The Bridges' phone records show the following calls made to companies that make barrels. Apparently, however, the Government was not able to connect Nichols or McVeigh with a purchase from either of these companies:

CALLS MADE TO BARREL COMPANIES

DATE	TIME	MIN:SEC	CALLED FROM	CITY	CALLED TO	CITY
10-19	10:36 a.m.	00:56	Payphone at Denny's Restaurant	Wichita, KS	SDS, Inc.	El Dorado, KS
10-19	10:49 a.m.	00:00	Payphone at Denny's Restaurant	Wichita, KS	Coffeyville Recon.	Coffeyville, KS
10-19	10:50 a.m.	00:00	Payphone at Denny's Restaurant	Wichita, KS	Coffeyville Recon.	Coffeyville, KS
10-19	10:51 a.m.	00:00	Payphone at Denny's Restaurant	Wichita, KS	Coffeyville Recon.	Coffeyville, KS
10-19	10:53 a.m.	00:37	Payphone at Denny's Restaurant	Wichita, KS	Coffeyville Recon.	Coffeyville, KS
10-19	11:22	02:23	Payphone at Korner Mart	Benton, KS	Grief Bros. Recon.	Winfield, KS

K. THE RYDER TRUCK

The Prosecution
A key part of the Government's case is based on activities they ascribe to McVeigh in the days just prior to the bombing. These activities include McVeigh checking into the Dreamland Motel in Junction City, Kansas on the Friday before the bombing (14 April), renting the Ryder truck in Junction City on Monday (17 April), mixing the bomb in the truck at nearby Geary Lake on Tuesday with Nichols (18 April) and delivering the bomb in Oklahoma City on Wednesday (19 April). They presented witnesses and phone records to try to establish these facts, as follows:

The Government presented evidence to show that McVeigh checked on a Ryder truck rental as early as 05 April 1995 with the Ryder agency in Lake Havasu, Arizona. The call was placed from the Imperial Motel in Kingman, Arizona at 3:43 p.m. The Prosecution called Helmut Hofer, owner-operator of the motel to the stand. He testified that McVeigh had stayed at his motel from 31 March 1995 through 12 April 1995. He verified that the number from which the call to Ryder was made was a number at his motel. He identified McVeigh in the courtroom.

The Prosecution then showed a phone record for 14 April 1995 to the Ryder Truck Rental in Junction City, Kansas, made from the J and K Bus Depot, also in Junction City. According to Prosecutors, McVeigh left Kingman, Arizona on 12 April and drove to Central Kansas in his Pontiac. The car gave him problems on the way, and he stopped and bought an oil filter in Arkansas City, Kansas at a Wal-Mart store on the 13th. By the time he arrived in Junction City on 14 April, he decided to buy a different car and went to an acquaintance, Thomas Manning, at the Firestone store. Here he bought the Mercury Marquis. The Government contention is that, while McVeigh was waiting on the Mercury to be serviced, he walked to the J & K Bus Depot about a block away and used the payphone. The Bridges' phone record shows a call to Nichols' house for 54 seconds at 9:51 a.m. There was also a call to the Ryder Truck Rental in Junction City at 9:53 a.m. This call lasted seven minutes and 36 seconds. The Prosecution read a deposition from Manning which stated that McVeigh disappeared for about 15 minutes while at the Firestone store.

The Defense

The Defense called Arthur Wells III, a Firestone mechanic, as a witness. He testified that, while he was working on the Mercury Marquis, Manning and McVeigh stood right outside the bay talking. Manning brought McVeigh over and introduced him. McVeigh stood by the Mercury and watched the work the entire time. Then, Wells took the car to Jim's 66 station to fill it with gas and was gone 10 to 15 minutes. He said that, when he left, Manning and McVeigh were in the repair bay talking. When he returned, they were still talking just outside the repair bay.

The Prosecution

Defense attorneys may have wished they did not call this witness. Under cross-examination from the Prosecution, Wells agreed that he did not know if McVeigh had left the premises before coming into the repair bay, or while Wells was filling the car with gasoline. He said when he returned, McVeigh got in the Mercury and left; and, when asked, said that McVeigh had not transferred anything (including a television set) from the Pontiac to the Mercury. He was quite adamant in his response.

The Prosecution

When arrested, Nichols had a receipt for an oil filter from the Arkansas City Wal-Mart in his billfold. His wife Marife testified that Nichols had stopped at Wal-Mart in Junction City and Manhattan to return a filter, but she did not think he had gotten the money back on it. (This filter would have fit McVeigh's car, but would not have fit Nichols' truck.) FBI Agent Louis Hupp testified that both McVeigh's and Nichols' fingerprints were on the receipt. This proved that Nichols must have seen McVeigh either on 13 or 14 April, contrary to what he told the FBI in interviews with them. He told them McVeigh had never been to his house in McPherson, Kansas and he had not seen McVeigh in months.

The Defense

The Defense made a valid argument for this event in their closing argument.

> *There is nothing to say in this evidence that's inconsistent with Tim McVeigh having dropped that oil filter and receipt on the porch, in the mailbox, out behind the shed, somewhere else. And there's no evidence of a face-to-face meeting. And you might*

look at me and say, "Well, wait a minute, what's the evidence that there wasn't a face-to-face meeting?" Well, I look back at you and say, "Who's got the burden of proof here?" The point is that if the circumstantial evidence, if the evidence points in either of two directions, the law says which way to cut.

The Prosecution
Prosecutors said that McVeigh stayed at the Dreamland Motel in Grandview Plaza, Kansas, on the edge of Junction City, just prior to renting the Ryder Truck. They called Eric McGown as a witness. His mother owned the motel, and Eric worked there when he was not in school. At the time of the bombing, Eric had just turned 17 years of age on 14 April and was a junior in high school. Eric testified that he did general maintenance, care of the pool and lawn, and desk clerk work. He and his mother and sister lived in an extension behind the office of the motel. His hobbies were computers and cars. He said his mother checked McVeigh into the motel on 14 April and gave him Room #25. McVeigh paid for four nights. He said he never saw McVeigh with anyone else. He identified McVeigh in the courtroom.

The Prosecution then turned to the motel records. Eric identified his mother's handwriting on the bottom part of the registration form. Jennifer McVeigh (Timothy's sister) had previously identified McVeigh's handwriting on the top of the form. McVeigh registered under his own name and gave his address as 3616 Van Dyke, Decker, Michigan. He identified his car as a Mercury with Arizona tag number L76-034. He put down one person and no pets.

The Defense
During the Nichols' trial, Eric's mother, Lea McGown, was called as a Defense witness. As part of her testimony, she stated that, on the day he registered, McVeigh was very neat and clean, but his car was very raggedy; he had a Michigan driver's license but Arizona tags; therefore, it made him somewhat suspicious, so she assigned him to the room closest to the office so she could keep an eye on him. She said she "noticed how the trunk opened, and he grabbed something and hold it with both arms." She said she saw McVeigh again that Friday or maybe Saturday driving out from the motel. She noticed his license plate was "hanging sideways, was only secured with one bolt."

The Prosecution
The motel phone records (and also the Bridges' records) showed four calls were placed from Room #25: Calls on 14 and 17 April were to Spotlight for a balance check. The two other two calls were made on 15 April to the Hunan Chinese Restaurant.

Yuhua Bai owned the Hunan Chinese Restaurant in Junction City, Kansas. She testified that, on 15 April 1995, she received a call from a customer ordering moo goo gai pan and an egg roll, to be delivered. He said his name was Kling. Bai commented to him, "Pretty like Chinese name. Could you spell for me?" She asked where he wanted it delivered, and he told her Dreamland Motel, Room #25. She identified a receipt for the delivery and noted that Jeff Davis was the man who delivered the food. She also said that she received money for the food when Jeff returned, so she would assume the delivery was actually made.

The Defense

The Defense at both trials called John Jeffrey Davis to testify. In addition to his job at the Hunan Restaurant for four years, he was also an alarms monitor and 911 operator under contract to the Government at Fort Riley. The Defense wanted to show that McVeigh may not have been the guest—or the only guest—in Room #25.

Davis said he arrived at the motel around 5:45, after having first made a delivery to a trailer park about three blocks from the restaurant. From there, he went through Fort Riley and to the motel. He said he had made probably 50 or more deliveries to the motel in the past. He said that, when he arrived, "there was a gentleman standing in the doorway of the first door to the left of the office," and "the door was already open." He checked the door numbers of the rooms next door to make sure he was at the right room. He parked in front of Room #25. He did not recall another car being parked in front of the room. He got out of the car with the bag of food and approached the man. He described the encounter as follows:

Q. *Did you have a conversation with the gentleman?*

A. *A short one. His food was fairly late at that point. He asked if I had had a problem getting out there due to the bridge being out. And I told him that no, I'd just gotten to work late and we were running a little behind.*

Q. *Was he angry or upset that his food was late?*

A. *No, he didn't appear to be.*

Q. *Was there any other conversation that you had with him?*

A. *We discussed the fact that it was fairly nice out that day; it had been rather dreary and rainy the week prior.*

Q. *Okay. And how was the individual dressed, if you recall?*

A. *Casually. I mean, he wasn't dressed in sweats and a T-shirt and looking scraggly and bummed out; but he was just casual dress: jeans, T-shirt type.*

Q. *Was he wearing a military uniform or camouflage...fatigues or anything?*

A. *No, sir.*

Q. *Okay. And where was he standing during this period that you had a conversation with him?*

A. *He was standing in the doorway.*

Q. *How close did you get to him?*

107

A. Oh, close enough to hand him the food at arm's reach—three feet.

Q. How long did you stay there in conversation with him?

A. Two to three minutes.

Davis said that, when the FBI came to the restaurant, they showed him two sketches. He was not able to identify either as being the man he had seen at the motel. When they showed him a photo line-up later, he could not identify any of those individuals either. The following testimony was given:

Q. What did you tell the agents concerning the description of the individual as it compared to the photograph in the newspaper of Mr. McVeigh?

A. That there were several things that didn't fall in line and made me believe that it was not Mr. McVeigh that I delivered to.

Q. All right. The individual that you saw and talked with..., what was his hair color, if you recall?

A. It was a very dark blond, light brown.

Q. Was it short, in a burr haircut?

A. No, it was not.

Q. Was it—can you give the jury an idea of what length of the hair it was and how it was combed or styled?

A. It wasn't styled. It was fairly -- it looked like he'd been kind of just lounging around in his room. And the length, two inches on top, above the collar in back.

Q. Style was not a good word to use. How was the hair? Was it combed, or unkempt, tousled, or what?

A. I would -- I would go with unkempt and tousled.

Q. And was that different than what you saw in the newspaper photo of Mr. McVeigh?

A. Yes.

Q. What about any facial characteristics of Mr. McVeigh—excuse me—of the person that you saw at the room that night that was different from the photo that you saw of Mr. McVeigh, just the facial characteristics?

A. The nose was not the same. The ears.

Q. What was different about the nose?

A. Mr. McVeigh has a rather prominent nose, and his ears stick out from his head, as opposed to laying flat up against his skull.

Q. And the individual you saw at the motel, what was different about his nose and his ears?

A. His nose was not a prominent feature of his face, and his ears didn't appear to me to be larger than average.

Q. Okay. Anything about his mouth?

A. Not specifically.

Q. Anything about the width of the face?

A. He had a fairly slender face with what a—what I would term a severe jaw line, squared off.

Q. Let me clarify the record here. When we say "he," I'm talking about the person at the room.

A. Yes; correct.

Q. The person at the room that you saw had a slim face?

A. Yes.

Q. And you saw the photograph of Mr. McVeigh?.... And he has a slim face?

A. Yeah, rather slim.

Q. Were they both similar in their slimness?

A. Yeah. I—That's not how I judge who I delivered to....I took the face as a whole, and it did not match up with the pictures I was shown.

Q. Okay. And you saw this picture on Sunday, the, what, 23d of April?... And you had seen the individual at the room on the 15th, eight days before?

A. Yes.

Q. So is it accurate to say that your memory was fairly fresh at that time?

A. Yes.

Davis said that the delivery stood out in his mind because, due to the bridge being out, he had had a discussion with his boss as to which way he needed to go. Also, he said, most of their deliveries were to the opposite side of the office where the long-term guests stay. The testimony continued:

Q. Okay. Now, have you had a lot of meetings with the Government since that time, Mr. Davis?

A. Yes.... A dozen or more.

Q. And where have they taken place?

A. In various locations. Been out here once to talk with them. Several meetings in Junction City at my apartment. I met with them on occasion down at the police department, also.

Q. Okay. And this is over what period of time?

A. Initially—the initial month following the delivery and the bombing, probably, oh, once every other day, like the first week. And then it slowly dropped off.

Q. Did it pick up again at some point in time?

A. Yes.... The grand jury empaneled down in Oklahoma City. And also the—shortly after ABC ran the composite that I worked on with Miss Boylan....

Q. Okay. What's been the tenor of those meetings? How would you characterize the meetings?

The Prosecution: Objection.

The Court: Sustained.

OKBIC Note
The point of these last questions from the Defense was to elicit testimony regarding what Davis saw as coersion from the FBI to change his memory of the motel guest. He said they would ask questions like, "It could have been McVeigh, couldn't it?" over and over again. (For a copy of the Jeanne Boylan sketch based on Davis' description, see her book, *Portraits of Guilt*.)

The Prosecution
Prosecutors asked Davis why he could remember the guest's face so well when Boylan was doing the composite drawing, yet he only had a sketchy memory when he talked to the FBI. His only information then was that the man was 28-29 years old, approximately six foot tall, had short, sandy hair, weighed about 180 pounds, had a clean-cut manner and no mustache.

In Boylan's book, she said that Davis told her that, when he was standing in front of the motel door, he could see into the room and saw McVeigh sitting on the bed. The Prosecution questioned him about this:

Q. ...You told the officers on Friday, April 21, that one thing you were sure of is that there was one man and one man only in Room 25. Is that correct?

A. Correct.

Q. Have you ever, Mr. Davis, said to anybody that there was more than one person in that room?

A. No, sir.

Q. Mr. Davis, take a look at this dark-haired woman back here at the second table. Have you ever met her before?

A. Not to my knowledge, no.

Q. Do you remember in September of 1996, on an occasion that Mr. Woods asked you about, staying at the Burnsley Hotel?

A. Yes.

Q. Mr. Davis, do you remember meeting the bartender at the Burnsley Hotel?

A. Yes.

Q. Did you in that visit to Denver, Mr. Davis, tell the bartender you saw two people in Room 25?

A. No, sir, I did not.

Q. You deny that?

A. Yes, I do.

Q. Do you deny in equal fashion, Mr. Davis, having made the statement to Jeanne Boylan, the composite artist that you spent several hours with, in April of 1996, that Tim McVeigh, in addition to your composite person, was in Room 25?

A. Yes, I emphatically deny that.

The Defense
The questions about "this dark-haired woman back here at the second table," were apparently a ruse. The Defense questioned her identity:

Q. Mr. Davis, follow-up on the question--I'm not quite sure what he was asking. The dark-haired lady: Was that the bartender at the Burnsley?

A. No. I do not believe so.

The Prosecutor: I agree with that, your Honor.

Ms. McGown, in her testimony, also recalled an incident that showed other people to be in McVeigh's room. She said it was her practice to walk the motel grounds to make sure everything was okay. On Saturday or Sunday night, she made her rounds after midnight; and, as she walked past Room #25, she heard voices. She said,

A. ...So on my way back I decided to walk very slow by the door and the window to hear better. And I could hear several voices in the room because the seating is right next to the window, and I could hear the voice on the window side talking and the answering voice right across where the bed is, and the TV is to your left side against the bathroom wall.

Q. Okay. From listening to the voices, could you determine how many people were talking?

A. I know by [sic] sure it was two people and possible [sic] three.

Q. And did you recognize Mr. McVeigh's voice?

A. I do believe the voice on the window was Mr. McVeigh's.

Q. All right. Did you recognize the other voice or voices?

A. Not clearly.

Q. How would you describe the other voice?

A. Kind of velvety deep voice.

Q. And that's the description you gave the law enforcement authorities. Is that correct?

A. Yes, sir.

Q. Had you heard the voice before, the velvety deep voice?

A. I don't recall.

Q. Do you recall whether or not you told the law enforcement authorities that this voice sounded like the one that had called Mr. McVeigh two or three times previously while he was staying there?

A. It could be the same voice.

Ann Puett and her husband owned and operated Bell Taxi in Junction City. The dispatcher received a call on 17 April 1995 for a pickup at the Stop and Shop in Grandview Plaza, a few blocks from the Dreamland Motel. Ms. Puett said that each taxi driver maintains a trip sheet for each shift he works. The sheet is used to record the driver's name, starting mileage, date and taxi number. As he works his shift, the driver records each fare: the number of passengers, pick-up location, drop-off location and the amount of the fare. The times of pick-up and drop-off are not recorded. At the end of his shift, he turns in the sheet and the money at the office where it is put into a safe. The next morning the trip sheets and money are checked against the dispatcher's records. The information is recorded in the computer and the trip sheets are filed by date for a period of one year. A trip sheet for 17 April for driver David Ferris was identified and shown. This sheet showed a fare (#20) for one passenger, picked up at Grandview Plaza and dropped at McDonald's South in the amount of $3.65. Puett said McDonald's is four to five miles from the plaza.

The Government introduced the Bridges' phone record to show a call placed to Bell Taxi on 17 April at 3:29 p.m. from the Stop and Shop pay phone in Grandview Plaza. They asked Puett about a regular pickup the taxi company makes each weekday at the Westwood School in Junction City between 3:30 and 4:00 p.m. On 17 April, David Ferris' trip sheet showed he made the pick-up at the school immediately after the pick-up at the Stop and Shop. This established the approximate time of pickup at Grandview Plaza to be between 3:29 and 4:00 p.m.

The Defense
Puett said that whichever taxi is dispatched to the school each day is determined by the proximity of the cab to the school at the time pick-up is scheduled. She agreed that sometimes the taxi may arrive a few minutes early or late. The Defense pointed out that, by looking at the fare sheet, there is no way "we know when the call came to dispatch the cab to the Grandview Plaza.... Nor does it tell us what time the fare was picked up.... Nor does it tell us what time the fare was delivered to McDonald's...." Puett agreed.

The Prosecution
David D'Albini, manager of McDonald's restaurant at 6th Street and Interstate-70 in Junction City was called next. His restaurant maintained time-lapse surveillance tapes. The Prosecution introduced a video tape and still photos from the tape for 17 April 1995. At 3:49:02 p.m., the tape shows a customer at the counter, getting money out of his pocket. He has a crew cut and is wearing a dark shirt over a light T-shirt and light-colored jeans. He remains in the film until 3:49:07 p.m. at which time the film captures a different camera image for five seconds. There are seven cameras, so it takes 35 seconds to get back to the first camera. The next time this customer is seen is at 3:57:06. He is coming from the dining room area in the back corner. At 3:57:08 he is walking in the direction of the door and appears to be looking at his watch. At 3:57:12 he is almost to the door and is shown in the film for the last time. Mr. D'Albini said that the time on the film could be off as much as two minutes plus or minus. He also said that the Ryder truck rental facility is directly down the street from his McDonald's, about one-and-a-quarter miles.

The Defense
D'Albini said that the Ryder facility is over a hill and has access to Interstate-70. He agreed that access to Interstate-70 can be obtained from Grandview Plaza and the Dreamland Motel, from the McDonald's restaurant, and from the Ryder rental facility.

The Defense then asked about the flagpole at McDonald's. D'Albini said that they tried to fly the flag every day; however, if it was raining they did not fly it. From the film, he agreed that, on the afternoon of 17 April, McDonald's was not flying its flag.

During Closing Argument at the end of the trial, the Defense pointed out that McVeigh could not have called for a cab from the Plaza Stop and Shop at 3:49 p.m. and been at the McDonald's counter, four-to-five miles, away at the same time.

Eldon Elliott owned the Ryder truck rental agency down the street from McDonald's. It was housed in the same facility as Elliott's Body Shop and shared the office area. Elliott was shown a copy of phone records for his company. He identified a call received at his business on 14 April at 9:54 a.m., which lasted seven minutes and 34 seconds. He said this call came in on the Ryder rental line. (As noted above, the Bridges' phone record showed a call from the J and K Bus Depot payphone to the Ryder truck agency at Elliott's on 14 April, placed at 9:53 a.m. This call lasted seven minutes and 36 seconds.)

The next day, 17 April, Elliott was at work. Only the truck rental portion of the business was open on Saturdays, so he was there alone. He said that about 9:00 a.m. a customer came in and told him that his name was Kling and he had received a price quote from Vicki Beemer the previous day and wanted to go ahead and reserve the truck. Elliott asked him for his license and recalled that it was in the name of Bob Kling with an address in Redfield, South Dakota. The birthdate was listed as 19 April 1970. Instead of just making the required $80 deposit, Kling paid the full cost of the rental. When asked if he wanted insurance on the truck, Elliott said Kling told him, "I'm not going very far, [and] I'm a good driver. I drive these deuce-and-a-halves out at Fort Riley. I don't want no insurance." Elliott completed the reservation form and Kling signed it. Elliott gave Kling the back copy and kept the front two.

OKBIC Note
The FBI could not find McVeigh's prints on this reservation form.

The following Monday, 17 April, Kling arrived at the rental agency to pick up the truck. Vicki Beemer assisted him with the rental and gave him the contract to sign. At the end of the transaction, Elliott said she called him into the office and asked him to do an inspection on the truck and make a note of any damage before the customer took possession. Elliott said that, when he entered the office, "Vickie Beemer was there and handed me the contract. McVeigh was standing there. There was another gentleman standing in the corner, and I had one of my mechanics [Tom Kessinger] was setting [sic] at a chair."

The Defense
The other "gentleman standing in the corner" mentioned in the paragraph above was the subject of a fair amount of testimony. Part of that is transcribed below:

Q. Well, he was in there at the same time. Do you know who that person is?

A. No.

Q. Did you conduct any business with him that day?

A. No.

Q. I take it you don't let strangers loiter around this small reception room you've got there.

A. No. I wouldn't do that, but I don't know when he come in, because I wasn't in the office, or I would have knew [sic] about it and I would have knowed [sic] what he was there for.

Q. Well, I take it you don't know what he was there for?

A. I don't know what he was there for.

Q. You didn't see who came in with Kling, if anyone?

A. No.

Q. And did you see him leave?

A. No.

Q. Did you see this other fellow conduct any business while you were in the office?

A. No.

Q. Did you recognize him?

A. No, I did not.

Q. Wasn't one of your regular customers?

A. No.

Q. Did you rent any more trucks after the one with Kling?

A. Not that day.

Then the Defense compared this testimony with previous statements he had made:

Q. Now, the grand jury asked you if Kling was with somebody. Do you remember that?

A. Yes.

Q. And you said, "Yes, he was."

A. Yes.

Q. Now, you didn't say there was just somebody else standing there. You said there was somebody with Kling.

A. Right.

Q. And you were under oath then? Sir?

A. Yes.

Q. And this is several months, nearly six months after the bombing, so you've had time to reflect and think. Is that right?

A. Right....

Q. And then the grand jurors asked you if you could tell them about the second man, didn't they?

A. Yes.

Q. Now, at that time you told them that you really couldn't tell them what he looked like. Right?

A. That's right.

Q. But you said, "I remembered that he had a hat with blue stripes or like lightening on the side of it; and I noticed that, but I didn't pay no attention to him."

A. That's right.

Q. Now, was he talking to Kling?

A. They was saying something when I came back in, but I don't know what they said.

The Prosecution
On his way outside to perform the truck inspection, Elliott said he asked Kling if he had changed his mind about wanting insurance and was told no. When he finished the inspection, Mr. Elliott came back into the office and went over the inspection report with Kling and had him initial it. Kling put the initials RDK and signed the rental agreement as Robert D. Kling. Elliott positively identified McVeigh as being the man who called himself Bob Kling on Saturday, 15 April, when he reserved the Ryder truck and on Monday, 17 April, when he picked up the Ryder truck.

The Defense
The Defense brought up prior testimony from Elliott to discredit his identification of McVeigh:

Q. Okay. Now, when you were interviewed on the 19th by Mr. Crabtree, did you describe the hair of Kling as being light brown, short, military-style haircut?

A. Yes, I think I did.

OKBIC Note
When he testified before the Grand Jury, Elliott said, "Golly, I can't remember. I really can't remember what color his hair was."

The Defense
The cross-examination resumed:

Q. Now, what did you say about Kling's complexion?

A. I said he was about medium complexion, about like mine, or maybe just a little bit darker....

Q. So you think that Tim McVeigh's complexion is darker than yours?

A. It was at that time...

OKBIC Note
McVeigh is fair complected, and was not darkly tanned at the time of his arrest.

The Defense
Cross-examination continued:

Q. Okay. Now, when you were asked by the grand jury what Kling looked like, wasn't your response, "Well, he was probably my height, a little bit taller. I'm about 5' 10""?

A. Right.

At one point in his interrogations, Elliott stated that the reason he thought McVeigh was about 5' 10" was because he was leaning slightly on the counter, which made him appear shorter than he was. The Defense questioned him about this:

A. He was 5' 10", 5' 10" or 11" or maybe just a little taller; but he was a little taller than me, I thought, because after thinking about it, leaning on the counter, he would have had to have been just a little taller than what I said.

Q. Well, did you tell the grand jury that he was leaning on the counter?

A. I don't remember if I did or not.

Q. Or is the business about leaning something that you have remembered since your grand jury testimony?

A. No, sir.

Q. Is it something that you remembered since your grand jury testimony because Mr. McVeigh has now been measured?

A. I really don't know how tall Mr. McVeigh is, sir.

Q. Well, the description that you gave of Mr. Kling to the grand jury under oath back in August of '95, is that the description that you remember?

A. That's what I remember; that he was around 5' 10", 5' 11".

Q. Standing?

A. Where I seen him, and he was leaning on the counter a little.

Q. Did you tell the grand jury he was leaning on the counter?

A. I don't remember whether I told the grand jury that or not, sir.

Q. Now then, do you remember that at the eyewitness hearing, when I was visiting with you, you said that he was leaning against the counter?

A. Right.

Q. When is the first time that you told one of the FBI agents or the prosecutor that you remember that Kling was leaning against the counter?

A. I don't remember when it was.

The Defense pointed out that Elliott had not been asked to attend the live line-up in Oklahoma City to see if he could identify Kling, and had not been shown a photo spread until 08 June 1995. They asked if he knew why, and, of course, he had no answer.

Vicki Beemer was called to testify for the Defense in both trials. She said she answered the call on Friday morning, April 14, asking to reserve the truck. The customer identified himself as "Kling." She described the conversation:

Q. And just tell me what you remember about that conversation.

A. I remember that when he called in, he asked about renting a Ryder truck. I remember that he told me he was going to be going to Omaha, Nebraska. When I asked him the size of truck that he was interested in, he asked me how many pounds does a 15-foot truck hold. And with that, I had to get up and walk around my desk to the chart that was hanging on the wall to see how many pounds a 15-foot truck would hold. I noticed that it would hold—I think it was something like 3400 pounds. I came back to the phone and I told him it would hold around 3400 pounds.... He then said, "I need a truck that will hold 5,000 pounds." I again got up and walked around and noticed that he would need a 20-foot truck—would accommodate him. And I came back and I told him this.

Q. This chart you're looking at, Beemer: ...Did it also have like two-bedroom house, three-bedroom house, or something like that on it?

A. We have that. I don't know that it's on that chart. We have a—another chart that shows a 10-foot truck will hold so many rooms, a 15-foot truck will hold so many. You know, each truck tells how many size—or how many rooms each size will hold. I'm not sure if it's on that chart or not.

The Prosecution
The Defense asked Beemer if she remembered releasing another truck rental to a customer at 8:20 a.m. on 17 April to go to Michigan that day. She no longer had a memory of it, but the FBI 302 report from 08 May 1995 showed that she had told the FBI about this rental at that time. It was the only other rental that day. The FBI report also showed that only one bodyshop customer had come in on the 17th.

The customer known as Kling came in on 17 April about 4:15 to claim his truck. Ms. Beemer said that a body shop employee, Tommy Kessinger, was in the office taking his break when Kling came in with another man. The Defense questioned her about Kling and the other man:

Q. Did he have anyone with him?

A. Yes, sir, he did.... I don't know who he was. It was just another man.

Q. All right. Did they come in together?

> A. Yes, sir, they did.
>
> Q. Did you see how they got there?
>
> A. No, I didn't.
>
> Q. So you don't know whether they walked, or drove, or somebody dropped them off?
>
> A. No, sir, I don't.

Beemer said Kling came right up to the counter, but she could not recall exactly where the other man was standing. The questioning continued:

> Q. All right. And at that time, what did you estimate Mr. Kling's height to be?
>
> A. I estimated it to be around 5' 10", 5' 11", about the height of my husband....
>
> Q. Now, how was he built?
>
> A. There again, he was medium to slender build, which was kind of like my husband, also.
>
> Q. What type of haircut did this individual have?
>
> A. It was a very short, military-type haircut.
>
> Q. Do you remember any of his facial features?
>
> A. No, I do not.
>
> Q. Have you been able to identify him—well, have you been able to identify him?
>
> A. No, I have not.

During the course of the rental transaction, Kling provided his license and furnished a destination address in Omaha, Nebraska. Beemer printed the rental agreement, had Kling sign it, asked Elliott to perform the safety inspection, and had Kling sign the inspection sheet. The keys were normally left in the truck for the customer. It operated both the ignition and the locks.

Beemer said that Kling and his companion left together. She could not recall what either one was wearing and could not recall if the second man wore a cap. The Defense asked her about her testimony before the grand jury when she said that the second man wore a cap. She explained,

> What I did at the grand jury was characterize John Doe 2, and what I thought that meant was to characterize him according to what I have seen on TV, what everybody had said that he had looked like, what it [sic] was read in the paper, what was seen on

the TV. It was not a description from my memory. It was a characterization.... What I was doing—The grand juror asked me to characterize John Doe 2. I had already said several times in my grand jury testimony that I did not know what this guy looked like.

Beemer said she was "very certain" that there were two men.

She also testified that she (accompanied by her husband), Elliott and Kessinger met with the FBI at Fort Riley about 4:00 in the morning on 20 April to talk to a sketch artist. The artist first talked to Kessinger. While the others were waiting on him, Ms. Beemer recalled that "Eldon said to—My husband and I were standing, or setting there—and he said, 'That guy had a beard, didn't he?' or 'Didn't that guy have a beard?'—something to that effect." She said she responded, "I have no idea." After the sketch artist had completed his drawings based on descriptions furnished by Kessinger, and after Elliott had been called in to look at the sketches, they were shown to Beemer. She was asked if there were any additions or deletions she could make to the sketches, and she told them no. Regarding Kling's likeness, she commented, "I didn't know if I've ever seen him before." She was asked, "Are you able to identify him today?" She answered, "No, I can't."

OKBIC Note
The Defense contends that Kessinger confused the individual who rented the vehicle on 17 April with two individuals who came to the shop the following day (Michael Hertig and Todd Bunting). The cap described above that the second man wore is similar to a hat that Bunting said he wore to Elliott's on Tuesday, although Elliott says that Bunting's hat is not the one he remembers. In regard to the sketch, the Defense said, "And the description he gave of the acne-faced individual is clearly not Tim McVeigh."

OKBIC Note
Tony Ward whom ATF informant Carol Howe identified as John Doe #2 does have a pocked complexion. (Source: *The Oklhaoma City Bombing and the Politics of Terror,* David Hoffman, Feral House, 1998k, pg. 232)

The Defense
Since the Prosecution's case included the assertion that McVeigh left McDonald's restaurant and walked to the Ryder rental agency, Elliott was asked about the weather conditions when he went outside to inspect the truck:

Q. And this fellow, Kling—Mr. Kling—didn't follow you outside, did he?!

A. No.

Q. Was it raining?

A. It was real light mist.

Q. Right light mist. Well –

A. Not real wet. It was just a real light mist....Now, so since it was misting, as you say, I take it you didn't dally too long outside?

A. No, I did not.

Q. When you saw Kling inside, did he look wet?

A. I didn't pay that much attention to him.

Q. When you looked into his face and—and you handed him—you have this business transaction, you didn't notice whether he was wet?

A. His face wasn't wet, no.

Q. Okay. How about his clothes?

A. I didn't even look at his clothes.

Q. You didn't even look at his clothes?

A. No.

Q. How did you miss that?

A. I didn't pay any attention to his clothes, maybe I should say.

Q. Did he have a raincoat on?

A. I don't know.

Q. Well, you looked at this other gentleman's clothes because you noticed his hat, didn't you?

A. I just glanced at his hat, and that's all I glanced at.

Q. Well, you knew enough as to color, and you described the flashes on it or lightening on it, didn't you? Stripes?

A. It was because it was something different.

Q. Yeah. Was it wet, or was it dry?

A. I did—I don't know.

Q. Did Kling have on a raincoat?

A. I don't know.

The Defense recalled for him the testimony he had given before the grand jury:

Q. Well, did you tell them it was a real light mist, or did you say it was a light mist?

A. Light mist.

The Defense directed attention to the papers McVeigh had signed. Twice during the cross-examination, they came back to the reservation form and then the contract. The first part of the testimony dealt with Saturday, the second part with Monday:

Q. Well, let me ask you something. Does this fellow Kling have gloves on?

A. No, he did not.

Q. Well, then, we ought to be able to find Mr.McVeigh's fingerprints on this --

The Prosecution: Objection, your Honor.

The Court: Sustained.

Q. When you saw Mr. Kling on Monday, did he have gloves on?

A. I don't—I don't know as I paid that much attention to his hands.

Q. Mr. Elliott, did he have gloves on Monday?

A. I can't remember.

Q. Can't remember. Is that the type of thing you would remember?

A. I don't remember that.

Q. Did he sign something Monday?

A. Not in front of me.

OKBIC Note
Notice that in his earlier testimony (a few paragraphs above), Elliott said that, when he came back from the truck inspection, he went over the form with Kling and Kling initialled it. However, Vicki Beemer said it was practice that she took care of having the customer read and initial the inspection sheet.

The Defense
Elliott confirmed that, while he was outside on Monday inspecting the truck, he noticed a full-sized, light-colored sedan parked in the front portion of the lot. The car did not belong to any of his employees. No one else was at the shop besides Kling and "this other fellow that was with him." Elliott, however, offered the conjecture that the car could have belonged to the customer who picked up a Ryder truck at 8:30 that morning, or that it could have belonged to someone who just left the car there for the day. The Defense elicited the information that the sedan was gone when Elliott closed at 5:00 p.m.

OKBIC Note

In McVeigh's "Petition for Writ of Mandamus" dated 25 March 1997 (to command the Government to produce the exculpatory material requested by the Defense) (see pg. 487-494), the Defense provided the following eyewitness account by Mr. Mistry (first name unknown), the manager of the Great Western Inn in Grandview Plaza, Kansas:

> The manager of the Great Western Inn at Grandview Plaza, Kansas, told the FBI that he observed the composite sketches of John Doe #1 and #2 when they were released, and stated that one of the sketches looked like a man who had checked into the motel on Monday, April 17, 1995 or Tuesday, April 18, 1995, the same time Tim McVeigh was staying at the Dreamland Motel. According to Mistry, the man was driving a Ryder rental truck which he parked in front of the motel and the man reminded Mistry of a "Moslem" and had a Middle Eastern accent. Mistry advised the FBI that the composite sketch of John Doe #2 "looked just like the man he described as having checked into the Great Western Inn on April 17, 1995 or April 18, 1995. (D.E. 2191 at 23.)

The Prosecution

During the four days that McVeigh was at the Dreamland Motel, Eric McGown said he only saw one Ryder truck at the motel. He said he saw McVeigh three times: (1) McVeigh was standing beside the Mercury Marquis. They had a short discussion about cars and weather. The car was parked directly in front of Room #25 and had Arizona tags on it. (2) McVeigh was driving a Ryder truck and backing up next to the pool. Eric's mother sent him to tell McVeigh not to park in that spot. McVeigh was polite and moved the truck across the motel driveway and parked under the sign. Eric said the truck was medium sized, not the newest model, had a different compartment for the cab, and had a trailer portion. After he saw the Ryder truck, he did not see the car again. (3) McVeigh was standing behind the truck trying to close the rear tailgate. Eric said he did not see any moving boxes or luggage in the truck to indicate McVeigh was in the process of moving. He said he could not remember for sure which days he saw McVeigh.

The Defense

The Defense homed in on contradictory statements made by Eric McGown in his court testimony and FBI 302 reports:

> Q. Well, then I'll ask you, sir, if on April 25, 1995, you didn't tell FBI Special Agent Mark Bouton that you saw a yellow Ryder truck being driven by Tim McVeigh, the man who was a guest at that time in Room 25 of the Dreamland Motel, arrive at the Dreamland Motel at about 4:00 p.m. on Sunday afternoon, April 16, 1995. You saw this Ryder truck when it [sic] returned from eating at a restaurant from Manhattan, Kansas, with his [sic] family on Easter Sunday?
>
> A. I said I thought I saw it, but I was never sure of that date or the next day.
>
> Q. So Special Agent Mark Bouton made a mistake?
>
> A. I do not know what he wrote down. All I know is what I said.

Q. And you don't remember seeing this when you were in the U.S. attorney's office two days ago?

A. No, I do not.

Q. Now, you were working on the swimming pool, weren't you?

A. That week, yes.

Q. And you also associated the swimming pool with seeing the Ryder truck, didn't you?

A. Yes.

Q. And you worked on the swimming pool on both Sunday and Monday, didn't you?

A. And on a few other days after school, yes.

Q. All right. But you only had Easter Sunday one day, didn't you?

A. Easter Sunday is only one day.

Q. Yes, sir. And you only left on that Sunday, April 16, to go eat in Manhattan, didn't you?

A. Correct.

Q. You didn't go to Manhattan on Monday, did you?

A. I don't recall what I did Monday.

Q. Mr. Bouton -- I'm sorry -- Mr. McGown, you are aware, are you not, that the statements as reflected in the FBI 302's that you gave on April 21 and April 25 are inconsistent with the theory that Mr. McVeigh rented the truck on Monday? Aren't you?

A. If that's the case, it is. I'm not aware of that.

Q. You're not aware of it?

A. I'm not aware of anything that's not dealing with what I remember.

Q. Well, doesn't this deal with what you remember?

A. That's—what they think is what they think. What I remember is what I remember.

Q. Now, one other thing: You said that you always ask for identification when someone checks in the motel.

A. *Yes. That's required that we have to have a form of identification.*

Q. *I understand it may be required. I just want to be sure that your testimony under oath is that you always ask for identification.*

A. *Yes, I always ask to see a driver's license --*

Q. *And your mother does?*

A. *I do not know what my mother does. All I know is what I do.*

Q. *So your mother might not always ask?*

A. *I do not know. That's her, not me. If you want to ask her that question, you call her here and ask her that question.*

OKBIC Note
Eric McGown was called as a witness during McVeigh's trial only. The Prosecution chose not to have him testify in Nichols' trial.

The Defense
Numerous witnesses were called by the Defense to testify that they saw a Ryder truck at the Dreamland Motel before the date and time prosecutors said that "Kling" rented a truck. Their testimony follows: Ms. McGown said that, on Easter Sunday, 16 April, she saw McVeigh shortly before 11:00 a.m. She and her daughter were on their way to church. McVeigh was standing by his car and said hello to her daughter. After church they returned home and got ready to go to the Carlos O'Kelly Restaurant in Manhattan, Kansas. She said that Eric, Kathleen and Renda Troung, a friend of Kathleen, went to the restaurant with her. She identified a receipt from the restaurant showing that she paid the bill at 2:34 p.m. It took about 30 minutes to drive back home. Upon returning to the motel, she took no note of whether or not McVeigh's car or the Ryder truck was there; but, later that day, she saw him in a Ryder truck parking by the pool and told Eric to tell him to park the truck by the motel sign. The following morning, she got up around 5:00 and saw the truck. Later that day, she noticed the truck was gone and made a notation on the maid's slip so the maid, Hilda Sostre, could clean the room. But Sostre came in later and said somebody was in the room.

LeaMcGown said she again saw the truck on Tuesday around 4:00 in the morning. She heard car doors slamming and got up to see what was going on. She saw David King standing with a group of young people in the parking lot in front of Room #24 on the other side of the office from Room #25. Across the parking lot, under the sign, she saw McVeigh in the Ryder truck with the cab door open and the dome light on. He was looking down at something in his lap; she assumed it was a map. That was the last time she saw McVeigh or the Ryder truck.

Hilda Sostre was a maid at the Dreamland Motel. On 17 April, she arrived at work around 8:00 to 8:30 a.m. and noticed a Ryder truck in her usual place to park. She said she saw a man walking toward the truck. She described him as medium height, good build, black hair, long nose and brown-like skin. She thought he might be Spanish. She said he resembled the second John Doe #II sketch. Thirty minutes later, the truck was gone. Around noon, she went to Room #25 and knocked on the door. The guest opened the door. She asked him if he wanted a clean towel. He said no and closed the door. As she was walking away, he opened the door again and said he would like a clean towel after all, so she exchanged his used towel for a clean one. She identified this guest as Timothy McVeigh.

The following calls to and from the Dreamland Motel were found on the Bridges' calling card:

DREAMLAND MOTEL PHONE CALLS ON DARRYL BRIDGES CREDIT CARD

DATE	TIME	MIN:SEC	CALLED FROM	CITY	CALLED TO	CITY
04-15	09:36 a.m.	00:00	Dreamland Motel	Junction City, KS	Terry Nichols' Home	Herington, KS
04-16	03:08 p.m.	03:02	Payphone at Tim's Amoco	Herington, KS	Terry Nichols' Home	Herington, KS
04-17	09:25 a.m.	00:57	Dreamland Motel	Junction City, KS	Terry Nichols' Home	Herington, KS
04-17	03:29 p.m.	00:30	Payphone at Plaza Stop & Shop	Junction City, KS	Bell Taxi	Junction City, KS
04-17	10:35 p.m.	00:52	Payphone at Kansas Airport	Kansas City, KS	Dreamland Motel	Junction City, KS

OKBIC Note

Eleven minutes after this last phone call there was a call on the Bridges' card from the Kansas City Airport to Lana Padilla's home. Terry Nichols was at the airport at that time putting his son on an airplane to go back home to Las Vegas.

The Prosecution

Federal prosecutors maintained that McVeigh and Nichols mixed the bomb in the Ryder truck on 18 April at Geary Lake, just south of Junction City on Highway 77. Nichols maintained that he had loaned his truck to McVeigh on that day, and was, himself, attending an army surplus sale at Fort Riley.

Agent Scott Crabtree testified that he interviewed Nichols on 21 April 1995 and asked him to tell them about any contact he might have had with Tim McVeigh. He said Nichols told him that he was at the Defense Reutilization and Marketing Office (DRMO) at Fort Riley and that he

> ...had expected Tim McVeigh to come back and pick him up; that he did not appear; that he went to another building, one that he had to sign into; spent some time there; and after he put in a bid, came outside; and sometime after that, Tim McVeigh returned and picked him up....

> Q. ...did he tell you how he and Mr. McVeigh had supposedly parted ways on Tuesday morning?
>
> A. Yes, sir, he did.
>
> Q. What did he say?
>
> A. That after Mr. McVeigh had picked him up, that they had returned back to McDonald's in Junction City; that they had gotten out of the vehicle and that was it, and that he hadn't seen him since.
>
> Q. Did Mr. Nichols indicate that Mr. McVeigh said anything memorable when he got out of the vehicle at McDonald's?
>
> A. Not on that occasion.
>
> Q. Do you remember the words that Mr. Nichols used to describe his parting of ways with Mr. McVeigh?
>
> A. He said Mr. McVeigh got out of the vehicle, and that was it. And that he hadn't seen him since.

Stephen Smith, FBI agent, provided testimony about his interview with Terry Nichols and their conversation regarding the DRMO. Agent Smith said Nichols told him that he and McVeigh "made plans to meet at approximately 7:30 at the McDonald's in Junction City that Terry Nichols had dropped Timothy McVeigh off [at] the previous morning," meaning that this was the same McDonald's where Nichols said he dropped McVeigh in the wee hours after picking up McVeigh in Oklahoma City on Easter Sunday. No reason was given as to why that location was chosen to meet at again. Additional testimony follows:

> Q. According to his statement to you, did, in fact, Mr. Nichols and Mr. McVeigh get together at that McDonald's?
>
> A. Yes. Mr. Nichols said that Terry—that Timothy McVeigh had told him that he was not in a big hurry, so they waited around; so Terry Nichols waited at home for approximately an hour and decided to meet Mr. McVeigh at the McDonald's at approximately 7:30 a.m. on that date.

OKBIC Note
The McDonald's tapes did not show McVeigh at the McDonald's again after the day McVeigh is alleged to have rented the Ryder truck.

Testimony resumes:

> Q. Was he with anyone?

A. No, he was not.

Q. What did the two men do after they met at the McDonald's according to Mr. Nichols?

A. According to Mr. Nichols, he picked up Timothy McVeigh and they got back on I-70 heading east and got off at K-18, which is a highway; and they went through Ogden, Kansas, and went up to the post at Fort Riley, going that direction.

Q. If you take that route starting at McDonald's and following it the way you've described it, how long does that trip take?

A. Approximately 20 minutes.

Q. Approximately what time, then, would Mr. Nichols have arrived at DRMO on that morning?

A. A little bit before 8 a.m.

Q. Did Mr. Nichols tell you whether he had ever been to an auction at that same facility prior to April 18?

A. No, he had not.

Q. Tell us what Mr. Nichols told you he did once he was dropped off by Mr. McVeigh at the DRMO.

A. Mr. Nichols got out of the -- got out of his pickup truck and looked at items for sale in a building and was—they decided to meet up—to have Timothy McVeigh come back at approximately noon that same day. When Timothy McVeigh did not show up at noon, Terry Nichols went into another building where he had to sign-in in order to look at items inside that building, also....He...then looked at the items that were for sale inside and bid on some of those items and came outside after approximately an hour of looking at those items, and Mr. McVeigh showed up shortly after that....

Q. According to his statement to you, when he linked back up with Mr. McVeigh, where did the two men go?

A. The two men -- Mr. Nichols drove Mr. McVeigh back to the Junction City area and dropped him off at the same McDonald's on South Washington Street.

Q. Did Mr. Nichols tell you what he did once he dropped Tim McVeigh off?

A. Yes. He said that he dropped Tim McVeigh off at the McDonald's in Junction City and that he, Terry Nichols, went back to the Manhattan area in order to pick up mail at a Mail Boxes Etc., where he had a mailbox.

Q. If you were at Fort Riley and wanted to go to Manhattan, what's the most direct route?

A. Just to continue on either I-70 or go the back route to Manhattan. Junction City is not in between Manhattan and Fort Riley.

Q. According to Mr. Nichols' statements, he went out of his way to drop Tim McVeigh off at the McDonald's before tracing his route to go back to Manhattan?

A. Right. Mr. Nichols drove from the DRMO on post at Fort Riley back to Junction City and then basically had to go back through Fort Riley to get to Manhattan....

Q. Again, what errands, according to Mr. Nichols, did he run in Manhattan that afternoon?

A. He said Mr.—Mr. Nichols said that he had picked up his mail at the Mail Boxes Etc., and then he went back to Herington, Kansas, and ran some more errands in Herington before arriving at home in Herington after 5:00.

Nichol's wife, Marife, testified about that day. She said her husband had been gone when she awoke, and she first saw him about noon. He had lunch, then said he had to go to the DRMO at Fort Riley for an auction of military surplus items.

Mary Garza, an employee of DRMO was the chief of the Distribution Branch in April, 1995. She referred to a diagram of the DRMO area and told a little about their procedures. First a customer would go in a door to area A02 and get a catalog and sign in. There are "banners indicating that's the area to go to." (However, she said, if, for some reason, a customer did not want to follow the signs and sign-in, and instead wanted to go straight to the outside yard, there was nothing to physically prevent their doing that.) They would look around the inside area, then the lady at the desk would direct them to the other areas where merchandise for sale was located. "They would have to exit back out of here and go through this fence, the gate, and see this property right there and there." The Prosecutor spent a little more time on the sign-in sheet:

Q. I want to turn back to Government 1956, which is the sign-in sheet that was admitted a couple minutes ago. And I want to show you page 11 from that sign-in sheet. Would you please read the third name on this 11th page.

A. Terry Nichols.

Q. And can you read the time that the sign-in reflects.

A. It looks like 12:50....in the afternoon....

The time-date stamp on the sheet showed an actual time of 12:37 p.m. The Prosecution then asked if she had reviewed the entire sign-in log for 18 April. She had, and said she had found no sign-in entries in the name of Joe Rivers, Joe Kyle, Ted Parker, Terry Havens, Joe Havens or Mike Havens. There was also no record to reflect that Nichols had been at the DRMO prior to 12:50 that day.

The Defense
The Defense showed Garza a DRMO catalog which had been introduced by the Prosecution. It had several items circled in it with a price written out beside the listings of those items. They corresponded with the ten items Nichols bid on that day. (Seven of those items were located in the outside area at the auction.)

William McDonald was called to the stand. He was retired from the U.S. Army as a sergeant-major. After retirement, he went to work for the DRMO. He testified that, on sale days, it was part of his duties to ensure that people did not go into the areas where non-sale materiel was stored. He said he kept a pretty close watch on the area and that no one would be able to stay in there for more than 15-to-20 minutes before he would have seen them and made sure they left.

The Prosecution
Carolyn Marin was at the DRMO on Tuesday, 18 April, with her husband and child. She said they arrived around 11:40 and went inside where they signed in. There were just two rows of things inside—a portion on the right side had been roped off. They looked around for about 15-to-20 minutes, then went outside to view sale items at the side of the building. She said they only stayed in that area about two minutes because it had tires and lawn mowers and things of that nature that they were not interested in. Next they went to the area where vehicles were being sold. They found one they liked and spent 10-to-15 minutes looking it over. They bid on the car and a couple of other items. Total, they were there for about an hour which, she said, was sufficient time to see everything they were interested in. She said they passed by the warehouse about 12:30 and did not see anyone standing in front waiting on a pickup.

The Defense
Darrell McCaleb was called by the Defense. He said he had been attending DRMO auctions about once a month for the past two-and-one-half years. He was there on 18 April, having signed in at 10:50 a.m. At that time, he noticed that there was no one manning the sign-in desk. He signed in anyway. He said that during the course of time he has been attending the auctions, he had observed that, on a number of occasions, the person at the sign-in table would leave the area.

Robert O'Connell said he had been to the DRMO sales eight-to-ten times. He usually looked at things like tents, canisters for fuel and the trucks. Often, he said, he did not go inside, so he did not sign in. He also said that, whenever he goes, he also looks at the area where future items will be going on sale to see what might be available in the future. He said he had never been approached and asked to leave this area.

The Prosecution
O'Connell had signed in to the DRMO at 2:34 p.m. He said he spent about an hour-and-a-half there that day. The Prosecution asked if he was aware that the DRMO closes at 3:00 p.m. on viewing days. O'Connell said,

> *I have heard a figure of 3:00. I am relatively sure that figure's not accurate. I do not know. I honestly don't. I've heard that figure passed around. I do not know whether it's accurate or not.*

The Prosecution
Kerry L. Kitchener, from Wakefield, Kansas (18 miles northwest of Junction City) worked for the Kansas Department of Wildlife and Parks. He was responsible for Maintenance at Geary Lake: cleaning and painting rest rooms, picking up trash along the highway, cutting tree limbs, etc. He also performed creel surveys at the lake to determine the kinds and size of fish being taken from the lake. He conducted a survey in 1995 from March until September or October. He parked by the boat ramp during the study. He said that at no time during his survey did he see a Ryder truck at the lake. He said he conducted the survey in accordance with the following schedule:

KITCHENERS' SURVEY SCHEDULE

DATE	ARRIVAL TIME	DEPARTURE TIME
4-10	1:30 p.m.	3:30 p.m.
4-11	8:00 a.m.	10:00 a.m.
4-13	4:00 p.m.	6:00 p.m.
4-16 (Easter)	4:00 p.m.	5:30 p.m.
4-17	7:30 a.m.	9:30 a.m.
4-19	5:00 p.m.	7:00 p.m.

He said that on 18 April (the day the bomb is supposed to have been mixed), he was not working at Geary Lake; he was at the wildlife area.

The Defense
The Government set up a roadblock at Geary Lake to stop vehicles and see if any of the people from the area had seen a Ryder truck at the lake on 18 April. The FBI made numerous reports of people who claimed to have seen a Ryder truck at the lake in the week before the bombing. They did not call any of these witnesses to testify, but the Defense did, as follows:

James Sargent, medically retired from the military, was out-processing from Fort Riley on 10 April 1995. He finished at 11:30 that morning and decided to go fishing at Geary Lake. After stopping for lunch, said that he arrived at the lake about 2:00 p.m. and looked across the jetty where he saw a Ryder truck sitting alone. He said it was medium-sized with no overhang over the cab. He saw a black man at the lake and went down and fished with him. Later, an older white man also joined them. They also saw two men in a paddle boat who were military and exchanged comments with the older man whom they seemed to know. Later, around 6:00 p.m., two vehicles approached the truck, a dull-red primer-colored pickup and a white car. When shown the Ryder brochure, he identified the three-bedroom truck. He said he also saw the truck at the lake on 11 April about 7:30 p.m. and again on the 12th.

Elwin L. Roberts, an engineer with BG Consultants in Manhattan, was picking up samples at Hamm's Quarry on 17 April and drove by Geary Lake about 10:00 that morning. He said he saw a Ryder truck with an older brown pickup behind it parked at the lake. He said the truck had a slipover front, meaning the box did not go over the cab front, but came down behind it.

The Prosecution
Prosecutors pointed out that, in previous testimony, Roberts had said the truck was parked by some restrooms, but there are no restrooms in that area.

OKBIC Note
It was later shown in Court that the area where the truck was reported seen does have a large sign with a roof over it which could easily be taken for restrooms.

The Defense
Rickey D. Glessner, also an engineer with BG Consultants, reported seeing a Ryder truck at the lake on Easter Sunday around 10:00-11:00 a.m. on his way to his folks' house in White City, Kansas. He described it as a 20- to 24- foot truck with a "grandma's attic" over it. He said he did not see the truck on his return.

Raymond Siek, a senior citizen, was attending his sister's funeral with his wife, son and daughter-in-law in Herington, Kansas on 17 April. They left the funeral about 3:30 p.m., and as they went by Geary Lake, he said he saw a Ryder truck backed up to the edge of the lake. Parked next to it was a pickup truck. He said it was raining, and two people were standing next to the truck talking. He commented to his son, " I wonder what those idiots are doing down there in the rain."

The Prosecution
Prosecutors elicited the information that the pickup truck was dark blue or black with a shell on top. Mr. Siek also said that, on 19 April, he went to pay his sister's gas bill and saw a man come out of the the gas company and get into a pickup that looked similar to the one he had seen at the lake. He said, when he saw pictures of Terry Nichols on TV, he thought Nichols was the same man he had seen at the gas company.

The Defense
Kevin Ray Siek, Raymond's son, also testified about seeing the Ryder truck at the lake on the 17th. He said it was blue and was pulled out on one of the jetties.

Sharen Diane White from Lost Springs, Kansas (six miles south of Herington) was on her way to the Wal-Mart in Junction City. As she passed by the lake, she saw a Ryder truck facing the exit. She picked the three-bedroom model from the brochure. She said this occurred about 9:30 a.m. on 13 April 1995. She was certain of the date from the date she wrote the check to Wal-Mart. She said she saw a Ryder truck later that day as she was getting ready to pull out of her driveway. As it went by, the passenger stared at her and even leaned out the window and stared back at her. She could not see the driver. When she saw McVeigh on TV, she thought he was the man she had seen.

The Prosecution
The Government emphasized that White had not contacted the FBI with this story until a year after the alleged incident. White said she had not wanted to get caught up in all the 'hullabaloo" and notoriety.

The Defense
On redirect, the Defense pointed out that White had asked the FBI for anonymity when making the report to them.

Kelly Gulker was returning to Milford, Kansas on Monday, 17 April, after visiting his brother in Wichita Falls, Texas for Easter. As he was traveling on Highway 77 about 4:30 p.m., on the southeast side of Geary Lake, he saw a Ryder truck. He said he did not remember what the truck looked like.

The Prosecution
Prosecutors made the point that, in previous discussions, Gulker had said the truck had a cab-over and that he had seen something blue next to the truck.

The Defense
Charles William Farley worked for the Fort Riley Outdoor Recreation Center, which rented boats, campers and camping equipment to base personnel. He was a mechanic and provided renters with hunting and fishing information. He said he went to Geary Lake on 18 April, arriving just before 6:00 p.m. He did not see a Ryder truck at that time; but, about 10 minutes later, when he retraced his route, a Ryder truck was there. In front of it was an old, green and white, heavy, brown car, possibly an Oldsmobile 98 or a 225 Buick. A two-ton 1950-53 farm truck was parked about 10 feet away. He described the farm truck as a flat-bed with stakes on the sides and said it was

> *Loaded, completely loaded. White bags sticking up even above the—the fence, the rails. It looked like it was completely weighted down. That was my initial thought was that it had -- that it had broken down and it was just bottomed out on the sprin. Thought the thing had been broken and, hence, the Ryder truck, and they were just going to unload the thing....*

He said a man was standing behind the farm truck and three men were standing between the Ryder truck and the brown car. He thought he would stop and see if they needed help; but, as he went around them, he saw a man walking beside the farm truck give him a dirty look, so he did not stop. He said the bags looked like ammonium nitrate.

Farley said that, after the bombing, he contacted the FBI, but got no help. A couple of weeks later, an agent came to the Recreation Center and Farley told him, "Sir, I believe I'm the one that you want to talk to."

The Prosecution
Farley stated that one individual he saw had "blue jeans, the long hair, black T-shirt with writing on it [and was a] kind of stocky fellow. You know, he was—I wouldn't call him fat, but he was pretty

well—pretty well put together." Farley also said the man was 25-30 years of age and wore a folding knife in a leather case on his hip. The man who sneered at him was described as older, having a beard, no mustache, and wearing slacks and a short-sleeved sport shirt. He said "something to the effect of 'We've got to get this done,' or 'We've got to get going.' 'We've got to get moving.' Something like that."

Beth Wilkinson

The Prosecution
The Prosecution attempted to show that Farley had lied to investigators, and that he made contradictory statements. The cross-examination did not get the response they had hoped for:

Q. ... Were you by yourself when you were at Geary Lake on April 18th?

A. No, sir, I was not.

Q. Who were you with?

A. My daughter was with me.

Q. Mr. Farley, earlier, you told us that you went from work to the store and then directly to Geary Lake. Is that right?

A. Yes, sir.

Q. Was your daughter at work with you?

A. Yes, sir.

Q. The whole day?

A. No, sir. I picked her up after school.

The Defense
On redirect, Farley explained that he had not mentioned his daughter to begin with because "she's mildly mentally handicapped and she doesn't need this."

Robert William Jaynes from Herington worked as a diesel mechanic at Fort Riley. The Saturday before Easter he was at Lake Geary. He said he saw a Ryder truck by the first boat dock on the first fishing pier before 2:00 to 4:00 p.m. It was a 16-24 foot truck with no cab-over. It was facing south, and there were no other vehicles around. From the brochure, he identified the three-bedroom truck.

Lenard White was a partner in Aerotech Engineering, a company that makes airplane parts. He and his wife Diana were in Junction City visiting his son who had just been discharged from the Army. They stayed in Room #29 at the Dreamland Motel on Saturday evening, 15 April. They saw no Ryder truck; however, the next morning, White said he did see a Mercury with Arizona plates parked by the office in front of Room #25.

Diana White, the data controller for Wichita Area Technical College, said that, on Easter morning, she went to the motel office to get her husband a cup of coffee. She saw an old, faded, yellow Mercury with Arizona tags parked either in front of Room #25 or one room over. She said she had owned a car that color in 1977 and that it "was a favorite color of 1977." She said she commented to her husband, "Can you believe that they drove that car from Arizona?" and she pointed out the tag to him.

The Prosecution
In cross-examination, both of the Whites conceded that they left the motel Easter Sunday morning and did not know if the Mercury was at the motel after that time.

The Defense
Renda Troung said that her mother was in the military, and, in April 1995, she was living at Fort Riley and helping her father clean their quarters for a permanent change of station (PCS) move. She later moved in with the McGowns to finish out the school year before rejoining her parents. On Easter Sunday, the McGowns asked her to go to dinner, and Ms. McGown and Kathleen picked her up. She said she saw a Ryder truck at the motel parked in front of the motel sign. She picked a three-bedroom truck from a brochure as the one she had seen at the motel.

Dan Harris, an architect from Enid, Oklahoma identified a scale model of the Dreamland Motel as a model he had constructed for the trial. This model was used by witnesses to point out pertinent sites.

In April 1995, Herta King lived in Junction City, Kansas, and her son lived at the Dreamland Motel in Room #24. On Easter Sunday she took an Easter basket to him on her way to dinner with a friend. She said that, when she pulled into the motel, she saw a Ryder truck parked right next to the sign, blocking the view of her son's car, an old, green, American car. She selected the three-bedroom truck from the brochure as the truck she had seen. She commented, "It doesn't make sense that McVeigh rented the truck on Monday morning when a Ryder truck was there already on Sunday."

The Prosecution
Upon cross-examination, King said that, when she went back to the motel later, she did not see the truck. When she had seen it earlier, she had not seen anyone walking to or from it. She said she had rented a 20-foot truck before, and it was bigger than this truck.

The Defense
Anthony Rockwood is a meteorologist in Denver, Colorado. He said that rain intensities are determined by a combination of visibility and the accumulation of precipitation; and, yes, weather between stations can be estimated. He introduced into evidence the hourly weather observations

from four Kansas cities: Manhattan to the north, Salina to the west, Emporia to the southeast and Fort Riley, also north, of Junction City. All four of the locations had readings of cool temperatures, rain showers, overcast and an east wind. They all showed rain showers for nine-and-one-half hours or more that day during the late morning and into the evening. Fort Riley, which is right at the edge of Junction City, reported at 3:55 p.m. that it had overcast skies, light rain showers, fog and an east wind. Based on these reports, Rockwood gave the opinion that Junction City would have had the same weather conditions on April 17 as these other reporting stations. He also referred to Doppler radar photos taken in five minute increments maintained by the National Climatic Data Center, beginning at 3:52 p.m. through 4:18 p.m. These were of Junction City itself and showed the presence of rain, increasing somewhat in intensity. Therefore, The Defense surmised, it would have been raining at the time that McVeigh was supposedly walking from McDonald's to Elliott's to rent the Ryder truck. Yet, when the person who actually rented the truck arrived at Elliott's—about a mile away from McDonald's, he was not wet.

L. FINAL SUMMATIONS

The major events as presented by the prosecution are put in chronological order below:

SUMMATION TIMELINE

DATE	EVENT	SOURCE
22 Sep 94	McVeigh rents storage shed #2 from Mini Storage in Herington, Kansas under name "Shawn Rivers." Pays through 22 May 95.	Helen Mitchell, employee
30 Sep 94	Nichols quits job at Donahue ranch. Leaves early (around noon) that day.	Timothy Donahue
30 Sep 94	Nichols buys 1 ton of ammonium nitrate from Mid-Kansas Co-op.	Gary Showalter, salesman
02 Oct 94	Nichols leaves hired-hand house at Donahue Ranch about 7:00 p.m.	Timothy Donahue
02 Oct 94	McVeigh & Nichols rob rock quarry to obtain components for bomb.	Government theory
04 Oct 94	McVeigh and Nichols in Kingman, AZ	Michael Fortier
04 Oct 94	McVeigh rents storage locker at Northern Storage in Kingman, Arizona to store explosives from rock quarry.	Jodi Carlson, employee
17 Oct 94	Nichols rents Unit #40 at Boots U-Store-It in Council Grove under name "Joe Kyle."	Sharri Furman, employee
18 Oct 94	Nichols buys second ton of ammonium nitrate from Mid-Kansas Co-op.	Fred Schlender
05 Nov 94	Nichols robs Roger Moore to finance bombing.	Roger Moore and search of Nichols' house
07 Nov 94	Nichols rents Unit #37 from Boots' U-Store-It in Council Grove under name "Ted Parker."	Sharri Furman, employee
???	McVeigh & Nichols obtain barrels to hold bomb.	Agent Jeffrey Hayes
14 Apr 95	McVeigh rents room at Dreamland Hotel.	Eric McGown
16 Apr 95	McVeigh drives Mercury Marquis to Oklahoma City and stashes it in an alley. Nichols picks him up & takes him back to Junction City & drops him at McDonald's.	Terry Nichols
17 Apr 95	McVeigh rents Ryder truck to transport bomb.	Eldon Elliott
18 Apr 95	McVeigh & Nichols mix bomb in Ryder truck at Geary Lake.	Government theory
19 Apr 95	McVeigh drives to OKC & detonates truck bomb in front of Murrah Building.	Government theory
19 Apr 95	McVeigh arrested south of Perry, Oklahoma & taken to Noble County jail.	Trooper Charles Hanger

The Defense

In addition to reiterating the arguments given above, the Defense, in Nichols' trial, spent a considerable amount of time talking about the phone calls. Part of that summation follows: l

> So if all you had were calls that supposedly were made from Terry Nichols' house, you might get the idea that maybe Terry Nichols might have some knowledge of that. Of course, if you looked at the whole pattern of calls that were made during that time that McVeigh was staying, you would see that even that is an inference that wasn't supported by the evidence. And why not? Because all of the calls were made during times that Mr. Nichols was expected to be out working for Mr. Donahue. As soon as it gets close to the noon hour, the phone calls stopped, and Mr. Donahue says and Marife Nichols says that Terry Nichols worked pretty much from 8:00 in the morning till the sun went down....

The Defense also spent much time discussing Michael Fortier and his testimony. Portions of that discussion follow:

> Let's go back to Government Exhibit 553, page 65, and watch what happens... sometime before October 31. He said Tim McVeigh came by his house and said, "I'm waiting for Terry." "Doggone it, he's not here."

> The prosecutor referred to this episode in closing argument. "When he gets here, you tell him to take the stuff out of the shed and meet me in New Mexico." Michael Fortier told you under oath that was at 20 minutes after 4. It was about 4:00 when McVeigh left, and it was about 20 minutes later that Terry Nichols arrived. And Fortier says, "I gave him a key that McVeigh had given me."

> Here's a call in the morning. This is the 29th of October. It's the only relevant date. Here's a call in the morning at 9:52. Michael Fortier's house to Lana and Leonard Padilla. Now, Lana Padilla is Terry Nichols' former wife. It's a place where he sometimes would stay when he was visiting his son, Josh.

> Then there's another call from Las Vegas, Nevada, to Michael Fortier's house. The only person in Las Vegas, Nevada, who, ever, is shown to call the Fortiers' house, because he was at that time working with Timothy McVeigh in the gun show business, is Terry Nichols. It's the only one. And that call is made at 5:58 p.m. Central Daylight Time. And Las Vegas is 90 miles away from Kingman, Arizona. There's no way that Michael Fortier's time works, and the telephone calls prove it.

The Defense drew a comparison between the explosive items found at Nichols' house and those found at Fortier's house:

> On redirect examination, when the prosecutor asked him, "You didn't have any barrels, did you," he said, "No, except for the three 55-gallon barrels that I had in back of my

house." Barrels that are never tested by the Government. Nobody cut a piece out of his and sent them up to Tony Tikuisis in Canada....

Well, let's see what Michael Fortier did, because the prosecutors have said that you're supposed to believe Michael Fortier. This is a man that had this Primadet that Mr. McVeigh gave him.... This is a man that had guns that Mr. McVeigh gave him to sell. This is a man that has ammonium nitrate. This is a man that has blasting caps. This is a man who helps Mr. McVeigh get false ID. This is a man who heard about the plan. This is a man who was offered $10,000 and then lied to by Tim McVeigh 'cause he never got his 10,000 to drive and case the building and get the guns; this is a man who says he saw Storage Unit No. 2 in Herington, Kansas; and when the door was opened, he looked inside and all he could see were mattresses.... Well, he cleans up pretty good. You saw his picture before. But even after they cleaned him up, I asked him, I said, "How about this fellow Jason Hart? Isn't he your dealer?" "No, he's not my dealer. I bought from him a few times. He's not my dealer." Mostly Hart gave it to him. And then we had Hart's testimony summarized, and he said, "No, no. I was his dealer, and I stopped after a while because he was using more than he was selling." Now, his lies to you on that score were not the first lies that Michael Fortier told you. Let's take a look at how Michael Fortier was made into a witness to come before you.

Marine Corps builds men. The FBI builds witnesses.

First, in the wake of the bombing, on the 21st of April, 1995, according to Patty Edwards,...Mr. Fortier came out of his house and went next door to James Rosencrans's house, another one of his dope-dealing friends.... And Patty Edwards hears him say, "Tim's the one who did it. Tim's the one who did it."

Now, after that, Michael Fortier begins to hear his name, and he begins to get a lot of newspapers. We're not talking about somebody who heard about a terrible event and bought all the newspapers at their local store. We're talking about a fellow who for days and days and days and weeks and weeks and weeks is able to follow on newspapers and television exactly what law enforcement is doing, who's been arrested, what the evidence is, all of that information, gathering it bit by careful bit. And what's he doing while he's gathering all the information bit by bit? Is he going to the police station to tell them what he knows? Well, he's going to the police station, but he's bragging to his friends that he stands toe-to-toe with the FBI agent and tells them things, and on his phone that the FBI agent had a tap on using all those colorful methamphetamine-esque language and four-letter words and so on. And then as he talks, he begins to see that there's a future for him in this, not a future going to law enforcement and telling them what he knows, not a future telling about some storage shed in Arizona so they could maybe test that in any kind of a hurry, not a future telling about any guns in his house, not a future telling about Primadet, not a future telling what he knows about Tim McVeigh because he wasn't telling that. No, he's got a future. And he told you what that future was. "I'd sit there and pick my nose and flick it at the camera, flick it and then kind of wipe it on the judge's desk. Yeah, really, ha-ha; or

> 'Wait, just a second, pull my finger,' to the lawyer asking me questions, 'Come here, pull my finger. I'm the key, the key man, the head honcho, Colonel Klink.'" Well, you heard the tapes.... This is a man who speculated about getting a cool million. This is a man who had bad words to say about CNN because he [sic] didn't pay them [sic]. This is a man who talked about book contracts and movie contracts and all the rest of it. And this is a man who the Government says is the witness that you're supposed to believe. Because why? Because he's the only one who ever says that he heard Timothy McVeigh say, "Yes, I'm going to go and bomb that Murrah Building."
>
> ...Now, in order to believe what Michael Fortier says, you have to believe two people. One is that Michael Fortier ever heard it. And second of course, you have to believe that Timothy McVeigh, the person he says said it, was telling the truth.
>
> ...Michael Fortier says that Timothy McVeigh says that he and Terry wanted to do something violent, blow up a building. Are we supposed to believe Timothy McVeigh when he says that and not believe everything else Timothy McVeigh said? What is there that corroborates...that version of events? Nothing. Nothing. Not even any evidence that Terry Nichols was in a position to hear any such things, had it been spoken.
>
> And what is it that contradicts it? What contradicts it is that in March of 1995, ...Fortier says McVeigh was getting desperate. He tells Michael Fortier: "Terry Nichols won't go through with it; I'll have to force him to do it." Well, if you're going to take what Timothy McVeigh said to Michael Fortier, let's take the whole thing.

Michael Fortier

> ...And the Judge is going to tell you that you look at the testimony of somebody who uses dope or uses methamphetamine, this particular drug, this drug that keeps you up all night, this drug that causes you to hallucinate, this drug that causes your perceptions of reality to be distorted.

The Defense then talked about what motive Michael Fortier would have to lie.

> This is a man that had this Primadet that Mr. McVeigh gave him;.... this is a man that had guns that Mr. McVeigh gave him to sell. This is a man that has ammonium nitrate. This is a man that has blasting caps. This is a man who helps Mr. McVeigh get false ID....And yet, you know, he hasn't been charged with conspiring.... He heard about it. The Government said they were going to charge him with every single thing he did. And he's not charged with conspiring. Neither is Kevin Nicholas, of course, in whose house McVeigh stayed for all of that time.

His testimony was bought and paid for. It was bargained for, not with money but with a coin that only the Government has the ability to print and to hand out; and that is immunity from punishment. Not immunity from all punishment, but you heard him say that he expected to be out—the guideline sentence for him, he doesn't know what it will be, but his guideline sentence is under three years. You heard him say that he had seen on the television and the radio that there was a death penalty involved here maybe. You heard him say that it was the most important thing in his life to go home to his children.

M. THE VERDICTS AND SENTENCES

1. Timothy McVeigh

The Jury went into deliberation at 9:34 a.m. on 30 May 1996. On 02 June, at 1:32 p.m., the Jury returned with its verdict. The Judge read the verdict:

Count One--Conspiracy to use a weapon of mass destruction: Guilty.

Count Two--Use of a weapon of mass destruction: Guilty.

Count Three--Destruction by explosive: Guilty.

Do you find that the Government proved beyond a reasonable doubt that the crime or crimes committed by the defendant, Timothy James McVeigh, as found above, resulted in the death of one or more of the persons named in the indictment? Yes.

Was the death of such person or persons a foreseeable result of the defendant's criminal conduct? Yes.

The Judge then read counts four through eleven, first degree murder of eight Federal Agents. McVeigh was found guilty on each charge. The Judge then polled the Jury individually on their verdict. He asked each juror, in turn, "Was this and is this your verdict?" All jurors answered, "Yes." The Judge then told them,

Members of the jury, you have determined by your verdict that the evidence established the guilt of Timothy McVeigh on these charges beyond a reasonable doubt of crimes for which death is a possible punishment. Whether Mr. McVeigh should be put to death for these crimes is a question to be answered by the jury serving as the conscience of the community. Although Congress has given this responsibility exclusively to the jury, the applicable statute and the Constitution command that you must exercise your discretion by following a specific procedure and give careful and thoughtful consideration to information characterized as "aggravating and mitigating factors" to be presented now in a court hearing that is in a sense an extension or continuation of the trial... there...there will be a hearing tomorrow, at which time I will hear some issues that are appropriately going to be raised by the lawyers so that we can have some—they can have some advance information with respect to the Court's ruling on what will be permitted to be heard by the jurors in connection with the penalty. And there will be a whole new set of instructions that will given to you as you address the question of the penalty to be imposed.... This is a solemn responsibility that is given to you; and it is, indeed, a most serious obligation that rests upon you to decide this next question.

The Jury returned with their recommendations for sentencing on 13 June. The Judge read the following Special Findings from the jury. They applied to all eleven counts:

Under Section I, Intent to Cause Death:

Question 1: The defendant intentionally killed the victims. Answer: Yes.

2: The defendant intentionally inflicted serious body injury that resulted in the death of the victims. Answer: Yes.

3: The defendant intentionally participated in an act, contemplating that the life of a person would be taken or intending that lethal force would be used against a person, and the victims died as a result of that act. Answer: Yes.

4: The defendant intentionally and specifically engaged in an act of violence, knowing that the act created a grave risk of death to a person, other than a participant in the offense, such that participation in the act constituted a reckless disregard for human life and the victims died as a direct result of the act. Answer: Yes.

Section II, Statutory Aggravating Factors:

1. The deaths or injuries resulting in death occurred during the commission of an offense under 18 United States Code Section 844(d), Transportation of Explosives in Interstate Commerce for certain purposes. Answer: Yes.

2. The defendant, in the commission of the offenses, knowingly created a grave risk of death to one or more persons in addition to the victims of the offense. Answer: Yes.

3. The defendant committed the offenses after substantial planning and premeditation to cause the death of one or more persons and to commit an act of terrorism. Answer: Yes.

4. The defendant committed the offenses against one or more federal law enforcement officers because of such victims' status as federal law enforcement officers. Answer: Yes.

Section III, Non-statutory Aggravating Factors:

1. The offenses committed by the defendant resulted in the deaths of 168 persons. Answer: Yes.

2. In committing the offenses, the defendant caused serious physical and emotional injury, including maiming, disfigurement, and permanent disability to numerous individuals. Answer: Yes.

3. That by committing the offenses, the defendant caused severe injuries and losses suffered by the victims' families. Answer: Yes.

Mitigating factors in Section IV:

1. Timothy McVeigh believed deeply in the ideals upon which the United States was founded. Number of jurors who so find: Zero.

2. Timothy McVeigh believed that the ATF and FBI were responsible for the deaths of everyone who lost their lives at Mt. Carmel, near Waco, Texas, between February 28 and April 19, 1993. Number of jurors who so find: 12.

3. Timothy McVeigh believed that federal law enforcement agents murdered Sammy Weaver and Vicki Weaver near Ruby Ridge, Idaho, in August, 1992. Number of jurors who so find: 12.

4. Timothy McVeigh believed that the increasing use of military-style force and tactics by federal law enforcement agencies against American citizens threatened an approaching police state. Number of jurors who so find: 12.

5. Timothy McVeigh's belief that federal law enforcement agencies failed to take responsibilities for their actions at Ruby Ridge and Waco and failed to punish those persons responsible added to his growing concerns regarding the existence of a police state and a loss of constitutional liberties. Number of jurors who so find: 12.

6. Timothy McVeigh served honorably and with great distinction in the United States Army from May, 1988, until December, 1991. Number of jurors who so find: 10.

7. Timothy McVeigh received the Army's Bronze Star for his heroic service in Operation Desert Storm in Kuwait and Iraq. Number of jurors who so find: 12.

8. Timothy McVeigh is a reliable and dependable person in work and in his personal affairs and relations with others. Number of jurors who so find: 2.

9. Timothy McVeigh is a person who deals honestly with others in interpersonal relations. Number of jurors who so find: 1.

10. Timothy McVeigh is a patient and effective teacher when he is working in a supervisory role. Number of jurors who so find: 12.

11. Timothy McVeigh is a good and loyal friend. Number of jurors who so find. Zero.

12. Over the course of his life, Timothy McVeigh has done good deeds for and helped others, including a number of strangers who needed assistance. Number of jurors who so find: 4.

13. Timothy McVeigh has no prior criminal record. Number of jurors who so find: 12.

With respect to the provision of extra spaces to write in additional mitigating factors, if any, found by any one or more jurors, the jury has answered, "none" with respect to both of those and stricken them out.

Recommendation, V: The jury has considered whether the aggravating factors found to exist sufficiently outweigh any mitigating factor or factors found to exist; or, in the absence of any mitigating factors, whether the aggravating factors are themselves sufficient to justify a sentence of death. Based upon this consideration, the jury recommends by unamimous vote that the following sentence be imposed:

The defendant, Timothy James McVeigh, shall be sentenced to death.

2. Terry Lynn Nichols

The jury at Terry Nichols' trial began deliberations on 16 December 1997 at 2:14 p.m. They arrived at a verdict at 4:39 p.m. on 23 December, as follows:

Count 1--Conspiracy to use a weapon of mass destruction: Guilty.

Count 2--Use of a weapon of mass destruction: Not Guilty.

Count 3--Destruction by explosive: Not Guilty.

> *If you find the defendant guilty of one or more of the crimes charged in these three counts, then answer the following question: Do you find that the Government proved beyond a reasonable doubt that the crime or crimes committed by the defendant, Terry Lynn Nichols, as found above resulted in the death of one or more of the persons named in the indictment? Yes.*
>
> *If your answer is yes, then answer the following additional question: Was the death of such person or persons a foreseeable result of the defendant's criminal conduct? Answer: Yes.*

The Judge then polled each Juror individually and asked, "Were these and are these your verdicts?" Each Juror answered, "Yes." The Judge told them that,

> *...because the offense of conspiracy to use a weapon of mass destruction under Count One does, by statute, provide that a person found guilty of that crime could be sentenced to death, it was required of you that you proceed to the hearing of additional information, because you also found in your verdict that deaths did result and that these deaths were foreseeable. And that was what, under the statute, made possible the imposition of the death sentence.*

The Judge told the jurors that with respect to the sentencing, they had a choice among three options: (1) death, (2) a sentence of life imprisonment without the possibility of ever being released, and (3) any lesser sentence provided by law to be decided by the Court. The Judge also said that "before considering the aggravating and mitigating factors,... you must focus on the question of intention...."

The Jurors were not able to come to a unanimous decision on the sentence; therefore, the Judge discharged the Jury and went with the third option of having the Court decide the sentence. He told them that,

> *...this is a final decision, both with respect to your verdict on the charges and with respect to the—what amounts to the decision that the specific intent has not been proved to the satisfaction of all 12 of you beyond a reasonable doubt. Therefore, there can be no death sentence.*

At the sentencing hearing, the Judge made the following additional comments:

> *Terry Nichols has been proven to be an enemy of the Constitution. And accordingly, the sentence that I am going to impose will be for the duration of his life and is based upon my view that anyone, no matter who that person might be, or what his background might be, who participates in a crime of this magnitude, has forfeited the freedoms that this government is designed to protect and defend. That is the rationale for this*

sentence. I do not do this in the thought that I have no choice because the guidelines say life is the appropriate sentence. I would impose this sentence regardless of the guideline.

The Judge then imposed sentence:

The defendant, as to Count One, is hereby committed to the custody of the United States Bureau of Prisons to be imprisoned for the duration of the defendant's life and for the concurrent terms of six years each on Counts Four through Eleven.
The defendant is ordered to make restitution to the General Services Administration in the amount of $14,500,000 (the original cost of the Murrah Building), restitution payable immediately and the Court requiring the defendant to notify the Court and the Attorney General of any change in his economic circumstances that might affect the ability to pay restitution.

The defendant will also pay the special assessment of $450 for Counts One and Four through Eleven, also payable immediately. No costs of confinement and no fine will be ordered because of the amount of the restitution that has now been ordered.

Chapter IV.

THE EYEWITNESSES

A. OVERVIEW

Many, many witnesses reported seeing Timothy McVeigh or John Doe #2 with one or more individuals prior to, or following, the Murrah Building bombing. The FBI, at first, was interested in their stories; but, as the Government began to develop its theory of what had transpired, it chose to ignore many of these witnesses and even tried to cast doubt on the veracity and sanity of some of them. The majority of these witnesses were interviewed by the FBI. Few were called to testify in the federal trials. Therefore, many of their stories have not been widely heard. Those who were called to testify often gave different accounts by the time the FBI and prosecutors finished drilling them on their testimony; therefore, some of what appears below is different from stories the witnesses told years later. Some of these witnesses have given affidavits to the OKBIC, but have requested that their names not be made public. OKBIC has honored those requests. They are identified in the report by fake initials only, with the exception of those who have since gone public with their accounts.

B. PRIOR TO APRIL, 1995

1. Summer, 1992

a. **Catina Lawson** was an acquaintance of Timothy McVeigh during the summer of 1992. She and a friend, **Lindy Johnson**, had graduated from high school and were sharing an apartment before starting college in the fall. Timothy McVeigh was often part of the group from Fort Riley with whom the girls socialized. As a result of this association, the FBI was provided with a picture of Lawson, Johnson and McVeigh coming out of a liquor store in Junction City. Lawson's mother admits that the three of them are depicted in the photo. Another picture showed what the FBI thought was a picture of Lawson and McVeigh at the senior prom. The male in the prom picture shows a strong resemblance to McVeigh, but Lawson's mother says that the picture is of Lawson and Eric Green, a soldier from Fort Riley whom Lawson dated for about two years and corresponded with for another year.

Lawson has stated that she observed McVeigh with Andreas Strassmeir and Michael Brescia at these same parties. These individuals were identified by FBI informant, Carol Howe, as part of the white-separatist compound called Elohim City in far Eastern Oklahoma. (Source: Witness interview by Glenn & Kathy Wilburn, an Oklahoma City couple who lost their grandchildren in the bombing and began their own investigation.)

b. Connie Smith, Catina Lawson's mother and a resident of Herington, Kansas, remembers meeting McVeigh in the summer of 1992. She was in her car and saw her daughter with a group of people behind the Cardie's Corner Convenience Store. Lawson waved her over to meet a new girlfriend of hers. McVeigh was there with Michael Brescia. In the fall of 1993 and spring of 1994, Smith remembers Lawson being home for holidays and getting together with her friends. McVeigh and Strassmeir were at some of their gatherings. She told Kathy Wilburn, when shown a picture of Strassmeir, "If his name is Andy, then he's been to my home."

According to Smith, in the summer of 1994, she observed Strassmeir at an arts-and-crafts fair in Herington, Kansas in the proximity of a booth where anti-Government literature was handed out to the public and where army surplus was being sold. She said she also saw McVeigh come out of the building later in the day.

Smith also recalled an instance in late summer 1994. Lawson told her about being at a "pasture party" with a group of people, including McVeigh, who were drinking beer. An older man known as "Ace," a quarter-master at Fort Riley, drove into the pasture and parked a distance away from the group. McVeigh went out to meet with him and they talked for about 10 minutes. Smith said she had seen Ace on occasion at the local diner with Terry Nichols. She described him as approximately 45 years of age and about 5' 2" in height, nice build, dark brown hair with a little bit of gray, business-type haircut, dark mustache, and short sideburns, slightly olive-toned complexion, preppy dress.

Robert Jacks

(Source: Taped OKBIC interview, 19 Aug 97 & interviews by the Wilburns)

2. July 1994

In July 1994, **William Maloney**, a realtor in Cassville, Missouri, received a call from an individual inquiring about a parcel of remote property in the Ozark Mountains. The person identified himself as Tim McVeigh. The realtor asked if the last name was spelled M-C-V-E-Y, and the caller said, "That's close enough." After discussing characteristics of the property, McVey said he would get back with the realtor. (Source: Taped OKBIC interview)

3. November 1994

On 02 November 1994, three men arrived at **William Maloney**'s realty office in an older four-door vehicle. Two of the men came into the office to discuss a remote piece of property. One of these two, identifying himself as Robert Jacks, did most of the talking. He told Maloney, "I just go by Jacks." Another man who worked for Maloney at the time, **Joe Lee Davidson**, was also at the office when the three men came by. He stated that Jacks was "the one that was in charge and control of what was going on." A second man used the name Terry Nichols, but took little part in the conversation. The third man, who stayed in the car most of the time, briefly stepped into the office doorway and had a conversation with Maloney. The realtor noticed a glimmering from a filling on the right side of his mouth, a detail which the FBI later confirmed was consistent with a filling McVeigh has. (Source: Correspondence from Maloney to OKBIC)

4. Early 1995

a. "Mr. A"

In the months preceding the bombing, "**Mr. A**" observed Timothy McVeigh and others at Cardie's Corner Convenience Store in Herington, Kansas on several different occasions. "Mr. A" said he also talked to Terry Nichols numerous times and gave him "quite an education… unfortunately [on] blowing up tree stumps [and] fertilizer and stuff." He also told of another man from the area with whom he was acquainted; they had talked during the week before the bombing while having a meal at the Santa Fe Diner. "Mr. A" alleges that this man told him about joining a militia and that "he was going down to Oklahoma to do a field exercise."

"Mr. A" overheard discussions regarding what type of truck was best to use to make a truck bomb. At one point, one of the men in McVeigh's company asked "Mr. A," "What kind of truck would you use to make a truck bomb?" He told them he would use a farm truck. (Source: Taped OKBIC interview)

b. Larry Wild also saw McVeigh at Cardie's Corner the night that discussions occurred about building a bomb. Wild said that McVeigh was with "three dark-complected guys." He described one of the men as "…about 5 feet, 10 inches, with dark hair combed straight back." He noted that the person he saw had more prominent cheekbones than the man depicted in the FBI sketches. There was also a man with "baggy jeans, a powder-blue jean jacket, sloppy." He was a "big, big-built Mexican with a big nose, kind of." Wild asserts that, an evening or two before the bombing, he saw "a Ryder truck, Nichols' truck, 10 or 12 guys, a Chevy Cavalier and an old four-door white-with-orange Chevy sedan with a license tag that ended in the numbers 3-1-6 behind Cardie's Corner." (Source: OKBIC taped interview & *The New American*, 13 May 96, pg. 38)

C. PRIOR TO FRIDAY, 14 APRIL 1995

1. After the composite drawings of John Doe #1 and #2 were released on 20 April 1995, people in the Junction City, Kansas area reported having seen the two men together on several occasions. **Miguel Cruz**, who works at the IG Sports Bar, said he had beaten one of them at pool twice. **Bob McDowell** said that he had seen them the previous week at a local convenience store and at Yesterday's Bar on Washington Street. He said that one guy "looked intense" as he waited for McDowell to finish playing a video game so he could play. **Sylvia Niemczyis** said the pair bought gas several times over the previous two months at the Texaco Food Mart where she worked. She relayed that "They came in a couple of times a week. They were clean cut. Casual. No problems." (Source: *The Washington Post*, 22 Apr 95, Pg. A12)

2. "Ms. B," a federal employee, was taking the elevator to the second floor of the Murrah Building when she encountered two men dressed in janitor uniforms. When the doors opened, she thought it odd that the two did not get in, but turned and walked away. She has identified one of the "janitors" as McVeigh. (Source: *The New American*, 13 May 96, p. 37)

3. 31 March or 07 April

Dr. Paul Heath was the Public Affairs Officer for the Veterans Administration (VA) at the Murrah Building. He has reported that McVeigh and two other individuals visited his office on Friday, 31 March or Friday, 07 April 1995 and has described the encounter in detail numerous times to investigators and journalists. Heath heard the bell ring at the front desk of the foyer in the VA office and came forward to find a man he said was McVeigh standing in front of the desk. Two other individuals stayed in the background while Heath and McVeigh carried on a conversation. Heath asked how he could help them and where they were from, and McVeigh responded that they were veterans looking for construction work. McVeigh told him that he had been staying out west, but that he was "from New York." Heath said he knew people from a small town in Oklahoma with the name McVeigh and asked if he was related to them. Heath said McVeigh's response was unusual and specific:

McVeigh: "How do they spell their name?"

Heath: "M-C-V-E-Y."

McVeigh: "Oh no. Remember, Dr. Heath, my name is spelled M-C-V-E-I-G-H."

They continued to converse. One of the two John Does asked to use the telephone, and Heath told him where it was and how to dial out. The third individual sat silently in a chair in the foyer without interacting with the others. (Source: Witness interviews with Glenn Wilburn and Charles Key, and media)

Dr. Paul Heath

4. 07-14 April

    a. **Max Albin** was in the Hot Iron Bar, in Dwight, Kansas sometime during the week between 07 and 14 April 1995. He observed Timothy McVeigh and a person with whom Albin was acquainted, "Mr. C," come into the bar. "Mr. C" approached Albin and stated something to the effect, "Look for something big to happen on the 19th." Albin also observed three other individuals come into the bar and meet with McVeigh and "Mr. C." He has stated that two of the individuals resembled Robert Jacks and Gary Land who were held as possible suspects by the FBI following the bombing. (Source: OKBIC interview)

    b. In the week before the bombing, **Jane C. Graham**, a public housing specialist with Housing and Urban Development (HUD), and the president of American Federation of Government Employees (AFGE) Local 3138, saw three men on the second level of the Murrah Building parking garage standing just west of the double doors leading to the elevator, behind an old station wagon. She thought maybe they were with the phone company because they were holding what looked like cream-colored, short pieces of telephone wiring. They also had a set of plans which she assumed to be plans of the building, and they were arguing about something to do with the plans and pointing to areas in the garage.

She said one of the men was about 6 foot 1 inch tall, with very dark collar-length hair and a mustache. He was wearing black cowboy boots and hat, jeans, and a jacket. The other two men were described as about 5 foot 8 inches with brown hair and wearing jeans. One of them, she said, had a brown plaid, short-sleeved shirt and obviously lifted weights. Graham told that, as she studied the men, they also watched her. One man spoke to the other, then took the wiring and paper bag to the station wagon and put them in the back seat area. She said they watched her until she went through the double doors to the elevator. (Source: Letter from Jane Graham, 15 Nov 96) (Appendix pgs. 416-418)

Jane Graham

5. 10-12 April, 8:00 a.m.

    a. Georgia Rucker routinely took her son to school at approximately 8:00 on weekdays and passed by Geary Lake on Highway 77. She said she saw a Ryder truck (a four-bedroom model) parked at the lake on the 10th, 11th, and 12th of April. On Tuesday, the 11th, she noticed two vehicles parked by the truck. School was not in session on Thursday, Friday or Monday, but on Tuesday, 18 April, she again saw the truck. (Source: Nichols trial transcript, pg. 12606-15)

    b. James Sargent retired from the Army on 10 April 1995 at Fort Riley. He out-processed that day and, finishing early, went to Geary Lake to fish. As he was moving to another location at the lake at around 2:30 p.m., he saw a Ryder truck parked by the jetty. He observed two vehicles approach the truck: a dull, red-primer pickup and a white car. He did not see if these two vehicles actually stopped by the Ryder truck. Sargent passed by the lake on 11 and 12 April and saw the Ryder truck parked there on those occasions also. (Source: Nichols trial transcript, pg. 12391-97)

OKBIC Note: McVeigh, reportedly, was in Kingman, Arizona at the time of this sighting.

6. 10-16 April, Various Times

Shane Boyd, a helicopter mechanic on contract with the Government, was working at Fort Riley and staying in room #28 at the Dreamland Motel. On Monday, 10 April, at about 6:00 a.m., he saw a three-bedroom Ryder truck with a 20-25 foot flatbed trailer behind it, making a U-turn in the parking lot. The truck and trailer were gone when he returned about 3:15 p.m. He continued to see a similar Ryder truck at the motel the rest of the week both early morning and afternoon. The last time he saw the truck was Sunday morning, 16 April. (Source: Nichols trial transcript, pg. 11957-62)

D. FRIDAY, 14 APRIL 1995

1. 14 April, 4:00 p.m.

Lea McGown is the owner of the Dreamland Motel in Junction City, Kansas. She was on duty at the counter on 14 April when Timothy McVeigh registered as a guest. He recorded his car as a Mercury with Arizona plate number LCC034 and his address as 3616 N. Van Dyke, Decker, Michigan (the address of James Nichols, Terry Nichols' brother). McVeigh checked into Room #25 under his own name. (Source: Nichols trial transcript, pg. 11817-18)

Dreamland Motel

2. 14 April, 6:00-7:30 p.m.

On Friday evening, **Shane Boyd** was cooking chicken on the outdoor barbecue pit in front of his room. He had fixed more than he and his wife could eat; so, when the door to Room #25 opened, he asked the occupant if he would like some of the chicken. The man ignored him and got in his car, a yellow Mercury, and left. Boyd identified this man as Timothy McVeigh. He said the last time he saw the Mercury was Sunday after Easter dinner, 16 April. (Source: McVeigh trial transcript, pg 11962-65)

3. 14 April, 11:00-11:30 p.m.

Elenora Hall and a female friend went to Denny's Restaurant in Junction City, Kansas around 11:00 p.m. on Friday. There were two Ryder trucks parked out front. As they were going into the restaurant, Hall saw a man by a bush near the door who appeared to be waiting and hiding. He was shaking and appeared to be "scared." She looked at him and their eyes held contact for a moment. She described him as being 5'7" or 5'8" tall, approximately 26 years old and clean-shaven. He had "an olive complexion and...long, straight, dark hair that came down to the neck.... He was kind of a stocky person, but not flabby or anything like that, just solid." He wore tennis shoes, brand new jeans and a white T-shirt with sleeves.

Hall and her friend went into the restaurant to wait for another friend who was going to join them. As their friend arrived, the man and a second man came in behind her and sat at a table. She described the second man as over six feet tall, about 40 years old, with poor posture and wearing a brown "UPS-type jacket" like those worn in the forties and a hat. He was white but looked like he could be part Mexican or Indian. (See Paragraph E.3. below for more.) (Source: OKBIC interview, 26 June 97)

4. 14 and 17 April

a. "**Ms. D**" owns a pawnshop in Oklahoma City. She states that McVeigh and two other men came into her shop on 14 April and again on 17 April. (Source: KFOR-TV Interview, 05 June 95)

b. Three women ("**Ms. E**," "**Ms. F**" and "**Ms. G**") worked in a store in a northwest area of Oklahoma City where a brown pickup truck, matching the description in the FBI all points bulletin (APB), was often seen at another neighborhood business. All three say that McVeigh, accompanied by two other men speaking a foreign language, came into their store on both 14 and 17 April. (Source: KFOR-TV interview, 05 June 95)

OKBIC Note: The driver of the brown pickup truck became a John Doe #2 suspect and was questioned by the FBI. He told authorities that he was employed both as a house painter and by a local restaurant. He claimed that, on the morning of the bombing, he was painting a garage on Northwest 31st Street. He produced a time sheet to prove that he had reported for work at 8:08 a.m. This suspect also asserted that he worked a second job as a janitor at a restaurant three nights a week, from 10:00 p.m. to 8:00 a.m., and would not have had time to participate in the bombing. Other witnesses claim that the suspect's story isn't true. Their accounts follow:

1). "**Mr. H**," who lived next door to the house on Northwest 31st Street said he was home that day, and nobody was painting that house.

2). "**Mr. I**" was a co-worker of the John Doe #2 suspect. He stated that John Doe's company did not use handwritten time sheets. Instead, a time clock had been used for the previous five or six months. He also said that the man in question was working at a different house, six blocks away by ten o'clock the morning of the bombing—but he wasn't there at 8:30 a.m. "Mr. H" stated, "They was out there acting like they was painting on that garage all morning. They didn't know I was already there before." "Mr. H" also stated that beginning "approximately. two or three weeks before the bombing," he often saw a "brown Chevrolet pickup, about a '94 model, with tinted windows and the bug shield" parked outside the office where he works.

3). "**Mr. J**" was assistant manager at the restaurant where the suspect worked part time. He said that the suspect had not worked from 17 to 20 April. The suspect reapplied for his job in May, then quit again in June.

4). "**Mr. K**," a former co-worker of the John Doe #2 suspect, says that he had drinks with the man at a bar on Northwest 10th Street and Indiana. The suspect claimed that he had never been in a bar on 10th Street, and that he is Moslem and therefore does not drink.

NOTE: See a copy of a police report on Appendix pg. 495 where this individual was arrested for being under the influence of alcohol and in control of a motor vehicle.

E. SATURDAY, 15 APRIL 1995

1. 15 April, 5:00-6:00 a.m.

Barbara Whittenberg and her husband owned the Santa Fe Trail Diner in Herington, Kansas, two blocks from Nichols' house. She related that Terry Nichols had been in the diner on many occasions for coffee or meals. He was quiet and sat alone unless his son Josh was with him. McVeigh had also been in previously on numerous occasions, but he was always in the company of teenagers, which included Lindy Johnson (See paragraph B1 above). Nichols and McVeigh never sat together; in fact, they sat in different rooms.

On 15 April, Whittenberg said she arrived at the restaurant sometime between 5:00 and 6:00 in the morning. A Ryder truck and an old beige, four-door sedan with Arizona tags were parked in the lot when she arrived. She went inside and to the back of the restaurant. When she came back to the front, there were three people sitting at a table close to the door: Nichols, McVeigh, and a third man resembling John Doe #2. She said the third man "looked Hawaiian. His skin was an olive color,...He was muscular built. He didn't have hardly a neck; so, you know, he was a body builder is what he looked like. He had a wide forehead, his eyes were set in a little bit....His nose was wide....The lips was thicker....His ears were set low on his head...."

She said she tried to make conversation with them, but they were not very communicative. When asked where they were going, the Hawaiian-looking man answered, "Oklahoma." Whittenberg stated that, "At that point, McVeigh looked at him, and a bucket of cold water was thrown on the conversation, and I knew to get out.... And then they got up and they all three left."

(Source: OKBIC taped interview)

2. 15 April, 8:45 a.m.

Eldon Elliot, the owner of Elliott's Body Shop and a Ryder truck rental facility in Junction City, Kansas first saw Bob Kling on the morning of Saturday, 15 April. He said Kling came into the Ryder rental facility to reserve a 20-foot truck for the following Monday. He refused insurance, saying he was a careful driver and accustomed to driving big trucks out of Fort Riley, which is about five miles north of Junction City. He stated that he would be traveling to Omaha and then to Iowa. He paid cash for the truck rental and asked that it be ready by 4:00 p.m. Monday. (Source: McVeigh trial transcript, pg. 8007-8059)

OKBIC Note: During testimony before the Federal Grand Jury, Mr. Elliott described Kling as around his own height of 5'10" and having a medium complexion like his own, maybe a little darker, half-an-inch-long hair, military style; he could not remember the color. Kling "kind of had like a little wrinkle or drawn-in on his chin." He said he spoke to Kling "face-to-face" across the counter.

OKBIC Note: During McVeigh's trial, Elliott testified that McVeigh was Kling and appeared shorter than his actual height because he had been leaning on the counter. He also suggested that the mark on his chin "might have been a shadow from the light or something."

3. 15 April, Noontime

Elenora Hall (paragraph C.3. above) saw the same man she had seen the previous night standing outside Denny's Restaurant door. On 15 April, at a grain elevator across from her house, she observed the same man. It was just after noon, when the business had closed and all the employees had left for the day. The man was in a Ryder truck parked by the elevator where the stairs connect rather than by the loading dock, and the door to the back of the truck was open.

Eldon's Body Shop

There was no furniture inside, and he was loading a single, very heavy, large bag into the truck with some difficulty. He looked her way and stared at her for a time. Later she checked with the owner of the grain elevator who told her that he had no idea who this man might have been or what he could have been doing. She said that this man was not McVeigh and did not resemble the John Doe #2 sketches much. (Source: OKBIC interview, 26 Jun 97)

4. 15 April, 2:00-4:00 p.m.

Robert Jaynes, a mechanic at Fort Riley, saw a Ryder truck at Lake Geary on Saturday, 16 April between 2:00 and 4:00 p.m. He identified the truck from a Ryder brochure as the three-bedroom model, 20-foot long with a truck front and no cab-over. (Nichols trial transcript, pg. 112695-98)

5. 15 April, 3:30 p.m.

On Saturday, 15 April, at about 3:30 p.m., **Shane Boyd** (paragraph C.2. above) left his room at the Dreamland Motel and went to the vending machine by the office to get a soda. On his return, a man was walking toward him and seemed to have come from one of the rooms between his room and the office, which would have included room #25. He described the man as "Hispanic, approximately 5' 6", 180 to 200 pounds, short, short haircut, seemed like he was in the military." He wore a "tan shirt, blue jean shorts down to the knees, no facial hair or anything like that, no jewelry or any scars or anything." (Source: Nichols trial transcript, pg. 11967-70)

6. 15 April, 5:30 p.m.

Jeff Davis delivered Chinese food to a "Bob Kling" at the Dreamland Motel, Room #25 at 5:30 p.m. on 15 April. Davis testified that someone—not McVeigh—was at the motel door and took the delivery. (Source: McVeigh trial transcripts, pg. 10321-24)

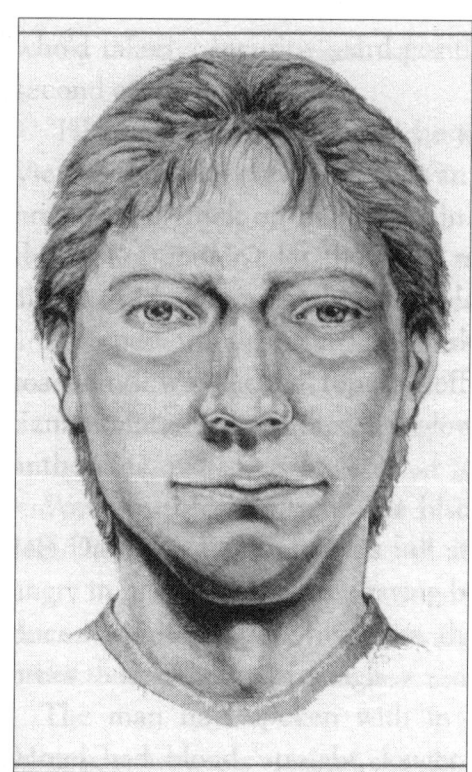

Jeff Davis Delivered Chinese Food To This John Doe At The Dreanland Motel

OKBIC Note: In her book, sketch artist Jeanne Boylan tells of meeting with Davis and producing a sketch of this man—John Doe #4. (Source: *Portraits of Guilt*, Jeanne Boylan, Pocket Books, 2000, pg. 259-262)

7. 15 April, Time Unknown

"**Mr. and Mrs. L**", husband and wife bartenders in Oklahoma City, reported serving beer to McVeigh and a dark-haired man on Saturday, 15 April. The dark-haired man "fit the description of John Doe No. 2...and spoke in broken English with a Middle-Eastern accent." (Source: *The New American*, 13 May 96, pg. 38) When shown surveillance photos of the John Doe suspect in the brown pickup truck, "Mrs. L" "positively identified him as the 'drinking buddy' of McVeigh" (Source: *The New American*, 04 Sep 95, quoting a KFOR-TV newscast)

8. 15 or 16 April, Just Before Midnight

Shortly before midnight, on Saturday or Sunday night, **Lea McGown** was making rounds outside her motel. As she approached Room #25, she heard voices inside. Since there was supposed to be only one guest in the room, she paused by the window and listened. She said the voices were coming from the opposite side of the room from where the television was located. There were at least two, and possibly three male voices. (Source: Nichols trial transcript, pg. 11837-38)

F. SUNDAY, 16 APRIL 1995 (EASTER SUNDAY)

1. 16 April, Just after Midnight

Connie Hood was visiting a friend in room #22 at the Dreamland Motel shortly after midnight. As she was walking to the room, the door to room #23 was flung open and a man inside eyed her and quickly closed the door. She described him as "about 5 foot, 9-10 inches, medium build, olive complexion, with thick, wiry, dark hair." The man strongly resembled the John Doe #2 sketch but had fuller features. (Source: *The New American*, 13 May 96, pg. 38)

2. 16 April, 9:30-10:30 a.m.

Leonard and Diana White were guests at the Dreamland Motel. Sometime between 9:30 and 10:30 a.m. on Easter morning, they saw an old, faded, late-model yellow car in front of Room #25. The couple noticed the rundown condition of the car and that it had an Arizona tag which was properly attached to the auto. The Whites do not remember seeing a Ryder truck in the parking lot. (Source: McVeigh trial transcript, pg. 10200-03 & 10215-19)

3. 16 April, 10:00-11:00 a.m.

On Easter Sunday, between 10:00 and 11:00 a.m., **Rickey Glessner**, with BG Consultants, an engineering firm in Manhattan, Kansas, was on his way to his parents' house in White City, Kansas. As he passed by Geary Lake, he saw a 20- to 24-foot Ryder truck with a "grandma's attic" (cab-over) at the lake close to the highway. (Source: Nichols trial transcript, pg. 12645-50)

4. 16 April, 12:30-1:00 p.m.

Nancy Jean Kindle, worked as a waitress at Denny's Restaurant in Junction City, Kansas. On Easter Sunday she was helping the hostess and took a seating request from a man named McVeigh. She identified this man in court as the defendant, Timothy McVeigh. She said he was in the company of two other men, one of whom she described as around 5'7" and "scraggly;" she could not describe the other man, but said that neither of them was Terry Nichols. (Source: McVeigh trial transcript, pg. 10707-09)

5. 16 April, 12:45-1:00 p.m.

Herta King took an Easter basket to her son in Room #24 of the Dreamland Motel at approximately 12:45 p.m. on Easter Sunday. As she pulled into the motel, there was a Ryder truck blocking the view of her son's room so that she could not see his car. The truck was a 20-foot model like one which she herself had rented before. Later that evening, around 7:00-8:00 p.m., King returned to the motel to bring Easter dinner leftovers to her son and noticed that the Ryder truck was gone. (Source: McVeigh trial transcript, pg. 10707-09 & 10766-70)

6. 16 April, Afternoon

After church on Easter Sunday, **Renda Truong** of Junction City, Kansas went to dinner with the McGowns, owners of the Dreamland Motel. Truong is not sure if it was before or after going to dinner that she saw a Ryder truck parked under the sign at the Dreamland Motel. She mentioned the truck in a conversation with Lea McGown. Truong is certain of the day because it was the only time she visited the motel that week. (Source: McVeigh trial transcript, pg. 10180-85)

7. 16 April, 3:30 p.m.

Easter Sunday, 16 April, is also the day **Terry Nichols** states he received a phone call from McVeigh asking for a ride back to Junction City because he had experienced problems with his car. (The Government contends that McVeigh was stashing his "get-away" car.) Nichols said that the call from McVeigh came around 3:00 p.m., and Nichols left for Oklahoma City shortly thereafter. Since a Denny's waitress (see next paragraph) reports seeing McVeigh at a Texaco station in Junction City at 4:30 p.m., and since a call from Tim's Amoco in Herington, Kansas was made to Nichols' home at 3:08 p.m. using the Bridges' calling card, there is a question about the origin of that telephone call--Kansas vs. Oklahoma. (Source: Testimony of Agent Stephen Smith during Nichols trial, pg. 9906-07, based on his interrogation of Nichols)

8. 16 April, 4:30 p.m.

Nancy Kindle (the waitress who seated McVeigh at Denny's Restaurant) saw McVeigh again at a Texaco station around 4:30 p.m. They said hello as she was walking in and he was walking out. Kindle does not remember seeing any vehicles in connection with McVeigh at that time. (Source: McVeigh trial transcript, pg. 10710-12)

9. 16 April, 8:00 p.m.

A trip from Herington, Kansas to Oklahoma City takes about five hours, driving down U.S. Highway 10. **Terry Nichols** told the FBI that he arrived in Oklahoma City at 8:10 p.m. and drove around in the downtown area looking for McVeigh, finding him in an alleyway on Northwest 8th Street, "standing in a light rain with Terry Nichols' TV set and a green laundry bag." He did not see McVeigh's car. (Source: Transcript of Agent Stephen Smith's testimony at Nichols trial, pg. 9915, based on his interrogation of Nichols)

G. MONDAY, 17 APRIL 1995

1. 17 April, 1:30 a.m.

Terry Nichols and Timothy McVeigh arrived back in Junction City, Kansas around 1:30 a.m. on 17 April. According to FBI Agent Stephen Smith, Nichols said that "he dropped Mr. McVeigh off at a closed McDonald's at—on Washington Street in Junction City, Kansas, and that Mr. McVeigh had said that he would call a friend." Nichols said that, as he was leaving, McVeigh was "walking towards a Denny's that was open up the street." (Source: Transcript of Agent Stephen Smith's testimony at Nichols trial, pg. 9922-23, based on his interrogation of Nichols)

2. 17 April, 8:00 a.m. & Noon

Hilda Sostre was a maid at the Dreamland Motel. On 17 April, she came to work between 8:00 and 8:30 a.m. after having been off over the weekend. She said there was a Ryder truck parked in her normal parking place. As she walked to the office, she saw a man walking toward the truck. She saw him approach the door to the truck, but did not actually see him open the door. She described him as having a "good build...black hair...long nose...brown skin." She thought he was Spanish. When she came out of the laundry room a little later, he was gone. About noon that same day, she went to clean room #25. She said she knocked on the door and asked the guest if he needed a towel. He told her no and closed the door. As she was walking off, he reopened the door and said, "No, I think I need some towel (sic)." She told him she would have to have the used one in exchange, and he went back inside and retrieved it. She identified this man as Timothy McVeigh. (Source: Nichols trial transcript, pg. 11918-26)

When she entered Room #25 on 17 April, "McVeigh and the vehicles were gone, but someone was still in the room." (Source: William F. Jasper interview with Sostre)

3. 17 April, 10:00-10:30 a.m.

Elwin Roberts, an engineering technician with BG Consultants, went to Hamm's Quarry near Herrington, Kansas on Monday, 17 April, "to take some samples." On his way back to the office in Manhattan, Kansas, between 10:00 to 10:30 a.m., he passed by Geary Lake where he saw an older brown pick-up truck parked behind a Ryder truck. He said the Ryder truck had a "slipover" front with no cab-over. (Source: Nichols trial transcript, pg.12636-40)

4. 17 April, 3:29 p.m.

Dan Ferris, a cab driver in Junction City, Kansas, said that, on 17 April, at 3:29 p.m., he picked up a fare at the Shop 'n' Stop in Grandview Plaza and dropped him at the McDonald's Restaurant South, about a 10-minute drive. He identified this person as Timothy McVeigh. (Source: Nichols trial transcript, pg. 11873-76)

5. 17 April, 3:57 p.m.

A video-tape at McDonald's Restaurant in Junction City shows McVeigh inside at 3:49:02 through 3:57:12 p.m. on 17 April. The video shows McVeigh wearing light-colored jeans and a dark shirt over a light T-shirt. (Prosecutors contend that, even though it was raining that day, McVeigh walked from McDonald's to Elliott's rental facility, "a little over a mile away, to rent the Ryder truck." Records show that "Bob Kling" was at Elliott's Body Shop and rented the Ryder truck at 4:16 p.m. that day. Elliott said that he paid no attention to Kling's clothes, but Kling's face was not wet when he saw him at his place of business.) (Source: Nichols trial transcript, pg. 11894-11910 & McVeigh trial transcript, pg. 8013-14 & 8021)

6. 17 April, 4:16 p.m.

Three employees of Elliott's Body Shop and Ryder Truck Rentals in Junction City, Kansas saw the person who rented the Ryder truck that carried the truck bomb. Their accounts follow:

    a. Employee, **Thomas Kessinger,** reportedly got the best look at "Bob Kling" and the man who accompanied him when the Ryder truck was rented on 17 April. He described Kling as "5'10", weighing 175 to 185 pounds, green or brown eyes, and with a rough complexion or acne." He said the second individual "was wearing a black T-shirt, jeans, and a ball cap colored royal blue in the front and white in the back. He also stated that John Doe 2 had a tattoo on his upper left arm. Kessinger was the source of the John Doe #1 and #2 sketches, which were completed on 20 April 95 and released to the public. (Source: McVeigh Writ of Mandamus, pg. 40)

OKBIC Note: Even though Kessinger was the source of the John Doe #1 sketch, he was not called to testify at either trial. Was this because the Government did not want him cross-examined regarding John Doe #2?

    b. Vicki Beemer, an employee of Elliott's Body Shop, at 1430 Golden Belt Boulevard, Junction City, Kansas, completed the Ryder truck rental contract for Bob Kling on 17 April at 4:19 p.m. Supposedly, McVeigh, using the name "Bob Kling" and John Doe #2 rented a 20-ft. Ryder truck. Beemer said Kling was "around 5'10," 5' 11," about the height of my husband; he was medium-to-slender build;...[his hair had] a very short, military-type haircut." Source: McVeigh trial transcript, pg. 10391-94)

The John Doe II With McVeigh (Alias "Bob Kling") When He Rented The Ryder Truck

c. Eldon Elliott (paragraph E.2. above) was at the office on Monday, 17 April, when Kling came to pick up the Ryder truck. Elliott said he was called into the office by his helper, Vicki Beemer, so he could perform the pre-rental inspection of the truck. He remembered asking Kling if he had changed his mind about getting insurance. He also recalled a man with Kling who had on a blue cap with white stripes on the side. (Source: McVeigh trial transcript, pg. 8050-54)

7. 17 April, Afternoon

Connie Hood (paragraph F.1. above) and her husband, **Donald Hood**, were visiting a guest in Room #22 at the Dreamland Motel on 17 April. She saw a Ryder truck arrive, driven by the man who had stuck his head outside of Room #23 the previous day. She entered Room #22 while her husband waited outside. He saw a man resembling John Doe #2 come from the office of the motel and get into a Ryder truck on the driver's side. About the same time, he saw McVeigh come from his room and get into the Ryder truck on the passenger's side. The two men then left in the truck. Mr. Hood described the first man as "about 5 feet, 9 inches, olive complected, with dark, brown hair combed straight back." (Source: *The New American*, 13 May 96, pg. 38)

8. 17 and 18 April, Time Unknown

Mr. Mistry (first name unknown) was the manager of the Great Western Motel in Junction City, Kansas. This motel is located in Grandview Plaza, down the road from the Dreamland Motel. Mistry reported to the FBI that the composite sketch of John Doe #2 resembled a man who stayed at his establishment on Monday and Tuesday, 17 and 18 April 1995. He stated that the man was driving a Ryder truck, and described him as having a Middle Eastern accent and bearing a great resemblance to the John Doe #2 sketch.

OKBIC Note: The FBI seized all related records from The Great Western Motel. The motel has since changed ownership, and OKBIC has been unsuccessful in finding anyone who knows how or where to locate this witness; therefore, no further information is currently available on this evidence. (Source: McVeigh Trial, Writ of Mandamus, page 100)

9. 17 or 18 April, Before Noon

Debbie Nakanashi worked for the U.S. Postal Service at their Center City office at Northwest 5th Street and Harvey, diagonally northwest across the intersection from the Murrah Building in downtown Oklahoma City. She was at work sometime between 9:00 and noon, "a day or two before the bombing," when McVeigh and another individual entered the Post Office. She described the second man as shorter with dark hair. She said the dark-haired man asked where he should go to fill out a federal job application. She mistakenly gave him the address of the main Post Office for postal jobs, rather than the Office of Personnel Management for other federal jobs. He did not thank her and started to walk away. She corrected herself and pointed to the window, telling them that they should apply at the Federal Building, catty-corner from the post office. She said they did not even glance out the window, but started out the door.

Nakanashi said she stayed home the rest of the week and spoke of the incident to the postal counselor who was calling employees to check on their well-being. Later that evening, she was visited by two agents from the Oklahoma State Bureau of Investigation (OSBI). The following week she spoke with OSBI and FBI agents and Postal inspectors. She said she spoke with at least seven different sets of agents. At one point she was shown a photo lineup and picked out McVeigh. (Source: Handwritten statement from Debbie Nakanashi, undated)

The FBI brought in Jeanne Boylan, a nationally known and very accomplished sketch artist, who drew a likeness of John Doe #2 based on Nakanashi's description. Within a week the sketch was removed from the APB. As Nakanashi put it, she "spoke with the John Doe #2 that has ceased to exist." (*Portraits of Guilt*, Jeanne Boylan, Pocket Books, 2000, pg. 210-216)

H. TUESDAY, 18 APRIL

1. 18 April, 1:30-2:00 a.m.

Rick Sinnett, a clerk at the Sav-a-Trip convenience store in Kingman, Kansas (approximately 25 miles west of Wichita) saw a Ryder truck pull into the parking lot and park beside one of the gas pumps. Two men, McVeigh and another man, got out of the truck. The second man pumped gas into the vehicle and McVeigh entered the store where he paid for the gasoline. The other man entered and bought a turkey and Swiss sandwich from the deli case. Sinnett described the second man as stocky, 5'8" to 5' 9", 180-185 pounds, blue-gray eyes, early-to-mid twenties, light complexion, and two-to-three inch long, light-brown, straight hair. (He did not think this man looked like the John Doe #2 sketches.) After the two men walked back outside, they seemed to be arguing about something, with McVeigh doing most of the talking. The second man went to the Ryder truck and got in on the passenger's side. McVeigh went around to the rear of the car carrier.

As the Ryder truck left the parking lot, two other vehicles came from behind the store and followed the truck—a brown pick-up truck and a white, or off-white, four-door car. "One vehicle pulled in behind the Ryder truck, and the other pulled alongside the Ryder truck," Sinnett related. All three vehicles headed west on Highway 54. (Appendix pg. 501)

Sinnett said the Ryder truck was towing a car carrier, the size that a full-size car would fit on. A large plastic circular tank was on the carrier. It was the width of the carrier and between six and eight feet tall. The tank was 85 to 90 percent full of liquid. (Source: Taped interview and written correspondence from Rick Sinnet to OKBIC)

2. 18 April, 4:00-5:00 a.m.

Lea McGown (paragraph D.1. above) saw McVeigh at the Dreamland Motel around 4:00 a.m. She had been awakened by noise from some area teenagers in front of the motel. She went into the office and looked out a window to see what was going on. She saw McVeigh sitting in a Ryder truck with the driver's door open and the dome light on. He appeared to be looking at a map. The teenagers left, so she went back to bed. When the alarm woke her again at 5:00 a.m., she went to the office to make coffee. Glancing out the window, she noticed that the Ryder truck was gone. That was the last time she saw McVeigh or the Ryder truck. (Source: Nichols trial transcript, pg. 11834–36)

3. 18 April, 5:50 p.m.

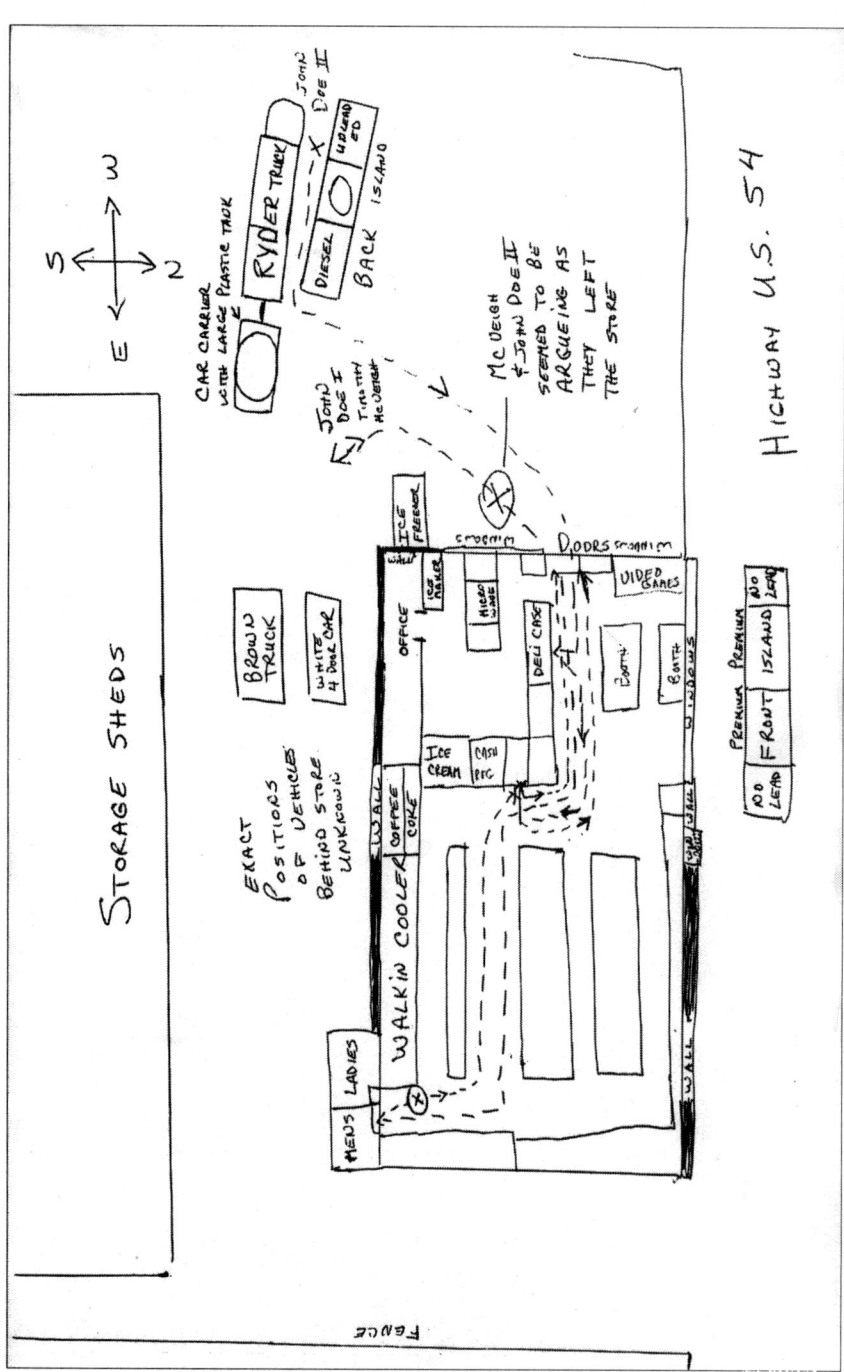

Map drawn by Rick Sinnett of McVeigh, a John Doe, and the three vehicles traveling together.

While driving around Geary Lake with his daughter, **Charles Farley**, who worked for the Outdoor Recreation Center at Fort Riley, observed a Ryder truck with three other vehicles and five men at Geary Lake at 5:50 p.m. on 18 April. He said a pick-up truck was loaded down with what appeared to be bags of ammonium nitrate. (Source: Nichols trial transcript, pg. 13652-73)

4. 18 April, 7:00 p.m.

Customers of the Cattle Baron's Steakhouse in Perry, Oklahoma (about 80 miles north of Oklahoma City) saw McVeigh and someone who resembled John Doe #2 having a beer at the restaurant on the evening of 18 April. According to *The Dallas Morning News*, owners, **Terry and Judi Leonard**, recalled a Ryder truck in their lot around 7:00 p.m. but paid little attention to the occupants. (Source: *The New American*, "The Trail of John Doe No. 2," 13 May 96, pg. 39)

5. 18 and 19 April

Rose Johnson was a maid at the Great Western Motel and cleaned rooms 107 and 110 on 18 and 19 April. She said the two men who occupied those rooms looked like the composite sketches of John Doe #1 and #2 that had been released shortly after the bombing. She reported that both rooms had been slept in and the showers had been used. (Source: *The Washington Post*, 22 Apr 95)

OKBIC Note: The FBI dusted the rooms for fingerprints, which are most likely part of the 1034 fingerprints that have not been run through their data bank.

I. WEDNESDAY, 19 APRIL (PRIOR TO THE BOMBING)

1. 19 April, 12:00-2:30 a.m.

Frederick Wade Skrdla, a gas station attendant at Cimarron Travel Plaza in Billings, Oklahoma, sold gas to a man fitting Timothy McVeigh's general description between midnight and 2:30 a.m. on 19 April, the morning of the bombing. The truck pointed in a northerly direction, although the witness did not see which direction the truck headed when it left. The Travel Plaza is 80 to 85 miles north of Oklahoma City. (Source: McVeigh preliminary hearing, 18 Feb 97,)

2. 19 April, 7:00 a.m.

Ms. M, the owner of a cafe in Mulhall, Oklahoma, reportedly saw a Ryder truck parked outside her business at 7:00 a.m. the morning of 19 April. This store is located on Rt. 77 in Oklahoma, approximately 45 miles north of Oklahoma City. (Mulhall is also close to the location where McVeigh was arrested by an Oklahoma Highway Patrol officer following the bombing.) (Source: OKBIC interview)

OKBIC Note: An employee of the store was subpoenaed to testify, but was not called to the stand.

3. 19 April, Early Morning

"**Mr. N**" a farmer, saw a Ryder truck on 19 April shortly after the sighting at the cafe. It was on the side of the road on Route 77 south of Mulhall, Oklahoma, heading south in the direction of Oklahoma City. He stopped and asked the occupants of the truck if they needed assistance and got a cold response from the two men, so continued on. (Second-party source received by Charles Key)

4. 19 April, 8:00 a.m.

Leonard Long was taking his daughter to school, driving east on Northwest 5th Street in downtown Oklahoma City. He encountered a brown pick-up truck with tinted windows, driving erratically. The driver yelled at him as they passed. Long described the two passengers: "one white male with sharp features and a dark-complexioned stockier man." He last saw the truck heading south toward Interstate-35. (Source: Glen Wilburn interview and J.D. Cash, *Media Bypass* article, Feb 96)

5. 19 April, 8:02-8:05 a.m.

Morris Kuper, an employee of Kerr-McGee Oil Company, saw a light-colored, pre-1980 Ford car, "most likely a Mercury," in the parking lot used by company employees. He stated he had never seen the car in the lot before. He observed two men approach the vehicle. As they were by the front bumper, they separated, the driver going to the driver's side of the car, the other man going to the passenger's side. Kuper parked his car and got out. The two men were standing by their car with the doors open, preparing to enter the car. Kuper and the men looked at each other from about 30 feet away. He described the men as follows:

> The driver of the car was a white male, probably 6—I'd say 6' 1" or 6' 2", weighed 180, 190 pounds. He was not a very heavy-set person. He was not a real skinny person, but he wasn't—He was just kind of the average guy. You know, he wasn't real muscular. He had short, light-colored hair—neat. He was wearing a white or light-colored T-shirt with dark pants. The other man was about 5' 8", 5' 9", stockier build. He was also wearing a light-colored shirt, dark pants. He was dark-complected, and I won't say nationalities. I'll just say dark complected -- I had sunglasses on. His hair was dark. It was not real long. It was somewhat short but kind of average. I mean, it wasn't out of place. And I say he was muscular because his T-shirt was full. You know, the arm filled up the shirt. There wasn't a lot of loose sleeve like the other man had a lot of loose sleeve on him. (Source: Nichols trial transcript, pg. 12815-21)

6. 19 April, 8:30 a.m.

Kyle Hunt, a bank vice-president from Tulsa, Oklahoma, saw a Ryder truck and a car resembling McVeigh's driving on Broadway in downtown Oklahoma City, moving slowly. Hunt remembers seeing two passengers with McVeigh, who was driving. He did not see the people inside the Ryder truck. (Source: Taped interview with Glenn Wilburn)

7. 19 April, 8:35 a.m.

David Snider, a warehouseman who worked south of the Murrah Building, flagged over a Ryder truck he believed was there to make a pick-up. Standing on the loading dock, he was at eye level with the passenger of the truck, and his description fit that of McVeigh. The driver, he said, did not fit the John Doe #2 profile. (Source: OKBIC witness interview)

8. 19 April, about 8:40 a.m.

James Linehan, an attorney from Edmond, Oklahoma, just north of Oklahoma City, watched as a yellow Mercury ran a red light at the intersection of Northwest 4th Street and Robinson. It then turned north on Harvey and sped into the underground parking garage at the Murrah Building. He glimpsed facial features that made him think the driver may have been a woman. He could not say if other passengers were in the car. (Source: The *Oklahoma Gazette*, 13 Feb 97, p. 8)

9. 19 April, 8:40 a.m.

David Snider

North of the bombsite, **Mike Moroz**, a tire store employee, walked out to help the driver of a Ryder truck who, he assumed, was looking for directions. The driver had on a baseball cap, worn backward. Moroz noticed that there was a passenger in the truck who was wearing a blue baseball cap. Moroz gave the driver directions to the Murrah Building. Four days later, Moroz participated in a police lineup to identify the passenger in the truck. He picked McVeigh and one other person out of the lineup. His identification led to the arraignment of Timothy McVeigh. (Source: OKBIC witness interview and FBI 302 reports)

OKBIC Note: Moroz was not called as a witness before the Federal Grand Jury or for the criminal trials.

10. 19 April, 8:45 a.m.

In the store on the first floor of the Regency Towers apartment building on Northwest 5th Street, one block west of the Murrah Building, **Danny Wilkerson** sold McVeigh two sodas and a pack of cigarettes. (McVeigh does not smoke.) Wilkerson saw McVeigh return to a Ryder truck which he described as a smaller version of the FBI-identified Ryder truck—one with a compartment over the cab. McVeigh and another male then drove around the block and back in front of the Regency Towers. They parked on the other side of the street to use the pay phone. (Source: OKBIC witness interview)

OKBIC Note: A short clip from the videotape taken at the Regency Towers showed a Ryder truck driving by just minutes before the bomb exploded.

11. 19 April, 8:50 a.m.

While parked across from the Murrah Building, **Leroy Brooks** saw a Ryder truck and a Mercury Marquis on the same street and block that Danny Wilkerson last saw the Ryder truck, but moved up several spaces toward the Murrah Building. Both drivers got out of their vehicles and appeared to exchange "a small object." Upon returning to his car from a visit to the Post Office, Brooks noticed the Ryder truck had now moved up one block, positioned in front of the Murrah Building. (Source: OKBIC witness interview)

12. 19 April, 8:45-8:55 a.m.

Gary Lewis stepped out into an alley on the south side of the Journal Record building, directly north across the street from the Murrah Building. He noticed a light-colored car in a "no parking" zone with a dark-complected or possibly Middle-Eastern man in the passenger seat. After going to his car, the witness walked back down the alley, and was almost hit by the light-colored car as it sped away. The car's license plate, not a brown Arizona tag, but a white tag, he said, dangled by a bolt. The vehicle passed Lewis on the driver's side, and Lewis saw the driver whom he identified as McVeigh. (Source: *The Dallas Morning News*, & witness interviews with KFOR-TV & the Wilburns)

13. 19 April, 8:55-8:59 a.m.

"**Mr. O**," is an attorney who was traveling west on Northwest 6th Street, on his way to the Oklahoma County Courthouse. As he neared the intersection of Northwest 6th Street and Robinson, he was approached from the rear and passed by a vehicle similar to the Mercury Marquis owned by McVeigh. The vehicle stopped at the light at Robinson alongside the attorney's vehicle, and the attorney saw a single occupant in the car, described as having a dark complexion, possibly a Middle-Eastern male. (Source: OKBIC interview)

This John Doe was seen by David Snider. He was driving a Ryder Truck and McVeigh was a passenger.

14. 19 April, Shortly before the Bombing

"**Ms. P**" told about a friend who was in front of the Murrah Building shortly before the bombing. She had pulled into a parking space right in front of the building to wait while her husband ran some papers inside. As she was waiting for her husband to return, a man with a crew cut "tapped on her window" and asked her to move her car "so he could pull his truck up into that space." She ignored him, but soon he asked again. About that time her husband returned and they drove off. In her rearview mirror, she saw the Ryder truck pull into her parking space. A few minutes later, the bomb exploded. (Source: OKC Central High School alumni newsletter, *45 Cardinal Quill,* pg 4)

15. 19 April, 8:58 a.m.

Rodney Johnson, a paramedic, drove a delicatessen truck at the time of the bombing. He was driving in front of the Murrah Building at 8:58 a.m. on 19 April when he had to abruptly brake for two men who were quickly crossing the street from the direction of the Murrah Building going to the Journal Record Building parking lot. Johnson notified the FBI that night and described the suspects—his descriptions matching those of the soon-to-be-released sketches of McVeigh and John Doe #2.

Johnson described McVeigh as wearing a white T-shirt and army fatigues. (When arrested, he wore a tan T-shirt over a white T-shirt with blue sleeves, black jeans and a blue windbreaker.) Johnson described the John Doe with McVeigh as being 5'7" to 5'8", 170 pounds and muscular, with dark, slicked-back hair. He wore a dark warm up suit with a stripe down the side, and a leather or heavy jacket with a hood.

OKBIC Note: It is important to point out that Johnson came forward with his statement before any press releases or sketches related to the John Does in this case were shown by the media. (Source: OKBIC witness interview and FBI 302 report)

Johnny's Tire Shop. McVeigh stopped here approximately twenty-five minutes before the bombing to ask for directions. A John Doe was with him in the passenger seat.

16. 19 April, 9:00 a.m.

a. Only moments before the explosion(s), bombing victim **Daina Bradley** was inside the Murrah Building on the first floor at the Social Security Office with her mother, her two children, and her sister. Bradley was there to change her son's social security card. She looked out a window and saw a Ryder truck parked by the front door. As she watched, two men got out of the truck. The man on the driver's side immediately walked across the street. She described him as a white male. The second man got out of the truck on the passenger's side, went to the rear of the truck, then back toward the front, "and proceeded to walk very fast forward in front of the truck…. He went back on the sidewalk and left." He left in a different direction from the other man.

The next thing Bradley remembers happening is that the bomb exploded, killing her mother and her two children, and severely injuring her and her sister. Bradley was trapped in the Murrah Building for five hours. Doctors had to amputate her leg to free her from the rubble of the building and get her to a hospital.

She described the passenger in the truck as being an "…olive-complexion man with short hair, curly, clean-cut. He had on a blue Starter jacket, blue jeans, and tennis shoes and a white hat with purple flames." She testified that the hat was a baseball cap. She also said that he did not wear eyeglasses or gloves, nor did not have a mustache or beard. She said she saw him from a side view. When she was shown a sketch of John Doe #2, she identified him as the man she had seen on the passenger's side of the truck. (Source: McVeigh trial transcript, pg. 10451-65)

Rodney Johnson saw McVeigh and John Doe II just minutes before the truck bomb exploded.

b. Candy Avey, who had just parked her car outside the Murrah Building and was on her way into the building to visit the Social Security Office, described her experience. "I was blown **back** [emphasis added], wrapped around the [parking] meter, and my face hit the car," she said. She also stated that she had broken her arm and jaw. There had been a man walking in the door in front of her whose "arm was blown off." She commented that he was in such shock that he did not seem to realize it and just kept helping others around him. (Source: *Time*, 01 May 95, pg. 59)

J. WEDNESDAY, 19 APRIL (FOLLOWING THE BOMBING)

After the explosion, many witnesses reported seeing suspicious Middle-Eastern men in the vicinity of the Murrah Building. Timothy McVeigh was also reported being seen at different locations—some of them impossible to reach in relation to other witness timeframes cited. (This led to speculation that a McVeigh look-alike was in Oklahoma City the morning of the bombing.) OKBIC has chosen not to select a particular time sequence as being the correct one, which would cause some witness statements to be discarded; therefore all the known witnesses' stories are included below.

OKBIC Note: Several people associated with this case have been identified as being McVeigh "look-alikes"; Catina Lawson's boyfriend Eric Green, Peter Ward from Elohim City, and an ATF agent. A photo of this ATF agent with two other federal agents in Waco, Texas during the ATF/FBI siege of the Branch Davidian complex at Mount Carmel in April 1993 can be found as Appendix pg. 450. The ATF confirmed that the man does work for them and is assigned to the Western region. (Source: Thomas Reisinger, *Soldier of Fortune*)

1. 19 April, Moments Following the Bombing

Within moments after the blast, **Kay Herrin Clark** was crossing Broadway near the Murrah Building when she was almost hit by two men driving a brown pick-up truck. She distinctly remembers they looked Middle-Eastern; and on the driver's face was a "chilling look of fear or anger." (KFOR-TV interviews, Jun 95)

2. 19 April, 9:10 a.m.

"**Mr. Q**" had been working in the Journal Record Building across the street from the Murrah Federal Building. After the explosion, he was helping a fellow employee exit the Journal Building using the front door. "Mr. Q" saw a tall "Arab-looking man" standing at the intersection of Northwest 6th Street and Harvey, looking back toward the bombed Murrah Building with "a big grin on his face." (Source: Witness interviews with the Wilburns)

3. 19 April, 9:30-9:40 a.m.

Bombing survivor and a branch chief with HUD, **Germaine Johnston** had left the Murrah Building and was on her way to the Kerr-McGee Building to find her husband. It was between 9:25 and 9:35 a.m. She was headed south from Fifth Street in a north-south alley between the two Southwestern Bell buildings. She encountered two men in the alley (one tall and the other shorter and darker) leaning against an older model, faded-yellow, four-door Mercury Marquis. Johnston said she and her husband used to drive a 1977 Mercury Marquis about that same color. The taller man asked her, "What happened? How many people were killed?" Later, when she saw McVeigh on TV, she was immediately struck with the thought that he was the man she had seen in the alley. She described the shorter man as approximately 5' 8" and 165 pounds. (Source: OKBIC witness interview and Nichols trial transcript, pg. 12847-55)

OKBIC Note: If Johnston saw McVeigh and the John Doe at the time indicated, McVeigh must have driven with great speed to have been to mile marker 202 on Interstate-35 by 10:17 a.m.

4. 19 April 19, 9:45 a.m.

Former Oklahoma City Councilman **Jack Cornett** was standing on the northwest corner of Hudson and Robert S. Kerr Avenues in downtown Oklahoma City waiting for a family member at approximately 9:45 a.m. shortly after the bombing. A man came up beside him and commented, "Maybe it got all the inspectors." Cornett turned to face him and the man immediately turned away. Sensing that something was wrong about this man, Cornett began to pursue him on foot. They headed west on Kerr Avenue.

When Cornett reached the corner of Kerr and Walker, he came upon a policeman, Officer Gore, and asked for help. He received none. Cornett came upon another police officer and, again, asked for assistance, receiving none. He eventually lost sight of the individual. He felt that the man went into the Oklahoma County Jail at Kerr Avenue and Shartel. Shortly thereafter he saw an older white four-door car come out an alleyway and turn onto Kerr Avenue at a high rate of speed. There was only one person in the car, and he believes it was his suspect.

Cornett called U.S. Marshal Crawford's office with this information at approximately 10:15 that morning. The Marshal's Service did not return his call. He then contacted FBI agent Joe Gray, followed by FBI headquarters in Washington, D.C. Receiving no further contact from them and believing his information was being ignored, Cornett then made an appointment with Bob Ricks, head of the Oklahoma City FBI office and provided this information to him. Cornett stated he was never contacted again by the FBI.

Cornett states that the man he chased was:

> *approximately 30 years old, 5'6" to 5'7"... had dark features, which appeared to be Arabic ... wore no hat or tie, had on an open shirt and a brown leather jacket vest with blue trim. The man's hair was dark and he may have had slight facial hair.*

K. CONCLUSIONS

The above evidence shows clearly that Timothy McVeigh had at least one other accomplice in the bombing. The individuals have been seen in McVeigh's company too many times in both Kansas and

Oklahoma to be just innocent bystanders; however, the FBI has chosen to ignore the existence of any other perpetrators besides McVeigh and Nichols. When will the other guilty parties be identified and punished?

Chapter V.

DAMAGE TO THE ALFRED P. MURRAH FEDERAL BUILDING

A. OVERVIEW

The Alfred P. Murrah Federal Building was considered a low risk facility for a terrorist attack. One guard was assigned to rove among four federal office buildings Monday through Friday from 6:00 a.m. to 8:00 p.m. According to Jim Boyd, a security specialist for Federal Protective Services, a branch of the Government Services Administration (GSA), a security review had been performed six weeks before the bombing and no need for change had been found (Source: *The Daily Oklahoman*, 21 Apr 95, pg. 8). This low-risk perception helped to make the Murrah Building a "soft target" and likely contributed to its selection by the bombers.

News reports said that President Clinton called Oklahoma Governor Frank Keating on the afternoon of 19 April and advised him that three anti-terrorist teams were en route to Oklahoma City. KFOR-TV reported "right now they are saying this is the work of a very sophisticated group. This is a very sophisticated device. It has to have been done by an explosives expert."
(Source: Tape of KFOR-TV broadcast, 19 Apr 95)

The FBI reported that the bombing of the Murrah Federal Building was caused by a single 1200 pound bomb made of ammonium nitrate (AN) and fuel oil (FO), contained inside 55-gallon barrels and exploded within a 20-foot Ryder rental truck parked in front of the Murrah Building, and this bomb alone caused the horrific damage that was done to the building. However, as people began to question this theory, that story changed (See paragraph C below). Additionally, other witnesses tell of hearing a second bomb; other experts assert that the bomb the FBI describes could not possibly have caused the amount of damage that occurred to the building. These arguments are presented in this chapter.

B. WITNESSES TO THE EXPLOSION

People from around the Oklahoma City metropolitan area report hearing either one or two distinct explosions; others heard nothing. The witness accounts vary considerably, depending upon their location in relation to the bomb(s). Several people reported having felt a sensation that allowed them time to get under their desks before the bomb exploded, supporting the theory that there may have been supplementary charges in the building. Following are the stories of some of the witnesses:

OKBIC Note: Reporter, Tara Blume,, said that she had spoken to several people who stated "that is how they survived it—by climbing under their desks." (Source: KFOR-TV broadcast, 19 Apr 95)

1. Jane Graham

Graham, an employee with Housing and Urban Development (HUD), was in her office on the ninth floor of the Murrah Building. She felt an initial shock which she thought was an earthquake. Eight to ten seconds later she felt a force (much different from the first) come from the central east portion of the building, and then a massive explosion ripped the floors to the roof. The blast knocked her back toward the west and knocked her unconscious for a few moments. When she opened her eyes, there was heavy black smoke and the sky could be seen from the rupture. (Source: OKBIC interview)

2. Jack Gobin

Gobin, an employee with the U.S. Department of Agriculture, was working at his desk in the Murrah Building the morning of the bombing. He told KFOR-TV in Oklahoma City that at first he thought it was an earthquake, but then the windows in his office blew in. He said he got under his desk and was not hurt. (Source: KFOR-TV broadcast, 19 Apr 95)

3. Man on the Street

A KFOR-TV commentator asked a man walking down the street at the bombsite what he had experienced. He told her, "I came out from under the desk and there just wasn't any building left around me. The whole office area was gone." (Source: KFOR-TV, 19 Apr 95)

4. Brian Espe

Espe, who worked on the 5th floor of the Murrah Building, stated, "I went under a table and the ceiling started to fall in." (Source: KFOR-TV, 19 Apr 95)

5. Virgil Steele

Steele was employed by Mid-Western Elevator Company which serviced the elevators in the federal complex. At the time of the bombing, he was northwest (about a mile north and about one-half mile west) of the Murrah Building. He recalls hearing a loud rumble and, upon immediately exiting the building he was in, seeing "two pillaring billows of smoke dust" and a "streak of light." He described the sounds as follows:

> *I exited the building probably a minute, or maybe even two, from the time I first heard the first rumble....It actually wasn't just one rumble; it was more like a clap of thunder—a very loud clap of thunder, followed almost simultaneously with a—a more of a—explosion-type boom, maybe even a two-percussion boom that—that followed the first one....We could feel it on—on Twentieth, at Twenty Thousand Classen Center.*

We could feel the shock wave from this thing.... And then, that's when we went to the [Murrah] building. (Source: Virgil Steele deposition, 27 Apr 98; Appendix pg. 532-3)

6. Lt. Col. George Wallace, Retired

Wallace is a retired fighter pilot. He spent 26 years in the U.S. Air Force, . At the time of the explosion, he was at his home, nine miles northwest of the Murrah Building. He described the sound as "a sustained, loud, long rumble, like several explosions." He related the sound to "a succession of bombs being dropped in the distance by B-52s." (Source: *The New American*, 07 Aug 95, pg. 22)

7. Jim Guthrie

Guthrie, an employee of the Veterans Administration recalled, "I felt a boom and was picked up off my feet and thrown under a water fountain." He also remembered hearing a second explosion and covering his ears. (Source: *The Washington Post*, 23 Apr 95)

8. Michael Hinton

Hinton was on a bus at approximately the intersection of Northwest 5th Street and Robinson when he felt an initial force tip the bus. Seconds later another wave came and almost tipped the bus on it's side. "I thought it was going to tip us over. There were definitely two episodes." (Source: OKBIC interview with Hinton)

9. Diane Dooley

Dooley stated she was at a third floor stairwell and heard a second explosion. (Source: *The Washington Post*, 23 April 1995)

10. Charles Watts

Watts is an attorney who was in the Federal Courthouse immediately across the street from the Murrah Building. He is also a Vietnam veteran who has experienced the effects of being within one hundred feet of B-52 air strikes. He described his experience as follows:

I was up on the ninth floor...with nothing between the two buildings. We were on the south side, in the foyer, outside the courtroom. It was 9:00 or just very, very shortly thereafter. Several lawyers were standing there talking and there was a large explosion. It threw several of the people close to me to the floor. I don't think it threw me to the floor, but it did move me significantly, and I threw myself to the floor, and got down, and about that time, a huge blast, unlike any thing I've ever experienced, hit....A second blast. There were two explosions. The second blast made me think that the whole building was coming in. (Source: *The Oklahoma City Bombing and the Politics of Terror*, David Hoffman, Feral House, 1998, pg.156)

11. Robert Dennis

Dennis, a 51-year-old Air Force Reserve lieutenant colonel, worked as a U.S. district clerk in the Federal Courthouse. He was in the Murrah Building when the bomb went off. He had just concluded a meeting with the Murrah Building manager and was heading toward the elevator. He described the bomb as follows:

> *It didn't sound like thunder. It was just a large bang, sort of "poof." I suppose I might have been temporarily unconscious because I'm not aware of the building falling. I didn't know what was happening. It was just kind of a strange, strange feeling....When I got out and saw the front of the building it was just unreal. The building wasn't really there.* (Source: Air Force News Service)

12. V. Z. Lawton

Lawton worked for HUD on the eighth floor, central/west portion of the Murrah Building. At the time of the explosion, he was sitting at his desk reviewing paperwork. The blast came from behind and hit him in the back of the head. He remembers the event this way:

> *I felt the building shake and could not imagine what was causing it. Then debris began falling from above me. The lights went out, and then something hit the back of my head and, the next thing I remembered, I was on my hands and knees on the floor. I never heard the bomb go off. When I stood up, I could look straight up into the sky; and, over the debris, I could see that the front of the building was gone.* (Source: Personal written statement to OKBIC)

13. J. D. Reed

Reed, an appraiser for Oklahoma County, worked in the county office building two blocks south of the Murrah Building. He recounted the following:

> *I was settled at my desk for a normal day [9:00 a.m.], when I heard a whistling noise, much like that of a jet engine. Less than a second later, I heard a deafening explosion and felt the building shake as if it were collapsing.* (Source: Oklahoma County Assessor Newsletter, Mass Media, Vol. 2, No. 4, 19 Apr 96 & Parker & Parsley Petroleum USA, Inc. company newsletter, Workin' Interest, 19 Apr 95) (Appendix pg. 485)

14. Arlene Blanchard

Blanchard heard nothing, no blast or explosion. She was badly injured. (Source: OKBIC interview with Blanchard)

15. Clark Peterson

Peterson was on the fourth floor of the Murrah Building, center portion. He wrote,

At 9:02 AM, an electric spark appeared by my computer and everything turned black. Propelled objects raced throughout the darkness amid the sound of moaning metal. I caught a glimpse of a terrified girl with both arms straight up in the air. We were apparently falling, but I did not realize what had happened until a minute or two later. (Charles Key interview with Peterson)

C. THE OFFICIAL STORY

Initially, the bomb was said to be around 1,000 pounds of a mixture of ammonium nitrate and fuel oil (ANFO). KWTV in Oklahoma City reported that "John Magaw, director of the ATF, has estimated the bomb size to be 1,000 to 1,200 pounds which would put it in the range of the bomb that was responsible for the World Trade Center bombing." The story later changed to a 4,000-pound ANFO bomb. Then during the trial of Timothy McVeigh, the story changed again to a 4,000 pound mixture of ammonium nitrate (AN) and nitromethane, (NM) a high performance racing fuel. (Source: Numerous local and national media reports and McVeigh trial, pg. 11298)

OKBIC Note: Oddly enough, the ATF seems to have known that it was a car bomb within just minutes after the explosion. Tiffany Bible, a paramedic who arrived at the scene at about 9:07 a.m., immediately struck up a conversation with an ATF agent. Having made an assumption that there must have been a natural gas explosion, she told the agent that she could not believe "that a gas explosion has caused this much damage to the building." He responded that the damage had been caused by a car bomb. It was much later in the day that news sources reported that a crater had been found, which would be indicative of a truck bomb. CNN reported that the bomb had left "a crater eight foot deep outside the building." (OCBIC interview with Bible & CNN broadcast, 19 Apr 95)

D. REPORTS OF OTHER BOMBS

After the rescue efforts had begun, there were reports of other bombs being found within the Murrah Building. The building was evacuated at least twice due to these reports. The Government denied that there were any other bombs found inside the building, but witnesses and news broadcasts told a different story. At one point, Toria Tolley with CNN reported,

> *There is still a danger of another huge explosion. Police have confirmed two more bombs have been discovered in the building. Authorities say one of the bombs has been found and disarmed. A bomb squad is reportedly dealing with the other one at this time.*

Later, KWTV reported,

> *A third explosive device, another bomb—We don't know if it's three or four—but perhaps another bomb has been found inside that federal building. They are moving everyone back once again. This would be the fourth time that this has happened.*

The Government labeled these reports as misinformation caused by the confusion which surrounds an event of this magnitude. However, official government records, as well as the original witnesses and media reports, tell a different story::

1. *Firehouse Magazine* Reports Four Bomb Scares

Firehouse Magazine, in their September 1995 issue (Appendix, pgs. 376-377), listed four bomb scares occurring at the Murrah Building at the following times:

> 10:00 a.m.
> 10:22 a.m.
> 10:45 a.m.
> 13:51 (1:51 p.m.)

2. *Oklahoma Final Report* Affirms Two Bomb Scares

The *Oklahoma Final Report* published by the City of Oklahoma City in July 1996, lists only two bombs:

a. Bomb Scare at 10:29 a.m.

According to the *Oklahoma Final Report*, the bomb scare occurred at 10:29 a.m. and happened as follows:

> *A rescue worker who was leaving the Murrah Building had told a GSA worker that he had seen a suitcase on the second floor that looked suspicious and could be a bomb. The GSA worker spread the word of a possible bomb and contacted a firefighter, who reported to the Fire Command Post, which in turn reported the possible bomb to the Police Command Post. Once the evacuation was complete, Oklahoma City Police, Oklahoma Highway Patrol, and Oklahoma County Sheriff Bomb Squads entered the building with special canine units. They searched for a suitcase or any possible explosive, they did not find a suitcase. The all clear was given at 11:22 a.m.*

b. Bomb Scare at 1:30 p.m.

The *Oklahoma Final Report* said that the second bomb scare occurred at 1:30 p.m. The report states the following:

> *1:30 p.m.: Suspicious crate found in Murrah Building.*
>
> *1:48 p.m.: Murrah Building evacuated; bomb squads to investigate crate*
>
> *2:02 p.m.: All clear given – rescue operations resume.*

OKBIC Note: The above reference does not state whether or not a bomb was found.

3. Dr. Randall Heather

Heather is a terrorism expert who was interviewed by Kevin Ogle of KFOR-TV in Oklahoma City on the morning of 19 April 1995, shortly after the bombing. During the interview, Heather made the following comments:

> *I know that there had been a threat called into the FBI last week. It's a great stroke of luck that we actually have got diffused bombs. It's through the bomb material that we will be able to track down who committed this atrocity.... Usually, when there is a bomb of this type,... sometimes they can get small pieces of the device and trace it back. It's my impression that we will have an entire actual diffused device. And that will be, for the FBI and the other investigative agencies, a tremendous help. It's a great leap forward in finding out who committed this act.*

4. Toni Garrett

Garrett was a nurse who was working in the identification and tagging of bodies. She states that "Four people—rescue workers—told us there was a bomb in the building with a timing mechanism set to go off ten minutes after nine." Garret stated the she was told by witnesses that it was an active bomb and that they "saw the Bomb Squad take it away." (Source: *The Oklahoma City Bombing and the Politics of Terror*, David Hoffman, Feral House, 1998, pg. 26).

5. Dick Miller

Miller, an Oklahoma City Fire Marshal, confirmed Garrett's story. In speaking of the bomb, he stated that a box marked "High Explosives" "had a timer on it." According to author, David Hoffman, "The timing mechanism apparently had been set to detonate at ten minutes after nine. Apparently it had malfunctioned due to the initial blast." (Source: *The Oklahoma City Bombing and the Politics of Terror*, David Hoffman, Feral House, 1998, pg. 26)

6. Oklahoma City Police Officer

Hoffman also tells of a Police Officer who started to walk into the building when a fireman yelled, "Hey, idiot, that's a bomb!" The officer looked around and saw a box surrounded by police crime tape. The fireman yelled to him again, "There's one over there and another over there! We're waiting for the bomb squads to come back from hauling off the others." (Source: *The Oklahoma City Bombing and the Politics of Terror*, David Hoffman, Feral House, 1998, pg. 26)

7. Another Oklahoma City Police Officer

According to Hoffman, Investigator Phil O' Halloran contends that he has an Oklahoma City police officer on tape stating that "one of the bombs found in the building was two to three five-gallon containers of mercury fulminate—a powerful explosive—one not easily obtainable except to military sources." (Source: *The Oklahoma City Bombing and the Politics of Terror*, David Hoffman, Feral House, 1998, pg. 27)

8. Tiffany Bible

Bible, an EMSA paramedic who was on the scene at approximately 9:06 a.m., overheard a conversation that took place after the 10:22 a.m. bomb evacuation. Two men whom she believed to be a county deputy sheriff and an ATF agent discussed finding a bomb attached to a natural gas line in the Murrah Building. (Source: Affidavit of Tiffany Bible, 23 Jan 98; see Appendix pg. 435)

Oklahoma Govenor Frank Keating

9. Oklahoma Governor Frank Keating

In a television interview shortly after the bombing, Gov. Frank Keating, a former FBI agent and previously "number two at Justice" (and, therefore, previously over the ATF, the Secret Service and the U.S. Marshal's Office) said, "The reports I have is [sic] that one device was deactivated and, apparently, there's another device; and obviously, whatever did the damage to the Murrah Building was a tremendous, very sophisticated explosive device." (Source: *The Stan Solomon Show* in Indianapolis, IN, interview with Gov. Keating's brother, author Martin Keating, 21 Aug 97 & *The New American* quoting from the film, *Cover-Up in Oklahoma*, produced by the Citizens Information Network in Fort Worth, Texas)

10. Oklahoma Highway Patrol Radio Dispatch Logs

The highway patrol dispatch logs clearly show that there were two bombs found in the Murrah Building after the blast. The following entries can be found:

> 10:29 a.m. *There is another bomb on the south side of the bldg. Need to get away as far as possible.... Evacuate the area of the bldg immediately....*
>
> 10:37 a.m. *OC Fire Dept. confirms they did find a second device in the bldg.* (Source: *The New American*, 20 Jul 98, pg. 13) (See Appendix, pg. 373.)

11. DoD Atlantic Command

A DoD Atlantic Command memo from Norforlk, Virginia dated 20 April 1995 also shows two additional explosives were found. (Source: *The New American*, 20 Jul 98, pg. 13) (See Appendix, pg. 408 and 440.)

OKBIC Note: Retired Marine Lt. Col. Roger Charles, who investigated the bombing for ABC's 20/20 and for OKBIC has noted, after reviewing official communications, that nowhere is there a correction to the information concerning bombs being found. Normally, a correction would have gone back through official channels to be recorded in the logs.

12. Joe Harp

Joe Harp is a retired CIA operative who now lives in Texas and told the following story. On the day of the bombing, he was in the Murrah Building at about 11:00 a.m. and observed members of "the fire department EOD" removing two devices and placing them in the bomb disposal unit (Appendix pg. 524). He described the devices as military olive-drab in color and the size of round five-gallon drums. He also stated that, upon his arrival, he knew that the explosive device that caused the damage to the building was not an ANFO bomb because he could smell sulfur in the air that reminded him of the gas-enhanced "Daisy Cutter" bombs that were used when he was in Vietnam. (Source: *The New American*, 20 Jul 98, pg. 14)

13. Dr. Tom Coniglione

On the morning of the bombing, Coniglione, introduced as the medical director of Saint Anthony's Hospital in downtown Oklahoma City, told broadcasters that, "at the present time, the medical teams downtown are unable to get into the wreckage to retrieve more of the injured because of the presence of other bombs in the area. I've been told by the police department that just as soon as those bombs are defused, they will permit the medical teams to enter." (Source: KFOR-TV, 19 Apr 95)

E. SEISMOGRAPHIC EVIDENCE

Seismographic equipment in Oklahoma City and Norman recorded the explosion(s) that occurred at the Murrah Building. The Seismograph in Oklahoma City is located at the Omniplex Science Museum which is 1.7 miles from the Murrah Building. The seismographic equipment in Norman is located at the University of Oklahoma, 16 miles from the Murrah Building, and is maintained by the Oklahoma Geological Survey (OGS).

The original seismograms were seized as evidence by the FBI shortly after the bombing. Copies have been made available to the scientific community. They show two separate events on the Oklahoma City seismograph, and three separate events on the Norman seismograph. These two seismograms have been widely discussed and debated by geophysical scientists immediately after the bombing and in subsequent interviews and forums. Their findings are presented next.

1. Oklahoma City Forum

A forum was hosted by the Oklahoma Geophysical Society of Oklahoma City on 20 November 1995. The speakers were Dr. Raymon L. Brown of the OGS and Dr. Thomas L. Holzer of the U.S. Geological Survey (USGS) out of Menlo Park, California, representing the Government. During the course of their research, they conversed back and forth and, somewhat, shared information; however, it appears that the Government wasn't entirely forthcoming with the information it had. Dr. Brown, at one point during his presentation, made the following comments:

> *And one thing that Tom [Holzer] had me looking for was a low velocity zone and I'm speculating, and Tom never told me—I was not totally aware of what their group was doing, and, I've always felt, Tom, that you were under a gag order of sort—because he was working on the case and couldn't tell me everything. I just know I had to find a low velocity zone.*

Holzer and Brown presented their findings and conclusions regarding their analyses of the seismic data to the forum. Their analyses are based on a comparison of the seismograms from the day of the bombing with seismograms from the day the building was imploded. They also explained what their conclusions were based on and how and why they interpreted the data as they did.

Holzer, in his opening remarks, took the position that (a) the "records are consistent with a single bomb" and (b) he doesn't "think you can use the records to argue that there were multiple explosions." He based his opinion on air wave data. In comparing the **explosion** seismograms to the **demolition** seismograms, he stated, "So even though they only used a rather modest amount of dynamite to **demolish** the building, it was able to generate an air wave that was recorded at the Ompliplex site." Thus, he attributes the first event on the seismic record at the Omniplex on the day of the bombing to the blast and the second event to airwave. (Appendix pgs. 422-434)

In speaking of the possibility of multiple bombs, Holzer also stated,

> *However, that doesn't mean that you can't preclude it because you can have small explosions that are sort of hidden in it. So the bottom line is I don't think you can use the seismic records to argue that there were multiple explosions. You have to come up with independent evidence for that. But it doesn't totally preclude it because small explosions could be hidden in it; and one could speculate about what a small explosion is."*

Brown agreed with Holzer that the second event recorded on the seismograph at the Omniplex on the day of the **bombing** was an airwave. He explained the added signal seen at Norman:

> *I agree that wave propagation artifacts can be used to explain the dispersions of this very high amplitude signal that arrived at the Omniplex. It spread out into the two signals that were received at Norman.*

Brown, however, disagreed with Holzer on another issue. On the day of the **demolition**, the USGS had brought in four instruments and placed one at the building site, one at the Omniplex, one in Norman, and the fourth about halfway between the Murrah Building and Norman. In regard to those **demolition** records, Holzer sees a small pulse followed by a larger pulse about five seconds later. He stated, "The energy is being primarily input five seconds into the record; and, more important, that energy is coming from the demolition of the building." These two pulses represent the implosion and the collapse of the building. He considers this record to be consistent with the bombing record, meaning that, on the **bombing** seismograph from the Omniplex, he also sees two pulses within the first event—a pulse for the bomb and another pulse for the collapse of the building. He stated,

> ...that Omniplex record [of the **demolition**] mirrors almost everything that [actually] took place at the [**demolition**] site on the day of the **demolition**.
> What I think I see is a wind shirr wave coming in from the first small explosion; and now I see shirr waves coming in from the larger explosion used to really bring the building down. Then you see a hesitation—which we also saw in the USGS records right at the site [from the instruments placed at the Murrah Building on the day of the demolition]. Then you see what I call three quarters of the building collapsing; and another hesitation; and then the elevator complex coming down; and, finally, you see the east wing swinging—the last portion of the building that was to fall.

On the copy of the bombing record received from the FBI, there was a white-out area that had not copied well. By "connecting the dots" and filling in the blank spaces, Dr. Brown reconstructed what he thinks the original record looked like. In regard to the reconstructed record, he sees the bomb as the first pulse and the collapse of the building as the third pulse. He concludes that the second pulse must be the result of another energy source. In accordance with this theory, he stated,

> It [the **demolition** record] looks like a direct correlation with the event [the **demolition**]. It would seem that this [same] type of thing occurred on the day of the **explosion**.... The truck bomb was no longer active after about three seconds. It was decaying; the pressure was falling; and, it was no longer radiating a pressure. And you've got this extra period of activity that took place after the truck bomb had ceased to be active. You've got to explain, then, "Where does the energy come from?". In fact it seems to gather more energy for the latter event....How do you get so much energy in this latter period of activity without having something explosive to contribute to that energy?...

> Notice that this central pulse is much higher than the pulse that was caused by three-fourths of the building collapsing, and the last and weakest pulse on the day of the **explosion** is comparable in amplitude to that signal...It looks like three-quarters of the building was not available on the day of the **demolition**, so how do you get so much energy in this latter period of activity [on the bombing record] without having something explosive to contribute to that energy?...I am not convinced that collapse is an explanation for the activity.

2. Oklahoma Radio Network

There was a subsequent radio interview on 18 February 1997 at 3:00 p.m. between Mike McCarvel of the Oklahoma Radio Network and Dr. Raymon Brown. When asked his opinion now, after studying the data for 20-21 months, Dr. Brown expressed that the data still does not give a definitive answer, but his conclusions have not changed.

He again compared the data from the **explosion** with data from the **demolition** and concluded that the eight to 10 seconds of activity recorded on the first event of the **bombing** record cannot all be bomb activity because the bomb only lasted two-to-three seconds. He also has a problem believing that the second pulse on the first event is the building collapse because it generated a much greater pulse (and would only have been for one-fourth of the building) than the pulse on the **demolition** record for three-fourths of the building. He put it as follows:

The Omniplex seismometer on the day of the **explosion** *[the bombing], indicated what I see as three separate pulses [within the first event] that took place over a total period of eight to ten seconds. And this, the first pulse is the only one that can possibly be associated with the truck bomb; and, surprisingly, it was not the largest.*

Now the rest of the activity could either be the result of building collapse and/or an exaggerated collapse due to demolition charges.... One of the enigmas, or one of the problems I had explaining that second event as building collapse was that the portion of the building that was collapsing was about a quarter of the building. And yet, on the day of the **demolition** *three-quarters of the building was collapsed—the rest of it. And that didn't make as big a pulse as the second pulse that was observed on the day of the* **explosion***.*

F. INDEPENDENT REPORTS AND EXPERT OPINIONS

1. Brigadier General Benton K. Partin

General Partin is retired from the U.S. Air Force with 31 years service. He spent 25 of those years in research design, development, test and management of weapons development. He has been trained in the chemistry of explosives, explosive train design, warheads, terminal ballistics fuses, wave shaping, propellants, and numerous other weapons, rocket and aerodynamics disciplines. He holds a B.S. in Chemical Engineering, an M.S. in Aeronautical Engineering, and completed the academics for a PhD in Statistics with a minor in Operations Research.

About two weeks after the 19 April 1995 bombing of the Murrah Building in Oklahoma City, Partin did a bomb damage analysis and concluded that the building could not possibly have been collapsed the way it was by 4,800 pounds of ANFO as claimed by the FBI. Partin arranged an appointment with Senator Don Nickles' assistant, Lee Morris, in an effort to get an independent investigation. Morris suggested it might be possible to get the National Guard to conduct such an investigation. Two days later, Morris told Partin that there were "differences of opinion" with respect to what had happened in Oklahoma City. Partin, therefore presumed that nothing was going to be done.

Partin then prepared a six-page technical analysis based on information available in the media. This report indicated that the FBI's single-truck-bomb theory was "beyond credulity" and strongly urged "that the U.S. Congress take steps to assure that evidence in Oklahoma City be independently evaluated by a collection of demolition experts from the private sector before the building is demolished," and questioned "Why the rush to destroy evidence?" Partin's extensive weapons credentials were included in the report.

On 17 May 1995 (29 days after the bombing), Partin hand-delivered the report, addressed to Senator Don Nickels at his office, with 23 information copies to other senators. Additionally, he addressed a report to Congressman Frank Wolf and hand-delivered it and 31 information copies to other congressmen. The response was little more than a "black hole." Congressman Wolf responded that he had forwarded his report to the FBI (an apparent source of disinformation) for their information and action. One senator responded that he was withdrawing his co-sponsorship of the counter-terrorism legislation and would work to clean it up.

Brigidier General Benton Partin U.S. Air Force (Retired)

Later, Partin was invited to Oklahoma City to brief his analysis to certain members of the Oklahoma legislative body, survivors of the bombing and the media. While in Oklahoma City, he had the opportunity to review hundreds of photographs taken throughout the building cleanup and sanitization process. These photographs and others provided pictographic confirmation of his earlier scientific analysis. He prepared an amplified bomb-damage analysis with photographs included, dated 30 July 1995, and hand-delivered copies to the offices of all 535 senators and congressmen. Each report had an independently addressed cover letter, which was essentially an executive summary. Using the Senator Trent Lott cover letter, another thousand information copies were distributed to media outlets across the country.

Partin's analysis determined that "the damage pattern on the reinforced concrete superstructure could not possibly have been attained from the single truck bomb," and that supplemental demolition charges were used to bring the building down. He cites many inconsistencies between the Murrah Building debris and the conditions that should have been observed if only a single truck bomb had been used without supplemental demolition charges. (Appendix pgs. 378-396) Several examples are listed below:

     a. The explosive damage potential drops off more rapidly than an inverse function of the distance cubed. Maximum explosive energy would have been released if the whole explosive charge had been put in a spherical configuration and detonated from the center. The blast wave pressure from 4800 pounds of ammonium nitrate and fuel oil (ANFO) would have fallen off to about 375 pounds per square inch by the time it hit the first column. That would be far below the 3500-pound compressive yield strength of the concrete. Therefore there would have been no brisance damage in the entire building. But there was photographic evidence of brisance damage on at least four column junctures. (There were numerous reports of other charges that were found that did not detonate.)

     b. The much smaller and closer columns, B4 and B5, are still standing while the much larger and farther column A7 is down.

     c. "The large header across the front of the building at the third floor was not blown back into the building as one may expect....It came straight down."

Bishopsgate Crater

d. "Columns B2, B4 and B5 all have the sheetrock and furring strip finish still intact on the second and third floors except where damaged by falling debris."

e. "A high detonation velocity **contact** explosive leaves a relatively smooth but granular surface (brisance) with protruding, bare reinforcement rods as was seen in some of the columns of the Murrah Building. Any structural collapse damage from the truck bomb would have been characterized by cracks and rough fracture surfaces."

The Murrah Building was demolished on 23 May 1995 without ever having been officially investigated by demolition or explosives experts. As Partin stated in the cover letter attached to the report he sent to all members of Congress:

No government law enforcement agency should be permitted to demolish, smash and bury evidence of a counter-terrorism sting operation, sabotage or terrorist attack without a thorough examination by an independent, technically competent agency.

If an aircraft crashed because of a bomb, or a counter-terrorism sting or an FAA Controller error, the FAA would not be permitted to gather and bury the evidence. The National Transportation Safety Board would have been called in to conduct an investigation and where possible every piece of debris would have been collected and arrayed to determine cause of failure.

To remove all ambiguity with respect to the use of supplementary demolition charges, the FBI should be required to release the high quality surveillance color TV camera tape of the Murrah building bombing on April 19, 1995.

OKBIC Note: The FBI answered a Freedom of Information (FOI) request saying they had the surveillance photographs, but they were not releasable.

Partin's analysis concluded that 4,800 pounds of ANFO in the Ryder truck could not have alone collapsed the building the way it was. He provided the following comments to OKBIC:

The FEMA/ASCE Report used crater size to estimate a truck bomb blast equivalence of 4,000 pounds of TNT, which would have had the blast equivalence of 14,800 pounds of ANFO. However, the crater diameter used by FEMA was 28 feet, while the scaled diameter was only about 16 to 18 feet. The 4,000-pound equivalence of TNT has to be exaggerated, if based on the pictured crater and the parametric data used by FEMA-ASCE.

OKBIC Note: A strange comment was made to General Partin by the FBI Chief of the Oklahoma Bombing Investigation, Danny Defenbaugh. While pointing to the picture in Partin's report, he said, "Suppose I told you that was not the crater."

In the book American Terrorist: Timothy McVeigh and the Oklahoma City Bombing," the authors, Lou Michel and Dan Herbeck, claim that, in April 1999, they had "more than seventy-five hours" of interviews with McVeigh in which he gave "the first complete, candid no-holds-barred account of his story." However, in April 2001, Herbeck told Partin that he "did not interview McVeigh;" that the interviews were by "the other guy."

In The American Terrorist, McVeigh is quoted as saying many things that he would have known were not true. For example: no other John Does, no Middle-Eastern accomplices, etc. Attorney

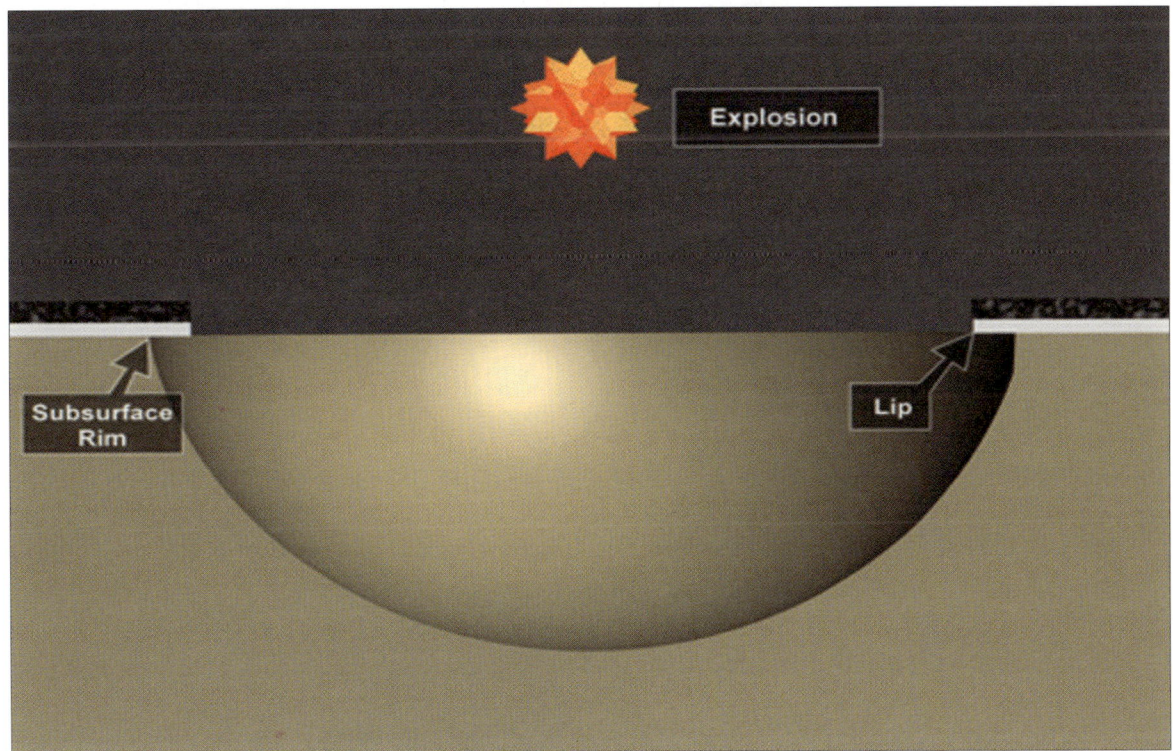

Crater Showing Concrete Lip Extending Inward From the Subsurface Rim (Figure A)

Stephen Jones said, after many years as his lawyer, that McVeigh was a "mule" in the effort. The question needs to be addressed: Did either Michel or Herbeck interview McVeigh?

The book says McVeigh's truck was 7,000 pounds of ANFO and nitromethane. If the composition were correctly balanced and properly prepared, the 7,000 pounds of ANFO/nitromethane would have the blast equivalence of approximately 7,000 pounds of TNT. The 7,000 pounds of TNT would have the blast equivalence of 26,000 pounds of ANFO.

There is a unique characteristic signature of a crater generated by a large explosive charge a few feet above a concrete road, runway, etc. The crater always has a concrete lip extending

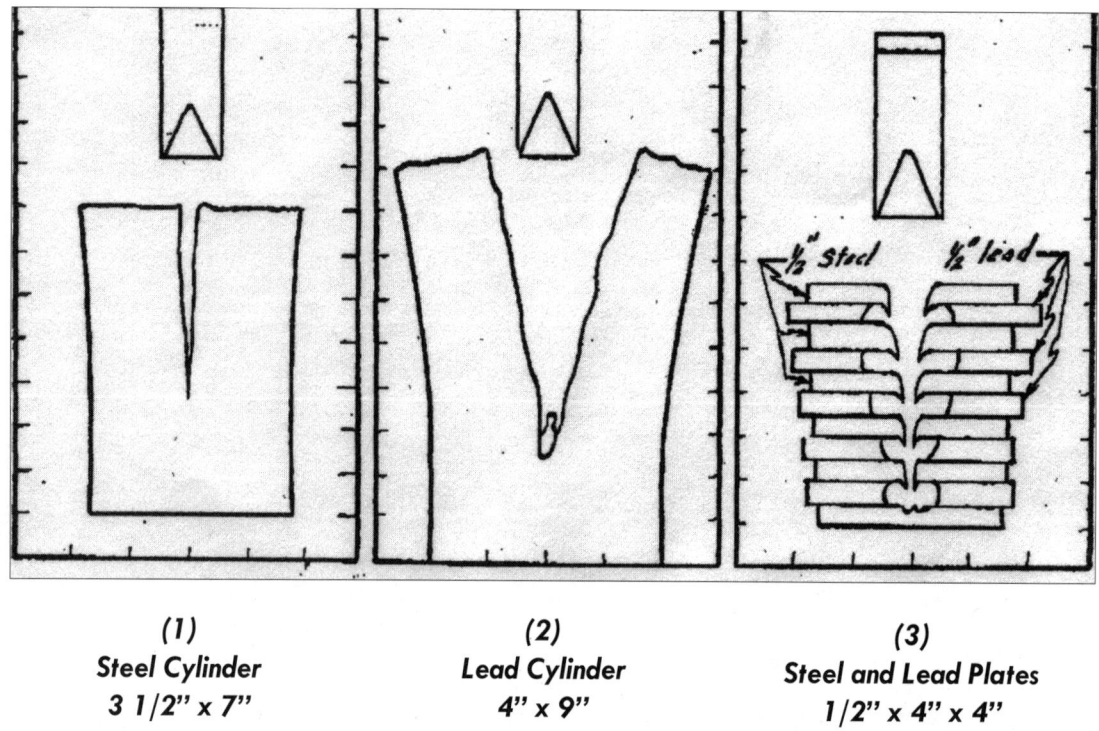

(1)
Steel Cylinder
3 1/2" x 7"

(2)
Lead Cylinder
4" x 9"

(3)
Steel and Lead Plates
1/2" x 4" x 4"

Comparison of Jet Penetration into Lead and Steel (Figure B)

inward from the subsurface rim; i.e., the subsurface rim is kinematically rammed back under the concrete or concrete and asphalt. (See Figure A.) This same phenomenon is shown (photograph pg. 184) for a vehicle bomb crater in the United Kingdom The crater picture from the Oklahoma City bombing does not have this characteristic lip; however, the lip could have been knocked off to make the crater appear bigger or for safety reasons.

The same phenomenon is shown for firing a shaped charge into a layer of steel over lead, as also shown in figure "(3)" above.

(From *Report on Shaped Explosive Charges*, Benton K. Partin, Captain, USAF, 16 Aug 54)

The following table summarizes the varying claims of bomb size and displays whether or not that claim is compatible with the crater size as shown in photographs taken at the bombsite:

CLAIMANT	POUNDS OF ANFO EQUIVALENCE	POUNDS OF TNT EQUIVALENCE	INTERNAL DEMOLITION CHARGES	COMPATIBLE W/CRATER SIZE	ASYMMETRY PROBLEM
FBI	4,800	1,300	No	Yes	Yes
Partin	4,800	1,300	Yes	Yes	No
FEMA-ASCE	14,800	4,000	No	No	Yes
McVeigh Book	26,000	7,000	No	No	Yes

2. Eglin Air Force Base

A series of Armament Directorate tests were conducted by Wright Laboratory at Eglin Air Force Base in Florida against simulated conventional urban buildings. This study was conducted to demonstrate the capability of explosive devices against cast-in-place concrete structures with steel reinforcement bars. The report states that "air blast alone was singularly ineffective in causing major damage to the Eglin test structure." (Source: Eglin AFB/WL/MN letter to General Partin, no date) (Appendix pg. 374-375)

3. Robert Frias

Robert Frias of Frias Engineering in Arlington, Texas, reviewed the tests conducted by Eglin AFB (Appendix pg. and made the following assessment:

> *The test facility...was similar to the Murrah Building in many respects but structurally not as strong....Additionally, the explosive force of the tritonal used in the first test was more powerful than what could have been expected from the truck explosives in the Murrah Building incident.* (Source: Letter, dated 05 Feb 97)

4. Sam Cohen

Cohen is retired after a 40-year career in nuclear weaponry. He was assigned to the Manhattan Project at Los Alamos, New Mexico, during World War II, and later developed the technical slant military concept of the neutron bomb in 1958. He provided a statement, dated 29 June 1995, to OKBIC, giving his professional opinion on the bombing which rejected the ammonium nitrate bomb theory. (Appendix pgs. 541-542) He wrote,

> *I believe that the demolitions charges in the building were placed inside at certain key concrete columns* [and] *did the primary damage to the Murrah Federal Building. It would have been absolutely impossible and against the laws of nature for a truck full of fertilizer and fuel oil—no matter how much was used—to bring the building down.*

5. Roger Raubach

Raubach holds a Ph.D. degree in Physical Chemistry which deals with rates of chemical reaction and the heat-energy relations involved in reactions. (The evaluation of explosives and their properties falls within the realm of the physical chemist.) He summarizes the two properties of explosives, power and brisance:

> *Power* [is] *the ability to move or displace matter, as in heaving dirt or rock in either mining, construction, or agriculture. Brisance, on the other hand, refers to the ability of an explosive to shatter, crack, or destroy structures. Brisance, in general, is directly related to the velocity of the shock wave generated by the detonation.*

Raubach has extensive experience in the use of ammonium nitrate in industry and specifically in mining applications. (Appendix pg. 520-521) He asserts that

> *The possibility of an ammonium nitrate fertilizer bomb, regardless of size, demolishing a reinforced concrete structure at a twenty or thirty foot standoff not only strains the limit of credibility but exceeds it by a considerable margin....Ammonium nitrate...[is] not "fast" enough to shatter concrete and break steel reinforcing rods.*

(Source: Letter to Charles Key, 28 Jun 95)

6. Dr. C. Frederick Hansen

Hansen has been a research scientist with the National Advisory Council for Aeronautics (NACA) and the National Aeronautics and Space Administration (NASA). In addition to studying properties of shock-heated air, he was involved in research using explosives to accelerate velocities. He has been a professor of Physics, Aeronautics and Astronautics, Science and Chemistry in major universities in the United States, India, and Taiwan. His teaching credentials include graduate courses in high-energy shock wave properties.

Hansen reviewed the report of General Partin and agrees with his assessment. In a letter to Charles Key dated 13 February 1998, he states that "Everything considered, it is hard to avoid the conclusion that only an explosive detonated right at the column could have sheared it." (Appendix pg. 515-519) He goes further to include pressure increase that occurs when a shock wave is reflected. The reflected wave "approaches a limit of eight times the incident pressure." He explains that

> *T-bar reinforced concrete columns require blast pressures that exceed several thousands of pounds per square inch [psi]. At Column B3, which was demolished, a 500,000 psi initial pressure wave would have reduced to about 30 psi 57 feet from the explosion ...and if the reflected wave were 8 times greater, this would still be far short of the 3500 psi or more required to exceed the yield strength of the column.*

7. Robert G. Breene, Jr.

Breene is the editor of the *Latin American News Syndicate* in San Antonio, Texas. His previous experience has been as a professor of physics at West Virginia University; a visiting scientist at Max Planck Institute in Munich, Germany; president of Physical Studies, Inc. (a consulting firm in applied research and theoretical physics); theoretical physicist with the U.S. Air Force (USAF); and as a fighter pilot and test pilot with USAF. He has published numerous books and over 50 articles in the scientific literature of six countries.

In an e-mail sent to Charles Key on 24 May 1996, Breene states that "evidence indicates that a vehicle bomb alone could not have done the structural damage suffered by the Murrah Bldg." For comparison, he cites the following examples which were multi-storied, reinforced-concrete structures with vertical-strength members. (Appendix pgs. 510-513)

a. National Security Department (DAS) Building in Bogota, Columbia

> *In 1989 Colombian terrorists detonated a vehicle bomb near the entrance to the DAS headquarters building in Bogota [Photo pg. 372]. The vehicle was parked next to the*

curb, the curb separated from the building by a one-meter sidewalk and a short set of stairs for a total separation of two to three meters from curb to façade. Thus this bomb was much closer to the building than was the Oklahoma bomb. The blast wiped the façade off the building, its vertical support columns unaffected.

b. U.S. Air Force Facilities in Saudi Arabia

The bombing in Saudi Arabia 25 June 1996 of the Khobar Towers (Photo pg. 373), which housed U. S. Air Force personnel, is another example. Damage was the result of a vehicle bomb. The façade was wiped off, but the vertical strength members were essentially unaffected. As reported in *The New American*, "The eight-story Khobar Towers structure is of much lighter construction than the nine-story Murrah building and was targeted by a bomb of considerably greater size and power, yet sustained markedly less damage. The Khobar building was of simple slab construction and had none of the heavy column supports found in the Oklahoma building." The bomb in the Murrah Building explosion was also much smaller. As the *Air Force Times* reported on 08 July 1996, "the tanker truck was probably loaded with 20,000 pounds of explosives." (Source: Robert Breene analysis and *The New American*, 05 Aug 96)

8. Ernest B. Paxson

Paxson has over 40 years experience as an aerospace engineer in the field of structural mechanics and dynamics. Part of that time was devoted to the topography of failed structural systems and structural components. At the Fort Leonard Wood, Missouri, U.S. Army Corp of Engineers, he was also trained in the use of explosives to destroy different types of structures. In a letter to Charles Key, dated 05 November 1999 (Appendix pg. 530-531), Paxson wrote,

A 4800 lb ANFO truck bomb is an extremely inefficient way to bring down a reinforced concrete structure. It might blow a hole in the curtain wall closest to the truck, but it would hardly affect the massive supporting columns of the building....To be assured of destroying any structure, one would have to place a sufficient amount of explosive charge in intimate contact with the pertinent supporting members.

Paxson also explained the topographies of structural elements and affirmed his opinion on the Murrah Building:

Structural elements present different fracture surface topographies depending on three main factors...[1] loading conditions, [2] type of material out of which structure was built, and [3] geometry of structural system or element.

For instance, a slowly applied load to failure of a structural element made out of a ductile metallic material will result in a different fracture surface pattern from that obtained when the same element is loaded cyclically [repeated load applications] to failure. If that same element is loaded to failure with a high rate loading such as impact, shock, or explosive force, the fracture surface geometry will again be different from the two situations just previously described.

The damage pattern of any structure will indicate how the loading conditions which caused failure were applied. In the case of the OKC Murrah Building, the failure pattern demonstrated to me that individual charges were placed on each of the failed columns inside the building.

9. Robert D. Vernon

Robert D. "Bob" Vernon is president of Microlithic Technologies, a firm that specializes in computer-based image analysis and data-visualization services for Cultural Resource Management (contract archaeology) firms and provides consulting engineering to high tech companies. Vernon is a chemist (B.S., East Texas Baptist College) with over thirty-five years of experience in failure analysis, engineering, and troubleshooting in microelectronics and process control industries.

Vernon has performed an in-depth analysis of photographic, seismic, and blast/brisance data associated with the bombing of the Murrah Building. His report appears on the following pages.

EVALUATION OF PUBLISHED EXPLANATIONS CONCERNING THE STRUCTURAL COLLAPSE OF THE ALFRED P. MURRAH FEDERAL BUILDING

" People in an open society do not demand infallibility from their institutions, but it is difficult for them to accept what they are prohibited from observing."
Supreme Court Justice Warren Burger

By Robert D. Vernon, Microlithic Technologies

EVALUATION OF PUBLISHED EXPLANATIONS CONCERNING THE STRUCTURAL COLLAPSE OF THE ALFRED P. MURRAH FEDERAL BUILDING

By Robert D. Vernon, MicroLithic Technologies

Introduction

Anyone who attempts to understand the events of 19 April 1995 in Oklahoma City soon discovers that theories as to what happened to the Murrah Building abound. Explanation attempts range from the frankly bizarre to serious scientific studies by eminent experts. And not all of the "experts" are in agreement.

Obviously, not all of these wildly diverse explanations can be correct. This report documents a *pro bono*, independent attempt to filter what has been published through a highly skeptical sieve of physical evidence and scientific analysis.

The credibility of much that has been published is suspect because the work bears the unmistakable stamp of some form of political or social agenda. However, it must be acknowledged that some of the most thorough investigation and reporting has been done by publications that are openly political—such as the *New American*. In such instances, extreme care has been taken to separate information from opinion, or, even, propaganda. Other publications—especially on the Internet—appear to consist of fact-free speculation, and—not a few instances of outright disinformation have been observed.

As much as is humanly possible, personal feelings and political inclinations have been set aside in an attempt to ascertain **what** happened to the Murrah Building and **how** the collapse occurred. No attempt was made to speculate on **who** was involved in causing this disaster—or **why** this reprehensible crime was perpetrated upon the good citizens of Oklahoma City.

It is the goal of this study to arrive at a single, plausible explanation. Wherever evidence inconsistent with that explanation remains, it will be delineated.

All who have attempted to develop an understanding of the Murrah Building's destruction have faced an almost insurmountable barrier: very little physical evidence remains to be examined. No one can fault the fact that structural materials were removed from their original resting places during heroic rescue and recovery efforts. However, the fact is that those same evidentiary materials were immediately removed from the crime scene—and quickly buried. And then, over serious objections, the remaining structure was demolished and the remains of the building were bulldozed, transported to multiple dumpsites, and buried.

More to the point, government agents who had custody of the crime scene failed to share—or, in some instances, even document—pertinent information on the damage to the building. As will be shown, they may have actively obstructed even official structural studies. Sadly, to many Americans, government agencies who had access to the facts acted in such a manner as to leave an overpowering impression that the true nature of what happened to the Murrah Federal Building on 19 April 1995 has been hidden from the citizens of these United States.

Although the full truth may never be known, this report is, simply, an attempt to dispose of some of the informational clutter.

TABLE OF CONTENTS

Abstract	**197**
Disclaimer	**198**
Executive Summary	**199**
A. Published Explanations	199
B. Primary Conclusions	200
C. The Bottom Line	201
D. Unresolved Issues	202
A. THE MURRAH BUILDING AND ITS MAJOR STRUCTURAL ELEMENTS	**204**
1. Nomenclature Conventions Employed in This Report	204
2. General Description of the North Face of the Murrah Building	205
3. Detailed Description of the Major Structural Elements	205
B. THE EVIDENCE—GENERAL DESCRIPTION OF OBSERVED DAMAGE	**211**
C. AIR BLAST VERSUS BRISANCE	**212**
1. Brisance--High Velocity "Cutting" Charges	212
2. Air Blast—Truck Bomb	213
D. FAILURE MODE AND MECHANISM	**215**
1. General Descriptions	215
2. Common Failure Mode of the Three Main Columns	216
3. Analysis of Labeled Details of Photo 1	219
4. "Lifting Failure" Mechanism	221
E. SEISMIC DATA	**221**
1. Two Large Explosions	221
2. "First Motion" Seismic Signals	222
F. THE CRATER—DISPUTED EVIDENCE	**224**
1. The "Missing" Crater	224
2. The "Flooded" Crater	225
3. The "Huge" Crater	225
4. The "Official Crater	227
5. The "Misrepresented" Crater	227
6. The "Two-Part" Crater	228
7. The Actual Crater	229

G. THE CRATER AS EVIDENCE—EVIDENCE "OWNED" BY THE FBI	**231**
1. Exposure Conditions for the Crater	232
2. The Defense Team's Visit to the Crater	234
3. The Crater Rim	235
4. FBI Agent Williams and the "Apparent Crater"	235
5. OIG Conclusions Regarding Williams' Report	235
H. CRATER DIMENSIONS AND BLAST RADIUS	**236**
I. THE LAST-HOUR "RACING FUEL" BOMB	**239**
1. ANFO	239
2. ANNM	239
J. REVIEW OF THE FEMA/ASCE BPAT REPORT	**242**
1. BPAT Composition	242
2. Evidence of Obstruction and Disinformation	243
3. Impact of Obstruction and Disinformation on BPAT Conclusions	247
K. POSSIBLE STRUCTURAL VULNERABILITY TO AIR BLAST DAMAGE	**249**
L. EVIDENCE NOT CONSISTENT WITH A SINGLE AIR BLAST	**253**
M. CONCLUSIONS	**255**
N. RECOMMENDATIONS	**256**

TABLE OF FIGURES

Figure 1	North Face of the Murrah Building -- Showing Portico	204
Figure 2	Plan View with Office Tower Coordinates and Nomenclature Conventions	206
Figure 3	Typical Structural Features Associated with the Portico -- Looking West	207
Figure 4	The Main Header or Transfer Beam -- Highlighted in White	208
Figure 5	Interlaced Rebar at Column-Header Junction -- Without Stirrup Ties	210
Figure 6	Structural Damage Associated with Failed Column G16[A7]	217
Figure 7	Structural Damage Associated with Failed Column G24[A3]	218
Figure 8	Scale Schematic of Plywood Covering and Actual Crater	231
Figure 9	Brisant Blast Radius -- Elevation View	237
Figure 10	Brisant Blast Radius -- Plan View	238
Figure 11	Wall Column Behind Column G20[A5]	250
Figure 12	Wall Column Supporting South End of Lateral Beam	252
Figure 13	Mechanism of Failure for Wall column	254

Photo 1	Structural Damage Associated with Failed Column G16[A7]	219
Photo 2	Structural Damage Associated with Column G24[A3]	220
Photo 3	Flooded Crater Covered with Floating Debris on Afternoon of 19 April 1995	226
Photo 4	Crater on Day 10 -- with Residual Lip and Tread Imprint of Tracked Excavator	227
Photo 5	Tracked Excavator Parked in Crater -- with Perspective-Corrected Grid	228
Photo 6	Crater Covered with Plywood -- Floral Arrangement at Corner of 16' Square	230
Photo 7	Caterpillar Track with Perspective-Corrected Grid	233
Photo 8	Brisance-Damaged Structural Material	244
Photo 9	PUSHED-Over Wall Column	249
Photo 10	Destroyed Top of Wall Column	251

Exhibit A	Seismic Data	223

ABSTRACT

Results of an independent photogrammetric analysis of publicly-available photographic and video evidence of structural damage to the A.P. Murrah building are presented. Published theories postulating possible causes of the structural collapse are assessed to determine their fit to observed damage patterns. Additional evidence from eyewitness accounts and audio and seismic recordings is evaluated to arrive at a scenario that most nearly fits the accumulated evidence. Recommendations for improving information collection on and understanding of future building collapses are offered.

DISCLAIMER

This report is restricted to discussions of **what** physical damage was done to the A.P. Murrah building and of possible physical causes thereof. No attempt is made to postulate **who** may have been responsible for the murderous act(s) that caused the building's collapse or motives therefore. However, persistent allegations that evidence has been withheld, obscured, concealed, falsely reported, and deliberately destroyed cannot be ignored.

EXECUTIVE SUMMARY

EVALUATION OF PUBLISHED EXPLANATIONS CONCERNING THE STRUCTURAL COLLAPSE

OF

THE ALFRED P. MURRAH FEDERAL BUILDING

By Robert D. Vernon, MicroLithic Technologies

A. PUBLISHED EXPLANATIONS

Medical Examiners' reports indicate that at least 90 percent of the lives lost in the bombing of the Murrah Building were due directly to the collapse of the building; *i.e.* the collapsing building itself was the primary instrument of death. Little, if any attention, however, was given by on-site federal investigative agencies to the actual mechanism of structural failure. Worse, there appeared to be a concerted effort to hurriedly remove all traces of damaged structural elements from the crime scene. Federal agencies' inadequate documentation and reporting of structural failure evidence plus the needlessly precipitous demolition of the building and removal and burial of failed structural materials gave strong appearance that a government-perpetrated cover-up had taken place.

This questionable handling of the crime scene and the physical evidence related to 90 percent of the casualties coincided with a growing atmosphere of citizen mistrust of the Federal Government. The resulting theories led to development and publication of numerous—often bizarre—explanations or hypotheses as to what actually damaged the building, and as to what type of structural failures actually occurred.

Explanations ranging from plasma-beam or electromagnetic pulse space-borne weapons to a single truck bomb of widely varying size, composition and power were published in various media. Some of the other theories between these two extremes were Tesla-like discharges from the earth, exotic "barometric" bombs, miniature nuclear devices, multiple bombs in a (nonexistent) basement, fuel-air "daisy-cutter" bombs, supplemental contact charges at critical structure points, and a pair of large bombs. Obviously, not all were correct.

Exhaustive photogrammetric analyses were performed on several hundred of the many photographs that were available in the public domain (and outside government control). Each of the published hypotheses was tested against the results of these analyses. Most published explanations were quickly eliminated because they simply failed to fit the physical and photographic evidence. For a time, a fuel-air device explosion over the parking lot was considered (and supported by preliminary image analysis) as a possible source of a second large explosion. As additional photographs taken from different viewpoints were analyzed, however, it became clear that the originally perceived possible signature of an air blast was invalid. Furthermore, seismic records were determined to provide no conclusive evidence of a second large explosion. The fuel-air explosive explanation was thereby eliminated.

Two hypotheses remain outstanding: (1) structural failure due to air blast from the truck bomb alone (the "official" explanation) and (2) structural weakening and initiation of collapse by small contact charges—immediately followed by blast damage from the truck bomb leading to catastrophic structural failure (per Partin, et al).

B. PRIMARY CONCLUSIONS

1. Number of explosions: One large device—possibly preceded by smaller explosions:

- Unequivocal physical evidence of a large, vehicle-borne explosive device parked to the northeast of column G20[A5] was observed.

- No substantial *physical* evidence of a second large explosion was confirmed (either inside or outside the Murrah Building).

- Published seismic records do not constitute convincing evidence of a second large explosion.

- A persistent and consistent residual body of seismic, audio, witness testimony, and structural damage evidence consistent with one or more small explosions occurring approximately four seconds prior to the large explosion exists and is reported.

2. Viable Explanations for Collapse:

Two potentially-viable theories as to the agent(s) and mechanism(s) of structural failure remain to be proven—or disproven:

a. A single truck bomb—possibly combined with structural vulnerabilities in the Murrah Building

- Credibility of government statements of bomb composition and size: poor—due to:

  - Progressive charge size inflation from 1200 pounds of ANFO to over 5600 pounds of ANNM over the span of two years.
  - Claimed bomb yield is inconsistent with actual crater dimensions

  - Evidence of main charge composition: Circumstantial only—no validated analytical data.

- Credibility of FBI Lab analysis: Poor to Negative—based on findings by the Office of the Inspector General (OIG) of the Department of Justice (DOJ).

- Credibility of government-published crater size: Extremely Suspect—at least 27 percent to as much as 77 percent overstated (Improper basis for device-yield calculation errors in several subsequent reports).

- Validity of federally (FEMA) funded study: Questionable—due to restricted access to the scene and dependence on inflated crater dimension data supplied by on-site agencies.

- Other non-government studies: Questionable—due to reference to inflated crater-diameter figures and/or dependence on brisant removal of column G20[A5] via hypothetical and contested 11X reflected-force multiplication to explain initiation of collapse.

- Structural flaws: A previously unpublished possible structural vulnerability to sub-brisant air blast damage was identified during this study and is reported.

   b. Additional demolition charges at critical structural points—preceding the truck bomb by approximately four seconds

- Seismic records from the Omniplex on **both** 19 April and 23 May 1995 show approximately four (4) seconds of small-amplitude earth motion ("first motion") **preceding** a much larger signal.

- The amplitude of the small first motion seismic signal on 19 April is of the same order as that produced by approximately 150 pounds of explosives on 23 May during demolition of the building.

- The small first motion observed on 19 April is totally **inconsistent with** the high-amplitude impulse first motion seismic signature typically produced by an above ground explosion of a single large device.

- Two audio recordings from 19 April both ostensibly exhibit a sharp "crack" impulse 4.2 seconds prior to the sound of a large explosion (or "boom"). High detonation-velocity charges produce a "crack," not a "boom."

- Multiple survivor testimonies of earthquake-like shaking prior to the large blast are on record.

- Disintegrated concrete with smooth fracture-termination signatures typical of localized high-brisance damage were documented on critical structural members.

C. THE BOTTOM LINE

Neither of the two outstanding explanations for the structural collapse is conclusively proven; nor can either be eliminated without further intensive study of materials now closely held by the Federal Government.

D. UNRESOLVED ISSUES

- What happened 4.2 seconds before the large explosion? (How did the explosion of 5600 pounds of ANNM produce the same first motion seismic characteristics as did the explosion of 150 pounds of implosion charges?)

- How (by what mechanism) did the otherwise undamaged main 3' x 5' x 200' transfer beam become separated from the supporting columns—leaving three cleanly sliced 21-inch gaps where the concrete is totally missing?

- How was it possible for the crater to fall well inside the corners of a 16-foot square of plywood (8 sheets in a 2 x 4 array), yet be reported as 28 or 32 feet across?

- Why was access to evidence of the size and nature of the crater deliberately withheld from the defense team? Was this a violation comparable to the recently revealed withholding of evidence documents by the FBI?

- If column G20[A5] was removed by brisance, how could the bomb that made only an 18-foot crater have done it? And by what mechanism could two other identical columns—as much as 50 feet from the truck—have suffered virtually identical damage?

- What caused the collapse of internal column F24[B3]?

- Why was the Federally chartered, FEMA-funded BPAT investigation team kept 200 feet from the building?

- What justified the immediate transportation and burial prior to the implosion—without documentation—of the main structural elements?

- Why was the site "sanitized" of heavy structural remnants prior to demolition?

- What was the **real** reason for the rush to demolish and bury the building—before it could be independently examined and analyzed? Who—at all levels—was involved in, and responsible for, approving the demolition?

- Why was the crime scene—including the crater—bulldozed immediately following the implosion?

- Why have Federal and Oklahoma agents persisted in a campaign to label citizens who ask reasonable and honest questions like these as "conspiracy theorists," "crackpots" or "off the reservation"?

It is the intention of this report to dispose of conspiracy theories, not to create or propagate them. However, considering the foregoing list of unresolved issues, it should be expected that, lacking a new attitude of openness on the part of the Justice Department and the FBI, citizen mistrust of Federal agencies and their motives will persist.

> *" People in an open society do not demand infallibility from their institutions, but it is difficult for them to accept what they are prohibited from observing."*
> *Supreme Court Justice Warren Burger*

EVALUATION OF PUBLISHED EXPLANATIONS CONCERNING THE STRUCTURAL COLLAPSE OF THE ALFRED P. MURRAH FEDERAL BUILDING

A. THE MURRAH BUILDING AND ITS MAJOR STRUCTURAL ELEMENTS

1. Nomenclature Conventions Employed in This Report

Confusing variability was encountered in published reports as to floor numbering and as to which side (north or south) of the Murrah building was the front. For purposes of this report, the Murrah Building's main office tower will be described as viewed from Northwest Fifth Street, facing the severely damaged north face, which will be referred to as the "front". On the north side, entry was at the slab level; accordingly, the slab or grade level will be referred to as the "first" floor (Fig. 1). Another point of confusion encountered in published reports relates to references to a "basement". There was no basement under the first floor of the **main office tower.** Because Northwest 5th Street sloped upward to the east from North Harvey Avenue to North Robinson Avenue, only the midpoint

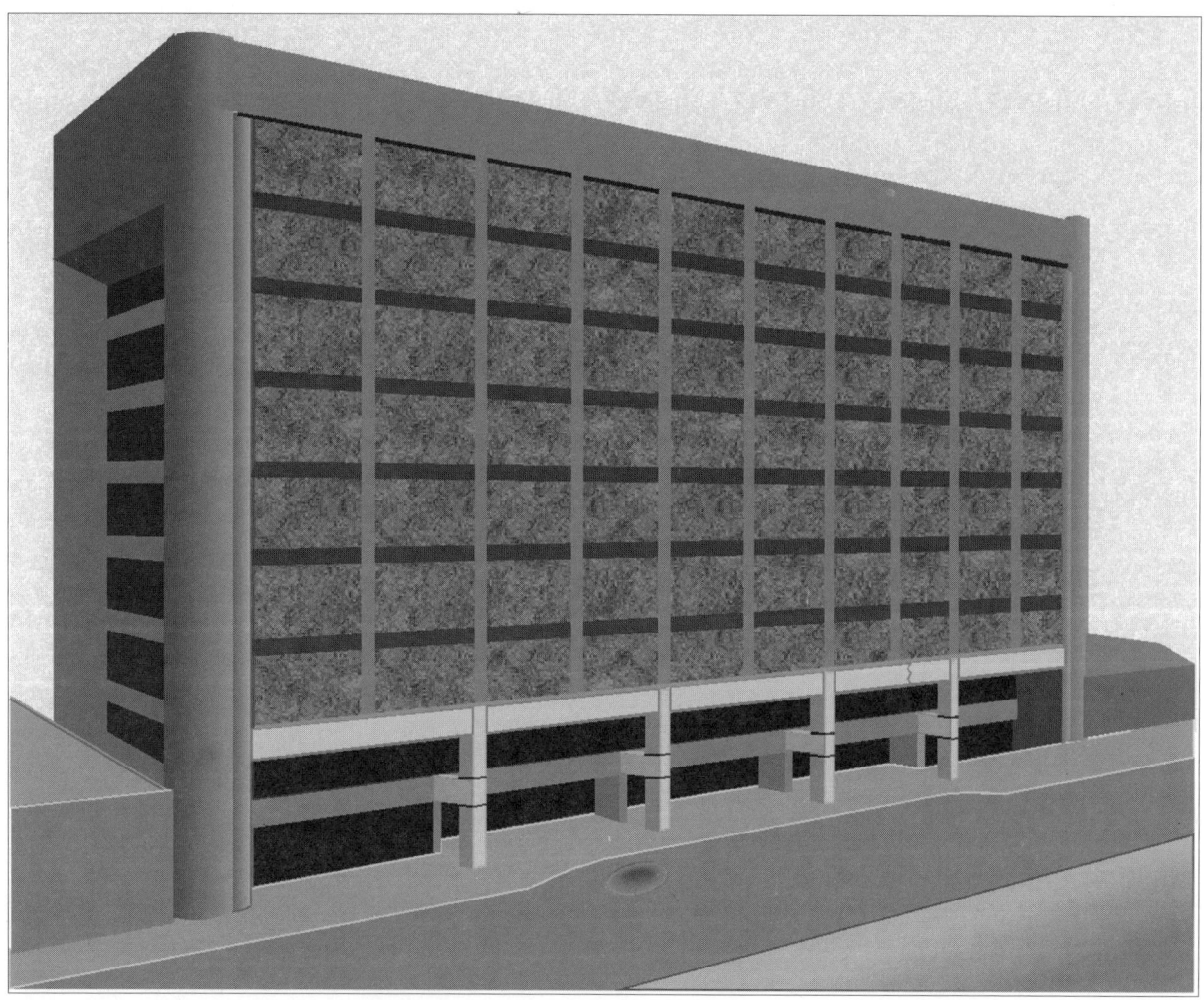

North View of the Murrah Building -- Showing Portico (Figure 1)

of the first floor of the office tower—immediately opposite the north entrance—was at the same level ("grade") as the street. The west end of the first floor was above grade (street level); and, conversely, the east end of the first floor was below grade—or set into the side of the hill. It was this below-grade eastern section of the first floor that was perceived and described by rescuers as being a basement. This misperception was exacerbated by an early Associated Press drawing that erroneously showed three levels of basement below the southern half of the office tower. (There were three basement levels of the parking garage south of the office tower, under the courtyard.)

The architect's drawings of the Murrah complex employ a Cartesian grid coordinate system, (with its origin in the southwest corner of the complex) for designating column locations. It consists of numbered north-south lines, with numbers increasing from west to east, and lettered east-west rows, with letters increasing from south to north. The main office tower of the building was bounded by grid lines 10 through 26 and rows E through G. (Fig. 2)

In the report of General Benton Partin (Appendix pg. 378-398), he employed a unique coordinate system with its origin in the northeast corner. For reader convenience, the corresponding "Partin" coordinate will be appended in brackets to the architect's coordinates. For example, the row of columns supporting the north face of the building will be referred to as the "G[A]-row", with the G[A]-row column in line with (north of) the failed internal column referred to as "G24[A3]" (Fig. 2).

2. General Description of the North Face of the Murrah Building

The north face of the office tower of the Murrah Building (Fig. 1) was distinguished by a portico formed by recessing the first and second floor glass walls. The first floor walls were set back 20 feet, and the second floor was set back 10 feet. Support for the upper floors was provided by a transfer spandrel or "header" which spanned the entire 200-foot width of the tower, and which, in turn, rested on the four large G[A]-row columns. Vehicular access to the portico was enhanced by a curb inset which allowed vehicles to approach to within seven-and-a-half (7.5) feet of the outer row of columns. These architectural features significantly contributed to the vulnerability of the Murrah Building to a vehicle-borne bomb attack.

3. Detailed Description of the Major Structural Elements

To assist in discussion of the following, a scale drawing of a typical G[A]-row column structure and associated support elements (viewed looking west) is provided (Fig. 3).

a. The Main Header Beam

Aside from the concrete slab upon which it stood, the Alfred P. Murrah Federal Building's single most massive and critical structural member was the reinforced concrete "spandrel" or "transfer beam" or "header beam" ("main header") that spanned the G[A] (north) face of the building at the third floor level (highlighted in white in Fig. 4).

Upon it rested the weight of all 637 feet of upper columns along the north face, the north ends of the upper seven floors and roof, and the northern glass fascia of the building. Its complete collapse

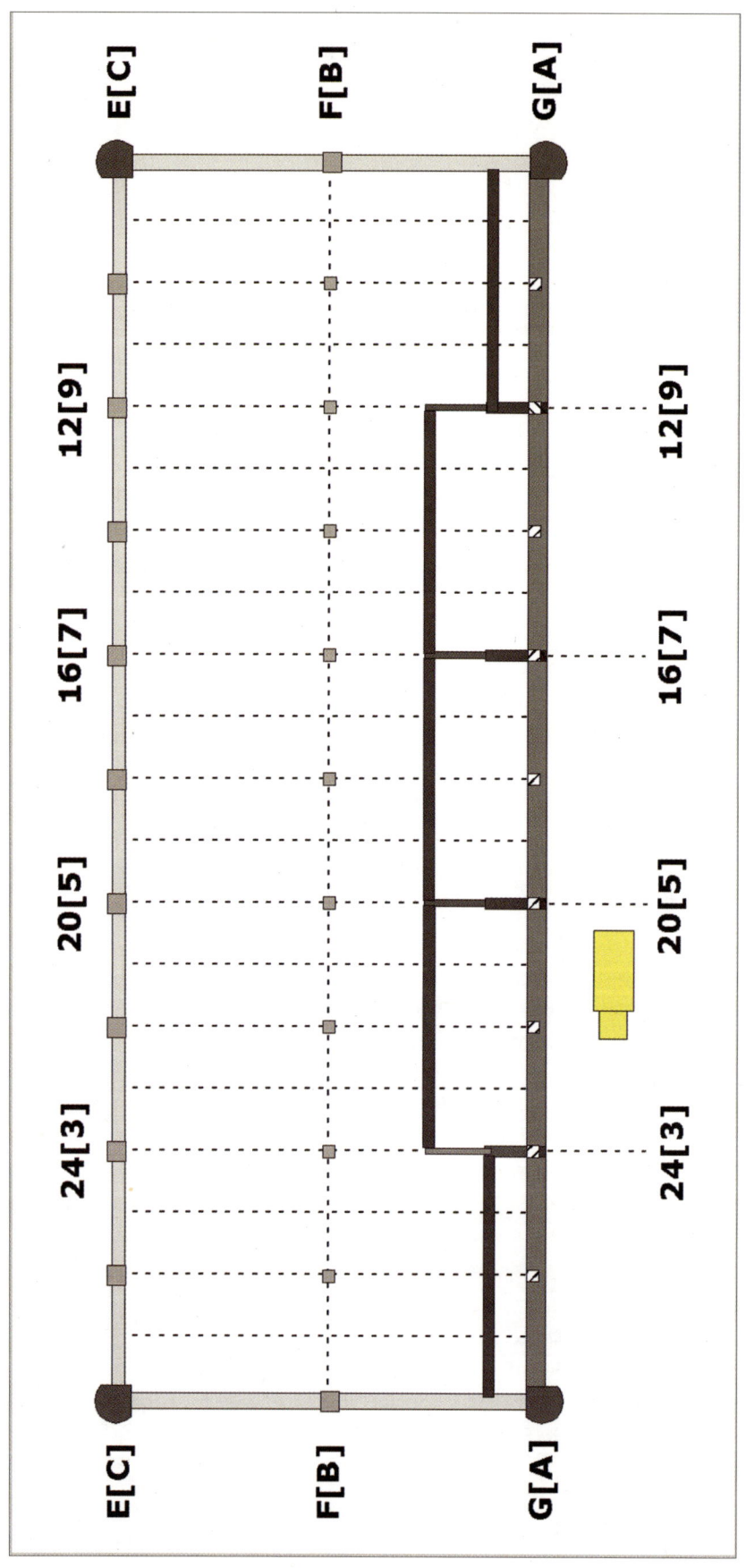

Plan View with Office Tower Coordinates and Nomenclature Conventions (Figure 2)

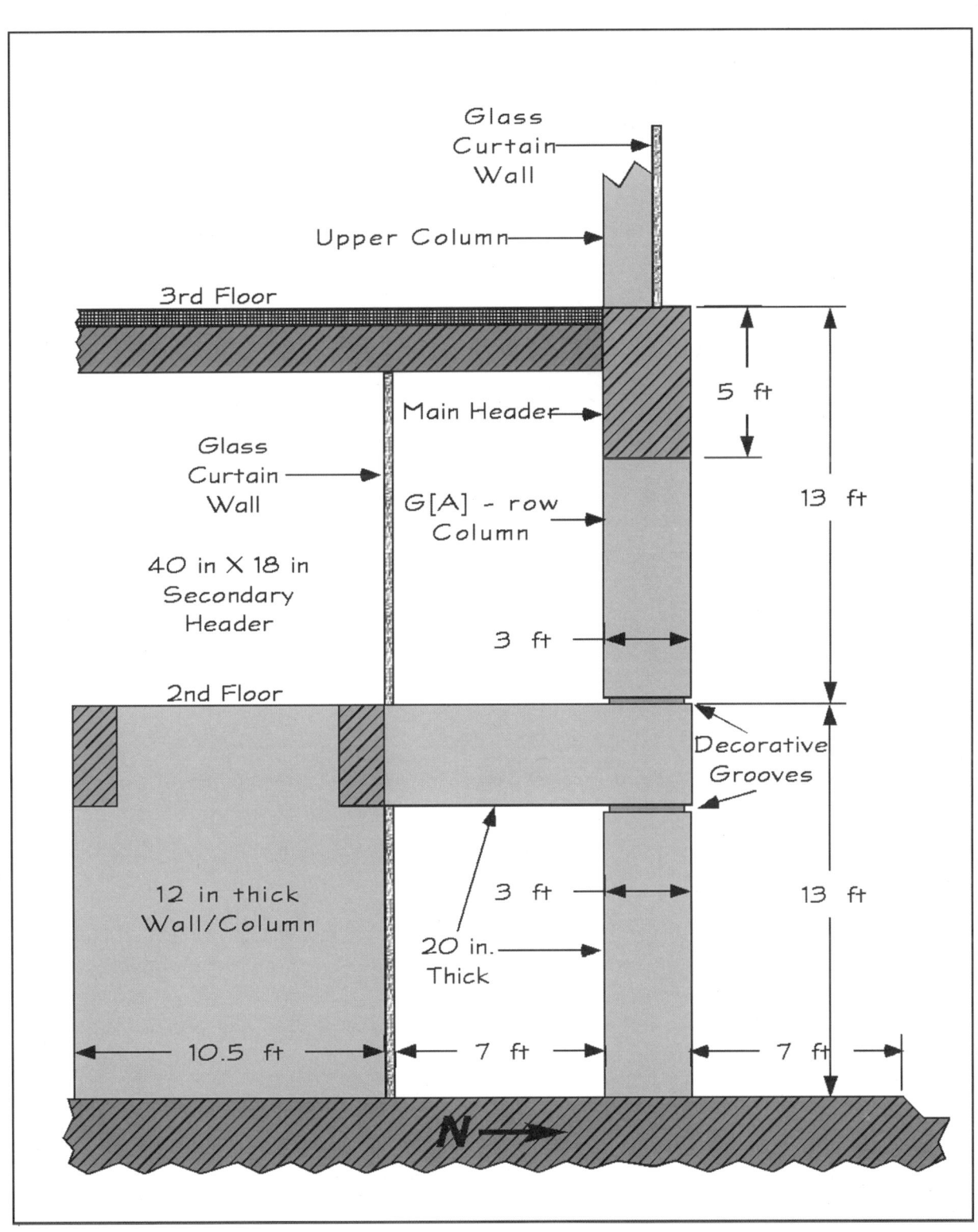

Typical Structural Features Associated with the Portico -- Looking West (Figure 3)

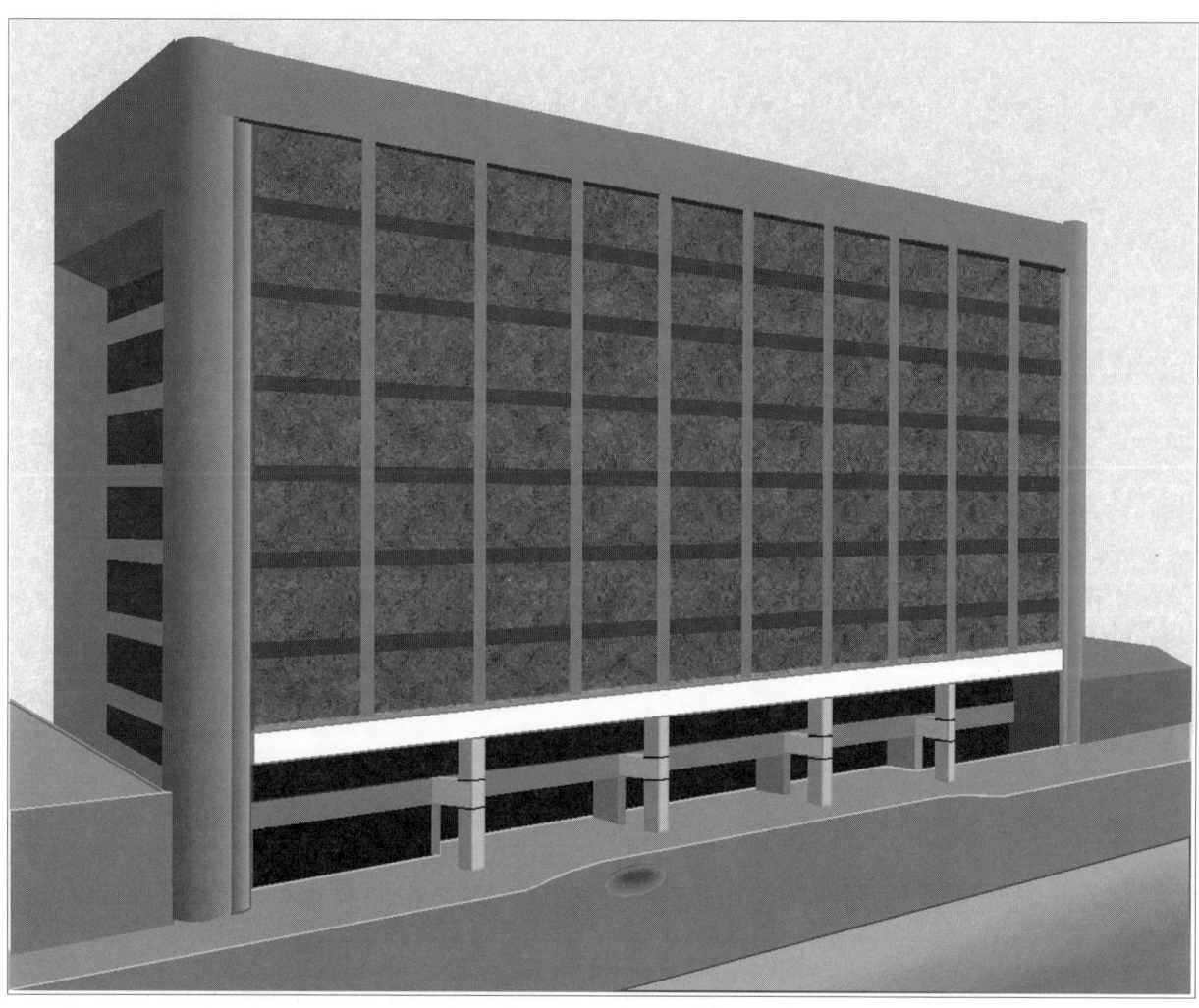

The Main Header or Transfer Beam -- Highlighted in White (Figure 4)

would have been sufficient to bring down the entire northern half (exclusive of the end walls) of the Murrah Building's main office tower.

The header beam measured five (5) feet tall, was three (3) feet thick, and was 200 feet long. In addition to being anchored at both ends, it rested upon—and was, via rebar, integrally connected to—four massive, reinforced concrete columns spaced along row G[A] at regular intervals of 40 feet. Its upper surface was at the third floor level. The header was formed from over 110 cubic yards (eleven cement-mixer truck loads) of concrete, which weighed approximately 450,000 pounds or 225 tons.

To gain a personal sense of the massive scale of the main header beam and its position relative to the oft-mentioned "truck bomb," the reader is invited to perform the following "thought experiment":

> Envision yourself standing in the end zone of a football field. In front of you, with its end on the goal line, is a concrete wall five feet tall and three feet broad. It

extends away from you for two-thirds of the length of the field. Walk out onto the field alongside the wall to the 23 yard line (70 feet), then turn and back away from it for ten feet. Now imagine the wall levitated as high as the peak of the roof of a two-story home. Your eyes are now are at the approximate center of the "Ryder Truck bomb", and you are looking up at the closest point on the massive header beam from a line-of sight distance of 26 feet.

b. The Four External Columns

Each of the "four massive, reinforced concrete columns spaced along row G[A] at regular intervals of 40 feet" mentioned in paragraph a above was 21 feet tall (the 26-foot height of two 13-foot stories minus the five-foot height of the header). Reinforcement in each column consisted of twenty pieces of #11 (1.4 inch diameter) rebar tied together at close intervals by "stirrups," as shown in Figure 3-9 of the ASCE-FEMA/BPAT Report (Appendix pg. 378-398). This column rebar extended down through the slab into concrete footings and extended up through the five-foot height of the main header, and was integrally cast therein (Fig. 5). Each column was three feet deep (north to south) and was 20 inches thick. Upon these four columns rested most of the 225-ton weight of the main header beam.

c. The Horizontal Bracing Beams

A report by the National Academy of Science described the G[A]-row columns as "...shattered eight meter tall columns that were unsupported for two floors". Quite the contrary: at the second-floor level, the G[A]-row columns were braced by horizontal beams the same 20-inch thickness as the columns and forty 40 inches tall, which extended back (southward) seven feet from the columns to where they joined—and were supported by—reinforced concrete support walls ("wall columns") upon which the recessed second floor also rested).

d. The Second Floor Transfer Beam

Parallel to the main header, but inside the porch or portico, was a set of smaller horizontal transfer beams at the second-floor level that supported the northern edges of the recessed second floor. These "secondary headers" were 18 inches thick and 40 inches tall. They, like the horizontal beams from the columns, were supported by the four "wall columns."

e. The 12" "Wall Columns" or "Column Walls"

Support for both the second-floor headers and the horizontal beams from the G[A]-row columns was supplied by four 13-foot tall by 10.5 foot deep load-bearing "column walls" that, like the G[A]-row, were centered on the 12, 16, 20, and 24 grid lines. The entire weight of the second floor headers, plus that of the southern end of the column-bracing beams, was borne by concrete sections that were approximately 12 by 18 inches. As indicated, these wall junctures may have constituted serious structural weak points.

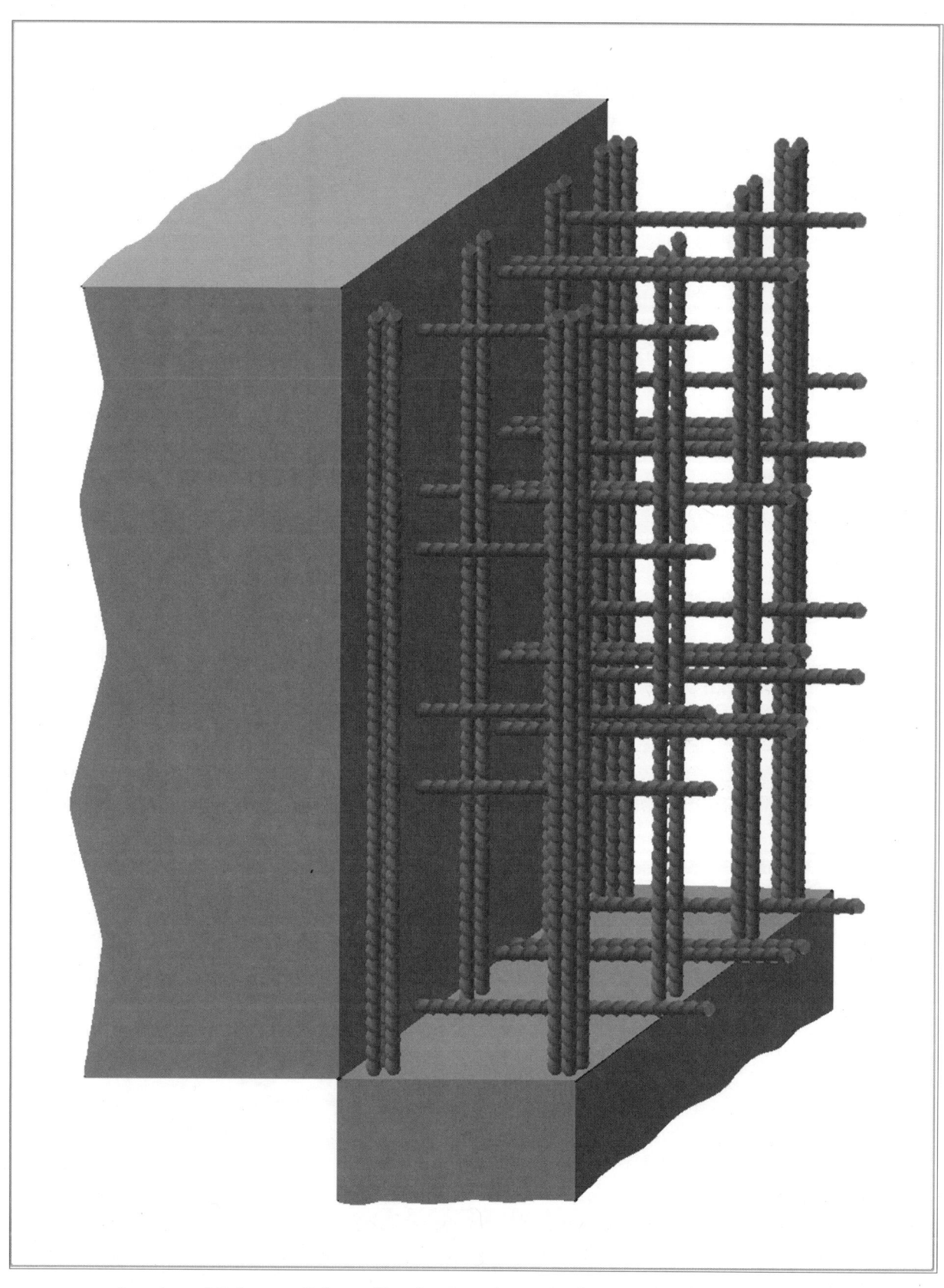

Interlaced Rebar at Column-Header Junction -- Without Stirrup Ties (Figure 5)

f. The Decorative Grooves

Approximately one-inch square, sharp-edged decorative grooves marked the junctions of the horizontal beams with the columns and the junctions of the columns with the header. Partin pointed out instances (Appendix pgs. 378-398) where these fragile, decorative features remained unmarred, though in close proximity to totally destroyed concrete. At some locations, however, the decorative grooves apparently coincided with rebar shear ties; these instances may have acted as stress concentrators.

B. THE EVIDENCE—GENERAL DESCRIPTION OF OBSERVED DAMAGE

Testimony by prosecution explosives expert Linda Jones described the truck bomb as being of a "heaving or pushing" nature.

> *I think overall my first impression of the building and the crater was that the damage had been caused by an explosive that would have a pushing and a heaving effect; for example, like the sort of explosive that would be used in quarrying, to give a general idea, yes* (Source: McVeigh trial transcript, pg. 9890)

Such a low-velocity, "pushing and heaving" explosive would have lacked the 'brisant' or shattering levels of energy required to have pulverized one of the columns—as claimed in other reports.

However, it is generally accepted that the portions of the Murrah Building that collapsed did so under the influence of gravity after critical support structures were weakened or destroyed. A report published by the structural engineering firm, EQE International, specifically states that

> *The explosion collapsed columns of the first few floors at the rear [sic] of the building, the north side, and one center line column [F24], and gravity brought down the structure above.* (Source: http://www.eqe.com/publications/revf95/oklahoma.htm)

It is now known that the portions of the Murrah building that collapsed did so vertically, and that there was little transport of building materials toward the south (back into the building) due to blast. The same EQE International report specifically states that:

> *According to Mark Ghilarducci, Incident Support Team (IST) leader, from the Office of Emergency Services in California, through the help of Geographical Information Systems software, rescuers concluded that the building fell straight down by comparing the original location of workstations to where they were found.*

> *Learning that the building fell straight down and [was] not pushed to the side because of the blast helped focus the search effort.* (Source: http://www.eqe.com/publications/revf95/oklahoma.htm)

Three of the G[A]-row columns were destroyed—in virtually identical fashion—and the section of the main header supported by them fell, bringing down all seven upper floors and the roof across most of the north face.

Total collapse of internal column F24[B3] caused all floors and the roof in the two adjoining bays to collapse in the section known as the "bite", where collapse extended almost to the south wall.

In order to determine the possible mechanisms of the Murrah Building collapse, the following evidence was analyzed in this report: (1) the effects of air blast versus brisance, (2) failure modes and mechanisms, (3) seismic data, and (4) the dimensions and properties of the crater.

C. AIR BLAST vs. BRISANCE

For the purposes of this discussion of explosive damage to a reinforced concrete structure, explosive action can be relegated to two applicable categories: brisance and blast.

1. Brisance--High-Velocity "Cutting" Charges

Brisance is the technical term that characterizes the **shattering** effect of high explosives on hard materials. Perhaps the most familiar example of brisance is the action of demolition charges placed against—or within—reinforced concrete structural members of a building undergoing demolition. Such charges couple a high-velocity shock wave directly into the concrete. In that portion of the concrete where the combination of direct and internally reflected shock wave pressure exceeds the compressive strength of the material, the concrete completely disintegrates. In effect, the concrete is dissociated back into its constituent materials of sand and powdered limestone. Many types of gravel or crushed-rock aggregate within the concrete are frequently pulverized as well. Brisant failure is failure of the bulk concrete material.

The lingering image of a building that has undergone implosive demolition is that of a cloud which totally obscures the scene. That cloud is not smoke; it primarily consists of the concrete that has been reverted to powder by explosive brisance. One of the impediments to rescue was large quantities of pulverized-concrete dust.

At the point at which shock-wave energy, propagated through the body of the concrete, drops below the compressive strength of the concrete, a fracture termination with a distinctly smooth and granular and rounded surface is formed. By contrast, fracture terminations due to tension or shear failure typically are sharp and jagged, with rough, uneven surfaces.

Properly coupled and directed brisance energy can produce almost surgically clean and precisely localized destruction of concrete structural members. Expert prosecution witness Linda Jones, addressed this phenomenon in testimony:

> *[These military explosives or other very high explosives that are meant to shatter]...can be used—well, in the military they'll be used as shells for firing at tanks or other targets. They can also be used in some demolition work. You can—It's all very clever. You can use them to almost cut surgically. You could have, for example, with a plastic explosive, you could roll it out like a putty and wrap it 'round a structure. When you set off that explosive, you can cut through, for example, like a bridge support or a girder. (Source: McVeigh trial transcript, pg. 9893-94)*

Increasing the velocity of detonation increases the brisance capability of an explosive device. The effective brisance of an explosive is also a function of the quantity of explosive and the range to the target.

Regardless of the explosive under discussion or its velocity of detonation, **brisance is a short-range effect.** Unless the explosive is in intimate contact with the target, energy must be transmitted to the target through intervening air. Because of the cubic falloff of explosive energy with distance, even very high explosives have a severely limited effective brisance radius.

The **characteristic signatures of brisant damage** in reinforced concrete are as follows:

- Sharply localized total concrete disintegration
- Clean, exposed reinforcement steel ("rebar")
- Smooth, rounded, powdery fracture terminations.

2. Air Blast—Truck Bomb

Blast or "air blast" (energy transmission through air) is the mechanism upon which any explosion depends for exerting damaging **force when detonated at a significant distance from the target.** Unlike the sharply localized—and typically directional—effects of brisant damage, air blast exerts its influence relatively uniformly upon all exposed surfaces. With air blast, sharply localized damage usually occurs only if there is a structure-based concentration of force—or a structural weakness.

a. Pushing and Heaving Effect

Prosecution expert Linda Jones described the pushing and heaving effect of an explosive:

> *If we think of an explosive of a quarrying operation where what you want to do is bring down a rock face to produce fairly large materials for—I don't know, as aggregate or whatever, then you will use a certain type of explosive, one that will heave and push, rather than shatter the material into little tiny pebbles.*

b. Uniform and Non-Selective

An air blast wave is, in essence, a gust of wind—an extremely fast-moving, highly-compressed and, near the blast center, superheated gust of wind. Unlike an ordinary wind gust, however, the duration of an air blast wave is measured in thousandths of a second (milliseconds). Air blast force is typically uniform; it consists of a rapidly expanding sphere radiating out from the explosion center. Air blast is, by its very nature, non-selective in its effects.

Blast force is measured in units of force divided by units of area—expressed in this report as pounds per square foot. The pushing effects of air blast couple energy best into objects with large surface areas; the larger the area, the greater the effective pushing force. Objects with small cross-sectional areas facing the blast experience little pushing force. Walls broadside-on to a blast receive maximum impulse; walls that are edge-on to a blast may remain relatively untouched.

As an analogy, the bare masts of a sailboat interact hardly at all with the wind. Hoisting of the large-area sails, on the other hand, provides a large area to be acted upon by that same wind, and sufficient force is generated to move the hull through the water at a speed that can be a significant fraction of that of the wind.

Like the boat's bare mast, the narrow columns and transfer beam supporting the Murrah Building were minimally affected by the blast wave. Conversely, sufficient force was coupled into the large-area floors and walls to cause massive damage as far up as the fourth floor. It is generally accepted that, even if none of the columns had collapsed, the air blast from the truck bomb would have caused significant casualties due to disrupted floors and from flying fragments of the glass curtain wall.

c. Cubic, Then Square Pressure Falloff Function with Distance

As a blast wave radiates out from the blast center, its pressure diminishes proportional to the cube of the distance. Each time the distance doubles, the pressure is divided by a factor of eight. At distances beyond the initial sphere of expanding gas produced by the explosive, the energy propagates outward as a simple shock or sound wave, whose energy decays as the square of the distance. Each year, several incautious youngsters experience a validation of the inverse cube law: in contact with, or very near to a hand, even a small firecracker can inflict painful injury. At even a few inches distance, however, it is hardly felt.

The implications of the inverse cube law are significant: There were massive structural elements in the Murrah Building that failed—at distances from the truck bomb where the blast pressure was far below their compressive yield strength. Some of those sharply localized failures occurred in elements that were unscathed in areas between the truck bomb explosion and the point of failure. For those failures, we must seek some explanation other than simple air blast as their cause.

d. "Snap" Failures in Concrete

Failure in concrete structural elements due to the pushing or heaving effects of air blast are distinctly different from compressive failures caused by brisance. Instead of crumbling into dust, concrete elements usually fail at the points where they connect to other elements. Large, flat concrete panels may be "dished in" at the center, with fractures radiating out to the corners. Walls may be pushed over, remaining largely intact, except where they break away from floors or ceilings. Blast-induced failures are fractures, not disintegration of the bulk material.

e. Characteristic Signature of Air Blast Damage

The signature of air blast is very visible, widespread damage, large objects pushed from their at-rest positions, and jagged fracture terminations in brittle materials like concrete.

D. FAILURE MODE AND MECHANISM

1. General Descriptions

To describe a failure completely and precisely, practitioners of reliability physics employ two formal terms: the **mode** of failure (or "**failure mode**") and the **mechanism** of failure (or "**failure mechanism**").

a. Failure Mode

The mode of failure is a term that describes the article in its failed state. For example, the failure mode of a tire whose failure resulted in an automobile accident might be, "the tread was separated from the carcass of the tire."

b. Failure Mechanism

Failure mechanism, on the other hand, is a complex analytical term that describes -- as precisely as possible -- **how** and, more importantly, **why** a failure occurred. For the aforementioned tire, an appropriate failure mechanism might be

> At highway speed, and on pavement at temperatures over 100 degrees F, flexure of the nylon plies relative to the steel belt caused heat buildup, which, in turn, softened and weakened the tread/carcass bonding layer to the point that catastrophic failure in the form of tread separation occurred. Further analysis reveals that the bonding layer was improperly formulated during manufacturing.

When arriving at a proposed failure mechanism, several factors are considered:

- Stress condition(s) under which the failure occurred
- The as-built structure of the failed item(s)—Including all materials and components
- Built-in or designed-in weaknesses or flaws, if any
- Anomalies in the manufacturing or construction process, if applicable
- Interactions within the structure, which could have contributed to failure
- Effects of aging, if applicable

c. Failure Mode Class

When a number of similar failed items exhibit the same failure **mode**, they may be treated as a failure **class.** In order for failures to exhibit a common failure mode, a common failure mechanism—incorporating one or more of the following common factors and contributors to failure—must exist:

- A common, inherent, or designed-in vulnerability or weakness
- A common manufacturing or materials defect(s)
- A common (similar magnitude) stress condition(s)

The failure modes of the three main exterior columns and the adjoining regions of the main header beam appear to be virtually identical. They can, therefore, be treated as a **failure-mode class**.

2. Common Failure Mode of the Three Main Columns

Figure 6 schematically depicts the failure mode common to three critical locations: columns G16[A7], G20[A5], and G24[A3]. From approximately the second floor level up to the third floor level—including the volume of concrete through the main header beam which encompasses the column rebar—the concrete is missing, (depicted in red), leaving only bare rebar. Where visible, fracture terminations appear to be clean, smooth, rounded and granular. The large (three feet thick and five feet tall) main header appears to have been cleanly sliced through immediately adjacent to the decorative grooves in line with the east and west faces of the columns.

a. Column G16[A7]

At the westernmost column, G16[A7], all twenty pieces of #11 rebar within the column apparently separated from the transfer beam early in the collapse process. The lower (first to second floor) section of the column toppled directly north, landing on its outermost face, with the relatively straight column rebar extending out into the street (Photo 1). Early separation of the column rebar is indicated by the fact that the rebar appears to be relatively straight.

Figure 7 concisely illustrates the damage to column G16[A7] and adjoining structures inferred from photographic analysis.

Photo 1 is the best currently available overall photographic view of one of the three failed main external columns and the adjoining main transfer beam. It exemplifies the difficulty with disposing of General Partin's hypothesis that high-velocity charges were placed in intimate contact with the failed columns.

b. Column G24[A3]

At the other two columns, on the other hand, the rebar apparently remained enmeshed with the rebar of the header beam, and was bent downward with it as the header beam fell. All of the rebar in column G24[A3] apparently remained enmeshed with the header rebar (Photo 2). It is evident that a sizeable, very rounded, pillow-shaped chunk of concrete remained attached to the column rebar slightly above the second floor level, while the remainder of the rebar was stripped bare.

c. Column G20[A5]

At column G20[A5], most of the rebar followed the header down as it fell, but several of the twenty pieces of #11 rebar apparently separated from the header in mid-fall. Those pieces of rebar are bent back toward the header, but their third-floor ends are free, with their ends remaining straight.

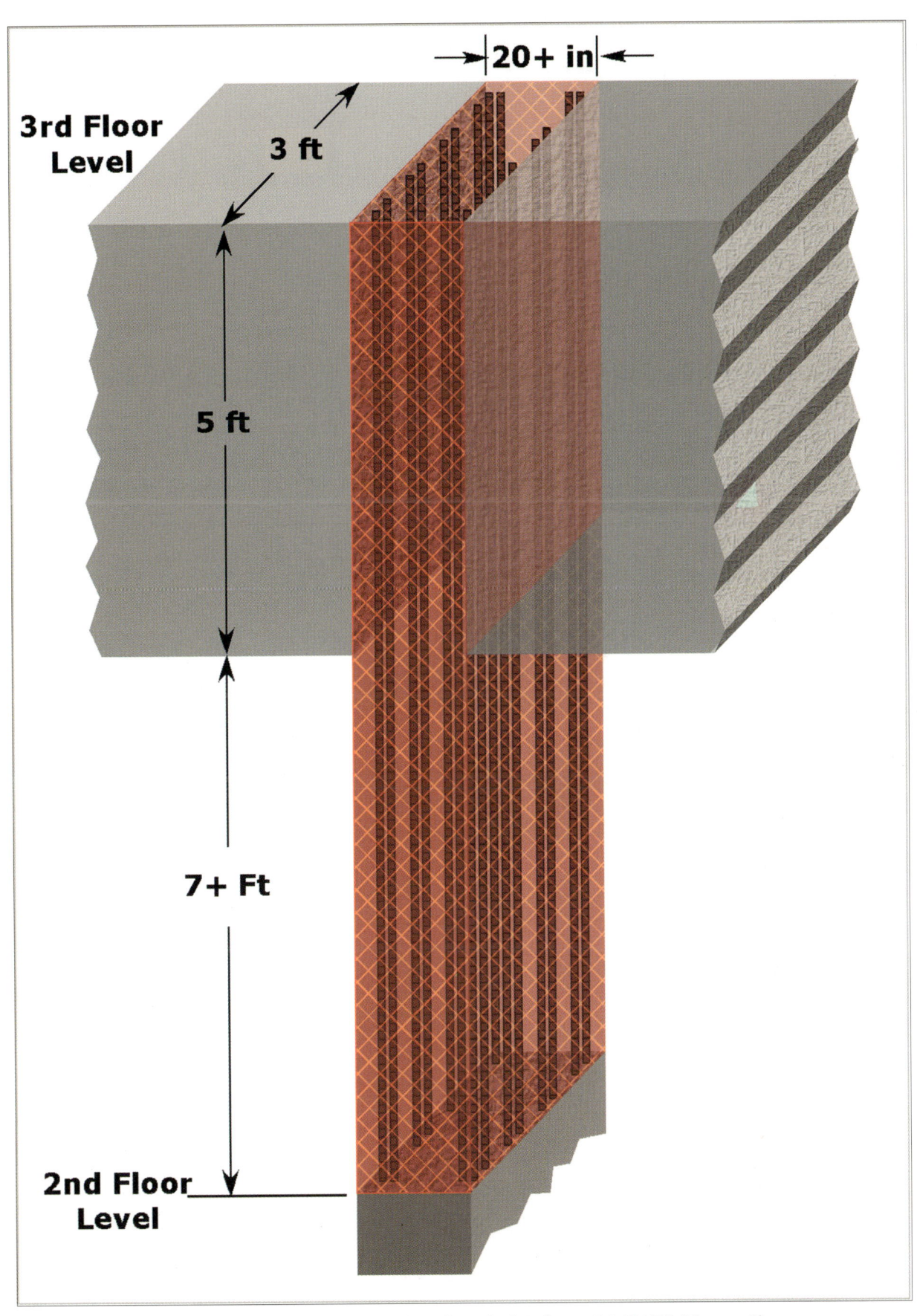

Structural Damage Associated with Failed Column G16[A7] (Figure 6)

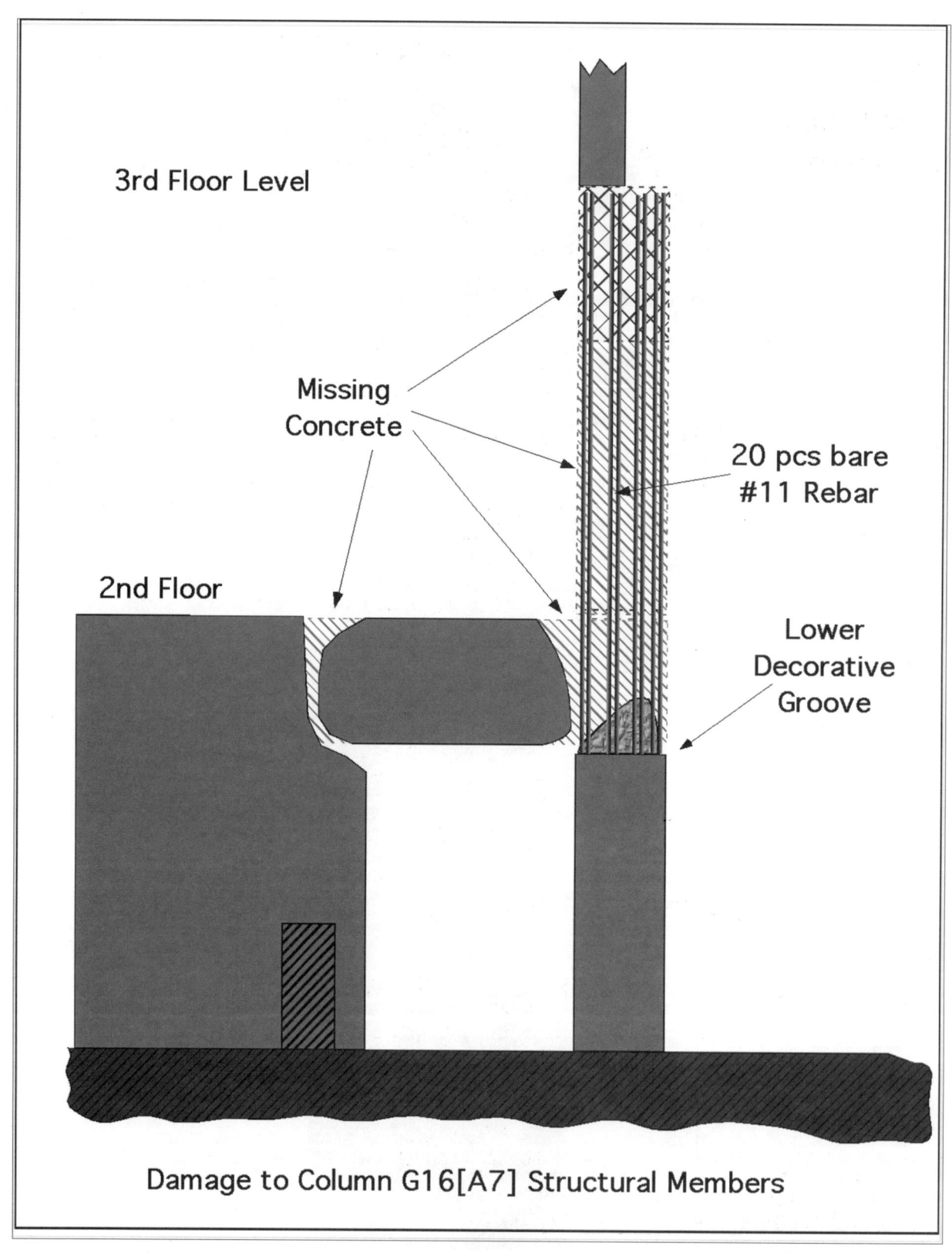

Structural Damage Associated with Failed Column G24[A3] (Figure 7)

Structural Damage Associated With Failed Column G16[A7] (Photo 1)

3. **Analysis of Labeled Details of Photo 1: "Structural damage associated with failed column G16[A7]"**

    a. Column G16[A7] at just below the second floor level. Note that the column toppled directly northward—approximately at right angles to the blast wave from the truck bomb.

    b. The lower of the two decorative grooves at the second floor level. (Column G24[A3] failed to almost the same level.)

    c. The cut-off (by rescuers) ends of the 20 pieces (13 feet long) of bare #11 (1.4-inch diameter) rebar that were within the column between the second floor level and the top of the main transfer girder or "main header." Note that intact stirrups are visible.

219

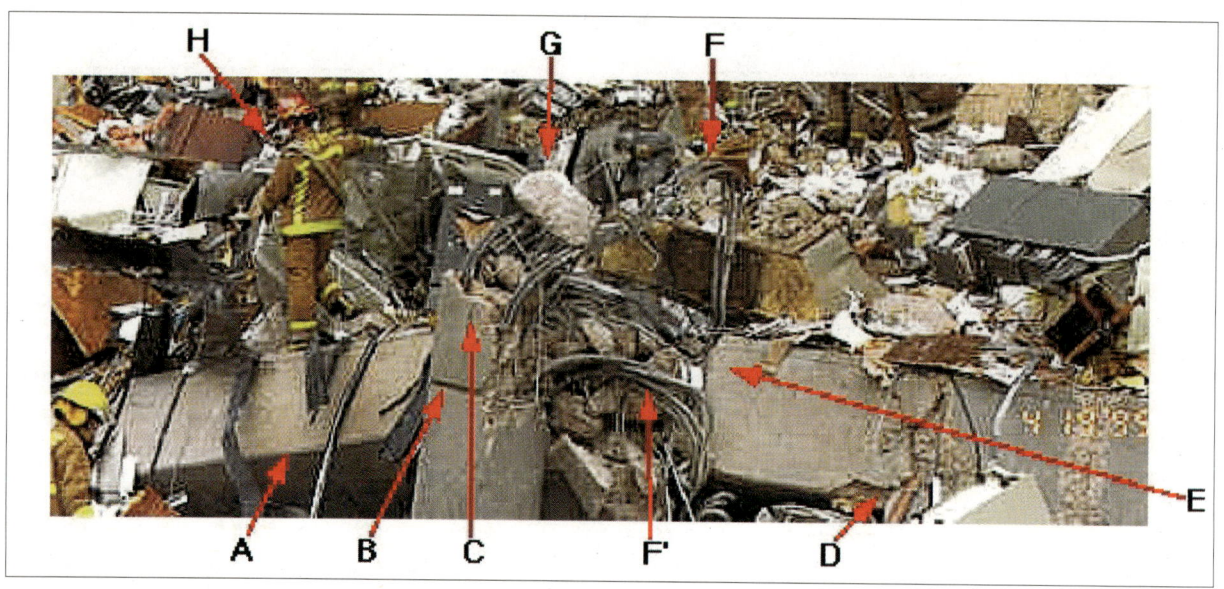

Structural Damage Associated With Failed Column G24[A3] (Photo 2)

    d. The (relatively undamaged) bottom of the main transfer or header beam. The rescuers are standing on what was the outer, vertical surface of the beam. The truck bomb was approximately 50 feet to the left.

    e. Imprints where the #11 rebar of the column passed through—and were cast within—the main transfer beam.

    f. Three instances of what certainly resembles the "smooth, rounded and granular" fracture termination surfaces described by Partin as typical of regions where a high-velocity compressive deformation wavefront (imparted by a very high-velocity contact explosive) drops below the compressive failure strength of the concrete. The triangular or pyramidal portion of concrete bounded by the column rebar and the lower decorative groove is particularly striking.

    g. One end of the 40" x 20 " x 7' horizontal beam that ran from between the two second floor decorative grooves on the column and the 12" x 10.5' x 7' "wall column" at the back of the portico.

    h. The 12 inch thick "wall column" that supported the inner end of the horizontal support beam at the second floor level. Note that its top is distinctly tilted over to the west (in the direction of the blast from the truck bomb. It has not been determined if the wall displacement was due to blast—or to forces imparted by falling debris. There is, however, (right below the "H" label) a small hole through the wall that appears to have been caused by a projectile striking it from the left (truck bomb) side. Also note that the "seat" which supported the horizontal beam is severely crumbled or eroded or blasted away. It is quite feasible that these relatively thin wall columns could have constituted points that were vulnerable to blast.

The other two main columns (G24[A3] and G20[A5]) apparently share a failure mode virtually identical to that shown above for G16[A7].

No one has identified a common, inherent, or designed-in vulnerability or weakness or a common manufacturing or materials defect at these failed locations. Given the great disparity in the locations of these three points of failure with respect to the truck bomb, it is difficult to envision how these near-identical failure modes could have resulted from a common (similar magnitude) stress condition directly imposed by the truck bomb's air-blast effects.

4. "Lifting" Failure Mechanism

One failure mechanism that has been postulated for the structural failure of the Murrah Building was that the blast pressure lifted the main transfer or header beam, and then allowed it to drop, thus crushing the main supporting columns. A simple "thought experiment" will suffice to dispose of this notion:

> Assume that the header beam is hanging free in space, not burdened by the weight of the upper seven floors, and not constrained against vertical motion by being integrally cast with the supporting columns. The surface area of the bottom of the beam is 600 square feet, and its weight is 450,000 pounds. Assuming then, that the bomb was directly beneath the beam, the blast would have to have exerted 750 pounds per square foot on the entire lower surface of the beam, to begin to lift the beam alone -- if it were hanging free in space.

Of course, in reality, the beam was burdened with the entire weight of the upper seven floor face of the building, plus at least a quarter of the weight of the upper seven floors. And it was firmly connected to the supporting columns by virtue of the fact that the twenty pieces of #11 (1.4 inch diameter) rebar which reinforced the columns continued up through the header beam and were integrally cast within it. The broken end of the header beam at column G16[A7] in photo (Appendix, pg. 409) clearly shows the impressions of the column rebar that had been integrally cast within the header beam.

Of course, the bomb was not directly beneath the header beam, not did it apply a force of 750 PSI along its entire lower surface. It is highly unlikely, therefore, that the main header beam lifted and then dropped, causing the total concrete disintegration observed at the header's junctures with the main columns.

Figure 6 schematically summarizes the characteristic common failure mode shared by columns G24[A3], G20[A5] and G16[A7]—and their junctures with the main header or transfer beam. In all three locations, the concrete was stripped away from the column rebar, from the second floor level up to and through the section of the transfer beam that enclosed the column rebar.

E. SEISMIC DATA

1. Two Large Explosions?

Many investigators have interpreted seismic recordings made at the Omniplex Science Center in Oklahoma City and at the Oklahoma Geological Survey station in Norman, Oklahoma as showing two large explosions shortly after 9:00 a.m. on 19 April 1995. This investigation, on the other hand, has found no physical evidence that indicates that two large explosions occurred.

The **second large** signal on the 19 April Omniplex seismogram appears at the exact time at which the sound wave or air shock from the explosion would be expected to arrive at the Omniplex. (Exhibit A) It has been claimed that the amplitude of the second signal is too large for an air-coupled impulse. In the experience of the author, such is not the case. The large amplitude of the second pulse is almost certainly due to enhanced signals generated and coupled into the ground by the vibrational response of surrounding buildings to the air blast.

Just such an event was recently recorded in California (personal communication with OGS seismologist, Dr. Raymon Brown). The shock wave (sonic boom) from the Space Shuttle returning to Edwards Air Force Base passed directly over downtown Los Angeles. Seismic signals generated by the shock wave as it passed over ocean and open ground were miniscule. However, as the shock wave passed over the built-up portion of Los Angeles, so much vibrational energy from building motion was coupled into the earth that seismologists at first interpreted the event as a major earthquake in the center of the city.

It is the opinion of the author that, if the 19 April truck bomb shock wave had traveled to a seismometer in open country with no buildings nearby, the second (air blast) signal would have been relatively insignificant in both amplitude and duration.

It is also likely that the most satisfactory interpretation of the two 19 April seismic events recorded in Norman is that they are the result of multi-path propagation of seismic signals. This phenomenon was well-explained by USGS seismologist Dr. Thomas Holtzer, and agreed with by Dr. Brown (see pgs. 179-182) who utilized additional seismic data recorded by additional, broadband seismometers as generated by the 23 May implosion of the Murrah Building.

2. "First Motion" Seismic Signals

Public clamor to "prove" that the 19 April seismic records showed two large explosions unfortunately served to distract seismologists from thorough analysis of the seismic records. As a result, a significant seismic indicator, "first motion," was overlooked. First motion refers to the amplitude and phase of the first few cycles of ground motion, and is the primary diagnostic parameter for distinguishing the seismic signal generated by an explosion from that of an earthquake.

Large, aboveground explosions, as seen on vertical-channel seismograms, are characterized by **a high-amplitude initial excursion, followed by rapid signal decay.**

Comparison of first-motion signals recorded by the Omniplex seismograph on 19 April, and on 23 May (during the implosion) (Exhibit A), reveals a most interesting phenomenon: in both cases, there are approximately **four seconds of low-amplitude signal preceding** the onset of **large amplitude signal.** The first-motion signal from the detonation of approximately 150 pounds of contact explosives during the implosion was low-amplitude — as expected from such an event. **However, the first-motion signal of the 19 April event was virtually identical in both duration and (low) amplitude to the first-motion signal generated by the supposedly smaller implosion charges on 23 May.**

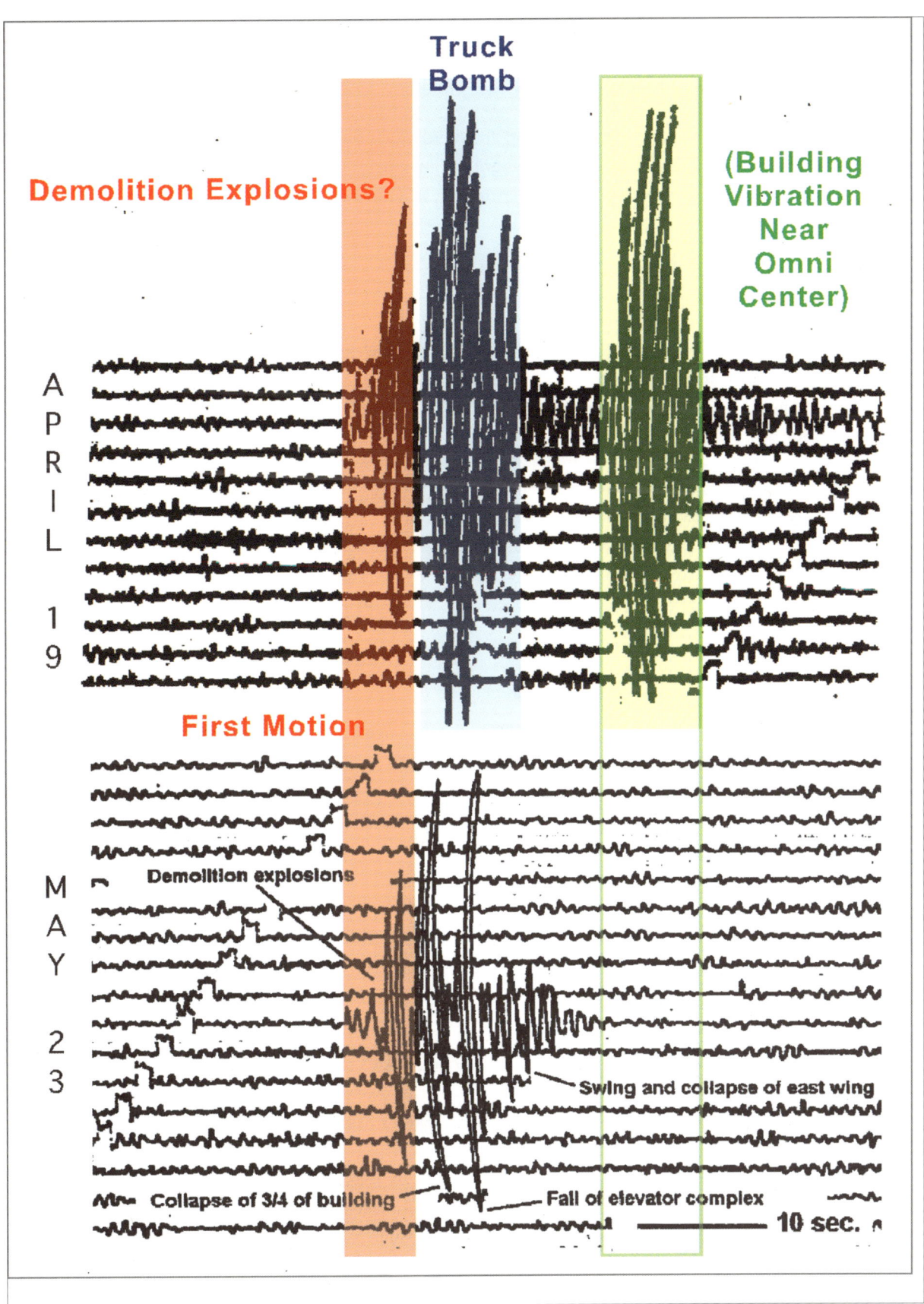

Exhibit A Seismic Data

One might reasonably question how the first-motion seismic signal generated by a (purported) 4,000- to 6,000-pound truck bomb appears identical to that from the detonation of 150 pounds of demolition explosives—as recorded by the same instrument.

Of all physical evidence examined during this investigation, it is felt that the **low-amplitude first motion** seismic signal from the 19 April event is the most credible evidence suggesting the explosion of small charges placed on exterior (portico) structural members of the Murrah Building prior to detonation of the truck bomb.

F. THE CRATER--DISPUTED EVIDENCE

Of all the items of physical evidence at the Murrah Building site, the crater, its location, and its dimensions are the single most significant indication of the location and performance of the explosive device that was allegedly contained in the Ryder truck. Yet no other item of evidence has been more widely misreported and misrepresented.

Early news reports and elaborate published news graphics erroneously represented the crater as being thirty feet or more in diameter and located in the middle of Northwest Fifth Street. Subsequently, published graphics erroneously placed the crater in line with columns G24[A3] and F24[B3]—well to the east of its actual position—inferring that the location of the truck bomb corresponded to the asymmetric pattern of collapse. A discussion of the various crater representations follows:

1. The "Missing" Crater

Some observers reported that no crater actually existed on 19 April (Day One). Some internet discussion groups and websites went so far as to claim that the crater that was finally revealed had actually been dug in the course of uncovering gas lines.

Several videotapes, produced and sold long after the event, perpetuated several of these errors, and some of them went to great lengths to claim that the crater was originally nonexistent. Even prosecution witness Linda Jones had difficulty identifying the crater in a 19 April photograph introduced into evidence by the prosecution, as shown by the following.

> Q. Now, Miss Jones, you said this was going to explain something about the damage of the building to the jury. Excuse me. If we could have the photograph for the jury.
>
> A. Here we can see the damaged face of the Murrah Building. And we can see that a bite—well, the bite that I spoke of has been taken out of this area of the building. And the front of the building has slid down. The crater, I think is under—generally about this area. But rubble and debris has fallen into it. (Source: Nichols trial transcript, pg. 11644)

It is true that the crater was not readily discernible in most of the aerial views from early news helicopter photographs or videotapes. Nor is the crater obvious in still pictures taken from elevated vantage points such as the Regency Tower apartment building. Even most ground-level photographs taken on 19 April 1995 show little evidence of a crater in Fifth Street.

Yet the crater was there—and in plain view.

2. The "Flooded" Crater

There is a simple—and well-documented—reason for the apparent invisibility of the crater in early photos: **The crater was filled with muddy water, and the surface of the water was covered with floating debris.** As a result, except upon direct examination, the crater closely resembled the rest of the debris field.

Photo 3, taken on the afternoon of 19 April (Day One), clearly shows the crater to be filled with reddish, muddy water, with floating debris covering most of the water's surface. The photographer, who worked in the building from Day One until the implosion, attributed the water to a damaged air conditioning chiller unit on the east (uphill) side of the building. As late as 07 May (Day 19), minutes of a meeting of the committee responsible for coordinating recovery and demolition activities recorded the following: "Water line broken and water coming into crater. Judy will call city."

Flooding of the crater with water obviously destroyed or severely compromised its value as a source of direct chemical evidence of the composition of the bomb. This fact has significance relative to subsequent FBI statements regarding the crater.

3. The "Huge" Crater

Early news articles reported that a crater as large as 40 feet in diameter existed in Fifth Street. Subsequent articles reduced the reported diameter to "over thirty feet." FBI Supervisory Special Agent (SSA) Dave Williams (who was in charge of evidence collection at the crime scene) stated in his deposed response to questions from the Office of the Inspector General's (OIG) investigators that "We have a 32-foot crater." (Source: *Whitehurst Review*, Case No. 9403575, DOJ OIG, pg. 117)

During her testimony in the Nichols trial, expert explosives witness Linda Jones, having reviewed **only** government-supplied videotapes, photographs and plans, and referring to a government-constructed model of the Murrah Building and its environs, testified about the crater:

> A. *The thing that impressed me most was the size. From the charts and the plans, it appeared that it was a big crater. It was of the order of 32 feet in diameter.*
>
> Q. *Does the size of the crater assist you in any way in determining the size of the bomb that was used?*
>
> A. *Very generally, yes.... It—the size and shape of the crater will depend very much on the size and the shape of the bomb, but a crater of that size would be created by a big bomb.* (Source: Nichols trial transcript, pg. 11640)

4. The "Official" Crater

The Federal Emergency Management Agency (FEMA) is required to perform a building security evaluation in the event of damage to a federal building. In evaluating the Murrah Building, FEMA obtained the assistance of the American Society of Civil Engineers (ASCE). Together they formed a Building Performance Assessment Team (BPAT) and filed a report of their findings and conclusions (to

Flooded Crater Covered with Floating Debris on Afternoon of 19 April 1995 (Photo 3)

be discussed in detail below). The opinions of FBI Agent Dave Williams and expert witness Linda Jones of a 32-foot crater notwithstanding, the "official" diameter of the crater as supplied to the blue-ribbon BPAT was—not 32 feet, but—28 feet.

5. The "Misrepresented" Crater

It is a matter of grave concern that persuasive evidence exists that the government misrepresented the size of the crater by grossly exaggerating its diameter. Even the "official" 28-foot diameter apparently overestimates the crater size by a large margin. If that is, indeed, the case, all estimates of the size and explosive power—and destructive potential—of the truck bomb based on government-published crater dimensions are seriously overstated.

6. The "Two-Part" Crater

According to dimensions cited in the BPAT report, the pavement of Fifth Street in the region of the

Crater On Day 10 -- With Residual Lip and Tread Imprint of Tracked Excavator (Photo 4)

crater was eleven inches of asphalt over seven inches of concrete, over packed soil. The actual imprint of the truck bomb blast on **the Fifth Street pavement and its substratum**, as revealed in photographs, was clearly composed of two distinctly different regions:

a. a central region, which clearly penetrated the asphalt and concrete pavement and displaced the underlying soil. The depth of this region was several feet. This region is referred to in this report as the "penumbra" or "actual" crater. Within this region, the truck bomb exerted sufficient brisance to destroy seven inches of concrete overlaid by eleven inches of asphalt. Although the pavement in this region was exposed to both direct blast and reflected energy, it was demonstrably smaller in diameter than the "official" diameter of 28 feet (Photo 4).

b. a larger, visible surrounding region, wherein the surface of the asphalt was visibly burned, scoured or "scuffed"—or covered with red soil ejected from the crater—but not penetrated. The depth of this region was only a few inches. Within this region, the truck bomb did not exert sufficient brisance to penetrate the asphalt—much less destroy seven inches of concrete. However, it was presumably the diameter of this minor, non-penetrating or "umbra" region that was reported as the 28-foot crater diameter by government representatives.

7. The Actual Crater

Tracked Excavator Parked in Crater - with Perspective-Corrected Grid (Photo 5)

Numerous photographic views of the crater, which exist in the public domain, were analyzed as a major part of this study. Examples described below are of particular significance:

      a. Photo 4 depicts the crater on 28 April 1995 (Day 10). Of particular interest is the position of the eastern edge of the crater, which is located approximately two feet west of the pedestrian ramp in the background. Notice the complex cribbing support of the ramp, whose right end rests on the angled fallen header beam just to the east of the former location of where upper column G22[A4] was supported by the header. Also of interest is the imprint of the tread of the Caterpillar Model 225B LC Tracked Excavator where the machine had earlier been positioned in the crater to use its pneumatic jackhammer attachment for cutting through the fallen main header beam (Photo 5). Attention is directed to the workers on the left, most of whom are standing in the red soil-stained superficial "umbra" region that was ostensibly included in the reported 28 to 32-foot crater diameter. It is also noteworthy that the worker on the right is standing on a relatively undisturbed surface—between the crater and the location of (destroyed) column G20[A5].

      b. Photo 6, an overall view of the north side of the Murrrah Building was taken through a window in the Journal Record Building by Oscar Johnson on Saturday, 22 April (Day Four). Notice that the pedestrian ramp cited above is already in position just to the left of center. Also note that the ramp almost certainly remained in the same location for the duration of its use—since shifting it even slightly to the left or right along the inclined header beam would have necessitated rebuilding its complex cribbing supports. The former location of column G20[A5] is to the right (west) of the hook sheave of the crane. The crater has been spanned with timbers, then covered with plywood. The majority of the crater has been covered with two rows of four sheets of plywood—an area of 16 feet by 16 feet. Judging from other views (and by the location of the same exposed, red soil-stained region which is described in paragraph "a" above), the crater extends no more than four feet to the right (west) under the four sheets whose long axis is parallel to the header beam.

A conclusive indication of the actual extent of the crater is the location of a floral arrangement, placed by rescuers on the red clay-covered area, at the corner of the 16-foot plywood square at the edge of the crater (Photo 6). Had the crater, as claimed by the FBI, extended beyond the 16 foot by 16 foot plywood cover, the floral arrangement would have been deep within the crater.

Figure 8 is a scale schematic that portrays the plywood covering and the actual crater, whose eastern edge begins two feet west of the fixed wheelbarrow ramp. Notice the icon, representing placement of the floral arrangement adjacent to the northwest corner of the 2-sheet x 4-sheet center section of plywood. Also shown are 28-foot and 32-foot diameter circles representing crater diameters published by the FBI and clearly revealing the fallacy of those claims.

Clearly, the absolute maximum diameter circular crater that could be covered by the plywood arrangement shown in Photo 6 and Figure 8 is less than 22.6 feet—the diagonal dimension of the 2-sheet x 4-sheet center section of plywood.

Crater Covered With Plywood -- Floral Arrangement at Corner of 16' Square (Photo 6)

Scale Schematic of Plywood Covering and Actual Crater (Figure 8)

G. THE CRATER AS EVIDENCE—EVIDENCE "OWNED" BY THE FBI

Given the absence of surviving witness surfaces in close proximity to the site of the truck blast, and the lack of positively identifiable explosives residue, the crater left in Northwest Fifth Street was the single-most significant remaining evidence of the nature and explosive power of the truck bomb. Given the importance of this crucial piece of evidence, it is striking that it was treated by the FBI with a curious combination of cavalier disdain and possessive parsimony.

1. Conditions to Which the Crater Was Exposed

The sequence of conditions to which this crucial item of evidence was exposed is worthy of note:

a. With the collapse of the building, the bottom of the crater was filled with debris of all sorts. On the eastern end, panels from the roof slid into and filled part of the crater.

b. Very quickly following the blast, the crater was flooded with water from leaking air conditioner chiller pipes (Photo 3). This basically destroyed any possibility of recovering uncontaminated explosives residues from the crater. In all likelihood, some erosion and slumping of the crater walls and lip occurred, and items in the crater bottom were coated with sediment during this period. According to daily meeting notes, this condition existed for several days.

c. The initial attempt to preserve this crucial item of evidence was via the ineffective expedient of tossing several colored tarps into the hole. As evidenced by various photographs, these tarps provided minimal and incomplete protection; indeed, they shifted locations over time.

d. During the rescue period, the crater was, for several days, bridged by timbers and covered over with sheets of plywood. As is noted above, the geometry of those coverings constitute convincing evidence of the relatively small actual size of the crater.

e. The following remarks are from an article, "Agents Rebuff Bomb Conspiracy Theories," by Diana Baldwin, interviewing FBI Agent Danny Defenbaugh, and published in *The Daily Oklahoman* on 13 December 1998:

> *Baldwin:* Some theorists also complain the crater was covered too quickly after the bombing. They say the FBI was hiding what really happened.
>
> *Defenbaugh:* Investigators weren't hiding anything from the public, only trying to protect the evidence that was water-soluble.

Any "evidence that was water-soluble" that was in the (flooded) crater ran away down the gutter (See Photo 3). There was no uncontaminated "evidence that was water-soluble" to protect. And covering the crater with casually tossed tarps or loosely stacked plywood would have been ineffective in protecting "evidence that was water-soluble"—had any such evidence remained in the crater.

Agent Defenbaugh is no mere public relations spokesperson—not only was he in charge of the entire Oklahoma City bombing investigation, he also worked, for a time, in the FBI Laboratory. His statement on protecting "evidence that was water-soluble" was not based on ignorance or lack of information. The only appropriate appellation for the above official FBI statement seems to be "Lie."

f. When it was deemed necessary to begin removal of the fallen main header beam between fallen columns G20[A5] and G24[A3], the crater was uncovered and a Caterpillar tracked excavator with a pneumatic cutting hammer tool-head attached was positioned with one

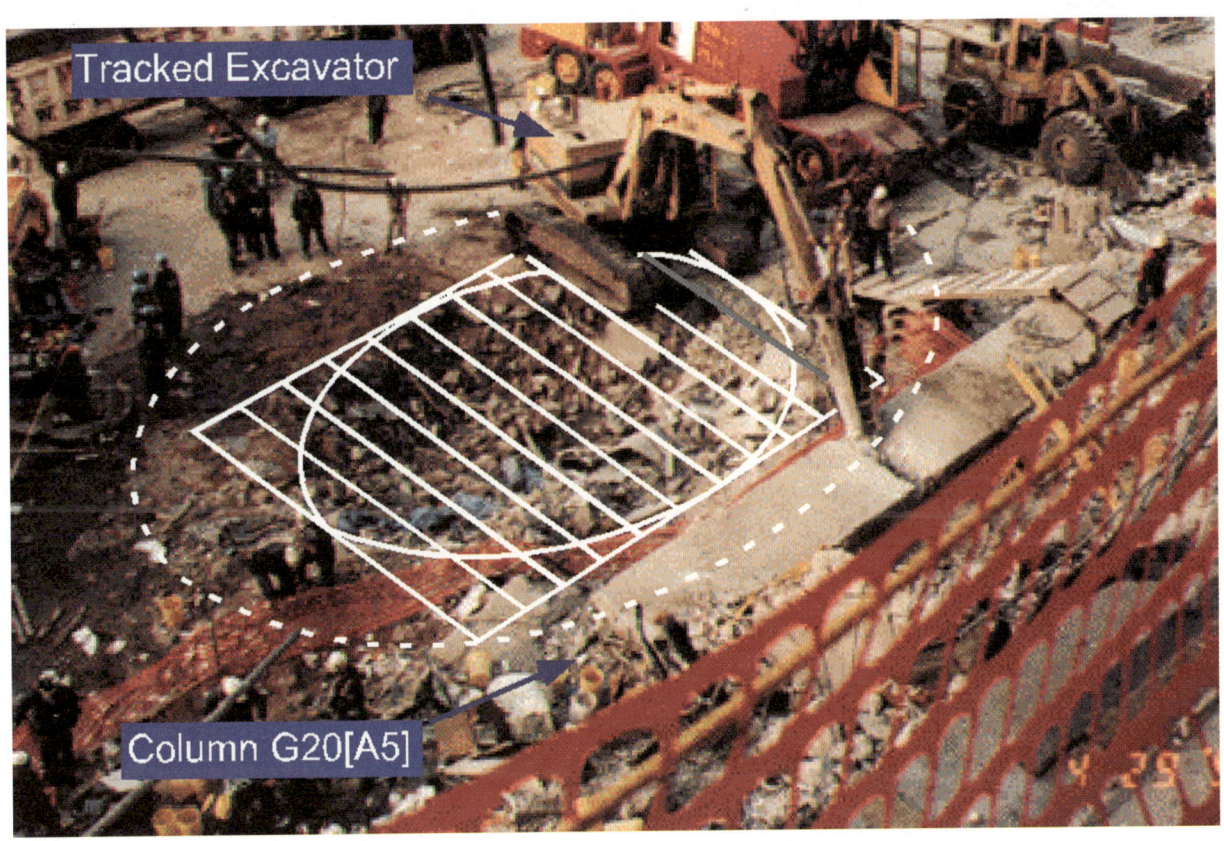

Caterpillar Track with Perspective-Corrected Grid (Photo 7)

track extending into and halfway across the crater (Photo 5). It is obvious that this gross violation of the evidentiary integrity of the crater was allowed to occur **before** FBI investigators removed the debris in order to examine and measure the bottom of the crater. It should be noted that any measurements of crater depth made prior to, or made without, removal of debris from the crater are, at best, only estimates of the actual crater depth. (However, the width of the tread on the tracked excavator can serve as a useful indicator of the scale of the crater.)

Superimposed on Photo 7 is a perspective-corrected grid based on the width of the Caterpillar track as a unit of scale. The long dimension of the crater is equivalent to eleven track widths. Even if the excavator were equipped with 27-inch wide "high flotation" tracks for operation on soft terrain, the equivalent crater diameter would be only 24.75 feet—still significantly less than the FBI's claimed 32 feet.

g. At some time following the intrusion of the tracked excavator into the crater, it is reported that FBI evidence-gathering personnel finally excavated the bottom of the crater. Witnesses have claimed that this was done in secrecy—at night. Through personal experience with archaeological excavations, this investigator can attest that excavation by means of artificial illumination (especially mercury vapor) is extremely poor practice because color perception of soil features is distorted and small items may be overlooked. It must be noted that this investigator has not personally seen any photos of the crater with the debris removed—because, immediately following the FBI's excavation, the crater was backfilled with sand.

2. The Defense Team's Visit to the Crater

As Sid Woodcock, one of Stephen Jones' colleagues, stated prior to the defense team's visit to the bombing site,

> *They're going to have the place clean as a whistle.... We won't find a scrap of anything of evidentiary value. What we really need, though, is the crater, access to the crater. We want the exact dimensions—the circumference, the depth, take our own pictures and so forth. But I'll bet you my last dollar that they'll have it covered over before we get there.* (Source: *Others Unknown*, Stephen Jones & Peter Israel, Public Affairs, N.Y., 1998, pg. 44)

And that is precisely what happened. The defense team, according to Jones, met with overt hostility from the FBI agents at the site, being told, "We're not here to give you a tour." Concerning the crater, Jones wrote,

> *And, yes, the crater was covered. Our hosts refused to uncover it for us or to let us do it for ourselves. It was not the first, and it would be far from the last time that I found myself wondering what was so dangerous about letting us take a look at something related to the case. If the government was so certain with regard to its theory of what happened, what did they have to fear from uncovering the crater for us? What possibly could be buried that they might not want us to find?* (Source: *Others Unknown*, Stephen Jones & Peter Israel, Public Affairs, N.Y., 1998, pg. 44 & 45)

A reasonable answer to Jones' query would be that what "they might not want us to find" apparently was the true nature of the crater itself—its relatively diminutive actual size, as compared to the FBI's inflated claims.

Why was access to the evidence of the size and nature of the crater deliberately withheld from the defense team? Was this impropriety not comparable to the recently revealed withholding of thousands of evidence documents from the defense by the FBI?

3. The Crater Rim

A sufficiently large explosion over concrete and asphalt will characteristically recess the compacted soil and gravel under the crater rim. The only recess under the crater rim visible in the Oklahoma City crater is in a small segment of the crater's circumference that occurs approximately two feet to the west of the pedestrian ramp. At the time Photo 4 was taken, the pictured crater did not consistently exhibit the rim geometry of a large explosion over concrete and asphalt. Had rescue efforts or other activities collapsed the lip, thereby enlarging the crater beyond its original limits? Or had soil slumping during the time the crater was flooded caused the lip to collapse?

4. FBI Agent Williams and the "Apparent" Crater

In his response to charges leveled against him in the report of the DOJ OIG's audit of his laboratory work and his reports on the Oklahoma City bombing, an enigmatic reference to crater dimensions was submitted by FBI SSA David Williams:

> *In nearly all cases, no chemistry examinations or laboratory findings are available initially, and in some cases never are known. It is therefore necessary to provide a timely estimate upon reasonable and prudent technical data and observational data used within the explosives community which may include: apparent crater/actual dimensions.*

"Apparent crater" versus "actual dimensions"? or "Apparent crater" and/or "actual dimensions"? What does this mean? This investigator is at a loss to explain why an examiner would imply that a physically accessible crater's dimensions could be anything other than those which were measurable—unless that examiner intended to leave himself room to claim that the crater size was other than that which could be measured.

5. Inspector General's Conclusions Regarding SSA Williams' Report

The OIG report was the result of an investigation performed at the FBI Lab as a result of accusations of improprieties made by lab chemist Dr. Frederic Whitehurst. Whitehurst had claimed that the lab reported unfounded conclusions and slanted results to favor the prosecution. An excerpt from the OIG report shows their findings against Supervisory Special Agent (SSA) Dave Williams. The paragraph conveys an impression of negativity:

Conclusion

> *Williams' report contains several serious flaws. His opinion as to the VOD of the main charge was unjustifiable; his statement of the VOD of ANFO was incomplete; his categorical identification of the main charge as ANFO was inappropriate; his estimate of the weight of the main charge was too specific and based in part on improper grounds; his conclusion as to the containers for the main charge was unjustifiably categorical; his categorical identification of the initiator for the booster was improper; his conclusions concerning a non-electric detonator, the fuse, and the time delay were scientifically insupportable; his conclusions were not supported by the contents of the report; and he included some AE dictation in a selective or confusing way. These errors were all tilted in such a way as to incriminate the defendants. We are troubled that the opinions in Williams' report may have been tailored to conform to the evidence associated with the defendants. We conclude that Williams failed to present an objective, unbiased, competent report.*

By presenting those same words on a point-by-point basis and highlighting the negative syntax, the scathing nature of the OIG's total condemnation of Williams' work becomes painfully clear (reformatted and presented on the following page with emphasis added):

> *Conclusion*: Williams' report contains **several serious flaws**.
> [1] His opinion as to the VOD of the main charge was **unjustifiable**;
> [2] his statement of the VOD of ANFO was **incomplete**;
> [3] his categorical identification of the main charge as ANFO was **inappropriate**;
> [4] his estimate of the weight of the main charge was **too specific**
> [5] and **based in part on improper grounds**;
> [6] his conclusion as to the containers for the main charge was **unjustifiably categorical**;
> [7] his categorical identification of the initiator for the booster was **improper**;
>
> his conclusions concerning
> [8] a non-electric detonator,
> [9] the fuse, and
> [10] the time delay were **scientifically insupportable**;
>
> [11] his **conclusions were not supported** by the contents of the report; and
> [12] he included some AE dictation in a **selective or confusing way**.
> [13] These errors were all **tilted in such a way as to incriminate the defendants**
> [14] We are troubled that the opinions in Williams' report may have been **tailored to conform to the evidence** associated with the defendants.
> [15] We conclude that Williams **failed to present an objective, unbiased, competent report.**

H. CRATER DIMENSIONS AND BLAST RADIUS

The single best measure of the yield of the explosive device in the Ryder truck--and of its ability to destroy concrete by brisance at a distance--is the diameter of the primary portion of the crater that **penetrated the pavement** of Northwest Fifth Street. In other words, it is that portion of the crater wherein *concrete was actually destroyed* that is the only *de facto* evidence of the capability of the bomb to cause compressive concrete failure due to brisance.

As has been shown, photographic evidence indicates that the concrete-destroying crater diameter was a maximum of 18 feet. Figures 9 and 10 are based on the best photogrametric evidence of the location, diameter and depth of the actual, concrete-destroying crater.

Figure 9 is an elevation view--to scale--of the 20-foot Ryder truck, parked immediately against the curb, and of the structural elements associated with column G20[A5]. Based upon the diameter of the crater and the height of the bomb center above ground, a projected radius of brisant-energy blast is scaled to be 10.3 feet.

Brisant Blast Radius - Elevation View (Figure 9)

Brisant Blast Radius - Plan View (Figure 10)

Even if the bomb centerline were directly in front of column G20[A5], the brisant-level energy would not have reached the outer face of the column.

However, as seen in the plan view (Figure 10), the center of the crater (and the bomb) was at least 10 feet to the east of column G20[A5]. Actual "standoff distance" or range from the center of the blast to the center of column G20[A5] was 16.4 feet.

Therefore, the best physical evidence (the concrete-penetrating crater's location, diameter and depth) indicates that, well before the blast wave reached the closest major structural member, column G20[A5], energy levels of the blast had fallen well below the brisant energy capable of causing compressive concrete failure.

I. THE LAST-HOUR "RACING FUEL" BOMB

On the day of the bombing, television broadcasts quoted government officials who were saying that the explosion was caused by an ANFO bomb weighing between 1000 and 1200 pounds. This figure changed to 4000 pounds of ANFO when the Government located purchases purportedly made by Nichols for two tons (4000 pounds) of ammonium nitrate.

1. ANFO

ANFO is the acronym for an ammonium nitrate (AN) and fuel oil (FO) slurry. ANFO solves the major problem with ammonium nitrate as an explosive: its tendency to pick up water vapor from the air, which results in the explosive failing to detonate when such an attempt is made. This condition is rectified by mixing 93 percent (by weight) ammonium nitrate with seven (7) percent fuel oil, or kerosene. The kerosene keeps the ammonium nitrate from absorbing moisture from the air. An ANFO explosive also requires a large shockwave to set it off.

Dupont recommends a ratio of 93 percent AN to seven (7) percent FO by weight—hardly any oil at all. More oil makes the mixture less explosive by absorbing detonation energy, and excess fuel makes detonation by-products health hazards as the mixture is oxygen poor. Note that commercial fertilizer products do not work as well as the porous AN prills that Dupont sells, because fertilizers are coated with various materials meant to seal them from moisture, which keep the oil from being absorbed.

2. ANNM

Very shortly prior to the beginning of opening arguments in the McVeigh trial, the Government once again changed their allegations as to the composition of the truck bomb. According to news reports, the stimulus for this major change in the prosecution's claims was an article in *Playboy Magazine*, published 11 March 1997. Based upon statements in *Playboy*, purported to have been made by McVeigh to his defense attorneys, the FBI descended upon racetracks in the Dallas, Texas area and found an instance where an individual had purchased three drums of nitromethane racing fuel. Although the seller was unable to identify the buyer, the prosecution insisted that the buyer of the nitromethane was McVeigh. (Source: *Rocky Mountain News*, "Prosecution Made the 11th Hour Change," 16 May 97)

The FBI claimed that McVeigh had purchased the above-mentioned three 55-gallon drums of nitromethane racing fuel at a racetrack in Ennis, Texas, approximately 35 miles south of Dallas. Correspondingly, the prosecution changed the composition of the bomb actually alleged at trial from ANFO to ANNM: 4,000 pounds of ammonium nitrate fertilizer (AN) mixed with 165 gallons of liquid nitromethane (NM).

As noted above, the fuel oil in an ANFO mix is used primarily to inhibit moisture absorption by the ammonium nitrate. Fuel oil, used in this manner, does relatively little to increase the explosive yield over that derived from the rapid thermal decomposition of ammonium nitrate alone.

Nitromethane, on the other hand, is described as "the simplest explosive nitro compound." (Ref: *http://www.cyberhost3.com/nitronic/research8/shelly.html*).

Properties of Nitromethane

Composition	CH_3NO_2
Specific Gravity	1.139
Density	9.682 pounds per gallon
Flash point	95°F
Auto-ignite point	785°F

When mixed with ammonium nitrate, nitromethane significantly increases the explosive power, as described in *Mississippi v. Brewer*, (No. 93-KA-00676 COA) (Ref: http://mslawyer.datasync.com/mssc/ctapp/960917/93676.html):

> *Also, the materials bearing the brand name "Kinepak" were shown to be a liquid (nitromethane) and a powder (ammonium nitrate), which, when combined as specifically intended by the instructions furnished by the Kinepak manufacturer, would produce, according to the State's expert, 'a very high explosive, very shock sensitive explosive.'*

Data published by the supplier of "Kinepak" explosives in Carrollton, Texas claim that the velocity of detonation (VOD) of their proprietary nitromethane/ammonium nitrate mixture is 21,500 fps—within the middle of the VOD range for TNT.

There is also information in published scientific studies (Ref: http://www.aps.org/ BAPSSHOCK97/abs/S1700.html#SG1.005) that combining nitromethane with other nitrogen-bearing compounds, specifically amines, greatly increases its sensitivity to shock. One (thankfully, now deactivated) "Anarchist's Cookbook" webpage actually listed ratios for combining nitromethane with specific amines or aniline to produce a shock-sensitive mix that is "[t]o be detonated with a #8 cap". (Ref:http://home1.swipnet.se/~w-19872/files/anarchy/bombbook1.txt)

That same "Anarchists' Cookbook" internet source also stated that "solid nitromethane explosive" is composed of two parts of nitromethane liquid to five parts of ammonium nitrate, or a liquid-to-solid ratio of 0.4:1 by weight.

According to that same source (mixing instructions deleted), "This is supposed to be 30 percent more powerful than dynamite containing 60 percent nitroglycerin, and has 30 percent more brisance."

If one assumes that the 0.4:1 weight ratio cited above is the stoichiometrically optimum ratio of nitromethane to ammonium nitrate for maximum explosive yield, then the quantities of materials alleged by the FBI to have been in the possession of McVeigh, *et al*, were ideal for creating a powerful bomb.

Three 55-gallon drums of nitromethane	1597.45 pounds
Eighty 50 pound bags of ammonium nitrate	4,000 pounds
Weight ratio (1597.45 lbs/4000 lbs)	0.399:1

It would appear to be beyond coincidence that the combination of three drums of nitromethane with eighty bags of ammonium nitrate (0.399:1 ration) almost perfectly matches the 0.4:1 or two to five ratio specified in the cited "Anarchists' Cookbook" internet reference.

According to the purported "defense chronology document:"

> *The morning before the bombing, Nichols and McVeigh made the bomb with ammonium nitrate and nitromethane, a liquid fuel for race cars, at Geary State Fishing Lake, near Nichols' home in Kansas. They measured the fuel using a bucket on a bathroom scale.*

It was alleged that Nichols and McVeigh progressively assembled an arsenal of bomb ingredients.

McVeigh allegedly purchased eight 50-pound bags of ammonium nitrate from a store just east of Manhattan, Kansas, then 10 bags in McPherson and six more in a town 20 miles south. **(400 + 500 + 300 = 1200 lbs.)**

Allegedly, McVeigh and Nichols later bought 80 more bags in McPherson, Kansas. **(+4000 lbs.)**

Total maximum available ammonium nitrate = 5200 lbs.

According to the document, on 18 April, Nichols joined McVeigh at a storage area. After collecting the component materials from storage sites, the two traveled to Geary Lake and began making the bomb. They used 13 plastic drums, pouring 350 pounds of ammonium nitrate and seven 20-pound buckets of nitromethane into each. A mixture of 140 pounds of nitromethane and 350 pounds of ammonium nitrate constitutes a ratio of exactly 0.4:1--or exactly the 2:5 ratio advocated on the "Anarchist's Cookbook" website.

However, three drums nitromethane = 1500 pounds—which would yield only 10.74 (rather than 13) 40-pound batches at the 0.4:1 ratio.

In reality, mixing six (6) buckets of nitromethane per seven (7) bags of ammonium nitrate would yield a weight percent of 25.3 percent. (The NM/AN ratio used in the commercial binary explosive, Kinepak, is 24 percent.)

The bottom line: 5200 pounds of ammonium nitrate plus three (3) drums of nitromethane does not follow the "Anarchist's Cookbook" formulation, but it would have made a 6700-pound bomb with explosive power at least equivalent to commercial binary (Kinepak) explosive.

The resulting device could have had an explosive yield approaching that of three tons (6,000 pounds) of TNT. If that size device had been exploded in a Ryder truck over the pavement of Northwest 5th Street in Oklahoma City, one would have expected a crater significantly larger than eighteen feet in diameter to result. The ANNM bomb and the size of the crater do not appear to match.

According to the website of VP Racing Fuels, the alleged supplier of the nitromethane racing fuel, (*http://www.vpracingfuels.com/main.html*) they supply nitromethane in bright blue, closed top steel drums. Such closed-top drums would have been worthless as vessels for mixing the bomb. The FBI went to considerable effort to document and report a large area **diesel fuel spill** at Geary Lake, where the (now-discredited) ANFO bomb was supposedly mixed. However, as far as has been determined, the FBI has never reported finding the three empty, bright blue painted, steel nitromethane drums.

J. REVIEW OF THE FEMA/ASCE BPAT REPORT

Considerable effort was expended by this author and associated investigators in attempts to locate and obtain at least one credible report that quantifies how air blast could have caused the damage observed to have been inflicted upon the structure of the Murrah Building. One of the most thorough and authoritative publicly available engineering reports **based upon a single air-coupled blast** was produced by representatives of the American Society of Civil Engineers (ASCE). The study, entitled *The Oklahoma City Bombing: Improving Building Performance Through Multi-Hazard Mitigation,* was performed and published under the Building Performance Assessment Team (BPAT) process of the Federal Emergency Management Administration (FEMA).

1. BPAT Composition

Beyond question, the ASCE members who participated on the BPAT were eminently qualified representatives of the civil engineering discipline and were teamed with experts from FEMA, the General Services Administration (GSA), the U.S. Society of Civil Engineers (USACE) and the National Institute of Standards and Technology (NIST). They were supported by the resources of major universities and world-class civil engineering firms, and also received assistance from various on-site entities—including the FBI.

2. Evidence of Obstruction and Disinformation

The Oklahoma City Bombing: Improving Building Performance Through Multi-Hazard Mitigation contains a wealth of useful architectural and engineering drawings and data tables. The analyses employ "best practice" engineering principles to arrive at logical conclusions based on available starting data. Unfortunately, it is evident that the BPAT's initial assumptions were based on government-supplied information that was deliberately falsified and distorted. The eminent ASCE experts on the BPAT were, evidently, victims of obstruction and disinformation perpetrated by those agencies that controlled the crime scene and had custody of—and responsibility for—accurately and truthfully curating and reporting the evidence.

These actions by federal agencies so effectively thwarted the BPAT in their efforts to obtain accurate, factual information that the resulting report not only contains inaccurate analyses, but may well have reached dangerous conclusions, such as:

- At best, the report grossly overestimates the quantity and power of explosive in the truck bomb, and, consequently, the damage caused by air blast to the Murrah Building's structure.

- It reaches conclusions that directly contradict those presented in government witness testimony and FBI Laboratory reports.

- At worst, it recommends mitigation strategies that focus on improving resistance to air blast while ignoring the imminent danger of designs that feature critical structural members openly exposed to placement of contact explosives.

a. BPAT Forbidden Access to the Murrah Building

On 05 May (Day 17), the first day following the end of victim remains recovery and four days prior to BPAT arrival, the minutes of the building control team's daily planning meeting included the following statement regarding their first item of business:

> Restrict to workers—no agencies or ASCE personnel allowed inside building.

That this stratagem was, indeed, enacted is confirmed by a disclaimer in the BPAT report's "Executive Summary:"

> Visual inspection of the [Murrah Building] structure was limited to observation from a distance of 200 feet.

Safety concerns may have justified restricting BPAT access to selected, unstable areas of the building's interior. Keeping them outside a 200-foot fenced exclusion zone was—and remains—indefensible.

b. Structural Members Selectively Removed Prior to BPAT Arrival

All identifiable traces of the failed north-face structural members of the Murrah Building were selectively removed prior to arrival of the BPAT. As stated in the report's "Executive Summary":

> The BPAT visited the area around the Murrah Building during the period of May 9 through 13, 1995 [Days 9-13], three weeks after the blast occurred on Wednesday, April 19 [Day 1].

Photo 8 provides direct evidence of selective removal of brisance-damaged structural materials at least one week prior to arrival of the BPAT. Note the following examples:

Brisance-Damaged Structural Material (Photo 8)

- The temporary plywood covering has been removed from the blast crater, which is clearly visible—still filled with rubble. This dates the photo on, or shortly prior to, 01 May (Day 12), when the crater was filled with sand.

- The section of main header between columns G16[A7] and G20[A5] has already been removed. (Removal was arguably justifiable to facilitate access to the remaining debris pile.)

- One of the two cranes available for human remains recovery has been commandeered to be used for removing the stub of column G16[A7]. At the time of the photograph, the area surrounding G16[A7] had already been completely cleared (swept clean) of debris; the stub of column G16[A7] does not appear to present any impediment to further victim-recovery work.

Note: Up until 11:50 p.m. on 04 May (the end of Day 15), recovery of victims' remains was reportedly top priority.

- The stub of column G16[A7] bears clear evidence of high velocity brisant damage; its removal and disposal could be construed as tampering with crime scene evidence.

- Availability of the stub of column G16[A7] for examination by the BPAT could have significantly altered reported conclusions as to its mode and mechanism of failure.

- As far as can be determined, neither the stub of G16[A7] nor any other identified portion of the remains of columns G20[A5], G24[A3] or F24[B3] nor any identified portion of the main header beam were made available to the BPAT for direct examination.

Immediately across 5th Street to the north of the damaged face of the Murrah Building was a parking lot that was within the cordoned area under the control of the FBI. It would have been simple and convenient for the cranes to have boomed around 180 degrees and to have placed recovered sections of the G[A]-row columns and header in positions akin to those in which they were found. Such "proximate reconstruction" is common practice in aircraft crash analysis. Instead, all critical structural evidence of the cause of the Murrah Building's collapse was hauled away and buried—in a secure area—with unseemly haste.

In other words, the site was evidently "sanitized" of all evidence of brisant damage on an expedited schedule—prior to BPAT arrival.

c. Samples Provided to BPAT Lacked Origin and Identity

The samples supplied to the BPAT for strength-of-materials analysis lacked provenance and identity. As stated in BPAT report section 2.2,

> *Inspection of remaining pieces of concrete debris revealed that there were a few "chunk" samples and sections of spandrel beams near the parking lot of the [Sheriff's Department] Firing Range. Also, a few pieces of deformed reinforcing bar were stacked near the concrete debris. Sheriff's personnel confirmed that the concrete and the reinforcing bars had come from the Murrah Building.*

d. BPAT Supplied with Inappropriate Photographs.

The photographs published in the BPAT report are singularly uninformative, and, in several cases, are manifestly misleading. Far superior images of structural damage and of the nature of the blast crater were available in the public domain.

- At paragraph 2.2 in the BPAT report, it is stated that "...photographs taken soon after the explosion by several law enforcement agencies were reviewed." As exemplified by Figures 1-14, 3-12, and 3-13 (Appendix pgs. 399-405), early images are singularly uninformative as to the condition of the structural elements under study. In the cited figures, all structural elements are obscured by rubble; even the marked locations of the G[A]-row columns are debatable.

- In both of the photographs of the blast crater published in the BPAT report (Figure 1-13, "Aerial view of damaged building," and Figure 3-1, "Blast crater [covered by tarp]"), the crater is obscured by a plastic tarpaulin. (Appendix pgs. 399-405)

- Photographs of sheets of blue plastic spread over a debris field do not constitute quantifiable evidence of either the size or location (or existence) of a blast crater. At best, such images are uninformative; at worst, they can be deliberately misleading.

- Surprisingly, the report makes no attempt to explain the collapse of interior column F24[B3].

- Superior images showing both the crater's size and configuration (photo 4) and its location (Photo 6) were available in the public domain.

- It is improbable that the law enforcement agencies responsible for evidence recovery failed to photographically document both location and condition of the crater and the collapsed structural elements as they were uncovered. Failure to record and maintain such documentation could only be construed as evidence of gross investigative incompetence. Withholding of such evidence from a federally chartered analysis team might be construed as conspiracy to obstruct or to conceal.

e. BPAT Provided with Erroneous Crater Dimensions

The BPAT was apparently provided with a deceptive description of the crater's dimensions, as explained below:

- As seen in photo on page 408, the true, penetrating "umbra" portion of the blast crater is surrounded by a larger "penumbra" area, consisting of shallow, superficial erosion that does not penetrate the pavement. The person in the red jacket and yellow hat is standing just inside this "penumbra" region. Note that the true, penetrating crater is considerably smaller, and that it extends eastward to within approximately two feet of the wooden pedestrian ramp. The tracks where the tread of the yellow backhoe/jackhammer intruded into the crater are useful indicators of scale.

- In the photo on page 407, most of the long dimension of the true penetrating portion of the crater has been covered with eight (4'X8') sheets of plywood—an area 16 feet square. (Recall that the crater begins approximately two feet west—to the right—of the pedestrian ramp). Although a small section of the crater may extend westward under the sheets of plywood to the right, **the actual, penetrating crater cannot reasonably be construed to exceed 18 feet in its longest dimension.**

- The same "penumbra" area where the person in the red jacket was standing (see photo, pg. 408) remains uncovered and visible (see photo, pg. 407) to the right of the four plywood sheets.

- The BPAT report at 3.2.1 states that "In this report, the engineering survey of the crater forms the basis of this inference.... The crater was approximately 28 feet in diameter and 6.8 feet in depth, as shown in Figure 3-2." (Appendix pgs. 399-405)

- One can only deduce that "the engineering survey of the crater" (cited without source or attribution and not available to this author) represents the entire 28-foot diameter of the (non-penetrating) "penumbra" region as the diameter of the crater. In reality, the actual penetrating diameter of the crater was approximately eighteen feet—or less. It should be noted that Figure 3-2 is merely an artist's line drawing based upon the overstated 28-foot dimension reported to BPAT as the diameter of the crater. (Appendix pgs. 399-405)

- Further evidence that it was the non-penetrating "penumbra" region that was reported as the crater diameter exists in Figures 1-26 and 3-3 in the BPAT report. (Appendix pgs. 399-405)

- The members of the BPAT were misled by being supplied with a diameter dimension for the crater that was at least 1.64 times the longest dimension of the actual, penetrating blast crater.

3. Impact of Obstruction and Disinformation on BPAT Conclusions

a. Erroneous Crater Dimensions Result in Inflated Quantity of Explosives

The BPAT based its estimate of the quantity of explosives upon the misleading description of the crater's diameter and depth. BPAT Report, Section 3.2.1 states that

> As shown in table 3.1, the detonation of a spherical charge of trinitrotoluene (TNT, the standard by which the energy of various explosives is measured) weighing approximately 4,000 pounds at 4.5 feet above 18-inch-thick pavement on soil results in a crater whose dimensions are consistent with those measured at the Murrah Building site.

The very foundation upon which all further BPAT blast loading calculations were based—an explosive charge equivalent to 4,000 pounds of **TNT**—was a deceptively overstated crater diameter.

Per FBI Laboratory testimony and report at the McVeigh/Nichols trials, the quantity of ANFO purportedly produced and detonated by the defendants was 4,000 pounds. One must assume that data placed into evidence in capital trials by the Department of Justice is the best that can be obtained. Since TNT and ANFO have significantly different explosive yields and effects, at least one of these two government-funded reports is incorrect.

b. Inflated Quantity of Explosive Results in Erroneously Reported Cause for Column G16[A7] Failure

Dependence upon the inflated estimate of 4,000 pounds of TNT resulted in reporting of a marginal air-blast-induced shear failure in column G16[A7].

In section 3.2.3, "Blast Analysis of Columns G24[A3], G16[A7] and G12[A9]," the BPAT report describes the failure condition for column G16[A7]:

> "As shown in Table 3-2, the slant range (distance from the explosion to the column mid-height) is greater for column G16[A7] than for column G24[A3]. At this distance of 50 feet the blast pressure is still 642 psi. According to an analysis similar to that performed for column G24[A3], this loading **just reaches** the shear capacity. This implies an incipient brittle failure which is consistent with the conditions shown in figure 3-13." (Emphasis added.) (Appendix pgs. 399-405)

Whereas the BPAT's calculated pressure (from 4,000 pounds of **TNT**) at column G16[A7] is 642 pounds per square inch (psi), General Partin's calculated pressure for 4,800 pounds of **ANFO** at column G16[A7] was "in the 25 to 35 pounds per square inch region."

According to the BPAT's own calculations, a lesser air blast (from 4,000 pounds, or, even 4,800 pounds of **ANFO**—as opposed to 4,000 pounds of **TNT**) **would have been insufficient** to have caused column G16[A7] to fail in shear.

It should also be noted that the cited Figure 3-13 does not actually show any evidence of the remains of column G16[A7], which was still buried under several feet of rubble at the time Photo 3-13 was taken. In fact, the roof panels—complete with window washer support stanchions—have yet to be removed from the rubble covering the G16[A7] location. It is not apparent that the figure even points to the correct location for column G16[A7]. (Appendix pgs. 399-405)

As shown in Photo 1, after removal of the rubble overburden, the stub of column G16[A7] was found to have fallen directly to the north, was resting on its narrow (20-inch) side, and was supporting the western end of the header segment between columns G16[A7] and G20[A5]. Not only did the column fall at a right angle to the supposed shearing force reported in BPAT section 3.2.3 above, it was not displaced laterally to the east as it would have been if air blast from the truck bomb had caused it to fail in shear. This is further indication that photographs of the uncovered structural elements may have been withheld from the BPAT.

c. BPAT Members Were Not at Fault; They Were Misled by the FBI

The prestigious members of the ASCE Building Performance Assessment Team (BPAT) who prepared what is now called the "FEMA Report" should not be faulted for these errors. Since they were prevented from approaching the Murrah Building, they apparently were forced to rely upon materials and information supplied to them by the FBI.

K. POSSIBLE STRUCTURAL VULNERABILITY TO AIR BLAST DAMAGE

The 12-inch thick X 10.5-foot deep X 13-foot tall "column walls" or wall columns" that supported the inner ends of the heavy horizontal beams extending behind the main (G[A]-row columns may have posed a catastrophic vulnerability to air blast. Not only were they considerably thinner than the 20-inch thick columns and the beams they supported, unlike the columns, they presented a large surface area upon which air blast could exert force.

As shown in Figure 11, the wall column behind column G20[A5] was almost directly in line with the blast; it remained upright and relatively unscathed.

The wall column behind column G16[A7] faced the truck blast at an angle of 66.5 degrees. As seen in Photo 9, the top of it was pushed over westward sufficiently to dislodge the support beam and secondary headers that it supported. However, air blast might not have been the sole cause of this displacement. In Photo 8, it can be seen that the wall was impacted by a projectile object, coming from the direction of the truck blast. The impact was energetic enough to drive a hole entirely through the wall's 12-inch thickness. Of course, it is also possible that the wall's displacement could have been caused after the fact by forces imparted to it by falling debris.

Likewise, the wall column behind column G24[A3] faced the blast at an angle of 54.2 degrees, but it was substantially closer to the truck bomb. Until Photo 10 was discovered, it was believed that this wall column, in the G24[B3] line, had been completely destroyed. From Photo 10, it appears that the top of this wall was not only pushed eastward, the wall was destroyed down to about shoulder height.

If, indeed, the wall column in the 24[3] grid line were destroyed prior to the building's collapse — either by air blast or by contact charge — its failure might well have initiated the majority of the collapse pattern observed — including collapse of internal column F24[B3].

Figure 12 illustrates the critical importance of the relatively thin column wall behind column G24[A3]. It, alone, supported the south (inner) end of the heavy lateral beam

PUSHED-Over Wall Column (Photo 9)

249

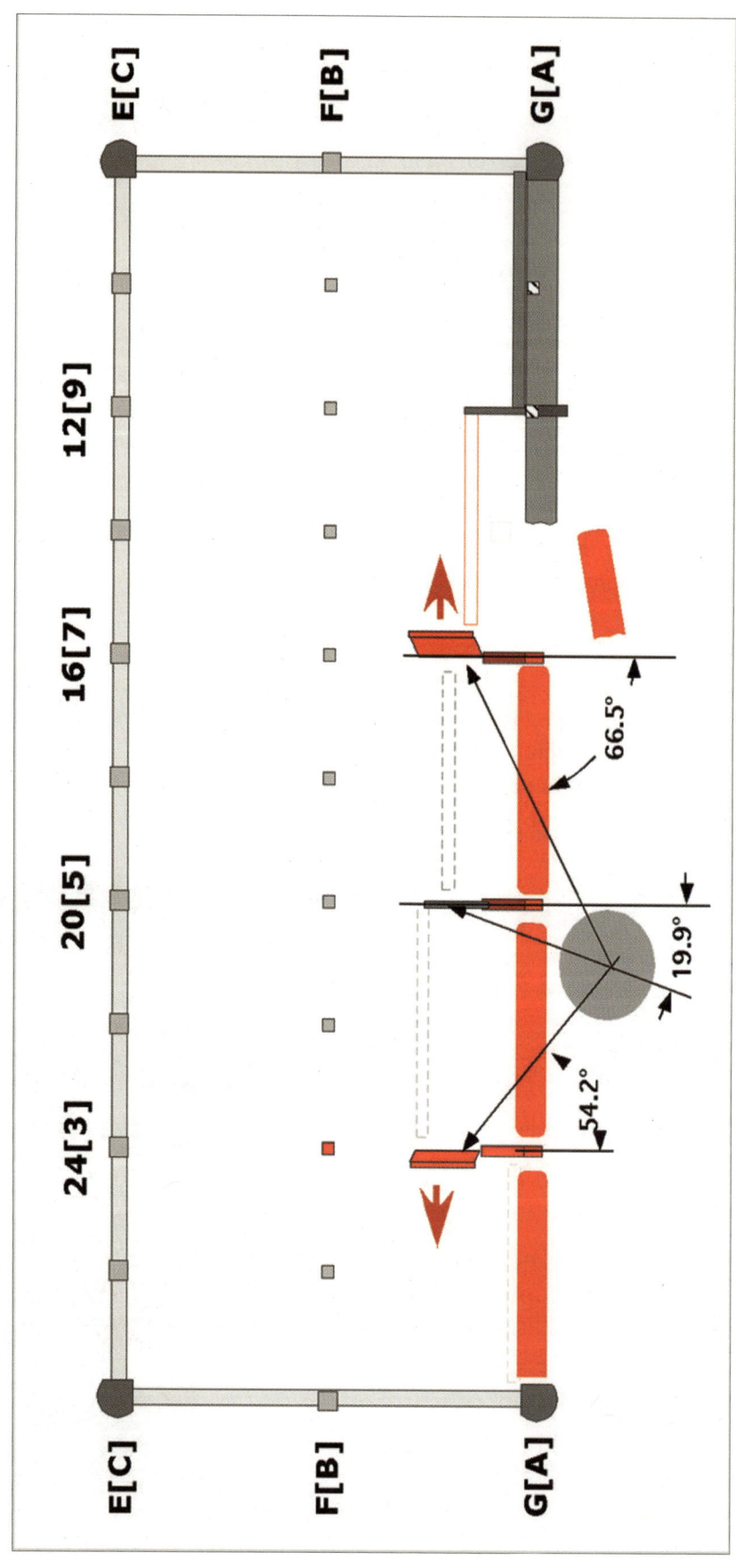

Wall Column Behind Column G20[A5]
(Figure 11)

Destroyed Top of Wall Column (Photo 10)

that was integrally cast with major column G24[A3]. Also illustrated is the fact that column G24[A3] and the main header beam atop it at those coordinates were connected back to internal column F24[B3] through the floor beams.

Hinman and Hammond show that internal column F24[B3] failed at the slab and third floor levels. Unlike the failed external columns, internal column F24[B3] was not pulverized between the second and third floors, and its failures at the slab and third floor appear to have been in shear. (These observations are at odds with Partin's postulated "cutting charge" at F24[B3]). (Appendix pgs. 378-398) Hammond (personal communication) also stated that he had observed a failure at E24[C3] where the floor beams had pushed the E[C]-line (southern) wall of the building outward (southward). (Source: *Lessons from the Oklahoma City Bombing — Defensive Design Techniques*, Hinman and Hammond, ASCE Press, figure 1.14[a])

Figure 13 illustrates a possible vulnerability and failure mode associated with the wall column in the 24[3] grid line. (Displacements are exaggerated for illustrative purposes.)
If the 24[3] grid line wall column were destroyed, the inner end of the massive 20-inch X 40-inch X 7 foot horizontal beam could have rotated downward, placing a destructive, shearing torque on its attachment with column G24[A3]. Failure of the column could have propagated upward, and initiated displacement of the main header beam at the third floor level.

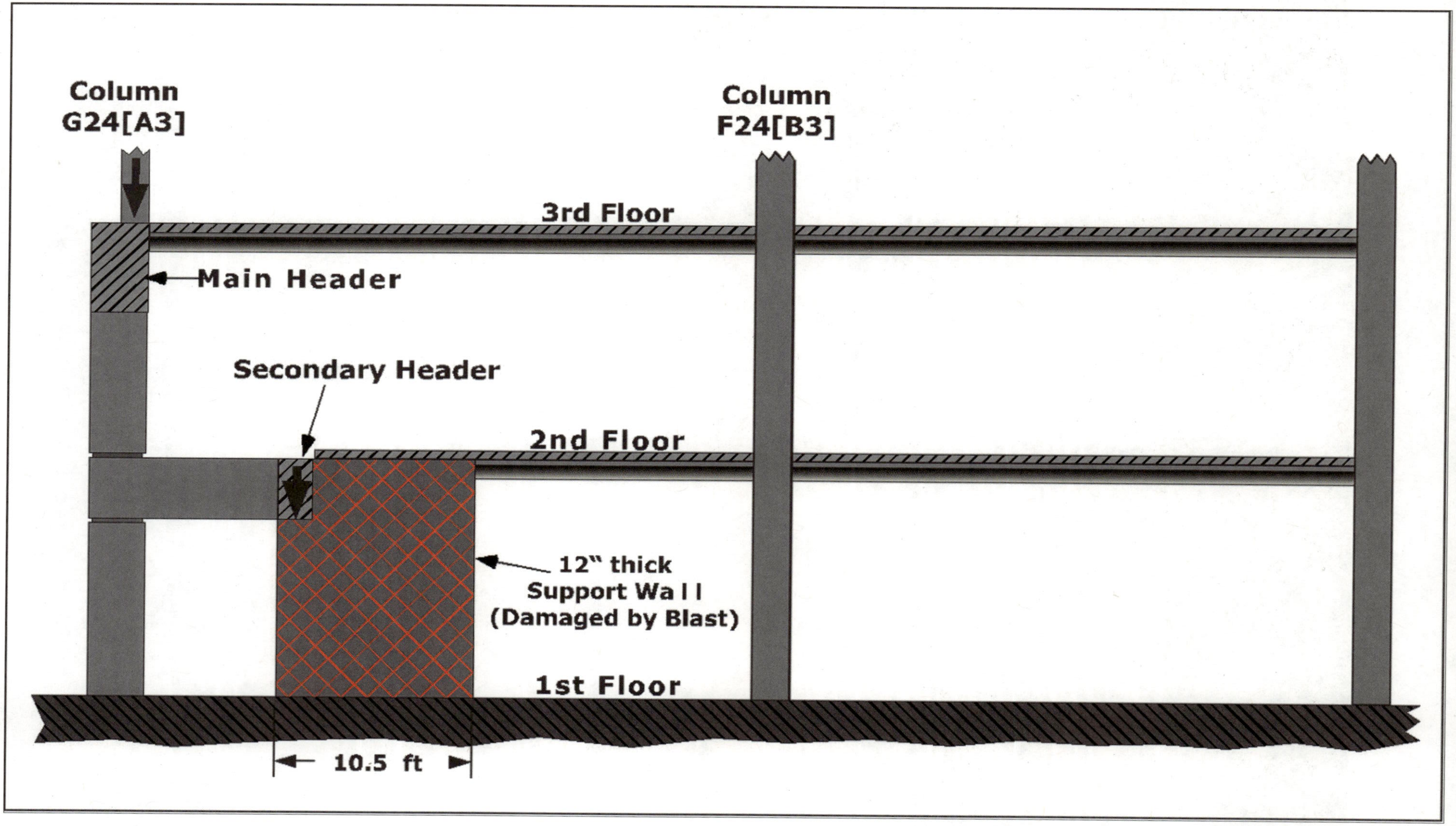

Wall Column Supporting South End of Lateral Beam (Figure 12)

It is well known that the off-center, downward thrust of upper columns caused the top of the main header to roll inward. (The entire fallen header rotated inward ninety degrees.) The resulting inward thrust may have been propagated inward through the floor beams, causing shear failure of column F24[B3], as reported by Hinman and Hammond. Failure of column F24[B3] could then have allowed the floor beam to thrust farther southward, causing the E[C]-line failure observed by Hammond.

The exact mechanism by which the main header beam became detached at its connections with the G[A]-row columns, as shown in Figure 6, remains unclear. What is clear, is that such separation **did** occur at the junctions of columns G24[A3], G20[a5] and G16[A7] and the main header (or transfer) beam—allowing the broken beam to rotate inward and then fall..

If the mechanism of failure illustrated in Figure 13 is valid, then the destruction of the 24[3]-grid line wall column (possibly aided by the failure of the 16[3]-grid line wall column) could have resulted in the exact, asymmetrical pattern of collapse that occurred on 19 April 1995.

L. EVIDENCE NOT CONSISTENT WITH A SINGLE AIR BLAST

It may prove possible to develop a scenario whereby the air blast from the truck bomb alone caused the observed damage to the Murrah Building. However, there remains a set of evidence that is more consistent with General Partin's theory that precise, small, high-velocity charges at critical locations weakened the building prior to the truck bomb explosion. Some of those outstanding items are:

1. At least six survivors reported that the building shook, and they had time to think an earthquake had occurred, and to seek cover — before the truck bomb blast blew in the windows and lifted the floors beneath their feet.

2. At least two audio recordings made outside the building reportedly have sharp "crack" impulse signals approximately four seconds prior to the sound of the truck blast. (This investigator has observed that high-velocity explosives like C4 make a sound more closely approximating that of an electric discharge than the rolling "boom" commonly associated with lower-velocity explosives.)

3. The nearly identical failure modes described for the main header (or transfer) beam at its junctions with columns G24[A3], G20[A5] and G16[A7], and the disintegration of the second-to-third floor concrete on those columns, closely resemble the "cutting charge" damage described by General Partin.

4. No satisfactory explanation has yet been put forth as to how the main header beam became free to move independently of the three destroyed columns, with which it was integrally cast.

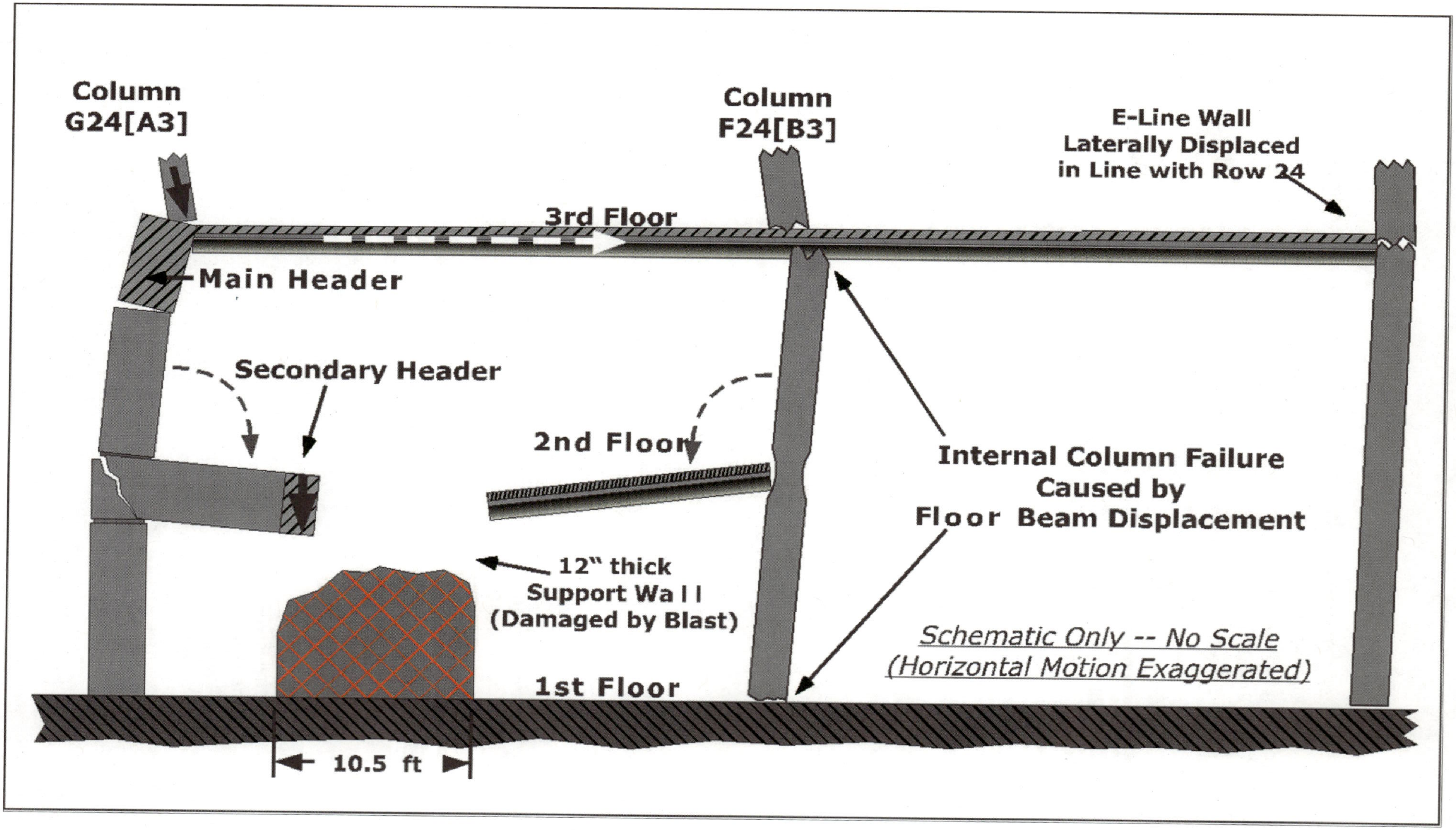

Mechanism of Failure for Wall Column (Figure 13)

5. The first few seconds of seismic signal on the Opmniplex seismograph for both the bombing and the demolition are strikingly similar. The 19 April 1995 first-motion signal more closely resembled the signal from demolition charges than it did that typical of a large, low-velocity, above-ground explosion.

Perhaps, years from now, future archaeologists will excavate the sites where the structural evidence of the Murrah Building's destruction lies buried. And, perhaps, then, the validity or fallacy of the "multiple bombs" theories will finally be proven. Until then, America will be left with the above tantalizing indications that, perhaps, what caused the collapse was quite different from the official "one truck, one bomb" explanation.

M. RECOMMENDATIONS

A primary reason that development of this report faced near-insurmountable uncertainties—indeed, its true *raison d' etre*, was that the conditions and positions of key failed structural elements of the collapsed Murrah Federal Building were very inadequately documented. And that such first-hand documentation as exists remains possessively held by the FBI.

Modern image analysis techniques enable extraction of much valuable information from photographs. Photos are invaluable records, but they can only capture a specific instant in time. Most photos examined for this study were taken while the structures of interest were still buried—or shortly after they had been removed; thus, they contributed little to the understanding of collapse mechanisms.

In a scenario wherein rubble must be removed slowly to protect victims, exposure of structural evidence is necessarily gradual and piecemeal. Failure documentation must be paced accordingly.

An additional resource that is recommended for inclusion in future scenarios of structural collapse—whether accidental or deliberate is **Forensic Engineering Documentation Teams (FEDTs)**. It is strongly recommended that these teams **NOT** be a part of—or under control of—law enforcement agencies. FEDTs would be a component of Urban Search and Rescue (USAR) teams, but should bear no direct responsibility for rescue or structural stabilization. (That does not infer that their input would not be invaluable aids in those efforts.)

Documentation produced by FEDTs should be open and public records.

Recommended staffing, equipment, and training should include:

- Registered Professional Engineers — who are qualified to testify as expert witnesses
- "Total Data Station" computerized, laser-based surveying and data-recording equipment
- Powerful laptop computers with full CAD capability
- Photographers and videographers
- Several time-lapse video recording units fixed from diverse viewpoints
- Training to include courses in data recording techniques used in modern field archaeology

It is fervently hoped that America will never suffer another terrorist tragedy like the attack on the Murrah Building. However, America's structural infrastructure is aging, and natural disasters are inevitable. Documenting the vulnerabilities in our buildings is but a first step in enhancing America's safety.

N. CONCLUSIONS

Most of the published hypotheses as to what caused the collapse of the Murrah Building simply do not fit the available evidence, and may be discounted.

It is beyond question that a very powerful truck bomb was detonated on Northwest Fifth Street near the north face of the Murrah Building. Certainly, that device, alone, would have caused tremendous damage and loss of life, even if the main structure of the building had remained intact.

There is no incontrovertible evidence that the blast from the truck bomb destroyed one—much less three—of the structural columns by brisance alone. However, it remains possible that, acting upon designed-in vulnerabilities of the Murrah Building, the truck bomb could have caused the structural collapse examined in this report.

However, there remains a significant body of evidence that is inconsistent with the effects of a single, air-coupled explosive blast. That body of evidence is consistent with the scenario, first proposed by General Benton Partin, that small, high-velocity contact charges may have been exploded on or near the junctures of columns G16[A7], G20[A5], and G24[A3] with the main transfer beam some seconds prior to explosion of the truck bomb..

Neither of these two outstanding explanations for the extensive structural collapse of the Murrah Federal Building is conclusively proven; nor can either be eliminated satisfactorily without further intensive study of evidentiary materials now closely held by the Federal Government.

Bogata, Colombia

Khobar Towers, Saudia Arabia

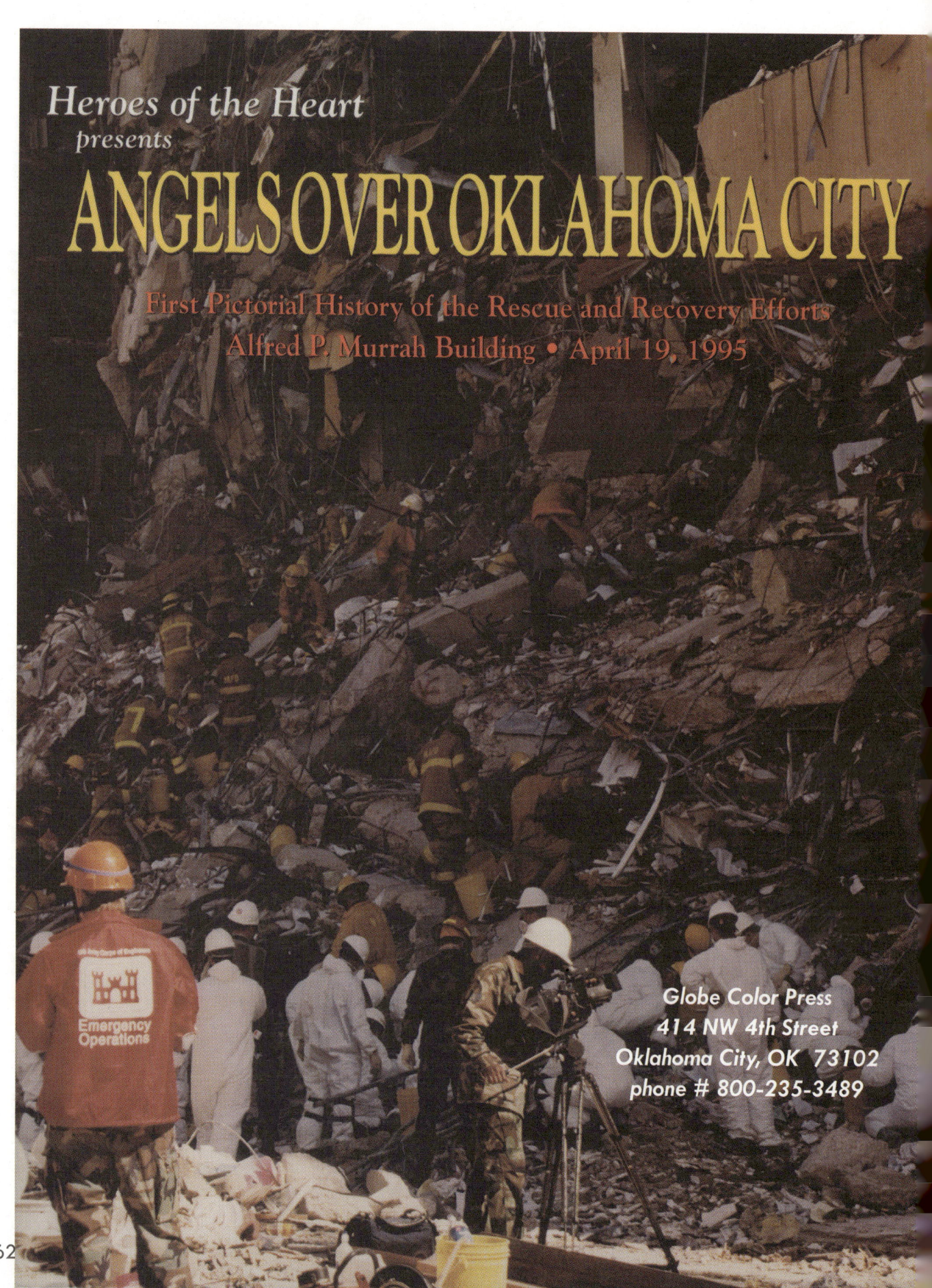

Chapter VI

PRIOR KNOWLEDGE

A. OVERVIEW

As the initial shock of the bombing wore off, many people in Oklahoma City began to recall pieces of conversations they had had or overheard which they realized indicated that the Federal Government had prior knowledge of an impending attack on the Murrah Building—or at the very least, a general warning of an attack in the Oklahoma City area. Locations across the country had been put on alert that day. There were bomb scares in Ft. Worth, Texas. The Internal Revenue Service in Boston, Massachusetts and federal buildings in Omaha, Nebraska and Wilmington, Delaware were evacuated. Across the country steps were taken to increase security at federal sites. (Source: KFOR-TV broadcasts, 19 Apr 95)

Locally, reports began to surface of phone calls and memos various government agencies had received prior to the bombing. Employees of local government agencies advised that they were alerted to be in a state of readiness for an undisclosed event. Witnesses also claimed that there was an increased law enforcement presence in the vicinity of the Murrah Building on the morning of 19 April 1995 before the bomb went off.

William Jasper in *The New American*, tells of meetings he was invited to attend with bombing victims who were concerned that they were being lied to by officials and that certain events surrounding the bombing were being covered up. He was provided with three tapes of telephone conversations recorded by a rescue worker. The caller was trying to dissuade the rescue worker from "rocking the boat" with his concerns over allegations of prior knowledge. The caller or callers admitted to a "failed sting operation" and told the rescue worker that his actions had conse-quences—that he could be jeopardizing the lives of undercover agents. (Source: *The New American*, 28 Oct 96)

Mr. Jasper has also received testimony from an Oklahoma law enforcement officer who said that, "at a mandatory daily security briefing at the Murrah Building, the assembled group were told, 'in no uncertain terms' by one of the lead federal officials that, for 'security reasons,' it was necessary to provide the public with 'disinformation' regarding certain aspects of the case, and that this 'official line' was not to be contradicted by any of those in attendance." (Source: *The New American*, 28 Oct 96)

This chapter presents the accounts of those who came forth with information regarding the prior knowledge issue. There are too many to be ignored.

B. PRIOR WARNINGS PROVIDED BY GOVERNMENT INFORMANTS

1. Carol Howe, ATF Informant at Elohim City

Carol Howe, a debutante from an affluent Tulsa family, was accosted by three black men who chased her onto a roof and pushed her off in February, 1994. She suffered severe damage to both her heels. After this incident, she called the racist hotline where she met a man named Dennis Mahon, former Imperial Dragon of the Ku Klux Klan. She became his lover, but later filed a domestic protective order against him when he threatened her. Shortly afterward she became a paid informant for the ATF. She was recruited in 1994, and began undercover work in August. Her primary job was to report on the activities of known members of the White Aryan Resistance, the Ku Klux Klan, and the white-separatist compound of Elohim City in Eastern Oklahoma. Having already visited Elohim City in the past with Dennis Mahon, she resumed her acquaintance with him and, again, was accepted into the compound. Upon arrival, she began providing monthly reports to her "handler," Agent Angela Finley-Graham out of the Tulsa ATF office. During the course of her undercover work, she submitted some 70 reports and routinely submitted to polygraph tests with "the government's own documents indicating she passed, 'showing no deception on her part in any polygraph examination.'" (Source: *McCurtain Daily Gazette* of Idabel, Oklahoma & ABC News Primetime, 10 Dec 97)

Carol Howe

Approximately two months before the Oklahoma City Bombing, Ms. Howe reported that members of Elohim City were making plans to bomb federal buildings and assassinate politicians. Howe reported that members of this group had begun staking out federal buildings in Oklahoma City and Tulsa. One of these individuals was identified by Howe as Dennis Mahon; the other was identified as a West German national, Andreas Carl Strassmeir (also known as Andrew and Andy). In her reports, she advised that these two men had made trips to Oklahoma City in November and December of 1994, and again in February 1995 to inspect the federal building. She also advised that militants within their group were advising that action needed to be taken by April 19th. (Source: ABC News *Primetime* Interview, 10 Dec 97; *Others Unknown*, Stephen Jones & Peter Israel, Public Affairs, NY, 1998, pg.183-197; *The McCurtain Daily Gazette*, 16 Mar 97, pg. 16))

2. Cary Gagan, ATF Informant

Cary Gagan has been part of the criminal element and has served time in prison. He states that, due to his ability and reputation for obtaining false identification papers, he was approached by Arab-looking individuals who offered him $250,000 to help them in a bombing plot. Gagan usually met with these individuals in and around the Kingman, Arizona, area. He knew them as Omar and Ahmad. They were often in the company of an unidentified third man.

In September 1994, Gagan informed the U.S. DOJ in Denver, Colorado, that he had been approached by these men to take part in the bombing of a federal building somewhere in the Midwest. He said the plot included Latin American conspirators. Gagan was given a letter of immunity by the Justice Department (Appendix pg. 410), and he continued to meet with the individuals who recruited him. On 17 March 1995, Gagan met with these people in a motel room in Las Vegas, Nevada where they examined drawings of the Murrah Building. Three times Gagan was sent by the group to Oklahoma City to case the building. He said he reported these occurrences to Justice Department officials in Denver.

OKBIC Note: Mr. Gagan filed a civil lawsuit against the Government for withdrawing his immunity without advising him and for attempting to prevent him from testifying in the criminal and civil trials resulting from the Oklahoma City bombing. He alleged that the Government took this action in order to cover up their wrongdoing in not acting on the bomb warnings he had provided to them.

(Source: Letter from Gagan to FBI, 19 Sep 94; Letter from Gagan to Joseph Hartzler, Dept of Justice, 16 Feb 97, and Gagan lawsuit, Civil Action No. 97-S-308, filed in U.S. District Court in Colorado)

3. German Bundesnachrichtendienst (BND)

The German BND is the equivalent of the American Central Intelligence Agency (CIA). According to William Northrop, former Israeli intelligence officer, the BND sent a warning to the U.S. State Department. (Source: *The Oklahoma City Bombing and the Politics of Terror*, David Hoffman, Feral House, 1998, pg.156)

OKBIC Note: Historically, when the State Department learns of a credible threat, it shares that information with the general public through airlines, travel agents, local Chambers of Commerce, etc. The FBI, however, selectively shares threat information with other law enforcement agencies at its own discretion.

4. Saudi Major General

According to an FBI 302 report, a Saudi major general responsible for protecting the Saudi royal family sent a warning to former CIA Counter-terrorism Chief Vince Cannistraro. In turn, Cannistrato contacted Kevin L. Foust, one of the FBI's leading counter-terrorism agents. "Ironically, the information was given to Foust on the same day as the bombing." The Saudi claimed to have seen a list of targets within the United States, and asserted that, at the top of the list, was the Murrah Federal Building in Oklahoma City, followed by the Immigration and Naturalization Service (INS) in Houston, Texas, and the FBI office in Los Angeles,

California.. (Source: *Others Unknown*, Stephen Jones & Peter Israel, Public Affairs, N.Y., 1998, pg. 199-203)

C. GENERAL WARNINGS BY GOVERNMENT BEFORE BOMBING

1. Government Warns of Possible Islamic Attacks

According to a newspaper report, the U.S. Marshal Service warned federal agencies and judges of their concern for an Islamic fundamentalist attack. The article stated,

> U.S. law enforcement authorities have obtained information that Islamic terrorists may be planning suicide attacks against federal courthouses and government installations in the United States. The attacks, it is feared, would be designed to attract world-wide press attention through the murder of innocent victims.

(Source: *New Jersey Star-Ledge*, 15 Mar 95)

Former ATF Director John McGaw

2. Statement of Increased Vigilance by ATF Director

At a news conference held on 25 May 1995, ATF Director John Magaw was asked if any preparations had been taken by government agencies because of the significance of 19 April. His response was "I was very concerned. We did some things here in headquarters and in all our field offices throughout the country to try to be more observant." (Source: *The New American*, 11 Dec 95, pg. 7)

3. Warning to Judge Wayne Alley

In an interview with his hometown newspaper, *The Oregonian* (see pg. 420-21), U.S. District Judge Wayne Alley of Oklahoma City said that he had received a warning. The news article reported:

> The judge said the bombing came just a few weeks after security officials had warned him to take extra precautions. "Let me just say that within the past two or three weeks, information has been disseminated that indicated concerns on the part of people who ought to know that we ought to be a little more careful," he said.

Alley was cautioned to be on the lookout for "people casing homes or wandering about the courthouse who weren't supposed to be there, letter bombs. There has been an increased vigilance." (Source: *The Oregonian*, 20 Apr 95)

OKBIC Note: ATF agent Luke Franey tried to convince bombing survivors and family members that the ATF had no prior warning. He said, "No, there was no alert or any concern on our part about the significance of that day." (Source: *Media Bypass*, Jun 96, pg 33

OKBIC Note: U.S. District Judge Alley was originally assigned to preside over the Murrah bombing case. On 01 December 1995, a decision of the 10th Circuit Court of Appeals substituted Judge Richard Matsch for Judge Alley because his office and staff had been hurt by the bombing. Subsequently the trials of Timothy McVeigh and Terry Nichols were moved to Denver, Colorado, because the defendants had been "demonized" In Oklahoma. (Source: *The New American*, 11 Dec 95, pg. 8-9)

Federal Judge Wayne Alley

4. Warning to Oklahoma City Fire Department

Harvey Weathers, a deputy fire chief with the Oklahoma City Fire Department reported that the FBI issued a warning the week prior to the bombing for them to be on alert. However, the head of the Oklahoma office of the FBI, Bob Ricks, was quoted denying that any call was made:

> *Ricks discounted reports that the FBI had alerted police and fire officials late last week to possible threats. However, Harvey Weathers, Assistant Fire Chief, said the Oklahoma City Fire Department did receive a report on Friday, April 14, about "some possibilities of some people entering the city over the weekend". He did not elaborate.*

(Source: *USA Today*, 20 Apr 95) (See Appendix pgs. 437-438.)

Weathers also gave this information to Glenn Wilburn in a face-to-face interview in the fall of 1995. Wilburn first went to the Fire Department's main offices and talked to Chief Charles Gaines. Wilburn asked Gaines about receiving any information prior to the bombing suggesting they be on alert. Gaines responded that he did "not remember anything like that."

Wilburn then went to Chief Weathers' office and asked him the same question. Weathers answered, "Yes, we got a call from the FBI about the possibility of some people entering the city over the weekend that we should be aware of.". Wilburn then said, "You might find it interesting to know I just left Chief Gaines office and he said he didn't know anything about it." Weathers replied, "Well, I'm not going to lie for anybody. That's what happened."

On 31 December 1998, the Oklahoma County Grand Jury reported that

Fire Chief Charles Gaines received a telephone call allegedly from "Gilmore with OSBI" on April 14, 1995, with a warning to be aware of something that may happen on April 15, 1995. The caller was not specific. It was not unusual to receive such calls. Chief Gaines passed the call on to Dispatch with instructions to notify the chiefs and safety officers.

(Source: Glen Wilburn Interview with Chief Gaines and Chief Weathers)

D. OKLAHOMA CITY POLICE DEPARTMENT RECEIVES TIP

State Representative Charles Key was contacted by an Oklahoma City Police dispatcher named Calena Flo Groves, who volunteered information concerning a call she had taken on approximately 12 April 1995. The caller told Groves that he had overheard two men discussing a bomb plot. The man also said he had heard the name Nichols mentioned by the two men. The conversation was overheard in a fast food restaurant or convenience store in the downtown area. When police officers did not arrive to take his statement, the man called again and talked to Groves two or three more times. Groves told interviewers Roger Charles and Charles Key that she did not believe the caller was impaired or unbalanced, as depicted in the police report, which was not filed until after the bombing. (Source: OKBIC taped interview with Calena Groves)

Attempts to acquire the dispatcher records under an Oklahoma Open Records Act was at first acknowledged, and then ignored, by the Oklahoma City Police Department. These records were, however, turned over to the Oklahoma County Grand Jury. The Grand Jury handled this report as follows:

> *We also learned of a telephone call made from a pay telephone at a Taco Bell on April 12, 1995, at 4:00 p.m. to 911. The call was taken by an Oklahoma City Police Department dispatcher, and she recalls it was a bomb related call and was categorized as a signal 8, meaning a mentally ill person. We received an audio-tape of the telephone call. Police officers responded to the Taco Bell and talked to the individual who made the call. His address was a home that cares for the mentally disabled. The dispatcher with 20 years experience, felt the caller knew about a bombing that was to occur, but had no specifics and never mentioned a Federal Building. We listened to a tape of the call and there was nothing specific mentioned.*

The Grand Jury apparently did not call the witness to testify and did not attempt to discern how he had acquired the information or from whom.

E. CONVERSATIONS SHOW PRIOR KNOWLEDGE

1. Congressman Istook Reportedly Says "We knew"

In October of 1997, a call was taken at the office of Oklahoma State Representative, Charles Key. The unidentified caller said he and another man had information regard-

Deputy Reserve Sheriff David Kochendorfer

ing prior knowledge of the Oklahoma City bombing. Approximately two weeks later, the caller, Don Hammons, accepted an invitation to be interviewed. He also brought with him another witness, David Kochendorfer. Both men are, and were at the time of the bombing, Reserve Deputy Sheriffs for Oklahoma County. (See Appendix pg. 412-413.)

Kochendorfer and Hammons were working on the northwest perimeter of the Murrah Building on 19 April 1995. Their job was to ensure that unauthorized persons did not enter the area and thereby disrupt the rescue process. The two Reserve Officers saw U.S. Congressman Ernest Istook and a female associate approaching their position at sometime between 9:30 and 10:30 p.m. Hammons and Kochendorfer stood approximately 30 feet apart.

The Congressman walked over to Kochendorfer, and the woman walked to a position close to Don Hammons and began taking photographs with the camera she was carrying. Photographs were prohibited, but since the woman was with the Congressman, Hammons allowed her to proceed, admonishing her to not take photos of any personnel. The reason for this was that undercover agents who did not want to be photographed were in the building.

As they conversed about the tragedy of the event, the woman stated that she had overheard talk of a warning in Congressman Istook's office on 09 April 1995. Hammons states that he distinctly remembers the 10-day time gap related to the bombing on the 19th. The woman gave Hammons her business card with her home telephone number written on it so he could contact her for copies of photos she had taken of the reserve officer. The card identified her as Lana Tyree, an Oklahoma City attorney.

Deputy Reserve Sheriff Don Hammons

At the same time, Congressman Istook and Kochendorfer had a separate conversation. Kochendorfer was in uniform and had on a yellow raincoat and a wide-brimmed hat similar to those worn by the highway patrol. The Congressman was standing shoulder-to-shoulder with Kochendorfer and said, "We knew this was going to happen. We blew it." Kochendorfer responded, "Excuse me, sir?" Istook repeated, "We had information about a fundamentalist, right-wing Islamic group operating out of Oklahoma City and we knew this was going to happen. We just blew it." Istook then turned to look at Kochendorfer and

Congressman Ernest Istook

his uniform and asked, "Aren't you highway patrol?" Kochendorfer replied, "No, deputy reserve officer." The congressman walked away from Kochendorfer with no additional comment.

(Source: Taped OKBIC interviews with Hammons and Kochendorfer)

OKBIC Note: Congressman Istook and Lana Tyree vehemently deny having any knowledge of the Murrah Building bombing. In a press release, Congressman Istook stated, "It is garbage and a total fabrication to suggest that I have information that the government supposedly had prior knowledge of the Murrah Building bombing. Any such suggestion is the product of somebody's sick and warped imagination." (Source: *The New American*, 16 Feb 98, pg. 12) KTOK Talk Radio, hosted by Mike McCarville, interviewed Charles Key and Istook. In a poll conducted of listeners, over 900 callers responded, with over 55 percent believing the deputies rather than Istook. (Source: *The New American*, 16 Feb 98, pg. 14)

OKBIC Note 2: Both reserve deputy sheriffs have recorded their statements on audio and video tapes, signed affidavits, testified under oath before the Oklahoma County Grand Jury and were willing to take lie detector tests. Congressman Istook declined offers to take a lie detector test. (Source: *The New American*, 16 Feb 98, pg. 16)

2. ATF Agents Say They Were Tipped

a. Agent Tells EMSA Paramedic ATF Not in Office

Tiffany Bible, a paramedic with the Emergency Medical Service Authority (EMSA), arrived on the south side of the Murrah Building four-to-five minutes after the bombing. She recalls having thought that there must have been a natural gas line explosion. She approached an entrance to the building where an ATF agent was standing and asked how a gas line explosion could do that much damage. The agent replied that it was the result of a car bomb. (This conversation took place sometime before 9:15 a.m.) Bible expressed concern because there were fellow agents of his in the building. The agent responded by saying, "No, we weren't in there today." (Source: Sworn affidavit of Tiffany Bible, 23 Jan 98)

b. ATF Agent Says Phone Page Told Them Not to Come to Office

Bruce Shaw's wife worked in the Murrah Building at the Federal Credit Union. Shaw had been at work when he both heard the blast and learned of the bombing. He and his supervisor, Tony Brasier, rushed to the scene. When they arrived, they came upon an ATF agent with a hand-held communications device. Shaw asked the agent if he would inquire about the status of his wife. The agent stated that it was too early for information such as that, but he made the attempt anyway. Then Shaw asked the whereabouts of any local ATF agents because he and his wife knew them, and they would help him find his wife. The agent responded that the agents were tipped on their pagers not to come into the office that morning. (Source: News media interviews with Shaw immediately after the bombing; OKBIC interview and Bruce Shaw's signed affidavit: *Media Bypass*, Jun 96, pg. 37))

c. Two ATF Agents Discuss Page to Not Come In

Attorney Lana Tyree

Katherine E. Mallette, an Emergency Medical Technician, Intermediate, with EMSA responded to the explosion at the Murrah Federal Building between 10:30 and 11:00 a.m. As her ambulance was waiting to transport victims to area hospitals, two ATF agents walked by her ambulance, and she heard one of the agents say to the other, "Is that why we got the page not to come in today?" (Source: Signed affidavit of Katherine Mallette)

OKBIC Note: The ATF has vehemently denied that they had prior knowledge. ATF Director Magaw stated that most of the agents were either in court or were "out working on the street" at the time of the bombing, and that "you will never find any time, unless you're having some office meeting of some kind, where all 15 or 17 people will be in that particular office." Other people who worked in the building, however, said that, on a normal day at 9:00 a.m., the ATF contingent was considerably more than the five people who were supposedly in the office that morning. (Source: *The New American*, 11 Dec 95, pg. 7)

In an apparent effort to put the issue to rest, ATF Resident-Agent-in-charge (RAC) Alex McCauley and DEA agent David Schickendanz were credited with being in a free-falling elevator and barely escaping with their lives. They say that they had entered the elevator on the eighth floor of the Murrah Building just before any explosion occurred. Then, they claim, the explosion caused the elevator to 'free-fall' to the third floor where, after four attempts, they forced the doors open and escaped. (Append. pg. 406-7)They say they then began to help victims of the bombing. (Source: *The New American*, 17 Feb 97, pg. 15)

OKBIC Note: The morning of the bombing, there were both General Services Administration (GSA) and Midwestern Elevator Company inspectors on the scene of the bombsite. Midwestern Elevator held the service contract for the Murrah Building. Employees of the company were present in the building daily and were familiar with the elevators. The Midwestern technicians inspected the elevators immediately and found that five of the six elevators were stopped between floors with their doors blown inward, which caused "the safety mechanisms to freeze them in place." J.D. Cash in the *Gazette quoted* Duane James, the elevator maintenance man, as saying that, "Once that occurs, the doors cannot be opened—period." James said that the elevators are equipped with safety switches which prevent excessive speed. None of the switches had been tripped. They were only able to get the sixth elevator and a freight elevator in working order to help with the rescue effort. GSA inspectors and Midwestern technicians have stated in interviews with various media, and in sworn affidavits and/or testimony that there was no evidence of (1) free-falling elevators, (2) persons in any of the elevators who then forced their way out, or (3) failure of the safety mechanisms built into the system. Duane James, put it this way:

> *If you fell six floors and it was a free fall, it'd be like jumping out a six-story building. I'd ask them how long they were in the hospital and how lucky they were to survive.*

ATF Special Agent-In-Charge Dallas Region-Lester Martz

(Source: *The New American*, 11 Dec 95 & 13 May 96; ATF Newsletter & ABC news program 20/20, 17 Jan 97))

OKBIC Note: Oscar Johnson, president of Midwestern Elevator, said that two of his technicians and a GSA inspector were in the tunnel under the street going from the courthouse (across the street south of the Murrah Building) to the Murrah Building when the explosion occurred. They were at the elevators, checking them, within a couple of minutes of the blast. (Source: The New American, 11 Dec 95, pg. 6)

OKBIC Note: Lester Martz, Special-Agent-in-Charge (SAC) of the ATF Dallas Region, regarding the story about McCauley and Schickendanz free-falling, apparently "threw them to the wolves" later. He told *Media Bypass* that "Maybe Agent McCauley just imagined he free-fell." (Media Bypass, Jun 96, pg. 36))

3. Corrections Center Inmate Overhears Plan to Evacuate Building

Jeffrey H. Broyles, an inmate of the Hobart, Oklahoma Correctional Work Center in Kiowa County, reported that, on 19 April 1995, he was in the custody of United States marshals being transported from the Oklahoma County Jail to the McCloud, Oklahoma Correctional Facility. Sometime between 8:30 and 8:40 a.m., a radio dispatch came in. At the end of it, the female officer made a statement to the male officer, "I wonder why they're going to evacuate the Federal Building." At approximately 8:50 a.m., another dispatch came in. The male officer made the comment, "Well, now they're not going to evacuate it." Approximately one week after the bombing, he told this story to the FBI and OSBI. (Source: Sworn affidavit of Jeffrey H Broyles, 10 Dec 97.)

4. Reports Indicate State Government Had Prior Knowledge

a. Highway Patrol Stops Ryder Truck Four Days Before Bombing

On 07 December 1997, a Pittsburg, Pennsylvania attorney (who wishes to remain anonymous) e-mailed Charles Key to report an incident he feels shows prior knowledge of the Oklahoma City bombing by state authorities. He reported that

> I have clients in Ohio who have an adult babysitter who, with two of her female relatives moved a load of household goods from California to Ohio. Their route took them through Oklahoma City several days BEFORE the explosion. They had rented a Ryder Truck for this trip and, as they drove near Oklahoma City, they were pulled over by several Oklahoma state troopers.... You can imagine their shock when a few days later the explosion occurred and it was revealed that a Ryder truck was involved.

At Key's request, the attorney made contact and spoke to the oldest of the women, the mother of the other two women. He reported,

> These women are scared.... They are seriously concerned for their safety, and it is not some militia fringe element they worry about—It's the FBI. The mother told me she has been interviewed by the FBI and has given sworn statements.... She said the stop occurred four days before the explosion. There were three Oklahoma State Police cars involved, but there was no search. The first trooper who approached did so with gun drawn. After a few questions regarding who the women were, where they were coming from, and where they were heading, they were told they could go. No explanation, no tickets, just a frightening stop and the shock of the explosion days later.

(Source: OKBIC Correspondence with Pennsylvania attorney)

b. Call Allegedly Made From Governor's Office Regarding Triage

V.Z. Lawton worked for the Department of Housing and Urban Development (HUD) and lost part of his hearing in the Murrah Building bombing. He also is a board member of the OKBIC. In November 1997, Lawton was visiting his son who was serving in the military and stationed in Germany. While there, Lawton took a tour of the Black Forest where he met a fellow traveler, a female army captain, who told him the following story:

> You know, something odd happened to us prior to the bombing. I work at Walter Reed Medical Center. In the days leading up to the bombing, our office received two phone calls. This person identified himself as a "Pentagon" or "Congressional liaison to the Governor of Oklahoma's office." He asked to speak to a doctor in our office about medical protocols. He asked specifically

about "triage for victims of blast overpressure." After what happened in Oklahoma a few days later, we thought this call was very odd.

The doctor requested by the caller was not available, so the woman handed the telephone to her immediate supervisor who asked if he could call him back or deliver a message to the doctor. The caller declined and said that he would call back later. Immediately after the call, she discussed the incident with another officer and a sergeant who were standing there. They all agreed the call "was weird."

A second call was made to this office, and the caller talked to the captain's supervisor. Both calls were reported to their commanding officer, an Army colonel. Notes of the conversations were made by one of the Army officers; however, over time, these notes have been misplaced and have yet to be located.

OKBIC interviewed the Army officers extensively over a period of months. Each related that calls had been received in their office prior to the Oklahoma City bombing. The female captain stated that the caller had specifically asked what types of injuries could be expected and what types of medical treatment would be required for blast overpressure.

OKBIC also interviewed the female captain's supervisor, a PhD at the hospital. He also confirmed the telephone calls and remembered that the call was in response to a liaison to the Oklahoma Governor's office, and that they wanted triage information for blast overpressure. He remembered the calls coming in three-to-four days before the Oklahoma City bombing.

(Source: Taped interviews with the three witnesses)

OKBIC Note: OKBIC did try to gain access to the Oklahoma Governor's phone records, but were told FEMA pays that office's phone bill, and we would have to go through them. On 18 May 1998, OKBIC hand-delivered a complete summary of this information, including the names and telephone numbers of all three witnesses to the Oklahoma County Grand Jury for further investigation. There is no indication that grand jurors checked or investigated this call for themselves. To our knowledge, none of these witnesses ever testified before the Grand Jury. In their Final Report, the Grand Jury said,

> *Another strange call was reportedly made to the Respiratory Research Unit of Walter Reed Army Institute of Research, Washington, D.C. The call was made on Monday, April 17, 1995, by a person who identified himself as being a Pentagon Congressional Liaison Officer representing the Governor of Oklahoma. The caller was inquiring about how to treat victims of a blast and what type of medical team and equipment would be required to treat such victims. None of the persons involved could recall the caller giving his name. None of them could recall any specific reference to a bombing in Oklahoma City. We were unable to find the source of this call.*

OKBIC Note: If the Grand Jury had subpoenaed telephone records and staff of the Governor's office, they might have been able to get to the bottom of these calls.

5. Calls to the U.S. Department of Justice

According to an FBI 302 report, on 19 April 1995 at 9:32 a.m. eastern standard time (EST), a call was placed to the Department of Justice in Washington, D.C. James Miller, a receptionist in the Executive Secretariat, took the call on the so-called "nut line." Fellow employee, Kimberly Tolson, was standing by his desk, as well as a courier from the Criminal Division, Russell Stuart Green, who had just made a delivery. Since Miller was busy on the phone, Tolson signed Green's log acknowledging receipt of the delivery. As soon as he completed the call, Miller told the other two people about his call. He said the caller stated

> *I'm nobody special. The federal building in Oklahoma City has just been bombed. I'm standing across the street from it. I can see it from where I'm standing.*

Green asked Miller to time-stamp his delivery log so he could leave. About an hour later, Miller learned that a bomb had actually detonated in Oklahoma City and advised his supervisor of the call he had received.

The following day, Green returned and had the delivery log with him. He noticed a discrepancy in time: The time-stamp at the time of the call the previous day was 9:38 a.m. EST (9:32 allowing for a noted six-minute adjustment for the clock being fast.) In Oklahoma City, the time would have been 8:32 a.m. central standard time (CST)—30 minutes before the explosion at 9:02 a.m. This obviously meant that someone who knew of the bombing had made the call—but not from Oklahoma City—and had obviously not considered the time difference when he made the call.

The FBI interviewed both Tolson and Green who told basically the same story. On the 302 report, Green was quoted as saying that, once Miller got off the phone, he stated, "There's been a bombing in Oklahoma City." Tolson also related a similar recollection, where she remembers this call and conversation happened as she was preparing for a 10:00 a.m. EST mail pickup for DEA.

(Source: *Others Unknown*, Stephen Jones & Peter Israel, Public Affairs, N.Y., 1998, pg. 211-221)

OKBIC Note: FBI 302 reports show an interview date of 27 April 1995, but a file date of 28 Feb 96.)

On 30 December 1998, the Oklahoma County grand jury reported:

> *Among the many rumors brought before the Grand Jury, was a report of a telephone call allegedly made to the Department of Justice in Washington, D.C.,*

stating the caller was across the street from the Murrah Building which had just been blown up. This call was supposedly made thirty-eight minutes prior to the actual bombing. The Justice Department employee who took the call, later worked out the timing of the telephone call he had received from Oklahoma City. He was able to determine the time based on a package delivery. The actual time was determined to be after the bombing.

OKBIC Note: No other explanation or proof was offered by the grand jurors to account for the change in Miller's time stamp or the recollection of the other two witnesses. The jurors were given the Government version of events and simply took the Government's story as fact. To our knowledge, James Miller and the other witnesses to this forewarning never testified before the Oklahoma County Grand Jury.

OKBIC Note: The Grand Jury failed to question why, if this caller was standing across the street from the Murrah building after it had just blown up, he didn't call 911 instead of the Justice Department.

F. BOMB SQUAD SIGHTINGS INDICATE PRIOR KNOWLEDGE

1. Bomb Squad Member Says They Searched Federal Courthouse

Randall A. Yount, working as a park ranger for the Oklahoma Tourism and Recreation Department, felt the explosion from his house in Bethany, Oklahoma, a suburb west of Oklahoma City. He immediately turned on the television and heard news of the bombing and the need for emergency assistance; so he put on his uniform and went downtown, arriving at 9:23 a.m. An Oklahoma Highway Patrol officer saw him walking in the downtown area and offered to give him a ride to the bombing area. The trooper dropped him at the Southwestern Bell Building where the Highway Patrol was setting up a command post in the parking lot. Yount was subsequently partnered with a trooper to help at the Murrah Building. While in the telephone company parking lot, Yount saw a marked Oklahoma Bomb Squad white truck with a trailer behind it. Sitting in the truck was an acquaintance of his named Terry. Terry told him, "Yeah, we've been down here since early this morning looking. We got word that there was going to be a bomb, and we thought it was going to be the courthouse. We went over everything and couldn't find anything." (Source: OKBIC Interview & Randy Yount's sworn affidavit)

2. Mother of Victim Sees Bomb Squad

Renee Cooper's infant son was in the daycare center on the morning of the bombing and was killed in the blast. She says she saw several men in dark jackets with the words "Bomb Squad" written on them standing in front of the Federal Courthouse, across the street south of the Murrah Building, at 8:05 a.m. (Source: *The Oklahoma City Bombing and the Politics of Terror*, David Hoffman, Feral House, 1998, pg. 332)

OKBIC Note: According to David Hoffman, reporter J.D. Cash was told by Bomb Squad Captain Robert Heady, that "We don't wear those type shirts." Hoffman also reports that Deputy Sheriff Melvin Sumter made a videotape "at the scene of the blast [that] shows Bomb Squad members, along with the captain, in T-shirts with words "BOMB SQUAD" in large silver-white letters written across their chests." (Source: *The Oklahoma City Bombing and the Politics of Terror*, David Hoffman, Feral House, 1998, pg. 333)

3. Local Attorney Sights Bomb Truck

Dan Adomitis, an attorney in Oklahoma City, was on his way downtown for a 7:30 a.m. charity board meeting. Driving down Hudson Street which is a block-and-a-half west of the Murrah Building, he noticed a fairly large truck with a trailer behind it. According to Adomitis, "It had a shield on the side of the door and it said 'bomb disposal' or 'bomb squad' below it. And I really found that interesting. You know, I'd never seen anything like that in person." (Source: ABC News 20/20 Interview by Tom Jarriel, 17 Sep 97)

4. Employee of County Assessor's Office Sights Bomb Squad Truck

J. D. Reed, an employee with the Oklahoma County Assessor's office, also saw the Bomb Squad truck parked on the east side of Hudson Street in front of the county courthouse on 19 April prior to the bombing. He commented on how unusual it was to see this vehicle. He recalled,

> *I was settled at my desk for a normal day [9 a.m.] when I heard a whistling noise, like that of a jet engine. Less than a second later, I heard a deafening explosion and felt the building shake as if it were collapsing. "How far will this floor fall?" I remember wondering. As the shaking subsided, I ran to the window to investigate. Had an airplane struck the building? There was no sign of it. I looked for the Bomb Disposal Unit, but it was gone. Had they mistakenly set off an explosive while trying to disarm it? What was it???*

[Source: Article from a special edition of *Mass Media*, 19 Apr 96 (Oklahoma County Assessor's Newsletter)

5. Board of Elections Employee Sees Bomb Squad Truck

Norma Joslin, a 30-year employee of the Oklahoma County Board of Elections stated that she saw the Bomb Squad truck parked on the east side of Hudson Street in front of the county courthouse. She says she commented to a co-worker on the unusual nature of this sighting and speculated that they would probably know why it was there soon enough. (Source: *The New American*, 11 Dec 95, quoting an article in *The Watchman*.)

6. Private Investigator Sights Possible Bomb-Search Team

Claude Criss is a private investigator and part-time employee for the Oklahoma county courts. On the morning of the bombing he also noticed something unusual. As he was driving down Harvey Street, a half block from the Murrah Building, and came to the corner of Harvey and McGee, he saw four to seven paramilitary individuals with arms and three police dogs going through the bushes of the courthouse across the street from the Federal Building. When asked, he agreed that the dogs looked like sniffer dogs, "the type they use for bomb searches." (Source: ABC News 20/20 interview by Tom Jarriel, 17 Sep 97)

OKBIC Note: According to David Hoffman, the driver of the Bomb Squad truck, Deputy Sheriff William R Grimsley, states that he "left the county jail at 7:00 a.m., stopped at the nearby courthouse for a few minutes to take care of an errand, went to McDonald's for breakfast, then drove to the bomb training site 10 miles away." (Source: *The Oklahoma City Bombing and the Politics of Terror*, David Hoffman, Feral House, 1998, pg. 333)

OKBIC Note: Then-Oklahoma County Sheriff J. D. Sharp tells a different story. He stated, "I can assure you from the testimony of the witnesses and the bomb commander that our unit was not anywhere near the Murrah Building the morning of the blast" (Source: KFOR Channel 4 interview, 21 Nov 95). Sharp later claimed that Deputy Grimsley picked up the truck around 7:00 a.m. and drove directly to the department' training center. (Source: The Oklahoma Gazette, 13 Feb 97)

OKBIC Note: The FBI conducted a raid on an Oklahoma City mosque just prior to the bombing. There has been speculation that they gained information from the raid to alert them to the possibility of the Oklahoma City bombing. The FBI borrowed Arabic linguists from the U.S. Army on the day of the bombing to monitor and interpret Arabic wiretaps. A witness in the downtown Oklahoma City area says his neighborhood was full of FBI and ATF agents picking up documents as the dust cloud from the explosion deposited them on city streets. He also said he overheard agents on the payphone in front of his business speaking in Arabic. (Source: *SOURCE Investigative eJOURNAL*, Vol III, Issue 3, Jun 98)

OKBIC Note: Did the raid on the mosque give the FBI prior warning of the Oklahoma City bombing? Is that why witnesses saw Bomb Squad trucks and searchers in the vicinity of the Murrah Building before the bomb exploded? (For more information on this incident, see Chapter VII, page 281.)

G. S.W.A.T. SIGHTING SUGGESTS PRIOR KNOWLEDGE

Photojournalist Pat Carter was in downtown Oklahoma City on Harvey Avenue , 100 to 200 feet from the Murrah Building on 19 April 1995. It was 30 minutes to an hour after the bombing. He said he saw a half dozen ATF agents on the corner of Northwest 6th Street in front of a parking garage wearing their special weapons assault team (S.W.A.T.) gear—bullet-proof vests and black uniforms. He said he knows what kind of dress the ATF wears on crime-scene investigations like the Murrah Building, and they normally have on their blue windbreakers. He commented that "these guys were obviously part of a 'bust' that turned to [expletive deleted]!... The feds had this deal wired from the beginning." (*Media Bypass*, Jun 96, pg. 36)

H. TRIGEN CORPORATION

In downtown Oklahoma City, a company log from Trigen Companies, which produces steam energy, shows curious event. On 16 April 1995, three days before the Oklahoma City bombing, a boiler apparently blew up. at 2315 hours (11:15 p.m.) the police pounded on the contraler room window. An employee was told that they (the police) had received a report of a "major explosion and possible terrorist takeover of the building." A policeman indicated they would notify the bomb squad. The employee explained that the situation wa under control. (Source: Trigen watch log, Appendix p. 436)

I. CONCLUSIONS

Federal, state, county and city officials were obviously given some kind of warning prior to the bombing. How specific that warning was we do not know. It could have been a general alert to be more vigilant, as government spokespeople have said. With some government agencies, this may be true. But with other government entities, the threat seems to have been more specific. The presence of the Bomb Squad in the downtown area that morning and the page to the ATF agents telling them to not come into the office supports this conclusion. We question why government agencies have tried to quash these reports, have provided disinformation, and have tried to discredit the witnesses. Is it to cover up the fact that they knew but did not let other workers in the building know? Or is there some other motivation? (For taped conversation on government sting operations, see ps. 535-540.)

Chapter VII.

THE SEARCH FOR JOHN DOE AND OTHERS UNKNOWN

A. OVERVIEW

Government agencies gathered a very large amount of information and evidence that clearly point to other individuals who may have been involved in the Oklahoma City bombing; however, for reasons unknown to the general public, they chose to ignore that evidence and did not pursue the arrest and prosecution of these individuals. In fact, at the trials of McVeigh and Nichols, the Government selectively culled out those witnesses who might have shed some light on these "Others Unknown."

This chapter deals with specific information regarding other possible participants in the Oklahoma City bombing. The information demonstrates that other individuals were involved, and that Federal Government officials obtained information which validated that fact. The following data is taken from actual Government documents, from investigations by private investigators hired by OKBIC.

B. THE MIDDLE-EASTERN CONNECTION

Immediately after the bombing, reports surfaced of suspicious-acting Middle-Eastern individuals seen in the vicinity of the Murrah Building shortly before or after the bomb went off. As a result of these reports and the arrest of Timothy McVeigh, many witnesses surfaced who had seen the potential culprits in the days and weeks leading up to the bombing. They described them in different ways: Middle-Eastern, Arabic, or dark-complexioned. Several of the witnesses have already been mentioned in the chapter on "Eyewitnesses," such as the account given by Mike Moroz and his co-worker who state that they saw and spoke with McVeigh at Johnny's Tire Store approximately 30 minutes before the blast. They both state that McVeigh had a passenger in the Ryder truck resembling the John Doe II sketch and possibly being of Middle-Eastern extraction (Source: OKBIC witness interviews and FBI 302 reports). Another man, an employee of the Journal Record gave an account of almost being run down just before the blast by McVeigh and his passenger whom he described as possibly being Arabic. (Source: *The Dallas Morning News* & Interview with Glenn and Kathy Wilburn). Daina Bradley, who was in the Social Security office at the Murrah Building when the blast occurred, describes an individual of possible Arabic descent getting out of the Ryder truck and walking away toward the east. (Source: McVeigh Trial, pg 10451-10465). Another witness, Kay Herrin Clark, described a brown pickup truck almost running her over and coming so close that she could clearly see the driver, who fit a Middle-Eastern description. (Source: KFOR-TV broadcast, Jun 95) Other events also point to a possible Arab connection: (See Appendix pg. 419.)

NBC News correspondent Tom Brokaw interviewed Neil Livingstone, a leading terrorist expert. Livingstone stated that Islamic fundamentalists often "go where security is the weakest," and Oklahoma has "so many people involved in the oil industry and quite a few students from Middle-Eastern countries who are studying various types of engineering."

I. Arabic Linguists from U.S. Army Loaned to FBI

According to *SOURCES Investigative eJOURNAL*, the FBI had a secret eavesdropping operation underway in Oklahoma City before the bombing. A prior raid on a mosque in Oklahoma City may have been the catalyst for the operation. Arabic linguists from the U.S. Army were loaned to the FBI with approval from the Secretary of the Army to listen to and interpret wiretap tapes. This order was soon revised at the direction of the Secretary of Defense to allow the linguists to listen to live conversations. Under the Posse Comitatus Act, Executive Order 12333 and DOD 3025.1, the military may not participate in civilian law enforcement activity, including live wiretap monitoring; however, in order to protect the President, an exception is made under DOD 5525.5, encl 4. A.2.(e)(6).

A witness in Oklahoma City, Andy Edt, who owns Midwest Customs in the downtown Oklahoma City area, told of activity on the morning of the bombing. His shop is approximately one mile from the bombsite and four blocks from the Evidence Control Center. He remembers the smoke from the bombing coming toward his shop and bringing with it "papers falling from the cloud like snow." His neighborhood "was 'wall-to-wall' with FBI and DEA agents as they picked up federal documents." He said that the payphone in front of his shop had a lot of activity that day. Walking by, he heard a caller, who was wearing a blue windbreaker marked "FBI" on the back, speaking in a Middle-Eastern dialect. He said the agent did not look Middle-Eastern, but spoke the language very well. The next afternoon, he said, he heard one or two other men in FBI jackets talking in Arabic on the payphone.

OKBIC Note: The FBI and DEA agents must have already been in-place in the downtown area at the time of the bombing if this witness' recollection is correct and the agents were picking up documents as they fell from the cloud of smoke.

It is not known if there is any connection between the bombing of the Murrah Building and this eavesdropping activity; however, according to the *SOURCES* article, "among the tens of thousands of documents the government turned over to McVeigh's defense attorneys were references to the spying operation and to an assassination plot by Islamic extremists." The article further states that the Army Forces Command (FORSCOM) memos and situation reports (sitreps) that prompted the McVeigh defense investigation were examined by Terry Prosch, a public affairs spokesperson at FORSCOM, and he verified their authenticity.

The article also cites another document, dated 22 April 1995, signed by Captain Mark E. Austin at FORSCOM. The memo was sent to the FBI to determine "if the linguists were still needed, as there had been an 'arrest of a domestic suspect in the OKC incident.'" The FBI responded that the linguists were being used "to monitor wiretaps of radical fundamentalist Islamic organizations in an effort to protect the President from possible attack during his attendance of the memorial service in OKC on Sunday, 23 April."

The loan of the Army linguists was requested by the FBI on the day of the bombing, and they arrived at the Pentagon at midnight —15 hours after the bombing. From there they were deployed to FBI regional offices in Phoenix, Boston, Detroit, Houston, San Diego, Los Angeles, Tampa, Newark, Chicago and New York City.

(Source: SOURCES Investigative eJOURNAL, Volume III, Issue 3, Jun 98)

OKBIC Note: Did the raid of the mosque uncover a plot to blow up the Murrah Building—which would mean that there truly is an Arab connection to the Oklahoma City bombing? What did the Arab conversations concern to cause such a furor? Were there discussions of other bombings that were planned? We may never know, but it leads one to speculate. And the speculation occurs because our Government has so little faith in its people that it thinks it has to keep unpleasantness from us for our own protection and peace of mind—the "What you don't know can't hurt you" mentality—except that this time it did hurt us—to the tune of 168 people dead.

2. Nichols and Possible Arab Connections

A key Iraqi terrorist was Ramzi Yosef who was convicted of conspiracy in a plan to blow up eleven U.S. commercial jet planes at the same time. He was also indicted for masterminding the attack on the World Trade Center in New York City. Additionally, he was responsible for placing a bomb on Philippine Airlines flight 434 in December 1994. Terry Nichols may have met with him or his followers during his trip to the Philippines in November 1994. The U.S. Government investigated this lead following the bombing.

Terry Nichols first went to the Philippines in 1990 after he found Marife Torres in a mail-order bride service. They married in the Philippines, after which Nichols left almost immediately for Michigan, while Marife waited for a visa in order to join him. Marife returned to the Philippines several times over the next few years. So did Nichols—but not always when Marife was there. He said he was looking for business opportunities.

In September 1994, Marife returned to the Philippines for six months to go to college, she has said. Nichols joined her in November at the beach house she was renting in Cebu City (her hometown). He said he spent most of his time on the beach with his daughter. After he went back home on 31 January 1995, Marife broke her lease and went to live in a boarding house in Cebu City. Most of the residents of the boarding house were Muslim students from the Philippine island of Mindanao, home of 500 or more radical Muslim fighters. Nichols called the boarding house 71 times after he returned home—12 of these calls were made after Marife had left the Philippines.

Stephen Jones has a theory on Nichols' visit to the Philippines. Is he correct? Did Nichols go to the Philippines to receive training in how to build a bomb? (An FBI 302 report cites that a neighbor of Marife's parents said Marife's father told him he saw Nichols with a book on building bombs. When questioned by the Philippine National Police, Marife's father admitted it was true.)

(Source: *Others Unknown*, Stephen Jones & Peter Israel, Public Affairs, 1998, pg. 121-128 & Nichols' Trial, pg 13830-13937)

C. THE WHITE EXTREMIST CONNECTION

In the Oklahoma City bombing investigation, leads to "Others Unknown" seem to point in many different directions—to Middle-Eastern accomplices, to extremist organizations in Arizona, Michigan and Elohim City and to German, Russian, and Japanese extremists. It seems confusing and preposterous to assume that all these elements came together to plan and carry out the bombing of the Murrah Federal Building—until one realizes that cooperation between these groups takes place on a frequent basis. The question arises: With all that separates these groups, including political ideology, cultural and ethnic differences, an innate distrust of one another and often opposing agendas, why would they cooperate on any joint venture? Because, they have two things in common—a hatred for the U.S. Government and a hatred for the Jews. (This section of the Report is based on information gleaned from an OKBIC investigator's visit to Germany and discussions he held with officials in Germany.) (See Appendix pg. 451-462.)

1. Cooperation Among U.S., German and Middle-Eastern Extremists

The Stockholm Revisionist Historian Conference held in Sweden in November 1992, is an example of these diverse groups coming together for a common cause. (This movement disputes many of the incidents of history, including denial of the very existence of, or at least the full extent of, the Holocaust.) Organized by Ahmed Rami, formerly of "Radio Islam," the Conference was attended by numerous Nazi and neo-Nazi figures as well as by members of Hezbollah and Hamas (Arab extremist groups), Japanese extremists, and Pamjat (a Russian extremist group).

Nazi-Middle Eastern collaborations go back at least as far as World War II. After the war, former Major General Ernest Rhemer fled Germany and settled in the Middle East where he set up intelligence operations for several Arab countries. He played a prominent role over the next several decades in coordinating German right-wing activity with the Arab world. (Rhemer is also prominent in the "revisionist scene.")

Other Nazi and neo-Nazi figures have actually been implicated in Middle Eastern special weapons procurement and terrorist activity since the 1960's:

     a. An elderly Swiss Nazi named Francois Gernaud has reportedly masterminded several airplane hijackings for the Palestine Liberation Organization (PLO).

     b. An "old line" Nazi named Antoine Eyerle, with two corporations previously operating near Munich, was convicted in Germany on 20 July 1994 for trading nuclear and SCUD rocket detonation technology to Iraq.

     c. A former Nazi scientist, Volker Weissheimer, helped recruit former Nazi and East German scientists to work on Libyan and Iraqi chemical weapons projects.

     d. The Odessa organization had numerous documented meetings with representatives of various Arab organizations. Odessa, which was comprised of former German SS officers, was formed to assist Nazis in escaping the Allies after World War II. Most of these Nazis relocated to South America.

     e. During the 1980's, a neo-Nazi named Odfried Hepp attacked several U.S. military installations in Germany with bombs. Hepp was later found to have been financed by Al Fatah, a terrorist organization founded by Yasir Arafat.

There are numerous documented instances of militant neo-Nazi party members who also held membership in the PLO and/or the Popular Front for the Liberation of Palestine (PFLP): Odfried Hepp who went to prison in Germany, and Udo Albrecht, a German neo-Nazi mercenary, are but two examples.

The U.S. involvement with defending Israel during the Gulf War generated high levels of neo-Nazi hostility, which have not dissipated since the Gulf War. The U.S. support of Israel during the Palestinian violence makes the U.S. a continued object of neo-Nazi/Middle Eastern displeasure. According to a research book, *Europas Braune Saat*, the Schiller Institute, a subsidiary of American Lyndon LaRouche, (an extremist American political organization) mounted a massive propaganda effort in Germany against America's entry into the Gulf War. Michael Kuhnen founded the Anti-Zionist League, which formed relationships between Nazis and Arab groups. He was succeeded by a man named Hubner who organized campaigns for Saddam Hussein during the Gulf War. (Hubner has connections with Kirk Lyons, attorney for Andrew Strassmeir, and numerous other militant individuals and organizations.)

During the Gulf War, Michael Kuhnen, then a top German neo-Nazi figure, negotiated a contract to provide Iraq with 100 German neo-Nazi volunteers and later with an additional 100 American and British neo-Nazi volunteers to fight for Iraq in the Gulf War. Kuhnen died before he could fulfill this contract, so a French neo-Nazi leader named Michael Faci stepped in and provided an unknown number of "storm troopers" who did indeed fight with Saddam's army during the Gulf War.

After the Gulf War, President Bush began a program of resettlement of Iraqi prisoners to the U.S. This program was continued and expanded by President Clinton (see Appendix, pg. 475-477). Additionally, there are scores of Middle-Eastern students attending colleges and universities in the United States, with the University of Oklahoma having one of the largest Arab populations. As a result, there are now large pockets of Middle-Eastern individuals residing in the U.S. Many are law-abiding citizens and visitors, but many also are likely "plants" from government-sanctioned extremist organizations in their respective countries of origin, here at the ready to participate in any terrorist actions their organizations desire.

At the time of the Oklahoma City bombing, the trial for the bombing of the World Trade Center in New York City was taking place, in which several Syrians and their leader in America were charged with conspiracy for blowing up the building. This trial had the Arab terrorist community at a fever pitch, and many experts say that the Murrah Building also has the earmarks of a Middle-Eastern terrorist attack.

(Source: OKBIC investigation and discussions with officials in Germany & *The Oklahoma City Bombing and the Politics of Terror*, David Hoffman, Feral House, 1998, pg 126)

Timothy McVeigh often traveled the gun show circuit and mixed with white extremists from across the country. He is known to have contacted various paramilitary groups and to have been associated with many of their members. His known associates, Terry Nichols and Michael Fortier also were known to fraternize within these organizations. ATF informant Carol Howe, who infiltrated the organization at Elohim City, said that people within the compound had been talking about blowing up a federal building and had been casing the Murrah Building. She also stated that Dennis Mahon, a part-time resident of Elohim City, received a phone call at his Tulsa apartment shortly before the bombing from a "Tim Tuttle," an alias used by McVeigh. A phone call was made on the Bridges' calling card from Arizona to Elohim City the week before the bombing. The caller asked for "Andy," which is a nickname used by Andreas Strassmeir, a German national who was head of security at Elohim City, and who has admitted to having met McVeigh (see pg. 405). A long-time friend of McVeigh, Michael Brescia, was a resident of Elohim City at the time of the bombing. Therefore, there is good reason to think that McVeigh may have been working with a white extremist organization. There are numerous other connections to extremist organizations which will be shown below.

2. Ties to Russia, South America, and Other Countries

In addition to these connections, there are also possible ties to Russia, Columbia, Mexico, the Philippines and other foreign countries. As noted above, Terry Nichols frequented the Philippines and made numerous calls to a boarding house there, even after Marife was back in the U.S. Cary Gagan, in the following paragraph, tells of meeting someone who looked like Nichols at a meeting he attended with a terrorist organization. Gagan and another witness below tell separate stories of meetings with conspirators from various countries wherein they believe the Oklahoma City bombing plot originated.

a. Government Informant Tells of Multi-National Plot

Cary Gagan claims to have been involved with conspirators to the Oklahoma City bombing. He contacted the U.S. Marshal's Office in Denver, Colorado to advise them that he had been approached by two men who were planning to blow up federal buildings in Denver, Colorado, as well as other cities around the country. On 14 September 1994, Gagan met with a man named Richard from the FBI and with David Floyd, a U.S. Marshal, and provided a description of the two terrorists. He also met with James Allison, head of the criminal division with the U.S. Attorney's Office and signed a letter of immunity to work as a Government informant within the ring of conspirators.

Gagan is a graduate of the University of Northern Colorado and holds a bachelor's degree in Recreation and a liberal arts degree with a teacher's certificate in Physical Education and English. He also has a criminal background and has served time for theft and criminal impersonation, and has served probation for insurance fraud. In the 1980's, Gagan had experience in Mexico City where he worked with U.S., Soviet and Syrian connections and drug cartels. He is known for being able to provide forged identification documents.

Toward the end of May 1994, Gagan stated that he met with two Arab men, Omar and Ahmad, in Henderson, Nevada, a suburb of Las Vegas. He described Omar as being short and heavy with no facial hair and in his early thirties; and Ahmad was described as being five foot ten or eleven, nice looking and younger. Also present were four or five other people including someone he said looked like Terry Nichols and some Latin-looking individuals. Gagan pointed out that the people came from a variety of backgrounds: Irani, Iraqui, Columbian, Irish and neo-Nazi. They had a large supply of money and an elaborate network for smuggling and gathering information. They met at various locations, one being the Player's Club, an upscale apartment complex in a Las Vegas suburb. Omar and Ahmad became his contacts. Sometimes there was another man present. Gagan described him as 6'2 and handsome. He "wore a suit, [was] a banker type and Latin," and may have been the "money-guy." They had plans to blow up a federal building and wanted Gagan to transport some explosives in his suitcase when he flew back to Denver. At that point, Gagan contacted federal authorities.

In January 1995, Gagan said, he was supposed to move some explosives in a second-hand mail truck which had been repainted so it again looked like a U.S. Postal Service mail truck. He asserted that, in the back of the mail truck, were 50 duffle bags with "laboratory something" written on them, full of "sodium or ammonium nitrate." There were also "a mixer in there that said LELY" and "something called sodium azide chemicals," and "some stuff from a place in Las Vegas called Sandex." Gagan called the FBI to alert them so they could follow and make arrests, but the FBI did not get back with him.

On 17 March, Gagan said he attended a meeting with the terrorists at the Hilton Inn South in Greenwood Village, Colorado. His Arab contacts and one other person were present at the meeting. On the table were architectural drawings of the Alfred P. Murrah Federal Building with the name, "J. W. Bateson Company [architect], Dallas, Texas" on the bottom of the drawings. They spoke of important dates: 17 March 1992 (bombing of Israeli embassy in Argentina); and 12 April (significance unknown). They asked Gagan to identify federal judges and to obtain their addresses and photos. He hand-delivered a note concerning this meeting to the FBI on 27 March 1995.

Then, over the 4th and 5th of April 1995, Gagan traveled by car from Las Vegas to Kingman, Arizona with a member of the terrorist organization to deliver a package to an unknown individual driving a brown or maroon pickup. On the way back to Las Vegas, Gagan was told that a federal building would be bombed within a couple of weeks. When he asked if it would be in Denver, he was told, "Maybe." Gagan had previously been to Oklahoma City to check out security and the fifth floor of the Murrah Building. He believes there was a small network looking at different parts of the building. Gagan realized that Denver was probably not the site because it was a "hard target" (18-story concrete and set back from the road), while Oklahoma City was a "soft target."

Upon his return to Las Vegas on 05 April, Gagan flew to Denver to provide updated information of an imminent bombing of a federal building to his Government contacts. On 06 April, he had a note hand-delivered to Tina Rowe of the U.S. Marshal's Office providing information and asking her to contact him. She did not do so.

(Source: Letter from Gagan to FBI, 19 Sep 94; Letter from Gagan to Joseph Hartzler, Dept. of Justice, 16 Feb 97; Gagan lawsuit, Civil Action No. 97-S-308, filed in U.S. District Court in Colorado; and Gagan deposition with Stephen Jones, 20 Jul 95)

b. Mexican-Russian-PLO Plot Detailed

Michele Torres, the daughter of a former Communist Party official, Hirram Torres, in Mexico City, had been raised to assume a position in the Communist Party; but, at age 17, she rejected her upbringing and fled to the United States. In her recounting of events, Torres stated that, in the winter of 1992, she overheard her father and others discussing a bombing plot against the United States. She believes this plot culminated in the bombing of the Alfred P. Murrah Federal Building.

At the time, her father was working in the office of the PLO in Mexico City. He was speaking with two Arab men, one from Palestine and another from either Jordan or Iraq. Her father asked them what they thought of the new plan, and one of the men said that a Russian officer suggested that they blame American white supremacists and the neo-Nazis. By blaming Americans, they would appease both the Arabs and the Communists. According to Torres, her father told his visitors that he had tried to contact some neo-Nazis to help him, but they refused to do so. He said that they did not want to get involved with Communists, but he was going to blame them anyway by hiring some "white guy" to act as a neo-Nazi to help his Arab accomplices.

Torres also said that the plan was to bomb an office building in the middle of the country, and it had to involve children. She explained that there had to be children involved because of the emotional impact it would cause. She said that she had "listened to this kind of conversation" all her life and that her father had killed many people. She stated, "He was involved."

Ms. Torres' story corroborates a possible Arab, neo-Nazi, and Russian link to the bombing. As preposterous as it sounds, her story ties in with other reported events. Dennis Mahon was being paid by the Iraqis to stir up dissent among the white supremacists during the Gulf War, Cary Gagan met with Oman and Ahmad in Mexico City; and Timothy McVeigh, an alleged white supremacist, was reportedly seen with an Arab in Oklahoma City shortly before the bombing. (See below for information on these individuals.)

(Source: OKBIC interview with Ms. Torres)

OKBIC Note: Michele Torres' interview tapes were voice stress-analyzed and indicated she was telling the truth.

D. ORIGINAL APB ON 19 APRIL 1995

Directly after the bombing on 19 April 1995, an FBI all points bulletin (APB) went out concerning a brown Chevrolet pickup truck with suspects appearing to be of Middle-Eastern origin. An APB is the initial announcement on radio frequencies used by law enforcement to identify suspects for pursuit and apprehension and to request assistance from all other law enforcement agencies. The APB was played on news broadcasts and reported in numerous publications. It read as follows:

> *Be on the lookout for a late model, almost new, Chevrolet, full-size pickup. It will be brown in color with tinted windows, smoke-colored bug deflector on the front of pickup...Middle-Eastern male, 25 to 28 years of age, six feet tall, athletic build, dark hair and a beard.... Driver of the vehicle was not identified. Subjects were last seen heading north on Walker at a high rate of speed.... Authorization FBI.*

(Source: *The New American*, 14 Sep 98, pg. 24)

The source of the APB was a female eyewitness in downtown Oklahoma City who provided an affidavit to the FBI on 20 April 1995 (unsealed on 09 November 1995) swearing to these events. This witness states that she was standing near the Murrah Building shortly after the explosion and saw two men of Middle-Eastern appearance, wearing blue jogging suits, running from the vicinity of the Murrah Building to a late-model brown Chevrolet pickup parked near the building. A third man was driving the truck.

A follow-up APB from the Oklahoma Highway Patrol, issued at 2:28 p.m. on 19 April 1995, stated at the end, "Vehicle may be a rental car from National Car Rental Systems DFW Texas. Possible tag of PTF54F Texas." (Source: *The New American*, 14 Sep 98, pg. 22)

Mysteriously the FBI pulled the APB without any explanation later the same day. Yet, apparently, as late as the middle of May 1995, they still believed that there was a John Doe #2. According to a late edition of *The New York Times*, Steven G. Colbern, an admitted acquaintance of Timothy McVeigh, was arrested on federal weapons charges, and "officials in Washington" said they hoped that Colbern could help "clear up the mystery of John Doe No. 2." (See below for more information on Colbern.)

(Source: *The New York Times*, 14 May 95)

E. THE SEARCH FOR MIDDLE-EASTERN CONSPIRATORS

After the APB was issued, neighbors of a Middle-Eastern man with a brown pick-up truck suspected that their neighbor might be the man whom authorities were looking for. They reported their suspicions to the FBI in Oklahoma City, and a manhunt for the individual got underway. He and several other Arab suspects were looked at as possible accomplices. The Oklahoma City KFOR-TV news team of Jayna Davis and Brad Edwards also looked into this area. (Source: KFOR-TV broadcasts and *The New American*, 01 Sep 95, pg 13)

In their investigation, KFOR-TV interviewed several international terrorism experts who expressed their beliefs that the bombing had "the hallmarks of other bombings...carried out by Islamic terrorists." These experts included Steve Emerson, who wrote and produced the PBS special, *Jihad in America*; which exposed terrorist networks in the U.S.; Laurie Myllroie, former professor at both Harvard and the U.S. Naval War College, who is an expert on Iraq and Islamic terrorism; and Taylor Jesse Clear, former Foreign Service Officer, later assigned to the Counter-Terrorism Directorate in the U.S. Department of Defense. (Source: Al-Hussaini Hussain vs. KFOR-TV et al, Case No. CIV-97-1535-L, U.S. District Court for the Western District of Oklahoma, Partial Judgment entered by Judge Tim Leonard, 17 Nov 99, pg. 9) (See Appendix pgs. 478-484.)

On 21 April, The *Dallas Morning News* reported that, on the night of 19 April, federal agents searched a Dallas apartment where they confiscated several boxes and duffel bags. Three men of Middle-Eastern descent were questioned in Oklahoma City and Dallas in connection with the search. They had been riding in a Chevrolet sports utility vehicle whose license plate belonged to a Chevrolet Cavalier that had been rented at the Dallas-Fort-Worth Airport by one of the men. This man was a resident of New York City, but was originally from Pakistan. (Source: *The Dallas Morning News*, 21 Apr 95)

The following day, FBI Special Agent Henry Gibbons signed a sworn affidavit before U.S. Judge Ronald L. Howland seeking an arrest warrant to detain Abraham Abdullah Ahmad for questioning. (Source: FBI Agent Henry Gibbons' signed affidavit)

1. Abraham Abdullah Ahmad

Two hours after the bombing, a Jordanian national, Abraham (also spelled Ibrahim or Abrahim in some accounts) Abdullah Ahmad was on an American Airlines flight which left Oklahoma City for Chicago, then on to Rome, Italy and finally to Jordan. Airline employees who observed Ahmad in Oklahoma City prior to flight thought he was "acting nervous;" so they contacted the American Airlines National Security Office in Dallas, Texas, who, in turn, contacted the Chicago office of the FBI. Ahmad was detained in Chicago at approximately 12:30 p.m. and was questioned by FBI Agent Chuck Miller. Ahmad contended that "he was traveling to Jordan to discuss his father's planned marriage. He also advised that he was born in Jordan but is a naturalized U.S. citizen." After the interview he was allowed to continue on his trip. He had missed his original connection to Rome, but obtained a flight to London, England.

Meanwhile, Ahmad's luggage continued on the original flight to Rome. Italian officials searched it and found "(a) multiple car radios; (b) a small tool kit and other tools, consistent with use for both explosive devices and normal electronic repair and installation; (d) blue jogging pants and a blue jogging jacket with a floral pattern around the neck; (e) black sweatpants; (f) video cassette recorder, and (g) solder."

When Ahmad arrived in London, authorities determined that he was "ineligible for entry into or transit through England," so they informed the FBI Command Center in Washington, D.C., and returned him to the United States. The FBI then obtained the arrest warrant. When Ahmad arrived back in Chicago, he was again interrogated and released.

(Source: FBI Agent Henry Gibbons' signed affidavit)

Why was Ahmad not investigated further before being released? He was acting suspicious at the airport; his vehicle and his blue jogging suit matched the description given by the original APB witness; his luggage contained potential bomb-making materials; and his return from Jordan could not be assured. He is connected with at least two other potential suspects in this case: Al-Hussaini Hussain (also known as Hussain Al-Hussaini) and Samir Khalil.

2. Samir Khalil

Ahmad's neighbors also pointed to another suspect, Samir Khalil, at whose property management office, a brown pickup truck with tinted windows and a bug shield had been seen. "At one time the federal government thought Khalil might have connections with the Palestine Liberation Organization (PLO)." (Source: Al-Hussaini Hussain vs. KFOR-TV et al, Case No. CIV-97-1535-L, U.S. District Court for the Western District of Oklahoma, Partial Judgment entered by Judge Tim Leonard, 17 Nov 99, pg. 9)

Khalil came to the U.S. on an Israeli passport. He says that he was born in Jerusalem but came to the U.S. from Libya where he grew up. He has amassed a considerable real estate empire consisting largely of HUD housing he rents as low-income units. His ex-wife, Carole

Sue Khalil, (divorced 01 February 1994) worked for the U.S. Department of Agriculture and was killed in the Murrah Building bombing.

Worth noting is a police report dated 03 July 1995, which was filed by Khalil's ex-secretary, Sharon Twilley. In the report, Twilley said she had spoken to KFOR-TV and to the FBI concerning Khalil's employee Al-Hussaini Hussain. Khalil fired her in a rage and then tried to immediately kick her out of one of his HUD houses which she was renting. She forced him to give her a 30-day eviction notice. At 3:00 the next morning, someone came to Twilley's house and fired three shots into her bedroom window and one into her car. She called the police. A neighbor said he saw an Iranian-looking man run from the house and get into a white, extended-bed Toyota pickup like that driven by the landlord (Khalil). Khalil was arrested, but then not charged due to a "lack of evidence." (Source: Oklahoma City Police report, 03 Jul 95) (Appendix pg. 506-509)

3. Al-Hussaini Hussain

Al-Hussaini Hussain

The suspect Ahmad was friendly with one of Khalil's employees, Al-Hussaini Hussain, a recent "refugee" from Iraq who had served in the Iraqi army. He came to Oklahoma City in 1994. An eyewitness identified Hussain from a photograph as the individual driving the brown pickup truck down Robinson that almost ran her over immediately after the bombing. "Law enforcement persons expressed their opinions to [reporter] Davis that Al-Hussaini looked like the sketches of John Doe #2.... [He] has a tattoo of an anchor and snake on his left arm." Hussain claimed that, at the time of the bombing, he was painting a house for his employer in Oklahoma City, and produced a timesheet to prove his claim. However, his co-workers disputed his alibi, and the person who prepared the timesheet later admitted she fabricated it. (Source: Al-Hussaini Hussain vs. KFOR-TV et al, Case No. CIV-97-1535-L, U.S. District Court for the Western District of Oklahoma, Partial Judgment entered by Judge Tim Leonard, 17 Nov 99, pg.10-11)

Hussain, was reportedly seen at a bar in Oklahoma City drinking beer with McVeigh the Saturday before the bombing (Source: KFOR-TV and *The New American*). These witnesses participated in a photo line-up and picked out Hussain (Source: Al-Hussaini Hussain vs. KFOR-TV et al, Case No. CIV-97-1535-L, U.S. District Court for the Western District of Oklahoma, Partial Judgment entered by Judge Tim Leonard, 17 Nov 99, pg. 11)

Hussain refuted the charge, saying that he is Muslim and his religion forbids alcohol. However, a police report on 03 June 1995 (Appendix pg. 495) shows him passed out behind the wheel of a vehicle which had crashed into a curb and was still in "drive" when police officers arrived at the scene. Officers smelled a strong odor of alcohol on his person and found an open beer can in the car. He was given a blood-alcohol test which resulted in a .21 blood-alcohol concentration. This incident occurred just a couple of hundred yards from the bar where Hussain says he has never been. (Source: Oklahoma City Police citation)

4. Middle-Easterners and the Brown Pick-Up Truck

a. Pickup Truck Rented in Dallas

In accordance with Stephen Jones, McVeigh defense attorney,

> *FBI officials in Washington, speaking anonymously, suggested strongly the investigations were focusing on Middle East terrorists . . . among the leads being investigated was a television report of three males of Middle East origin who rented a brown Chevrolet pickup at the Dallas-Fort Worth International Airport. Witnesses have reported seeing three men driving away from the blast area in a similar pickup.*

(Source: Petition to Honorable Richard P. Matsch for Writ of Mandamus for Timothy McVeigh trial, 25 March 1997, page 25,)

b. Truck Abandoned in Oklahoma City

Joe Royers, his wife and 18-year old son lived at the Woodscape Apartments at Northwest 39th and Meridian in Oklahoma City at the time of the bombing. A cul-de-sac is at the back of the apartments and backs up to an old abandoned restaurant, which means it is basically out of sight. This cul-de-sac is rarely used by residents except for those who live at the rear of the apartment complex. Mr. Royers maintains that the brown pickup truck seen speeding away from the bombing site was abandoned at this apartment complex. The following is the Royers' account of events:

About two weeks after the bombing, the FBI interviewed Mr. Royers regarding a yellow pickup truck that had been backed into the cul-de-sac and left abandoned. According to Mr. Royers, about 2:00 that afternoon, he left his apartment and got in his car, which was parked in the cul-de-sac. A man knocked on his car window, showed him FBI identification and asked to speak to him. The agent showed him three photographs of a yellow pickup truck and wanted to know if Royers had seen it. He told them he had.

The FBI agent also interviewed Mrs. Royers. She described the vehicle as being "a real loud, noisy, kind of beat-up looking pickup truck." She saw its driver "straight ahead," 10 to 15 feet away. She described the driver as "olive complected, wavy black or dark hair, and—not kinky or nappy like a black person would have, but more—maybe Italian or something like that or Middle Eastern or whatever." Her husband said the truck had "everything stripped off of it" and was canary yellow "with these great looking wheels and brand new tires on it."

Mr. Royers asked the agent if this had "anything to do with what happened in downtown Oklahoma City?" He was told something to the effect, "Do you remember the APB that was put out? They were looking for a brown pickup truck seen speeding away from downtown Oklahoma City. This is the brown pickup." The agent told him that under the yellow paint, there was brown paint. There were no tag numbers, no stickers—nothing to identify it. They had finger-printed it from top to bottom and had found one print. Royers looked at the photographs again, and he could see where the truck had been over-sprayed on the chrome bumper. The FBI had impounded the pickup, and Brown's Wrecker Service towed it. Royers was informed that it had been towed to either 50 Penn Place on north Pennsylvania Avenue (where FBI offices are located) or to south Eastern (where there is a big Government parking lot).

OKBIC Note: During cross-examination in the Nichols' trial, FBI agent James Elliott answered questions about a yellow Chevrolet pickup truck that was brought into the Evidence Recovery Center, a warehouse in downtown Oklahoma City. He testified that

> It was recovered—It was a stolen vehicle, as it turned out, and was returned to an individual. I don't know all the ins and outs of why it was brought there. I know it was examined, and the vehicle—I was present when it was being examined. The vehicle identification numbers and all the identification numbers had been destroyed except for one number.

On the morning of the bombing, Mr. And Mrs. Royers were both home and felt the blast from the bomb. After he knew what had caused it, Mr. Royers went outside with his son's portable police scanner. He ran into a Middle-Eastern man coming down the stairs, and, "kind of in jest," said, "Oh, boy, all this excitement is more than my old heart can take." The man just looked at him, then looked away and kept walking. The apartment the man came from was rented at the time by a man with the last name of Ahmad (not Abraham Abdullah Ahmad discussed above). According to the Royers' son, there were six or seven people in and out of the apartment all the time. Their subsequent conversation with the apartment manager revealed that the Ahmads had skipped out, owing rent on the apartment, sometime between 01 May and 01 June 1995.

The following day, 20 April, Mrs. Royers flew to Chicago. Her husband took her to the airport about 6:30 that morning. Upon his return to the apartment, the yellow pickup passed by him. He did not get a look at the driver because Royers' car sits low to the ground, and his attention was on the truck and the wheels because they did not seem to belong together—and the truck just "definitely did not fit in our parking lot where we live" because "most of the cars are like, you know, Honda Accords, and they're upscale-type vehicles," he commented.

On 22 April, Mrs. Royers returned from Chicago, and Mr. Royers returned on the 23rd from Texas where he had gone. Then on the next evening, 24 April, Mrs. Royer was walking her dog when she saw the yellow pickup pull in with the same driver and back into a parking space in the cul-de-sac. As he was backing the truck, he looked at her, then stared straight ahead. (Mr. Royers said the FBI found her description of how the truck was parked to be consistent with the way they found it.)

On the morning of 25 April, Mr. Royers again saw the yellow pickup truck while he was walking the dog. That evening the truck was impounded by the FBI. It had been reported to the police by a man employed by the apartment complex. The police, apparently, reported it to the FBI.

After the FBI visit, Mrs. Royers asked an acquaintance, an art teacher, to sketch a likeness of the pickup driver based on her description. The only thing she did not like about the completed drawing was the nose. This was **not** the same individual seen in the John Doe #2 sketch. The Royers called the FBI to tell them about the sketch they had made, but the FBI agent never returned their call. Therefore, they contacted Dave Ballew at KWTV in Oklahoma City, a CBS affiliate. Ballew did a local news story on the Royerses that aired on a Sunday.

OKBIC Note: The Tuesday after the program aired, Ballew was fired, ostensibly for using an audio from NBC regarding the all points bulletin.

Three months later on the 26th of July, while walking the dog, Mrs. Royers said she again saw the man from the yellow pickup, and their eyes met. This time he was driving a car. She took down his license plate number, and a friend ran a check on it. It belonged to a red Honda Prelude out of Piedmont, Oklahoma (a small community northwest of Oklahoma City). The car that the tag was on was not the car it was registered to.

Knowing that the man she saw was probably connected to the bombing, that he had driven through the parking lot again three months after the yellow truck had been impounded and that he knew she had seen him, Mrs. Royers became afraid for her safety and went to stay in Tennessee for awhile.

(Source: Taped interview with Glenn Wilburn & William F. Jasper)

F. THE SEARCH FOR WHITE SUPREMIST CONSPIRATORS

Timothy McVeigh, Terry Nichols and Michael Fortier all held similar anti-Government views. Many of these same views are held by white-supremacist, para-military and militant extremist groups. McVeigh, Nichols and Fortier were reported to have associated with people from these groups, though there is no record that they ever formally joined any of them. McVeigh especially is linked to people associated with some of these organizations. There has been much speculation that McVeigh was working with one or more of these organizations to blow up the Murrah Building and that much of his financing came from them. Some of the major possibilities in this area are given below:

1. Stephen Colbern

Stephen G. Colbern was arrested on an outstanding federal weapons charge from California on 13 May 1995 for possession of a knife, an assault rifle, a silencer, two loaded pistols, and a device to convert a semi-automatic weapon to fully automatic. The arrest occurred in Oatman, Arizona, a small mining town about 20 miles southwest of Kingman, Arizona. (Timothy McVeigh had periodically stayed with Michael Fortier in Kingman, and Colbern admits to knowing McVeigh under his alias of Tim Tuttle.) When agents searched Colbern's trailer house and an outbuilding in Oatman, they found a laboratory for making the drug methamphetamine, several cases of ammunition (including cases holding link-belt rounds for machine guns), cases of rifle and handgun bullets (some stamped "China"), unspecified stolen medical supplies, and several boxes of documents which, the FBI said, included "some interesting paperwork."

At the time of his arrest, Colbern had been living in Oatman for about four months, working as a dishwasher and cook's helper at the Oatman Mining Company's Food and Spirits Restaurant. Formerly he was a research associate in DNA studies at Cedars-Sinai Research Institute in Los Angeles, California. He holds a degree in chemistry from the University of California at Los Angeles. He grew up in Oxnard, northwest of Los Angeles, where an acquaintance said that "He did talk about explosives....He was just interested in those sorts of things. He just liked making things go boom." He was described as being "very strange, very smart, kind of nerdish, kind of lonerish." Another person said he was "very quiet, kind of a loner, and very strong." A third person said that Colbern had expressed anti-Government and pro-Nazi sympathies, and he was convinced that Colbern "was not too happy with our government."

Witnesses state that Colbern had been out of town for two or three weeks at the time of the Oklahoma City bombing. However, one of Colbern's roommates, Preston Scott Haney, said, "...he was sitting right next to me when the bomb went off. And he was here the week before and the week after." However, his boss, Lou Mauro, said Colbern had been gone the week of the bombing, explaining that he had to visit his mother who had had a stroke in Los Angeles, and that he did not return until the weekend of 22 April.
(Source: *The New York Times*, 14 May 95)

OKBIC Note: On the day of the bombing, was Colbern in Oatman with Preston Scott Haney or in California visiting his mother—or—was he in Oklahoma City?)

2. The Kehoe Brothers

The Kehoe Brothers, Chevie (age 22 at the time of the bombing) and Cheyne (age 18 in 1995) are white supremacists. Chevie Kehoe, of Colville, Washington, and his friend, Daniel Lee, were charged in a federal case in Arkansas for "participating in the Aryan Peoples Republic" and "using robbery and murders" to "foment revolution and create a whites-only nation." Daniel Lee, also known as Danny Graham (age 22 in 1995), is from Yukon, Oklahoma, a small town just west of Oklahoma City on Interstate-40, and just east of El Reno, which houses the federal penitentiary where McVeigh was incarcerated before being transferred to Denver. (Source: *The Daily Oklahoman*, 07 Jan 98, pg. 3)

Cheyne Kehoe claims that his older brother Chevie knew about the Oklahoma City bombing before it occurred. A former motel manager in Spokane, Washington makes the same claim. He said that several days before the bombing, Chevie had mentioned there would be something happening on the 19th and it would "wake people up." The manager said that, on 19 April 1995, about 45 minutes before the bombing, Chevie came in wanting to watch CNN. When the bombing was reported, Chevie was characterized as ecstatic. In an interview with *The Spokesman Review,* a newspaper in Spokane, Washington, the manager quoted Chevie as saying, "It was about time." The motel manager also claimed that Chevie arranged to have a man named Tim stay at the motel several months before the bombing. He stated, "I'm 75 percent certain it was him, McVeigh, but I could be wrong." (Source: *The Oklahoma Gazette,* 18 Feb 98)

The Kehoe brothers and their father were charged in a series of crimes across the Midwest. At 1:30 p.m. on 15 February 1997, Cheyne and Chevie Kehoe opened fire on police officers in Wilmington, Ohio, about 45 miles northeast of Cincinnati. According to police officers, they had been stopped for a routine registration check when they began firing, using semi-automatic weapons. They escaped but abandoned the Chevrolet Suburban they were driving. A search of the vehicle produced six guns, more than 4,000 rounds of ammunition, bullet-resistant vests and a large amount of military-type gear.

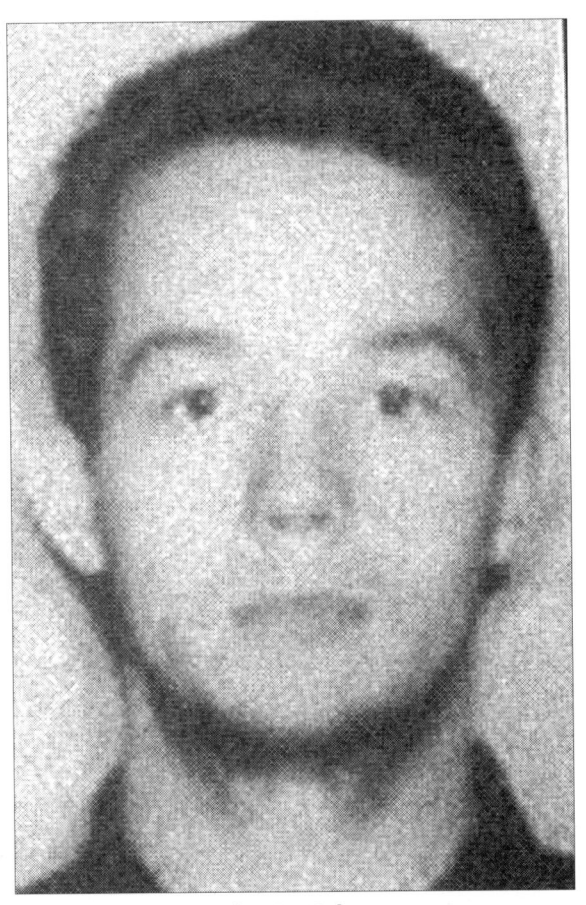

Chevie Kehoe

A check on the Suburban revealed that it was registered to a Sean Michael Haines, known as a youth leader for "The Aryan Nation" in Spokane, Washington. Haines had been arrested in Sioux Falls, South Dakota two months earlier. When stopped for a traffic violation, authorities had found an AR-15 rifle in his possession. Sheriff Jay Winters suspected that it might be one of more than $40,000 worth of weapons and munitions that had been stolen in April 1995 from William Mueller, a gun-parts dealer from Tilley, Arkansas. Mueller, his wife and eight-year old daughter had been murdered and their bodies found by a fisherman in a bayou near Russelville, Arkansas. Haines told authorities that he had swapped for the gun with Chevie Kehoe the previous summer.

On 12 December 1996, Haines was held over for a $50,000 bail hearing. He disappeared on 30 December without ever having posted bond. Chevie Kehoe and Danny Lee were later charged with these murders.

A second Mueller gun, a .45-caliber pistol, was recovered in the spring of 1996 in a Seattle pawnshop. The man who pawned the pistol told police that he had purchased the gun from Kirby Kehoe, Cheyne and Chevie's father.

On 19 February 1997, a 16-count indictment by a county grand jury charged Cheyne and Chevie with assault, attempted murder and other charges. The Kehoe brothers took flight and avoided authorities during a manhunt that stretched across several western states. They were believed to have made their separate ways back to a local campground where their wives and children were staying, and, from there, drove to Indianapolis in a white camper which they abandoned in Casper, Wyoming. (A search of the camper turned up components for bombs, but no detonators.) Police believe that a white car with Montana license plates picked up the Kehoes and their families and traveled to a separatist compound in Belen, New Mexico, the hometown of Peter and Tony Ward of Elohim City. (The Ward brothers were identified by ATF informant Carol Howe as being John Doe #1 and #2.) From New Mexico, the Kehoes and their families went north to their usual haunts in eastern Washington and western Idaho.

Four months after their indictment, on 16 June 1996, in Coleville, Washington, Cheyne Kehoe turned himself in after a brief negotiation between authorities and a family friend. His older brother Chevie was arrested without incident a day later in Cedar City, Utah. Chevie was taken to Salt Lake City where he was arraigned on federal charges: unlawful flight to avoid prosecution, several charges of possession of stolen firearms, and one count of unlawful possession of a machine gun. Cheyne was charged with attempted murder, felonious assault and carrying a concealed weapon. Soon after this, Cheyne began to implicate his older brother, saying Chevie was the one involved in the Mueller murders. (See Appendix pg. 502-503.)

The Kehoe brothers, their father and Daniel Lee were indicted in July 1998 on 57 separate crimes, including five murders   Additionally, Lee and the Kehoes were charged with setting off a bomb in front of City Hall in Spokane, Washington in April 1996.

(Source: *The Oklahoma Gazette*, 18 Feb 98; & *AP*, 21 Jan 98)

OKBIC Note: How did Chevie Kehoe know in advance about the Oklahoma City bombing? Was he part of the plot? Did the robbery of Mueller help finance the bombing?

3. Elohim City

Elohim City (Hebrew for "City of God") is a compound in eastern Oklahoma just off Interstate-40 near Muldrow, Oklahoma, close to the Arkansas border. It consists of 240 acres of largely undeveloped land, and houses between 25 and 30 families. Robert Millar, a Canadian, is its founder and leader. Elohim City is listed in the publication *Terrorist & Extremist Organizations in the United States* as preaching white supremacy, polygamy and the overthrow of the U.S. Government. Millar has said that they are "racial purists." They believe the white race to be God's "chosen people."

Elohim City, reportedly, has close ties with other extremist groups, including "The Christian Identity Movement" and "The Covenant, the Sword and the Arm of the Lord" (CSA). The CSA's second-in-command, Terry Noble, who later left the militia movement, has said that, prior to Millar becoming involved with their organization, Elohim City had no weapons; but that changed after their association, and the CSA provided Elohim City residents with weapons training. Many of the members of these groups and people on their fringes stayed at Elohim City either as residents or guests. (Source: Television production, "The Fifth Estate," by the Canadian Broadcasting Corporation)

In the days and weeks before the bombing (19 April 1995), Elohim City was rife with people who had motives to strike a blow against the United States. And 19 April held special significance to many of them who would have felt that retaliation was appropriate and 19 April was the perfect date. The significant events attached to this date were (1) the start of the American Revolution (19 April 1775), (2) the government raid on the CSA (19 April 1985), (3) the Government raid on the Branch Davidians in Waco, Texas (19 April 1993) and (4) the execution of Richard Snell (19 April 1995). Biographical sketches on some of the Elohim City residents/guests follow:

a. Richard Snell

The CSA had strong anti-Government feelings and was dedicated to the violent overthrow of the U.S. Government. According to Terry Noble, in 1983, the CSA was planning to bomb the Alfred P. Murrah Building in Oklahoma City. CSA leader, Jim Ellison, and another influential CSA member, Richard Snell, had decided it was the perfect building for their purposes because it housed many Government agencies, had little security, and would cause a big impact because it would not be an expected target. They planned to use a rocket launcher for the attack.

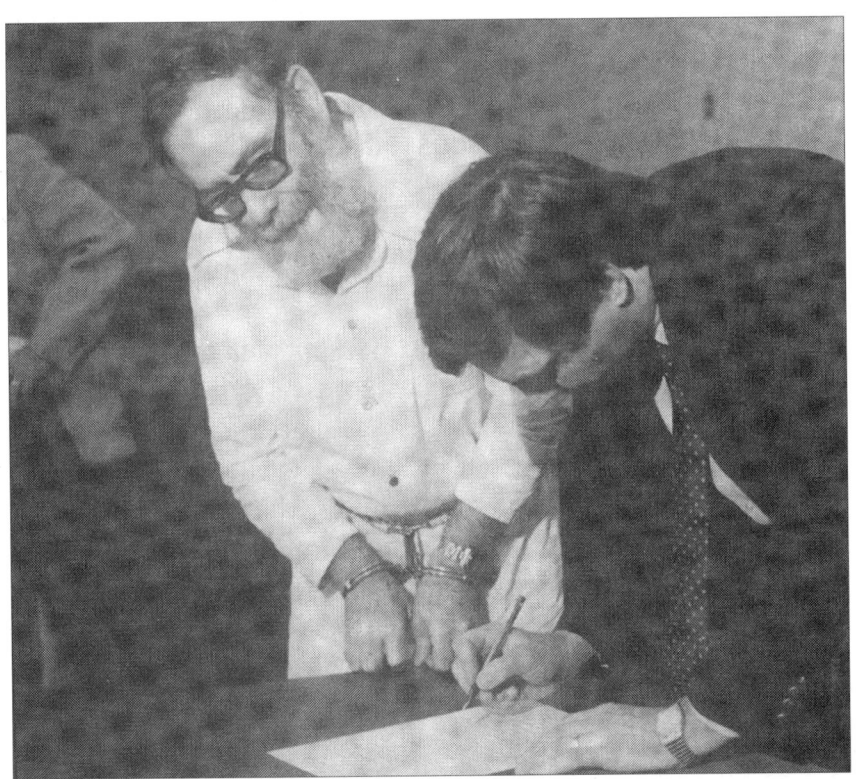

Richard Snell (left), April 19, 1995, the day of his execution

On 19 April 1985—exactly 10 years before the Murrah Building bombing—the Government conducted a raid on the CSA, and their Arkansas compound was surrounded by federal agents. Millar from Elohim City went to Arkansas to lend moral support. The compound eventually surrendered. Leaders Jim Ellison, Terry Noble and Richard Snell were arrested.

Snell was later convicted and sentenced to death for the murder of a pawn-broker he erroneously thought to be Jewish. While awaiting execution in Arkansas, he wrote a newsletter for the militia. On his list of "approved visitors" was his "spiritual advisor," Robert Millar.

Snell's execution took place on 19 April 1995—the very day of the Oklahoma City bombing. Millar had warned the Government that 19 April was a bad day to execute Snell and advised delaying the execution. Snell himself predicted that there would be catastrophic events on that day. He said the governor would regret not changing the date. He also warned of a bomb. On the day of his execution, Snell's "death watch log" reported that, at 12:20 p.m., Snell asked that the TV be turned on. He watched coverage of the Oklahoma City bombing. The 12:30 report said that he smiled and chuckled as he was watching the coverage.

One of his last statements before he was put to death was, "Governor, look over your shoulder. Justice is coming!" He also stated, "Snell has victory. I am at peace." Millar took Snell's body to Elohim City for burial. Several members of the CSA now reside at Elohim City.

Terry Noble, interviewed by "The Fifth Estate," said that older leaders of the militia movement had been pressuring younger members to do something dramatic during their lifetime. He believes the militia was behind the Oklahoma City bombing. McVeigh's attorney, Stephen Jones, theorized, "Did someone decide to give the old man [Snell] a going-away gift?"

(Source: Television production, "The Fifth Estate," by the Canadian Broadcasting Corp.)

b. Andreas "Andy" Strassmeir

Andreas Strassmeir (also known as Andrew Strassmeyer) is a German national whose grandfather helped found the Nazi Party in Germany but whose father was Secretary of State for West Germany and a member of the Christian Democrat Coalition. Strassmeir himself was a former lieutenant in Germany's Panzer Grenadiers (similar to the U.S. Special Forces) and was trained in military intelligence (Source: *The Oklahoma City Bombing and the Politics of Terror*, David Hoffman, Feral House, 1998, pg. 122).

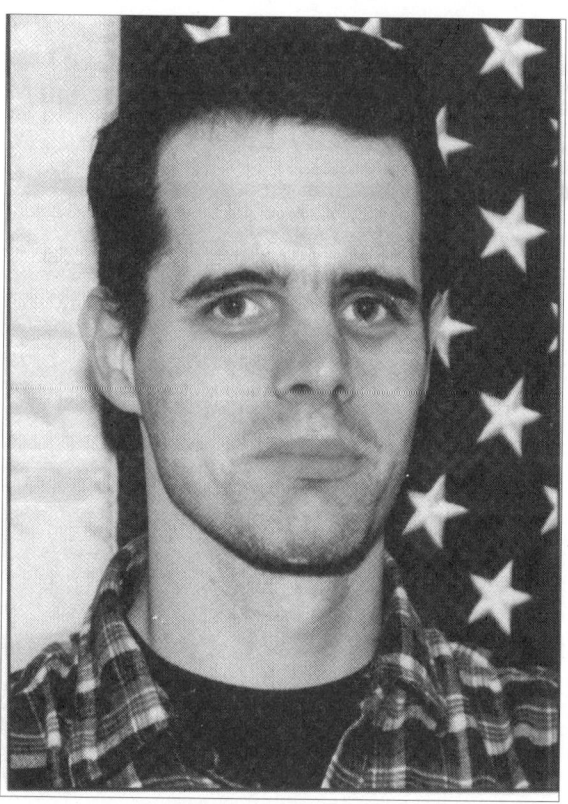

Andreas Strassmeir

Strassmeir first visited the United States in 1989. In 1991 he again came to the U.S. on a three-month visa (which was never extended). An acquaintance, retired USAF Col. Vincent Petruskie, tried to help him get a job with the DEA or the Department of Treasury, but apparently was unsuccessful. Strassmeir then went to Texas where he landed a job with a computer company. While there, he became associated with the extreme fringes of the Christian right.

(Source: *The Secret life of Bill Clinton*, Ambrose Evans-Pritchard, Regnery Publishing Co., 1997)

According to journalist and author Ambrose Evans-Pritchard, Strassmeir was associated with the Texas Light Infantry. In an interview with a member of this organization, Evans-Pritchard says he learned that some members of the group thought that Strassmeir was an ATF informant, so they followed him one night. Strassmeir was seen going into a federal building where the ATF office was located. There were electronic locks on the door, and they saw Strassmeir punch in a code. The door unlocked and he went inside. *(Source: The Secret Life of Bill Clinton, Ambrose Evans-Pritchard, Regnery Publishing, Inc., 1997, pg. 81-82)*

Ambrose Evans-Pritchard says that Strassmeir had a Special Status of "AO" in the Immigration and Naturalization Service (INS) computers. (He did not explain what status AO meant.) As of 28 April 1995, AO showed on all his entries into the United States; but, a "printout dated March 18, 1996, shows that somebody had gone back into the system and altered the entries," deleting the AO. *(Source: The Secret Life of Bill Clinton, Ambrose Evans-Pritchard, Regnery Publishing, Inc., 1997, pg. 81)*

In February 1992, Strassmeir was given a traffic ticket outside of Elohim City. His car had no license plate and was impounded. The trooper searched the car and found a briefcase that contained what he "suspected were classified government documents." The tow truck operator, Kenny Pence, then became "inundated" with phone calls from people in the Government to release the car back to Strassmeir. Pence said he received calls from a military base in the Carolinas and from the State Department. (Source: The *Oklahoma Gazette*, 13 Feb 1997)

According to *Media Bypass* magazine, a high-level FBI source told them that "ATF computer 'indices' reflect 'substantial' intelligence-gathering activities in which Strassmeir participated." He further stated that "Either Andy is their snitch or he is under investigation and has been for a long time.... And considering the fact that it was Strassmeir that McVeigh made the call to...well, why do you suppose he wasn't interviewed right after that became known?...Could it be that Andy's being protected?" (Source: *Media Bypass*, Sep 96, pg. 13)

OKBIC Note: The phone call referenced above is reflected on the Bridges calling card record, showing that a call was made from McVeigh's motel in Kingman, Arizona to Elohim City on 05 April 1995 at 3:43 p.m. (Source: McVeigh trial, Exhibit 554). Rev. Millar at first denied that they had received a call from McVeigh; but, when confronted with the phone records, he said that conversations with members had revealed that a call might have been received for an individual named "Andy," a nickname for Strassmeir. Strassmeir admits to meeting McVeigh and selling him a military knife at a gun show McVeigh attended with Roger Moore. He also thinks he may have given a business card to McVeigh with his Elohim City phone number. (Source: Various news broadcasts)

Strassmeir may have actually met McVeigh earlier than the gun show. Although he claims that he has never been to Herington, Kansas, Catina Lawson and her mother, Connie Smith, tell of McVeigh, Strassmeir and a friend named Michael Brescia attending parties at their homes during the summer of 1992. (Source: OKBIC interviews with Catina Lawson and Connie Smith) (Page 148 in the chapter on "Eyewitnesses" gives more on this association.)

Strassmeir came to Elohim City in 1992 where some say he became Chief of Security in weapons training. Joan Millar (Millar's daughter-in-law) described Strassmeir as having "a very exact manner, always walking as if on parade, never relaxed." She said that Strassmeir was not in charge of security, but only of training for the security patrols. (Nichols trial transcript, pg. 13709-13731

In late 1993, German officials were concerned with the activities of Strassmeir, so FBI Director Louis Freeh and another individual went to Germany to meet with German internal security officials. The German officials said that Strassmeir had been "nation hopping" between Germany and the U.S. and that they were concerned with his association with the neo-Nazi movement. The FBI advised the Germans that they were monitoring his activities, but because of First Amendment considerations, there was nothing they could do. (Source: *Others Unknown*, Stephen Jones & Peter Israel, Public Affairs, 1998, pg. 152)

Michael Brescia

c. Michael Brescia

According to correspondent Ambrose Evans-Pritchard in *Foreign News*, 30 June 1996, Michael Brescia is "tanned, tattooed, and muscular." Some witnesses say that he is John Doe #2.

Brescia comes from a Catholic family in Pennsylvania where his father was a battalion chief in the Philadelphia Fire Department. He was an Eagle Scout and attended a private high school. A rock musician, he formed "a speed metal band" named "Cyanide" (Source: *The Oklahoma City Bombing and the Politics of Terror*, David Hoffman, Feral House, 1998, pg121). For college, Brescia attended La Salle University in Philadelphia where he studied finance and was a member of Delta Sigma Pi fraternity. Fraternity brother, George Ralko, told

Evans-Pritchard that Brescia was "a very outgoing, likeable guy, but he tried to set up a white supremacy group on campus." The fraternity threatened to revoke his membership and told him "the fraternity wouldn't tolerate that kind of behavior."

In his third year at LaSalle, Brescia dropped out and told friends he was taking a job offer in Oklahoma. He actually joined the community in Elohim City where he shared a house with Andrew Strassmeir. Eventually, he married the granddaughter of Millar, Elohim City's leader.

(Source: *The Secret Life of Bill Clinton*, Ambrose Evans-Pritchard, Regnery Publishing, Inc., 1997, pg. 100-105)

On the day following the bombing, Brescia was identified to the FBI as John Doe #2 by Catina Lawson, a college student and acquaintance of both McVeigh and Brescia. She often attended parties in Kansas that McVeigh also attended. Her mother, Connie Smith, confirms the identification. Lawson said she told the FBI that the sketch was a man named "Mike" whom she knew in Kansas, but because she could not remember his last name at the time, they (the FBI) made her feel ignorant, as if she did not know what she was talking about. Later, when shown a picture of Michael Brescia by a family member of one of the bombing victims, she immediately identified him as the man she had told the FBI about. She contacted the FBI again, but they did not return her call. (Source: OKBIC interviews with Lawson and Smith)

OKBIC Note: Not until February of 1996 did the FBI talk to Lawson again. As of that date, they had still not talked to Brescia. It is unknown if they have ever spoken to him regarding the bombing.

OKBIC Note: McVeigh, Strassmeir and Brescia were seen at the Lady Godiva strip club in Tulsa, Oklahoma on 08 April 1995. Five women who worked at the club were interviewed. At least one waitress and two dancers positively identified the three men from photographs. The waitress was caught on tape with the dressing room camera on 08 April telling another employee about her customer who told her, "You're going to remember me on April 19, 1995. You're going to remember me for the rest of your life." He reportedly told her his name was Timothy McVeigh. (Source: Canadian Broadcasting Corp. television production, *The Fifth Estate*)

OKBIC Note: Brescia was living at Elohim City at the time of the bombing. Andreas Strassmeir claimed that, on 19 April, Brescia was attending a clemency rally for Wayne Snell in Little Rock, Arkansas. And on the day that the Ryder truck was rented, according to Joan Millar, wife of Bruce Millar (Rev. Millar's son), Brescia was in Elohim City "helping to prepare the grave for Wayne Snell." (Source: *The Secret Life of Bill Clinton*, Ambrose Evans-Pritchard, Regnery Publishing, Inc., 1997, pg. 104)

OKBIC Note: Elohim City's leader, Millar, asked Strassmeir and Brescia to leave the compound about three months after the bombing. According to Dennis Mahon (see below), Brescia went to live in Canada (Source: *The New American*, 28 Oct 96). Strassmeir's attorney, Kirk Lyons of Houston, Texas and North Carolina, admitted he spirited Strassmeir out of the

U.S. via Mexico, France and then Germany. He said it would be easier to defend Strassmeir in Germany than from a federal prison in the U.S. (Source: *Others Unknown*, Stephen Jones & Peter Israel, Public Affairs, N.Y., 1998, pg. 152)

d. Dennis Mahon

Dennis Mahon

Another resident at Elohim City was Dennis Mahon. He was the third person in authority in the White Aryan Resistance (WAR) movement and a former imperial wizard of the Ku Klux Klan. He has referred to the Oklahoma City bombing as a "fine thing." He also said, "I hate the federal government with a perfect hatred. If I had a nuclear bomb, I'd put it in a truck and drive it right up to the Capitol Building in Washington and blow it all up, me included...." (Source: T.V. program *Hard Copy*, as reported in The New American, 24 Jun 96, pg. 7)

Mahon had previously lived in Michigan, approximately 100 miles from the Decker, Michigan farm where Terry Nichols and his brother James lived, and where McVeigh had stayed for long periods of time. Mahon, reportedly, had "experimented with blowing up a vehicle loaded with ammonium nitrate." (Source: *Others Unknown*, Stephen Jones & Peter Israel, Public Affairs, N.Y., 1998, pg. 74)

Mahon and Strassmeir were close friends, and Mahon traveled extensively in Germany. Mahon was also an associate of Gary Lauck who was arrested in Germany for smuggling pro-Nazi propaganda into Germany, where this type of literature is against the law. In his manifesto, *Strategy, Propaganda and Organization*, Lauck described organizing worldwide extremist groups into a tight network and providing "military education with terrorist aims." He had frequent contacts with Islamic terrorist groups. Mahon seemed to take his message to heart. During Operation Desert Storm, he produced several videotapes opposing U.S. policy in Iraq. As a result, he admittedly received monthly allotments from Iraq. After Lauck's arrest, Mahon made several trips to Germany to help establish a chapter of WAR in Stockholm, Sweden to help smuggle terrorist information into Germany. Source: *Others Unknown*, Stephen Jones & Peter Israel, Public Affairs, N.Y., 1998, & *The Oklahoma City Bombing and the Politics of Terror*, David Hoffman, Feral House, 1998, pg156)

Canada and Britain banned Mahon from their countries because Interpol classified him as an "international terrorist." (Source: *Others Unknown*, Stephen Jones & Peter Israel, Public Affairs, N.Y., 1998, pg. 157)

Mahon was a friend and former lover of ATF informant Carol Howe. He met Howe after she called his "Dial-a-Racist" phone line. Howe went with him to Elohim City and infiltrated the compound. She reported that Mahon discussed with her "targeting federal installations for destruction through bombings, such as the IRS building, the Tulsa federal building, and the

Oklahoma City federal building." Mahon and Andrew Strassmeir made trips to Oklahoma City in November and December 1994, and again in February 1995. Howe accompanied them on the December trip. (Source: *McCurtain Daily Gazette* of Idabel, Oklahoma & ABC News Primetime, 10 Dec 97)

Due to Howe's reports, the ATF was planning a raid on Elohim City. Millar was aware of this potential, and admitted his fears to two local sheriffs, complaining of increased aerial over-flights of the compound. "Spotters" were stationed throughout the property to watch for law enforcement vehicular traffic, and police broadcasts were monitored. Reportedly, people within the compound had vowed that it would not become another Waco and that they would strike first in a "Holy War." Was the Murrah Building their first strike? (Source: *McCurtain Daily Gazette* of Idabel, Oklahoma & ABC News Primetime, 10 Dec 97)

OKBIC Note: In a series of ATF field reports dated 27 and 28 February and 06 March 1995, it is apparent that some ATF and FBI field and supervisory personnel at the state and regional levels became aware for the first time that each of the agencies had an agent(s) who had infiltrated Elohim City. After a series of quickly called meetings between Dave Roberts, Resident-Agent-in-Charge (RAC) of the ATF office in Tulsa, Steve Lewis, U.S. Attorney in Tulsa and Bob Ricks, RAC of the FBI in Oklahoma City, a decision was made to terminate the "sting operation" at Elohim City, and the ATF raid did not take place. However, with the validity of her reports proven, immediately after the Oklahoma City bombing, Howe was brought to the bombing command headquarters and paid to go back to Elohim City to gather more information—this time at the direction of the FBI. Her usefulness as an informant came to an end when her employment with the ATF leaked to the press and it became public that she intended to testify for the defense in the trial of Timothy McVeigh regarding the happenings at Elohim City. (Source: *McCurtain Daily Gazette* of Idabel, Oklahoma & ABC News Primetime, 10 Dec 97))

After McVeigh's arrest, while talking to journalist J. D. Cash, Mahon made a tape for McVeigh. Cash had told Mahon that he had a pass to visit McVeigh and would slip the tape to him. Part of the tape stated that McVeigh should "accept his 'sacrifice,' even if he was guilty by reason of entrapment." The journalist turned the tape over to McVeigh's attorney. (Source: The Secret Life of Bill Clinton, Ambrose Evans-Pritchard, Regnery Publishing, Inc., 1997, pg. 51)

e. Mid-West Bank Robbers

Elohim City has been a temporary home to six individuals charged in a series of Mid-Western bank robberies which allegedly were made for The Aryan Revolutionary Army to fund their activities. The spree of bank robberies began sometime prior to January

Richard Lee Guthrie

1994. In all, 22 banks and armored cars were robbed in seven states—14 or 15 of which happened before the Oklahoma City bombing. An estimated total of $250,000 was stolen over a two-year period.

There has been some speculation that these robberies helped finance the Oklahoma City bombing. Timothy McVeigh's sister, Jennifer, signed a statement on 02 May 1995 in which she stated that Tim had asked her to launder some one-hundred-dollar bills for him. He told her he had gotten them from his share of the proceeds in helping to plan a bank robbery.

The "Bank Bandits," as they were sometimes called in the press, were known to carefully case their targets. They wore Halloween masks and left dummy bombs, often disguised as baskets. Using fake birth certificates to acquire social security cards of dead people, they then obtained drivers' licenses under these fake names, usually in Iowa where procedures were somewhat lax. They also registered their cars to fake businesses as a way to avoid suspicion by authorities if stopped, and rented "safe houses" that were used as headquarters. The first was in Pittsburg, Kansas. The second was at 585 Reinhard Avenue on Columbus, Ohio's south side. They also rented storage lockers to keep weapons, explosives, fake identification, disguises and other gear. The original known leaders of these "Bank Bandits" were Richard Guthrie and Peter Langan. J.D. Cash gave the following information in articles in the *McCurtain Daily Gazette*:

1). Richard L. "Wild Bill" Guthrie, Jr.

With the help of a Government source (Shawn Kenney, a soldier from Cincinnati) Guthrie was arrested on 15 January 1996. With Guthrie's help, Langan was arrested three days later on 18 January 1996.

2). Peter "Commander Pedro" Langan

The son of a CIA employee, Peter Langan was arrested in November 1992 for the robbery of a Pizza Hut restaurant in Lavonia, Georgia. He supposedly was released as a result of Secret Service involvement on his behalf. Then, on 18 January 1996, Langan was again arrested, this time for the Midwest bank robberies. His arrest occurred after a brief shootout with police behind the Reinhard Avenue residence. He was charged with the 1994 bank robberies in Columbus and Springdale, Ohio.

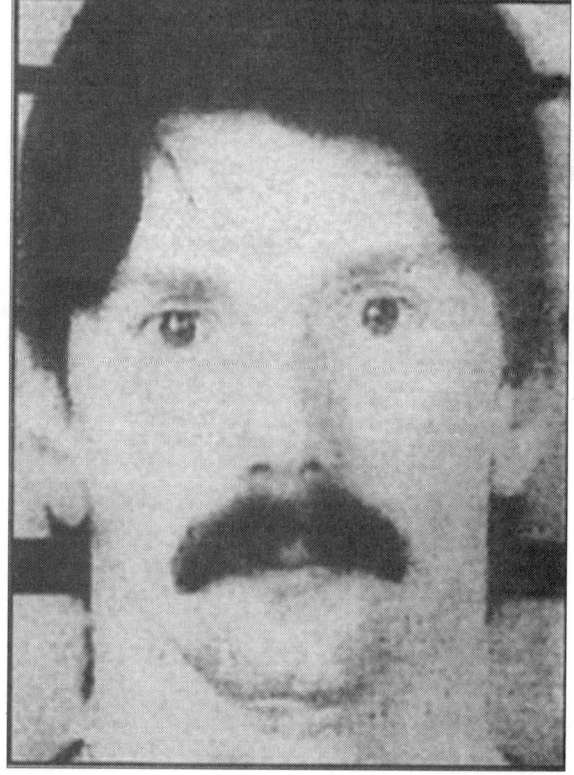

Peter Langan

In pre-trial hearings, it was brought out that the Government source, Kenney, had a long-standing relationship with Guthrie and Langan going back to 1991. He had been invited to join the gang in 1993, but declined because he had a wife and child. Kenney was said to have accompanied Langan and Guthrie in 1994 when they cased a bank near Cincinnati and armored cars in Arkansas. Reportedly Kenney even visited Langan in jail after Langan was arrested. Kenney denied all of the allegations. During pre-trial hearings, FBI agent Ed Woods said that he had interviewed Kenney a couple of weeks before Langan's arrest and Kenney had passed two polygraphs.

On 11 August 1996, Langan's attorneys asked that Guthrie be transferred from the Kentucky jail where he was being held to Ohio where Langan stood trial. The following day, Richard Guthrie was found hanged in his Kentucky prison cell. (Source: *Rocky Mountain News*, 19 Apr 98)

3). Mark Thomas

Mark Thomas is from Berks County, Pennsylvania. He was a part-time truck driver with an eighth-grade education. For the previous 25 years, he had been involved with such organizations as the Ku Klux Klan, the Aryan Nation and the Aryan Republican Army. He was the leader of the "Posse Comitatus" in Pennsylvania, another extremist organization, and had a farm in Longswamp Township near Allentown, Pennsylvania where he regularly hosted white-supremacist rallies. He has spent time at both Ruby Ridge, Idaho and Elohim City, Oklahoma, where he was the Thursday before the Oklahoma City bombing. At one time he had an internet site called *The Watchman*.

Thomas was arrested in January 1997 for conspiracy and for receiving proceeds from the bank robberies, and pled innocent. Then, on 18 February, he changed his plea to guilty and promised cooperation with authorities.

OKBIC Note: Upon hearing the news of Mark Thomas' cooperation with authorities, Dennis Mahon stated to the press that he "was disappointed he [Thomas] cracked so quickly," that he had "possibly ruined 25 years of development in the Aryan movement." Mahon, however, went ahead and sent funds to Thomas' wife who was pregnant at the time and also had a one-and-a-half year old child.

4). Kevin McCarthy

Later in February, Kevin McCarthy, originally of Philadelphia, pled guilty to robbing a Missouri bank and in helping to plan five other robberies. For more than six months, McCarthy cooperated with prosecutors to help convict at least two of his fellow bank robbers, Scott Stedeford and Peter Langan.

OKBIC Note: Both McCarthy and Guthrie gave information about another individual, previously unknown to have been involved in the Wisconsin robbery, Michael Brescia.

5). Scott Stedeford

Scott Stedeford, originally of Camden, New Jersey, was the first of the bank robbers to be sentenced in Iowa, a week previous to McCarthy's plea hearing. He was convicted of bank robbery in a West Des Moines, Iowa heist. A prosecution witness, Stephen Musich of Toledo, Ohio, testified about another bank robbery the gang had pulled in Sylvania, Ohio where he saw two of the masked bandits flee the bank. Jurors also heard an audio-tape made by Stedeford about details of a planned bank robbery in Minneapolis.

4. OTHER POSSIBLE ACCOMPLICES

There are other people and organizations with connections to McVeigh in one form or another who may have had involvement with the Oklahoma City bombing. Two of these are presented below:

a. The National Alliance

Records of the Bridge's debit card, owned jointly by McVeigh and Nichols, show a call from the Imperial Motel in Kingman, Arizona, where McVeigh was staying at the time, to the Ryder truck rental company in Lake Havasu, Arizona on 05 April at 3:43 p.m. Three minutes later, the call to Elohim City was made from the motel. At 10:44 p.m. and again at 11:03 p.m., calls were made to the National Alliance in Mohave Valley, Arizona. Both these calls lasted three minutes and 36 seconds. Another call on 06 April lasted three minutes and 22 seconds. Five more calls were placed on the 6th to the National Alliance and one on the 7th. These calls were either not answered or lasted only a few seconds each. The National Alliance is an extremist group headed by William Pierce. Pierce is the author of *The Turner Diaries*, the book characterized by the government as the "blueprint" for the Oklahoma City bombing. Was there a National Alliance involvement with the bombing? Or was McVeigh simply looking for a place to hide out afterthe bombing?

b. Robert "Jacks"

The FBI found the name Robert Jacks with numerous spellings in Marife Nichols' notebook. (Source: Nichols trial, pg. 7875) The FBI began searching for a Robert Jacks. According to *The Rocky Mountain News*, "the FBI has checked hundreds of people's backgrounds simply because their last names are Jacks, Jacques, Jacquez, or Jocques." They "analyzed statewide computer downloads of drivers' records, license photos, motor vehicle registrations and criminal rap sheets,... motel registration cards, military service rosters, immigration records and other data bases." Even records of magazine subscribers were examined. Several potential Robert "Jacks" were discovered:

1). Jacques at Lockport, New York

Two brothers who went to the same high school as Timothy McVeigh, were interviewed. They have a cousin whose first name is Robert, who was looked at as a potential suspect. He was eventually cleared by the FBI.

2). Robert Jacks in Arizona

Twenty days after the bombing, the FBI detained two older Arizona men in Carthage, Missouri, thought to have been acquainted with McVeigh. Their names were Gary Allen Land and Robert Jacks. They lived at the El Trovatore Motel in Kingman, Arizona from Christmas 1994 until early April 1995. During much of that time, McVeigh was visiting the Fortiers in Kingman. The final week of their stay, McVeigh was staying five blocks away at the Imperial Motel. The FBI questioned the two and then released them 18 hours later. In tracing their movements, it was found that they were often in areas where McVeigh could be found. At the time of McVeigh's arrest, the pair were at a motel in Perry, Oklahoma, just off the highway from where McVeigh was arrested by a highway patrol trooper. (Source: *The Rocky Mountain News*, 19 Apr 98)

OKBIC Note: Weldon Kennedy, the FBI's chief investigator for the bombing, mandated that all Gary Land and Robert Jacks leads go directly to him and not be filtered by subordinates—very unusual for a pair of insignificant cross-country drunks!

3). Robert Jacks in Cassville, Missouri

A Robert "Jacks" visited William Maloney's real estate office in Cassville, Missouri with Timothy McVeigh and Terry Nichols, according to Maloney. "Jacks" told him, "I just go by Jacks." The three men were interested in a piece of remote property in the Ozark Mountains in Missouri. However, this area, close to the Missouri-Arkansas border "has been home to privacy seekers ranging from well-armed isolationist groups to prosperous marijuana farmers," Maloney said. So he asked them, "Are you looking for a place to hide?" He said the three men "left the same day and never came back." Joe Lee Davidson, who worked for Maloney, said that Jacks "seemed to be the one that was in control and in charge of what was going on."

Robert Jacks

OKBIC Note: The land that Maloney showed this group on maps was just one-half mile from the Branch Davidian Compound, a sister organization to the group in Waco, Texas.

Pictures of Gary Land and Robert Jacks (the two men detained by the FBI) were shown on television. When Mr. Maloney saw them, he "knew they had the wrong person." They were older than the Robert "Jacks" he had seen, so he contacted the FBI. Based on Mr. Maloney's description, sketch artist Jeanne Boylan drew a likeness of the suspect. He was described as a muscular young man with a short haircut, full face and dark features, maybe Indian. Davidson agreed, adding, "maybe a little bit Hawaiian...."

OKBIC Note: A café owner in Herington, Kansas, Barbara Whittenberg, also reported seeing a man she thought to be Hawaiian in the company of Nichols and McVeigh. (See chapter on "Eyewitnesses.")

In a special television interview by Bernard Shaw of *Impact*, Maloney further described Jacks as having a "short cut hair, not plumb-down military, but short cut. Rather full lips. Clean shaven. Dark complected. He was dark-skinned." A CNN artist had seen the Jeanne Boylan sketch and made a sketch of his own. Maloney was shown this sketch. He said that "the nose is different when seen from the side. It's a long nose and it's sharp pointed and it was not wide like this." Maloney has also said that Jacks had a tattoo on the left arm about halfway between the wrist and elbow.

OKBIC Note: To our knowledge, the FBI has not shown their sketch of Robert "Jacks" to any of the eyewitnesses in either Kansas or Oklahoma City.

OKBIC Note: When shown the CNN sketch, Ms. Whittenberg stated, "It looks closer to him than any of them. This is the closest picture that I've seen yet." She said it resembles the person she saw by "about 75 percent."

4). Robert A Jacques in Cassville, Missouri

Terry Nichols owned property with an airstrip in Cassville, Missouri which he leased to a man in Wichita, Kansas. In October 1999, a piece of property just across the lake from Nichols' land was sold by a Robert A. Jacques from Wichita, Kansas. (Source: William Maloney)

5). Jacques in Rogers, Arkansas

This Jacques had stayed at a motel in Rogers, Arkansas on Labor Day weekend 1994 while visiting a friend. Rogers, Arkansas is 30 miles from Cassville, Missouri, home of real estate agent Maloney.

6). Robert Jacquez in Odessa, Texas

On 09 September 1997, the family of an Odessa, Texas man filed a wrongful death suit against the man's employer after his arm was torn off in an industrial accident from which he later died. His name was Robert Jacquez. He reportedly shared a post office box with a neighbor of Michael Fortier named Jim Rosencrans. Rosencrans lived in Odessa for approximately 18 months after the bombing. At last word, the FBI was supposedly trying to locate photographs of this Robert Jacquez to show to relevant witnesses.

OKBIC Note: Reportedly, there was a third person (unidentified) sharing the post office box with Jacquez and Rosencrans. According to the Odessa postmaster, no two or more people can share a post office box unless there is a relationship that connects them. What is that relationship in this case? Rosencrans asserts that he never knew Jacquez and doesn't know how he ended up sharing his post office box.

(Sources for Paragraph F.4.b.: OKBIC Interviews; various articles by Kevin Flynn of *The Rocky Mountain News*; *Nation* Newspaper, July 97; *Impact* television show by CNN, 09 Mar 97; *The Odessa American*, 09 Sep 97 & 28 Jan 98; & Nichols trial transcript, pg.14424)

G. Conclusions

With all the eyewitness accounts of a dark-complexioned man in the company of McVeigh in the days leading up to the bombing and on the morning of the bombing itself, it is inconsistent with reason to assume that McVeigh and Nichols were the only conspirators in the Oklahoma City bombing. Yet, the Federal Government wants us to accept that all the perpetrators have been brought to justice. The overwhelming number of eyewitness accounts dispute this. We at the OKBIC have not been able to determine who these conspirators are, but we have presented several possibilities. Only if the Government with its vast resources chooses to pursue the leads is it likely that these criminals will ever be brought to justice.

Chapter VIII

THE OKLAHOMA COUNTY GRAND JURY

A. BACKGROUND

Even though federal investigations into the bombing of the Murrah Building commenced immediately following the event, many interested parties began to question those investigations when it was evident that testimony by various witnesses was being ignored and/or distorted. Once Timothy McVeigh and Terry Nichols were apprehended and indicted, federal agencies appeared to have no further interest in pursuing leads that conflicted with or contradicted the cases they had developed against the two defendants.

In May 1995, Oklahoma State Representative Charles Key (R) requested that the Oklahoma State House of Representatives conduct hearings regarding the bombing, but his request was denied. A chain of events was set in motion that would encompass the next 18 months when Key and Glenn Wilburn filed a petition in the Seventh District Court of Oklahoma County on 27 October 1995, exercising their Constitutional right to impanel a grand jury to hear their evidence and bring appropriate charges. (Wilburn's two grandsons had perished in the daycare center when the Murrah Building was bombed.)

Oklahoma and New Mexico are the only two states where the State Constitution ensures the right of citizens to call for a grand jury. In Oklahoma, it is relatively common for multiple grand juries to be impaneled to consider evidence in a variety of cases at any given time.

Justification for resistance to the establishment of a grand jury was that it was too costly and because a duplication of efforts would be created since the same evidence would be heard that was presented in the federal trials. It is interesting to note, however, that a second trial for Terry Nichols in Oklahoma City was not considered to be too expensive.

Glenn Wilburn

Impaneling a grand jury in Oklahoma would have had no impact on the federal trials, which were ongoing at the time, because grand jury investigations are held to the highest standards of secrecy with evidentiary information sealed. "...the fact that the county grand jury might interfere with a federal investigation is not a ground for denial of the circulation of the petition. ("Grand Juries in Oklahoma: Where Are We Now?," article appearing in *The Oklahoma Bar Journal*, Vol. 68, No. 30, David W. Lee, 26 July 97).

313

Judge Daniel L. Owens

On 06 November 1995, Judge Daniel L. Owens of the Seventh District Court of Oklahoma County entered an order to quash the Amended Grand Jury Petition because, "...this Court sees no reason, as a matter of law, to attempt to reinvent the wheel and duplicate an investigation performed by the federal government."

For over a year, Key and Wilburn, through the court system, fought for their right to circulate a petition to seat a grand jury. They were thwarted at every turn until December 1996 when the Oklahoma Court of Appeals unanimously ruled in favor of their Constitutional right to pursue the seating of a grand jury. In its published opinion, the Court ruled that the request was a clearly protected Constitutional right. As a "published" opinion, a precedent was established and it will be used as a reference case in future litigation in regard to the State Constitution and statutes. (For Petition and Appeal documents, see Appendix pgs. 467-471.)

The following month, Oklahoma County District Attorney Robert Macy filed a brief with the Oklahoma State Supreme Court in an attempt to block the impaneling of a grand jury. However, on 12 February 1997, the Court unanimously ruled in favor of Key and Wilburn, upholding earlier court decisions.

Once the Court ruled that Key and Wilburn had the lawful right to circulate a petition to impanel a grand jury, they began their petition drive in mid-April. The 45-day deadline was successfully met with 13,500 signatures, more than double the 5,000 signatures required. Upon receipt of the petition, the Oklahoma District Court ordered that a grand jury be impaneled on 30 June 1997.

Two polls, taken independently of one another, revealed that the citizens of Oklahoma were not concerned about the cost; their concern was to continue the probe and put forth information that federal prosecutors were suppressing in the federal trials. One poll showed that 80 percent of those responding favored impaneling a grand jury, while the other poll showed that 90 percent did. In addition, according to *Spotlight*, 02 February 1997, Oklahoma City radio station KTOK took a public opinion poll and the results showed that 89 percent of Oklahomans supported impaneling a grand jury to probe the bombing independent of the Justice Department investigation.

Neither the courts nor the attorney general's office have the authority to deny citizens their right to a grand jury. It is a clear Constitutional and statutory right to which the citizens of Oklahoma are entitled. In this case, however, that right was consistently impeded by the legal machinations of those officials who ignored that they were elected to accommodate their constituency.

B. OKLAHOMA BOMBING INVESTIGATION COMMITTEE FORMED

The Oklahoma Bombing Investigation Committee (OKBIC) was established in April 1997 by Representative Key and other interested parties to investigate matters that government agencies had refused to consider, to process the petition drive, and to submit information to the Oklahoma County

Grand Jury. OKBIC is registered with the State of Oklahoma and the Internal Revenue Service as a non-profit organization, with all funds being generated through donations received from concerned citizens throughout the United States.

C. EFFORTS TO INTIMIDATE OKBIC

A week before the Supreme Court's ruling on 12 February 1997, a fax on "Drew Edmondson Attorney General of Oklahoma" letterhead was circulated and signed by Richard M. Wintory, Chief Deputy Attorney General, Criminal Division, to "...anyone interested..." [within Federal agencies]. The content of the fax was entitled, "A Plea to the Media From Oklahoma City -- Don't OJ Us," signed, "Many survivors and family members, Oklahoma City Bombing." A notation appearing on the fax said, "to be sent to *The New York Times*." The purpose of the fax was to secure signatures of survivors and was designed to rebut a program aired on ABC's "20/20." In this program, bombing survivors, family members of victims, and other witnesses were interviewed; several of those interviewed supported OKBIC's contention that certain federal entities had prior knowledge of the bombing.

The faxed response to the allegations referred to it as a "paranoid delusion" and accused *20/20* of sensationalism in an effort to enhance television ratings. The response further made a plea to the media to "...not cast aside the emotional health of fellow human beings for the sake of a story." Edmondson's propaganda counteroffensive was disguised as a spontaneous response from the bombing survivors.

Oklahoma Attorney General Drew Edmondson

V.Z. Lawton was one of many survivors who refused to sign the letter. A HUD employee at the time of the blast, he responded to Edmondson's solicitation of signatures by publicly denouncing the letter, "...the communication was loaded with lies and half-truths...I certainly could not sign it and I felt like a state attorney general could better spend his time supporting an effort to find the truth than this transparent effort at helping to hide it." (Source: OKBIC interview)

Jane C. Graham, another survivor, is a HUD employee and union president who expressed her anger at Edmondson's letter: "I am angry that the Attorney General's Office would play on the emotions of this office at HUD under the guise of keeping us posted on how they are proceeding and planning the case, causing further emotional turmoil in this office between employees." (Source: OKBIC interview)

The timing of the circulation of the fax appears to have been designed to further discredit the efforts of OKBIC and to have been distributed in retaliation for the OKBIC's victories through the judicial system.

Also in April, Oklahoma Attorney General Edmondson made yet another attempt to block OKBIC's request for an investigation by subpoenaing Representative Key, Ken Blood (another OKBIC member), and Key's secretary, to answer questions before a multi-county grand jury regarding donations received by OKBIC. Richard Wintory presided over the proceedings. The Grand Jury dropped all charges when it was proven that OKBIC had not violated any law under the Oklahoma Charitable Contributions Act.

D. LAW APPLICABLE TO CONDUCT OF GRAND JURIES

A grand jury is unique in its concept and application because, unlike a trial jury, no defense attorneys appear to represent a plaintiff or complainant. Witnesses are interrogated by prosecution attorneys and grand jurors are permitted to ask questions at the conclusion of the witness testimony. Attorneys are not permitted in the courtroom, although they can be available outside in order to be available to their clients for consultation. The grand jury is not held to the same standards as a trial court; there is more flexibility regarding conduct of the procedure. In a trial court, for example, hearsay evidence is not admissible. However, a grand jury is permitted to consider such evidence. The grand jury is an investigative body and acts independently of the judicial system, and the rules of evidence should not apply to grand jury proceedings. Grand Jurors have the right to subpoena witnesses and to ask questions of a witness once the prosecution has completed its interrogation. (Source: Evidence Subcommittee's Note following Okla. Stat. Tit. 12, Sec. 2103)

Even though the grand jury is supposed to be independent, the reality is that the only cases heard by a grand jury are those presented by the prosecutor. The prosecutor determines which witnesses to call and then interrogates them.

E. OKLAHOMA COUNTY GRAND JURY PROCEEDINGS

Judge William R. Burkett gave the following instruction to the Oklahoma County Grand Jury at the time of its impanelment: "You may not receive hearsay or secondary evidence. Evidence is 'hearsay' when it consists of a narration by one person of matters told to him by another. Judge Burkett's instruction was in complete opposition to existing case law. In 1978, the Oklahoma Legislature passed the Oklahoma Evidence Code, which repealed a statute that prohibited the grand jury from receiving hearsay or secondary evidence.

George Wallace, a local businessman and OKBIC member, was out of town when he received notice that a registered letter was being held for him at the post office. Upon his return, he went to the post office late in the day, signed for the letter, and accepted it. The letter served notice that he was to appear before the Grand Jury at 8 a.m. the following morning. He then called the District Attorney's office and talked to Assistant District Attorney Suzanne Gump, stating that the only information he had was hearsay. She informed him that he needed to bring all documents in his possession and, even though his testimony would be hearsay, it would be acceptable because there were 25 to 30 exceptions to the hearsay rule. (Source: OKBIC interview)

Gump's assurances that hearsay testimony would be acceptable is in complete conflict with Burkett's instructions to the Grand Jury. Evidently, the prosecution was selective in whose hearsay evidence would be put before the Grand Jury.

In January and February 1998, OKBIC founder Charles Key and two other OKBIC members, were subpoenaed to appear before the Grand Jury with instructions to provide "...any and all items relating to the bombing...specifically...information you personally have participated in collecting and visual recordings, sworn affidavits, written statements, interview summaries, possible witnesses...photographs and transcribed interviews..." The subpoenas further noted that the materials requested pertained only to those items that were "...personally collected or were provided to you by others ...investigating the incidents." Additionally, the subpoenas required that OKBIC members "...bring the names, addresses and any written or recorded statements of any additional witnesses you have..."

OKBIC complied with the subpoenas and submitted a list of 149 witnesses with pertinent information to the Grand Jury. However, only 49 witnesses on the list were ultimately called to appear. It is interesting to note that OKBIC was forthcoming and cooperative in providing all information requested by the Grand Jury. However, as early as October 1995, Representative Key had requested bomb squad records for 19 April 1995 from the Oklahoma County Sheriff's Department. Over a month elapsed before Key received a response, not from the Sheriff's Department, but from John M. Jacobsen, Assistant District Attorney, stating, "...we have advised the Sheriff that It is our opinion these records are not subject to the Open Record Act. "

Upon receiving Jacobsen's letter, Key questioned him to determine why those particular records were not subject to the Open Record Act. Jacobsen was evasive and never explained the reasoning behind the rejection of Key's request.

The last witnesses to testify were federal employees whose testimony had been blocked by the Tenth Circuit Court of Appeals because of concerns by Terry Nichols' and Timothy McVeigh's attorneys that such information could conceivably jeopardize their rights through the appeals process or in future criminal trials in Oklahoma. On 03 November 1998, the Court lifted the ban and the federal employees were released to testify.

F. ONE INDICTMENT ISSUED BY GRAND JURY

The lone indictment rendered by the Grand Jury was against David Hoffman, who was charged with jury tampering, a misdemeanor that carried a possible sentence of two years. This charge against Hoffman occurred because he had sent a copy of his book, *The Oklahoma City Bombing and the Politics of Terror*, with a cover letter to the home of each member of the Grand Jury. The letter purportedly urged the Grand Jurors to "...not let themselves be pushed around...do the right thing or face grave consequences." Allegedly, the word "grave" was

David Hoffman

underlined and the Jurors considered the statement to be threatening. The charges were subsequently dismissed, with Hoffman being assessed a fine and community service.

The dust jacket on Hoffman's book states, "forward by Representative Charles Key." In response, Key presented a press statement on 18 January 1998 in which he noted that he never gave Hoffman permission to include his name in the book, never wrote a forward to the book, and furthermore, disagreed with portions of it. The dispute between Key, Hoffman, and Hoffman's publisher, dates back to June 1997.

Despite all the evidence presented to the Grand Jury, the charge brought against Hoffman was the only indictment issued. Considering the length of time the Grand Jury was in session, and the cost of the proceedings, perhaps the Grand Jury felt compelled to issue at least one indictment in order to justify their existence.

During the 18-month period from 30 June 1997 to 30 December 1998, the Grand Jury served 133 working days reviewing the testimony of 117 witnesses and 1,909 related exhibits.

G. GRAND JURY FINAL REPORT ISSUED 30 DECEMBER 1998

In his statement following the issuance of the Final Report, Judge Burkett stated that Suzanne Gump and Pat Morgan, assistant district attorneys, and Larry Dellinger, investigator for the prosecution, had assisted the Grand Jury in sifting through "mountains of evidence." This certainly indicates that the prosecution determined which evidence would be provided to the Grand Jury and which evidence would be suppressed.

Assistant District Attorney Pat Morgan

Given the manner in which selective information was filtered to the Grand Jury by the prosecution, the end result was a foregone conclusion. From the beginning, when OKBIC sought investigation via a grand jury, District Attorney Robert Macy and Oklahoma Attorney General Drew Edmonson, collectively and separately, made every effort to discredit parties who expressed doubts about the investigation launched by federal, state, and local authorities immediately after the bombing. Judge Burkett continued that pattern when he instructed the jury to ignore "hearsay" evidence, contrary to established law.

Judge Burkett commented in his statement following the issuance of the Grand Jury Final Report that the outcome of the McVeigh and Nichols trials gave, "...all citizens a renewed confidence in the judicial system," and alluded to the outcome of the O.J. Simpson trial by way of contrast. If there were any truth to this statement, there would be no need for OKBIC's continued efforts in pursuit of the truth, and 475 survivors and families of bombing victims would not have engaged in civil lawsuits to pursue the truth. The first lawsuit was filed in Federal Court in April 1997 by 170 family members, and charged that the Federal Government "...knew or should have known" that the Murrah Building was the target of a bomb attack. Five families filed a second lawsuit. The third lawsuit was filed in State Court by 300 families and claimed, not only prior knowledge by the Federal Government, but also charged the Government with conducting a failed "sting operation." (Source: *The Washington Times*, 22 Jun 98)

Larry Dellinger

In conclusion, the Grand Jury Final Report stated, "This was an act that could have been carried out by one individual." It is difficult to understand how the Grand Jury could have interpreted the evidence to arrive at this conclusion. If, in fact, the explosive was a 4,000-pound ammonium nitrate-fuel oil (ANFO) truck bomb, it would be interesting to know how it could have been physically managed by one individual.

Rep. Charles Key's reaction to the Grand Jury Final Report was reported in *The Washington Times* on 11 January 1999: "...the only thing the Final Report lacked was an FBI signature at the bottom."

1. John Doe II

The Grand Jury's Final Report conceded that there were multiple John Doe #2 sightings. Approximately 26 witnesses testified that they saw John Doe #2 or Timothy McVeigh with John Doe #2. "Often the testimony of these witnesses conflicted with each other and...were reported after composites were shown on television or after Timothy McVeigh was led from the Noble County Jail on April 21, 1995." This statement may have been true in some cases, but was not cause to dismiss the testimony of all the witnesses.

The Grand Jury Final Report stated further, "Based on the descriptions of these witnesses John Doe #2 would have to be as follows: Height 5'3" to 6'3"; Weight 140 pounds to 210 pounds; Build: slim and skinny to stocky and muscular; Race: White, Hispanic, Middle Eastern or Asian; Skin color: white, olive, or dark; Hair color: dark blond, red, brown or black; Hair length crew cut, 2 inches long, or shoulder length; Facial hair: mustache or none."

Evidently, the Grand Jury seems to have assumed that descriptions of John Doe #1 and John Doe #2 were one individual only. They never considered that tere may have been multiple John Does, although they stated, "...in spite of all the evidence...we cannot finally put closure to the question of the existence of a John Doe #2."

2. Conspiracy/Prior Knowledge

The Grand Jury gave no credence to allegations that the Government had prior knowledge of the bombing; however, there is sufficient evidence showing that, indeed, there had been warnings of a terrorist strike in Oklahoma City before 19 April 1995.

Public statements were made by the ATF that a general alert was issued to federal offices throughout the country prior to the bombing. The alert emphasized that the date, 19 April, had significance to anti-government groups that celebrated it as "Patriot's Day," and it was the second anniversary of the end of the government's seige of the Branch Davidian compound in Waco, Texas.

Richard Snell, a leader in The Covenant, Sword and The Arm of the Lord (CSA), a white supremacist organization, was executed the same day as the bombing for the murder of an Arkansas pawn shop owner. Among his last words were, "Governor, look over your shoulder. Justice is coming," and, "Snell has victory. I am at peace." Robert Millar, the founder and leader of Elohim City, a white supremacist group, served as Snell's "spiritual advisor," and following his execution, Millar traveled to Arkansas to retrieve his body in order to have it buried at Elohim City. Thus, Snell's position as a martyr to anti-government and white supremacist groups was ensured.

Numerous reports were made stating that ATF employees were paged on their pagers the morning of the bombing and told not to report for work. Evidently not all employees were contacted, but it is significant that many of the employees were in "offsite meetings" or "out of town" at the time of the tragedy.

Rep. Charles Key stated, "We have always been very specific about the prior knowledge of the government...there's a mountain of evidence that shows they knew ahead of time and failed to warn the public." Continuing, he said, "We have never claimed the federal government bombed their own building. That's merely a propaganda campaign meant to discredit anyone who tries to bring the facts to light." For further information corroborating prior knowledge of the bombing by law enforcement agencies, refer to Chapter Six of this Report.

3. Elohim City

The significance of Elohim City, the small white supremacist compound in eastern Oklahoma, was diluted by the Grand Jury. In the Final Report, the Grand Jury concluded, "We have made every effort to try to identify any plausible connection between [Elohim City] and the bombing. In spite of a possible telephone call from Timothy McVeigh to Elohim City in April 1995, we have been unable to find such a connection."

ATF Special Agent Angela Finley-Graham's attorney, Richard O'Carroll, stated that ATF informant, Carol Howe's claims of warning the federal government about the bombing were "damnable lies," and "...is a figment of her imagination and just an opportunity for her to stay in the limelight." ATF documents clearly prove otherwise. Ironically, Howe has moved from her home, changed her identity and gone into hiding -- hardly the actions of a publicity-seeker searching for attention.

One must ask, why would the ATF refer the FBI to Howe and have her subsequently return to Elohim City immediately after the bombing to obtain further information if the ATF considered her information prior to the bombing to be "damnable lies?"

In her testimony before a Federal Court in Tulsa, Oklahoma, on 24 April 1997, ATF Agent Finley-Graham confirmed that prior to the bombing, Howe had told her of threats originating from Elohim

City to blow up federal buildings and assassinate politicians. Agent Finley-Graham reported on 28 February 1995 that, on the previous day, she had met with Howe to discuss further infiltration of Elohim City during the week of 05-11 March 1995. Finley-Graham's report was endorsed by her supervisor, Resident Agent in Charge (RAC) David Roberts, then forwarded to the Dallas ATF Field Office and ATF Headquarters in Washington DC. Roberts noted, "I concur with the recommendations of Special Agent Angela Finley (now Graham) to reactivate CI-183 [Howe]."

There is a further connection between McVeigh and Elohim City through his association with Andreas Strassmeir and Michael Brescia, who were residents at Elohim City and were acquaintances of Carol Howe.

4. The Elevators

According to the Grand Jury Final Report, the ATF did not have prior knowledge of the bombing, because at the time of the blast, DEA Agent Dave Schickendanz and ATF Resident-in-Charge (RAC) Alex McCauley, alleged that they were in an elevator that free-fell from the eighth floor to the third floor, and they were able to walk out to safety.

However, in a 20/20 interview with Tom Jarriel, elevator maintenance men Duane James and Oscar Johnson told Jarriel that they arrived on the scene 20 minutes after the explosion. James reported, "...several of us entered [the Murrah Building] and did a floor-by-floor search to see where the elevators were...we inspected each elevator..." Jarriel noted that photographs of the elevators were taken and the inspection was documented. The photos showed that all pulleys and safety cables were intact and operable and would have prevented the elevator from free-falling. James further stated, "...if you fell six floors and it was a free-fall, it'd be like jumping out a six-story building. I'd ask them how long they were in the hospital and how lucky they were to survive. " It is interesting to note that a General Services Administration inspector also testified before the Grand Jury that there was no evidence of a free-fall.

In a tape-recorded interview with J.D. Cash, the Special Agent in Charge of the Dallas Region of the ATF, Lester Martz, said, "Well, I have discussed this with the agent [McCauley]...maybe Agent McCauley just imagined he free-fell." (Source: *Media Bypass*, Jun 96 issue).

Since it is evident that McCauley and Schickendanz were not in the elevators, where were they? With the testimony before the Grand Jury, why did they conclude that the ATF agents had really been in the elevators?

Yet, subsequent to the alleged "free-fall," the ATF still felt an award was in order for Schickendanz, who received an award naming him one of the national policemen of the year. The award noted that he had survived a dramatic six-story free-fall.

5. The More-Than-One-Bomb Theory

Particularly troubling is the fact that in the earliest television broadcasts following the bombing, newscasters reported that as many as three bombs were found in the building and one had been removed by the bomb disposal unit for analysis. In later broadcasts on the day of the bombing, however, it was announced that the explosion was caused solely by one truck bomb, and there was never any further mention of multiple bombs.

The Grand Jury Final Report supports the prosecution's contention that only one bomb caused the devastation of the Murrah Building and the loss of 168 lives and countless injuries. The only comments regarding this topic in the Grand Jury Final Report pertain to various interpretations of seismographs and the intensity and scope of burns found on the victims and in the remains of the building. No mention is made in the Report that several occupants of the Murrah Building testified that they heard and/or felt activity immediately prior to the blast which allowed them sufficient time to seek shelter or protection.

One such witness, Jane C. Graham, a HUD employee, recalled the discovery of additional explosive devices following the initial explosion. Additionally, she asserts that she felt both bombs and is dismayed because the discovery of multiple explosives was subsequently denied and suppressed by the Government. She asks, "What's there to hide...why all this suppression of evidence and pressure on federal workers to shut up?"

The Final Report does not reflect that in both the Nichols and McVeigh trials, "...the government's 'expert testimony' on the bomb forensics fell apart..." (Source: *New American*, 01 Feb 99). Dave Williams was the FBI agent in charge of evidence collection at the Oklahoma bombing crime scene, and admitted to the Justice Department Inspector General's Office that he determined that the Murrah Building had been destroyed by an ammonium nitrate-fuel oil (ANFO) bomb because he knew that Terry Nichols had possessed fertilizer and diesel fuel, not because of scientific proof. (Refer to Chapter Three, "The Federal Trials of Timothy McVeigh and Terry Nichols")

Neither does the Final Report reflect that the Grand Jurors had access to the findings of military explosives expert General Benton K. Partin, neutron bomb inventor Sam Cohen, or NASA physicist Frederick Hansen, who have all stated that it would be physically impossible for the blast from an ANFO truck bomb outside the building to have caused the destruction of the steel-reinforced concrete columns without supplementary demolition charges inside the building.

The Grand Jury did not seem to be aware that it would be totally incompatible with physics experience for the columns in the building nearest to the truck bomb to remain intact while those further away from it collapsed.

Additionally, the Grand Jury failed to recognize the fact that prosecution witness Michael Fortier testified that, several months prior to the bombing, McVeigh and Nichols had failed to successfully detonate even a small milk jug of ANFO. In light of that testimony, it is inconceivable that they are credited with devising a bomb that was 100 percent effective in burning all of its explosive components; scientists have been unable to achieve those results even in laboratory settings using high-grade materials. (Source: McVeigh trial transcript, pg. 8244)

And, evidently the Grand Jury was not cognizant of the fact that shortly before the McVeigh trial, the prosecution was compelled to withdraw certain FBI experts as witnesses because of the report issued by the Justice Department OIG citing abuses and fraudulent practices at the FBI Crime Laboratory, specifically mentioning the Oklahoma City bombing investigation. In light of the conclusions drawn by the Grand Jury, it is evident that this most critical information was withheld from the panel.

6. The Sheriff's Bomb Truck

The Grand Jury Final Report stated that an "...Oklahoma County Sheriff's bomb truck was at the Oklahoma County Sheriff Office's Training Center, Northeast 36th and Air Depot, at the time of the blast and responded immediately." That location is approximately 10 miles from the bombsite, and it can be reasonably assumed that it would have taken upwards of 10 minutes for it to arrive in downtown Oklahoma City.

Prior to the bombing, at least seven witnesses reported seeing a white truck with "bomb disposal" or "bomb squad" on the side of it.

Dan Adomitis, Oklahoma City attorney, saw a large truck with a trailer marked "bomb disposal" or "bomb squad" on the side, along with a shield. (Source: ABC 20/20 interview with Tom Jarriel, 17 Sep 97)

J.D. Reed of the County Assessor's Office saw a bomb squad truck parked in front of the County Courthouse on the east side of Hudson Street prior to the explosion. At 9 a.m., he heard a "whistling" noise and looked out a window to determine its cause and noted that the truck was gone. (Source: Article appearing in special edition of *Mass Media*, the Oklahoma County Assessor Newsletter, 19 Apr 96).

Renae Cooper took her son to the daycare center in the Murrah Building and, upon leaving the building, saw several men wearing what appeared to be bomb squad uniforms. (Her son perished in the bombing.) (Source: *Media Bypass*, Jun 96).

Norma Joslin, a 30-year employee of the Oklahoma County Board of Elections saw a bomb squad truck on the east side of Hudson Street in front of the County Courthouse immediately prior to the bombing. (OKBIC interview)

Claude Criss, private investigator and part-time employee of the Oklahoma County Courts, also saw a bomb squad truck prior to the bombing. He observed bomb-sniffing dogs with their handlers on the south side of the Post Office building 30 to 45 minutes before the bombing. The Post Office is located approximately one-half blocks northwest of the Murrah Building. Criss was the only witness asked to take a lie detector test. (Source: OKBIC interview)

H. AFTERMATH

Federal Judge Matsch, who presided over the trials of McVeigh and Nichols, publicly reprimanded federal prosecutors for failure to pursue answers to many unanswered questions, and the jury forperson in the Nichols trial also lambasted the federal prosecutors for their "sloppiness and arrogance" in the handling of the investigation into the bombing.

The *Pittsburgh Post Gazette* published a 10-part series (22, 23, 24, and 29 Nov 98 and 01, 06, 07, 08, and 13, Dec 98) entitled, "Win At All Costs," which gave rise to media investigations throughout the country into our judicial system and prosecutorial misconduct.

The *Chicago Tribune* began a series on 10 January 1999, entitled, "Trial and Error". The first installment, "How Prosecutors Sacrifice Justice to Win," included an article focusing on Oklahoma District Attorney Robert Macy. Tribune reporter, Ken Armstrong, noted that while Macy has received numerous awards and recognition as a prosecutor and was re-elected to his fifth term in November 1994, he has been harshly criticized by various courts. At least four men convicted of murder have received new trials or sentencing hearings based upon appellate findings that Macy broke the rules of fair play; one of those cases was reversed, resulting in acquittal. And, at least 17 other defendants had trials in which reviewing courts stated that Macy or his trial partners acted improperly. However, in those cases, the courts either upheld the convictions anyway or ordered a new trial on some other basis.

The Daily Oklahoman (named "America's Worst Newspaper" by the prestigious *Columbia University Journalism Review*) continued attacking Charles Key and OKBIC for their continued pursuit of answers to unresolved questions. Articles praised the Grand Jury Final Report and featured comments only from bombing victims who agreed with it.

Bombing victims called OKBIC to report that their negative reactions to the Grand Jury Final Report were never printed. The only letters to the editor that were printed were those claiming that Charles Key accused rescue workers and local law enforcement of prior knowledge of the bombing and of failing to take action. Key submitted a written response to those accusations via certified mail to *The Daily Oklahoman* but his letter was returned to him unpublished. Regardless of erroneous statements in the media, OKBIC has continued to praise the efforts of rescue workers and law enforcement officials for their heroic efforts following the bombing.

Six years after the bombing, citizens continue to come forward in contacting OKBIC with information they have already provided to law enforcement authorities. In many cases, they felt that law enforcement was unresponsive to their information. Some witnesses have felt that their information was relevant, but they did not know who to report it to, and given the Government's stance that the crime was committed by only McVeigh and Nichols, they had a strong distrust of governmental officials.

Assistant District Attorney Suzanne Gump

Others delayed reporting their information to OKBIC because they had reported it to governmental agencies earlier, assuming they would be called to testify in the Denver trials. When they were not, however, they contacted OKBIC. Several witnesses complained about being mistreated by FBI agents as well as by some members of the Oklahoma County District Attorney's office. A frequent complaint was that Assistant District Attorneys Suzanne Gump and Pat Morgan "...ran this [the Grand Jury hearing] like a criminal trial."

Following the publication of the Grand Jury's Final Report, prosecutor Suzanne Gump was quoted by *The Sun*, "...many of the critics and would-be witnesses may say one thing to a conspiracy theorist and another one when put before a ruling body under oath." When asked why that might happen, Gump responded, "Maybe they want their 15 minutes of fame." Does this mean that Gump believes that some of the witnesses who were called to testify by her own office gave perjured testimony?

Although extremely disappointed that the Grand Jury he had worked so hard to establish was a rubber stamp of the federal grand jury, Key was not surprised at the outcome. In the 01 February 1999 issue of the *New American*, Key said, "...we had hoped at the beginning to be able to have an independent counsel appointed, which is allowed by state law. Since District Attorney Bob Macy had been so vocal and vehement in fighting our effort to impanel the Grand Jury, he should have recused himself and his office from handling the Grand Jury."

Key further explained that OKBIC "...could have appealed his decision, but then we would have faced the alternatives of prosecutors appointed by Attorney General Drew Edmondson or Governor Frank Keating, both of whom were even more adamantly opposed to our effort. We would still be tied up in appeals today."

Continuing, Key said, "...we had the deck stacked against us and we gave our best shot at using the legal processes available to us." He further voiced the expectation that when the OKBIC's final report is issued and "...fair-minded people have access to all of the compelling evidence we intend to present...they will have no doubt that others who were involved are still on the loose and they will demand an end to the cover-up."

The FBI repeatedly has stated that the bombing case is closed. Attorney General Janet Reno said, after the Nichols jury was unable to reach a sentencing verdict, that she had reviewed **all** the evidence in the case and was satisfied the right suspects were apprehended and convicted. (Emphasis added). It would have been impossible for Reno to have reviewed the "billions" of documents that Robert Macy claimed existed. The information she received would have been furnished to her by federal agencies, and most likely in a summary format. Her conclusions would, therefore, have been reached by reviewing only those materials federal agencies wanted her to see.

Perhaps the most revealing reaction to the Final Report occurred when a well-known Oklahoma City radio talk show took a poll, resulting in 60 percent of those polled rejecting the findings of the Grand Jury.

I. IMPROPRIETIES BY JUDGE WILLIAM BURKETT

Following the Grand Jury's Final Report, in a subsequent election, Burkett lost his seat on the bench, which precluded any attempts by OKBIC to censure him through the grievance process with the Oklahoma State Bar Association. Burkett breached his fiduciary duty in a number of ways:

1. By instructing the Grand Jury to disregard hearsay testimony even though case law allows for such testimony in a Grand Jury forum.

Judge William Burkett

2. By saying, in his statement following the publication of the Grand Jury Final Report, that Assistant District Attorneys Suzanne Gump and Pat Morgan, along with the investigator for the prosecution, Larry Dellinger, had "assisted" the Grand Jury in sifting through "...mountains of evidence." This would certainly lead one to conclude that the Grand Jury was presented solely with information provided at the discretion of the prosecution.

3. By stating that "...maybe (Representative) Charles Key should be indicted." On 15 September 1998, Burkett made this statement in a speech before an audience of 50 to 60 at a Kiwanis Club meeting, many of whom were Key's constituents. That same day, a primary election was held with Key on the ballot for re-election. Key responded in a complaint to the Court that Burkett's comments were "...improper and injudicious...also in violation of court rules for judges..." He continued by stating that Burkett's comments were in violation of Oklahoma statutes which prohibit judges from commenting about pending cases and grand jury investigations, particularly in cases where the judge is presiding.

4. By publicly stating that he had no intention of allowing the Grand Jury to reach any conclusion that would conflict with those reached by the federal government. The public was made aware of Burkett's support of the prosecution when he made this statement prior to the Grand Jury being impaneled, and even before he had been selected to oversee the proceedings. This comment was reported by Mike McCarvel on his radio show on KTOK, and Burkett never refuted it.

It is certainly obvious that Burkett behaved unprofessionally throughout the 18 months that the Grand Jury was impaneled. It is evident that he gave the greatest latitude to the prosecution while exercising his own beliefs and prejudices against anyone opposing his preconceived opinions and those of the Federal Government.

J. CONCLUSIONS

It took over one and a half years of legal roadblocks before a grand jury was finally impaneled to hear evidence relating to the bombing of the Murrah Building in Oklahoma City. Another 18 months elapsed before the Grand Jury issued its Final Report in December 1998. Almost four years had passed since the bombing, and still questions remained unanswered for which we may never know the truth.

The Grand Jury Final Report is a reflection of the Federal Government's conclusions and mirrors the findings in the Tim McVeigh and Terry Nichols trials. It is apparent that the only evidence the Grand Jury heard was what the prosecution wanted them to hear. From its inception, the Grand Jury was manipulated by the prosecutors, the Oklahoma County District Attorney, the Attorney General, and even the presiding judge. The Jurors were not allowed to hear from at least one hundred witnesses who were available to them. Justice has not been served in this case

Chapter IX

GOVERNMENT IMPROPRIETIES

A. FBI PUTS VICTIMS' RESCUE ON HOLD WHILE THEY RESCUE DOCUMENTS

The Times Union quotes a New York newspaper which tells of statements made by an Oklahoma City fireman and a police officer in the K-9 unit. According to their accounts, about 10 to 12 hours after the bombing, the FBI curtailed rescue efforts for the victims, allowing only 10 to 12 rescuers to continue work and limiting them to the lower right side of the building. Then 40 to 50 Government agents spent most of the night removing boxes from the areas, where the offices of the DEA and ATF had been located. (Source: *The Times Union*, Jacksonville, FL, 02 May 95) (Appendix pg. 411)

Danny Defenbaugh
FBI Agent in charge of
The OKC Bombing Investigation

B. FBI QUASHES REPORTS OF OTHER EXPLOSIVE DEVICES FOUND IN BUILDING

Many engineering and explosives experts have reviewed photographs of the bombing and have concluded that the building could not have received such extensive damage without the help of demolition charges attached to the supporting columns. Test blast studies on concrete buildings conducted by the Air Force support this contention. The FEMA report, August 1996, paragraph 2.5.7, reported that Engineer David Hammond, a FEMA consultant from Palo Alto, California, stated that "at least one column near the blast had been destroyed by brisance." (Brisance is not seen with an ANFO bomb but with explosive charges.)

Numerous reports of other bombs being found in the building have been reported. A Military Support of Civilian Authorities (MSCA) Update report, dated 20 April 1995, stated that "a second bomb was disarmed, a third bomb was evacuated." A FEMA HQ Command Center Status Report dated 19 April 1995 stated that, as of 12:30 p.m., "the FBI reports that two additional explosive devices have been found in the building. The first one found has been disarmed but the third has not been disarmed." Live television news broadcasts from the bombsite quoted officials who confirmed unexploded devices had been found inside the building. Dr. Tom Coniglione, introduced as the Medical Director of Saint Anthony's hospital, gave the following statement on KFOR-TV on the morning of the bombing: "At the present time, the medical teams downtown are unable to get into the wreckage to retrieve more of the injured because of the presence of other bombs in the area. I've been told by the police department that just as soon as those bombs are defused, they will permit the medical teams to enter." Rescue workers were evacuated from the building twice on the first day of operations because bombs had been found. According to The *New American* (Vol. 14, No. 15, 20 Jul 98, Pg13), the Oklahoma Highway Patrol dispatch log shows a call at 10:29 that morning. The entry states, "There is another bomb on the south side of the bldg. Need to get away as far as possible…." A 10:37 a.m. entry states that the "OC Fire Dept. confirms they did find a second device in the bldg." The article quotes a ForceCom entry at 11:57 a.m., which states, "Two more explosive devices were located vicinity the explosion site. Evidently intended for the rescuers." It also cites a videotape produced by Jerry Longspaugh of the Citizens Information Network in which Oklahoma Governor Frank Keating is seen stating, "The reports I have is [sic] that one device was deactivated and, apparently, there's another device; and obviously, whatever did the damage to the Murrah Building was a tremendous, very sophisticated explosive device." In a KFOR-TV interview by Kevin Ogle, 19 April 1995, terrorism expert Dr. Randall Heather spoke about finding a defused bomb in the building.

Toni Garrett, a registered nurse, was assisting with rescue efforts by tagging the dead. She tagged over 120 victims. She said that "there was [sic] a couple of people who had actually seen them remove the bomb when the bomb squad had come down to the Murrah Building." She was told that the bomb had a timing device on it "set to go off 10 minutes after the bomb had gone off that morning."

OKBIC Note: The Government quickly denied that additional bombs were found and claimed that the first bomb found at the Murrah building was actually an antitank weapon being used by the U.S. Customs' office in an undercover operation. County bomb squad member, Bob Heady, said it had been examined by a bomb technician from Fort Sill, Oklahoma and was determined to be unarmed. The Government claimed that the second bomb found was a desk clock that resembled a bomb. (Source: *The Daily Oklahoman*, 25 Mar 98)

Jayna Davis with KFOR-TV in Oklahoma City reported that the fire department told her that "in the basement, the ATF had some live training ordnance that could be considered potentially explosive…. However, "witnesses on the scene [said] that they overheard some firefighters that were first on the scene that there was the possibility of a secondary explosive device…and that that device may have been placed near the nursery." (The daycare center was on the second floor.)

C. ATF UNLAWFULLY STORES MUNITIONS IN A FEDERAL OFFICE BUILDING

During rescue efforts at the Murrah Building, several people reported seeing munitions which had been stored in the Building. Randall A. Yount, a Park Ranger for the Oklahoma Tourism and Recreation Department, was one of these. He was in uniform in downtown Oklahoma City shortly after the bombing. After exiting his car near Northwest 10th Street and Broadway, an Oklahoma Highway Patrol (OHP) car pulled up next to him, and the trooper offered him a ride. They made their way to the southwest side of the Southwestern Bell Telephone Building where an OHP command post was being set up. Within minutes, several other OHP vehicles arrived, and the troopers were paired off to begin searching the Murrah Building. One trooper did not have a partner, so the on-scene commander told Yount to pair with the odd trooper. They went to the Murrah Building and began placing tables and benches for a temporary morgue.

Yount said that, around 10:30 a.m., an ATF agent-in-charge instructed him and his partner to join with four of his agents and two U.S. marshals in forming a "fire brigade line." They were led down a short set of steps to the first-floor level where they had to pry open a door and remove large chunks of concrete to proceed farther into the building. He said they could hear the children from the daycare center crying and moaning and thought they were there to help rescue the children; so they "picked up the pace to clear the debris, thinking that [they]...were right on top of the kids."

They continued clearing debris until they came to a steel door that was jammed and had to be forced open. The room had concrete walls, was approximately 25 by 35 feet, and was "very much intact" except for a small amount of concrete debris. It was a vault-type room with one door, and contained wooden crates. He said the crates were filled with assorted weapons, bolt-action single shot rifles to fully automatic-type rifles.

The ATF agent in-charge called on his two-way radio and told the person at the other end that they had found the room and secured it. The troopers were then told that they would be removing the weapons to a white van which would transport the weapons to a secure area. The group leader told them, "If you have any problem with not discussing this, leave now." According to Yount, nobody left.

They began carrying out the crates which were "about five feet long, two feet wide, [and] two feet deep with the markings of 'U.S. ARMY' and 'EXPLOSIVES' on the crates. There were numbers stenciled on the crates, as well." He said there were 24 crates in all plus some shoulder-mounted missiles.

There was a second vault-type door in the area, which they forced open. The first man to look through the door with a flashlight commented, "There must be four or five floors here." Yount said he overheard one of the ATF agents say, "Yeah, my last inventory was 1200 pounds of C-4. That's what went up. The C-4 went off and detonated." (C-4 is a high-explosive material.)

Yount described the common wall between the two rooms as still standing, but bowed inward toward the first vault room they had entered. He said "it looked like the force of an explosion behind the common wall had bowed the wall inward," and the wall "looked cracked and rubberized." He stated that the ATF agents seemed "more interested in the second vault area then the first one that contained the crates and weapons."

To our knowledge, this situation was not investigated by Justice Department officials. No official sanctions were taken against any Government personnel for violating federal law and putting the lives of co-workers and visitors-to-the-building in jeopardy by storing munitions inside.

J. D. Cash with *The McCurtain Daily Gazette* in Southeastern Oklahoma said he talked to Assistant Fire Marshal Dick Miller. He said Miller, "in very clear terms, readily admitted that there were explosives removed from the Murrah Building immediately after the disaster, ...and it was those devices...that caused the evacuation of the rescue workers...." While the explosives were being removed, victims were left "bleeding to death and dying." Cash said Miller told him that the 2:30 p.m. bomb scare was called for the purpose of removing a 2' x 2' x 2' box marked "high explosives" which he witnessed and which he learned were percussion caps used for C-4. Cash said he has photographs of an arsenal room on floor nine of the building which was used by DEA and ATF to store munitions. He says he has four witnesses on tape who helped unload this room two weeks after the bombing. The room contained all sorts of firearms, thousands of rounds of ammunition, boxes marked "explosives," TOW missiles, and hand grenades according to his reports. (Source: OKBIC interview with J.D. Cash)

The Government came up with the story that these munitions were "nothing but training devices." Cash calls that "the most ludicrous excuse." One has to question why training devices would be stored in the federal building rather than at the training facility.

If Cash is correct, his information negates the stories about the bomb scares being caused by additional bombs set by the perpetrators. It does confirm, once again, that the Justice Department will go to any lengths to cover up its wrongdoing.

D. FBI FAILS TO RECORD OR VIDEOTAPE INTERROGATIONS AND INTERVIEWS

It is apparently against FBI policy to tape record interviews. According to the transcript of the Nichols' trial, FBI Agent Stephen Smith testified as follows:

> *It is not my practice to tape-record statements, and the FBI policy on tape-recording statements is that they are, as a general rule—Statements are not tape-recorded.*

The practice of handwritten note-taking lends itself to error. The interviewer's memory may be faulty after hours of interrogation. Notations of important information can be missed because, at the time, the importance may not be recognized. Agent bias can come into play. During testimony, words can be misinterpreted and taken out of context. The tone of voice in which the words were spoken can also change the meaning. The way a question is phrased can influence the answer received. Phrases and sentences spoken in a facetious or sarcastic manner usually mean the opposite of what is actually said; yet the agent can recite those words in court and give them whichever meaning he chooses.

Simply taking notes is an antiquated practice that had its usefulness in the pre-electronic age; but there is no excuse for its continued use in the "high-tech" world of today—unless the FBI is consciously wanting to "selectively edit" the interview. Defense Attorney Michael Tigar addressed his concerns over this situation in his closing remarks during the Nichols' trial:

> *Now, as the prosecutor told you, the interview is not recorded. It's not video-recorded and it's not tape-recorded. Whereas every major police department in this nation tape-records interviews with suspects, the FBI doesn't. The FBI wants to rely on the recollection of the agents. The evidence will show that one of the reasons they do this is because at trial, the Government wants to rely on the credibility of the FBI, as opposed to the credibility of the suspect being interviewed. The evidence will show that a tape recording of that interview would clear up those questions, would show a jury exactly*

what the suspect said and would clear up exactly how the FBI framed the question and in what context it was said. But we don't have a tape recording, and you don't have it in any FBI case. All you have is the recollections of the agents.

Along the same line, James Linehan, a witness in Oklahoma City who saw a Mercury Marquis in the downtown area go into the Murray Building parking garage about a half-hour before the bombing, told his story to the FBI. He grabbed a legal pad and started to draw a diagram. He said one of the FBI investigators "slammed a hand down on the pad and barked, 'Nothing in writing.'" (Source: The *Oklahoma Gazette*, 29 Apr 98)

E. FBI REFUSES TO RELEASE SURVEILLANCE TAPES AND SATELLITE PHOTOS OF OKLAHOMA AND KANSAS CONFISCATED AFTER BOMBING

Immediately after the bombing, the Government confiscated videotapes and satellite photographs relative to this crime. They included surveillance videos from the Regency Tower Apartment Building, the Southwestern Bell Telephone Building, the Journal Record Building and numerous other video cameras in the downtown Oklahoma City area, as well as tapes from Kansas, including the MacDonald's video. The Government has steadfastly refused to release these tapes to the public or the media. A court ruling on 03 June 1996 prohibited "the public disclosure of any discovery information exchanged by the parties;" therefore, the Government has not honored Freedom of Information requests for surveillance tapes. But the federal cases against Nichols and McVeigh are now completed, and the only open action against either man is the trial soon to take place in Oklahoma for Nichols' role in the bombing on state charges. So why is the Federal Government still maintaining jurisdiction over these items? A lawsuit is currently underway by author David Hoffman to try to force the release of these tapes. The release will probably not happen until after the Nichols' trial completes in Oklahoma; but, unless they are classified for national security reasons (and if that is the case, tell us that it is), there is no legitimate reason to withhold release after that. These photos have the potential to prove or disprove many eyewitness accounts of events in Oklahoma City on the day of the bombing and the days leading up to it. They could shed light on the issue of John Doe #2 and others who may have been involved in the bombing. If, as the Government claims, there is nothing of this nature on the tapes, then release them and set this issue to rest. (Appendix pg. 449)

F. FBI HOLDS NICHOLS' FAMILY IN CUSTODY WITHOUT LEGAL REPRESENTATION AND WITHOUT A WARRANT

When Terry Nichols turned himself in at the police station on 21 April 1995, his wife Marife and infant daughter Nichole were with him. The FBI came in within 10 to 15 minutes and immediately separated Terry and Marife and began questioning them. The interrogations lasted until late into the night. When they had finished with Marife, they allowed her to go to the basement for a quick good-bye with Terry, then took her to a motel in Junction City. She was not allowed to go home because, they told her, the bomb squad needed to go through the house first. The FBI stayed in an adjoining room in the motel; and, the next day, took her to a store and bought a few clothes for her.

They questioned her again that day. On Sunday, they took her back to the police station, apparently to get an okay to go back to her house. Marife was given Terry's personal items, including his wallet and coat. The FBI then took her to her house where she was told to pack some things. She said she packed some toys for Nicole and some clothes.

The FBI took her to another motel, because, they said, it was not safe to stay in her house. She stayed in that motel for three-to-four days, being interrogated each day. She testified that, in all, she was in FBI custody for 36 days, in different cities, including Junction City and Wichita in Kansas, Oklahoma City, and also somewhere in Missouri. The FBI interviewed her each of these 36 days.

Marife is from the Philippines and speaks broken English. She also is not familiar with U.S. laws. She was not given benefit of counsel during these interrogations. She was not under arrest; but, all the same, was not allowed to return to her home.

Nichols' first wife, Lana Padilla, and their son, Josh Nichols, received some of the same treatment according to Michael Tigar in his closing argument. When the FBI decided to question Padilla, they contacted the Las Vegas FBI office with instructions to pick up Padilla and Josh. The two were brought to the FBI office on Friday morning, 21 April 1995, and were immediately separated and put in different rooms. Tigar described the interrogations this way: "Teams of people interview the two of them. And they don't let them go back home for five days. They keep them in hotel rooms at night and not let them return home." (Source: Nichols trial, pg. 6456)

Again, Padilla and Josh were not served with a warrant and did not have benefit of counsel. Josh was only 11 years old, but was not allowed to have his mother present when he was questioned. What a frightening experience this must have been for him. Is this the kind of treatment we should expect from the FBI: Intimidation of children? Stepping on the rights of witnesses?

G. COURTS DO NOT HOLD THOSE WHO PERJURED THEMSELVES ACCOUNTABLE FOR THEIR TESTIMONY

Numerous witnesses who testified at trial altered their stories from their previous depositions and testimony. After hours and hours of "refining" their testimony with prosecutors prior to the trials, they "remembered" events and descriptions entirely differently than they had earlier. The Defense used their previous remarks to the FBI as recorded on FBI 302 reports, their testimony before the grand jury and their statements in depositions to impeach the testimony. Many of these occurrences have been pointed out in this Report in the Trial Summary chapter. In no instance were any of these witnesses charged with perjury or were the prosecutors or FBI agents charged with suborning perjury. A few of these situations are listed below:

    1. James Miller and Kimberly Tolson from the Secretariat Office within the Justice Department and Russell Stuart Green, a courier from Justice, told the FBI about Miller receiving a call on 19 April advising that a bomb had gone off in Oklahoma City. According to the 302 report, the call came in at 9:32 a.m. Eastern Standard Time. This would have been 30 minutes before the bombing (which occurred at 9:02 a.m. Central Standard Time) due to the one-hour difference in time zones.

On 20 August 1996, Defense counsel Stephen Jones requested access to these witnesses, as well any other relevant information and evidence surrounding this incident. Jones' request went unanswered. On 14 October 1996, Jones asked again, and again was not answered.

Later it was discovered that, on 16 October 1996, Special Agent Doyle was sent to re-interview Miller, with nothing new to add. On 15 November, a new agent and federal prosecutor Aitan Goelman re-interviewed him. On 19 October, Green was re-interviewed. On 25 November, Tolson was re-interviewed. Their stories changed then: Miller himself had signed the log sheet after receiving the phone call and had time-stamped it 10:26 a.m—18 minutes after the bombing. The delivery Tolson had signed for now had a handwritten date on it with no time-stamp. Green could no longer remember which delivery it had been. The Prosecution finally contacted the Defense and provided a copy of the "complete delivery log" on 10 December 1996. (Source: Article from *U.S.A.Today*, 20 Apr 95; *Others Unknown,* Stephen Jones and Peter Israel, Public Affairs, N.Y., 1998, pg 4-5 & 216-219.)

2. Prosecution attorney, Beth Wilkinson, told the Court that the Government had no evidence of foreign involvement in the bombing. However, an FBI 302 report said that on official of the Saudi Government had given a warning to Vince Cannistraro (former CIA counter-terrorism chief) who passed on the information to the FBI. The FBI 302 report listed the top three targets as the Murrah Building, Houston's Immigration and Naturalization Service (INS) office and the FBI office in Los Angeles. Additionally, as Wilkinson knew, a call was received on 19 April 1995 at the Los Angeles Crisis Center in which the NFI (an Islamic group) claimed responsibility for the Murrah Building bombing. This caller provided the same targets in the same order that were provided to Cannistraro. Wilkinson, apparently, dismissed her culpability by saying the informant was not credible. (The informant was credible enough that, according to the 302, he was responsible for developing intelligence to help prevent the Saudi royal family from becoming victims of a terrorist attack.) No action was taken against Ms. Wilkinson for misleading the Court in this matter. (Source: *Others Unknown, The Oklahoma City Bombing Case and Conspiracy,* Stephen Jones, Perseus Books Group, 1998, pages 199-203

3. According to Michael Tigar, Nichols' defense attorney, the FBI committed blatant perjury in obtaining the arrest warrant for Terry Nichols. According to Tigar's account in the closing argument, by 21 April 1995, the FBI had set up a Strategic Information Operations Center (SIOC) in Washington D.C., which was staffed by top senior officials of the FBI and Department of Justice. The SIOC had open phone lines to all the FBI offices involved in the investigation: Oklahoma City, Kansas City, Junction City, Las Vegas, and Detroit. Through the phone line, they were able to coordinate and distribute information as it became available so that everybody involved in the investigation could be instantly updated on events related to the case.

About noon on Friday, 21 April, Washington made a decision at the highest levels to arrest Terry Nichols as a material witness. A material witness warrant would allow them to keep Nichols in custody without bail until taken before the grand jury. So the FBI sent word to the Kansas City office and dispatched a Special Weapons Assault Team (S.W.A.T.) and a Special Operations Group (SOG), (a surveillance team), to Herington, Kansas to keep an eye on Nichols until they could obtain the warrant.

Somebody, however, leaked the story to the press that Terry Nichols and his brother James were wanted as suspects in the case. Terry Nichols heard the news broadcast and went to the police station about 3:00 that afternoon. The surveillance agents watched him go in; "but the agents didn't go in, because...[they] had come to the conclusion that Mr. Nichols was now holding the police officers hostage. That's the mind-set that we're dealing with." They had their supervisor in Kansas City call the police station and ask questions to determine if there was a hostage situation. Their supervisor was told that there was no danger and Nichols wanted to talk to them. (Defense Attorney Michael Tigar in Nichols trial, pg. 6462)

The agents then called their top Washington lawyer, Howard Shapiro, who told them to keep Mr. Nichols talking until they could get the warrant signed in Oklahoma City. So Washington knew the situation and would have notified all the pertinent offices that Nichols voluntarily went to the police station to talk.

Back in Oklahoma, the FBI continued with the arrest warrant. They drew it up and went to a judge and told him that "Mr. Nichols has attempted to flee the jurisdiction of the United States" and the warrant was needed because "it's impractical to secure his attendance in front of a grand jury any other way." The warrant was then issued at 4:45 p.m. and faxed to all offices out of Oklahoma City. "Yet they never tell Terry Nichols until the next morning when they conclude the interview." Defense Attorney Michael Tigar in Nichols trial, pg. 6464)

These FBI agents who lied to the judge were never brought before the judicial system to answer for their action. We are not sure if this falls within the laws of perjury; but, at the very least, it falls under "obtaining a warrant under false pretenses." These agents were also never reprimanded by the Justice Department—in fact, quite to the contrary, they were told to proceed with the warrant, knowing full well that they would have to lie to obtain it.

H. FBI FAILS TO FOLLOW-UP ON LEADS TO JOHN DOES

There have been dozens of people who contacted the FBI with information they thought was pertinent to the Oklahoma City bombing, just to have their statements ignored. A few of their stories follow:

1. FBI Fails to Follow Up on Call to Justice Department

Regarding the above related story of the call to the Justice Department telling of the bomb going off before it had actually done so, there is no evidence that the FBI pursued this lead to determine who it was that knew about the bombing ahead of time and, therefore, would have been involved in it. Instead, they chose to falsify documents and harass the witnesses into changing their story, so there would be no evidence that someone else had been involved.

2. FBI Ignores Three Different Kansas Law Enforcement Officials' Identifications

According to the *Boulder Weekly*, three different law enforcement officials from Kansas notified the FBI that a known anti-Government activist from their part of the state resembled John Doe #2. Jake

Mauk, sheriff in Shawnee County (about 50 miles east of Junction City), saw the sketch of John Doe #2, recognized him as the activist and alerted the FBI; but they failed to take any action. Suzanne James, an employee of the Shawnee County District Attorney's office also called the FBI about this same individual being John Doe #2. Additionally, she told them that she might know an informant who could help them. She said the Government seemed less than interested. They told her they had already investigated the individual as a result of Mauk's phone call. Russell Roe, assistant county attorney for Geary County, Kansas also identified the same man to the FBI as resembling John Doe. He further told them that the man had been exploding fertilizer bombs on his remote farm prior to the Oklahoma City bombing. Again the FBI, apparently, was not interested. All three of these witnesses come from an area close to St. Marys, Kansas, which is at the center of the Kansas Freemen movement. (Source: *BoulderWeekly.Com*)

3. FBI Ignores Jeanne Boylan's Recognition of Photograph

Jeanne Boylan, in her book, tells about being at the Command Post at Fort Riley to meet with Jeff Davis and provide a sketch based on his recollections from his delivery of Chinese food to Room #25 at the Dreamland Motel. Boylan was told to have a seat while they ordered lunch for themselves and her. She said that, as she started to eat the burger, she saw a "military photograph" of McVeigh pinned to the wall. With him in the photo was a dark-skinned man who matched "perfectly" with the man she had drawn after talking to Debbie Nakanasha at the Oklahoma City Post Office. She made this known to an agent who passed on the information to the commander and quickly closed his office door. When he returned, the agent scurried her out of the building, hamburger still in hand. (Source: *Portraits of Guilt*, Jeanne Boylan, Pocket Books, 2000, pg 214)

4. FBI Ignores Report of John Doe Sighting in Waurika, Oklahoma

Darvin Bates owned a restaurant in Waurika, Oklahoma. Two or three weeks after the bombing he called the FBI about a man who had come to work for him who claimed to be from Kingman, Arizona and knew a lot about the area. Bates said the man resembled John Doe #2. He says he called the FBI office three different times, but no one came to interview him. (Nichols' Trial, pg 13257)

I. OKC COMMAND POST ORDERS LEADS ON JOHN DOE #2 HELD IN ABEYANCE

Denver writer, Ryan Ross, states that an internal FBI memo called off the search for John Doe #2 sometime between mid-May and late June 1995. A copy of a sitrep from one of their agents regarding a lead received from a "Columbia airtel" dated 03 May 1995 states, "In view of the fact that the Oklahoma Command Post had directed all offices to hold unsub #2 leads in abeyance, San Francisco will conduct no further investigation regarding this lead."

J. FBI FAILS TO INVESTIGATE 1034 FINGERPRINTS

There were 1,034 fingerprints, 87 palm prints and 17 "impressions" that the FBI gathered as evidence. FBI fingerprint supervisor Louis Hupp said they ran these prints against the prints of 14 "known suspects" which included Nichole Nichols, age two, Jeffrey Martin (unknown to OKBIC) and James Lee Walters (also unknown). The list of names used to run the prints against was furnished to the fingerprint experts by their superiors. Mr. Hupp said that he "had discussions with...the command post in Oklahoma City as to the feasibility of doing computer searches and it was determined at that time that it best be put off until a later time."

The other 11 people whose prints were checked against the latent prints were (1) Timothy McVeigh, (2) Terry Nichols, (3) Michael Fortier, (4) Marife Nichols (Terry's wife), (5) Jennifer McVeigh (Timothy's sister), (6) James Nichols (Terry's brother), (7) David Paulsen (from Paulsen's Military Surplus), (8) Edward Paulsen (owner of Paulsen's Military Surplus and David's father), (9) Roger Moore (a gun dealer and friend of McVeigh whose house was robbed), (10) Karen Anderson (Moore's friend and partner) and (11) Kevin Nicholas (McVeigh's friend in Michigan with whom McVeigh stayed).

The FBI had gathered 26 prints from Room #25 at the Dreamland Motel room where McVeigh stayed, other prints from the Great Western Motel where employees reported John Doe #2 stayed, the Ryder truck agency where the truck was rented, the yellow Mercury Marquis that belonged to McVeigh, and an Easy Go convenience store in Newkirk, Oklahoma (significance unknown). If these areas were considered important enough to warrant the time to take the prints, then it would follow that the prints are important enough to run for computer matches.

Hupp said that later, "towards the very end of it [the investigation] when most of the evidence had been completed," they again discussed "the feasibility of doing computer searches, and it was decided by the command post here in Denver that those searches would not be necessary." Not necessary—when John Doe #2 had still not been identified; when evidence pointed to possible foreign connections; when Elohim City residents and visitors were identified as plotting to blow up the Murrah Building; when numerous witnesses saw four individuals with a Ryder truck at Geary Lake. What were they thinking—or trying to hide?

If the FBI were truly interested in determining if there was a John Doe #2 and, if so, who he was, then it surely would have run the prints. As of the date of Hupp's testimony (24 November 1997), these prints had still not been run. To our knowledge, they have yet to be examined. Is the FBI afraid that running the prints would force further investigation?

Kathy Wilburn and her late husband Glen lost two grandchildren in the blast and conducted their own investigation into the bombing. Kathy said that "she was told the fingerprints were not run for a match because the FBI didn't want to give Nichols' defense team more ammunition against federal prosecutors." (A "win-at-all-costs" approach.) She said Agent Jon Hersley told her they would run the prints after completion of the Nichols' trial. However, Chris Whatney, the federal spokesperson for the bombing investigation said there is no ongoing investigation. (Source: *The Daily Oklahoman*, 21 March 1998)

K. GOVERNMENT FAILS TO PURSUE LEADS ON ELHOIM CITY RESIDENTS

1. ATF informant Carol Howe told the FBI two days after the bombing that Andreas Strassmier had threatened action against the Government and that he had made three trips to Oklahoma

City in November and December 1994 and February 1995. Strassmier, a German citizen, had allowed his visa to expire years before, yet the FBI took no action to detain him for questioning. He returned to Germany in January 1996, and the FBI finally conducted a telephone interview with him and his attorney on 30 April 1996—a full year after the bombing. (*The Secret Life of Bill Clinton*, Regnery Publishing, Inc., 1997, pg 77-78)

2. Dennis Mahon from Tulsa, Oklahoma was a close associate of Strassmier. He had been a former Grand Dragon of the Klu Klux Klan and was a member of the White Aryan Resistance (WAR) movement. He traveled extensively in Germany, recruiting new members, and operated a "dial a racist" hotline. Both Canada and Britain had banned him from their countries because "Interpol had him classified as an international terrorist." Informant Carol Howe had hold the ATF that Mahon had talked to her about "targeting federal installations for destruction through bombings, such as the IRS Building, the Tulsa Federal Building and the Oklahoma City Federal Building." (Source: (1) Television production, "The Fifth Estate," by the Canadian Broadcasting Corporation and (2) *Others Unknown, The Oklahoma City Bombing Case and Conspiracy*, Stephen Jones and Peter Israel, Perseus Books, pg 156-160)

3. Michael Brescia, who bears a remarkable likeness to John Doe #2, was Strassmier's roommate at Elhoim City. He was identified to the FBI by Catina Lawson and her mother, Connie Smith, immediately after release of the John Doe sketches. They told the FBI that his name was Mike and that he had attended parties at their home in the summer of 1992 with Andreas Strassmier and Timothy McVeigh. Later, Lawson tried to call in with Michael's last name, but she said the FBI would not talk with her. It was not until February 1996 that the FBI contacted her again. As of that date, they still had not interviewed Brescia. These three individuals who had ties to each other, and two of whom are known to have ties with McVeigh, were ignored by the Government after the bombing. Their own informant advised the FBI of the information she had passed to the ATF regarding these men. Connie Smith independently tied Strassmier and Brescia to McVeigh. The FBI would have had to be "blind, deaf and dumb" to overlook these potential suspects. Why did they wait years before investigating these leads?

L. FBI LIES TO COURT

In pretrial discovery hearings, the Government said that Strassmier had never been the subject of investigation in the Oklahoma City bombing, but defense counsel provided documents showing that the FBI, as late as 11 January 1996, stated that Strassmier was wanted in connection with the bombing, that he should be detained and the FBI notified, and that he should be considered armed and dangerous.

M. FBI DENIES NICHOLS LEGAL REPRESENTATION DURING INTERROGATION

After Nichols made himself available to the FBI at the police station in Herington, Kansas, the U.S. Attorney's office was contacted by an attorney offering to represent Nichols. He was denied access to Nichols during the interrogation process. The Defense tried to make this point to the jury twice in its cross-examination of Agent Stephen Smith; but, both times, the Prosecution objected, and Judge Matsch sustained the objection. This denial for the attorney to see Nichols may not have been technically a failure to allow legal representation because Nichols had not yet been arrested; but it was certainly not in the spirit of the law.

N. JUDGE ILLEGALLY DISMISSES GRAND JUROR FOR "TRYING TO DO HIS JOB"

Hoppy Heidelberg, a prominent thoroughbred horse breeder from Blanchard, Oklahoma was called to sit on the federal grand jury that indicted Nichols and McVeigh. Heidelberg stated that he "believes the indictments are valid and that the prosecution proved its case." His disagreement with the proceedings stemmed from what he saw as the prosecution's attempts to limit the indictments to McVeigh and Nichols. He became concerned when the Government tried to convince the jurors that the identification of a John Doe #2 was the result of "misidentification and confusion" on the part of the Ryder employees who confused an "innocent Army private, Todd Bunting," (who also rented a Ryder truck at Elliott's) with the person who was with "Kling" when he picked up his truck. Heidelberg said, "That's what got my attention. They went to a hell of a lot of trouble to try and make John Doe No. 2 go away." According to *The New American* article, "New Charges of OKC Cover-Up," dated 27 November 1995,

> *Heidelberg accused the federal prosecutors of stymieing jury requests to subpoena witnesses, thwarting attempts of jurors to ask questions of witnesses, and engaging in "intimidation." If members of the jury had questions for any witness, the witness was sent out of the room and the jurors were then required to ask their question of the prosecutor, who would fetch the witness and ask the question in his own words....The prosecution would usually let it be known by his body language, facial expressions, and tone of voice that the jurors' questions were "unwelcome."*

According to this article, *Media Bypass* reporter, Lawrence Myers, broke the story of a juror's dissatisfaction with the prosecutorial tactics. Heidelberg was accused of being that juror and was subsequently dismissed as a juror by U.S. District Judge David L. Russell for violating his oath of secrecy during the grand jury proceedings. Heidelberg contended that he had not been the source of the leak.

The New American, "OKC Grand Juror Vindicated," 01 April 1996, reported that Heidelberg had not leaked the story. Instead, in September 1995, Heidelberg contacted a Nebraska attorney, John DeCamp, for legal advice regarding his options before the grand jury to arrive at the truth. DeCamp was unavailable to meet with him and sent his investigator instead. The investigator was in the company of a video producer. The video producer later related Hoppy's story to a group of people, which included a research director for *Media Bypass*, Troy Underhill. Underhill, in turn, passed the story to *Media Bypass* reporter, Lawrence Myers who printed the story.
On 05 October 1995, Heidelberg sent a letter to Judge Russell expressing dissatisfaction with the grand jury proceedings and the prosecution's attempts to limit discovery of John Doe #2. He listed certain witnesses he would like called as witnesses. A letter from Judge Russell to Heidelberg, dated 24 October 1995, dismissed him from the grand jury. Heidelberg was quoted in *The Daily Oklahoman* of 27 October 1995 as saying, "You don't fire a man for trying to do his job. You fire him for not doing his job. This is the exact opposite of what needs to be done...."

As seen above, federal prosecutors prevented the grand jurors from properly investigating areas they felt were important. They led the jurors down the path they wanted them to go and thwarted their attempts to thoroughly investigate any other possibilities: specifically, John Doe #2 involvement in the bombings. Judge Russell allowed this to happen.

O. GOVERNMENT IGNORES WARNING FROM GOVERNMENT INFORMANTS

1. Carol Howe

Carol Howe infiltrated the compound at Elhoim City in Muldrow, Oklahoma. Elhoim City is reputed to be a white-separatist quasi-religious organization with ties to many radical right-wing groups. Howe was a paid ATF informant. She sent reports to the ATF warning of a possible bombing of a federal building. She advised that the Murrah Building was a potential target. The ATF had planned a raid of the compound; but, when they learned that the FBI also had informants who had infiltrated Elohim City, they called off the raid. They apparently took no preventive action as a result of Ms. Howe's warnings.

2. Cary Gagan

Cary Gagan was an paid Government informant. He said he was approached by Middle-Eastern individuals who wanted him to assist them in a bombing plot. He contacted the Justice Department with this information and was given a letter of immunity to provide the Government with information. He said that three times he visited the Murrah Building to case it out. He also saw architectural drawings of the building in the possession of the conspirators. When he passed on the information, no action was taken on it, and nobody from the Government would contact him to verify his data. (Source: Ltr from Gagan to FBI, 19 Sep 94; Ltr from Gagan to Joseph Hartzler, Dept of Justice, 16 Feb 97, and Gagan lawsuit, Civil Action No. 97-S-308, filed in U.S. District Court in Colorado)

P. GOVERNMENT INTIMIDATES INFORMANTS AND WITNESSES

There have been so many stories told of attempts by the Government in general, and the FBI in particular, to intimidate witnesses. Carol Howe and Cary Gagan were not only intimidated but were harassed and subjected to retributive legal action.

1. Carol Howe

After the FBI learned that Howe intended to testify for the Defense in the trials, they painted her in derogatory terms: the ATF had terminated her as an informant three weeks before the bombing because she allegedly tried to commit suicide; she was no longer loyal or competent. However, this "incompetent" informant was reassigned too help the FBI activated on 21 April, just after the bombing, and was sent back to Elohim City through 03 May, 1995. On 08 May, she was approached again about returning to Elohim City, but refused because she had received a phone call warning her not to return there. She remained on the ATF books until late 1996. At one point, Howe thought her life to be in danger and asked the FBI for protection. In a threat assessment, her handler Angela Finley Graham, wrote, "This agent...can assert that this informant has not been overly paranoid or fearful during undercover operations." The request for protection, however, was turned down.

In January 1977, Howe's boyfriend, James Dodson Viefhaus, Jr., was arrested because he had a message on his answering machine, which threatened to blow up some more federal buildings. Allegedly, Howe's voice was also on the tape. The FBI obtained a search warrant and raided the house. The search yielded much the same type material as found in the seach of Nichols' and Fortier's homes: bomb-making materials and "how-to" manuals, as well as the answering machine tape. Both Howe and Viefhaus were arraigned, but the indictment named only Viefhaus.

But then, the media picked up on the story and Howe went public. She claimed that the reason she was not indicted was because she knew about Elohim City, and that the materials found in the search were things she had gotten for the ATF from Elohim City. In a possible effort to keep her quiet, approximately 30 days before the start of the federal trial of McVeigh, Howe was also indicted. (Appendix pg. 443-448)

The Justice Department filed the charges for allegedly making a bomb threat and for possessing a non-registered destructive device. A federal jury acquitted Howe of all charges in July 1997.

(Source: Writ of Mandamus section IV, pages 38-53)

2. Cary Gagan

Cary Gagan was another paid Government informant whose warnings were ignored. He had contacted federal authorities about a bombing plot by Arabs whom he had become involved with. He was given a letter of immunity by the U.S. Attorney's Office on 14 September 1994 which stipulated that (1) he must cooperate fully with federal authorities; (2) any information he provided would not be used against him in criminal proceedings; and (3) any false information provided would nullify the immunity and he would be subject to prosecution for any acts he had committed while under the immunity agreement. The Government revoked the immunity without notice on 01 February 1996, after Gagan agreed to testify for the Defense in the McVeigh trial.

Gagan filed suit against the Government, alleging they illegally revoked his immunity by unilaterally making the determination themselves to do so without any form of judicial review. The Government never polygraph-tested Gagan to determine if the information he was providing was truthful or not. They did no follow-up on the information he provided, apparently took no action as a result of his information, and did not return his phone calls. The suit also alleges that Gagan's attorney was told that the letter of immunity had been signed by Assistant U.S. attorney James Allison, when it had actually been signed by his secretary, creating an opportunity for the Government to later challenge the legality of the agreement. A third claim that Gagan makes is that the U.S. Marshal's Office for the District of Colorado and the FBI deliberately exposed the plaintiff as an informant by interviewing him in the public lobby outside the FBI office in plain view of the public. A fourth claim is that the U.S. Attorney's office "On August 10-11, 1995, falsely [stated] for public dissemination by the media (*Rocky Mountain News* and KMGH-TV) that Plaintiff [as the informant] had a 'history of mental illness.'" (Source: Letter from Gagan to FBI, 19 Sep 94; Letter from Gagan to Joseph

Hartzler, Dept of Justice, 16 Feb 97, and Gagan lawsuit, Civil Action No. 97-S-308, filed in U.S. District Court in Colorado)

3. Other Witnesses

Numerous witnesses in Oklahoma City and Kansas have said they felt a veiled threat from authorities to "keep their mouths shut."

    a. Debbie Burdick said she received a call from "John with the FBI" who told her not to talk to anybody about seeing a bomb truck in downtown Oklahoma City minutes before the explosion. She said she felt it was a warning. John also tried to intimidate her by implying that, if she told her story, she would be helping to acquit McVeigh and Nichols. He asked her, "Don't you think these people are guilty?" John also implied that, if she told the truth, she would be unpatriotic: "You love your country don't you?"

    b. Nancy Kindle, who was attending college nights, studying nursing, and who worked as a home health aid, also worked days at Denny's Restaurant in Junction City, Kansas. She testified during McVeigh's trial that, on Easter Sunday in 1995, she was helping the hostess at the restaurant, and saw a group of three waiting at the front. One of the men told her they wanted to sit in the smoking section and gave her his name, spelling it for her. She identified him as Tim McVeigh. This was about 12:30 that afternoon. She said she saw McVeigh again about 4:30-4:45 coming out of a gasoline/convenience store as she was going in. They said hello. Kindle provided this same testimony at Nichols' trial, but added that she had been harassed by the Prosecution after her previous testimony. She said,

> *They just -- I put them on speakerphone so my family could hear how they kept on asking me over and over if I'm sure I didn't remember some—or if I'm sure that that was the man I seen. And then it started to get me irritated because they had two of them on the phone talking back and forth; and finally, I said, you know, "I've had enough," you know, "I'm home," you know, "Can you—sorry—Can you please leave me alone!"*

    c. John Jeffrey Davis, who delivered Chinese food to McVeigh's room at the Dreamland Motel, had testified that the individual he delivered to was not McVeigh. He said that the FBI went over his testimony with him over 20 times, and he felt pressured to change his testimony. He gave the following account:

> *The process of giving an oral description of the person I delivered the food to, the number of times that that has been gone back over, rapidly in succession, and to still be asked that same question consistently when my answer remains consistent to me feels like the response they receive is not the one they would like and that we'll go over this again and again and again.*

    d. Randall A. Yount, discussed earlier in this chapter in regard to munitions stored in the Murrah Building, was also warned. He said he later discussed this event with an ATF agent from his church and was told, "You really need to let this rest. Let us handle it. We'll get to the bottom of it…. You need to let it rest, for your own safety." He said he also discussed it with an FBI agent who attends his church and received similar advice: "The best thing you can do for your own peace of mind and that of your family is to leave it alone." Yount said he "read between the lines" and took that to mean to "keep my mouth closed.."

       e. Attorney Jim Linehan reported to the FBI that he had seen a yellow Mercury enter the parking garage at the Murrah Building approximately 30 minutes before the bombing. Linehan stated, "The FBI positively wanted me to identify McVeigh in the vehicle. I wouldn't." (Source: *Oklahoma Gazette*, 13 Feb 97, pg. 8)

       f. Morris Kuper saw two men in the Kerr-McGee parking lot shortly before the bombing. When questioned by the FBI, he described one of the men as looking like McVeigh and the other as being dark-complexioned and muscular. The FBI asked if the second man could be Terry Nichols. Kuper told them no, but they continued to ask. (Source: Nichols trial transcript, pg. 12822)

Title 18 USCS 1512 provides criminal penalties for intimidation, physical force or misleading conduct directed at a witness. Government agents seem to be immune from the penalties of this law. Even when witness accusations are highly publicized, no action is taken by the Justice Department to bring charges against the accused agents or even to investigate the charges.

Q. ATF TELLS AGENTS TO NOT COME IN

Several reports have surfaced in which witnesses say that the ATF was told not to come to work on the morning of the bombing. Katherine E. Mallette, an Emergency Medical Technician, was waiting with her ambulance to transport victims to area hospitals. As two agents walked by, she heard one of them say to the other agent, "Is that why we got the page not to come in today?" Tiffany Bible, also a paramedic, was at the bombsite four-to-five minutes after the blast. She approached an ATF agent in front of the building and expressed her concern for the other ATF agents in the building. He told her, "No, we weren't in there today." (Source: Sworn affadavit, 23 January 1998) Bruce Shaw, whose wife worked in the Murrah Building, was at the site within a few minutes of the blast. He saw an ATF agent and, since he and his wife knew several agents, asked the whereabouts of the other agents so he could check with them about his wife. He was told that the agents were tipped on their pagers to not come into the office that morning. (Source: OKBIC Interview and News media interviews with Shaw immediately after the bombing)

R. FBI LAB FALSIFIES RESULTS AND SLANTS TESTIMONY TO FAVOR THE PROSECUTION

       1. David L. Kochendorfer, the reserve deputy sheriff who said he heard U.S. Congressman Ernest Istook say that "We knew this was going to happen" ("Prior Knowledge" Chapter), was interviewed by FBI Agent James F. Carlile on 26 January 1998. As a result of that interview, Kochendorfer wrote a letter to the Special Agent in Charge of the Oklahoma City office complaining about the way his information was handled. He wrote,

He [Agent Carlile] made comments during the interview and at its conclusion which led me to believe his report was not going to accurately reflect my feelings concering the manner in which Congresman Istook made the statement to me the evening of the bombing.

At the conclusion of the interview, Mr. Carlile indicated to me, his report would reflect that I felt Congressman Istook was just repeating "scuttlebutt" he heard that evening. I told Agent Carlile I disagreed with his assessment of the conversation.... I would like my statement to accurately reflect that I feel Congressman Istook...was forthright and momentous.

2. Dr. Frederick Whitehurst, a forensic scientist with the FBI crime lab, prepared a paper critical of procedures and criminal investigation results within the FBI lab. His paper is titled *Flagging the Defense and the Scottsboro Boys—Lessons Learned? Lessons Forgotten?* In this paper, he cites numerous incidences of sloppy, deceptive, and even falsified forensic test results. He spoke of the "pressures continually applied upon these scientists to 'interpret' their data in the 'appropriate' manner."

Dr. Whitehurst tried to convince the FBI lab to change the way in which it handled evidence and drew conclusions. When he was not successful, he contacted the Department of Justice's Office of the Inspector General (IG) in January 1996. According to a *Daily Herald* article dated 12 March 1998, the resulting IG report "blasted the world-renowned lab for flawed scientific work and inaccurate, pro-prosecution testimony in major cases including the Oklahoma City and World Trade Center bombings. Bromwich [the IG] recommended major reforms and discipline for five agents...."

Dr. Fredrick Whitehurst
Special Agent at the FBI Crime Lab

As a result of Whitehurst's allegation, a Congressional investigation ensued and Whitehurst was called to testify. He spoke of the World Trade Center bombing and was asked, "In other words, you began to experience pressure on you to say that the explosion was caused by a urea nitrate bomb?" His response was "Yes, that is correct."

Senator Charles E. Grassley addressed the Congress with the following comments. The comments are recorded in the Congressional Record of 25 February 1997, Vol. 143, No. 21:

Reports of alleged mismanagement within the Federal Bureau of Investigation have been in the news, recently. Most of the reports reflect issues in the FBI's vaunted crime lab. These allegations of mismanagement come on the heels of FBI management disas-

ters with Waco, Ruby Ridge, Filegate, and Atlanta, as well as others.... The average citizen is wondering if this premiere law enforcement agency is out of control....The issue is trust and confidence in the Nation's No. 1 law enforcement agency. And in the context of other, recent management fiascos at the FBI, skepticism is validly the order of the day.... So far, the FBI has responded to the allegations in a less than credible way.

First, they shot the messenger—Dr. Whitehurst, the lab scientist who first raised the allegations. Next, the FBI used the typical "everything's okay" strategy to make the public think there was no problem. But that was contradicted by the facts. Weldon Kennedy [deputy director of the FBI] said the problems in the lab wouldn't compromise any past, present, or future case. That statement raised a lot of eyebrows.... In my view, Mr. Weldon Kennedy is playing fast and loose with reality, with a purpose to mislead the public and mislead Congress. The simple fact is, it is much too premature for Mr. Kennedy to be making groundless predictions. For him to do so anyway shows a strategy to mislead.

Third, I have learned that it is not just Dr. Whitehurst who has alleged wrong-doing in the FBI crime lab. Others have as well....Finally, I fear the FBI has covered up the lab's shortcomings....

Mr. President, what we're seeing in the FBI lab issue is systemic. It reflects a culture that says the FBI is more interested in a conviction than they are in the truth. They don' reveal all the facts. Only enough to make their case. Finally, Mr. President, let me send a shot across the bow. There are rumors I'm hearing that the FBI intends to fire Dr. Whitehurst right after the IG report is released. My message today to the Bureau is, "you fire Dr. Whitehurst, and you will cause a protracted battle with the Congress over the integrity of the FBI's leadership.

In the Congressional Record of 06 March 1997, Vol. 143, No. 28, Sen. Grassley further addressed the Congress:

The FBI's defense—some would say cover-up—is slowly unraveling. Last week, we discovered that it wasn't just Dr. Whitehurst that has raised serious concerns. Another respected scientist, Dr. William Tobin, had raised equally serious allegations in 1989. He alleged that an FBI agent tampered with evidence and made a series of false statements while testifying in court proceedings....The FBI covered up this matter.

In the past 2 weeks, two additional cases... appear to reveal similar improper behavior by FBI agents testifying in Federal cases....Last week, the Miami Herald ran a story about a Florida case reviewed by the IG....The testimony of evidence linking Mr. Trepal to this murder may have been tainted by an FBI lab supervisor.

And now there's a third case, Mr. President. The Associated Press reported yesterday that the IG found similar problems in the VANPAC case.... According to the AP, the IG report states that "a lab witness overstated test results during the trial." And that's not all. In addition to overstated testimony in VANPAC, the report found the lab lacked databases to support its conclusions, used unvalidated tests, lacked written test procedures, inade-quately documented why it discounted test results that undercut its conclusions, and lacked any record for some tests."....

Whitehurst asked that a special, independent, or outside counsel review the matters. But the FBI chose another course. It did not empanel an independent review. Instead, the mat-ter was assigned to two attorneys within the Office of the General Counsel. They reported directly to Mr. Shapiro and Mr. Freeh (the Director of the FBI)...What is amazing to me is that neither Mr. Freeh nor Mr. Shapiro recused himself from the decision-making role with respect to the review. After all, they had prosecuted on the cases—the VANPAC case—in which Dr. Whitehurst alleged [that] misconduct had occurred.

I have now obtained a redacted copy of the results of that review....The first thing they did was fire at the messenger. On the very first page, the FBI notes that Dr. Whitehurst could be disciplined for providing information about the lab's misconduct to Congress. You see, Mr. President, providing information to Congress—and I'm quoting the FBI—"violates FBI and DOJ regulations." Were you aware, Mr. President, that FBI and DOJ regulations override the first amendment guarantee of the people's right to petition Congress?

OKBIC Note: According to the *Daily Herald*, 12 March 1998, Dr. Whitehurst filed suit against the Justice Department for spreading false and derogatory information to discredit him. *A & E Investigative Reports*, "The FBI Under Fire," reported that Whitehurst was suspended and filed suit for "violating the whistle blower's law which protects employees who reveal wrong-doing." In the 1998 settlement, Whitehurst agreed to resign from the Bureau and was awarded a total of $1.6M. According to the *Daily Herald*, this settlement included $300,000, an agreement to pay Whitehurst (age 50) annual payments equal to the salary and pension he would have earned had he continued to work until retirement age (57 years) plus his attorney fees which amounted to $258,580..

It is the contention of OKBIC that this same type of subterfuge was used by the FBI during the Oklahoma City bombing investigation. It decided on a strategy and culled out all evidence that did not support that strategy. It failed to scientifically investigate forensic evidence, i.e., 1034 latent fingerprints they collected which might have indicated other possible accomplices. It coerced and threatened witnesses so they would support the FBI strategy. Agents gave slanted and incomplete testimony in court and misleading answers to Defense probes. They failed to provide exculpatory evidence to the Defense, and only did so after repeated letters and compulsion by the Court. It failed to follow up on leads to "Others Unknown" because other involvement did not fit their scenario. They deceived the American public on this and did so with deliberateness and foresight.

S. FBI DECIDES ON TYPE OF BOMB WITHOUT PROPER SCIENTIFIC EVIDENCE

The Government decided what type of bomb had exploded as early as 21 April 1995. An article dated 21 April in *The Daily Oklahoman* quoted FBI agent, Weldon Kennedy as saying, "Analysts determined that a homemade mix of fertilizer and fuel oil, possibly several thousand pounds of it, created the blast...."

The Justice Department's IG report found that the conclusions reached on the bomb by Agent Dave Williams from the FBI lab lacked scientific bases. They highlighted similarities between Williams' reports on the bombs in Oklahoma City and at the World Trade Center in New York City, which were based on conjecture and foreknowledge of the defendants.

OKBIC Note: During the trial, Agent Burmeister testified regarding lab results. His supervisor, Dave Williams was greatly criticized by the IG report; yet, Judge Matsch refused to allow the IG's conclusions into the trial, thus preventing the jurors from knowing that much of the scientific evidence was suspect, or that the evidence Burmeister presented may have been affected by his superior's influence. In Section C of the IG report, Agent Williams was highly criticized for his testimony during the World Trade Center bombing trial held September 1993 through March 1994. According to the IG report, Williams based his "expert" opinion that urea was the main ingredient in the bomb, in part, on the evidence that urea nitrate had been found in searches associated with the defendants. The IG said that this was "comparable to a firearms expert identifying the caliber of a spent bullet based on the mere fact that a suspect had a handgun of a particular caliber."

They assessed the "scientific" analysis performed, as follows:

> *It appears Williams may have worked backward—that is, he may have first determined the result he wanted [here, that the defendants could have produced 1200 pounds of urea nitrate, the amount he estimated was used in the bombing] and then tailored his testimony about yield to reach that Result. We are deeply troubled by this possibility....We find that Williams testimony about non-laboratory yield was invalid and beyond his area of expertise.*

The IG report also found problems with the method of arriving at velocities of detonation (VOD). They pointed out conflicting conclusions reached by Williams to support his suppositions in the World Trade Center bombing and his suppositions in the Oklahoma City bombing. The IG report stated that, in reporting on the World Trade Center, Williams emphasized that

> *the pitting and cratering within a radius of 4 feet from the seat of the explosion, whencombined with only heaving without pitting and cratering within 8.5 feet, showed a velocity of detonation of 12,000 to 16,000 feet per second.*

> *...Moreover, in the Oklahoma City case, Williams found pitting and cratering 12 feet from the seat but nevertheless estimated the VOD to be 13,000 feet per second in the case, effectively under-cutting the primary basis he claimed for his VOD opinion in the World Trade Center case.*

In his report for the Oklahoma City case, Williams' determination of the VOD was based on "examina-tions of the crater, explosive damage to the bomb-laden vehicle, witness buildings, automobiles, victims and other local witness materials." The IG found that Williams' specific VOD "lacked an adequate scientific and empirical basis."

Williams' determination that the Oklahoma City bombing was caused by an ANFO bomb also lacked scientific backup. He acknowledged that, "although ammonium nitrate crystals were found at the post-blast scene, there are many explosives in the range of 12-14,000 feet per second that have ammonium nitrate in them." He admitted that "he reached this conclusion, in part, because Terry Nichols…purchased ammonium nitrate and diesel oil prior to the bombing."

The IG stated that, "without the evidence of these purchases, Williams admitted he would have been unable to conclude that ANFO was used." By basing an opinion about the main charge of an explosion, "in whole or in part, on prior knowledge of the explosive components purchased by a defendant…is misleading and presents the case in a way most incriminating to the defendants." The IG further stated that, "Had Williams explicitly stated in his report that the ANFO opinion was based on the defendant's purchase, the opinion could have been appropriately discounted as a non-expert conclusion that seeks to match the characteristics of the explosion with evidence associated with the defendants."

The IG also found that Williams' estimate of the bomb size—4,000 pounds—was "flawed." Williams said that, "by other things, including the crater size, the blast damage, breakage, building damage, I can estimate it's approximately 4,000 pounds." The IG asked, "That's not based on searches or anything? Your conclusion as to 4,000 pounds, is that based on anything that was recovered in the searches or receipts or what they ordered?" Williams responded, "Yes, it is—It's not solely based—My estimate of 4,000 pounds is not solely based on the receipts."

OKBIC Note: In the Oklahoma City bombing case, the size of the bomb kept changing: on 20 April 1995, *The Daily Oklahoman*, in an article titled "Scores Killed in Bomb Blast; State Stunned," page one, stated that "officials estimated the device had 1,000 to 1,200 pounds of explosives. Shortly, it became 4,000 pounds. But once the Government was able to tie Nichols to the possible purchase of 4,800 pounds of ammonium nitrate, that became the size of the bomb.

Other errors the IG found in Williams' conclusions were:

    1. Because Williams concluded that the bomb was ANFO, a container was necessary to hold the bomb. Since white plastic barrels and white plastic barrels with blue trim were found at Nichols' home, it was determined that similar barrels had been used to hold the bomb. The scientific analysis of the plastic shards found at the bombsite did not include determining the radius of curvature, so "it is virtually impossible to know that the containers definitely were 50 gallon barrels that were white or white with blue trim."

    2. Williams concluded that "[t]he initiator for the booster[s] was either a detonator from a Primadet Delay system or sensitized detonating cord." (Primadet was found at Nichols' house.) The IG said that since these items were not found at the crime scene, "We conclude that it was improper for Williams to render a categorical conclusion identifying the initiator for the booster."

    3. Williams concluded that the initiator for the Primadet was a non-electric detonator (Such fuses were found at Nichols' home.), and the time delay was approximately two minutes and 15 seconds, based on a videotape showing the Ryder truck appear near the Murrah Building two-minutes and 15 seconds before the explosion. Williams postulated that a three-foot cord would be needed, based "on his assumption that the perpetrator had a military background." No evidence of a non-electric detonator was found at the scene. Therefore, the IG concluded that "it was improper for Williams to render a categorical conclusion identifying the initiator for the booster."

(Source: Department of Justice Office of the Inspector General report, *Whitehurst Review*, Case No. 9403575, 19 Mar 96)

The problems with the FBI lab appear to be systemic. They start at the top of the Bureau and filter down. The Director of the FBI, after prosecuting on the VANPAC case, appointed himself as the reviewing agent on the investigation into the FBI's handling of the case. He tried to mislead Congress on problems within the Bureau, and defended the FBI's actions in such ill-conceived actions as Ruby Ridge and Waco. The FBI is apparently more concerned with "getting their man" than with truth or justice. They appear ready to go to any lengths to make their case and to cover up their mistakes. Their power is such that they "get away with it." Nobody wants to think that this premier law enforcement agency in the U.S. is above the law, but events in the last several years show that to be true. When will the people demand of Congress that the FBI and Justice Department become accountable? How many more "fixed" trials and witness intimidations and botched raids are we willing to put up with?

T. FBI FAILS TO TAKE RESIDUE SAMPLES FROM BOMB SCENE FOR COMPARISON WITH EVIDENCE

The FBI Evidence Recovery Team failed to take any samples of the soil or ground coverings in the Murrah Building or surrounding areas where evidence was recovered. Samples would have served the purpose of providing a baseline for residue levels on evidence recovered. These levels could have been compared to levels found on evidence to determine if the levels were significant or possibly just contamination from the site. FBI agent Steven Burmeister said that "there is also the complication that there is a lot of contamination of items by dirt and debris at the scene. For example, there will be a lot of dust. In general, a lot of dirt." When questioned by the Defense whether the FBI had taken any soil samples, Agent Burmeister said,

    A. Well, I have no reason to believe that the ground itself had nitrates on them.

    Q. But you didn't check, did you?

    A. It's typically not a procedure that I would actually take.

Therefore, the FBI was aware of the possibility of contamination from the scene, but took no measures to collect soil and dust samples for comparison. They then testified in court about nitrate residues found on evidence they collected.

U. GOVERNMENT FAILS TO SECURE BUILDING AFTER WARNINGS

The Government received warnings of a general nature from outside sources of a threat to federal buildings. Former intelligence officer, William Northrop, revealed that the German BND had sent a warning to the State Department (Source: *The Oklahoma City Bombing and the Politics of Terror*, David Hoffman, Feral House, 1998, pg.156). The U.S. Marshal Service sent an alert to federal agencies and judges that "Islamic terrorists may be planning suicide attacks against federal courthouses and Government installations in the United States designed to attract worldwide press attention through the murder of innocent victims (Source: *New Jersey Star-Ledger* article on 15 March 1995). U.S. District Judge Wayne Alley of Oklahoma City advised that he had received a warning "within the past two or three weeks...to take extra precautions. (Source: *The Oregonian*, 20 April 1995). Harvey Weathers, a deputy fire chief with the Oklahoma City Fire Department reported that the FBI issued a warning the week prior to the bombing for them to be on alert (Source: *USA Today*, 20 April 1995). Apparently, no action was taken at the Murrah Building to step up security. The only action seems to have been to warn law enforcement agencies of the warning.

At a meeting held at the Wilburns' home with blast victims, Agent Luke Franey was asked if any preparations had been taken by government agencies because of the significance of 19 April, "Was the ATF on some kind of special alert?" He responded that "No, there was no alert or any concern on our part about the significance of that day." His boss, ATF Director John Magaw told a different story, however. In a CNN interview, he stated, "I was very concerned about that day and issued memos to all of our field offices—They were put on alert." When Wilburn asked him where his agents were that day, he said, "Some were out on assignment , and some...were out of town." A surprised U.S. attorney said, "I thought they were at a golf tournament." But Franey insisted they were working in the field. (Source: *Media Bypass*, June 1996, pg 33)

Why were only law enforcement and Justice Department officials at the Murrah Building alerted? If other workers in the building had been notified, there could have been hundreds of sets of eyes "on alert." Also, workers would have been aware of the potential danger and could have made an informed decision for themselves whether or not to go to work that day, as Judge Wayne Alley did.

V. FBI CANCELS APB ON MIDDLE-EASTERN SUSPECTS

The original sketches of John Doe #1 and #2 were released on 20 April 1995. The Justice Department reported on 21 April that he was still at large. However, as early as 26 April, the FBI was saying that they might never find John Doe #2—that he might have been killed in the blast. However the APB had been cancelled the same day it was issued.

W. GOVERNMENT IGNORES THOSE WHO WITNESSED SUSPECTS IN BUILDING BEFORE BLAST

Jane Graham with HUD worked in the Murrah Building. The week before the bombing, she saw three men with wires and tools and building plans in the garage. She had assumed they were telephone company employees. After the bombing, she thought maybe otherwise, so she contacted the FBI and spoke with Joe Schwecke. They made an appointment for 05 September 1995. Schwecke did not show for the meeting. Graham called again and made another appointment for the following week. Again Mr. Schwecke did not show up. On 12 September, in the Office of Native

Americans/HUD, she said several agents were there interviewing people, asking a set series of questions regarding the bombing. She was interviewed by a female agent. When told they were finished, Graham told the agent that she was not finished—that she wanted to know why no one had asked questions about the week before the bombing and if anyone had seen anything suspicious. Her feelings were that "the FBI was not interested in any time other than the Monday or Tuesday the week of the bombing!!!! And only if the responses pointed directly to McVeigh." She said that, when she first told her story, the only question asked was "Was one of the men McVeigh?"

X. U.S. ARMY TAKES ACTION AGAINST MEMBERS ASSISTING WITH RESCUE

Arlene Blanchard with the U.S. Army recruiting office told about a sergeant first class and a captain from battalion headquarters (BN HQ), who were assigned to the Medical Examiner's Office during the rescue and recovery effort. They provided information and pictures from inside the building to Mrs. Blanchard's husband who took the pictures to the FBI's bombing investigation operations director. As a result, the FBI interviewed the two military men, which, Blanchard said, enraged Battalion Commander LTC Regis Carr. He told his people that it was not their job to investigate the bombing or to help with the investigation. In retaliation, LTC Carr downgraded the sergeant's medal and denied any medal for the captain, while making sure all other BM and Recruiting Company soldiers (including himself and the sergeant major who were not even in the building when the bombing occurred) received the highest-possible medals and awards. The captain was relieved of command and forced to retire.

Blanchard also told about two Army sergeants who remember seeing Timothy McVeigh in the BN HG office in the Murrah Building. She said these sergeants were "soon 'conveniently' transferred to other **remote** commands." (Emphasis added.) Blanchard told this story on ABC's *Nightline* program, then was told by military officials she could not talk about what happened to anyone else.

She herself was subjected to intimidation by the U.S. Army. She had talked to ABC's *Nightline* program about John Doe #2. She was given a direct order by the Battallion Commander, the Battallion Sergeant Major, and the Brigade Public Affairs "bird" colonel not to talk to the press again. This direct order was given in the presence of agents from the FBI, the ATF and the Army CID. The Army CID told her that she was "ruining their investigation by going on national TV and talking about John Doe #2." Although now retired, she was still a member of the Ready Reserve. She said she received a veiled threat that, if she talked to the press again, she would be "called up" and put back on active duty status. She would then be subject to the Uniform Code of Military Justice and would be brought up on charges of disobeying a direct order and would be court martialed. This was while she was still recovering from her injuries. She also feels that the Army took retaliatory action against her when she applied for medical retirement as a result of her injuries. She was initially given a 10 percent "**Non-job related**" disability, even though she was in uniform and at her normal duty station. (Due to efforts of her congressman, Frank Lucas, and his staff member, Phillip Davis, she has now been awarded 40 percent disability.)

Y. JUDGE MATSCH CHOOSES TO IGNORE REMARK SHOWING JUROR WAS BIASED

During McVeigh's trial, Judge Matsch constantly cautioned jurors that they were to remain impartial until all the evidence had been presented, and told them not to talk about the case among themselves. But, when one of the jurors complained to the court clerk that another juror had made the comment, "I think we all know what the verdict should be," Matsch chose to ignore the remark. Match thought it would be too difficult to question jurors on what had been said; so, without questioning, he decided that "the thing, in context, is joking around." Judges handling McVeigh's appeal thought the juror should have been excused. Judge David Ebel said the circumstances were no different than if the juror himself had written a note to the judge saying he had heard enough and knew the defendant was guilty. The judge would immediately dismiss that juror. Judge Mike Murphy felt that Matsch should have held a hearing to determine the impartiality of the juror. He commented that it looked like the prosecutors were afraid to hear the juror's answers. (Source: *The Daily Oklahoman*, 29 April 1998)

Z. FBI 302 REPORTS REFLECT ERRONEOUS WITNESS STATEMENTS

Witnesses have stated that the FBI 302 reports did not accurately reflect the information they had provided to the FBI. Oklahoma City Reserve Deputy Sheriff Kochendorfer said that, when he told the FBI about a U.S. Congressman telling him that "We knew this was going to happen," the FBI agent told him his 302 report would reflect that Kochendorfer thought the congressman was just repeating scuttlebutt. Kochendorfer wrote the RAC in Oklahoma City to ensure that there was a record of his true remarks (Appendix pg. 414). John Jeffrey Davis, who delivered Chinese food to McVeigh's room at the Dreamland Motel, said the person who took the food was not McVeigh. At trial, he was questioned by the prosecution about statements made to the FBI about fearing for his safety. The FBI agent apparently recorded that Davis told him that he was concerned for his safety if he changed his statement regarding the identity of the man in Room #25. Davis said he had not told the agent that he was afraid—the agent had asked him. Davis had then told him that, some day, the door to a delivery room might open and he might be facing a shotgun. Davis said this statement was made in a sarcastic manner. The agent, however, did not indicate on his report that it was a facetious remark. An FBI 302 report on Charles Farley, who saw a Ryder truck, other vehicles and several men at Geary Lake on 18 April, recorded that Farley knew one of the vehicles was a three-quarter-ton truck because it had eight lug nuts on the wheel. Farley said he did not tell them eight, but six.

AA. GOVERNMENT IGNORES SIGHTINGS OF RYDER TRUCK AND OTHER VEHICLES

The Government case had a piece missing: Where was the bomb mixed? So, to bolster their case, they decided that the bomb must have been mixed at Geary Lake outside of Junction City, Kansas. The lake is partially visible from U.S. Highway 77, so the FBI set up a roadblock to stop residents in the area to see if anyone had seen a Ryder truck at the lake on Tuesday, 18 April 1995, the day before the bombing. What they heard was that there were over 20 sightings of a Ryder truck at the lake the week before the 18th. Some of the witnesses reported seeing several individuals around the Ryder truck, as well as other vehicles, such as a dark blue pickup. So what did the prosecution do with this information? They chose to ignore it. Instead, they called one witness, Gary Kitchener, who had not seen a Ryder truck at the lake. Kitchener worked for the Kansas Department of Wildlife and Parks. In April of 1995, in addition to his normal maintenance work at the lake, he was performing creel surveys to determine the kinds and size of fish being taken from the lake. His schedule for the study during this time period was for approximately two hours a day, with the times varying, on the 10th through the 13th, and on 16, 17 and 19 April. He testified that he did not see a Ryder truck at the lake at any of these times. So, because he did not see a truck prior to 18 April, no truck was at the lake. Since there were at least 20 other sightings, it begs the question: Was Mr. Kitchener really at the lake doing his creel studies or was he only professing to do them while he was off doing other business on county time? Or was he just unobservant? At any rate, since he was not at the lake on 18 April to see whether or not a Ryder truck was there, the Government apparently felt that this proved their case that the bomb was mixed at Geary Lake on the morning of 18 April by Timothy McVeigh and Terry Nichols. (Obviously, the other 20 or more sightings were caused by mass hallucination.)

BB. FBI KEEPS FEMA INVESTIGATORS 200 FEET FROM BUILDING

FEMA sent a Building Performance Assessment Team (BPAT) to Oklahoma City 09-13 May 1995 to investigate the damage caused to the Murrah Building. The team was composed of American Society of Civil Engineers and Government engineers. In their investigation, they were not allowed to physically inspect the structure or the crater. As stated in their official report, "Physical inspection of the structure was limited to visual observation from a distance of approximately 200 feet." The BPAT was allowed to examine the rubble of the building, which had been taken to the Oklahoma County Sheriff's Training Center for storage; but this review did not show them which column pieces had been where in the building. They had to rely strictly on photographic evidence for this information. (Source: Fema Report, *The Oklahoma City Bombing: Improving Building Performance through Multi-Hazard Mitigation*, page 1-1)

OKBIC Note: Since recovery efforts had still been ongoing until 04 May 1995, the week before FEMA's arrival on 09 May, and since the building had been shored up for rescue/recovery efforts, why was it so imperative that FEMA not be allowed inside the building, or even within 200 feet of it? What was the FBI afraid they would find?

OKBIC Note: The architect who designed the Murrah Building, said that the building could be saved—"after all, two-thirds of it is underground parking, which is not seriously damaged." (Source: The Daily Oklahoman, 21 Apr 95, pg 11)

CC. GOVERNMENT DESTROYS CRIME SCENE BEFORE PROPER INVESTIGATION OF BLAST DAMAGE

The Government imploded the Murrah Building on 23 May 1995, 33 days after the bombing. General Benton K. Partin had asked that the demolition be delayed until explosives experts could examine the building. The request was denied and the demolition proceeded on schedule. The Government obviously did not want experts to determine the cause of the building collapse.

OKBIC Note: When questioned by the *Daily Oklahoman* about scientific experts' opinions that the Murrah Building must have had contact explosives placed on the columns, FTI special agent Danny Defenbaugh made the following comments:

> *Along with one of those theories are a number of individuals who are saying, 'OK, I never went on site. I never saw the Murrah Building. I never saw the crime scene, and I never saw any of the damage... But I saw all these pictures that were given to my by the public...' but I can tell you right now this is exactly what happened.*

Yet, this is "exactly what happened" to the FEMA/ASCE BPAT personnel who were kept 200 feet from the crime scene and had to base their assessment on pictures.

DD. GOVERNMENT DETERMINES REVENGE FOR WACO WAS MOTIVE WITHIN MINUTES OF BLAST

Paramedic Tiffany Bible said she was talking to an ATF agent at the bomb scene a few minutes after the bombing and pondered why someone would blow up a building in Oklahoma City. She said he answered that "the Murrah Building was bombed because of Waco" and it was targeted because "the person in charge in Waco was transferred to Oklahoma City." This statement supports the belief of many that the ATF was very aware of the potential danger that 19 April held, but failed to share that information with other occupants of the building.

EE. PROSECUTORS DELIBERATELY TRY TO MISLEAD JURORS

When Jeff Davis was called by the Defense to testify in the Nichols' trial, he stated that the person he delivered Chinese food to in Room #25 at the Dreamland Motel did not look like Timothy McVeigh—supporting the contention that others besides McVeigh and Nichols were involved in the bombing. The prosecutor asked him if he had ever told anyone that he had seen McVeigh sitting on the bed in the room that night. Davis said that he had not. The prosecution then had Mr. Davis look at "this dark-haired woman back here at the second table" and asked if he had ever met her before. When he told them no, they asked if he remembered staying at the Burnsley Hotel in Denver and talking to the bartender. He was then asked if he had told the bartender that he saw two people in Room #25. Again he answered no. The prosecution asked, "You deny that?" He replied, "Yes, I do." The Defense next asked if the dark-haired lady was the bartender. Davis said he did not believe so. After comments from the defense, the prosecution admitted that she was not the bartender. This was a deliberate ploy by the prosecution to confuse and deceive the jury. Judge Matsch did not reprimand the prosecutor for this behavior.

In other instances during the trial, the prosecution led the jury to believe that witnesses had refused to answer FBI questions when, in actuality, the FBI had never asked the questions. An example follows; Agent Stephen Smith is giving testimony about Nichols' interrogation:

> Q. You told the jury that Mr. Nichols said he had driven by "that building," the Murrah Building. Did he explain to you how he came to use that description?
>
> A. Yes. He said that he had driven past "that building" a couple of times, and it was obvious in the context of the interview that it was the Alfred P. Murrah Federal Building.

> Q. *Did he tell you why he remembered that building in particular?*
>
> A. *No, he did not.*
>
> Q. *Did he tell you whether he had ever been downtown in Oklahoma City on 5th Street past the Murrah Building prior to Easter Sunday?*
>
> A. *No, he did not.*
>
> Q. *Did he give you any basis for explaining why he even recognized the building in order for him to describe it to you?*
>
> A. *No, he gave no basis.*

Apparently, federal prosecutors have missed the point that their job is to arrive at the truth—not neces-sarily to get a conviction. One wonders if their job appraisals are tied to conviction percentages—or is it only their egos?

FF. OKLAHOMA COUNTY DISTRICT ATTORNEY'S OFFICE BELITTLES GRAND JURY

Rick Sinnett, who saw a Ryder truck and trailer at the convenience store where he worked in Kingman, Kansas, was called by the Oklahoma County D.A.'s office to question if Mr. Sinnett would honor a subpoena to appear before the Grand Jury if the subpoena were mailed rather than served in person. He told the caller that, yes, he would honor it. The caller made the statement to him that he "did not know why he was having to do this, that Charles Key was pushing this and that nothing would come of it and that it was a waste of time." (Source: Signed affidavit, 25 Aug 97)

GG. COURT PLACES TRIAL DOCUMENTS UNDER SEAL

During the trials of both Nichols and McVeigh, voluminous amounts of motions were placed under seal by Judge Matsch. Many of these covered items which, in our opinion, should have been open to the public, such as expenses filed by the defense attorneys. During the first 10 days of December in the Nichols' trial (the trials each lasted for several months), the following motions were sealed:

    20 Bench Conferences
     4 Portions of trial transcript
     4 Brief and Judge's ruling in support of Defenses' proposed jury instructions
     4 Granting prosecution motion regarding proposed jury instructions
     4 Issuance of Subpoenas in Forma Pauperies
     4 Witness travel
     3 Nichols' memorandum regarding possible witness invocation of their Fifth
         Amendment rights
     3 Nichols' motion to secure attendance of a witness under seal
     3 Nichols' memorandum regarding witness' testimony
     3 Ex Parte conference in chambers

    3 Copy of Writ of Habeas Corpus ad Testificandum for Defense witness
    3 Order allowing third party witness Writ of Habeas Corpus securing his presence
    3 Judge's orders granting motion regarding witness travel
    2 Memorandum for leave to file "Memmorandum and Offer of Proof of Testimony of defense rebuttal expert witness
    2 Granting of above motion
    2 Defense motion to strike expert testimony

HH. FBI REFUSES TO ACCEPT EVIDENCE FROM TELEVISION REPORTER

On 01 March 2001, FOX News program "The O'Reilly Factor," interviewed former KFOR-TV reporter Jayna Davis from Oklahoma City. During the interview she stated that the results of her investigation showed that Iraqi terrorist Osama Bin Laden had financed the Oklahoma City bombing. She asserted that an unidentified source observed Terry Nichols in the presence of terrorist Ramsi Yousef in the Phillipines, and that Yousef is funded by Bin Laden. She told of a Middle-Eastern terrorist cell living and operating in Oklahoma City. She also had in her possession 24 sworn statements of witnesses who had seen an Arab-looking person in McVeigh's company in the days before, and the morning of, the bombing

Davis went to the FBI in Oklahoma City with an offer to provide her investigative documentation to them. She had a notary with her and asked that they sign an affidavit confirming receipt. The agent spoke with his superiors in Devner, then refused to accept the material.

II. FBI FAILS TO PROPERLY SECURE EVIDENCE

When the FBI gathered evidence in Oklahoma City after the bombing, they failed to follow proper protocol. Items of evidence were bagged together, allowing for cross-contamination; items were moved, then replaced, to photograph them "in place;" a chain of custody was not strictly adhered to; and persons handling the evidence in the lab did not place their own initials on the items, but rather their supervisor's.

JJ. GOVERNMENT IGNORES SCIENTIFIC ANALYSES OF BLAST DAMAGE

Many independent scientists looked at the damage to the Murrah Building and concluded that an ANFO bomb could not possibly have caused the amount of damage done. An Air Force test at Eglin Air Force Base confirmed these results. Yet, the FBI did no investigation to determine if a different type bomb or explosive charges were used on the building.

KK. PROSECUTION WITHHOLDS DISCOVERY EVIDENCE FROM THE DEFENSE

Stephen Jones tells that the prosecution failed to provide requested formation in their possession to the defense as required by *Brady* obligations. Jones had to appeal to the Court more than once in order to get this accomplished. When Jones asked for information that the Government had on Andreas Strassmeir and Dennis Mahon, the prosecution wrote back, stating that, "At no time did the FBI consider Andreas Strassmeir or Dennis Mahon a subject of the Oklahoma City bombing investigation." This letter was written in 1997, but later Jones learned that the FBI was looking at Strassmeir and Mahon as early as 1995. Computer files provided by the prosecution regarding Carol Howe and Elohim City had virtually everyone's names spelled incorrectly so that when the defense did computer searches, they were not able to find the needed information. Prosecutor Beth Wilkinson told Judge Matsch that the prosecution "had **no** [emphasis added] evidence of foreign involvement in the bombing." Yet, among the FBI 302 reports the prosecution finally sent to the defense was a report on the warning sent by the Saudi Arabian official.

When the prosecution finally did send the 302 reports, they sent over ten thousand at one time, in complete disarray, with reports regarding one subject mixed throughout the entire batch. How many man hours were spent at taxpayer's expense to so thoroughly disarrange the files, and conversely for the defense to put them back in order? (Source: *Others Unknown*, Stephen Jones & Peter Israel, Public Affairs, N.Y., 1998, pg. 135-36, 149-53, 185-86, 190-98, 202-205)

OKBIC Note: According to the *New York Times*, "an unsigned message' was issued from FBI headquarters in Washington, D. C. to send in all items related to the Oklahoma City bombing to Oklahoma for archiving. The FBI archivists discovered, in March 2001, that thousands of pages of documents had not been turned over to the McVeigh or Nichols defense teams. They notified Special Agent Danny Defenbaugh (chief inspector for the OKBOMB Task Force and since named as the chief agent in the Dallas Office) who was in charge of the files cleanup. He reportedly did not advise his superiors of the problem until 07 May, knowing that McVeigh was scheduled for execution on 16 May. Surely this seasoned FBI agent (who had also worked in the FBI lab) was aware of the requirement to turn this evidence over to the defendant and his lawyers, yet he waited two months before advising anyone of the problem. (Source: *New York Times*, "What Happened to the McVeigh Evidence?" 13 May 01)

LL. PROSECUTORS DEFY JUDGE'S ORDER REGARDING INTERROGATION OF DEFENSE WITNESSES

During the McVeigh trial in Denver, the defense flew in witnesses who would testify for Timothy McVeigh. As the witnesses arrived at the Denver airport, prosecutors met them and whisked them off for interroga-tion. Defense attorneys complained to Judge Matsch, who told the prosecutors to refrain from this type action. Prosecutors then went to the witnesses' motels and cajoled desk clerks into providing them with room numbers; then went to the witnesse's rooms where they interrogated them. (Source: *New American* journalist William Jasper interview with McVeigh defense attorney Stephen Jones)

MM. GOVERNMENT FAILS TO CONTINUE JD #2 INVESTIGATION

At Nichols' pre-trial hearing on 25 March 1998, Federal judge Richard Matsch (who also presided over McVeigh's trial) said, "There are many unanswered questions. It would be very disappointing to me if the law enforcement agencies of the United States government have quit looking for answers in this Oklahoma bombing tragedy." His comments prompted FBI officials to say that they were working on it, but no specifics were offered.

However, on 03 May 1995, an FBI document states, "In view of the fact that the Oklahoma Bombing Command Post had directed all offices to hold unsub #2 [John Doe #2] leads in abeyance, San Francisco will conduct no further investigation regarding this lead." (See Appendix pg. 439.) This confirms that the search for John Doe #2 ended three years before federal agents told Judge Matsch they wre still working on it. (Appendix pg. 439)

NN. FBI FAILS TO FOLLOW-UP ON LEADS TO FEMALE ACCOMPLICES

Melvin Beale, an employee with the Oklahoma Natural Gas Company (ONG) in Oklahoma City, and formerly an Oklahoma City policeman for 21 years, saw McVeigh, a Spanish-looking male and two women in the ONG building. They were asking for directions to the Social Security Office (which was housed in the Murrah Federal Building). The women told him they were from Kansas, south of Manhattan and Junction City. The Spanish-looking man said he was originally from Kingman, Arizona, but had been stationed at Fort Riley. The four left and got into a yellow Mercury Marquis.

After the bombing, Beall tried to reconstruct the time of the encounter, and arrived at a date of 06 April 1995. He contacted several people in the FBI office, and was finally interviewed. He called back to provide the information that the women were from Kansas. He was told that Agent Tommy Ross would be given the information. Ross never got back with him. Just before McVeigh's trial, having seen witnesses on T.V., Beall advised that the three people at ONG were Michael and Lori Fortier and Jennifer McVeigh.(See Appendix pg. 543-547.) (Source: Beall's signed statement)

OO. Government Ignores Another Lead

Joe Hurley served as an informant for the Secret Service, beginning in 1992 when he notified them of a counterfeiting operation spearheaded by Wayne Waggoner and his family in Missouri. Waggoner offered to repay a loan to Hurley using counterfeit money. The Secret Service asked Hurley to arrange a trap for the Waggoners, but it never came to fruition. Afterwards, when the Waggoners plotted bank robberies and murders, Hurley notified the FBI and continued to serve as an informant. It was at the rural home of Waggoner where Hurley met Timothy McVeigh, and they practiced target shooting. Hurley said McVeigh was in disguise and was wearing an ill-fitting wig.

Two of Waggoner's sons and a third man reportedly robbed two people and beat them to death. The third man agreed to testify against the sons and was being held in the Osceola, Missouri jail. Waggoner made plans to blow up the courthouse and jail. He said he would use a rocket launcher, then cover up that fact by also using an ammonium nitrate-fuel oil bomb. He also wanted to blow up dams and armories in the area, and possibly the Branson Theater. Hurley and Waggoner traveled to the home of Waggoner's mother near Oklahoma City to dig up mortars and grenades that Wagner had buried there. Howeveer, they got "spooked" and did not complete the dig. Waggoner claimed to have worked for AMOCO Oil Company and to have been a mercenary in Bolivia, so was familiar with explosives. (Note that Timothy McVeigh had been trying to sell a rocket launcher in September 1993 that had belonged to gun dealer, Roger Moore.) Waggoner was arrested for trying to buy a rocket launcher from an FBI undercover agent.

Hurley contacted Don Higgerson with the ATF in Springfield and warned that bombings would still occur, that Dallas, Kansas City and Springfield were the most likely targets and "not to worry about Oklahoma City" since Waggoner had too many connections and family members in the area. In November 1994, Waggoner's cell mate informed the ATF that Waggoner was making threats against both their organization and Hurley. Hurley alleges that Waggoner's stepson, John Russell, was in on the bombing plot of the Osceola jail, and would have been willing to carry out Waggoner's threats. He said the last time he saw Russell, he had dyed his blond hair and whiskers black and had dyed his skin brown.

On 19 April 1995, Hurley contacted Higgerson and told him that there was a very good chance that it was Waggoner's people who had blown up the federal building. After seeing the sketch of John Doe #2 on television the day following the bombing, Hurley advised Higgerson that the sketch was a "dead ringer" for John Russell, who was free on parole at the time. Hurley's attorney, Mel L. Gilbert, said that the ATF appeared more interested in who else Hurley had told this to rather than in Hurley's information. Horley taped telephone conversations he had with ATF Agent Higgerson. He said Higgerson made 40 references to who else Hurley had talked to. Higgerson told him that his boss had been in Oklahoma City, and he would call him to find out what was going on there, and find out if he needed to follow-up on this, and "they'll probably say 'yes,' if there's people that they are looking for that are not in custody."

Attorney Gilbert said the FBI had been to his office, but not to interview Hurley, nor to listen to any tapes or to look at any transcripts; therefore, they had done no follow-up. When Hurley called other FBI offices, there was never any indication that a record of his previous calls had been made. Hurley tried to tell the FBI of McVeigh's connection with the Waggoners, but was told they did not want any more information. He then contacted "terrorist units from San Antonio to the Senate standing committee on terrorism," also the House of Representatives, the Pentagon and White House. No one was interested. The Government now calls him a "nut" and claims he was never a Government informant. (Source: "Anomalies" TV show in Springfield, MO, interview with Linda Eastburn, 31 May 01)

PP. FEDERAL JUDGE MAKES RULING WITHOUT READING EVIDENCE

A week after the execution of Timothy McVeigh, *The McCurtain Daily Gazette* revealed that U.S. District Judge Richard P. Matsch, who presided over the trials of McVeigh and Terry Nichols, had not read evidence related to ATF informant, Carol Howe, when he ruled that her testimony in Nichols' trial was "irrelevant."

According to an unsealed transcript of a closed-door session between Matsch and attorneys for the Justice Department and attorneys for Nichols, Matsch admitted that he had received Howe's file months earlier but had failed to read it. The session was held on 08 December 1997.

Howe was a paid informant for the ATF who notified her handler, Special Agent Angela Finley months before the bombing in Oklahoma City, that members of a racist commune at Elohim City, Oklahoma were planning to "bomb Government buildings and assassinate politicians." Two days after the bombing, in an interview with the FBI in Oklahoma City, Howe reported that Dennis Mahon had told her that federal installations such as the IRS Building, and federal buildings in Tulsa and Oklahoma City were the targets. She also reported that Mahon and Andreas Strassmier, a German military officer in charge of security at the camp, had traveled to Oklahoma City on three occasions to case the Murrah Building. The information provided by Howe was substantiated by audio and video tapes made pursuant to court-authorized wiretaps, "body wires," and hidden cameras that she carried and operated during visits to Elohim City.

The individuals named by Howe and provided to the FBI and ATF as being allegedly involved in the Oklahoma City bombing were never detained or questioned by either agency. The information Howe provided was kept secret by in the ATF office in Tulsa. Each month, Tulsa agents forwarded her information to the ATF office in Dallas.

Finley never disputed Howe's information, and in a lead sheet provided to the FBI, Finley attested to Howe's veracity, a fact confirmed by polygraph examination. The contract between the ATF and Howe as an informant was signed only after the polygraph results were known, substantiating the fact that Howe was truthful and loyal to the Government.

As a result of the decision Matsch made in the closed-door session, attorneys for Nichols were prohibited from opening Howe's informant file to show the jury that *after* the Oklahoma City bombing, she had been recruited by the Government to return to Elohim City. Jurors were thus denied access to more than 200 pages of statements, testimony, and handwritten notes Howe had supplied to the ATF, which set forth the intentions of those at Elohim City.

While a judge has the power to exclude the testimony of certain witnesses at trial, that power is perverted when it is applied indiscriminately, as it was in this case. Had Matsch read Howe's file and then ruled her testimony as "irrelevant," the defense could have objected, but would have concluded that he, at least, ruled on an informed basis. Instead, by ruling her evidence as "irrelevant" without having read the file, Matsch's actions were indefensible and demonstrated his bias against the Defense. The information contained in Howe's file shows a clear connection to the Oklahoma bombing. (Source: *WorldNetDaily*, 19 June 2001)

Chapter X.

RECOMMENDATIONS

OKBIC questions the extent to which the power of Government law enforcement agencies has been allowed to expand in recent years. Almost daily, the newspapers and magazines of this country contain results of investigations uncovering abuse and misuse of power by these agencies. This Report has highlighted many in the case of the Oklahoma City bombing, but there are others so numerous that it would take an entire set of books to reveal them all. Immediately brought to mind are the abuses perpetrated at Ruby Ridge and Waco. The agents involved in those raids had awards bestowed on them, and some were given promotions for the parts they played in the atrocities committed. Less publicized, but just as unjust, are the innocent people across the country who have been ruined financially, have been sent to jail on trumped up charges, or have had their characters assassinated by federal prosecutors and FBI, DEA, IRS, ATF, U.S. Customs, INS, and U.S. Marshal's Office agents.

In a series of articles, "Win at all Costs," in the *Pittsburgh Post-Gazette,* which ran from 22 November through 13 December 1998, reporter Bill Moushey provides the results of a two-year investigation, citing example after example of people caught up in "Government misconduct in the name of expedient justice." He provides details on how the Government "lied, hid evidence, distorted facts, engaged in cover-ups, paid for perjury and set up innocent people in a relentless effort to win indictments." One example tells about a woman who was lied to by federal prosecutors when they told her that her brother, held in custody, was dying, in order to persuade her to testify against him since he was going to die anyway. She was promised a reduced sentence in return; however, when the judge asked the prosecutor if he had a request for sentence reduction, the prosecutor made no such motion.

Another example cited a Government sting operation aimed at key NASA employees and contractors suspected of giving and taking bribes. The FBI set up a dummy company, registered it with Dunn & Bradstreet, and proceeded to involve a man with a small, struggling company in the marketing of their nonexistent "product." When they failed to snare the bigwigs they were aiming for, to justify the millions spent in the investigation, they charged the man with 21 counts of mail fraud and one count of bribery. All charges were eventually dismissed, but the legal fight cost him "his business, his life savings, his fiancée, and his health…."

Still another example cites a pilot who was flying cocaine into the United States as part of a U.S. Customs sting operation. The Justice Department brought charges against him. At trial, two Customs agents corroborated his story, but he was sentenced to life in prison anyway, and charges were brought against the Customs agents for perjury. They were eventually exonerated.

In yet another example, a farmer who filed a $250,000 crop insurance claim after his crop was destroyed by drought was charged with fraud. A Government expert testified that a neighboring farm did not suffer any drought damage. The farmer was convicted. It was later learned that the expert had never contacted the neighbor, and that, in fact, the Agriculture Department had approved a drought insurance claim for that same neighbor. It was also learned that prosecutors knew this information but withheld it from the defense. The farmer has been granted a new trial; but, in the meantime, has lost his farm to bankruptcy.

Dozens of other examples are provided in this newspaper series. They are merely a drop in a very large bucket of incidents of the common man being ruined by overzealous federal agents and prosecutors who are not held accountable for their actions.

A Government that will not protect its citizens will eventually reap the consequences. Congressional hearings and court cases that cover up the truth cause the average citizen to lose faith in the justice system. When group rights and individual rights are not protected, the situation becomes intolerable and people rise up against their Government. Apparently, this is the point McVeigh had reached—thus, the partial quote from Samuel Adams that was written on McVeigh's T-shirt: "When the Government fears the people, there is liberty; when the people fear the Government, there is tyranny."

It is only because people feel powerless against the Government and fear its abuses that they band together to protect themselves from it. If individual rights were respected, if Government agents were punished when they step on people's rights or break laws and if victims were reimbursed for their losses in these situations, there would be no more acts of internal terrorism, no perceived need to stockpile weapons; no more militias. Militia membership would dwindle and simply go away

The only body with the power to stop these abuses is the Congress of the United States. Through their control of funds and their audit process, federal law enforcement agencies can be held accountable for the billions of dollars spent yearly. (It has been almost 50 years since the Congress has performed an audit of the FBI.) The Congress also has the power to make or revoke laws which would make federal agencies more accountable for their actions. And, if necessary, the Congress also has the power to withhold these funds.

RECOMMENDATION ONE: That the Government Accounting Office (GAO) perform a thorough audit of federal law enforcement spending, to determine if the millions of dollars spent on sting operations are netting any "big fish" or if the funds are basically being wasted.

RECOMMENDATION TWO: That the Congress establish an oversight group, similar to the Consumer Protection Agency, staffed by attorneys and investigators, to be legal advocates for the common citizen in federal law enforcement abuse charges. (The average citizen cannot fight the Federal Government because it amounts to one against thousands in both money and manpower.)

RECOMMENDATION THREE: That supervisors of agents be held accountable and be subject to personal liability for failure to take disciplinary action against agents who abuse their power or break the law in the carrying out of their official duties.

RECOMMENDATION FOUR: That federal law enforcement officers be required to take an oath or sign a sworn affidavit regarding the basis for the issuance of a warrant, and that the officer be subject to the penalties of perjury for any false statements made.

RECOMMENDATION FIVE: That all FBI 302 reports of interrogations be read, signed and dated by the person interviewed.

RECOMMENDATION SIX: That the FBI lab establish written protocols to cover the recovery, tagging, transportation, chain of custody, testing, and analysis of forensic evidence. And that a system of internal self-inspection be implemented to ensure compliance with the procedures.

RECOMMENDATION SEVEN: That members of federal grand juries be instructed in their rights as jurors to call and question witnesses. Judges at grand jury proceedings should give the jurors more explicit instructions about their rights and should not allow the prosecution to run roughshod over juror's requests for additional evidence or witnesses. Jurors must be allowed to ask their own questions of witnesses.

RECOMMENDATION EIGHT: That periodic, unannounced inspections be performed of federal law enforcement offices to ensure that ordnance of any kind is not being stored in office buildings. And that significant fines be assessed to any agency found to be in non-compliance.

RECOMMENDATION NINE: That federal law enforcement officials be required to tape-record interrogations. This will result in more accurate information being provided at trial, and will remove one more obstacle to the truth and having a fair trial. It will also eliminate some of the harassment that witnesses say they are subjected to.

RECOMMENDATION TEN: That attorneys at law who are federal prosecutors be held to the same ethical standards as defense attorneys in the private sector. Should they violate any legal, moral or professional ethic or any federal, civil, or criminal law in the scope of their professional conduct, they should be held accountable to the extent that resulting consequences could be disbarment, disciplinary action, the levying of fines and/or penalties, and possible incarceration. Their position as federal employees should not protect them from prosecution to which civilian attorneys are subject.

RECOMMENDATION ELEVEN: That employees within a building—not just law enforcement personnel—be notified when a credible bomb threat is received against a building.

RECOMMENDATION TWELVE: That federal prosecutors be held in contempt and fined when they "play games" instead of forthrightly turning over discovery information to defense counsel. The name of the game should be "justice" rather than "convictions."

RECOMMENDATION THIRTEEN: That legislation be passed requiring any building which has been damaged by an act of terrorism or sabotage be thoroughly investigated by an independent, technically-competent agency before it is permitted to be destroyed, and that evidence from the building not be smashed, buried, or in any other way destroyed until these same experts have investigated that evidence.

RECOMMENDATION FOURTEEN: That the Government reimburse individuals or businesses who are victims of abuse for actual losses incurred and for punitive damages, and that the funds for reimbursement come from the budget of the agencies involved.

RECOMMENDATION FIFTEEN: That the Government fund both parties in civil proceedings where victims have incurred losses through abuse.

RECOMMENDATION SIXTEEN: That the 1,034 fingerprints from the Oklahoma City bombing investigation which were not processed through the FBI's computer databank be run, and the individuals identified be investigated as possible bombing accomplices.

RECOMMENDATION SEVENTEEN: That the Courts, in the Oklahoma City bombing case, order the immediate release of all surveillance tapes and photographs related to the Oklahoma City bombing under the Freedom of Information Act. Unless these tapes involve national security or an **open** federal investigation, there is no legal reason to keep them under wraps.

EPILOGUE

As we go to print, it has come to light that the FBI failed to turn over numerous tapes, lead sheets, and several thousand pages of documents to the McVeigh and Nichols defense teams at the time of their trials in 1997. Even when the FBI made this failure public and assured both defense teams that all files pertaining to the Oklahoma City bombing case had now been given to them, it was subsequently revealed that still more evidentiary materials had been withheld. This critical exposure of the FBI's arrogance and criminal negligence compelled Attorney General Ashcroft to admonish the FBI to locate every piece of evidence related to the case, even if it involved traveling around the world to achieve that end.

This situation reinforces the Recommendations listed in this Report, and has caused the need for more to be made. Moreover, we now feel, that a mechanism for judicial reform must be proposed that has a realistic chance of re-establishing justice and equality in the FBI. Therefore we propose the following:

THAT a panel be established to investigate the FBI and its practices and to make recommendations for reforms.

This panel should not be composed solely of bureaucrats, present or past politicians or Government contractors. Another blue-ribbon panel will simply rubber-stamp the FBI's previous actions and only serve to further undermine the confidence and trust in our Government by the American people. Just as was shown in the Office of the Inspector General (OIG) Report regarding the VANPAC case, Louis Freeh, in essence, investigated himself. As could be expected, he found no improprieties, although the OIG found many. For this reason, we can no longer accept the Government investigating itself. It is critical that a panel be established to impartially scrutinize FBI operations and procedures and make recommendations that can be implemented immediately.

OKBIC Note: The VANPAC case involved mail bombs being sent to four different locations. The FBI referred to the case as "VANPAC" because a federal judge, Robert Vance, was killed with a bomb mailed in a package. Dr. Frederic Whitehurst of the FBI laboratory, accused two laboratory employees of perjury, fabricating evidence, and obstructing justice with regard to the case.

For this task, we feel it is imperative that the panel include individuals known to have been involved in investigative work and to have looked at issues with a critical eye. People of both conservative and liberal persuasion must be included. They should come from the private sector and include representatives from several different disciplines, including, but not limited to investigative journalism, political watch organizations, academia and the legal field:

- Investigative journalists should include such people as Bill Jasper with *The New American*, Bill Moushy with the *Pittsburg Post Gazette*, Joe Farah with *World Net Daily*, Christopher Ruddy with *News Max.Com* (formerly with the *Pittsburg Post Gazette*), and Robert Novak with the *Chicago Tribune*.

- Political watch organizations such as the Heritage Foundation, CATO, the Judicial Watch organization and the Mackinac Institute for Public Policy could provide excellent representation.

- From academia we would suggest professors in the fields of political science, constitutional law, business ethics, accounting and economics.

- The legal field should include attorneys who specialize in both criminal defense and civil cases including those who have represented individuals victimized by Government and/or major corporations.

This panel must have the full cooperation of the Justice Department and the President, and should be vested with the authority to call witnesses to testify and examine any documents required in the pursuit of the truth (legitimate security issues excepted).

The Oklahoma City bombing case is literally the "straw that broke the camel's back," in a series of cases that have been grossly mishandled by what is supposed to be the premier investigation arm of our government. Congress supposedly has oversight responsibility for the FBI, but has failed to censure an out-of-control agency that answers to no one.

We want the citizens of this great country to become more involved, to take a stand, to make our government once again "of, by and for the **people**." Our elected officials, as well as appointed officials, must recognize the fact that they work for us — not the other way around. Write your elected representatives in Congress; voice your concerns; and let them know you want federal law enforcement agencies to be held accountable for their actions. Most importantly, **demand** a full investigation of the FBI.

Edmund Burke, noted eighteenth century British philosopher said, "The only thing necessary for the triumph of evil is for good men to do nothing." Let the tragedy in Oklahoma City serve as the impetus for our citizens to demand the Government our forefathers envisioned and established. Let it begin with an investigation that will result in justice for us all.

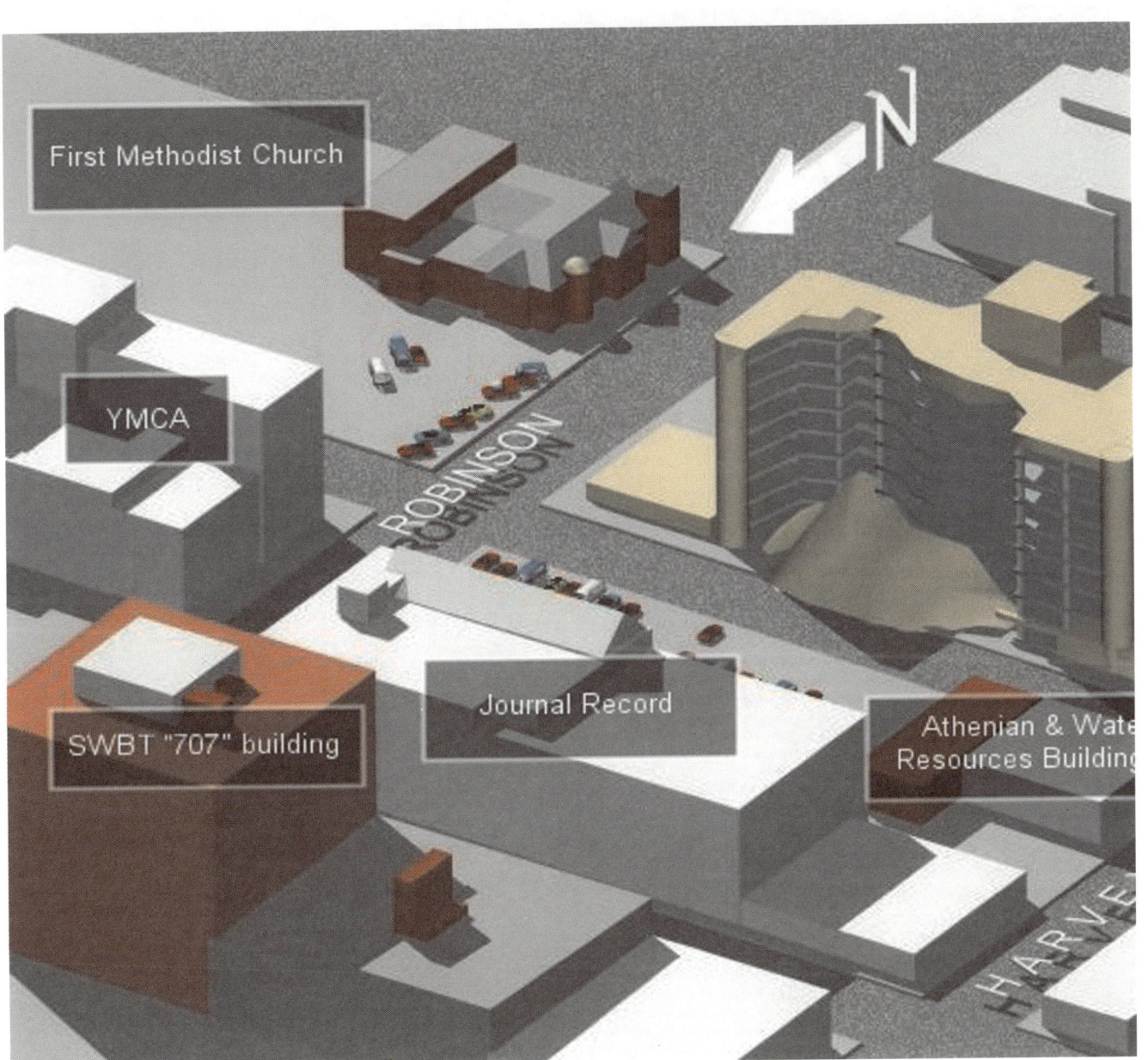

OKLAHOMA HIGHWAY PATROL
Okla

RADIO LOG — Call
RADIO DIVISION

OPERATOR _____ DISPATCHER _____ SHEET 1

MESSAGE, DISPATCH, AS TRANSMITTED

OF #36, CONT MADE WITH THE TRAINING CENTER TO GET #366, 668,
54 10-8 TO ASST WITH TRAFF CONTROL ON THE CROSSTOWN/
THOMPSON ON RADIO
MOSS ON RADIO LOG
R BOMB FOUND ON THE S- SIDE OF THE BUILDING/
HAS BEEN MOVED TO 5TH AND BROADWAY AT THIS TIME/OK
E DEPT CONFIRMS THEY DID FIND A SECOND DEVICE IN THE BLDG/OK
LL TROOPERS AND HAVE THEM MOVE ALL CIVILIAN PERSONNEL BACK 1 lk
DICAL PERSONNEL ARE MOVING TO 10TH AND HARVEY/RT
___ 6TH AND HARVEH VERY SHORTLY/OK
RUSH TPC/GO AHEAD/THERE IS ANOTHER BOMB ON THE SOUTH
SIDE OF THE BLDG NEED TO GET AWAY AS FAR AS POSSIBLE/BB
SUBFLT 3 AND LB EVACUATE THE AREA OF THE BLDG
IMMEDIATELY, EVACUATE THE AREA OF THE S SIDE OF TEH BLDG
IMMEDIATELY/BB
DID YOU HAVE ANY FURTHER?/NEG/BB
WANDA AT TRNG CTR ADV 10-39 AND THE TWO MEDICS ARE ALREADY
ON SCENE/BB
ADV ALL OUR PEOPLE APPROACHING THE COMMAND POST THAT THEY
NEED TO COME EAST ON 6TH TO HARVEY DONT TRY TO COME IN ANY
OTHER WAY/BB
WERE YOU OKAY/AFF/BB
ALL UNITS ENRT COMMAND POST NEED TO GO IN EAST ON 6TH TO
HARVEY DONT TRY TO IN ANY OTHER WAY/BB
10-8/BB
ADV CP WE POSS HAVE ANOTHER DEVICE/IF IT IS THE ONE ONE THE S
SIDE WE HAVE ALREADY GB'D IT/OKAY/DID YOU HAVE ANYTHING
FURTHER BESIDE THE ONE ON THE S SIDE?/NEG/BB
10-8/BB
THE FIRE DEPT HAS LOCATED ANOTHER DEVICE/AFF/BB
HAVE ALL UNITS MOVE CIVILIAN PERSONEL BACK ONE BLOCK/TB
ALL UNITS MOVE CIVILIAN PERSONEL BACK ONE BLOCK/TB

Courtesy New American Magazine

Figure 1: Cast-in-place Concrete Test Structure

Figure 2: Damage Resulting from External Detonation of 830 lb TNT Equivalent

Figure 3: Damage Resulting from Internal Detonation of 180 lb TNT Equivalent

Figure 4: Damage Resulting from Internal Detonation of 35 lb TNT Equivalent

OCFD Time Line: The First 36 Hours

4-19-95

09:02 a.m.	OCPD notified dispatch of an explosion. Primary backup phones down at Emergency Medical Service Agency
09:05	Engine 51, Truck 1, E 6, T 6, E 4, E1, Squad 1, Chief 1 Third alarm: Chief 3, Haz Mat 5, Deputy Chief, E 5, T 5, CS established, Sixth & Harvey.
09:10	601A designated IC.
09:11	Fourth & fifth alarms: E 4 on scene, all patients to Sixth & Robinson.
09:12	E 1 began fighting car fires.
09:14	T 7, E 10, E 7, T 8, E 8, Squad 17, T 24, Squad 18, Squad 21, Squad 34.
09:20	E 1, T 1, Squad 17 searched Water Resources, 1 patient.
09:27	First patients transported.
10:00	Electric, gas, water off, 601A ordered evacuation because of possible second device. Command post at Eighth & Harvey. Morgue on the south side of Federal Building.
10:15	Water Resources evacuated.
10:22	Building evacuated second time, Triage at Fifth & Robinson, staging at Seventh & Robinson.
10:27	Federal Emergency Management Agency (FEMA) offered Urban Search and Rescue (USAR) teams.
10:30	General alarm, T 10.
10:32	Six bodies recovered.
10:45	E 1, T 1 sent to Eighth & Harvey staging. Fire under control. Building evacuated, possible third device.
11:00	Staging moved to 10th & Harvey.
11:20	Outside perimeter controlled.
11:35	Rehab established at Eighth & Harvey.
12:09	E 11, E 19, T 19, E 21, E 15, T 15, E 22, T 22, E 30, T 30.
12:12	E 9, T 9, E 25, E 24, E 17. 12 transports from the building.
12:30	Shawnee FD loans OCFD ropes, generators, lights.
13:51	Report of fourth possible device.
17:00	227 injured.
18:22	Severe thunderstorm watch issued.
19:10	Sacramento & Phoenix FEMA teams dispatched. United States Fire Administration (USFA) investigators dispatched. Virginia Beach on standby.
19:18	28 doa's.
20:34I	D badges ordered.
22:30I	5-year-old female found alive.

4-20-95

01:00	Primary search above third floor complete.
06:45	Fences erected.
06:59	Southwestern Bell installed cell sites and provided 150 phones.
0730	Large contingent from FBI, ATF, U.S. Marshals, Oklahoma Highway Patrol, Military Police at scene.
13:32	Airspace restricted for five miles. Count stands at 38 doa, 200 missing, 423 injured.
17:44	Suspect composites released.
22:25	Doa #41 removed.

4-21-95

02:10	Respirators needed for rescue workers.

Firehouse/September 1995

Bomb Damage Analysis Of Alfred P. Murrah Federal Building Oklahoma City, Oklahoma

July 30, 1995

by

Benton K. Partin
Brigadier Gen. USAF (Ret.)

8908 Captains Row
Alexandria, Virginia 22308
703-780-7652

Benton K. Partin
Brigadier Gen. USAF (Ret.)
8908 Captains Row
Alexandria, Virginia 22308
703-780-7652

July 30, 1995

Sen. Trent Lott
United States Senate
487 Senate Russell Office Building
Washington, DC 20510-2403

Dear Sen. Lott:

The attached report contains conclusive proof that the bombing of the Alfred P. Murrah Federal Building, Oklahoma City, Oklahoma, was not caused solely by the truck bomb. Evidence shows that the massive destruction was primarily the result of four demolition charges placed at critical structural points at the third floor level.

<u>Weapons Experience</u>: I do not offer such an analytical conclusion lightly. I have spent 25 years in research, design, development, test and management of weapons development. This included: hands-on work at the Ballistic Research Laboratories; Commander of the Air Force Armament Technology Laboratory, and ultimately management responsibility for almost every non-nuclear weapon device in the Air Force (at the Air Force System command, Air Staff and the Office of the Secretary of Defense (OSD) levels). I was also the first chairman of the OSD joint service Air Munitions Requirements and Development Committee. (A more detailed resume appears at Tab 1.)

<u>Observations in Oklahoma City</u>: To verify earlier analysis, I visited Oklahoma City during the last week of June. There I had the opportunity to view hundreds of photographs taken throughout the cleanup operation as the layers of debris were cleared away. The photos present irrefutable evidence that at least four demolition charges were set off at four critical columns of the reinforced concrete structure at the floor level of the third floor.

<u>Conclusion:</u> Based on my experience in weapons development and bomb damage analysis, and on my review of all evidence available, I can say, with a high level of confidence, that the damage pattern on the reinforced concrete superstructure could not possibly have been attained from the single truck bomb. The total incompatibility of this pattern of destruction with a single truck bomb lies in the simple,

incontrovertible fact that some of the columns collapsed that should not have collapsed if the damage were caused solely by a truck bomb, and, conversely, some of the columns were left standing that should have collapsed if the damage had been caused solely by the truck bomb.

It is my hope and request that, as a Member of Congress, you will support a Congressional investigation to determine the true initiators of this bombing, which could not have occurred the way in which it has been portrayed as having happened. Further, it is requested that you defer action and reserve judgment on so-called anti-terrorism legislation that has serious civil liberties implications, and which would not be passed except for the Oklahoma City bombing until the causes of the Oklahoma City disaster are determined by independent investigators.

Both the Federal Building in Oklahoma and the Trade Center in New York (See New York Times, October 28, 1993, p. A1) show evidence of a counter-terrorism sting gone wrong.

No government law enforcement agency should be permitted to demolish, smash and bury evidence of a counter-terrorism sting operation, sabotage or terrorist attack without a thorough examination by an independent, technically competent agency.

If an aircraft crashed because of a bomb, or a counter-terrorism sting or an FAA Controller error, the FAA would not be permitted to gather and bury the evidence. The National Transportation Safety Board would have been called in to conduct an investigation and where possible every piece of debris would have been collected and arrayed to determine cause of failure.

To remove all ambiguity with respect to the use of supplementary demolition charges, the FBI should be required to release the high quality surveillance color TV camera tape of the Murrah building bombing on April 19, 1995.

It is my observation that the effort required to bomb the A. P. Murrah Federal Building in Oklahoma City pales in comparison with the effort to cover up evidence in Oklahoma and the media's withholding of vital information from the American people.

Sincerely yours,

Benton K. Partin
Brigadier Gen. USAF (Ret.)

BKP:aw
Enclosure

Contents

Report

    Bomb Damage Analysis Of Alfred P. Murrah Federal Building Oklahoma City, Oklahoma

Biographical Summary

    Tab 1 —   Benton K. Partin, Brigadier Gen., USAF (Ret.)

Graphics

    Tab 2 —   Building Cross-Section

    Tab 3 —   Potential Bomb Damage Profile from Truck Bomb and Demolition Charges

Photographs

    Tab 4 —   Building after Clean-Up

    Tab 5 —   Column A7 Failure

    Tab 6 —   Demolition of Columns A3, A5, and B3

    Tab 7 —   Demolition of Column A5

    Tab 8 —   Demolition of Column A7

Appendix

    Tab 9 —   Corroborating Assessment by Dr. Rodger A. Raubach
        —   Corroboration Assessment by Sam Gronning

Bomb Damage Analysis Of
Alfred P. Murrah Federal Building
Oklahoma City, Oklahoma

On April 19, 1995, the Alfred P. Murrah Federal Building, Oklahoma City, Oklahoma was bombed, causing extensive damage to the structure, the loss of 168 innocent lives, the victimization of the families of those who lost loved ones, hundreds of non-fatal injuries, and substantial property damage in the vicinity.

The media and the Executive branch reported that the sole source of the devastation was a single truck bomb consisting of 4,800 pounds of ammonium nitrate, transported to the location in a Ryder Truck and parked in front of the building. It is impossible that the destruction to the building could have resulted from such a bomb alone.

To cause the damage pattern that occurred to the Murrah building, there would have to have been demolition charges at several supporting column bases, at locations not accessible from the street, to supplement the truck bomb damage. Indeed, a careful examination of photographs showing the collapsed column bases reveals a failure mode produced by demolition charges and not by a blast from the truck bomb.

To understand what caused the damage to the Murrah Building, one needs to understand some basics about the use and nature of explosives.

First, blast through air is a very inefficient energy coupling mechanism against heavily reinforced concrete beams and columns.

Second, blast damage potential initially falls off more rapidly than an inverse function of the distance cubed. That is why in conventional weapons development, one seeks accuracy over yield for hard targets. That is also why in the World Trade Center bombing (where the only source of blast damage was a truck bomb) the column in the middle of the bombed-out cavity was relatively untouched, although reinforced concrete floors were completely stripped away for several floors above and below the point of the bomb's detonation (see *Time Magazine*, 3-8-93, page 35).

By contrast, heavily reinforced concrete structures can be destroyed effectively through detonation of explosives in contact with the reinforced concrete beams and columns. For example, the entire building remains in Oklahoma City were collapsed with 100-plus relatively small charges inserted into drilled holes in the columns. The total weight of all charges was on the order of 200 pounds.

The detonation wave pressure (1,000,000 to 1,500,000 pounds per square inch) from a high detonation velocity contact explosive sweeps into the column as a wave of compressive deformation. Since the pressure in the wave of deformation far exceeds the yield strength of the concrete (about 3,500 pounds per square inch) by a factor of approximately 300, the concrete is turned into granular sand and dust until the wave dissipates to below the yield strength of the concrete. This leaves a relatively smooth but granular surface, with protruding, bare reinforcement rods —a distinctive signature of damage by contact explosives. The effect of the contact explosive on the reinforcement rods themselves can only be seen under microscopic metallurgical examination. (The rods are inertially confined during the explosion and survive basically in tact because of their much higher yield strength and plasticity.)

When a reinforced concrete structure is damaged through air shock coupling and the pressure is below the compressive yield strength of the concrete, the failure mode is generally compressive structural fracture on one side and tensile fracture on the other — both characterized by cracks and rough fracture surfaces. Such a surface texture is very different from the relatively smooth granular surface resulting from contact explosives.

Analysis of Graphic Evidence

Tab 2 is a cross section view of the building looking from the west. The very large header or cross beam is shown at the north edge of the third floor. A large but smaller header is seen at the recessed north edge of the second floor with a brace beam extending out to the large columns in Row A. The front of the whole building is glass.

Tab 3 shows the architectural layout of the first floor of the Murrah Building and the location of the truck bomb with superimposed circles of roughly equal levels of damage potential. The explosive force drops rapidly (initially proportional to one over the distance cubed) as the shock front travels farther and farther away from the truck bomb. After the release wave, the shock front will propagate proportional to one over the distance squared.

The maximum possible yield from 4800 pounds of ammonium nitrate would be obtained if it were in a compressed sphere and detonated from the center. That would produce a 4.4 foot diameter sphere of detonation products at about 500,000 pounds per square inch. By the time the blast wave hits the closest column, the pressure would have fallen off to about 375 pounds per square inch. That would be far below the 3500 pound compressive yield strength of the concrete. Any column or beam failure from the truck bomb would therefore have been from blast wave structural loading and not from any wave of deformation in the concrete.

The basic building structure consists of three rows of columns (35 feet apart) with eleven columns in each row (20 feet apart). The four corner columns have an external clamshell-like structure for air ducts, etc. If we label the column rows A, B, and C from front to back, and number the columns 1 through 11 from left to right, then columns A_2, A_3, A_4, A_5, A_6, A_7, A_8, and B_3 collapsed, essentially vertically. Tab 2 shows a very large reinforced concrete header at the floor level of the third floor of column row A. Much larger columns extend from the header down for the odd-numbered columns, i.e., A_3, A_5, A_7, and A_9. The even- and odd-numbered columns extended from the top of the building down to the header. The foundation of the building is a heavy, reinforced concrete slab with no sub-levels.

From the potential damage contours on Tab 3, and assuming the single truck bomb, the pressure and impulse for collapsed columns B_4, B_5 and A_7 are all in the 25 to 35 pounds per square inch region. However, the much smaller and closer columns, B_4 and B_5, are still standing, while the much larger column A_7 is down. Column B_3 is down with 42 percent less pressure and impulse than columns B_4. These facts are sufficient reason to know that columns B_3 and A_7 had demolition charges on them. Moreover, there is not sufficient blast impulse at that range to collapse any of the three. In fact, columns B_2, B_4 and B_5 all have the sheet rock and furring strip finish still intact on the second and third floors except where damaged by falling debris.

The large header across the front of the building at the third floor of Row A was not blown back into the building as one may expect from such a large bomb. The header came straight down but rolled backward 90 degrees because the columns above the header rested off center toward the back.

Analysis of Photographic Evidence

A careful examination of photos showing the "A" row columns and the large header from the third floor reveals absolutely no air blast shock wave fracture, which is consistent with the pressure fall-off with distance from the truck bomb. The cleaned-up building structure (Tab 4) shows that the failure line across the roof goes all the way to the ground except around columns B4 and B5 at the second and third floor levels. Reinforcement rods stripped out of beams and floors extend straight down on all floors. Columns A3, A5, A7, and B3 collapsed straight down as the apparent result of demolition charges at the column juncture with the third floor for column B3 and with the third floor level header for columns A3, A5, and A7. The even numbered columns (A2, A4, A6, and A8) in Row A collapsed straight down because they were supported at the third floor by the header, which necessarily failed with the demolition of its conjunctions with columns A3, A5, and A7. When columns A2 through A8 collapsed straight down, the roof and floor fracture lines at all floors acted as an instant hinge line, which would have given all floors collapsing down a slight tug toward column row B. Because of the collapse of column B3, the floors were cropped closer to the north side of columns B4, B5, which resulted in damage by falling debris to sheet rock on columns B4 and B5 at the third floor level.

The so-called "pit" area behind columns B4 and B5 was caused either by the blast from the truck bomb pushing out the ceilings of the first and second floors or from the demolition charge on column B3. From the third floor it would look like a "pit" into which much debris fell. The blast pressure in this area would have been sufficient to exceed the ultimate yield design strength of the floor. There were large areas at this pressure being held only by the floor-thick, reinforced concrete around the 20-inch reinforced concrete columns in the B row. The floor of the first floor could not be blown downward, because it was a heavy concrete slab on compacted earth. The ceilings of the first and second floors nearer the truck between the A and B column rows could also have been blown upward initially.

Although the truck bomb had insufficient power to destroy columns, the bomb was clearly responsible for ripping out some floors at the second and third floor levels.

Photographic Evidence of Demolition Charges

Turning next to the demolition charges in the building, refer to the picture at Tab 5. Here you see column A9 with no spalling as one would expect with the blast pressures involved and the decorative indents are unmarred. Note also the grooves at the top of the column and across the header. When the demolition charge on column A7 went off, the charge instantly left a 40 foot cantilevered header supporting column A8. Cascading columns and beams from above probably snapped off the end with a clear structural fracture, including rugged cracks and rough surfaces. There is a large unseen beam extending from behind the column, between the decorative groves, back to the first floor header. This beam adds considerable rigidity to the lower odd-numbered columns in Row A.

Turning next to Tab 6, the stub of column B3 has been cleared, showing the bare reinforcement rods at the third floor level. The large header from the third floor level has fallen almost straight down with what appears to be demolition charge damage clearly evident to the right of column A3. The exposed reinforcement rods are clearly seen at the header end to the right of column A3. It appears that the demolition charge pulverized the header and columns out to about two feet from the juncture. Column A3 is standing there with the clean reinforcement rods clearly extended. Also, the architectural decorative band is clearly evident without blemish (indicating no blast damage in excess of yield strength). In this picture, the failure of the header at column A5 is still covered with rubble, and is not visible. However, the discontinuity in the slope of the header on either side of the column A5 location clearly shows that it failed in the region of its juncture with column A5.

Tab 7 shows the localized damage to the header at the position of column A5, the closest column to the truck bomb crater. The end of the beam on which the men are standing shows evidence of a demolition charge at its juncture with column A5. Several feet of the beam juncture appear to have been pulverized away by a demolition charge and the ends jammed together in the collapse. The blast pressure from the truck bomb would have been in the 400 pounds per square inch region — a factor of 10 below the yield strength of concrete.

Tab 8 shows the localized demolition damage at the juncture of column A7 and the header. The same telltale demolition charge evidence is clear. The straight edge of the decorative grove at the juncture can be seen on both the column and the header.

In my discussions with the building architect, who was on the scene as an advisor throughout much of the cleanup, he told me that the residual building was structurally sound and that the Murrah Building could have been rebuilt. This is totally consistent with the collapse of columns with demolition charges because the inflicted structural damage is more localized.

Discussions above have been limited to the reinforced concrete structure of the Murrah Building. Reinforced concrete columns are hard targets for high-explosive bombs. Structures that have large areas for blast loading and low mass can be destroyed at considerable range from a large blast. That is why glass, plaster, and light structures were destroyed at considerable distance from the Murrah Building, but not reinforced concrete columns. Five pounds of blast pressure will flatten most frame houses.

Seismograph Readings

Much has been said about seismograph readings. Was there more than one explosion? Most people I talked to in Oklahoma City heard two explosions relatively close together. Some close by said they didn't even hear an explosion. That is not unreasonable, when you consider that getting walloped by an intense shock wave is about like being hit across the ear by a 2" x 4". One would expect the demolition charges to have had an electrical or primacord interconnect. If so, it would be difficult to separate them on a seismograph. If delays were used, they would be discrete. If a sensitivity switch was used inside the building, the explosions would have been distinct. Bomb initiations could have been easily designed to go off either simultaneously or with separation.

Conclusion

The Murrah Federal Building was not destroyed by one sole truck bomb. The major factor in its destruction appears to have been detonation of explosives carefully placed at four critical junctures on supporting columns within the building.

The only possible reinforced concrete structural failure solely attributable to the truck bomb was the stripping out of the ceilings of the first and second floors in the "pit" area behind columns B_4 and B_5. Even this may have been caused by a demolition charge at column B_3.

It is truly unfortunate that a separate and independent bomb damage assessment was not made during the cleanup — before the building was demolished on May 23 and hundreds of truck loads of debris were hauled away, smashed down, and covered with dirt behind a security fence.

When the picture at Tab 4 was made, all evidence of demolition charges had been removed from the building site (i.e., the stubs of columns B_3, A_3, A_5, A_7 and the demolished junctures at the header with columns A_3, A_5 and A_7.

All ambiguity with respect to the use of supplementing demolition charges and the type of truck used could be quickly resolved in the FBI were required to release the surveillance camera coverage of this terribly tragic event.

BENTON K. PARTIN
8908 Captains Row
Alexandria, Virginia 22308
(703) 780-7652

Biographical Notes

<u>Thirty one years</u> active duty in the Air Force. Progressively responsible executive, scientific and technical assignments directing organizations engaged in research, development, testing, analysis, requirements generation and acquisition management of weapons systems. Assignments from laboratory to the Office of the Secretary of Defense.

<u>Personal contributions</u> made in the fields of research and development management, weapon system concepts, guided weapons technology, target acquisition aids, focused energy weapons, operations research and joint service harmonization of requirements. Retired as a Brigadier General.

White House appointed Special Assistant to the Administrator, Federal Aviation Administration. Personally designated to prepare the <u>White Paper on the Federal Aviation Administration for the 1989 Presidential Transition Team</u>. This included development of policy initiatives on FAA/USAF joint use of the Global Positioning System (GPS), operational life for commercial aircraft, anti-terrorism, airport and airway capacity, requirements in the FAA acquisition process and FAA leadership and management development.

Military Command Pilot and Command Missleman with 4000 hours (37 combat.)

<u>Education</u>: B.S. Chemical Engineering; M.S. Aeronautical Engineering; Ph.D. Candidate, Operations Research & Statistics (Academics Completed.)

<u>Publications/TV</u>

<u>Sino-Soviet Conflict, Competition and Cooperation:</u>
<u>Risks in Force Structure Planning</u>.
<u>A Reduced Upper Limit for Sequential Test Truncation Error</u>.
Frequent TV Talk Shows on the Voice of Freedom.

<u>Honors</u>: Distinguished Service Medal, Legion of Merit thrice, Distinguished Graduate - Air War College

<u>Community Affairs</u>:

Chairman, United States Defense Committee
Member of the Board, In Touch Missions International
Member of the Board, Front Line Fellowship
Founding Chairman of the School Board, Engleside Christian School
Washington Representative for the Association of Christian Schools International (1981-1983)
Chairman Fairfax County Republican Party (1982-1986)

<u>Lifelong Professional Challenge</u>: Continuing studies and analyses to anticipate and forecast the future course of world military/political/economic transforming processes.

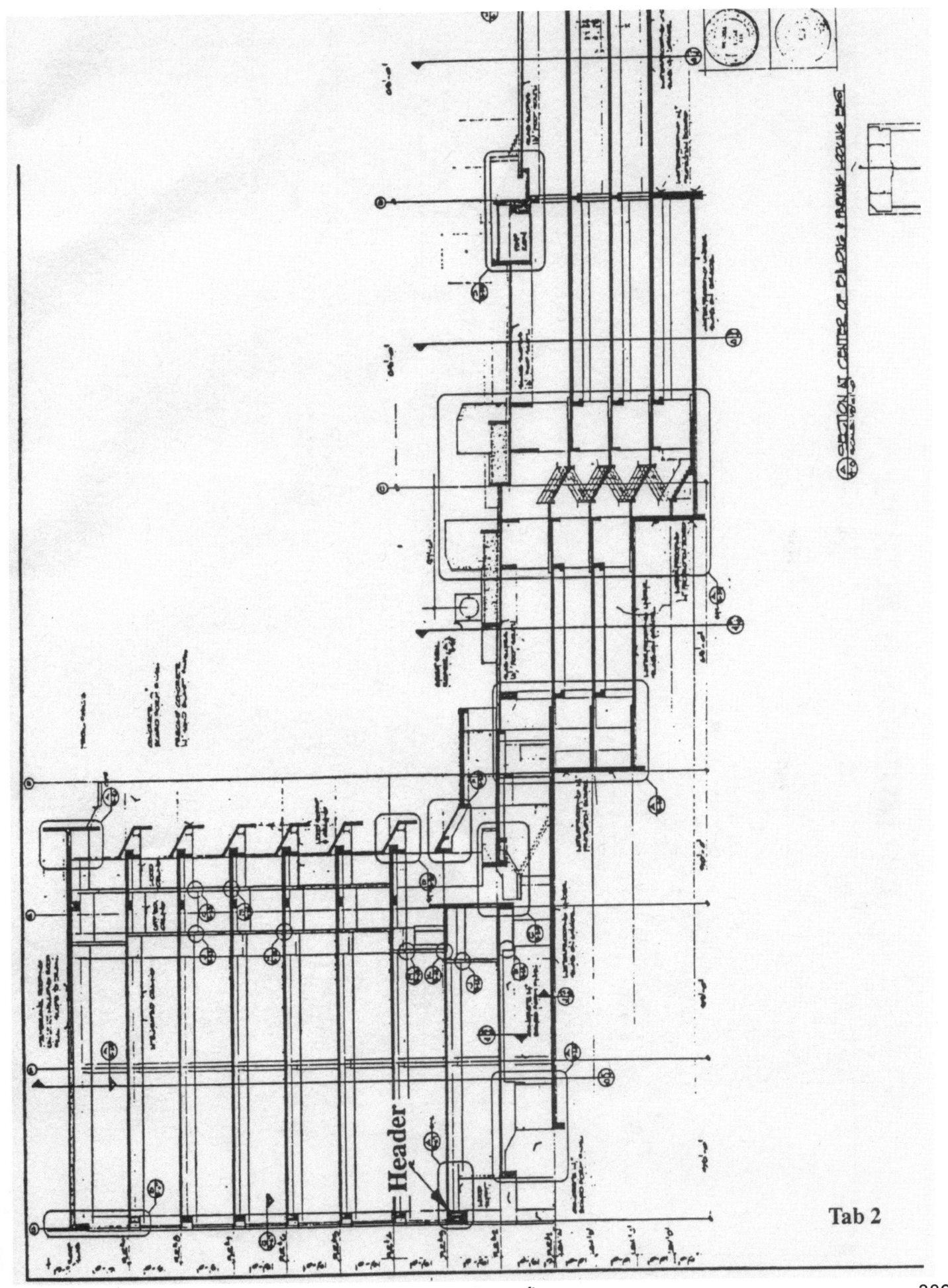

Appendix

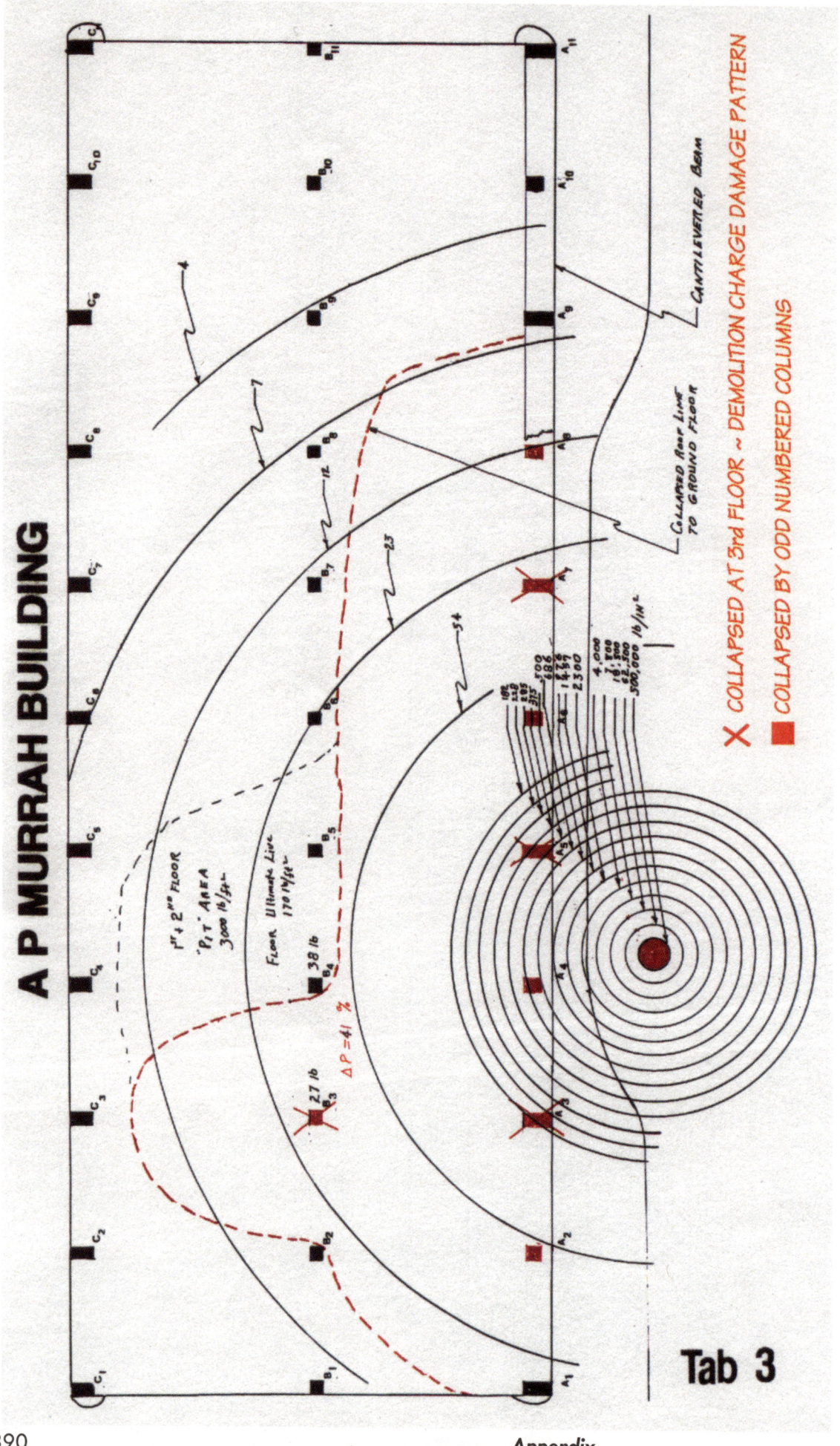

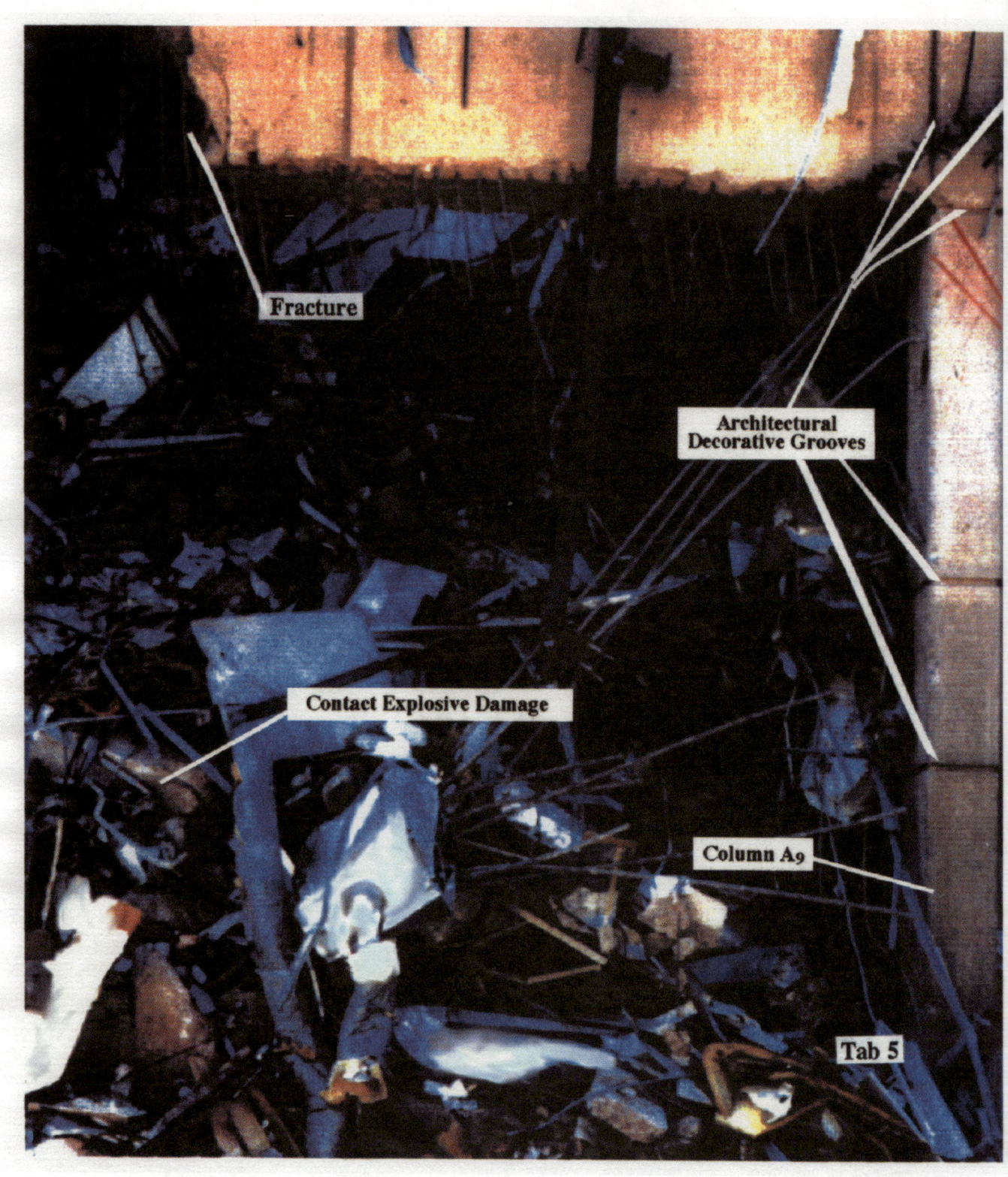

Appendix

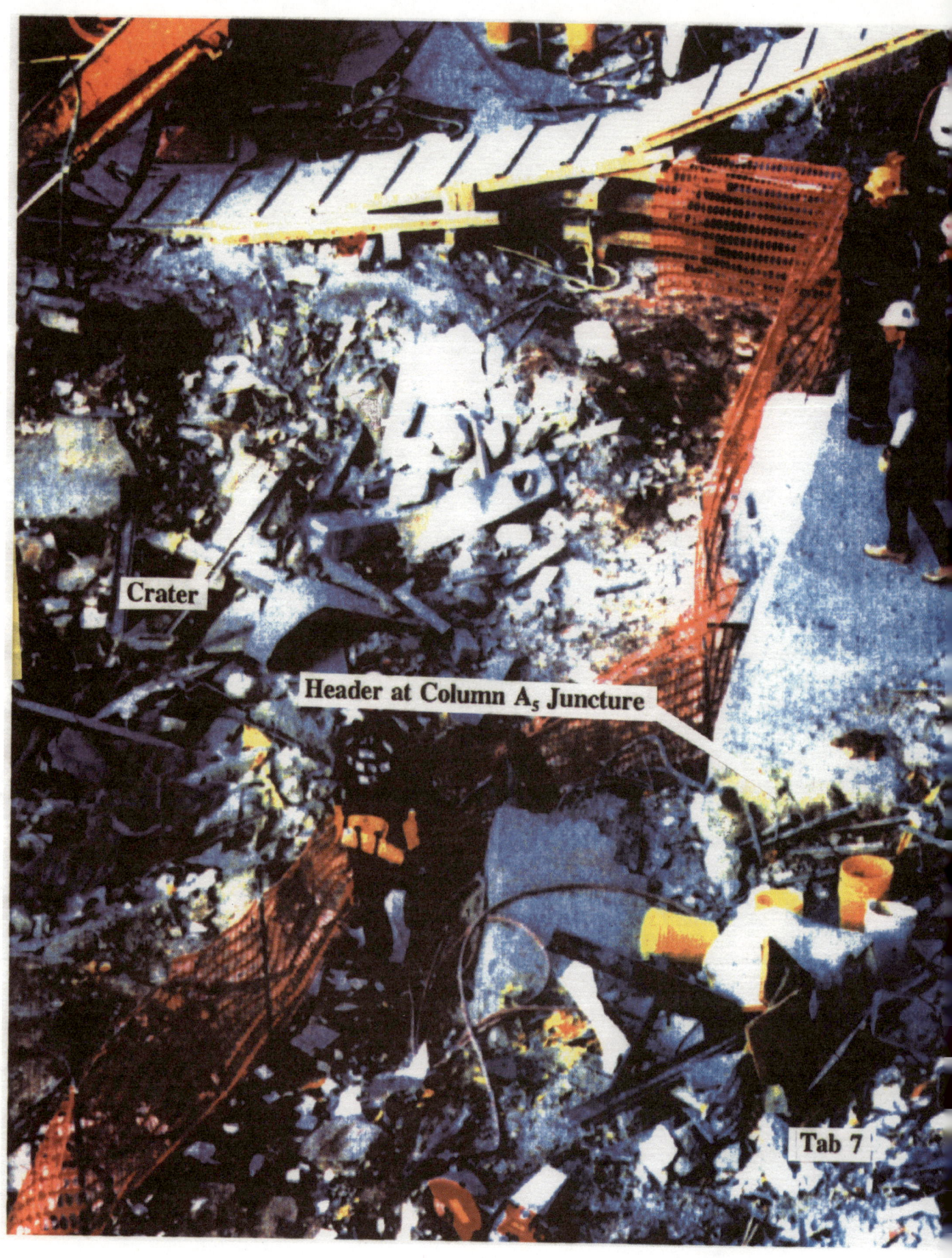

Rodger A. Raubach Ph.D
P.O.Box 3042 , Casper , WY. 82602-3042
Phone: (307)-235-5266 ; FAX: (307)-237-2500

18 July 1995

Brigadier Gen. Benton K. Partin
8908 Captains Row
Alexandria , VA. 22308

Dear Gen. Partin;

Earlier today I received a copy of your report on the bombing in Oklahoma City, entitled "Bomb Damage Analysis of the Alfred P. Murrah Federal Building,Oklahoma City". This report was dated July 13,1995.

I read this report carefully and examined the exhibits appended to the text. Your observations and photographic analysis are meticulous in the extreme , and you are to be commended for your insights regarding the effects of blast vs. distance from the detonation.

The major points of the report which I believe need to be emphasized are: (1) the fact that rebar reinforcing rods were broken but appear to be embedded in concrete;(2) very little concrete appears to have been crushed by the blast. These observations alone are at extreme variance with the hypothesis of a single large truck bomb containing ANFO. For the large (4800 lb.) ammonium nitrate bomb to have caused the damage, there would be huge amounts of sand generated from the crushed concrete around the columns wherein the rebar was fractured.

I took the liberty of checking with the leading concrete supplier in my area in order to confirm the compressive yield figure that you used,that being 3500 psi. What I was told about concrete was very interesting. A 3500 psi figure is extremely low for structural concrete. A properly mixed and cured structure of the type dealt with in your report would probably have a yield strength of 5600 psi.

In conclusion,General,I find myself in awe of the technical achievement that your report represents. I can find no scientific flaws in either your observations or your conclusions. I am,therefore,in full agreement with the conclusion of strategically placed small explosive charges being responsible for the destruction of the building.

We can only hope and pray that a few good men and women in our Congress will heed your report and take action that results in the punishment of the real guilty parties responsible for this heinous crime against the American people,and that these same few good people are able to stem the abrogation of any more of our Constitutional rights.

Please keep up the good work that you are doing for your countrymen.It is an honor to be able to correspond with you on this matter and perhaps to be of some small service to our country,the Constitutional Republic,to which many of us have sworn to defend to the best of our abilities.

If I may be of any further assistance,please contact me at any time. Looking forward to your response,I remain

Very Truly Yours,

Rodger A. Raubach   Ph.D.

Tab 9

UNIFORM TRAFFIC TICKET AND COMPLAINT

CASE NO. 09-24-414   DOCKET No. _____   PAGE No. _____   No. F 735922

ARKANSAS STATE POLICE

COUNTY OF Crawford

CITY OF _____

COMPLAINT AFFIDAVIT

THE UNDERSIGNED, BEING DULY SWORN UPON HIS OATH DEPOSES AND SAYS

ON THE 5th DAY OF Oct 19 93, AT 1:45 P.M.

NAME McVeigh Timothy J

STREET 6289 Campbell E

CITY - STATE Lockport, N.Y.

AGE __ BIRTH DATE 4/23/68   RACE W   SEX M   HT 6   WT 168

DRIV. LIC. No. NY-M03791582721200968   (DID UNLAWFULLY OPERATE)

VEH. LIC. No. 7NH-607   STATE NY   YR. __   MAKE Mer

UPON A PUBLIC HIGHWAY, NAMELY AT (LOCATION) I-540 Alma/Van Buren

EMPLOYED BY _____

Located in the city, village, township, county and state aforesaid and did then and there commit the following offense.

Leading Causes of Accidents				
SPEEDING (over limit) __ m.p.h. in __ m.p.h. zone)	☐ 5 - 10 m.p.h.	☐ 11 - 15 m.p.h.	☐ over 15 m.p.h.	
Improper LEFT TURN	☐ No signal	☐ Cut corner	☐ From wrong lane	
Improper RIGHT TURN	☐ No signal	☐ Into wrong lane ☐ Middle of Intersection	☐ From wrong lane ☐ Not reached intersection	
Disobeyed TRAFFIC SIGNAL (When light turned red)	☐ Past middle intersection ☐ Radar			
Disobeyed STOP SIGN	☐ Wrong place ☐ At intersection ☐ Between Traffic	☐ Walk speed ☐ Cut in ☐ On right	☐ Faster ☐ Wrong Side of pavement ☐ On hill	
Improper PASSING AND LANE USAGE	☐ Lane Straddling	☐ Wrong lane	☐ On curve	

OTHER VIOLATIONS Prohibited Passing

IN VIOLATION OF SEC. 27-51-307 (8)(4)

		CAUSED PERSON TO DODGE		TYPE ACCIDENT	PD PI FATAL
SLIPPERY PAVEMENT	☐ Rain ☐ Snow ☐ Ice	☐ Pedestrian ☐ Driver JUST MISSED ACCIDENT		☐ Ped ☐ Vehicle ☐ Hit Fixed Object ☐ Right Angle ☐ Head on ☐ Sideswipe ☐ Rear end ☐ Ran off Roadway ☐ Intersection	
DARKNESS	☐ Night ☐ Fog ☐ Snow				
OTHER TRAFFIC PRESENT	☐ Cross ☐ Oncoming ☐ Pedestrian ☐ Same direction				

AREA: ☐ Business ☐ Industrial ☐ School ☐ Residential ☐ Rural

HIGHWAY TYPE: ☐ 2 lane ☐ 3 lane ☐ 4 lane ☐ 4 lane divided

DO NOT WRITE IN THIS SPACE

"You may present this ticket to the Sheriff any time before the court appearance date and time shown below."

COURT APPEARANCE 24th DAY OF Nov 19 93 AT 1 P.M.

ADDRESS OF COURT Van Buren

I PROMISE TO APPEAR IN SAID COURT OR BUREAU AT SAID TIME AND PLACE

SIGNATURE _____

The undersigned further states that he has just and reasonable grounds to believe, and does believe, that the person named above committed the offense herein set forth contrary to law.

SWORN TO AND SUBSCRIBED BEFORE ME

THIS __ DAY OF __   (Badge No.) _____

F 735922

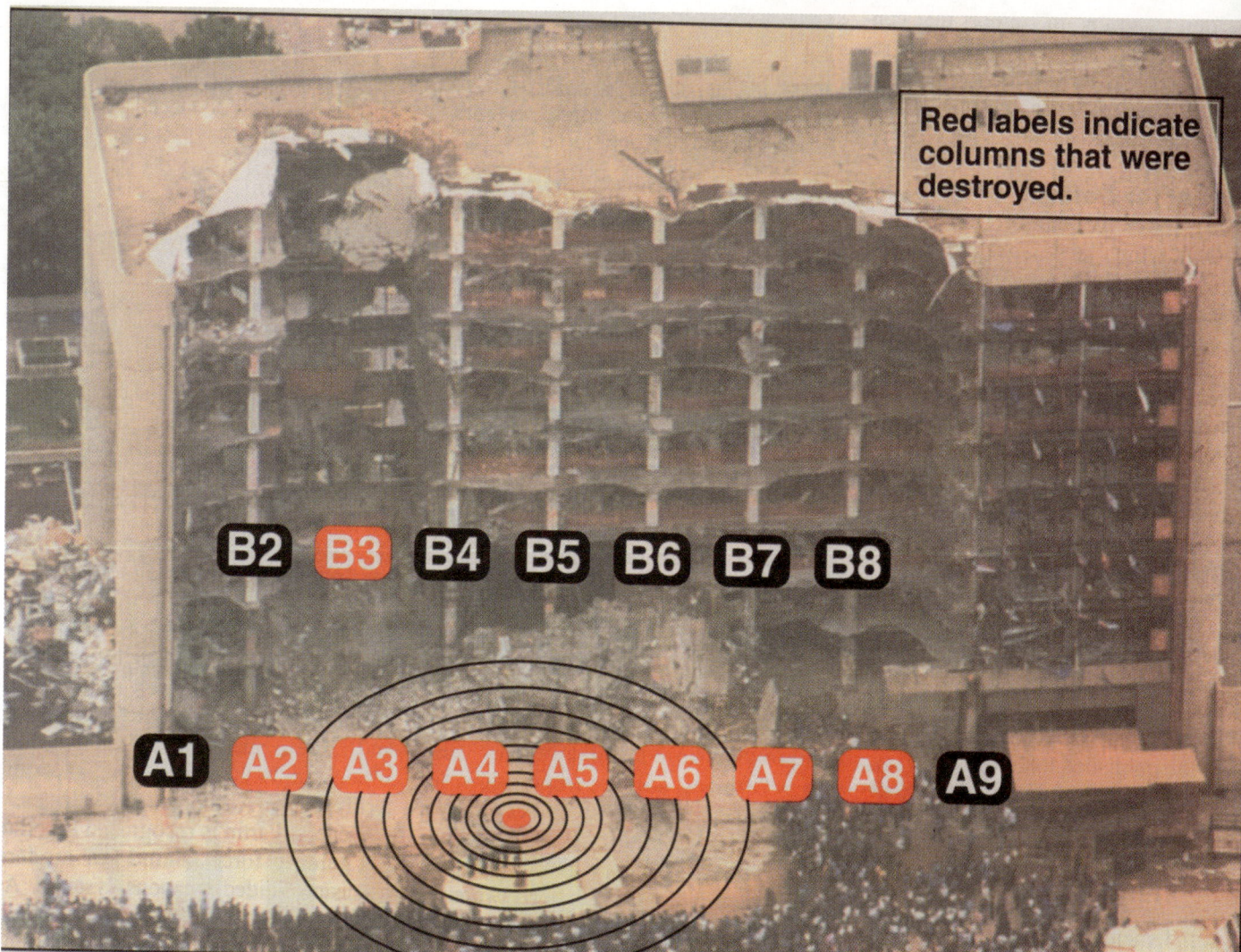

General Partin argues that the single-bomb explanation cannot account for the failure of column B3, which was further from the truck bomb than columns B4 and B5, which did not fail. He concludes that the asymmetrical nature of the damage to the Murrah building is one indication that demolition charges were used in the bombing.

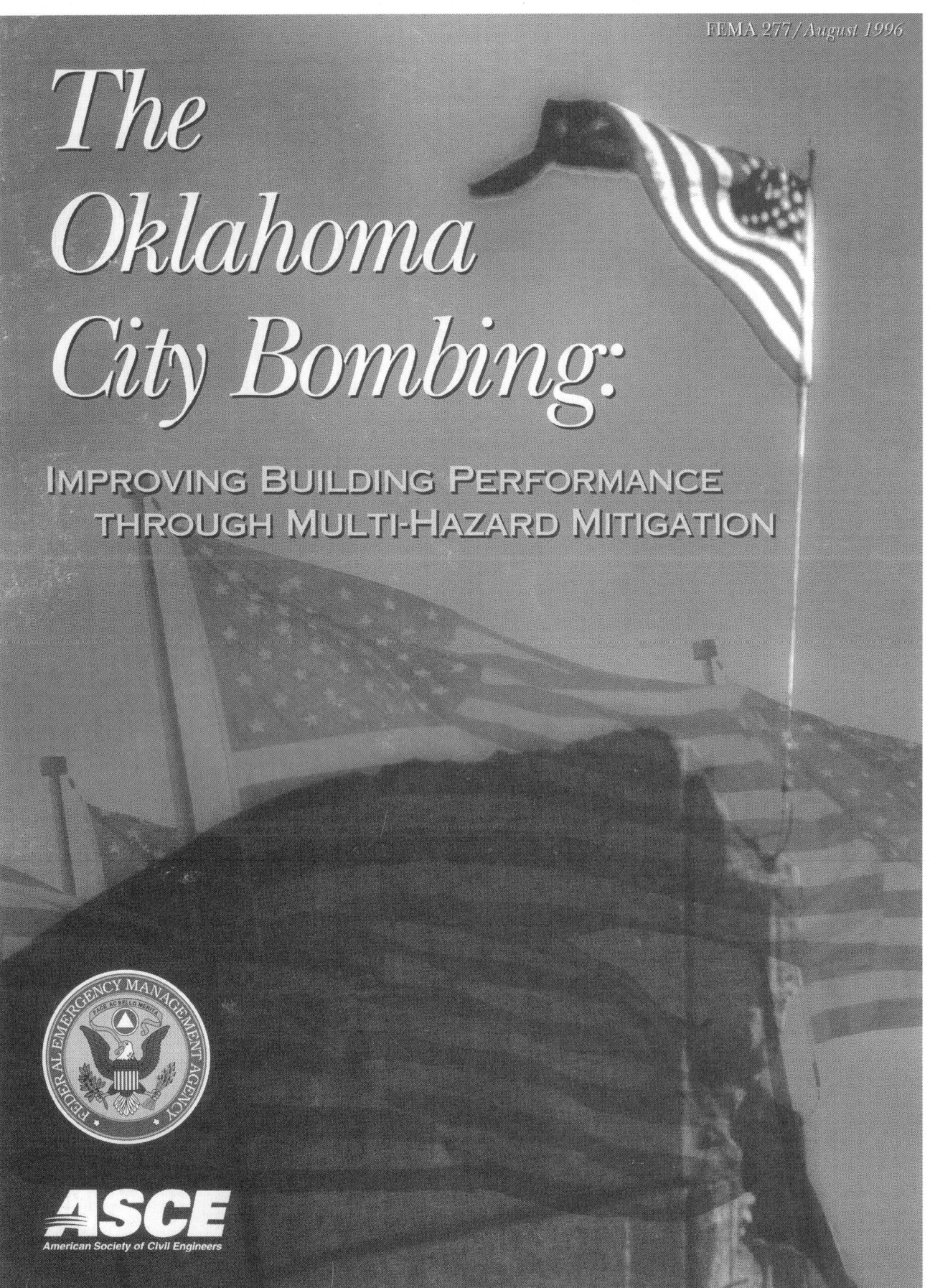

The FEMA Report is available free to the public. It can be ordered by calling 1-800-480-2520. Ask for Report # 277.

Appendix

Figure 1-14   Damage to north and east sides of Murrah Building.

Figure 1-15   Damage to southeast portion of Murrah Building.

1-18

Appendix

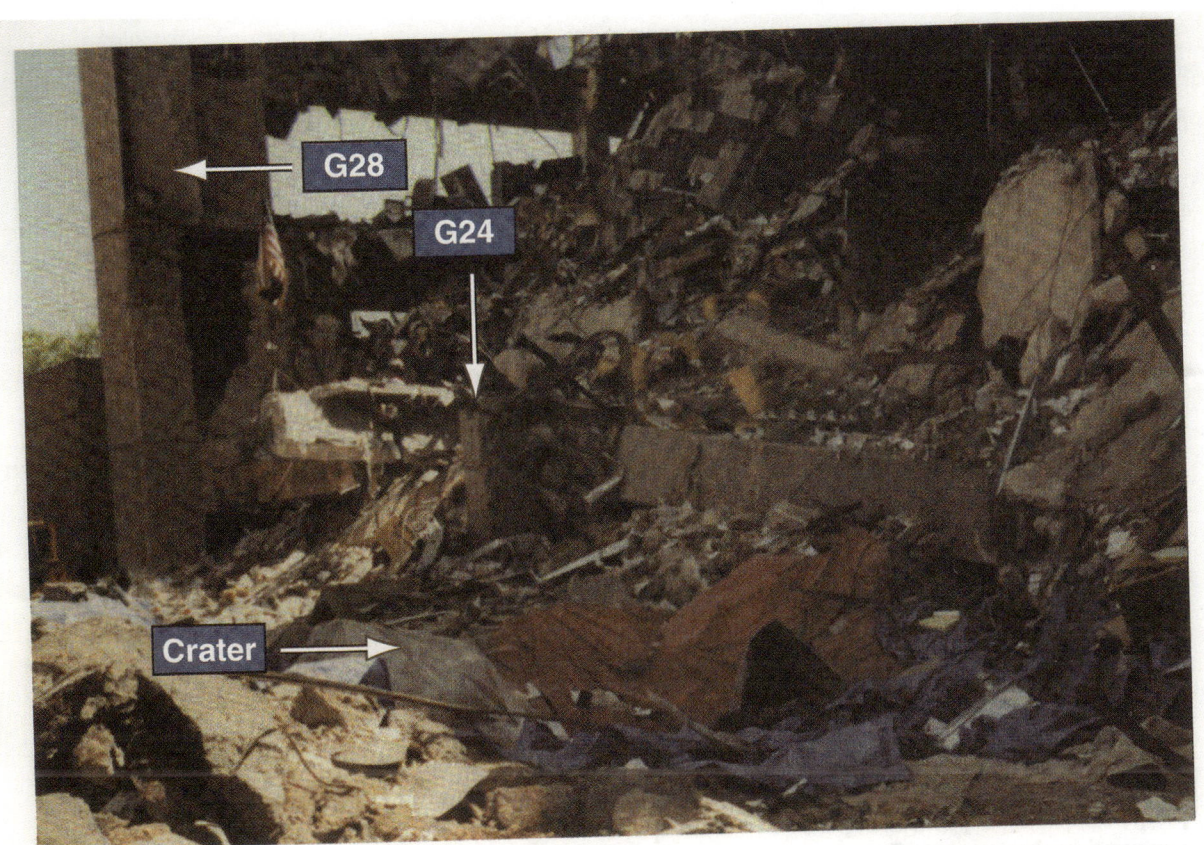

Figure 3-1 Bomb crater (covered by tarp).

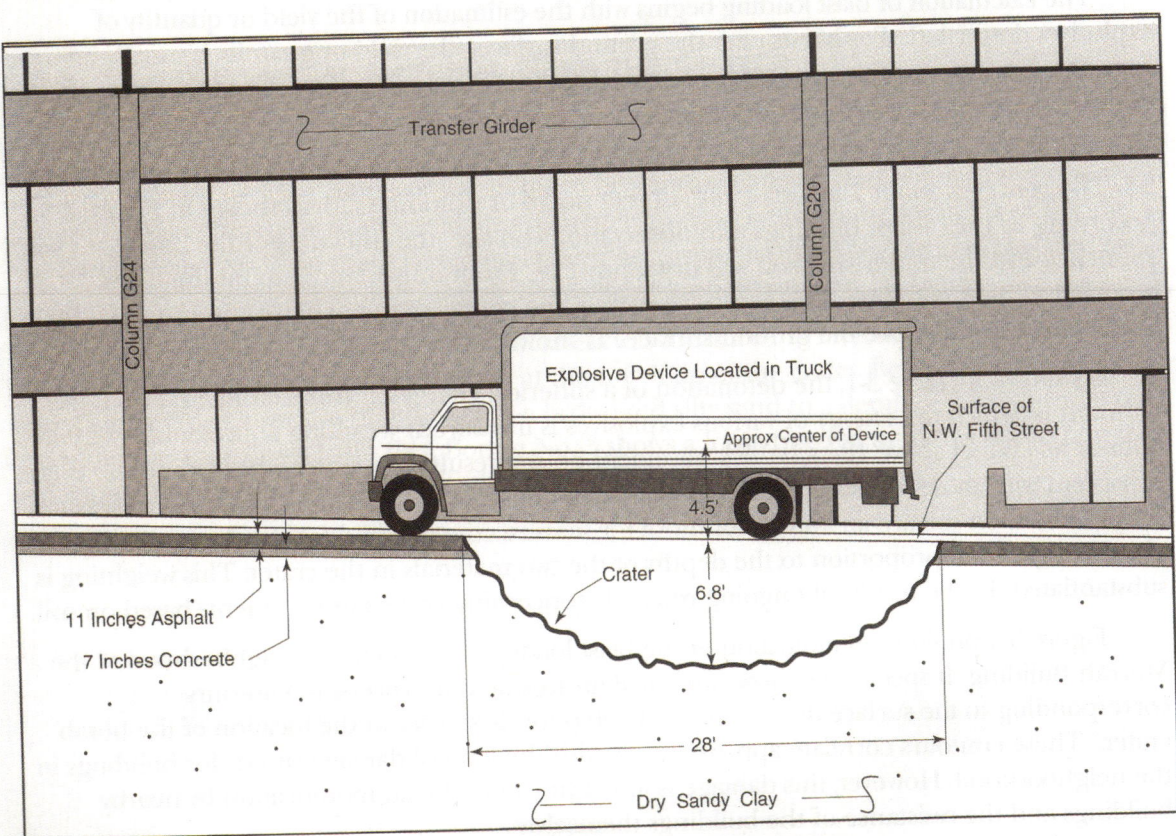

Figure 3-2 Approximate dimensions of crater at north face of Murrah Building.

3-2

ANALYSIS

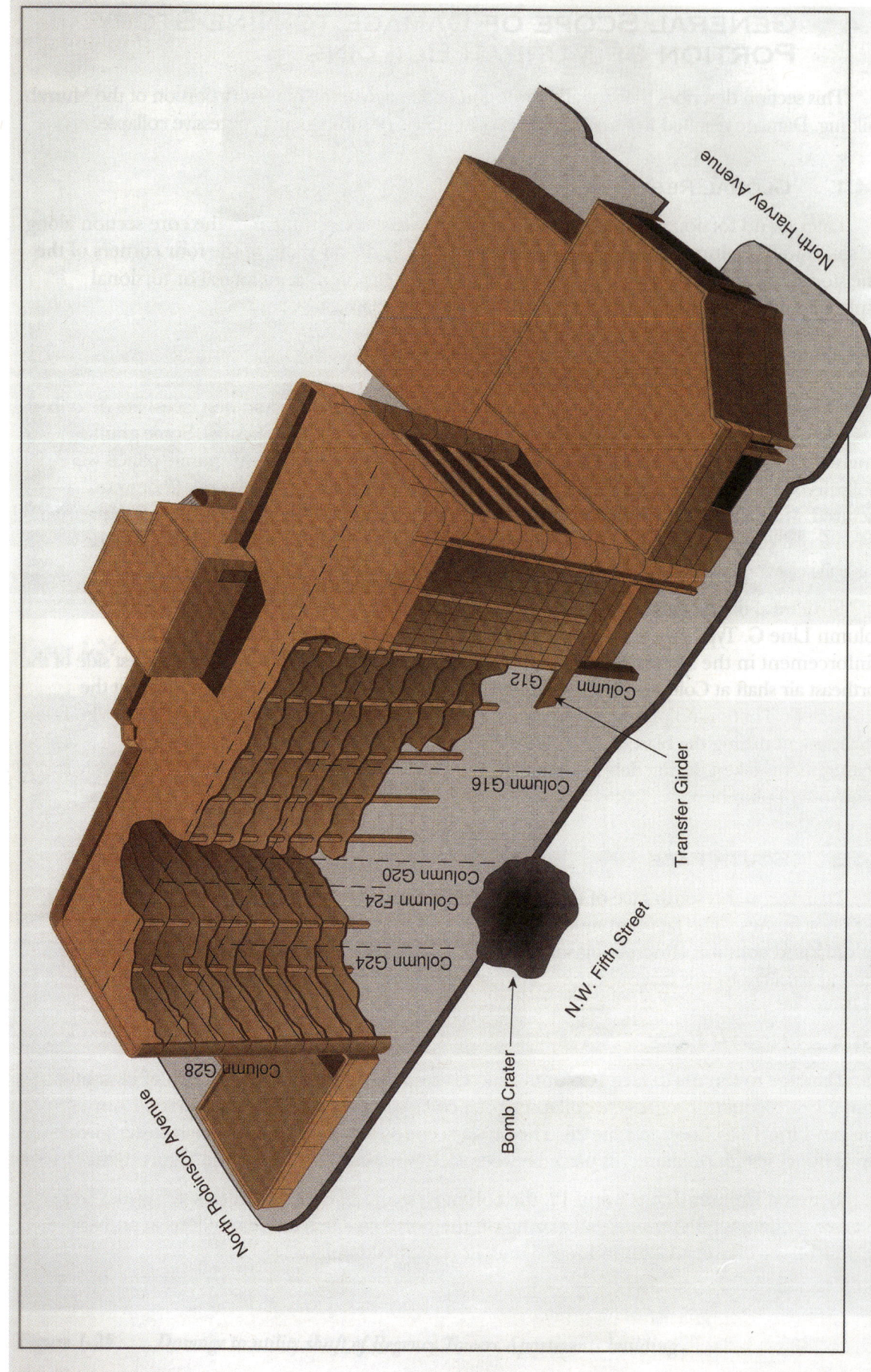

Figure 1-26 Failure boundaries of roof/floor slabs in Murrah Building.

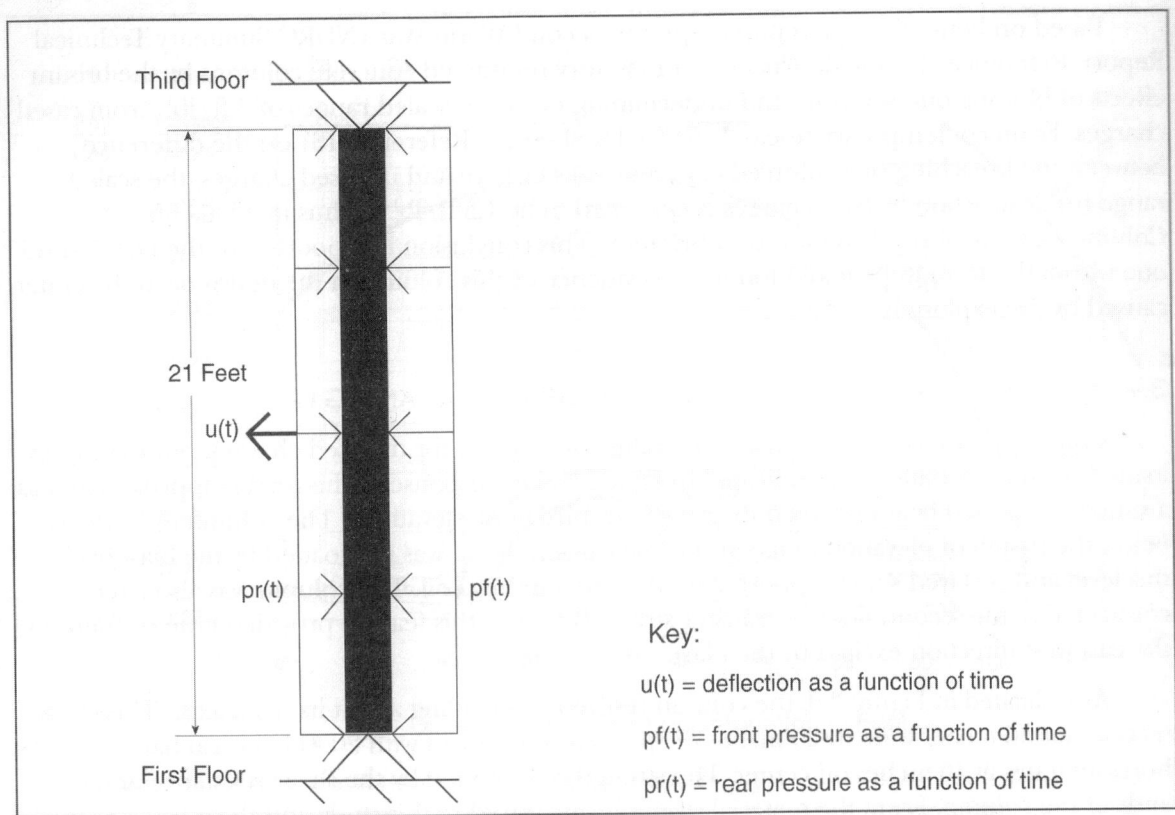

Figure 3-8 Model of Column G24 (singe degree of freedom).

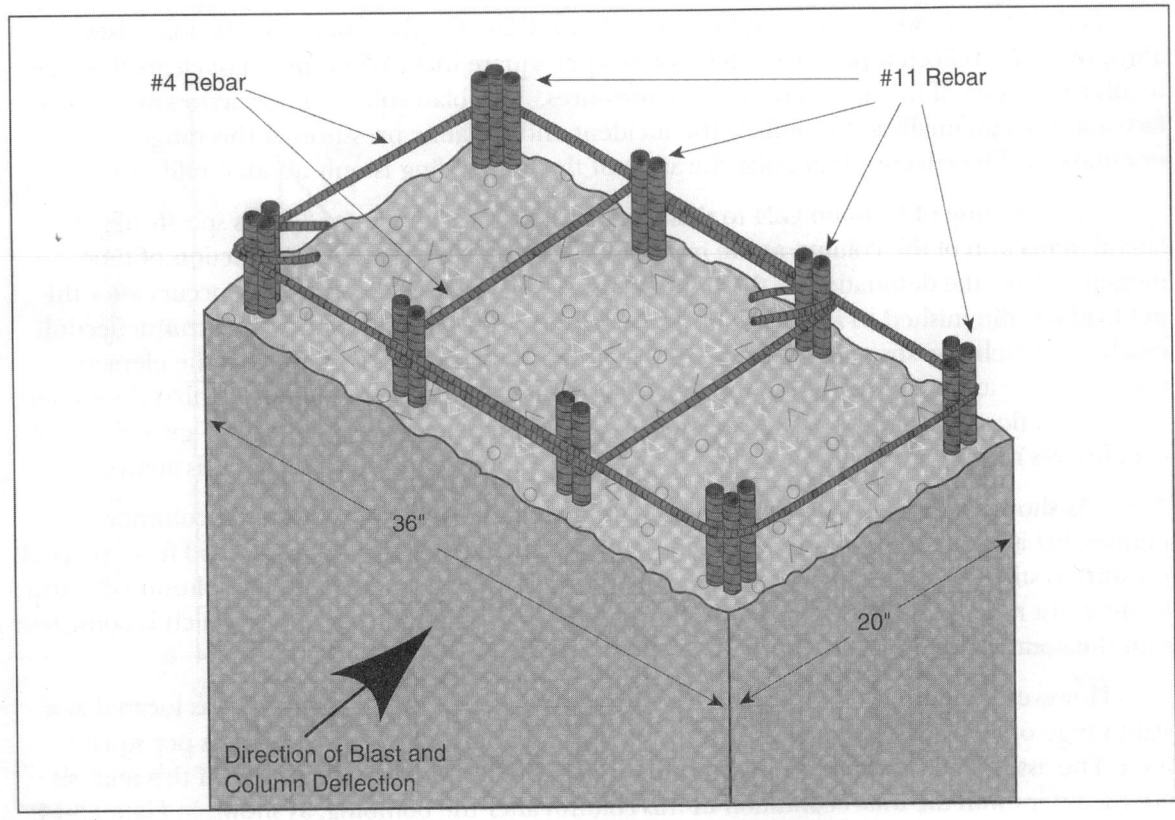

Figure 3-9 Cross section of Column G24.

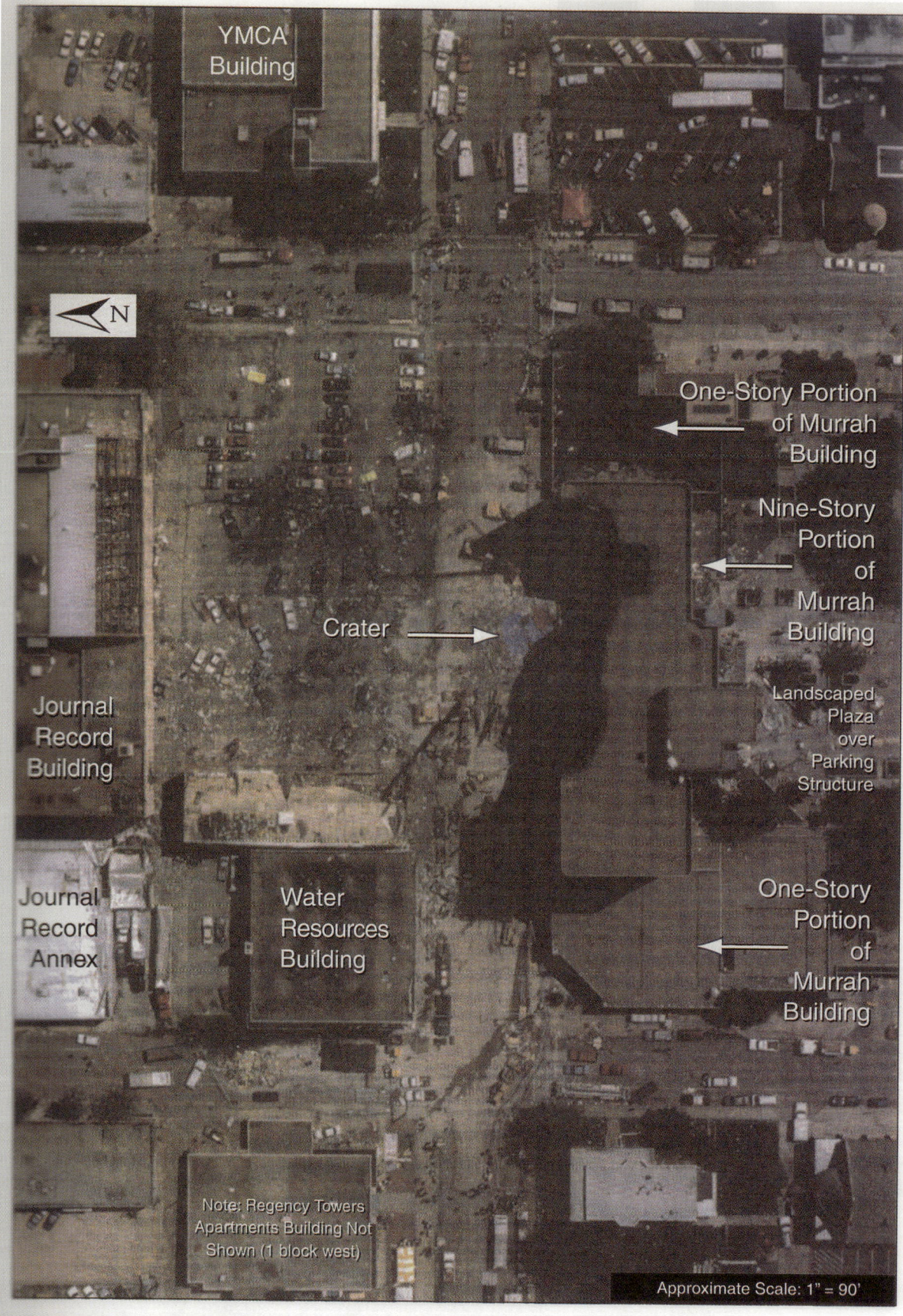

Figure 1-13   Aerial view of damaged buildings.

```
FD-822 (3-30-94)              Source: ATF-Tulsa, OK
                                      Confidential Informant
                              Prepared by: S/A Angela Finley


Information Control           Control Number: 6996


     In August 1994 this agent began an investigation of White
Aryan Resistance (W.A.R.) leader Dennis Mahon and Elohim City.
Confidential Informant has close ties with Mahon and has visited
Elohim City on numerous oca[?]tions (sic).  W.A.R. trains at
Elohim City and Posse Comitatus members also frequent Elohim
City.  ATF is primary enemy of all three ( sic) people.  Elohim
City's leader Robert Millar was contacted by McVeigh April 5,
1995 after he had contacted Ryder rental that day.


Assigned to: S/A Angela Finley    Date: 043095

Lead: Contact CI
```

McVeigh Phone Call To Elohim City

Department of the Treasury

ATF NEWS

For Immediate Release
Contact: Lester D. Martz

May 23, 1995
214-767-2250

ATF REFUTES RUMORS OF OKLAHOMA CITY EVACUATION

Dallas--Rumors that employees of the Bureau of Alcohol, Tobacco and Firearms (ATF) had evacuated the Murrah Federal Building prior to the April 19 bombing are entirely false.

Les Martz, Special Agent in Charge of the Dallas office, stated, "I strongly suspect that these malicious rumors are fueled by the same sources as the negative rhetoric that has been recently circulating about law enforcement officers. The facts are that ATF's employees in Oklahoma City were carrying out their assigned duties as they would any work day, and several of them were injured in the explosion."

Agent Martz continued, "There is a special bond within the law enforcement community. We worked side by side with agents from the Secret Service and the Drug Enforcement Administration who lost their lives in this devastating incident. The impact of this loss will be carried in our hearts forever. False rumors only serve to hurt the families of all the victims of this disaster. I am appalled that anyone would be so callous as to cause more pain to these fine people."

Several ATF employees were actually heroes on April 19. The following examples are well documented and refute any rumors to the contrary.

-- ATF's Resident Agent in Charge Alex McCauley was with a DEA agent in the elevator when the bomb exploded. The elevator dropped in a free fall from the eighth floor to the third. The two men were trapped in the smoke-filled elevator. The emergency buttons and the phone were inoperable. On their fourth attempt, they managed to break through the doors and escape from the elevator.

-more-

The agents made their way to the stairwell and brought with them 10 or 15 people they found along the way. At the second floor, the stairs were gone and they were all forced to shimmy down a sheet to a chain of rescuers who brought them out of the rubble. Agent McCauley then went to work helping victims and setting up a command center.

-- ATF Agent Luke Franey was on the phone on the ninth floor when the bomb exploded. He was knocked out of his chair and thrown across the room. When he gained consciousness, Agent Franey found that he could not escape, due to the structural damage of holes in the floor and fallen material. He found a hand-held radio and began transmitting for assistance. ATF agents and a highway patrol officer picked up the signal.

Agent Franey began recording his observations of the scene on a small tape recorder. He recorded the scene for investigatory purposes in terms of the color of the smoke around him and the directions of the fire and smoke. During the over one-hour time period that Agent Franey was trapped in the building, he managed to throw a radio receiver to the ground, giving him two-way communication with the investigators and rescue workers on the ground.

After a helicopter rescue of Agent Franey was aborted, he crawled out the window on a 45 degree ledge and made his way into another office. Trained in the martial arts, Agent Franey broke through three walls and found a stairwell. When he finally exited the building, Agent Franey began assisting rescue workers.

-- ATF's office secretary, Valerie Rowden-Matthews was at her desk when the explosion occurred. Her head was blown down against her desk from the impact. When she looked up, everything was gone. Ms. Rowden-Matthews stumbled out of the office and assisted a woman with a broken arm to escape the building.

-- ATF Inspectors Vernon Buster and Jim Skaggs were blown across their office on the ninth floor and covered with debris. Inspector Buster had a nail embedded in his arm. Both men were bleeding heavily from their heads. An officer from the Midwest City Police Department removed the debris, fashioned bandages from shirts, and stemmed the bleeding by applying direct pressure, before leading the Inspectors down the stairs for further medical assistance.

20 April 1995
CDR Mark Finch
J3323/4-5636

MSCA UPDATE

Oklahoma City Bombing Relief Operation

1. Situation (As of 0500L, 20 April):
    - At 191015 local a major explosion occurred in the Federal Building in Oklahoma City
    - One bomb from a car parked in front of the building with an estimated 1200 pounds of explosive is believed to be the source. A second bomb was disarmed, a third bomb was evacuated.

2. Sequence of events last 24 hours:
    - Established a Defense Coordinating Officer and element in Oklahoma City
    - Coordinated with DOMS and TRANSCOM to transport DOJ Crime Scene vans from Andrews AFB to Tinker AFB.
    - Coordinated with DOMS and TRANSCOM to move Urban Search & Rescue (US&R) Teams from Phoenix and Sacramento. Two more teams are scheduled to be transported this morning (Virginia Beach and New York City teams).
    - Sent EXORD for disaster relief operations establishing Tinker AFB as the Base Support Installation (BSI).
    - Provided two MEDEVAC helicopters and two dog teams for bomb threat support from Ft Sill.
    - Provided ambulances and rescue teams with dogs from Tinker AFB.

3. Summary of DoD support to date:
    - DCO and DCE
    - 2 MEDEVAC Helos
    - BSI
    - Dog Teams for bomb threat support
    - Ambulances
    - Rescue teams with dogs.

4. Anticipated taskings/events next 24 hours:
    - Complete transport of US&R teams.
    - Body Bags.

MEMORANDUM FOR:	Richard W. Krimm, Associate Director Response and Recovery Directorate
ATTENTION:	Chief, Federal Response Division
FROM:	Dell Greer, FCO/DRM
SUBJECT:	Situation Report (SITREP) No. 5
EVENT:	FEMA-3115-EM-OK
DATE AND TIME:	Period from 4-20-95 at 1145L to 4-20-95 at 2100L

1. SITUATION:

Most of the following situational information was obtained via media sources.

A major explosion occurred in the Alfred P. Murrah Federal Building in Oklahoma City at approximately 0905 CDT, causing severe damage. A car parked in the front of the building with an estimated 1200 lb. bomb is believed to be the source of the explosion. A second and third bomb were located in the building. The second bomb was disarmed and the third bomb was evacuated. The front third of the 9 story building was destroyed.

Federal agencies in the bombed building:

- Department of Defense
- Department of Transportation
- General Services Administration
- General Accounting Office
- Department of Health and Human Services
- Housing and Urban Development
- Department of Justice
- Department of Labor
- Office of Personnel Management
- Treasury Department
- U.S. Army, Air Force, and Marine Corps Recruiting
- Department of Agriculture
- Veterans Administration

United States Attorney
District of Colorado

Byron G. Rogers Federal Building
Twelfth Floor, Drawer 3615
1961 Stout Street
Denver, Colorado 80294

(303) 844-20..
FAX 844-67..

September 14, 1994

Cary James Gagan

Re: Letter of Immunity

Dear Mr. Gagan:

This letter is to memorialize the agreement between you and the United States of America, by the undersigned Assistant United States Attorney. The terms of this agreement are as follows:

1. You have contacted the U.S. Marshals Service on today's date indicating that you have information concerning a conspiracy and/or attempt to destroy United States court facilities in Denver and possibly other cities.

2. The United States agrees that any statement and/or information that you provide relevant to this conspiracy/conspiracies or attempts will not be used against you in any criminal proceeding. Further, the United States agrees that no evidence derived from the information or statements provided by you will be used in any way against you.

3. In return for this grant of use/derivative use immunity, you agree to fully and completely cooperate with all federal law enforcement authorities in the District of Colorado regarding your knowledge of and participation in any crimes and/or related activities. All statements and any testimony you give pursuant to this agreement will be protected by use/derivative use immunity as stated in paragraph 2 above.

4. If you make or give any false statements or testimony at any time, this agreement becomes null and void. The decision as to whether a violation of this agreement has occurred remains solely in the discretionary judgment of the Office of the United States Attorney for the District of Colorado.

5. If this agreement is violated, any statement made or testimony given by you during the course of this investigation and agreement will no longer be protected by any kind of immunity and you may be prosecuted for any crime of which the United States has knowledge, including knowledge ...ned by your own

Were papers Put before survivors?

The Florida Times-Union, Jacksonville, Tuesday, May 2, 1995

OKLAHOMA CITY — Hours after a truck bomb ripped apart the Oklahoma City federal building, some rescue workers were ordered to stop searching for survivors while federal officials removed boxes of documents, a New York newspaper has reported.

"You'd think they would have let their evidence and files sit at least until the last survivor was pulled out," one angry rescue worker told The Daily News.

"They had guys carrying out boxes while the rescue workers were forced to sit on their hands," said the worker, a member of a canine rescue squad who talked to the newspaper under condition of anonymity.

The rescue worker and an Oklahoma City firefighter, who also asked that his name be withheld, offered similar accounts in separate interviews.

The two said that about 10 to 12 hours after the April 19 blast, federal officials began limiting the number of rescue workers allowed in the building to about a dozen, confining them largely to the lower right side of the battered structure.

Meanwhile, 40 to 50 federal agents spent much of the night carrying dozens of boxes from the seventh and ninth floors, where the federal Drug Enforcement Administration and the Bureau of Alcohol, Tobacco and Firearms have offices.

The contents of the files were not known, but federal officials

(From Page A-1)

said they were looking into the possibility that alleged bomber Timothy McVeigh and his accomplices had targeted the nine-story building in an effort to destroy DEA or ATF investigation files.

FBI spokesman Gene Pogue called allegations that rescue workers were restrained by the feds "unfortunate," but refused other comment.

John Russell, a spokesman for the Justice Department, said: "Our first concern was retrieval of survivors. Documents and papers were secondary."

Oklahoma City Fire Chief Gary Marrs said smaller groups of rescuers were sent throughout the building nearly 12 hours after the blast, but he said he didn't know anything about the feds ordering that. He didn't explain why the search seemed to be scaled back.

The last survivor was pulled out of the wreckage about 11 p.m. EDT on April 20 — more than 36 hours after the blast tore through the Alfred P. Murrah Federal Building.

Outside the shaky ruins of the federal building yesterday, officials acknowledged the inevitable: It is time to give up the search for signs of life and switch to heavy machinery to remove bodies.

"I think they need to do whatever is necessary to ensure the safety of the rescue workers," said Jim Texter, whose wife, Victoria, was still missing. "Nobody wants to be responsible for more hurt."

The death toll reached 139, including 15 children. About 40 people were missing.

A still-grieving Oklahoma City focused on the fate of the missing. Marrs said a huge backhoe would be brought in to drag out debris from the hulking skeleton of concrete and steel.

Gov. Frank Keating said rescuers ed that everyone inside is dead. The concern now is for the crews that have been sifting by hand through debris with the threat of collapse always overhead.

"You reach a point where you don't jeopardize human beings in order to extract the dead," the governor said.

The machine was expected to begin work late yesterday or sometime today, Assistant Fire Chief Jon Hansen said. The work will begin as soon as rescue crews have removed all debris from areas deemed safe for them to be in, he said. Rescue officials and the governor met with families of the missing to discuss the decision.

The workers will use a machine that looks like a backhoe but is on tracks like a tank. Its big claw will lift debris inside the ruins and set it down outside to be searched by hand.

"It's frustrating because there's so much debris," police Sgt. Frank Koch said. "You know where they're at, and you can't get at them."

John Long, who was officially notified of his mother's death Sunday night, said the change in search tactics affected the mood of waiting families.

"This was the first time I had seen anything approaching despair on their faces," Long said. "We all know what we're waiting for, but we all need some closure. When I got to say goodbye to my mother last night, it was the first time I had had any peace in 11 days. I also felt a great deal of love for what those guys did to bring her back."

Sharon Parker, whose husband is lost in the debris, said she understood that it no longer is reasonable to expect firefighters to risk their lives by going into an unstable building to find persons who are probably dead.

more people to die in that building," she said. "I wish they didn't have to do it [with machinery], but I prayed on it and I know they have no choice."

Rescue worker Debi Croy of Menlo Park, Calif., said workers' attitudes haven't changed despite vivors is slim.

"We still have the same job to do," she said.

But the structural instability is worrying officials is more evident than it was a week ago, she said. Workers can't hear the but "we're a lot

Affidavit of Don Hammons Regarding The Bombing Of The Alfred P. Murrah Federal Building

State of Oklahoma   )
) SS:
County of Oklahoma   )

I, affiant herein, being of legal age and having been duly sworn, does hereby state as follows:

1) That my date of birth is September 26th, 1952.

2) That I reside at 5401 North Dewey, Oklahoma City, Oklahoma, 73118, Oklahoma County.

3) That I am a reserve deputy with The Oklahoma County Sheriff's Office.

4) That I was a reserve deputy with The Oklahoma County Sheriff's Office on April 19, 1995.

5) That I responded to the scene of the bombing of The Alfred P. Murrah Federal Building at approximately 12:30 PM on April 19, 1995, to give assistance in my capacity as a reserve deputy.

6) That sometime between 9:30PM and 10:30PM, on April 19, 1995, I was positioned northwest of The Murrah Building on the intersection of 5th Street and North Hudson providing a perimeter of security to the crime scene.

7) That sometime between 9:30PM and 10:30PM, on April 19, 1995, United States Congressman Ernest Istook approached my position with a female who identified herself as Lana Tyree.

8) That Ms. Tyree was taking pictures on the scene and I confronted Ms. Tyree and instructed her not to take pictures.

9) That Ms. Tyree stated to me that she was with Congressman Istook and that Mr. Istook wanted her to take pictures of the crime scene.

10) That Ms. Tyree made a statement to me that she was aware from Mr. Istook that a bomb threat had been called in on April 9th.

FURTHER, AFFIANT SAYETH NOT:

Don Hammons
Don Hammons

SUBSCRIBED TO AND SWORN BEFORE ME ON THE 12th DAY OF Dec, 1997.

Jim Grace
NOTARY PUBLIC

MY COMMISSION EXPIRES:

OFFICIAL SEAL
Jim Grace
Notary Public • Oklahoma
   and County
My Commission Expires Mar. 19, 2000

Affidavit of David Kochendorfer Regarding The Bombing Of The Alfred P. Murrah Federal Building

State of Oklahoma)
) SS:
County of Cleveland)

I, affiant herein, being of legal age and having been duly sworn, does hereby state as follows:

1) That my date of birth is February 21, 1943.

2) That I reside at 1413 Hollywood Avenue, Norman, Oklahoma, 73072, Cleveland County.

3) That I am a reserve deputy with The Oklahoma County Sheriff's Office.

4) That I was a reserve deputy with The Oklahoma County Sheriff's Office on April 19, 1995.

5) That I responded to the scene of the bombing of The Alfred P. Murrah Federal Building at approximately 9:30 AM on April 19, 1995, to give assistance in my capacity as a reserve deputy.

6) That sometime between 9:30PM and 10:30PM on April 19, 1995, I was positioned northwest of The Murrah Building on the intersection of 5th Street and North Hudson providing a perimeter of security to the crime scene.

7) That sometime between 9:30PM and 10:30PM on April 19, 1995, United States Congressman Ernest Istook approached my position and identified himself.

8) That Mr. Istook stated to me, "we knew this was going to happen and we blew it." And I stated to Mr. Istook, "Pardon me, how did you know this?" And Mr. Istook stated, "Well, we got word there's a undercover....a right wing Muslim Fundamentalist Extremist Group in Oklahoma City." Mr. Istook also stated that an information source thought that a Federal Building was going to be bombed.

9) That Mr. Istook asked me what department I was with, and I stated that I was with Oklahoma County.

10) That Mr. Istook made the statement, "Well, I thought you were with the Highway Patrol."

FURTHER, AFFIANT SAYETH NOT:

David Kochendorfer
David Kochendorfer

SUBSCRIBED TO AND SWORN BEFORE ME ON THE 9th DAY OF Dec, 1997.

Patricia Smith
NOTARY PUBLIC

MY COMMISSION EXPIRES:
11-27-99

Jan 27, 1998

Special Agent in Charge
Federal Bureau of Investigation
50 Penn Place, Suite 1600
Oklahoma City, Okla. 73118

Dear Sir:

On January 26, 1998, I was the subject of an interview conducted by James F. Carlile, Special Agent for the FBI at the Oklahoma County Sheriff Office. The interview was concerning the press conference in which I revealed the comment made to me by Congressman Ernest Istook about prior knowledge of a bombing of a Federal Building in Oklahoma City.

I feel, based on his demeanor, Special Agent Carlile was not completely objective during the interview. He made comments during the interview and at its conclusion which led me to believe his report was not going to accurately reflect my feelings concerning the manner in which Congressman Istook made the statement to me the evening of the bombing.

At the conclusion of the interview, Mr. Carlile indicated to me, his report would reflect that I felt Congressman Istook was just repeating "scuttlebutt" he heard that evening. I told Agent Carlile I disagreed with his assessment of the conversation.

I would like my statement to accurately reflect that I feel Congressman Ernest Istook made the statement to me "We knew this was going to happen and we blew it", he was forthright and momentous.

I respectfully ask this letter be part of my statement.

Thank you,

David L. Kochendorfer

U.S. Department of Justice
Immigration and Naturalization Service

MEMORANDUM OF INVESTIGATION

FILE NUMBER	TITLE:	CONTROL OFFICE
A74 602 286	STRASSMEIR, Andreas Carl	OKC

On 2/7/96, this office received a copy of an undated Freedom of Information Act (FOIA) request from the Dallas District (submitted by the New York Times) concerning SUBJECT. Said document was faxed to OKC FBI CASE CONTROL AGENT JOHN HIPPARD by OKC IA Pendley.

The writer received a call from OKC FBI SA LOUANN SANDSTROM (████████) this date who (1) Indicated that HIPPARD was no longer the point of contact for this case; (2) SUBJECT was out of the United States; (3) Asked whether or not SUBJECT could be legally admitted to the United States; and, (4) Asked about the status of our investigation against SUBJECT.

OKC OIC JOHNSTON and the writer called SANDSTROM and indicated that the SUBJECT was being investigated by the INS via a request from HIBBARD that if SUBJECT was encountered, to notify HIBBARD (and the writer) for further investigation concerning SUBJECT'S possible activity under FBI CASE NO. 174A-OC-56120, and for INS, SUBJECT'S status. OIC and the writer indicated that now that SUBJECT is out of the USA and not an overstay, it is unlikely INS would have any interest in him. In addition, since the purpose of the lookout was to locate SUBJECT and SUBJECT had already been seen in Germany (according to SANDSTROM), we inquired about whether the INS lookout should remain active. SANDSTROM indicated that the INS lookout should be canceled.

Action was taken by this office this date to cancel lookout on SUBJECT. Copy of cancellation to be placed in this file after action by PENDLEY. Copy of INS FOIA request faxed to SANDSTROM for FYI.

MIKE LOPEZ, DAL/FOIA, (████████) contacted this date concerning the FOIA request. LOPEZ indicated that he needed the original file to respond to the FOIA request.

OIC Johnston said that he would hand-carry the file to DAL and give it to J. RAMIREZ, DAL/ADD DD&P on 02/10/96. RAMIREZ would then give it to LOPEZ on 02/12/96. File transferred in CIS, sealed in envelope and given to JOHNSTON this date.

SIGNATURE: *Stephen C. Merrill*	DATE: 2/8/96
STEPHEN C. MERRILL INS SUPERVISORY SPECIAL AGENT	PAGE: 1/1

FORM G-166C (7/1/83; OKC: 4/28/94)

FILE: A:\166\STRASS

November 15, 1996

TO WHOM IT MAY CONCERN:

SUBJECT: MURRAH BUILDING BOMBING/INFORMATION AND MIS-INFORMATION WHAT IS THE REAL TRUTH, WHY ARE PEOPLE NOT BEING PUT UNDER OATH? WHY IS INFORMATION BEING SCREENED TO DETERMINE WHAT IS PUT OUT TO THE PUBLIC AND GIVEN TO DEFENSE? WHY DOES THERE APPEAR A UNIFORM CONSPIRACY TO ONLY GIVE PART OF THE FACTS/STATEMENTS/TRUTH ABOUT THE MURRAH BOMBING?

FROM: JANE C. GRAHAM
PUBLIC HOUSING SPECIALIST - FACILITIES MANAGEMENT
DEPARTMENT OF HOUSING AND URBAN DEVELOPMENT
AND
PRESIDENT, AFGE LOCAL 3138

This is my statement regarding the above. Approximately the last week of August, 1995, I contacted the FBI and spoke with a Mr. Joe Schwecke regarding the bombing and told him about events which I was aware of the week before the bombing. I made an appointment with him for Tuesday the 5th of September. HE never showed up. I again called and set up another appointment for the following week and that was never kept.

On September 12, (I believe this is the correct date), I had an interview with a female agent in the Office of Native Americans/HUD at 500 W. Main, OKC. There were several agents there asking a set series of questions regarding the bombing as she explained to me. These same questions were asked to everyone within a 10 block radius.

The questions were very basic, and few. When we were finished she said that was all and I said I was not finished. I told her of the previous report I had given Agent Schwecke and I wanted to know why no one asked questions about the week before the bombing and if anyone saw anything suspicious. APPARENTLY THE FBI WAS NOT INTERESTED IN ANY TIME OTHER THAN THE MONDAY OR TUESDAY THE WEEK OF THE BOMBING!!!! AND ONLY IF THE RESPONSES POINTED DIRECTLY TO MCVEIGH.

My question is why is it that they (FBI) were only interested if information was related to McVeigh? It appears that the FBI had an agenda which was to only target McVeigh and Nichols. The FBI conveniently dropped John Doe 2. Does the FBI believe that I as a citizen and a government employee and a survivor of the bombing, having been in the building at that time when it occurred, is so naive that I can't see through what has and is being orchestrated by Washington?

I contacted the FBI first by phone then by letter to inform them of three (3) men who I saw on the 2nd level of the parking garage the week before. The 2nd level of the parking garage is that level which is directly below the street level and customer parking.

These three men were standing just west of the double doors leading to the elevator, behind an older station wagon parked on the south side. They had a set of plans which appeared to be of the Murrah building. The reason I assumed the plans were of the Murrah building is they were obviously disagreeing on something and pointing to areas in the garage. Two of the men were approximately 5'8" and one man 6'1 or 2". Two men were brown hair, the tallest had very dark hair almost black and a mustache. He was wearing black cowboy boots, jeans and jacket and a cowboy hat. His hair was collar length. The other two men wore jeans one had a brown plaid short sleeved shirt and obviously lifted weights.

At first I thought as I studied them they were with the phone company because I saw what looked like telephone wiring. Cream colored but short pieces. He also had a paper bag with something in it. We had been having some telephone difficulty off and on in the building and that was the first thing that popped in my mind. But then I thought why would they be in the garage? They are always on a floor at the closet area when they are fixing a problem and would not be in the garage. Next I thought they must be with the gas company. There have been over the years gas leaks and maybe they were there for that purpose. As I studied these 3 men they were also watching me. At that time the man in the brown plaid shirt said something to the other man and he went to the station wagon and put the sack and wiring in the wagon behind the driver's seat and returned to the group. They watched me until I went through the doors to the elevator.

I had first thought of going up to them but thought they must have approval to be there in the building and they did have plans which they were discussing. The man in the brown shirt obviously knew what he was doing and was in charge even though you could tell there was disagreement among them. He reminded me of a surveyor or construction foreman except that I doubt that they would have been in that good of shape. These men were definitely physically well trained. I had intended to go to GSA but since I was in a hurry to get to work, I let it go by. Regrettably I wish now I had taken the time to go to GSA or to have gone up and talked to these men.

When I first told my story the only question asked was "Was one of the men McVeigh?" I told the agent absolutely not. Then I was asked can I positively identify the three men? I told him I didn't think I could be positive, and NO ONE HAD ASKED ME TO VIEW ANY PICTURES OF ANYONE. I WOULD BE VERY INTERESTED IN SEEING WHO WAS STAFFED IN THE ATF, FBI AND SECRET SERVICE PRIOR TO THE BOMBING AND IF THESE MEN I SAW WERE EMPLOYED BY ANY OF THESE AGENCIES.

I believe they were afraid I might be able to identify someone they did not want me to identify. I do have a good memory and I will continue to seek out and watch for these men to reappear and when I do I will confront them. This is not over.

Also, Germaine Johnston, who also works for HUD saw and spoke to McVeigh perhaps as much as 10 minutes after in the alley where he was "parked" sitting outside his car on the ground around on the passengers side along with John Doe 2. McVeigh asked her if anyone was killed. She replied, yes a lot were. At that point shaken, he got into his car and drove off by himself. John Doe 2 departed on foot. Now I ask you, does that sound like a man who was running? I don't think so. It sounds like a plan that went awry or something he did not know was going to happen.

These are just samples of stories which can be told and have not been given to the defense attorney. I DID FURNISH MY TESTIMONY TO JONES AS WELL AS FBI. GERMAINE FURNISHED HER'S TO THE FBI, THEY DID NOT GIVE THAT INFORMATION TO JONES. BUT HE HAS BEEN TOLD ABOUT IT AND SHE WILL BE INTERVIEWED BY ONE OF HIS ASSOCIATES.

THE IMPORTANT THING IS: THE TRUTH SHOULD COME OUT AND YOU HAVE A DUTY TO CALL A GRAND JURY TOGETHER TO SEE WHY MISINFORMATION IS BEING GIVEN AND SO MUCH OF THE TRUTH IS BEING HELD FROM THE PUBLIC.

THE GOVERNMENT MUST AND I SAY MUST TAKE RESPONSIBILITY FOR THEIR STING OPERATION GOING SOUR. YES, THEY HAVE A FINANCIAL RESPONSIBILITY FOR THE SUFFERING THEY HAVE CAUSED, DEATH AND DISMEMBERMENT OF PEOPLE. WE ARE NOT EXPENDABLE FOR THEIR CAUSE. JUST AS GSA INSTALLED PLATE GLASS WINDOWS A COUPLE OF YEARS BEFORE THE BOMBING TO SAVE SOME MONEY, LOOK AT HOW MANY PEOPLE THAT THEY KILLED BECAUSE OF COST SAVING MEASURES. THEY SHOULD BE HELD RESPONSIBLE ALONG WITH THE FBI AND ATF FOR THEIR STING OPERATION GOING SOUR -- OR DID IT? MAYBE THERE WAS A STING WITHIN A STING OPERATION TO ELIMINATE AGENTS WHO KNEW TOO MUCH.

Bonn to ask U.S. for crackdown on neo-Nazis

The German government is preparing to present a formal request to the United States to cooperate with German authorities in eliminating the links between Gary Lauck's NSDAP-AO organization in the United States and German neo-Nazis. Lauck, based in Nebraska, publishes a considerable portion of the neo-Nazi literature illegally circulating in Germany.

Previous attempts by Bonn to get the United States moving on the issue have failed, as American authorities told the Germans that Lauck is not violent and therefore his promotion of Nazi ideology cannot be prosecuted without violating his freedom of speech.

The Lauck problem was the subject of a report in the weekly *Welt am Sonntag* on Sept. 12, which pointed out that "by far the largest share of propaganda material of German neo-Nazis and skinheads is produced in the U.S.A." Lauck publishes a bi-monthly neo-Nazi journal, *Nazi Battle Cry*, which in its latest issue debates "the theoretical potentials of armed resistance against the German state."

In 1992 alone, German police found Lauck's propaganda in 72 searches of neo-Nazi residences, with one publication depicting a man with a swastika bombing a telecommunications tower.

The article quoted a German anti-terrorism expert: "For the FBI and CIA, Lauck is not interesting, because he is only a propagandist and not a violent person. If they would provide us with his address files, we could move against the people who are distributing his material in Germany illegally."

EIR September 24, 1993

U.S. racists' links to Germans probed

Los Angeles Times 12-15-93

WIESBADEN, Germany — Suspected links between extreme racist groups in Germany and U.S. hate organizations are under examination by the FBI, its director disclosed here Tuesday.

FBI Director Louis J. Freeh, completing 1½ days of meetings with cabinet ministers and top officials of BKA, the German counterpart of the FBI, stressed that the inquiry is just getting under way.

But his pledge to BKA President Hans-Ludwig Zachert, who provided leads for the inquiry, that it would be conducted "vigorously" marked the first official acknowledgment that the United States is investigating such trans-Atlantic links.

Equally significant, Mr. Freeh's statement illustrates the heightened cooperation that he and Ronald K. Noble, assistant secretary of the Treasury for enforcement, sought to achieve during meetings with their counterparts in Italy and Germany on a trip to the two countries that began Friday and ended Tuesday.

The move to share information came amid mounting concern over surging organized crime in the former Soviet Union and eastern bloc countries, fear that nuclear materials will fall into criminal hands, and attempts to counter racist violence by such groups as the skinheads.

The inquiry into any U.S. connection to what Mr. Zachert described as "xenophobic and racist attacks" in Germany has two aspects, officials explained. One involves "a particularly active person" in the Ku Klux Klan who is alleged to have played a role in the German violence.

Mr. Freeh, who is bringing back to Washington material that Mr. Zachert turned over to him on the case, described it as "an active case here in Germany which may have some connections, ramifications in the United States."

The second aspect are postcards sent with label addresses from the United States and Canada to German Justice Minister Sabine Leutheusser-Schnarrenberger urging her to resign for seeking to prosecute an individual accused of inciting neo-Nazi fervor, Mr. Freeh said.

Mr. Freeh directed Larry Potts, the FBI's assistant director for criminal investigations, to determine whether the bureau's guidelines permit looking into correspondence sent to a foreign official. Mr. Freeh, a former federal judge, noted that the U.S. Constitution affords strong protection for speech and the exchange of ideas "no matter how despicable those thoughts may be" and said he did not want the bureau to become "thought police."

Distributed by Los Angeles Times-Washington Post News Service

The Oregonian

OREGON'S NEWSPAPER SINCE 1850

"There are places in our national landscape so scarred by freedom's sacrifice that they shape forever the soul of America.... This place is such sacred ground."

— **PRESIDENT CLINTON**

• Blind teacher alters course

Remembering Oklahoma City

A12

Parents ca deal with s

Psychologists and counselors tell how a fears and lead them to put the Oklahoma C

By MAYA BLACKMUN
of The Oregonian staff

The news of the bombing in Oklahoma is the stuff of a parent's nightmare.

Children killed in their day-care center. Some children burned beyond recognition. Others injured and covered in blood.

These horrors leave parents dumbfounded. And such a tragedy raises questions and fears for young children.

How can parents explain such violence to their children, who may also be seeing, reading the reports in newspapers and hearing them on television and from friends and neighbors? Some may have seen the terrifying, unedited images soon after the explosion.

Child psychologists, counselors and others recommend these steps:
■ Find out how much the children already know and what they are concerned about. Monitor what they into tears, and couldn't take it."

Another nurse, Christine Johns, said: "Babies were wrapped around poles. I've never seen anything like it."

Her colleague, Bobby Johnson, 42 years old and the father of a 20-day-old son, had seen it before, but Wednesday's carnage still brought him to tears. "I was in Vietnam," he said "and I never thought I would see something like that again. But this is worse. It was awful. There was lots of blood and debris. Children's bodies were mangled and decapitated.

"I was shocked to think that someone could do that to small children," he said.

Kenneth "Sugar" Smith, a retired Oklahoma City police officer, was in an office less than two blocks from the federal building when the concussion hit, sending everyone into the street.

THE OREGONIAN, THURSDAY, APRIL 20, 1995

EXPLOSION IN OKLAHOMA CITY

Federal buildings in NW tighten up

Security is increased, and bomb threats prompt evacuations, while parents worry over their children in day care

"If they bomb San Francisco, we'll probably go across the street to the bar," said Ron Heard from his office at the Paralyzed Veterans of America Inc.

Tom Hallman Jr. and Stuart Tomlinson of The Oregonian's Crime, Justice and Public Safety Team contributed to this report.

If he'd been at work ... former Portlander says

Wayne Alley, a federal judge born in Oregon, takes the day to work at home and escapes the devastation from the blast

By DAVE HOGAN
of The Oregonian staff

A federal judge whose office faces the Alfred P. Murrah Federal Building across the street in Oklahoma City, Wayne Alley felt lucky that he didn't go to his office Wednesday.

Alley, who was born and raised in Portland, had taken the rare opportunity to work at home.

"Of all the days for this to happen, it's absolutely an amazing coincidence," Alley said in a telephone interview from his home.

The judge said the bombing came just a few weeks after security officials had warned him to take extra precautions.

"Let me just say that within the past two or three weeks, information has been disseminated ... that indicated concerns on the part of people who ought to know that we ought to go a little bit more careful," he said.

Alley, who started his law career in Portland, said he was cautioned to be on the lookout for "people casing homes or wandering about in the courthouse who aren't supposed to be there, letter bombs. There has been an increased vigilance."

He said he was not given an explanation for the concern.

Asked if this might have just been a periodic security reminder, he said, "My subjective impression was there was a reason for the dissemination of these concerns."

An FBI spokesman in Oklahoma told reporters during a news conference that he was not aware of any warning.

Not all of Alley's staff were as lucky as he was Wednesday. Some were in his suite of offices in the courthouse, which is across the street on the other side of the federal building from where the bomb exploded. Still, the force of the blast smashed the windows of his office and one of his law clerks was injured by the flying glass.

Alley attended Washington High School in Portland and was a law clerk for an Oregon Supreme Court Justice.

June 29, 1995

(1)

Dear Representative Key,

Attached seismograms from the Omniplex and station FNO near Norman are for both the demolition and the OKC explosion. Note that on the day of the blast the Omniplex record was saturated i.e. the instrument went off scale (the white area) for a period of ten seconds. Compare this to the signals from the demolition and collapse of the building. ⟹

OK GEOLOGICAL SURVEY ID:4053257060 JUN 29'95 10:11 No.003 P.02

None of the signals received during the demolition approached the intensity or magnitude of those received during the OKC blast.

The second signal at~~ the~~ Omniplex can ~~potentially~~ be interpreted to be an air blast signal. However, given the present uncertainty of the clock at the Omniplex, even this can be challenged.

Regardless of any subsequent explanation of all the seismic signals in terms of a "single event," the possibility for multiple ③ explosions has to be considered given the long duration (10 secs) of the first strong motion recorded at the Omniplex.

A single explosion is an unlikely explanation for 10 seconds of high intensity ground motion at the Omniplex.

— Raymon L. Brown

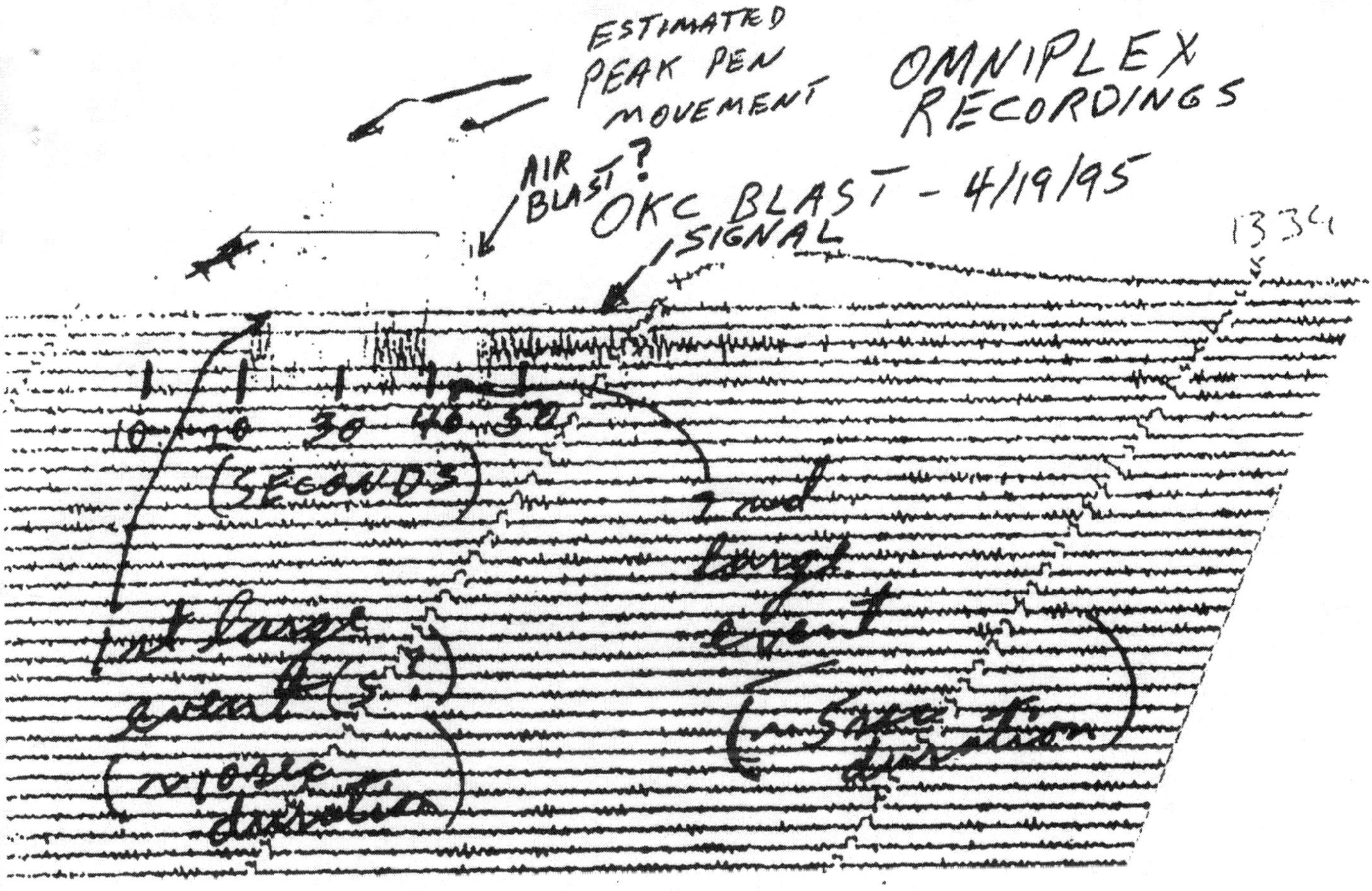

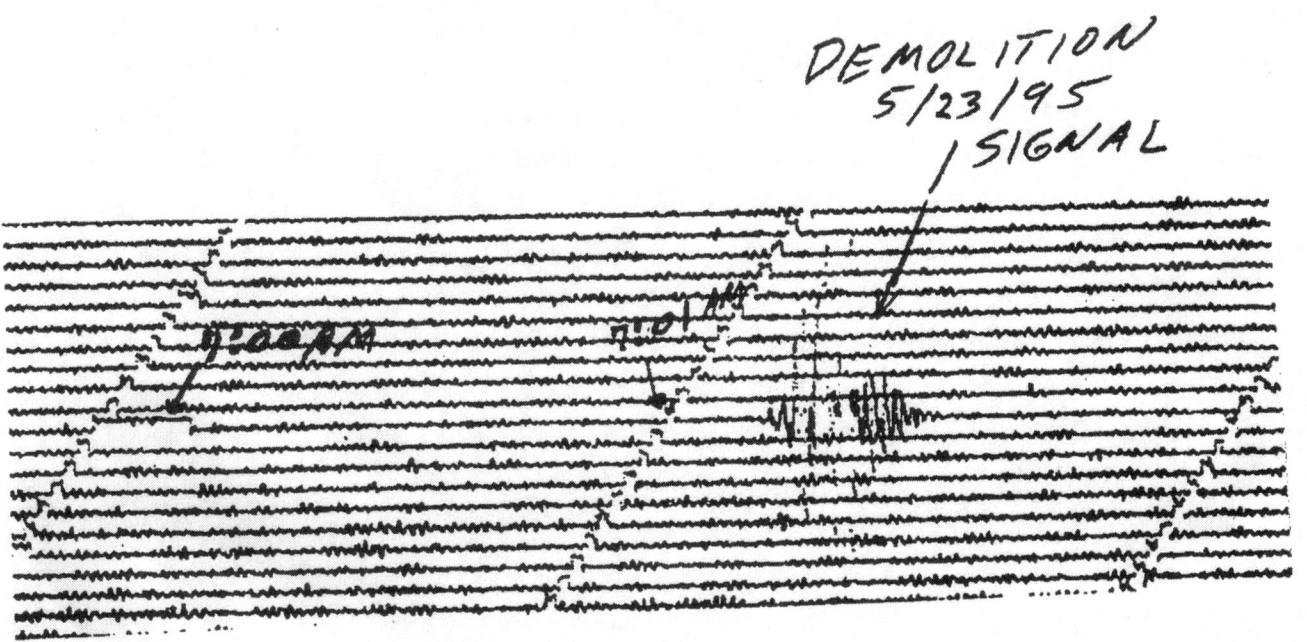

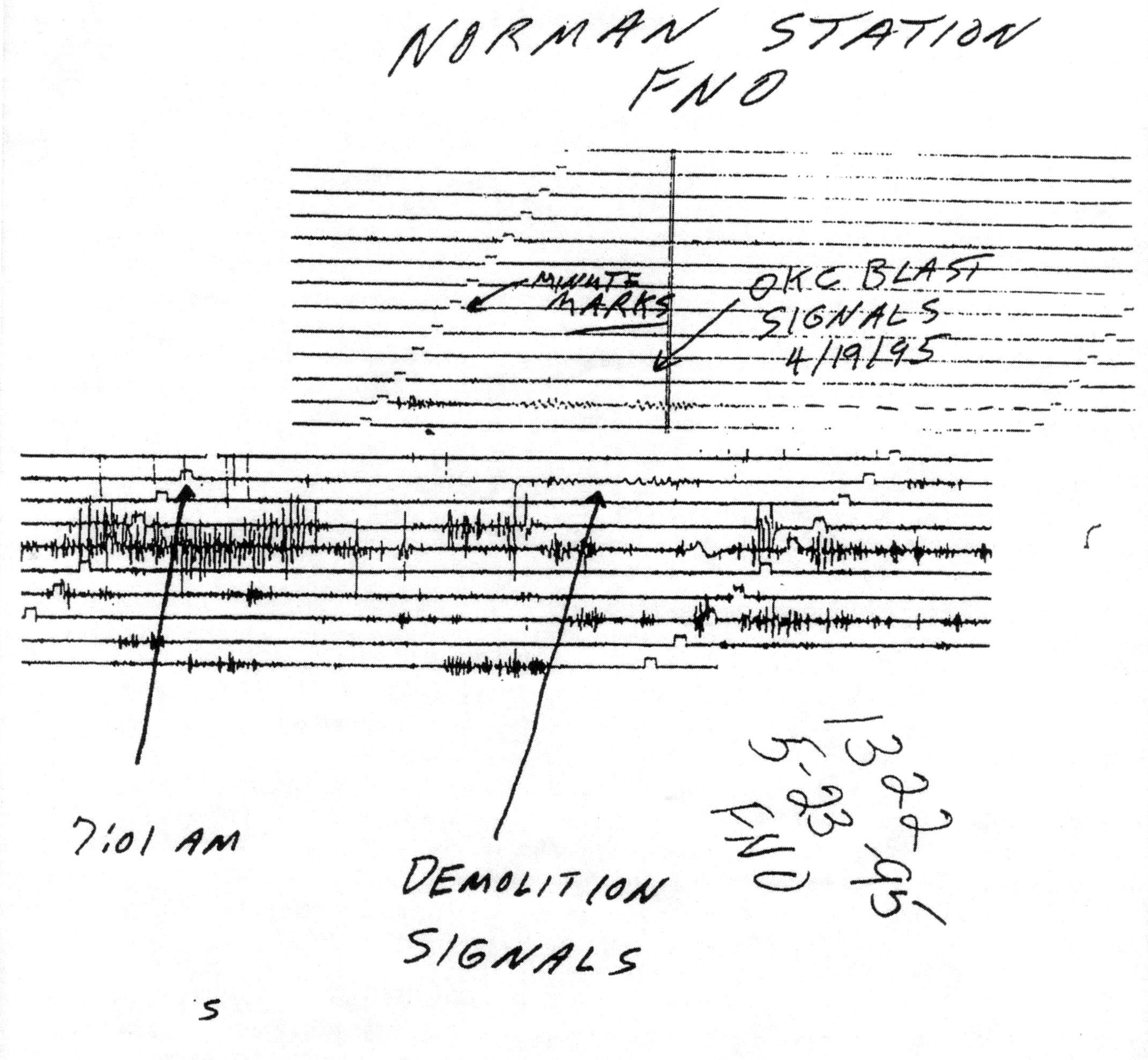

NORMAN STATION FNO

OKC BLAST SIGNALS
4/19/95

MINUTE MARKS

7:01 AM

DEMOLITION SIGNALS

1322
5-23-95
FNO

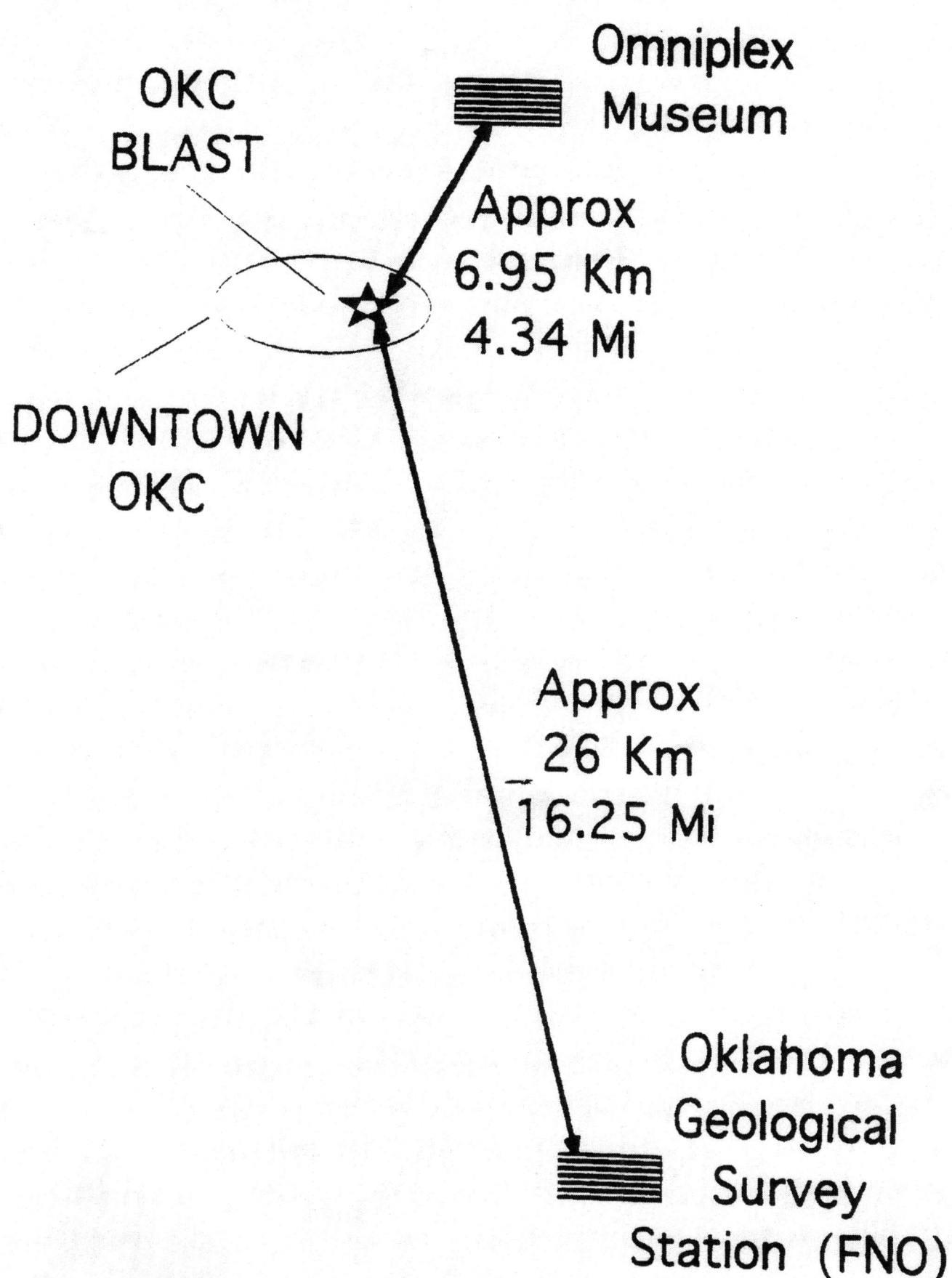

Appendix

OKLAHOMA GEOLOGICAL SURVEY

Energy Center Bldg.-Room N-131-100 East Boyd Street • Norman, Oklahoma 73019 • (405)-325-3031 • Fax: (405)-325-7069

July 10, 1995

State Representative Charles Key
Oklahoma

Dear Representative Key:

Attached you will find a schematic illustration of the seismograms recorded on the day of the OKC explosion (4-19-95). Initially, the relationship between these signals was not clearly understood. Thanks to the excellent data recorded by the U.S. Geological Survey, I think that I can give a preliminary interpretation of the signals recorded on the day of the blast.

The attached figure shows two high amplitude arrivals at the Omniplex Museum. The first signal to arrive is likely to be a type of wave called a p-wave which traveled through the ground to the Omniplex. Since the amplitude of p-waves is usually small compared to the later arriving S-waves and Rayleigh waves, the high amplitude signal which saturated the Omniplex for 10 seconds on the day of the blast can be interpreted to be the result of S-waves, Rayleigh waves and other waves traveling through the ground. After approximately 5-6 seconds, another high amplitude signal arrived at the Omniplex acting to saturate the seismometer. This signal appears to be an air blast. An air blast is a pressure wave which travels through the air at the speed of sound. When the pressure from the air blast is large enough, the air pressure pushes on the ground in such a way as to cause a seismometer to read a signal.

Identification of the second signal as an air blast and the first signal as shear, Rayleigh and other waves is an important step in the interpretation of the signals. Based upon the signals recorded during the demolition, the duration of the "ground wave" at the Omniplex is an approximate measure of the length of time of the seismic activity at the Murrah Building (10 seconds or less). The duration of the air blast is a measure of the length of time the air explosion was active. This means that the last 5 seconds (or less) of ground motion did not have an air blast associated it.

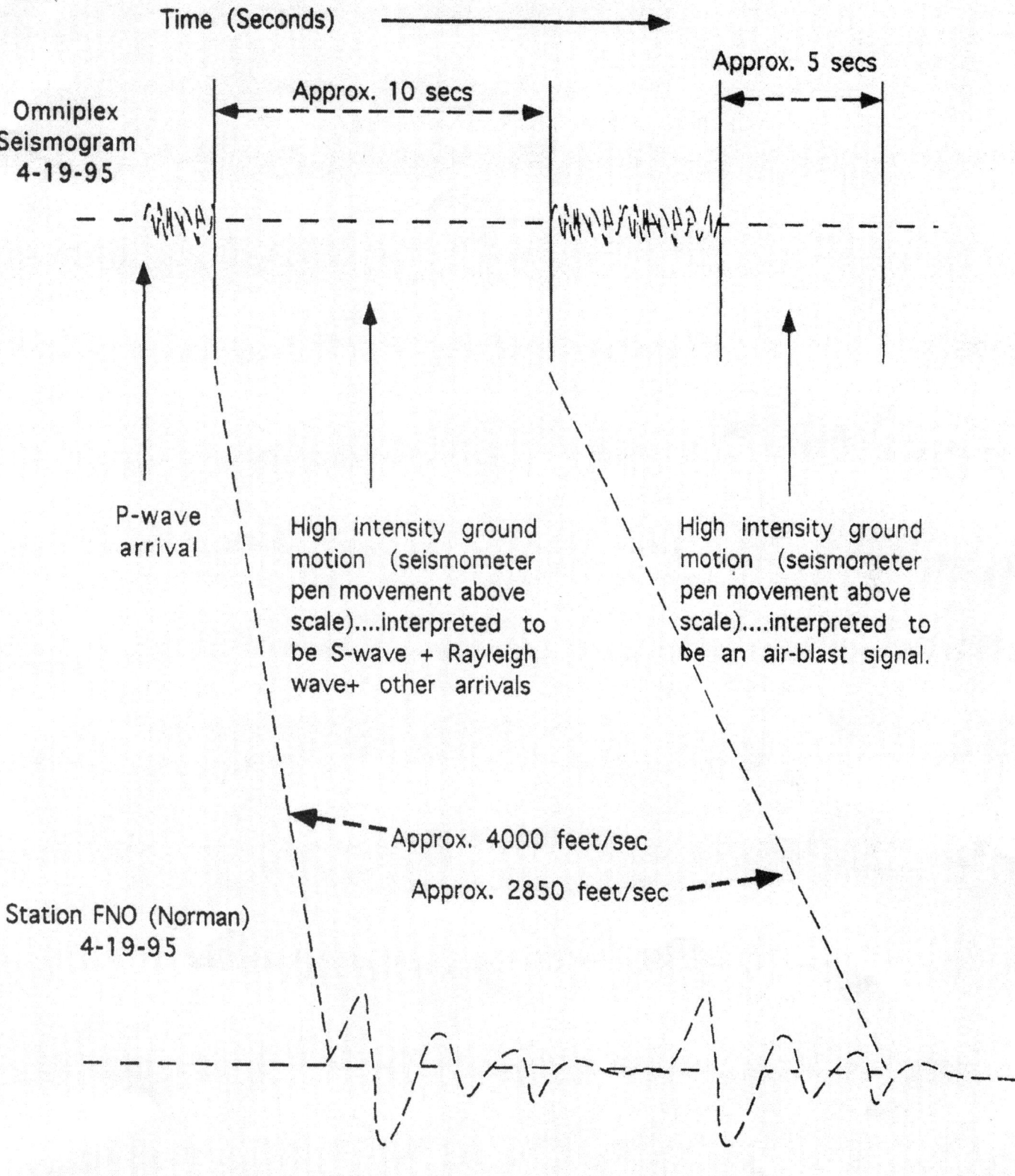

Appendix

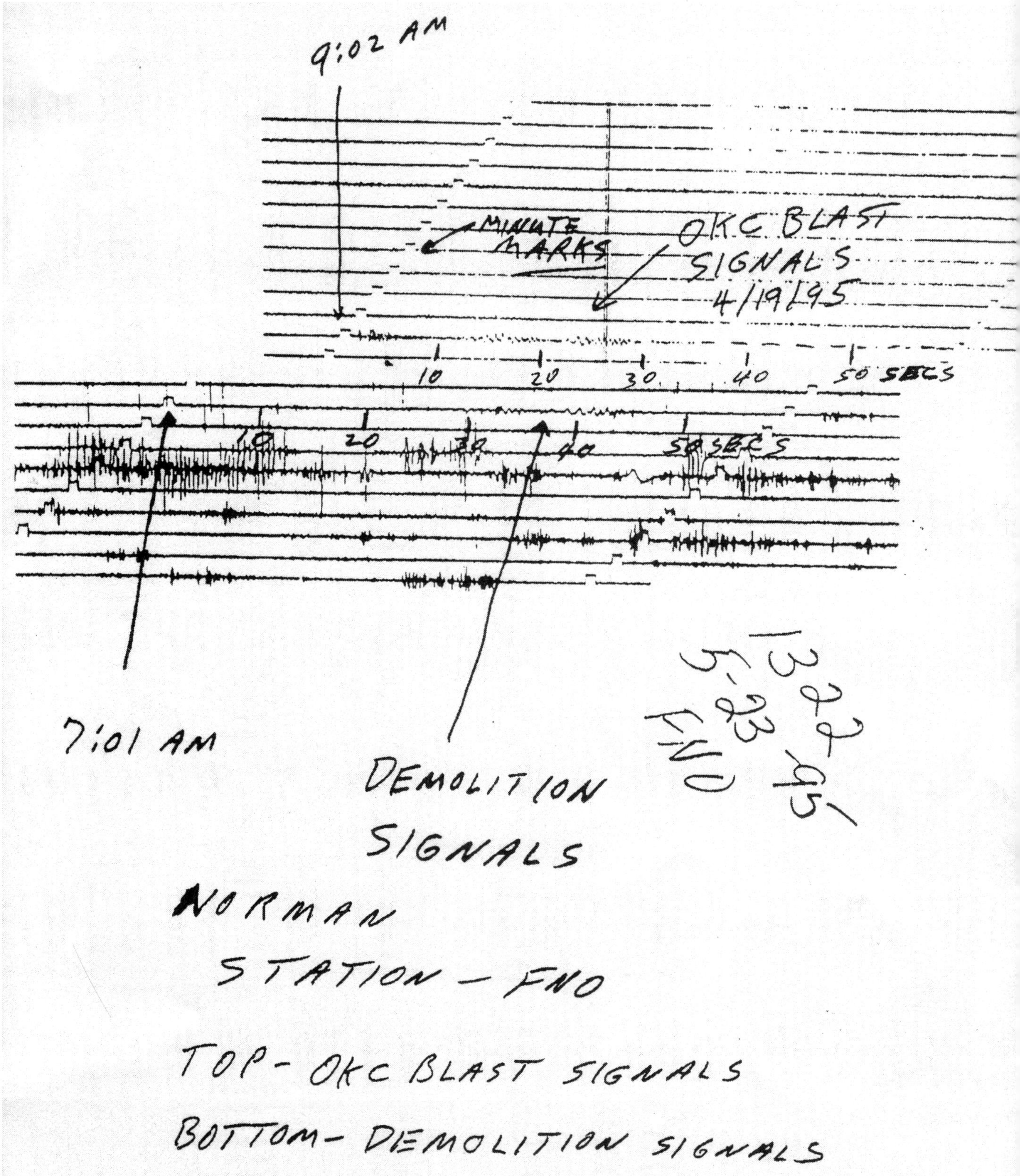

9:02 AM
MINUTE MARKS
OKC BLAST SIGNALS 4/19/95
10 20 30 40 50 SECS
10 20 30 40 50 SECS
7:01 AM
DEMOLITION SIGNALS
1322 5-23-95 FNO
NORMAN STATION – FNO
TOP – OKC BLAST SIGNALS
BOTTOM – DEMOLITION SIGNALS

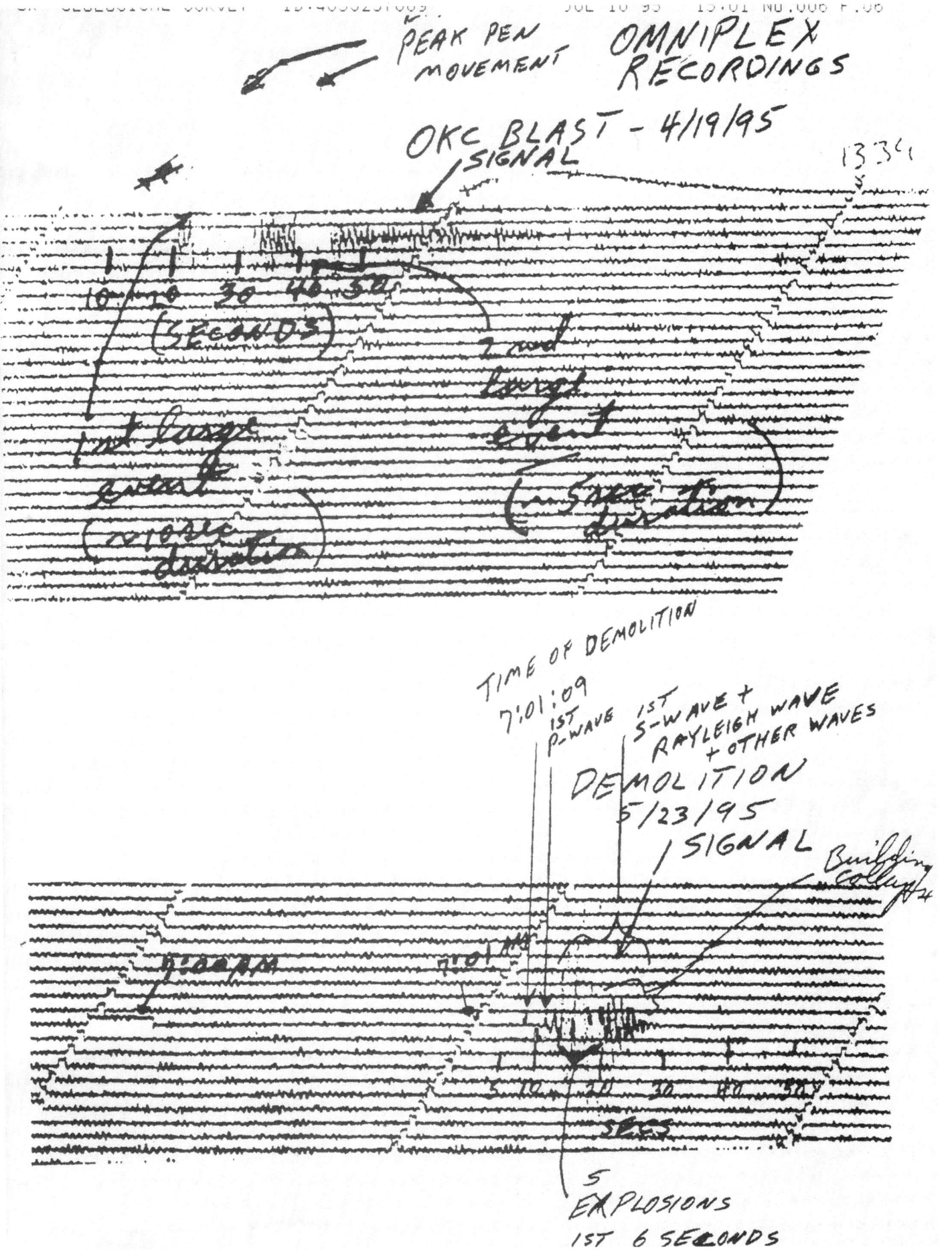

Appendix

June 29, 1995

Dear Representative Key, ①

Attached seismograms from the Omniplex and station FNO near Norman are for both the demolition and the OKC explosion. Note that on the day of the blast, the Omniplex record was saturated, i.e. the instrument went off scale (the white area) for a period of ten seconds. Compare this to the signals from the demolition and collapse of the building. ⟹

OK GEOLOGICAL SURVEY ID:4053257069 JUN 29'95 10:11 No.003 P.02

None of the signals received during the demolition approached the intensity or magnitude of those received during the OKC blast.

The second signal at the Omniplex can potentially be interpreted to be an air blast signal. However, given the present uncertainty of the clock at the Omniplex, even this can be challenged.

Regardless of any subsequent explanation of all the seismic signals in terms of a "single event" the possibility for multiple explosions has to be considered given the long duration (10 secs) of the first strong motion recorded at the Omniplex.

A single explosion is an unlikely explanation for 10 seconds of high intensity ground motion at the Omniplex.

— Raymon L. Brown

Affidavit of Tiffany Bible Regarding The Bombing Of The Alfred P. Murrah Federal Building

State of Oklahoma)
) SS:
County of Oklahoma)

I, affiant herein, being of legal age and having been duly sworn, does hereby state as follows:

1) That my date of birth is ▇▇▇▇▇▇68.

2) That I reside at ▇▇▇▇▇▇▇▇▇▇▇▇▇▇, Oklahoma City, 73114, Oklahoma County.

3) That on April 19, 1995, I was employed as a paramedic for the Emergency Medical Services Authority.

4) That immediately after the explosion at The Murrah Federal Building, myself and two Emergency Medical Technicians responded to the scene from Post 41, 2323 S. Walker.

5) That I arrived on the Southwest side of the Murrah Building by 9:07am.

6) That when I arrived on the Southwest side of the building I observed personnel from The Oklahoma City Fire Department, The Oklahoma County Sheriff's Office, and Agents from The Bureau of Alcohol Tobacco and Firearms along with other medical personel.

7) That I had a conversation with an ATF Agent and stated to him that I could not believe that a gas explosion had done this much damage to the building.

8) That the ATF Agent responded to me that the damage was not caused by a gas explosion and stated to me that the damage caused to the Murrah Building was caused by a "car bomb".

9) That I asked the ATF Agent why someone would blow up a building in Oklahoma City.

10) That the ATF Agent was visibly upset and responded to me that the Murrah Building was bombed because of Waco and that the reason the Murrah Building was targeted was because the person in charge in Waco was transferred to Oklahoma City.

11) That myself and the ATF Agent discussed the different agencies who had offices in The Murrah Building, including the ATF office and I said to the ATF agent, "Oh God there was people that you worked with in here?" and he responded, "No, we weren't in there today."

12) That the conversation between myself and this ATF Agent took place sometime between 9:07 and 9:15am.

13) That after the building was evacuated and we were allowed back on the scene, I observed another ATF Agent talking to another law enforcement officer and overheard this ATF Agent say that during the evacuation a fifty pound bomb was found attached to a gas line inside the Murrah Building.

14) That within the first twenty minutes that I was on the scene, I saw at least eight ATF agents on the South side of the building in clean black jumpsuits.

FURTHER, AFFIANT SAYETH NOT:

Tiffany Bible
Tiffany Bible

SUBSCRIBED TO AND SWORN BEFORE ME ON THE 23rd DAY OF July, 1998.

Jim Grace
NOTARY PUBLIC

MY COMMISSION EXPIRES:

OFFICIAL SEAL
Jim Grace
Notary Public ★ Oklahoma
Cleveland County
My Commission Expires Mar. 19, 2000

MACHINERY IN SERVICE

[redacted]	2	[redacted]	4	[redacted]	1
[redacted]	1	[redacted]	1&2 60	[redacted]	1&2
[redacted]	1&2	[redacted]	1	[redacted]	1
[redacted]	1	[redacted]			

NOTES:

2230	Relieved the watch
	Helping [redacted] with [redacted], etc.
2250	Safety lifted on [redacted] (in a large way)
	Just not enough [redacted] load.
	You get a lower [redacted] than [redacted] but since [redacted] aren't working right can't use them.
	Put # [redacted] & cooler on line
	Slow rolling [redacted]
2305	[redacted] on line
	[redacted]
2315	Police are pounding on control room window, checked with them and there report was of a major explosion and possible terrorist takeover of building. They said they were going to notify the bomb squad. I explained situation was under control & back to normal. They said in the future, to please pick a slower night for them for this to happen. He said y'all scared the SHIT out of the people in the Hotel (quote). We blamed it on the full moon, laughed, and on there way they went.
0000	Tore off strip charts
0030	Secured the power for [redacted] conductivity controller.
0100	Completed run hours.

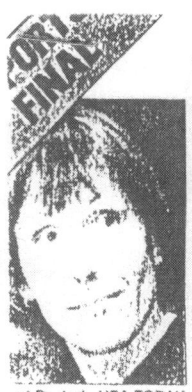

MARTINA SAYS HER RETIREMENT IS FOR GOOD

- STILL PLAYS DOUBLES, BUT 'I QUIT AT THE RIGHT TIME,' 1C
- PRO TENNIS COVERAGE, 5C

NAVRATILOVA: 'I'm stressing out,' 1C

YOUNG AMERICA SLIPS BY AMERICA³

SAILS ROUGH WATERS INTO LEAD OF DEFENDER FINALS, 1,9C

THURSDAY, APRIL 20, 1995

NEWSLINE

QUICK READ ON THE NEWS

WALL STREET: Dow Jones industrial average slips 28.36 points to 4207.49; Nasdaq index falls to 816.55; 30-year Treasury bond yield drops to 7.36%. 1,3B.

CONGRESSIONAL DISTRICTS: Supreme Court struggles with constitutionality of using race in drawing boundaries of congressional districts. 6A.

VIETNAM BOOK: Former Defense secretary Robert McNamara, left, says he'll donate some profits from his controversial Vietnam memoir. 9A.

McNAMARA: 'Open dialogue'

SIMPSON TRIAL: Judge Ito completes questioning jurors, alternates; defense says it expects current jury to remain intact. 6A.

PARTY CRASHERS: Some Georgia voters are fuming over Rep. Nathan Deal's switch from Democrat to Republican. So far, 3 defections to GOP in Congress since November elections, and more are expected. 8A.

HAT IN RING: Sen. Richard Lugar, R-Ind., is the eighth Republican to formally declare a run at 1996 presidency, pledging to replace federal income taxes. 8A.

GETTING AWAY: Record 92 million adults plan a family vacation this year — up 4% from '94; good economy could mean longer trips may be in store. 1D.

TODAY'S DEBATE: Corporate welfare. In USA TODAY's opinion, "Everybody's got an angle, a reason his business needs a break. But taxpayers can't afford it." 12A.

"A program which has kept people off welfare by yielding productive employment cannot ... be cited as corporate welfare," says Carl A. Nordberg Jr. 12A.

MONEY: Pressure, spotlight is on computer needs. 1B. U.S. trade deficit in goods and services shrinks. 1B.

SPORTS: Malone's 45 points lead Utah. NBA. 1,12C. USA TODAY's 1995 All-USA girls hoops stars. 1,10C.

LIFE: Can the King of Pop stay on top? 1D. Ad blitz for new Batman movie starts Friday. 1D.

USA TODAY

NO. 1 IN THE USA... FIRST IN DAILY READER

- 'No place is safe' from terrorism; 9-story hole in building, **Below, 1A**
- 'They're in heaven,' says of kids; doctor amputate leg; in

Terror in h

12 kids among 31 dead in

The woman, who had two children at the day-care center, was sedated through an intravenous needle in her neck, Tuggle said.

Only one doctor could reach her leg, so Andy Sullivan, who is smaller, amputated her leg at the knee, Tuggle said.

Massad said Sullivan cut a little bit, put clamps on arteries and veins, then cut some more, then used a saw to cut through the bone.

"She didn't have anything but her willpower to fight the pain," Massad said.

The amputation took about 10 minutes, but setting up took at least two hours, in part because rescuers were evacuated at least twice after reports surfaced that another bomb had been found.

The woman suffered other injuries and is in critical condition. Tuggle did not know whether her children survived.

Workers used a metal basket suspended from a construction crane to hunt for survivors.

Three people were rescued more than 12 hours after the explosion, but two of them died a short time later.

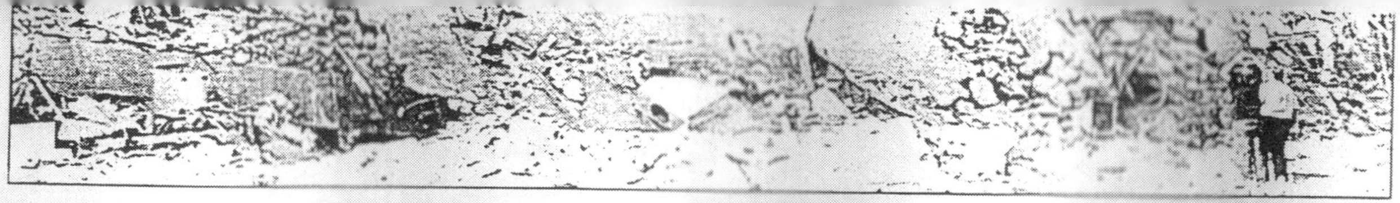

By David Longstreath, AP

DEVASTATION: The Oklahoma City blast was similar to a bombing that killed six and injured 1,000 at New York's World Trade Center.

Source: USA TODAY research

A 15-year-old girl was pul[led] from the rubble and rushe[d to] the hospital in critical co[ndi]tion.

Rescuers heard anoth[er] woman moaning in the ba[se]ment and began shouting [to] her. She told them two ot[her] people were trapped with [her] but she didn't know wheth[er]

An army of agents, experts following hundreds of leads

By Judy Keen
USA TODAY

Federal agents from around the country headed to Oklahoma City as the government launched a massive investigation into the car bombing that blew apart the Alfred P. Murrah Federal Building.

Special Agent Bob Ricks, who heads the FBI's Oklahoma City office, said the bureau had "hundreds if not thousands of leads," and was not making any assumptions. But officials made it clear they're treating it as a terrorist attack.

Despite the leads, Mayor Rob Norick said the bureau was desperate for help and he implored anyone who was in the building who might have information to contact the FBI.

A visibly angered President Clinton vowed: "Let there be no room for doubt — we will find the people who did this."

"When we do, justice will be swift, certain and severe," Clinton said.

Clinton said he had deployed a crisis management team under FBI direction that includes the Department of Justice, the Bureau of Alcohol, Tobacco and Firearms, the military and local authorities.

Attorney General Janet Reno said the FBI has established a command post in Oklahoma City that is in 24-hour contact with FBI headquarters and the Department of Justice.

Evidence response teams, explosive ordnance experts and agents experienced in bombing investigations were also sent from around the country to help in the tedious task of sifting for clues and interviewing witnesses.

Fifty more agents are to arrive today and more will be sent as needed.

Also, The Bureau of Alcohol, Tobacco and Firearms has sent two national response teams and a mobile command center. It's preparing to send up to 25 technicians today. The Secret Service is also sending explosives experts.

The explosion, similar to the terrorist car bombing that killed six people and injured 1,000 at New York's World Trade Center in 1993, came just after 9 a.m., catching most employees in their offices.

There was no immediate claim of responsibility for the attack, leaving authorities asking for help.

"It is not the place where you expect terrorists to strike," said Ricks. "Obviously their objective is to strike terror. They would just as soon rip you into pieces as look at you."

Ricks discounted reports that the FBI had alerted police and fire officials late last week to possible threats.

But Harvey Weathers of the Oklahoma City Fire Department said dispatchers received a report from the FBI on Friday about "some possibility of some people entering the city over the weekend." He did not elaborate.

Reno refused to talk about what the government suspects about the bombers or their motives. "We are pursuing all leads," she said.

Oklahoma Gov. Frank Keating said he was told by the FBI that authorities were initially looking for three people in a brown pickup truck. Keating said the people were of Middle Eastern descent. Keating later downplayed the report, sayi[ng] it was one of many leads bei[ng] checked.

Keating also said they we[re] checking whether the rental [of] a vehicle in the Dallas-Fo[rt] Worth area was tied to the e[...]

By David J. Phillip,

'CONCUSSION EFFECT': Experts suspect 'a cheap atomic bomb' was made with garden fertiliz[er] to rip open the building. Fragments at the scene will yield clues on the bomb's construction.

3A L.L.

↑ Prior Knowledge ?

174A-OC-55120
TPR:tpr

The following investigation was conducted by Special Agent (SA) THOMAS P. RAVENELLE:

Columbia airtel dated May 3, 1995, identified RICHARD DEHART, DOB 6/21/65, as a Phoenix resident and a possible look-alike for unsub #2 regarding captioned matter.

Phoenix determined a recent address for DEHART, but could not locate him. Phoenix directed San Francisco to attempt to contact the landlord for DEHART'S apartment to determine his whereabouts.

San Francisco made numerous attempts to locate the landlord ERNEST C. RENO, with negative results.

In view of the fact that the Oklahoma Command Post has directed all offices to hold unsub #2 leads in abeyance, San Francisco will conduct no further investigation regarding this lead.

Reference lead #10,220:

Referenced lead #10,220, San Francisco was directed to locate and interview LESTER SCANLON concerning his knowledge of STEVEN COLBERN. In view of the fact that COLBERN has been eliminated as a suspect in this matter, San Francisco will conduct no further investigation concerning lead #10,220.

requested a DCO and minimum staff for 24 hour operations for a minimum of three days. They are to report to Special Agent Webber. Contacted USA5 and spoke to Mr. Hendrix and Mr. Mangum.

1350 Received MG LaBoa's reply regarding e-mail log.

1345 C141 is on standby @ McGuire AFB for the VA US&R team.

1304 Both CA and AZ US&R teams are fully activated and enroute to the APOE (Travis AFB and Luke AFB, respectively). VA remains on alert (APOE is Norfolk NAS).

1259 LTC Gisler contacted USA5 EOC and informed them that although Tinker is trying to do the right thing, they are operating out of the loop and USA5 needs to corral them.

1258 Tinker AFB contacted Ft. Sill for 2 EOD teams (6 pax).

1245 2x bomb dogs, with handlers, from Ft. Sill ordered to deploy. Ft. Sill is sending 200 body bags.

1243 Chopped on ACOM message placing C141 on B alert and tasking TRANSCOM to prepare to transport the AZ US&R team, and possibly the CA and VA US&R teams. Only changes were the DTG of the incident.

1215 Called USA5, LTC Havelick, and advised him of Tinker's action regarding the EOD detachment. They were not aware of the action.

1211 Tinker AFB place the 61st EOD detachment from Ft. Sill on standby.

1211 The OK SRAAG stated that FEMA does not want a USA5 LNO.

1205 The following report was received: 2x UH-1Vs were requested from Ft. Sill at 0950S. The first took off at 1019S, the second at 1024S. Both are rigged with hoists.

1203 USA5 stated that the DCO is COL Barnhoft, from Ft. Sill, OK. USA5 has: LNOs notified and ready; offered assistance to FEMA; Regional Medical Planners notified. USA5 under modified alert until further notice. USA5 has requested 1xC12 on strip alert with possible stop at Denton, TX on way to OKC (A/C is for USA5 LNO and will pick up FEMA Region VI personnel, if needed).

1202 FEMA asked DOMS to provide transport for US&R teams; primary from Arizona, secondary from California and Virginia.

1157 Two more explosive devices were located vicinity the explosion site. Evidently intended for the rescuers.

DEPARTMENT OF THE TREASURY - BUREAU OF ALCOHOL, TOBACCO AND FIREARMS
REPORT OF INVESTIGATION (Law Enforcement)

RCS ATF R 3270.1

1. INVESTIGATION IS: ☒ SENSITIVE ☐ ROUTINE ☐ SIGNIFICANT

Page 1 of 2 pages

2. TO: Special Agent in Charge, Dallas Field Division

3. MONITORED INVESTIGATION INFORMATION (Number and Branch):
CIP: DALLAS FY-95
FIREARMS VIOLATIONS
REPORT 006

4. TITLE OF INVESTIGATION: White Aryan Resistence, W.A.R.

5. INVESTIGATION No. (Include Suspect No.): 53270-94-0124-B

6. TYPE OF REPORT: ☒ STATUS

7. BUREAU PROGRAM: ☒ TITLE I, ☒ TITLE II (FIREARMS); ☒ TITLE II (EXPLOSIVES); COLLATERAL (Request); COLLATERAL (Reply)

8. PROJECT(S): ☒ TERRORIST/EXTREMIST

9. DETAILS:

This is a 30 day status report in the investigation of the White Aryan Resistance and the violations of federal firearms and conspiracy laws in various counties in both the Northern and Eastern Judicial Districts of Oklahoma.

On January 29, 1995 CI-183 traveled to Elohim City. CI-183 then traveled with several individuals from Elohim City to Oklahoma City. Individuals that went were, Robert Millar "Grandpa," Zara Patterson III, Zara Patterson IV, Sarah LNU, Rachael LNU and Todd LNU. The purpose of the trip was to establish contact with another church, the Greater Cannon Baptist Church, at 731 N.E. 4th Street Oklahoma City, Oklahoma. The pastor of the church is Joe Cecil, a multiple convicted felon, who CI-183 met. CI-183 stated that Joe Cecil is an Indian male and that the rest of his congregation is mostly black and hispanic. When CI-183 inquired about this apparent mixing of the races, he/she was told that the members of Elohim City would unite with other races in order to create a more powerful adversary opposing the U.S. Government. The white supremacist issues are secondary to the anti-government attitude. It is believed by CI-183 that Robert Millar and Joe Cecil do some firearms trading. CI-183 overheard discussion between Millar and Cecil about going into business together.

On February 7, 1995 this agent along with TOO Pat McKinley and ASAC Tommy Wittman flew with OHP pilot Ken Stafford over Elohim City. Both photographs and video were taken.

10. SUBMITTED BY (Name): Angela Finley
11. TITLE AND OFFICE: S/A, Tulsa, Oklahoma
12. DATE: 02/28/95

13. REVIEWED BY (Name): David E. Roberts
14. TITLE AND OFFICE: RAC, Tulsa, Oklahoma
15. DATE: 2/28/95

16. APPROVED BY (Name): Lester D. Martz
17. TITLE AND OFFICE: Special Agent in Charge

DEPARTMENT OF THE TREASURY BUREAU OF ALCOHOL, TOBACCO AND FIREARMS REPORT OF INVESTIGATION - CONTINUATION SHEET (Law Enforcement)	PAGE 2 OF 2 PAGES
TITLE OF INVESTIGATION White Aryan Resistence, W.A.R.	INVESTIGATION NO. 53270-94-0124-B

DETAILS (Continued)

On February 8, 1995 this agent along with CI-183 traveled to Oklahoma City to identify the locations that CI-183 had been. CI-183 showed this agent the Greater Cannon Baptist Church which should be noted that this church is located in a predominately black part of the city. CI-183 then showed this agent the Jesus is Lord Garage & Salvage, 3308 N.E. 10th street, which is the workplace of Joe Cecil.

CI-183 showed this agent the Old West Lumbermill, which is owned by Don Bishop on the corner of 44th and Czech Hall Road in Mustang, Oklahoma. CI-183 stated that Millar spoke to Bishop about doing business since Millar has a sawmill at Elohim City.

CI-183 showed this agent the residence where the group stayed. It was at 717 N. Westchester Way Mustang, Oklahoma which is the residence of Millar's granddaughter.

From February 10 through February 24, CI-183 had personal matters to attend, therefore no investigative activity occurred on his/her part.

On February 22, 1995 this agent met with OHP Trooper Ken Stafford to exchange certain information regarding this investigation. Trooper Stafford indicated that the FBI also had an ongoing investigation regarding Elohim City.

On this same date, RAC David Roberts met with the United States Attorney for the Northern Judicial District of Oklahoma, Steve Lewis, to discuss this investigation.

On February 23, 1995 RAC David Roberts was contacted by FBI supervisor, Marty Webber, who stated that FBI Special Agent in Charge, Bob Ricks, would be available during the week of February 27 through March 03, 1995 to meet with ATF Special Agent in Charge, Lester Martz. Rac Roberts then contacted Dallas Division to request SAC, Martz meet with SAC, Ricks to discuss the investigation of Elohim City.

On February 27, 1995 this agent met with CI-183 to discuss future contact with members of Elohim City. It was determined that CI-183 would be visiting Elohim City during the week of March 5-11, 1995 for a duration of three to five days.

This investigation to continue.

Attachment: E/S Report of Use

Page 537

IN THE UNITED STATES DISTRICT COURT
FOR THE NORTHERN DISTRICT OF OKLAHOMA

UNITED STATES OF AMERICA,   )
    Plaintiff,   )
)
VS.   )   NO. 97-CR-05-BU
)
CAROL ELIZABETH HOWE,   )
aka "Freya",   )
    Defendant.   )

* * *

TRANSCRIPT OF PROCEEDINGS

JURY TRIAL

BEFORE HONORABLE MICHAEL BURRAGE, JUDGE

JULY 31, 1997

TRIAL TESTIMONY OF ANGELA GRAHAM

* * *

A P P E A R A N C E S:

FOR THE PLAINTIFF: MR. NEAL KIRKPATRICK
                          MR. KEVIN C. LEITCH
                          Assistant United States Attorneys
                          Page Belcher Building
                          333 West 4th Street, Room 3900
                          Tulsa, Oklahoma 74103

FOR THE DEFENDANT,   MR. CLARK O. BREWSTER
CAROL ELIZABETH HOWE: Brewster, Shallcross & De Angelis
                          2021 South Lewis Avenue
                          Tulsa, Oklahoma 74104

COURT REPORTER: KARLA S. McWHORTER
                          United States Court Reporter
                          P. O. Box 2251
                          Muskogee, Oklahoma 74402

KARLA S. McWHORTER
UNITED STATES COURT REPORTER

1 Q   And that individuals were coming from -- with
2 explosives from Pennsylvania and they were interested in
3 converting one particular individual's firearms to fully
4 automatic?
5 A   Yes, sir.
6 Q   Now, this is -- you conclude this report with, it's
7 requested that CI-183, Carol Howe?
8 A   Uh-huh.
9 Q   In light of all of this, go down to Elhoim City for
10 three months, that is your plan?
11 A   Yes, sir, that was part of the Elhoim City plan, what
12 they call the three, three, three plan, I think they come
13 out for three days, three weeks and then three months.
14 Q   Would you tell us what Carol was receiving as far as
15 compensation goes? Was it 25 dollars a day?
16 A   Yes, sir, about that.
17 Q   Do you think this was a pretty good place to send a
18 young woman about 23 years old in light of what was being
19 reported here?
20   MR. KIRKPATRICK: Objection, Your Honor, it's
21 irrelevant.
22   THE COURT: Overruled.
23 BY MR. BREWSTER:
24 A   She was comfortable going, sir, so I didn't --
25 Q   Now, in 1995 did Carol report to you that individuals

KARLA S. McWHORTER
UNITED STATES COURT REPORTER

of Elhoim City were interested in traveling to Oklahoma City?

A   Yes, sir.

Q   And did she indicate that they had white supremacy beliefs that were anti-government?

A   That members of Elhoim City did, yes, sir.

Q   And did you authorize Carol to go with Elhoim City individuals to Oklahoma City?

A   Yes, sir.

Q   And then when Carol returned, did she take you to Oklahoma City and show you the locations that they were interested in?

A   I took her back.

Q   Directing your attention, if I could --

MR. BREWSTER: Your Honor, if I may approach?

THE COURT: You may.

BY MR. BREWSTER:

Q   To Defendant's Exhibit 6-H for identification purposes, ma'am, does that appear to be the report that you authorized in February of '95?

A   Yes, sir.

Q   And this is the report that indicates that Carol traveled to or that, yeah, she traveled to Elhoim City and then traveled with individuals from Elhoim City to Oklahoma City; right?

A   Yes, sir.

Q   And therein after February you went with her and she showed you around where they were in Oklahoma City?

A   Yes, sir.

Q   Okay. Now, on February 22nd, does it indicate there was a meeting between various heads of departments of law enforcement with regard to Carol?

A   Yes.

MR. BREWSTER: We would move for the introduction, Your Honor, of 7-H.

THE COURT: Again, Counsel, I think I know what you are talking about, but I don't have one.

MR. BREWSTER: I'm sorry.

BY THE WITNESS:

A   Mr. Brewster, I apologize, but could you ask the question one more time?

MR. KIRKPATRICK: No objection.

THE COURT: 7-H will be admitted without objection.

BY MR. BREWSTER:

Q   My question is, did it come to be in February of 1995 that there was a meeting involving various heads of law enforcement regarding the Elhoim City investigation?

A   Sir, my report suggests that they were discussing having a meeting, but after I HAD been questioned about this previously, I asked my supervisor and there never was such a meeting.

KARLA S. McWHORTER
UNITED STATES COURT REPORTER

Q Does this report indicate on February 22nd, following your notes of February 22nd on this same date, RAC -- what does RAC stand for?

A Resident agent in charge.

Q Dave Roberts, who is that?

A My supervisor.

Q He is the head of the ATF in Tulsa, is he not?

A Yes, sir.

Q Met with United States Attorney for the Northern District, Steve Lewis.

A Yes, sir. I thought you were talking about the next paragraph, I apologize.

Q To discuss this investigation.

A Yes, sir.

Q Your supervisor met with the U.S. attorney's office to discuss the investigations this is the subject matter of your report; am I correct?

A Yes, sir.

Q And that on February 23rd, resident agent in charge, David Roberts, contacted by FBI supervisor, Marty Webber, who stated that FBI Special Agent in charge Bob Ricks -- where is he in charge?

A Oklahoma City, sir.

Q So we have got the head of Tulsa and the head of Oklahoma City, right, of FBI?

1   A   Yes, sir.

2   Q   And the head of ATF, Tulsa; right?

3   A   Yes, sir.

4   Q   Who stated that FBI special agent in charge, Bob Ricks, would be available during the week of February 27th through March 3rd, 1995, to meet with ATF special agent in charge Lester Marks? Where is he located?

8   A   He is special agent in charge of Durant, our division in Dallas, Texas.

10   Q   Resident Agent Roberts then contacted the Dallas division to request Special Agent in charge, Marks, meet with Special Agent in charge, Ricks, to discuss the investigation of Elhoim City; right?

14   A   Yes, sir.

15   Q   And that the concluding paragraph indicates that she is going to be -- Carol Howe will be visiting Elhoim City during the week of March 5th through 11th for three to five days; is that correct?

19   A   Yes, sir.

20   Q   So for purposes of understanding, this is just a little more than four weeks before the Oklahoma City bombing?

22   A   It was determined -- it says it was determined that she would be there during the week, but she wasn't. That is what your question was.

25   Q   My question is that was the plan, though, wasn't it?

KARLA S. McWHORTER
UNITED STATES COURT REPORTER

A CLOSER LOOK

Computer video still courtesy of KFOR-TV

KFOR-TV in Oklahoma City based this computer animation on detective Robert Jerlow's description of the surveillance video he claims was provided by the L.A. FBI office.

bomb, according to sources who have viewed an edited and enhanced version of the tape.

Agents in Washington and Oklahoma City declined comment concerning claims that the images of both McVeigh and John Doe No. 2 are clear in the video shot from the YMCA security camera, located across the street and just east of the federal building. Agents also declined to explain why no videotaped footage has ever been released to the public, which could help efforts to locate John Doe No. 2.

The charge that two FBI agents sought to profit from the tragedy could not come at a worse time for the bureau, surfacing as it does amid defense allegations of agents deliberately leaking false information about the case to the media, unrelated charges of misconduct at the FBI lab and congressional criticism over alleged racism and the improper use of deadly force.

The FBI has long maintained a global reputation as the premier law-enforcement agency on earth, and the vast majority of its agents are dedicated professionals. Still, 1995 will likely be remembered less than fondly by the bureau for many years to come.

The FBI's L.A. Field Office features about 700 agents assigned to Southern California and hundreds of support personnel, according to the Justice Department. Furthermore, Los Angeles is an aggressive and competitive media market, and reporters are always looking to develop relationships with field agents.

It is in this environment that a number of critical case details about the bombing were allegedly leaked to the media by agents or "anonymous sources" believed to work out of the L.A. office.

A recently retired agent with several years experience in Los Angeles said, "The news media seems to manage to penetrate the L.A. Field Office with impunity. It's like leak of the week around there sometimes."

> **Several cameras were damaged in the blast, including those stationed atop the nearby YMCA and Regency Towers. However, the tapes they provided reportedly included excellent footage of the Ryder truck and the suspects — McVeigh and John Doe No. 2 — leaving the vehicle.**

A "CRISIS OF CONFIDENCE"

The public relations staff at the Office of Public and Congressional Affairs (OPCA) at FBI Headquarters in Washington finds itself dealing with yet another crisis of confidence in the agency, according to sources in the Justice Department.

Despite FBI attempts to avoid public disclosure of the agent's name or supervisor, sketchy details of the investigation began surfacing in mid October. Among the unresolved questions, according to sources at FBI Washington, is how the agents in question came to possess the videotape in the first place.

"From what we understand, the (agents under investigation) did not have the authority to possess such a videotape or any other evidence from the OKBOMB case," said one FBI source. "Although a contingent of agents from Los Angeles did respond to the scene, these guys were not part of that detail. Their squad is not assigned to work on any aspect of the bombing investigation, other than some local leg work in Southern California running down minor leads. They apparently obtained a copy of the video

Robert Rodriguez, undercover ATF agent who tried to get bosses to call off the ill-conceived raid, was made scapegoat. He's now the first agent to ever sue the BATF. In photo he is escorted to Davidians' trial in San Antonio by case agent Davy Aguilera, left, and unidentified agent at right, who sat in press section of court with burp gun under his trench coat.
Photo: Bob Owen

Soldier Of Fortune Magazine

**INVESTIGATIVE REPORT
CONCERNING FACT-FINDING
TRIP TO GERMANY
APRIL 22-29, 1996**

Prepared for: *Representative Charles Key*

Prepared By: *John Michael Johnston, Esq.*
228 Robert S. Kerr Ave., Suite 620
Oklahoma City, OK 73102
Tel: (405) 235-4074
Fax: (405) 235-4084

Report Date: *May 15, 1996*

TABLE OF CONTENTS

                                                                                     Page(s)

INTRODUCTION 1

TOPIC I: *NEO-NAZI AND NATIONALIST HOSTILITIES AND MOTIVATIONS REGARDING THE UNITED STATES* 2

TOPIC II: *COLLABORATIONS BETWEEN GERMAN AND U.S. RIGHT-WING ORGANIZATIONS* 3

TOPIC III: 5

    A.   *HISTORY OF COLLABORATIONS OR CONTACTS BETWEEN GERMAN RIGHT-WING/NEO-NAZI GROUPS AND MIDDLE EASTERN POLITICAL OR TERRORIST GROUPS* 5

    B.   *EXAMPLES OF GERMAN AND/OR U.S. NEO-NAZI CONNECTIONS WITH EACH OTHER AND/OR WITH IRAQ* 7

TOPIC IV: *COULD ANDREW STRASSMEIR BE A GERMAN ESPIONAGE AGENT?* 8

INTRODUCTION

In connection with your investigation of the bombing of the Alfred P. Murrah Federal Building on April 19, 1995, you asked me to investigate several topics, to wit:

1. Would German and/or U.S. Neo-Nazi groups have any motive for an attack directed at the United States Government?

2. Is there a substantial amount of contact and/or communication between U.S. Neo-Nazi or Right-Wing individuals or organizations with Neo-Nazi groups in Germany?

3. If any Neo-Nazi figures were implicated in the Murrah Building bombing, is there any historical evidence that would suggest that Neo-Nazis might have collaborated with any Middle Eastern terrorist groups or with the government of Iraq?

4. Could a German citizen (Andrew Strassmeir) now living in Berlin, but at the time of the bombing living in Oklahoma, have been working undercover for any German intelligence or law enforcement organizations in attempting to penetrate Neo-Nazi terrorist plots in the United States?

During my trip to Germany, and thereafter, I have obtained pertinent information on each of these topics, which topics will be dealt with separately herein.

TOPIC I:
NEO-NAZI AND NATIONALIST HOSTILITIES AND MOTIVATIONS REGARDING THE UNITED STATES

In the former East Germany (at Gotha) I met with a private researcher who helped provide me with insights on Neo-Nazi attitudes and motivations toward the United States. The Neo-Nazi concept of "Teutonic Unity" (see attachment) is consistent with the strong nationalistic character of a segment of German society (beyond just the Neo-Nazi movement). This German nationalism was exemplified by the events preceding World War II and more recently during Reunification. In summary, the point was made to me that the Neo-Nazi community in Germany is proud that the "Fatherland" is now rid of half a million Russian soldiers (previously stationed in former East Germany). The Neo-Nazi right-wing now feels that only one enemy army of occupation remains to be dealt with — the United States Armed Forces.

In separate discussions that I had with a U.S. Army Colonel who has been stationed with the United States Army Headquarters in Europe (Heidleberg), I confirmed the existence of an undercurrent of Germany ultra-nationalism and hostility toward the United States and toward the U.S. military originating from the Neo-Nazi community.

A second ideological motive exists to expect animosities from Neo-Nazi groups. The Anti-Zionist Legion (see discussion *infra*) conceived by Michael Kühnen emphasizes a lasting common bond that exists between Nazis, Neo-Nazis and Arabs — hatred of World Jewry. The degree that the United States was intimately involved with defending indeed, the Clinton Administration's unwavering support of Israel during the recent Palestinian violence makes the United States a continued object of Neo-Nazi/Middle Eastern displeasure.

Ahmed Rami, European correspondent for *Al Shaab*, an Islamic newspaper, has urged in writing (April 1991) a "Western Intifada" against alleged Jewish dominance. Rami's call to action was reported in several right-wing German publications, including *Deutsche Rundschall, Remer Depesche*, and *Recht Und Wahrheit* which reportedly wrote:

> "One can say that the only winner of WW2 was the organized World Jewry...The organized World Jewry attained through Auschwitz, a never-before existing freedom to unrestricted development of power. Today, Jews control all important positions of power in the U.S.A."

TOPIC II:
COLLABORATIONS BETWEEN GERMAN AND U.S. RIGHT-WING ORGANIZATIONS

The United States-based "IHR" (Institute for Historic Review) is considered a collection point for Holocaust disputers, Neo-Nazis, Arabs, and other anti-Semites. The Revisionist History Movement (discussed *infra*) is a common thread between U.S., German and Middle East extremists.

An American who has figured prominently in the German Neo-Nazi scene, Gary Lauck of Lincoln, Nebraska, published a virulent Nazi-style newsletter/newspaper *N S Kampfruf* from P.O. Box 6414, Lincoln, Nebraska 68506. Since my return to the United States, I have been advised (but have not confirmed) that Lauck was arrested, based on information allegedly provided by Andrew Strassmeir, in Copenhagen, Denmark in approximately March of 1995 and is being/was extradited to Germany for prosecution under German Sedition statutes.

According to a research book entitled *Europas braune Saat*, initial contacts by the American Linden LaRouche's group with Iraq were made in the middle 70's. Later during the Gulf War, the cooperation strengthened and regular visits of LaRouche organizers to Iraq ensued. The activist Muriel Mirak Weissbach played and still plays a central role as an "envoy special" for the Near East. She returned in the summer of 1991 from an Iraqi trip marveling about the efficiency of the security forces — as soon as crowds gather, police forces were present immediately. According to the periodical "Neuen Solidaritat," she traveled in 1992 again to Iraq and met the Iraqi Minister for Public Works and Agriculture. She is quoted as saying: "Since the war, I have visited Iraq several times." Additionally, EIR (LaRouche publication) published an interview that Weissbach gave during another trip to see the Iraqi Minister for Trade, Dr. Mohammed Mehdi Salih. On a related subject, the LaRouche subsidiary, Schiller Institute, mounted (in Germany) a massive propaganda effort against America's entry into the Gulf War. The LaRouch organization named its propaganda campaign "Amerikaner gegen den Krieg/American against War."

The tenor of Neo-Nazi sentiment during the Gulf War was characterized by a quote from a Neo-Nazi Gulf War flier, titled *Impeachment gegen Präsident Bush*: "The horror of war has become a dismaying truth. George Bush has started a war in the Gulf region, that may lead humanity into the catastrophe of WW3...Bush compared Saddam Hussein frequently with Hitler, but who actually is the new Hitler?"

Around the time of the Gulf War, Michael Kühnen formed an "Anti-Zionist

Legion" in Germany. When Kühnen died he was succeeded by a man named Hubner. Reportedly, Kirk Lyons, Andrew Strassmeir's lawyer, has connections with Herr Hubner and has spoken with Hubner at several Neo-Nazi functions to the group "Deutsche Alternative." The group also organized support campaigns for Saddam Hussein during the Gulf War.

TOPIC III:

A. HISTORY OF COLLABORATIONS OR CONTACTS BETWEEN GERMAN RIGHT-WING/NEO-NAZI GROUPS AND MIDDLE EASTERN POLITICAL OR TERRORIST GROUPS.

While in Germany I met with two separate, private researchers who concentrate their research efforts on monitoring and analyzing the activities of right-wing and/or Neo-Nazi groups and individuals.

In the former West Germany I met with one researcher possessed of remarkable personal research materials and archives. The researcher provided me with extensive background on connections and collaborations between Middle Eastern nations and/or terrorist groups and German Nazi or Neo-Nazi individuals and organizations. According to this researcher, the origins of Nazi-Middle East collaborations go back at least as far as World War II. For instance, after World War II, former Major General Ernest Rhemer (who reportedly "cleaned up" after the famous assassination attempt on Adolph Hitler in the summer of 1944), fled Germany and settled in the Middle East where he set up intelligence operations for several Arab countries, including possibly Syria and Egypt. Rhemer also played a prominent role over the next several decades in coordinating German right-wing activity with the Arab world. As recently as 1993, Rhemer gave a lengthy interview to the Arab newspaper, *Al Shaab*. Rhemer is also prominent in the "revisionist scene" (addressed below).

Other Nazi and Neo-Nazi figures have actually been implicated in Middle Eastern special weapons procurement and *terrorist* activity, *e.g.*— since the 1960's, an old Swiss Nazi named Francois Genaud has reportedly masterminded several airplane hijackings for the PLO; an "old line" Nazi named Antoine Eyerle, with two corporations previously operating near Munich, was convicted in Germany on 20 July 1994 for trading nuclear and SCUD rocket detonation technology to Iraq; a former Nazi scientist, Volker Weissheimer, who received an original letter of commendation from Adolph Hitler during World War II for good work on "special weapons" projects, met with Dr. Ihsan Barbouti in London during 1983 and 1984 in order to help recruit former Nazi and East German scientists to work on Libyan and Iraqi chemical weapons projects; the (now defunct) "Odessa" organization, post-war successor to the S.S. had numerous documented meetings with representatives of various Arab organizations; and, during the early 1980's, a Neo-Nazi named Odfried Hepp attacked several U.S. military installations in Germany with bombs. Hepp was later found to have been financed by Al Fatah.

One propaganda project of the right-wing/Neo-Nazi movement is to foster "revisionist history" which history disputes many of the horrors of World War II, including denial of the very existence of, or at least the full extent of, the Holocaust.

A graphic illustration of the alliances between the German right-wing and Middle Eastern organizations occurred at the Stockholm Revisionist Historian Conference of November 28-29, 1992, in Sweden. The conference was organized by Ahmed Rami, formerly of Radio Islam and later a correspondent for *Al Shaab* newspaper. Along with numerous Nazi and Neo-Nazi figures the conference was attended by representatives of Hezbollah, Hamas, Japanese extremists, and Pamjat (Russia).

The researcher that I met with in Gotha (formerly East Germany) advised me that there are a number of documented instances of militant Neo-Nazi party members who also held PLO or PFLP[1] membership cards. Specific examples are Odfried Hepp (who went to prison in Germany at one time); Udo Albrecht (a German Neo-Nazi mercenary who was killed during the 1980's); and (FNU) Hoffman. Interestingly, Albrecht and Hepp had also been informants for Stassi (former East German Intelligence Service).

Another point of interest, this researcher did his Ph.D. on Neo-Nazi/PLO bombings of U.S. housing, cars and military facilities in Germany.

B. EXAMPLES OF GERMAN AND/OR U.S. NEO-NAZI CONNECTIONS WITH EACH OTHER AND/OR WITH IRAQ

During the Gulf War, Michael Kühnen, then a top German Neo-Nazi figure, negotiated a contract to provide Iraq with 100 German Neo-Nazi volunteers (who were to go to Baghdad *via* Copenhagen or Stockholm) as well as (later) an additional 100 American and British Neo-Nazi volunteers to fight for Iraq in the Gulf War.

However, Kühnen became ill and later died before he could fulfill this contract. Nonetheless, a prominent French Neo-Nazi leader named Michael Faci stepped in and provided an unknown number of "storm troopers" who did indeed fight with Saddam's army during the Gulf War. Supposedly, color videotape exists of these Neo-Nazi soldiers

---

[1] PFLP stands for Popular Front for the Liberation of Palestine.

in S.S. uniforms (and Michael Faci) being greeted upon their arrival in Baghdad by Iraqi Information Minister, Abdel Lateef Jassem.

Additionally, there were various rallies in support of Iraq during the Gulf War by prominent German Neo-Nazi groups under the leadership of Kühnen and Roland Tabbert.

Several German individuals (names not given) have apparently been convicted since the Gulf War of spying for Iraq on U.S. military installations during those earlier hostilities.

Most importantly to this investigation, the (East) German researcher told me that he has heard repeatedly in Neo-Nazi circles that John Doe # 2 (Murrah Building bombing) was an Iraqi agent.

TOPIC IV:
COULD ANDREW STRASSMEIR BE A GERMAN ESPIONAGE AGENT?

While in Berlin I conducted a partial interview of Andrew Strassmeir by telephone at his father's town home in Berlin (60 Nassauische Strasse). The purpose of the interview was, in part, to determine if Mr. Strassmeir was an agent of the German BND (or any other German intelligence agency) while he was in the United States. Several important points were made directly to me by Andrew Strassmeir during our discussion. Mr. Strassmeir admitted to me that he had indeed done undercover/informant work during his prior military service in the BundesWehr. However, Strassmeir said that he resigned his officer's commission in June 1988 and specifically denied being "undercover" at the time of the Oklahoma City bombing.

Mr. Strassmeir did confirm that several years ago he acted with (or on behalf of) a "retired" CIA man in writing a letter to the President of Lufthansa (German(Airlines concerning the possible purchase of a couple of Boeing 747 jumbo jets for "a small private airline in New York." Mr. Strassmeir revealed that he had known the CIA agent from the days that the agent was stationed in Berlin during the Cold War and prior to Germany's Reunification. Mr. Strassmeir stated that the former CIA agent approached him to write the letter because his (Andrew's) father was the Transportation Minister of Germany and the Strassmeir name would be well known to the President of Lufthansa.

Since my return to the United States, I have developed information that the retired CIA agent in question might be Vincent Petruskie of Manassas, Virginia and the airline in question might be Evergreen Air (which has sometimes been reported to be a CIA proprietary).

I have also developed information that Andrew Strassmeir had been a GSG9 while in the German Bundeswehr, which is an elite anti-terrorist "border patrol" (in the days of a divided Germany). I have also developed information that after officially leaving the German army, Mr. Strassmeir may have attended Schlierschied Military Academy in Hannover, Germany where he is said to have graduated on February 12, 1989 with a Certificate of Leadership signed by Frederick R. Adophus. I am still trying to determine if the Schliershied Academy is a training facility for espionage-type activity.

Certain interesting assertions and comments also arose out of two trans-Atlantic telephone discussions with Andrew Strassmeir's attorneys in the United States, but said discussions may be included in a subsequent report. Finally, Strassmeir's attorneys informed me that the United States Attorney General's office was not content with an *ex parte* written witness statement that Mr. Strassmeir tendered in the McVeigh/Nichols criminal case (a copy of which is attached hereto) and was trying to get a sworn statement from him in the near future (in Germany). It was also mentioned that Strassmeir might testify for the prosecution at the time of trial.

-END OF REPORT-

Houston Chronicle

Vol. 94 No. 211 — Friday, May 12, 1995 — 50 Cents ★★★

Friday
First-rate Brit film
With Hugh Grant as star, 'The Englishman' may get attention it deserves
Weekend Preview

Drubbed again
Suns have Rockets down 2-0 in series after 118-94 win
Sports

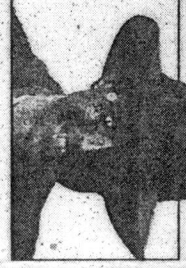

Home front
Pair's house, garden bring back the feel of an era gone by
Gardens section

Third suspect identified in Oklahoma bombing

By DAN THOMASSON and PETER COPELAND
Scripps Howard News Service

A third man wanted in the Oklahoma City bombing has been identified as Steven Colbern, a fugitive from a previous firearms charge. Colbern, aged 35 or 36, is described as 6-foot-1 and 195 pounds with green eyes, which roughly matches the description of John Doe II.

Law enforcement sources said Thursday night that Colbern was identified through his brown pickup. It was captured, by chance, on video taken from the state trooper's car that stopped Timothy McVeigh for speeding only 80 minutes after the blast.

"That trooper had a hell of a day," a federal investigator said.

An automatic camera in the car of Trooper Charles Hanger was taping the arrest of McVeigh. In the background was the image of the pickup, which also pulled over while McVeigh was being questioned. Sophisticated enhancement techniques were used to improve the video until investigators could read the license plate number.

The truck, registered to Colbern,

See BOMBING on Page 21A.

Stockman article accuses Clinton of using Waco to push arms ban

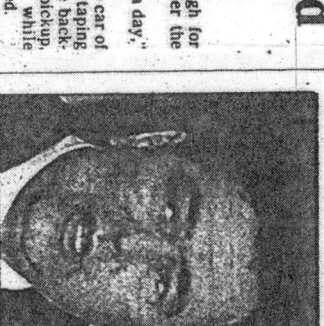

By BENNETT ROTH
Houston Chronicle Washington Bureau

WASHINGTON — Writing in the June issue of Guns & Ammo magazine, Rep. Steve Stockman suggested the government "executed" the Branch Davidians at Waco and President Clinton encouraged the confrontation to push through a ban on assault weapons.

"Bill Clinton and the gun-control lobby were not unhappy with the fiery end of the siege at Waco," he wrote. "Waco was to be a lesson to gun owners all over America. Don't own firearms that the government does not like."

The Friendswood Republican said that had Clinton been unhappy with the raid he would have had Attorney General Janet Reno "indicted for premeditated murder."

Stockman, who has emerged as

■ Dole won't follow Bush's path out of the NRA: Page 3A.

one of the most strident, anti-gun control advocates in Congress, is one of the principal sponsors of a bill to repeal the ban on assault weapons.

The congressman was recently embroiled in controversy when it was learned that he received a cryptic fax regarding the Oklahoma City bombing sent to him on April 19, the day of the bombing, by a woman working with a Michigan

See STOCKMAN on Page 21A.

Tracking a deadly disease

Ebola, a virus that causes hemorrhagic fever, is believed to have killed more than 100 people in Zaire.

Cell: invaded by worm-like virus

Clinton aides say Dole put nation at risk

Senate majority leader hit

Bombing
Continued from Page 1A.

contained traces of ammonium nitrate, believed to be the main explosive ingredient used in the bombing.

Colbern's age is unknown, but he shared a mail drop with McVeigh in Kingman, Ariz., sources said. The truck was found parked outside an abandoned mobile home in Kingman.

Colbern already was wanted on a federal firearms charge, officials said. He was arrested last summer in San Bernardino, Calif., for carrying a gun with a silencer. He was allowed to post bail but skipped.

The FBI revealed evidence Thursday that Terry Nichols, another of the alleged Oklahoma bombers, had amassed huge quantities of explosive material.

Storage sheds and a Ryder truck were rented using false names, and 80 bags of fertilizer — 4,000 pounds — were purchased during the weeks before the April 19 bombing.

Nichols heard the evidence against him at a hearing at El Reno, Okla., Thursday. His next hearing was set for May 18.

Although the information was not released until Thursday, Nichols, 40, of Herington, Kan., was charged Tuesday with destroying a federal building, a federal crime, and with aiding and abetting the bombing.

After the hearing, U.S. Attorney Patrick Ryan said, "Since the crime resulted in the loss of life, it would qualify for the death penalty."

The FBI affidavit said Nichols acknowledged that he was with McVeigh in downtown Oklahoma City three days before the explosion, but "denied involvement in or knowledge of the bombing."

And it said the FBI had obtained a letter from Nichols to McVeigh dated last Nov. 22, the day before Nichols left on a trip to the Philippines.

"In the letter, Terry Nichols tells Timothy McVeigh that he will be getting this letter only in the event of Nichols' death," the affidavit said. Nichols instructs McVeigh to "clear everything out ... liquidate" two of the storage lockers, the document said, adding, "Terry Nichols also tells McVeigh he is on his own and to 'Go for it!!'"

McVeigh, arrested in Perry, Okla., for speeding and carrying a weapon, was charged in the bombing. The address he gave police was a farm in Michigan owned by James Nichols, brother of Terry.

Terry Nichols turned himself in on April 21, but not before he took some of the ammonium nitrate in his house and "placed it on his yard as fertilizer."

"Nichols said that he did this after reading in several different newspapers that ammonium nitrate was used in the Oklahoma City bombing," according to the affidavit.

Nichols also said he hoped the FBI would not mistake household items" for bomb-producing materi-

als.

Meanwhile, FBI Director Louis Freeh told Congress that federal agents have had to be relocated after they received death threats from members of extremist militia groups. It was unclear from Freeh's remarks whether the threats were made before or after the bombing.

Also Thursday, the government awarded contracts to demolish the bombed building. Within 10 days, it will be destroyed by implosion, according to the General Services Administration.

Implosion is controlled explosion where debris collapses into the center of a building site rather than flying outward. Some Oklahomans have expressed concern that an explosion of any kind at the site might be psychologically damaging.

GSA said it has determined that the other common method of destroying a building, using wrecking balls, could pose a greater physical hazard to workers.

In another development, O.J. Simpson lawyer Johnnie Cochran Jr. filed a lawsuit in federal court in Oklahoma City against ICI Explosives U.S.A. Inc., the manufacturer of the fertilizer used in the bomb. The lawsuit, filed on behalf of four survivors but seeking class action status, seeks $50,000 per plaintiff on the grounds that the company didn't attempt to reduce the explosive potential of the fertilizer.

Newsday contributed to this story.

Demolition workers remove office equipment from the A.P. Murrah Federal Building in Oklahoma City on Thursday as they prepare to bring down the building.

Associated Press

Drowning
Continued from Page 1A.

stymied due to this code of silence.

"I publicly have compared hazing to gang activity in that it was violent activity, illegal and the participants become co-conspirators covering their illegal acts by observing a code of silence," Berdahl said.

Students connected to the Texas Cowboys — the vast majority of whom are selected from UT's 28 Greek fraternities — said they believe the public speculation of hazing is unfair and that their group has been judged before the investigation is complete.

But others claim such investigations will lead to a "slap on the wrists."

"The university will not do anything at all to embarrass or call attention to these young men," said a UT employee. "Hazing is still rampant within the organization. The fraternities are out of control. That, I guess, is an acceptable risk for UT administrators."

Higgins, authorities said, disappeared from the party about 2:30 a.m. on April 29. Although students told authorities they spent much of the night searching for Higgins, they failed to call police until 11:40 a.m. The body was found in 12 to 15 feet of water, with no signs of bruises or other injuries.

Authorities are trying to determine how Higgins, a minor, obtained the liquor and whether he was forced to drink alcohol or swim in the river. Forced alcohol consumption is considered hazing under state law, as is any type of physical activity that subjects a person to unreasonable risk of harm.

Jack Price, who represents Higgins' parents, said the incident has got the earmarks of hazing.

He said he was troubled by the Texas Cowboys' failure to notify authorities for more than nine hours, and that he was concerned pledges may have been forced to swim in what may have been a dangerous section of the Colorado River.

"From what we have learned, a number of the young men were taken down the bank of the river," Price said. "They were all dressed in cowboy boots and, as we understand, fully dressed it was a pretty steep bank, at midnight or after in a fairly treacherous river."

Price said a bend in the river caused a "fairly dangerous undertow," although it was not visible at the surface.

"I would think that if this was something imposed on the students that were there, it would amount to hazing," Price said.

Records show the Texas Cowboys — who dress in black hats and white shirts and serve as caretaker for "Smokey the Cannon" at UT football games — have been cited repeatedly for hazing violations since being founded in 1922.

A 1987 UT presidential commission report found the group continues "to permit hazing in some of its most blatant and offensive forms, including paddling and using cattle prods. The report added that many students believe the Texas Cowboys are "no longer considered destructable."

As recently as spring 1994 the Texas Cowboys were placed on probation for hazing violations in which members paddled pledges. The Cowboys were banned from three home football games.

But UT officials say hazing has decreased, especially since a 1987 state law adopted following the alcohol-poisoning death of a student.

"If you look at the history prior to 1987, I don't think anyone will argue with you that there was a long established tradition of hazing within the Cowboys," said James Vick, UT vice president for student affairs. But, he added, "I think most of those who have observed have felt many of the previous behaviors have been reduced or eliminated."

Vick said the most recent paddling incident that led to the Cowboys being placed on probation involved "a small cluster of students that were in one fraternity."

Higgins, a sophomore mechanical engineering major, is remembered as a good-natured and active student who served as an academic mentor to his Kappa Sigma fraternity brothers and a volunteer helping disabled children at Austin's Rosedale School.

"Gabe would serve as a big brother for the children," said Gloria Simonson, the Rosedale principal. "He would bring his guitar and sing and play music. He would do it one hour each week."

Simonson said Higgins and 31 other Cowboys volunteered to help the disabled students, accompanying them to a livestock show, providing Easter eggs and Halloween candy.

"I think we can't lose sight of the fact that these young men also have done a lot of good for a lot of people," Simonson said. "I hate for all of them to have a black cloud over them for one very, very unfortunate incident.

"And for that black cloud to blot out maybe all of the good they may have done for their four years in school."

Chronicle reporter Kevin Moran contributed to this story.

Virus
Continued from Page 1A.

to get to the United States, doctors could isolate the victim and prevent the spread of the virus. However, there is little they could do to save that person's life.

[...] ber of the family of filoviruses, has struck quickly and violently and then burned itself out as its victims died.

Researchers have not been able to find the source of the infection. That makes outbreaks impossible to predict or prevent.

But even in Zaire, Ebola is a minor health factor at this time, said DuPont, who heard about the outbreak while at meetings with the officials

---

But Bishop said Thursday that militia groups invigorated by the Congress last summer, more than a mitted no crime prior to the arrival officials.

direct and indirect contribution.

disagreements clearly rather than

It's A Matter Of Opinion.
Read Outlook.

The Chronicle
Houston's leading information source

vs.

TIMOTHY JAMES McVEIGH and TERRY LYNN NICHOLS,

Defendants.

REPORTER'S TRANSCRIPT
(HEARING ON MOTIONS - VOLUME VII)

Proceedings before the HONORABLE RICHARD P. MATSCH, Judge, United States District Court for the District of Colorado, commencing at 3:35 p.m., on the 14th day of November, 1996, in Courtroom C-203, United States Courthouse, Denver, Colorado.

Proceeding Recorded by Mechanical Stenography, Transcription

Produced via Computer by Paul Zuckerman, 1929 Stout Street, P.O. Box 3563, Denver, Colorado, 80294, (303) 629-9285

408

APPEARANCES

PATRICK M. RYAN, United States Attorney for the District of Oklahoma, 210 West Park Avenue, Suite 400, Oklahoma City, Oklahoma, 73102, appearing for the plaintiff.

JOSEPH H. HARTZLER, SEAN CONNELLY, LARRY A. MACKEY, BETH WILKINSON, SCOTT MENDELOFF, and VICKI BEHENNA, Special Attorneys to the U.S. Attorney General, 1961 Stout Street, Suite 1200, Denver, Colorado, 80294, appearing for the plaintiff.

STEPHEN JONES, ROBERT NIGH, JR., ROBERT WYATT, Attorneys at Law, Jones, Wyatt & Roberts, 114 East Broadway, Suite 100, Post Office Box 472, Enid, Oklahoma, 73702-0472, and JERALYN MERRITT, 303 East 17th Avenue, Suite 400, Denver, Colorado, 80203, appearing for Defendant McVeigh.

RONALD G. WOODS, ADAM THURSCHWELL, and REID NEUREITER, Attorneys at Law, 1120 Lincoln Street, Suite 1308, Denver, Colorado, 80203, appearing for Defendant Nichols.

* * * * *

PROCEEDINGS

433

MS. WILKINSON: Yes, Judge. What it is, it's the same story, I believe, as I told you this threat was -- the threat warning from the marshal service on March 15 was given to the -- the court family; and I believe after the bombing, Judge Alley made mention of the fact that he had received a general warning, you know, prior to the bombing.

MR. JONES: Well, I don't know that they are the same.

THE COURT: I see. But I mean, this is generated by the fact that there was some -- something in this newspaper in Oregon?

MR. JONES: He was interviewed by the Oregonian on the day of the bombing. He grew up in Oregon, and they called him because of the connection.

THE COURT: I see.

MS. WILKINSON: Your Honor, could I ask if Mr. Jones has interviewed Judge Alley?

THE COURT: Do you want to answer that, Mr. Jones?

MR. JONES: Well, if you'll consult your index of people I've interviewed, no, I haven't interviewed Judge Alley. He's interviewed me on a few occasions.

173 and 174 --

THE COURT: Well, have we left that open here? I'm not sure what the resolution of this has been. You don't have an interview report of anybody interviewing Judge Alley about this public statement? Is that the response?

434

MS. WILKINSON: I don't believe we do, your Honor, but I'd have to go back and check our index. As I said, we're working from the same index that we provided to Mr. Jones.

THE COURT: Yeah. Yeah. And I'm sure Judge Alley is equally available to the defense counsel as he is to the Government's counsel.

MS. WILKINSON: That was my point.

THE COURT: Yes. Well, I'll make it explicitly for you.

MS. WILKINSON: Thank you.

EXHIBIT "A"

95-7278-62
1726/0338
Blevins
OCT 30 19
DISTRICT COURT

In The District Court Of Oklahoma County

1995 OCT 27 P 3:04

State Of Oklahoma

CJ 95 7278-62

We, the undersigned, being duly registered voters in the county of Oklahoma County, call for a grand jury to be seated in the county of Oklahoma County according to Article 2, Section 18 of the Oklahoma Constitution. The purpose of the grand jury is to investigate the bombing of the Alfred P. Murrah Federal Building in Oklahoma City which occurred on April 19, 1995. The purpose of the grand jury also will be to investigate whether obstruction of justice, generally or specifically, has occurred or violation of Oklahoma Statutes Title 21 sections 421, 451, 452, 453, 454, 455, 456, 540, 543, 544, 545, 546.

Charles Key

Charles Key

Glenn Wilburn

Glen Wilburn

We, the undersigned, being duly registered voters in the county of Oklahoma County, Oklahoma petition the Court to immediately call a grand jury to be convened in the county of Oklahoma County according to Article 2, Section 18 of the Oklahoma Constitution for the following purposes:

1. To identify and indict persons who participated in the planning and/or carrying out of the bombing of the Alfred P. Murrah Federal Building in Oklahoma City, Oklahoma County, State of Oklahoma on April 19, 1995 which resulted in the deaths of Robert Neal Chipman, Katherine Louise Cregan, Anita Christine Hightower, Raymond Lee Johnson, Kathryn Elizabeth Ridley, Trudy Jean Rigney, and Charlotte Andrea who were killed away from federal property and, therefore, are not included by federal law in any federal indictments under the murder and/or racketeering and/or conspiracy laws of the State of Oklahoma, under Oklahoma Statutes, Title 21 & 22; and, in addition, to investigate into any and all other matters called to the attention of the Grand Jury.

2. To indict any person or persons who interfere with or provide false information to the Grand Jury in violation of Oklahoma Statutes, Title 21, sections 421, 451, 452, 453, 454, 455, 456, 540, 543, 544, 545, 546.

	SIGNATURE	ADDRESS	PRINTED NAME
1.			
2.			
3.			
4.			
5.			
6.			
7.			
8.			
9.			
10.			
11.			
12.			
13.			
14.			
15.			
16.			
17.			
18.			
19.			
20.			

IN THE SUPREME COURT OF THE STATE OF OKLAHOMA

IN RE: REQUEST FOR GRAND JURY)
)
CHARLES KEY and GLENN WILBURN,)   NOT FOR OFFICIAL
)   PUBLICATION
Appellants,)
)
v.)   No. 86,591
)
THE HONORABLE DANIEL L. OWENS,)
Presiding Judge, 7th Judicial District,)
)
Appellee.)

ORDER

Certiorari is Denied. The opinion of the Court of Civil Appeals is released by the Supreme Court for official publication pursuant to 20 O.S.1991 § 30.5.

Appellee's alternative prayer for this Court to invoke its superintending control over these proceedings and/or issue a stay is Denied as premature. This denial is without prejudice to a later presentation of a stay request before the Presiding Judge of Oklahoma County in the event a sufficient number of legal signatures are obtained to impanel a grand jury. Any subsequent request for a stay must be conducted in open court and a record made.

DONE BY ORDER OF THE SUPREME COURT IN CONFERENCE THIS 18th DAY OF FEBRUARY, 1997.

RELEASED FOR PUBLICATION BY ORDER OF
THE COURT OF CIVIL APPEALS

FILED
COURT OF CIVIL APPEALS
STATE OF OKLAHOMA
DEC 24 1996
JAMES W. PATTERSON
CLERK

IN THE COURT OF CIVIL APPEALS

STATE OF OKLAHOMA

DIVISION 2

IN RE: REQUEST FOR GRAND JURY.

CHARLES KEY and GLENN WILBURN,

    Appellants,

vs.

THE HONORABLE DANIEL L. OWENS,
Presiding Judge, 7th Judicial
District,

    Appellee.

No. 86,591

FOR PUBLICATION

APPEAL FROM THE DISTRICT COURT OF
OKLAHOMA COUNTY, OKLAHOMA

Honorable Daniel L. Owens, Trial Judge

REVERSED AND REMANDED WITH INSTRUCTIONS

Mark S. Sanford
Windham & Sanford, P.C.
Oklahoma City, Oklahoma   For Appellants

Robert H. Macy
District Attorney
John Jacobsen
Assistant District Attorney
Beverly A. Palmer
Assistant District Attorney
Oklahoma City, Oklahoma   For Appellee

...sidering the Petitioners' amended request, the district judge did not have the power to act as a super-legislature by rewriting legislative enactments to conform with his views of public policy. *Id.* Neither do we have such power and, therefore, cannot uphold the district judge's order.

In conclusion, we rule as a matter of law that Petitioners' amended request for a grand jury meets the statutory sufficiency requirements of 38 O.S.1991 §§ 101 & 102, and that the district judge has no discretion to prevent a sufficient petition from being circulated. Accordingly, we remand the cause to the district judge with directions to enter an order determining Petitioners' request to be sufficient and to allow Petitioners to proceed with the circulation of the petition for the requisite signatures.

GOODMAN, P.J., and STUBBLEFIELD, J., concur.

December 24, 1996

STATE OF OKLAHOMA   )
) ss
COUNTY OF OKLAHOMA)

AFFIDAVIT

I, HENRY C. GIBBONS, being duly sworn, do hereby state that I am an agent with the Federal Bureau of Investigation, having been so employed for 26 years and as such am vested with the authority to investigate violations of federal laws, including Title 18, United States Code.

Further, the Affiant states as follows:

1. The following information has been received by the Federal Bureau of Investigation on April 19-20, 1995.

2. On April 19, 1995, a powerful explosive device detonated in front of the Alfred P. Murrah Federal Building in Oklahoma City, Oklahoma, at approximately 9:00 a.m.

3. On April 19, 1995, a Special Agent of the FBI received information that a witness near the scene of the explosion saw to individuals running from the area of the Federal Building toward a brown Chevrolet truck prior to the explosion. The individuals were described as males, of possible Middle Eastern descent, approximately 6 feet tall, with athletic builds. One of the persons was further described as approximately 25-28 years old, having dark hair and a beard. The second person was described as approximately 35-38 years old, with dark hair and a dark beard with gray in it. The second person was further described as wearing

1

blue jogging pants, a black shirt and a black jogging jacket. A third person, not further identified, was believed to be in the brown Chevrolet truck.

4. At approximately 10:43 a.m. on April 19, 1995, an American Airlines flight left Oklahoma City en route to Chicago, Illinois. Aboard that flight was Abraham Abdallah Ahmed. Ahmed was scheduled to fly from Chicago to Rome, Italy and finally to Jordan.

5. American Airlines personnel in Oklahoma City observed Ahmed prior to the flight and thought he was "acting nervous." They called the American Airlines national security office in Dallas, Texas, who in turned notified the Chicago office of the FBI.

6. Ahmed was interviewed by FBI Agent Chuck Miller upon his arrival in Chicago at about 12:30 p.m. Ahmed stated that he was travelling to Jordan to discuss his father's planned marriage. He also advised that he was born in Jordan but was a naturalized United States citizen. He also said he was not scheduled to return to the United States until July 1995. Ahmed was observed to be approximately 5' 8" tall, weighing approximately 140 pounds, and wearing a moustache. His date of birth is July 15, 1963.

7. The luggage of Ahmed continued on the connecting flight from Chicago to Rome, Italy, while Ahmed remained in Chicago. The luggage was searched in Rome by Italian officials who discovered, inter alia: (a) multiple car radios; (b) a substantial quantity of shielded and unshielded wire; (c) a small tool kit and other tools, consistent with use for both explosive devices and normal

electronic repair or installation; (d) blue jogging pants and a blue jogging jacket with a floral pattern around the neck; (e) black sweatpants; (f) video cassette recorder; and (g) solder.

8. At the conclusion of the interview, Ahmed secured passage on a flight to London, England.

9. On April 20, 1995, British authorities informed the FBI Command Center in Washington, D.C., that they detained Ahmed in London and have determined that he is ineligible for entry into or transit through England and will be returned to the United States. Ahmed is expected to arrive at Washington-Dulles International Airport at 7:25 p.m. on April 20, 1995.

10. Based on the proximity in time of Ahmed's flight from Oklahoma City following the explosion to a destination outside the country, and his possession of multiple car radios, the wire, tool kit and tools, a blue jogging suit and black sweatpants, the testimony of Ahmed is required before a Federal Grand Jury investigating the April 19, 1995 explosion in Oklahoma City.

11. Ahmed's demonstrated intent to leave the country indicates that his testimony cannot be secured through the issuance of a subpoena.

Further your affiant sayeth not.

HENRY C. GIBBONS
Special Agent
Federal Bureau of Investigation

Update on Iraqi POW Resettlement

VFW 2/94

"Enemy Ex-POWS in Our Midst?" requires some clarification. I am still strongly pushing legislation to bar former Iraqi POWs from entering the United States.

The State Department continues to insist the U.S. has a *moral* obligation to accept Iraqi soldiers, particularly deserters. This is an insult to every American veteran. I hope your readers will join me in working to stop this offensive practice at once.

So far as I know, the promised review of our screening process — if it ever began — has not been completed. Despite passage of my amendment, the State Department is determined to get its way: It plans to admit at least 750 more former Iraqi soldiers during 1994.

I strongly urge your readers to let Congress and the White House know their feelings on this issue. If enough Americans voice their outrage, maybe even the State Department will hear it.

Rep. Elton Gallegly, U.S. House of Representatives, 2441 Rayburn Bldg., Washington, D.C. 20515

Copyright 1993 News World Communications, Inc.
The Washington Times

October 18, 1993, Monday, Final Edition

SECTION: Part A; NATION; UPDATE ON THE NEWS; Pg. A8

LENGTH: 522 words

HEADLINE: Congress lines up to oppose resettling Iraqi POWs in U.S.

BYLINE: Jerry Seper; THE WASHINGTON TIMES

BODY:
A "sense of the Congress" resolution calling on President Clinton to end a policy of granting refugee status to thousands of former Iraqi POWs and their families is gaining momentum in committee and is expected to be offered to the full House for a vote soon.

Started in September with 26 co-sponsors, the resolution by Republicans Don Manzullo of Illinois and Cliford Stearns of Florida now has 70 co-sponsors and is before the House Judiciary Committee. It asks the president to "terminate the policy of allowing resettlement of members of the Iraqi armed forces" in the United States.

"We're rolling out the welcome wagon to prisoners of war, yet our own veterans who fought there are having trouble getting any help," Mr. Stearns said.

The resolution says it is "inappropriate" for U.S. officials to resettle Iraqis in this country when Iraq remains in violation of numerous U.N. resolutions. It also says Iraqi forces are accountable for atrocities during the invasion and occupation of Kuwait and that Iraqi soldiers have continued to "violate the human rights of the native population of that nation."

The relocation policy also has been criticized in the Senate, where Virginia Republican John Warner's "sense of the Senate" resolution calling on Mr. Clinton to halt the program passed last month on a voice vote.

The nonbinding Senate measure created an exception for Iraqis who could demonstrate that they aided coalition forces during the Persian Gulf war and did not engage in war crimes in Kuwait.

The Washington Times, October 18, 1993

"I find it unconscionable that an Iraqi combatant soldier would be admitted into this country under refugee status and be given certain privileges and benefits and indeed a job at a time when many, many U.S. veterans ... cannot or have not thus far been able to get comparable benefits," Mr. Warner said.

Despite the Senate resolution and continued opposition in the House, the White House is committed to the resettlement of Iraqi prisoners of war, their families and others as recommended by the State Department.

"The United States agreed to settle some in the U.S. as authorized by President Bush, who consulted with Congress before he decided to do that," an administration official said. "That's a concern that the executive branch takes into consideration. At the same time, there's a humanitarian concern here. What happens to these folks?"

According to the State Department, 4,000 to 13,000 former Iraqi POWs have been declared refugees and designated as eligible for resettlement in the United States at taxpayer expense. They are among 39,000 Iraqis held at refugee camps in Saudi Arabia and include soldiers who took part in the August 1990 invasion of Kuwait and who fought U.S. forces in the Gulf war.

The Washington Times, October 18, 1993

More than 3,400 Iraqis - ex-soldiers, their dependents and others - have been settled in the United States. Another 4,600 are expected this year. The relocations are scheduled to continue through 1994.

The estimated cost of the relocations last year and this year is $60 million.

LANGUAGE: ENGLISH

LOAD-DATE: October 18, 1993

LEVEL 1 - 31 OF 162 STORIES

Copyright 1994 The Times Mirror Company

IN THE UNITED STATES DISTRICT COURT FOR THE
WESTERN DISTRICT OF OKLAHOMA

AL-HUSSAINI HUSSAIN, an individual,)
)
Plaintiff,)
)
v.) Case No. CIV-97-1535-L
)
PALMER COMMUNICATIONS, INC.,)
a Delaware corporation, d/b/a)
KFOR-TV CHANNEL 4;)
JAYNA DAVIS, an individual;)
BRAD EDWARDS, an individual;)
MELISSA KLINZING, an individual,)
)
Defendants.)

O R D E R

This matter is before the court on numerous motions. Plaintiff Al-Hussaini Hussain's action arises from certain news reports appearing on KFOR-TV Channel 4 in Oklahoma City in the months following the April 19, 1995 bombing of the A.P. Murrah Federal Building in downtown Oklahoma City, Oklahoma.

Defendants Palmer Communications (KFOR), Jayna Davis, Brad Edwards, and Melissa Klinzing have moved for dismissal and for summary judgment. The dismissal motion is primarily based upon plaintiff's documented and repeated failure to comply with certain orders of the court. In response to these motions, that whether these discrete statements are defamatory is an issue of law for the court. Plaintiff has failed to show how the depositions of the persons identified in his Rule 56(f) affidavit would create a genuine issue of fact as to whether the eleven statements are defamatory. Accordingly, plaintiff's request for more discovery pursuant to Rule 56(f) is denied and the court accepts as undisputed the following facts as stated by defendants (citations to the record are omitted):

1. On April 19, 1995, one or more persons bombed the A.P. Murrah Federal Building in Oklahoma City. The blast destroyed the building, killed 168 people, and injured hundreds.

2. Local, state, and federal authorities immediately began a massive manhunt for the perpetrators of the bombing.

3. A witness reported to the FBI that two Middle-Eastern looking men were seen running from the vicinity of the Murrah Building toward a brown Chevrolet truck. A third person was believed to be in the truck.

4. On April 19, the FBI issued an all points bulletin for authorities to be on the look-out for a late-model brown Chevrolet pickup truck with tinted windows and a smoke-colored bug deflector. The bulletin indicated that two Middle Eastern-looking men were believed to be in the truck.

5. Newspaper accounts the day after the bombing reported that a brown pickup and Middle-Eastern men were possibly involved in the bombing. For example:

　　a. The front page of the April 20, 1995 edition of *USA Today* contained a box entitled "Bomb attack at a glance," which said, in part, "Suspects: Reportedly 3 men, two described as having dark hair and beards, believed to be of Middle Eastern origin; officials said to be looking for brown Chevy pickup with tinted windows and a bug shield in the front."

b. The April 20, 1995 edition of *The Daily Oklahoman* contained a map of the area of downtown Oklahoma City surrounding the Murrah Building. Noted on the map was the description, "Suspect vehicle, brown pickup with tinted windows last seen on N Walker."

6. On April 20, 1995, the federal government issued an arrest warrant for "John Doe #2," who was described as of medium build, 5'9" to 5'10" tall, about 175-180 pounds, with brown hair and a tattoo on his left arm.

7. On the same day, April 20, authorities released composite sketches of two men believed to be involved in the bombing. The sketches were drawn by FBI sketch artist Raymond Rozycki based on descriptions provided by Tom Kessinger, a mechanic employed at Elliott's Body Shop in Junction City, Kansas. The FBI Facial Identification Fact Sheet regarding this John Doe #2 contained a different description than the arrest warrant, describing the man as 5'10" tall, of heavy build, and weighing 200 pounds.

8. During the time the defendants were investigating and producing the news reports at issue in this case, numerous experts on international terrorism expressed their beliefs publicly or to defendant Jayna Davis that the bombing in Oklahoma City bore many of the hallmarks of other bombings such as of the World Trade Center carried out by Islamic terrorists. Those experts included Steve Emerson, an author and producer of the PBS special "Jihad in America," a documentary exposing the terrorist networks in the United States; Laurie Myllroie, formerly a professor at Harvard and at the U.S. Naval War College, and presently at the Foreign Policy Research Institute in Philadelphia, who is an expert on Iraq, Islamic terrorist, and the World Trade Center bombing; and Taylor Jesse Clear, a

former Foreign Service Officer who in June 1995 was assigned to the Counter Terrorism Directorate in the U.S. Department of Defense and who is an acknowledged expert on terrorism and counterterrorism.

9. On April 20, 1995, federal authorities detained Abraham Ahmad, a Jordanian-American resident of Oklahoma City, in London, England, as a possible witness in the bombing. Ahmad was reported to have had duffel bags containing electrical tape, silicone, a hammer, tweezers, and a photo album with pictures of missiles and other weapons. Ahmad was reported to have left his home in northwest Oklahoma City approximately a half hour after the bombing and flown to Chicago, then London, en route to Jordan.

10. The defendant Davis interviewed Ahmad on April 22, 1995.

11. At about the same time as her interview with Ahmad, Davis interviewed Ernie Cranfield, who knew Ahmad. Cranfield told Davis that Ahmad had been to Cranfield's place of employment with unusual frequency in the days just before the bombing. Cranfield said that several of his (Cranfield's) co-workers were Iraqis who had been hired by his employer, Samir Khalil, in about November 1994.

12. At one time the federal government thought Khalil might have connections with the Palestine Liberation Organization (PLO).

13. Cranfield said that one of his Iraqi co-workers, al-Hussaini, had a tattoo on his left arm.

14. Cranfield also told Davis that he had seen a brown pickup truck with tinted windows and a bug shield at Khalil's place of business prior to the bombing.

15. The FBI questioned Cranfield in late April or early May 1995 about where al-Hussaini was on the morning of the bombing, and Cranfield told Davis he had been questioned.

16. Davis also interviewed Sharon Twilley, Samir Khalil's secretary. Twilley confirmed Cranfield's statements that Ahmad had visited Khalil's office several times a day in the weeks before the bombing, which was far more often than usual; and that she had also seen a brown pickup truck with tinted windows and a bug shield at Khalil's office. Twilley confirmed Cranfield's statements about the arrival of the Iraqi employees, including al-Hussaini, about November 1994. Twilley told Davis that Khalil had become unusually secretive after that.

17. The FBI also questioned Twilley in May 1995 about Khalil's and Ahmad's activities before the bombing. She provided a list of Khalil's Iraqi employees, including al-Hussaini, to the FBI. Twilley told Davis these things.

18. KFOR took surveillance photographs and videotape of Khalil and his Iraqi employees, including al-Hussaini. The photos were taken from a public street while the subjects of the photos were in public places.

19. On April 25, 1995, federal authorities issued an enhanced composite photo of John Doe #2. The full-face sketch shows the suspect wearing a ball cap.

20. On May 1, 1995, federal authorities released a third sketch of John Doe #2, a profile view of the suspect wearing a ball cap.

21. After comparing videotape and still photos of Khalil's Iraqi workers with the composite sketches of John Doe #2, and talking with law enforcement persons, Davis formed the opinion that al-Hussaini bore a strong resemblance to the composite photo of John Doe #2. Law enforcement persons expressed their opinions to Davis that al-Hussaini looked like the sketches of John Doe #2.

22. Al-Hussaini approximated the physical description of John Doe #2, and bears a strong resemblance to the composite sketch of John Doe #2. He has a tattoo of an anchor and snake on his left arm.

23. In their investigation of the bombing, Davis, defendant Brad Edwards, and other reporters for KFOR discovered several witnesses who believed that they had seen John Doe #2 in the company of Timothy McVeigh a few days before the bombing in a bar along N.W. 10th Street, or speeding away from downtown Oklahoma City moments after the bombing in a brown pickup truck with tinted windows and a bug shield. Each of these witnesses gave videotaped interview in which they described what they saw, picked al-Hussaini out of a photo lineup as the person they saw, and assured Davis on camera that they believed their observations enough to testify to them under oath before a grand jury.

24. KFOR shared the information it broadcast with the FBI and other authorities.

25. On several occasions when asked by KFOR, the FBI declined to clear al-Hussaini as a suspect or to say he was not a suspect; they did not indicate that KFOR's information was not accurate; and they did not try to dissuade KFOR from broadcasting its reports about a possible John Doe #2.

26. The FBI discouraged KFOR from interviewing al-Hussaini prior to the June 7, 1995 new report, saying agents were investigating his alibi. Therefore, KFOR did not interview al-Hussaini before the first news report on June 7, 1995.

27. After al-Hussaini had given interviews to other local media, Davis tried through Abraham Ahmad to arrange an interview with him, but he refused.

28. The plaintiff claims that at the time of the bombing he was painting a house for his employer in Oklahoma City.

29. The plaintiff's co-workers dispute his alibi.

30. The person who prepared a time sheet which the plaintiff showed to other media to substantiate his alibi later admitted she fabricated it.

31. KFOR broadcast five extensive news reports about a possible John Doe #2 in June 1995. Those reports were first broadcast on the following days: (a) June 7, 1995 at 10:00 p.m.; (b) June 9, 1995 at 10:00 p.m.; (c) June 12, 1995 at 10:00 p.m.; (d) June 14, 1995 at 10:00 p.m.; and (e) June 22, 1995 at 10:00 p.m. None of those reports used the plaintiff's name and his face was digitally concealed.

32. Following KFOR's first four broadcasts, the plaintiff contacted other media. He voluntarily allowed his name and picture to be broadcast by KOCO-TV (Channel 5) and KWTV (Channel 9); in news reports by those stations he voluntarily identified himself as the person in KFOR's news reports. The plaintiff also gave an interview to *The Oklahoma Gazette*, in which he voluntarily identified himself as the subject of KFOR's news reports.

33. In answers to interrogatories served on him by Davis, the plaintiff listed the statements in the news reports which he contended were false and defamatory. He confirmed in his deposition that those statements are the ones upon which his action is based: Those statements are:

In the news report on June 7, 1995:

    A.   "An employee of that business is this man (photo shown[1] of Mr. Hussain) who law enforcement officers agree with us strongly resembles the FBI sketches of John Doe #2."

    B.   "In fact, we know that the possible John Doe #2 is Iraqi."

---

[1] Plaintiff's face was digitally concealed any time it was broadcast by KFOR-TV.

A COMPANY NEWSLETTER

VOLUME 96, ISSUE 3

wednesday, april 19, 1995
a black day for us all
Contributed by J. D. Reed**

As usual, I pulled into the parking garage about 7:30 and made my way to the Oklahoma County Office Building, where I work as an appraiser for the County. Although it was unusual to see the Oklahoma County Bomb Disposal Unit parked outside the courthouse, I assumed it was routine business and thought no more about it.

I was settled at my desk for a normal day (9 a.m.), when I heard a whistling noise, much like that of a jet engine. Less than a second later, I heard a deafening explosion and felt the building shake as if it were collapsing. "How far will this floor fall?" I remember wondering.

As the shaking subsided, I ran to the window to investigate. Had an airplane struck the building? There was no sign of it. I looked for the Bomb Disposal Unit, but it was gone. Had they mistakenly set off an explosive while trying to disarm it? What was it????

Evacuating the building, we found everything in turmoil. Light fixtures and ceiling tiles were barely hanging; the ground floor was filled with smoke & dust; crowds of bewildered people already thronged the glass-covered street.

A buddy and I moved quickly toward the black smoke billowing into the sky. Computer paper and other office supplies were falling through the air. Emergency vehicles fought their way through the streets. Clearly this was more serious than even I had first imagined.

Rounding the southwest corner of the federal building, it was hard to focus on the destruction. There was so much confusion! Literally thousands of people were there, each with a personal guess of what had happened. The glass elevator was gone; there was absolutely no movement within the building; every floor was black and lifeless.

I stared at the building (still on the wrong side to see the full extent of the damage), trying to gather my thoughts and force some logic into the situation. Suddenly, I realized that I could see all the

AFTERMATH

Every day now as I drive to work, I see the vacant lots where buildings used to sit. I see boarded windows and missing bricks of buildings yet to be repaired or demolished. Each time I feel such sadness for the victims and for the friends and families left behind.

Wednesday, April 19, 1995, was a morning I shall never forget. History was on my door step scattering broken bodies and shattered lives – and mountains of debris, worth millions only moments before.

The unforgettable, unforgivable happened. The Alfred P. Murrah Federal Building, less than three blocks from my office, had been bombed.

** *J. D. Reed, husband of P&P's Kathy Reed (Acctg. Clk.), a county appraiser officing in the Oklahoma County Office Building, was definitely too close to the action here. We appreciate him for sharing his experience with us.*

THE BIGGEST HONOR I'VE EVER HAD was bestowed on me about two weeks later. I was one of six appraisers assigned to help the Governor's bombing task force and the Federal Emergency Management Agency (FEMA) organize a property damage assessment. We had to provide them with information on commercial structures around the Murrah building and surrounding areas. We visited buildings, talked with business owners and took pictures.

(continued on inside page)

way through the upper floors – I could see DAYLIGHT coming through the building!

The paramedics and firemen were already at work. [How could they move so quickly? They were there by the time we got down to the street!] Gurney crews were transporting bodies to ambulances. Injured were propped up everywhere.

An old man, with clothes covered in blood, was moaning and moving, obviously alive. Another man, so close I could have touched him, didn't look too bad but he never once moved. I watched his eyelids and his chest for movement. He never even twitched.

Whew! This was no place for non-medical personnel. I was in the way. My immediate shock had given way to a strong nausea. I made my way back to the county building where I learned that we had been released and encouraged to leave the area.

With all of the media around, there could be no doubt that Kathy was aware and worried. I made my way to the P&P office where everyone looked at me as if seeing a ghost. Then the questions started.

Still in shock, I guess, for several days, I tried to keep myself busy and my mind off the explosion, but I was drawn to the television set. Even after seeing all the turmoil in person and on TV, I could not comprehend the magnitude of the catastrophe. Why, why, WHY would anyone do this??

By Monday, we had to go back. It was hard to get to the parking garage, since all normal routes were blocked off. A horrible odor permeated the area; one like nothing I had ever experienced before. It resembled a decaying animal carcass, but this was clearly not the stockyards.

Not much work was accomplished this day. Some were afraid to return to the building. Everyone needed to talk it out. It was good therapy, so sharing feelings assumed priority.

IN THE UNITED STATES COURT OF APPEALS
FOR THE TENTH CIRCUIT

TIMOTHY JAMES McVEIGH,

    Petitioner-Defendant,

v.

                                    Case No. 96-_____
                                    (Case No. 96-CR-68-M below)

HONORABLE RICHARD P. MATSCH,

    Respondent.

PETITION FOR WRIT OF MANDAMUS OF PETITIONER-DEFENDANT, TIMOTHY JAMES McVEIGH AND BRIEF IN SUPPORT

MARCH 25, 1997

	Of Counsel
Stephen Jones, OBA #4805	Robert L. Wyatt, IV, OBA #13154
Robert Nigh, Jr., OBA #011686	Michael D. Roberts, OBA #13764
Richard Burr, FBA #407402	James L. Hankins, OBA #15506
Jeralyn E. Merritt, Esquire	Randall T. Coyne, OBA #549013
Cheryl A. Ramsey, OBA #7403	Amber McLaughlin, TBA #1374098
Christopher L. Tritico, TBA #20232050	Robert J. Warren, OBA #16123
	Mandy Welch, TBA #21125380
	Holly Hillerman, OBA #017055

RECEIVED
United States Court of Appeals
Tenth Circuit

MAR 25 1997

PATRICK FISHER
Clerk

TABLE OF CONTENTS

PAGE NO.

OVERVIEW 1

I. INTRODUCTION 4

STATEMENT OF MATERIAL FACTS 9

II. PHYSICAL AND POLITICAL MAGNITUDE OF THE DESTRUCTION OF THE ALFRED P. MURRAH BUILDING 9

    A. Immediate Effects of the Explosion 9

    B. The Response of the Federal Government 13

        1. The Government's Immediate Response to the Bombing 14

            a. Mobilization 14

            b. Evidence From Public Sources of Government Use of Intelligence Networks With Foreign Nations in the Investigation of the Alfred P. Murrah Building Bombing 16

            c. CIA and NSA Investigation Protocol 17

        2. Evidence of the International Scope of the Investigation and the Involvement of Organs of State Intelligence in Several U.S. Domestic Bombing Cases Including the Alfred P. Murrah Building 21

        3. The Investigative Focus Upon Foreign Terrorists 24

III. THE ARREST OF TIMOTHY McVEIGH 28

IV. THE GRAND JURY RETURNS THE INDICTMENT OF "OTHERS UNKNOWN" 29

V.	THE "OTHERS UNKNOWN" TO THE GRAND JURY		32
	A.	Elliott's Body Shop	32
	B.	Oklahoma City Eyewitnesses	34
	C.	Jeff Davis	35
	D.	Frederick Schlender	37
	E.	Legal Significance of the Existence of "Others Unknown"	38
VI.	PRIOR WARNING, ATF INFORMANTS, AND POSSIBLE "OTHERS UNKNOWN"		38
	A.	Elohim City	38
	B.	Dennis Mahon, Andreas Strassmeir and Carol Howe	44
		1. Dennis Mahon	44
		2. Andreas Strassmeir	47
		3. Carol Howe and the Bureau of Alcohol, Tobacco and Firearms	53
VII.	BEYOND ELOHIM CITY		79
	A.	Suspect I, Posse Comitatus, and Iraq	79
		1. Posse Comitatus	79
	B.	Saudi Report Concerning Iraq	81
	C.	FBI Special Agent Kevin Foust	82
		2. State Sponsorship Precedent	85
	D.	Israelis Present at the Bomb Site	89
	E.	A Subject of the Investigation in the Philippines	91

ii

VIII.	PROCEDURAL HISTORY OF DISCOVERY REQUESTS	101
	A. Introduction	101
IX.	GOVERNMENT EVASION OF ITS DISCOVERY RESPONSIBILITIES	111
	A. The Government's Restrictive Definition of *Brady*	114
	B. Counsel for the Government are Powerless to Effect Disclosure of Discoverable Information from National Intelligence Agencies	128
X.	AUTHORITY	137
	A. Judge Matsch's Denial of Mr. McVeigh's Discovery Motions is Reviewable Upon Petition for Writ of Mandamus	137
	B. Federal Rule of Criminal Procedure 16 Entitles Mr. McVeigh to the Requested Discovery Material	138
	C. The District Court Abused its Discretion by Denying Mr. McVeigh's Repeated Requests for *Brady* Material	142
	D. Standard for Guidance in Search	144
	E. Because the Material Sought by Mr. McVeigh is Material Both to Guilt and Punishment, the District Court's Abuse of Discretion Jeopardizes Both Stages of Mr. McVeigh's Capital Trial	146
X.	SPECIFIC RELIEF REQUESTED	152
	CERTIFICATE OF HAND DELIVERY	154

IN THE UNITED STATES COURT OF APPEALS
FOR THE TENTH CIRCUIT

TIMOTHY JAMES McVEIGH,

    Petitioner-Defendant,

v.

HONORABLE RICHARD P. MATSCH,

    Respondent.

Case No. 96-_____
(Case No. 96-CR-68-M below)

PETITION FOR WRIT OF MANDAMUS OF PETITIONER-DEFENDANT, TIMOTHY JAMES McVEIGH AND BRIEF IN SUPPORT

COMES NOW the Petitioner, Timothy James McVeigh, by and through the undersigned counsel, and moves this Court to:

1. Assume jurisdiction in this matter and issue a Writ of Mandamus to the respondent trial judge directing the respondent to enter the appropriate orders specifically requested herein; and

2. Issue a stay of the proceedings below pending resolution of this Petition in this Court or, in the alternative, allow jury selection to proceed on schedule, March 31, 1997, but stay the taking of evidence in the court below pending this Court's resolution of the Petition.

OVERVIEW

The McVeigh defense, based upon the material provided to it, suggests the following hypothesis: A foreign power, probably Iraq, but not excluding the possibility of another foreign state, planned a terrorist attack(s) in the United States and that one of those targets was the Alfred P. Murrah Building in Oklahoma City. The Murrah Building was chosen either because of lack of security (i.e. it was a "soft target"), or because of available resources such as Iraqi POW's who had been admitted into the United States were located in Oklahoma City, or possibly because the location of the building was important to American neo-Nazis such as those individuals who supported Richard Snell who was executed in Arkansas on April 19, 1995.

The plan was arranged for a Middle Eastern bombing engineer to engineer the bomb in such a way that it could be carefully transported and successfully detonated. There is no reported incident of neo-Nazis or extreme right-wing militants in this country exploding any bomb of any significant size let alone one to bring down a nine (9) story federal building and kill 168 persons. In fact, not even members of the left-wing militant groups such as the Weatherman were ever able to accomplish anything of this magnitude.

This terrorist attack was "contracted out" to persons whose organization and ideology was friendly to policies of the foreign power and included dislike and hatred of the United States government itself, and possibly included was a desire for revenge against the United States, with possible anti-black and anti-semitic overtones. Because Iraq had tried a similar approach in 1990, but had been thwarted by Syrian intelligence information given to the United States, this time the information was passed through an Iraqi intelligence base in the Philippines.

Operating out of the Philippines as a base, the state-sponspored terrorists, with the Murrah Building already chosen as the target, enlisted the support and assistance of members of the Radical American Right. The defense believes the evidence suggests that American neo-Nazis were chosen to carry out the bombing of the Murrah Building because of a shared ideological bent of hatred against the American government. It is possible that those who carried out the bombing were unaware of the true sponsor.

The evidence collected by the defense suggests that the desired ideology was found by the state-sponsored terrorists in Elohim City, Oklahoma, a small compound near Muldrow, Oklahoma, consisting of between 25 and 30 families and described as a terrorist organization which preaches white supremacy, polygamy and overthrow of the government. Elohim City was a haven for former members of The Covenant, The Sword and the Arm of the Lord ("CSA"), another extremist organization that had been raided by the federal government on April 19, 1995, exactly ten years to the day prior to the Oklahoma City bombing. One member of CSA turned on the organization and testified in court at the trial of Richard Snell and others who were charged in Arkansas with sedition in that they conspired to destroy the Alfred P. Murrah Building in Oklahoma City with a rocket launcher in the early 1980's. Snell was convicted on unrelated capital charges and sentenced to death in Arkansas. He was executed the day of the Oklahoma City bombing--April 19, 1995--and is buried at Elohim City. It is from this group of people that the defense believes that the evidence suggests foreign, state-sponsored terrorists groomed the most radical persons associated with Elohim City and extracted monumental revenge against the federal government by destroying the Murrah Building on the day of Richard Snell's execution and the anniversary date of federal raid.

But the defense hypothesis also entails evidence, very strong evidence, that the federal government, through the Bureau of Alcohol, Tobacco & Firearms, had an informant in Elohim City, an informant who warned federal law enforcement prior to April 19, 1995, that former residents, including the former chief of security, of Elohim City were planning to "target for destruction" federal buildings in Oklahoma, including the Alfred P. Murrah Building. The defense believes this scenario is true, that is is eerily similar to the World Trade Center bombing where the FBI had an informant infiltrate the terrorist group but failed to stop that criminal act, and that, absent judicial intervention, information concerning these matters in the possession of the federal government will be forever buried.

The defense for Mr. McVeigh is not engaged in a fishing expedition. As the information set forth in this Petition demonstrates, the McVeigh defense, using resources provided to it by the district court, has conducted a wide-ranging and increasingly narrow focused investigation. But without subpoena power, without the right to take depositions, and without access to national intelligence information, the McVeigh defense can go no further.

I. INTRODUCTION.

The Government of the United States is hiding from the defense and the trial court evidence and information that the government had a prior warning that the Alfred P. Murrah Federal Building in Oklahoma City (and possibly federal property in Tulsa) was very likely a target of a terrorist attack on or about April 19, 1995. This information came to the government from a variety of sources, including Carol Howe, a paid ATF informant for about 6 months, who infiltrated Elohim City and the Christian Identity Movement and who provided specific information prior to April 19, 1995, that an illegal German national, the grandson of one of the founders of the German Nazi Party, proposed to bomb federal buildings and installations and engage in mass murder. Information also came to the government through foreign intelligence services in the Middle East and from the government's own assets that an attack was being planned on the "heartland" of America.

The government responded to part of these warnings by conducting a superficial security examination of the federal building complex in Oklahoma City on the early morning hours of April 19, 1995.[1] But rather than admit that it acted, no matter how superficially or limited on this information, the government has chosen to deny, and maybe even withholding from the chief prosecutor, evidence of this prior warning from an informant it deemed reliable because she regularly passed polygraph tests. The defense has repeatedly sought by letter, motion, argument in chambers and in open court, detailed information which it knows the government has.

The district court has repeatedly advised the government, both in published opinions and in judicial statements, of the government's duty. The government has claimed it understood its duty. We submit the government has affirmatively misled the district court

---

[1] Several witnesses interviewed by ABC News *20/20*, including an attorney and a private process server, among others, claim to have seen law enforcement using sniffer dogs, as well as a "bomb disposal" or "bomb squad" unit truck near the Murrah Building in the early morning hours of April 19, 1995, shortly before the bombing. *See* attached Exhibit "D" (transcript of ABC News *20/20* broadcast, January 17, 1997). Oklahoma County Sheriff J.D. Sharp denied the presence of the Oklahoma County bomb squad truck, telling local media on the record that the county bomb truck was ten miles away from downtown and nowhere near the country courthouse. *See* attached Exhibit "E." However, the County Sheriff's office later stated that the bomb squad unit was in fact in downtown Oklahoma City the morning of the bombing for a routine training exercise. *See* attached Exhibit "H." This information was confirmed to the defense through discovery. *See* Exhibits "J" and "K." The presence of the bomb squad truck was commented on by several other persons and mentioned in a business newsletter of one downtown Oklahoma City business. *See* attached Exhibit "F"; ; *see also* Exhibit "G" (news account of witness in Oklahoma City who recalled that, "The day was fine, everything was normal when I arrived at 7:45 to begin my day at 8:00 a.m., but as I walked through my building's parking lot, I remember seeing a bomb squad.")

```
===============================================================
                  OKLAHOMA CITY POLICE DEPARTMENT
                           CRIME REPORT
===============================================================
Reported Date: 06/03/95    Time: 03:36
Code: AP1 MC               Type: APC              Case: 95-052264
Occurrence Date: 06/03/95-                        Rpts: 210401
Status:                    By: SATURDAY -
Location: NW. 8TH ST. /N. BLACKWELDER AV. , OK    Time: 03:36-
                                                  ID:   10
===============================================================
IMPOUNDED:          License: QHV255     State: OK  Type: A  Expires: 95
  Year: 86   Make: CADILLAC   Model: DEVILLE   Style: 4DR   Color: BRO
  Identifiers:
  Vin: 1G6CD6983G4327317
                            Disposition: ARROW #202249
=============================== SUBJECTS/ARRESTS ===============
ARRESTED:      ALHUSSAINI HUSSAIN H
  2116 NW. 32ND ST., OK                DOB: 09/09/65  Race: A  Sex: M
  Apt:       State: OK  Zip: 73112
  PCB:                         Hair: BLK  Eye: BRO   Phone: 405 557-0329   Adu/Juv: A
  Business Name: WESTERN SIZZLIN        Hgt: 508  Wgt: 150         Bld:
  5825 NW. 23RD ST.,
  OKLAHOMA CIT, OK                                    Phone: 405 946-1997

  Driver License: 018787609
  CII:              FBI:           OK   Social Security: (018787609)
                                        Booking Number:
=================== CRIME ANALYSIS ELEMENTS ====================
Age: 29
=========================== PROPERTY ===========================
 Number: 0001   Evid/Cust: C    Property Type: X   Cat: D   Article: SDL
Brand:          Model:          Serial: 018787609       Group Serial:
Color: APC                                Qty:          Value:
=========================== NARRATIVE ==========================
              WILL ROGERS DIVISION TELEPHONE REPORT

PROPERTY ROOM TAG #: 95-052264
-----------------------------------------------------------
 CUST    TYPE    CAT
 CODE    CODE    CODE    ARTICLE           BRAND/MAKE
                                           MODEL/NAME        QTY/VALUE
-----------------------------------------------------------
  E/C      X      D      OKLAHOMA DRIVERS LICENSE
                         #018787609
                                                                1

NOTES:

AR-ALHUSSAINI
================================================================
           S t a n d a r d   T r a i l e r  -  F i r s t   P a g e
================================================================
Reporting Officer: GAYMON, RODER   Number: 000768   Date: 06/03/95
Typed by: DDOE/S
```

INTERNATIONAL CRIMINAL POLICE ORGANIZATION
INTERPOL
U.S. NATIONAL CENTRAL BUREAU

U.S. DEPARTMENT OF JUSTICE   TELEPHONE NO: 202-616-9000
INTERPOL - USNCB   TELEFAX NO: 202-616-8400
WASHINGTON, DC 20530   NLETS ORI: DCINTER00

****

ROUTINE   PAGES TRANSMITTED (TOTAL): 3
DATE: 13 SEP 95   b7(C)

FROM: ████████████ SPECIAL AGENT, ATF INTERPOL REPRESENTATIVE
OUR REF:

****
TO: CHIEF, EXPLOSIVES DIVISION
ORGANIZATION: BUREAU OF ATF, HQ'S, WASHINGTON, D.C., ATTENTION
SAC, EXPLOSIVES TECHNOLOGY BRANCH
FAX NR: (202) ████████   PHONE NR: (202) ████████
YOUR REF: N/A   b2
_____

TO: UNIT CHIEF, EXPLOSIVES/BOMB DATA CENTER, FBI LABORATORY
ORGANIZATION: WASHINGTON, D.C.
FAX NR: (202) ████████   PHONE NR: (202) ████████
YOUR REF: N/A
****

REGARDING: OKLAHOMA CITY BOMBING
****

MESSAGE/INSTRUCTION: THE ATTACHED MESSAGE AND EXPLOSIVE DEVISE
SKETCH FROM THE ████████████ IS FOR YOUR INFORMATION AND
DISSEMINATION AS DEEMED NECESSARY. NO RESPONSE IS REQUIRED.

REGARDS.
END.

IN ANY REPLY, PLEASE QUOTE: 95-04-03501/████

ATTACHMENTS: MESSAGE AND EXPLOSIVE DEVISE SKETCH FROM THE
████████████

b7(D)

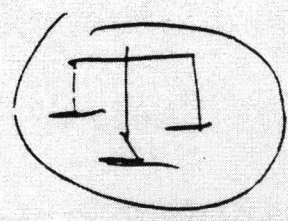

REWARD OF UP TO $2 MILLION

The Department of Justice is offering up to $2 million for information leading to the arrest and conviction of the terrorist criminals responsible for the bombing of the nine-story Alfred P. Murrah Federal Building in Oklahoma City on April 19, 1995. Two suspects are being sought in connection with this bombing. ~~They are:~~

xxxxxxxxxxx
   X
xxxxxxxxxxx

JOHN DOE 1

Description

Build: Medium
Height: 5'10"-5'10'
Weight: About 180-185 pounds
Hair: Brown, crewcut
Other: He is right-handed.

xxxxxxxxxxx
   X
xxxxxxxxxxx

JOHN DOE 2

Description

Build: Medium
Height: 5'9"-10'
Weight: 175-180 pounds
Hair: Brown
Other: Tatoo visible on his left arm below his tee-shirt. He is a possible smoker.

Both of these men should be considered armed and extremely dangerous. Citizens should not, therefore, attempt to take any action against them.

Anyone with information about these two men should provide it immediately to the nearest FBI office. Outside the United

U. S. Department of Justice — Translation
INTERPOL

===

Language: FRENCH   28 APRIL 1995   FAX

From: INTERPOL ▮

To: INTERPOL WASHINGTON

IMMEDIATE

BCN 5200/AC6/SR/PAY/3442   b7(C)   b7(D)

REFERENCE: GT/MRB/GI

FURTHER TO THE FILE CITED IN REFERENCE, AND MESSAGE BCN NR. 5095/AC6/3391/ST/FEN OF 26 APRIL 1995, CONCERNING THE PRESUMED AUTHOR OF THE ATTACK COMMITTED ON 19 APRIL 1995 IN OKLAHOMA CITY, AND WHO IS THE SUBJECT OF COMPOSITE SKETCH NR. TWO CIRCULATED BY THE F.B.I. - [b7(D) ▮▮▮▮▮▮▮▮▮▮▮▮▮▮▮▮▮] BECAUSE OF THE CIRCULATION CONCERNING THIS PERSON ON THE NATIONAL TERRITORY, PLEASE KEEP US INFORMED OF THE RESULTS OF THE INQUIRIES REQUESTED CONCERNING HIM.

THANKS FOR YOUR COOPERATION. END

INTERPOL ▮   Translator: ▮

                                        Date: 28 Apr 95

Who?

CRITICAL URGENT   b2 b7(C) b7(D)

FROM: INTERPOL WASHINGTON

TO: SECRETARY GENERAL, INTERPOL
ATTN: ████████/ANTI-TERRORISM GROUP

INFO: ████████
YOUR REF: IP/035/95/26-5 DATED 5 MAY 95

OUR REF: ████████
YOUR REF: DII/SD1/95/T612/TE-90/KT/ALK

REGARDING: UPDATE OF OKLAHOMA BOMBING TO INCLUDE NEW COMPOSITE SKETCH FOR "JOHN DOE" SUSPECT #2.

MESSAGE/INSTRUCTION: AS OF 05 MAY 1995, 167 BODIES HAVE BEEN RECOVERED FROM THE BOMBING SITE. TWO (2) INDIVIDUALS STILL REMAIN MISSING. OVER 500 INDIVIDUALS WERE TREATED FOR INJURIES CAUSED BY THE BLAST. RESCUE EFFORTS WERE CANCELLED DUE TO THE INSTABILITY OF THE STRUCTURE. IT IS NOW BELIEVED THAT THE EXPLOSIVES MIXTURE (AMMONIA NITRATE AND FUEL OIL) MAY HAVE WEIGHED AS MUCH AS 4,900 POUNDS. EVIDENCE CONTINUES TO BE GATHERED IN THIS BOMBING INVESTIGATION.

AS YOU ARE AWARE, BOMBING SUSPECT "JOHN DOE" #1 HAS BEEN ARRESTED AND IS IN CUSTODY. BOMBING SUSPECT "JOHN DOE" #2 IS STILL AT LARGE. A MASSIVE EFFORT IS BEING MADE TO LOCATE HIM. A THIRD COMPOSITE WAS RECENTLY MADE OF "JOHN DOE" SUSPECT #2. THE COMPOSITE IS A SIDE VIEW IMAGE OF HIM. HE IS DESCRIBED AS A WHITE MALE, LATE 20'S TO EARLY 30'S, MEDIUM BUILD, BETWEEN 5'9" AND 5'10", 175 TO 185 POUNDS, DARK HAIR WORN COMBED STRAIGHT BACK AND HAS A TATTOO ON HIS LEFT ARM BELOW HIS TEE-SHIRT SLEEVE. HE MAY ALSO BE A POSSIBLE SMOKER.

THEREFORE, AND FOR THE SAKE OF UNIFORMITY, IT IS REQUESTED THAT THE SG DIFFUSE THIS MESSAGE TO ALL MEMBER COUNTRIES AND PROVIDE THEM WITH THE ATTACHED COMPOSITE SKETCHES OF "JOHN DOE" SUSPECT #2 FOR TRANSMITTAL TO ALL APPROPRIATE REGIONAL ZONES. THIS IS A NEW COMPOSITE SKETCH OF "JOHN DOE" #2.

THE USNCB WOULD LIKE TO TAKE THIS OPPORTUNITY TO THANK THE SG AND ALL MEMBER COUNTRIES FOR THEIR EFFORTS, VIGILANCE, AND CONCERN IN THIS MATTER.

ADMINISTRATIVE:
BY SEPARATE FACSIMILE, THE SG WILL BE PROVIDED WITH NEW SKETCH FOR JOHN DOE SUSPECT #2 FOR DISTRIBUTION TO APPROPRIATE REGIONAL ZONES.
REGARDS.

IN ANY REPLY, PLEASE QUOTE:
FOR POLICE COURT/USE ONLY
INTERPOL WASHINGTON

U.S. Department of Justice

Federal Bureau of Investigation

Washington, D.C. 20535

FOR IMMEDIATE RELEASE
THURSDAY, APRIL 20, 1995

FBI, OKLAHOMA CITY:
(405) 232-8925

STATEMENT BY FBI SPECIAL AGENT IN CHARGE WELDON L. KENNEDY

Investigators have identified a vehicle that was used in connection with yesterday's attack on the Federal Building in Oklahoma City. Further investigation has determined that two white males were associated with that vehicle.

As a result, arrest warrants will be sought for these two males. Their exact identities are not presently known. Thus, the arrest warrants will be for two men, each identified as "John Doe."

The first man is medium build. He is further described as about 5'10"-5'11" tall, weighing about 180-185 pounds, with a light brown crewcut, and he is right-handed.

The second man is also medium build. He is further described as 5'9"-5'10" tall, weighing about 175-180 pounds, with brown hair, and a tattoo visible on his left arm below his tee-shirt sleeve. He is possibly a smoker.

Composite sketches of these two men have been prepared. We have copies here for everyone.

Both of these men should be considered armed and extremely dangerous. Citizens should not, therefore, attempt to take any action against them.

Anyone with information about these two men should provide it immediately to the nearest FBI office. They can also call phone banks we have specially established to receive their information. We urge people with information to call 1-(800) 905-1514. That number will be effective starting at 5:00 P.M. Eastern Daylight Time.

This information has been communicated to law enforcement at all levels -- domestic and international.

#####

Affidavit of Richard A. Sinnett Regarding The Bombing Of The Alfred P. Murrah Federal Building

State of Kansas   )
) SS:
County of Kingman   )

I, affiant herein, being of legal age and having been duly sworn, does hereby state as follows:

1). That I reside at 1307 Veach Street, City of Kingman, County of Kingman, Kansas.

2). That I received a phone call on July 25, 1997, from a person identifying himself as being with The Oklahoma County District Attorney's Office.

3). That this person told me that there was a subpoena issued to me from The Oklahoma County Grand Jury to testify before the Grand Jury regarding the bombing of the Alfred P. Murrah Federal Building in Oklahoma City.

4). That this person asked me if I would honor my supboena to appear by receiving service through the mail instead of having the subpoena served to me in person.

5). That I told this person that I would honor the subpoena and appear to testify by being served through the mail.

6). That this person made the statement to me that he "did not know why he was having to do this, that Charles Key was pushing this and that nothing would come of it and that it was a waste of time."

FURTHER, AFFIANT SAYETH NOT:

Richard A. Sinnett

Man: Brother Involved in Ok. Bombing

AP 21-Jan-1998 12:41 EST   REF5298

Copyright 1998. The Associated Press. All Rights Reserved.

The information contained in the AP news report may not be published, broadcast, rewritten or otherwise distributed without the prior written authority of The Associated Press.

WILMINGTON, Ohio (AP) -- A man sentenced for a videotaped shootout with police says he believes his brother, who is being looked at by agents for possible links to the Oklahoma City bombing, was involved in such an attack.

Cheyne Kehoe made the comment about older brother Chevie on Tuesday after he was sentenced to 24 1/2 years in prison.

"At this point, I do have knowledge of my brother's involvement in the bombing of a federal building," Cheyne Kehoe said in response to a reporter's question.

He refused to elaborate, saying he feared his brother. Federal investigators will interview Cheyne Kehoe as soon as possible, Ted Jackson, agent in charge of the FBI's Cincinnati office, said today. Chevie Kehoe, described as a white supremacist, faces both a trial in the shootout and federal charges in Arkansas, where he and two other men are accused of planning a revolt against the U.S. government. Those charges are not related to the Oklahoma City bombing. He pleaded innocent to those charges today in Little Rock and a trial was set for March 2.

Last week, FBI spokesman Ray Lauer said the agency was investigating claims by a former Spokane, Wash., motel manager who said Chevie Kehoe may have known in advance of Timothy McVeigh's plans to bomb the Oklahoma City federal building.

The FBI is trying to determine the credibility of the manager, who said Chevie Kehoe showed up at the motel on April 19, 1995, about 45 minutes before the bombing, and said he wanted to watch CNN. He reportedly was ecstatic when a news bulletin reported the blast.

The Spokesman Review newspaper in Spokane reported Friday that the motel manager quoted Kehoe as saying "it was about time." "Days before that, he had mentioned to me that there's going to be something happening on the 19th and it's going to wake people up," the manager told the newspaper on condition of anonymity.

Jeffrey Hoskins, Cheyne Kehoe's attorney, said his client told him at their first meeting that Chevie Kehoe was involved in a bombing. He said Cheyne Kehoe did not tell prosecutors and had not talked with federal agents about it.

Jerry McHenry, Chevie Kehoe's court-appointed attorney, said his client told him Friday that the reports were "outrageous accusations." "I don't put any stock in it at all," McHenry said Tuesday. "It's just another example of a desperate young man trying to help himself at the expense of his brother."

Cheyne Kehoe, 21, was convicted Jan. 12 on charges of attempted murder, felonious assault and carrying a concealed weapon for his part in a Feb. 15 gunfight that was videotaped by a dashboard-mounted camera in a state trooper's cruiser.

The officers escaped injury.

Chevie Kehoe, 24, is to stand trial Feb. 23 on similar charges. Chevie Kehoe had been held in the Warren County Jail at nearby Lebanon, but authorities there disclosed today that they had transferred him to Greene County on Dec. 30 because of allegations he was planning an escape.

His public defender, Kort Gatterdam, questioned today why Warren County authorities had not charged him with anything.

Cheyne Kehoe's lawyers said they will appeal his sentence.

"I'm very disappointed. I believe it's a sentence that was undue for the actions taken that day," Cheyne Kehoe said.

Judge William McCracken said that Cheyne Kehoe, who testified that he fired at a trooper and a deputy sheriff in self-defense, deserved the stiff sentence.

"The defendant has shown no remorse," the judge said. "The statements given by the defendant were self-serving."

☐

DAMO-ODS								19 Apr 95

MEMORANDUM FOR RECORD

SUBJECT: Linguist Support for the Federal Bureau of Investigation (FBI)

1. On 19 Apr 95, the FBI requested the use of ten linguists from the Document Exploitation Branch of the Defense Intelligence Agency (DIA). Support will be for a period of 30 days.

2. The linguists are required for immediate use in FBI field offices involved in the investigation of the 19 April bombing of the Federal building in Oklahoma City.

3. The Linguists will not participate in any law enforcement activities. Support will not involve any real time monitoring of electronic surveillance; only translation of tapes and documents.

4. The FBI will reimburse DoD pursuant to the provisions of the Economy Act.

5. This action was coordinated with SAGC (MAJ Strong), ASA IL&E (LTC Wells), and OSD Executive Assistant (LTC Godek).

6. The Secretary of the Army provided approval of this mission during a meeting with the Director of Military Support (DOMS).

						PLEZ A. JENKINS
						MAJ, GS
						Action Officer

DECISION

APPROVAL _____
DISAPPROVAL _____
OTHER _____

DEPARTMENT OF THE ARMY
HEADQUARTERS, FORCES COMMAND
FORT MCPHERSON, GEORGIA 30330-5000

AFOP-OC

22 April 1995

MEMORANDUM FOR RECORD

SUBJECT: Department of Defense (DoD) Linguist Support to the Federal Bureau of Investigation (FBI) in the Oklahoma City (OKC) Bomb Incident

1. As a result of the arrest of a domestic suspect in the OKC incident, the FBI was contacted by this office to determine if the DoD Arabic linguists were still required. Ms. Debbie Mauchas stated that they were being used to monitor wire taps of radical fundamentalist Islamic organizations in an effort to protect the President from possible attack during his attendance of the memorial service in OKC on Sunday, 23 April. She was informed that they were not provided for that purpose and that DoD soldiers are prohibited by the Posse Comitatus Act, Executive Order 12333, and DoDD 3025.1 from directly participating in law enforcement with civilian law enforcement agencies (LEA), to include real-time electronic monitoring. They are, however, excepted from these restrictions under DoD 5525.5 encl 4, para A.2.(e)(6) in order to protect the President.

2. This office contacted MAJ Jenkins at the Director of Military Support (DOMS) to inform him of the change in the linguist's mission. He stated that the original memorandum covering the mission could not be deviated from unless the FBI contacted the Secretary of the Army (SECARMY) and the Secretary of Defense (SECDEF).

3. This office contacted Mr. Richard Simmons of the FBI Special Operations Command Center at 211739ZApr95 and was informed that hte Director of the FBI, Mr. Free, had spoken directly with the SECDEF, Mr. Perry, and had agreed upon the change of mission for the linguists. This office contacted MAJ Jenkins to inform him of the change.

4. Direct questions concerning this matter to the undersigned at DSN 367-5872, COMM (404) 669-5872.

5. Coor SJA Comm'n.

MARK E. AUSTIN
CPT, EN
FORSCOM G3, MSCA

```
============================ Standard ████████ R e p o r t ===============
Reported Date: 07/03/95   Time: 03:52           Case: ████████   Page: █
Code: 21-1278 SS          Crime: WPN UNLAW INT   Class:
Occurrence Date: 07/03/95-   Day: MONDAY         -              Time: 03:52-
Status: AS ASSIGNED                  Closing Officer: 000183 EINHORN JAY
Location: 2814 NW. 41ST ST., OK                                 RD: 280
========================== INVOLVED PERSONS ==================================
INV PERS:    DAVE SWANSON                 DOB:            Race: W   Sex: M
   Apt:          State:      Zip:             Phone:
   POB:          Hair:       Eye:    Hgt:       Wgt:      Adu/Juv: A   Bld:
Business Name: F.B.I
   50 PENN PLACE           SUIT 1600
   OKLA CITY, OK 73116                                 Phone: 405 842-7471

INV PERS:    STRICKLAND JAMES             DOB:            Race: W   Sex: M
   Apt:          State:      Zip:             Phone:
   POB:          Hair:       Eye:    Hgt:       Wgt:      Adu/Juv: A   Bld:
Business Name: F.B.I
   50 PENN PLACE SUIT 1600
   OKLA CITY, OK 73116                                 Phone: 405 842-7471
=============================== NARRATIVE ===================================
   FOLLOW UP INVESTIGATION

CHARGE: ASSAULT WITH A DANGEROUS WEAPON 21-645

INITIAL CHARGE: 21-1278

SUSPECT: KHALIL, SAMIR SHARIF PM 1-6-42 BRO,BRO,507,150 SSN 448543465
         2104 NW 32 STREET, OKLA CITY 73112 SDL # 009225155

VICTIM : TWILLEY, SHARON KAY WF 4/24/60  (405) 946-9353
         2814 NW 41 STREET, OKLA CITY, OKLA 73112

WITNESS: MOORE, GLENN  WM 2-5-61
         2812 NW 41 STREET, OKLA CITY, OKLA (405) 947-8784

     ON 7-5-95 THIS DETECTIVE RECEIVED AN ASSIGNMENT FROM LT. ROBERT
HOLT TO CONDUCT A FOLLOW UP INVESTIGATION REGARDING AN ASSAULT WITH A
DANGEROUS WEAPON. THE FOLLOWING FACTS WERE OBTAINED THROUGH THIS
DETECTIVES INVESTIGATION AND REPORTS BY OTHER OFFICERS.

INTERVIEW WITH SHARON TWILLEY

     ON 7-5-95 I CALLED SHARON TWILLEY WHO ADVISED ME THAT OFFICER TYRA
NASH CAME OUT TO HER RESIDENCE AND TOOK A REPORT ABOUT THE POSSIBLE
SUSPECT SHOOTING IN HER RESIDENCE WHICH SHE RENTS FROM THE SUSPECT.

     SHARON TWILLEY STATED SHE WAS ASLEEP ON 7-3-95 AT APPROX 03:52 AM
WHEN SHE HEARD GUN SHOTS & ROLLED OUT OF BED AND CALLED 911 FROM THE
========================= Standard Trailer - First Page =====================
Reporting Officer: EINHORN JAY    Number: 000183   Date: 07/06/95  Time: 10:05
     Typed by: EINHORN            Number: 183      Date: 07/06/95  Time: 10:05
Approving Officer:
```

Standard Continuation Page

Reported Date: 07/03/95   Time: 03:52   Case: [redacted]   Page: 2
Code: 21-1278 SS   Crime: WPN UNLAW INT   Class: [redacted]

FLOOR.

SHARON TWILLEY STATED THAT HER NEXT DOOR NEIGHBOR GLEN MOORE HEARD SOME SHOTS FIRED & LOOKED OUT THE WINDOW & SAW THE SUSPECT RUN FROM HER RESIDENCE. SHARON STATED HE JUMPED INTO A WHITE TOYOTA PICK UP AND LEFT.

TWILLEY WAS ASKED HOW MOORE KNEW IT WAS THE LISTED SUSPECT. TWILLEY ADVISED SHE HAD ONLY LIVED THEIR FOR ONE YEAR. MOORE HAD LIVED IN HIS HOUSE FOR OVER TWO. MOORE RECOGNIZED THE SUSPECT AS THE LANDLORD WHO RENTED THE HOUSE OUT PRIOR TO TWILLEY LIVING THERE & KNEW HIM HAVING A WHITE TOYOTA PICK UP & HE SAID THAT WAS HIM MEANING THE SUSPECT.

TWILLEY STATED SHE SPOKE WITH MOORE THE EVENING OF 7-5-95. MOORE TOLD HER HE WAS NOW BEING FOLLOWED FOR BEING INVOLVED WITH TWILLEY'S CASE & DID NOT WANT TO BE INVOLVED NY FURTHER & REFUSED TO CALL THIS DETECTIVE.

TWILLEY STATED SHE WORKED FOR THE SUSPECT UNTIL AFTER THE BOMBING OF THE MURRAH BUILDING WHEN THE F.B.I. CAME OUT & QUESTIONED HER ABOUT THE SUSPECTS ACTIVITY. THE NEXT DAY SHE WAS FIRED. SINCE THAT TIME THE SUSPECT HAS TRIED TO KICK HER OUT OF HIS RENT HOUSE. HE HAD REFUSED TO ACCEPT HER CHECK & HAD TAKEN HER TO DISTRICT COURT & THE JUDGE ORDERED HIM TO SERVE A 30 DAY NOTICE. TWILLEY STATED THAT SINCE THAT TIME HER RESIDENCE WAS BURGLARIZED AND THEN THIS INCIDENT OF THE SHOOTING TOOK PLACE. TWILLEY STATED THE F.B.I. HAD SPOKE WITH HER A FEW TIMES SINCE SHE WAS FIRED & THEN IT ALL STARTED. TWILLEY STATED KHALIL WAS FURIOUS WHEN HE FOUND OUT SHE HAD SPOKEN TO THE F.B.I.

TWILLEY STATED WHEN THE FEMALE OFFICER CAME OUT TO TAKE THE REPORT SHE WAS VERY RUDE & STATED NOTHING WAS GOING TO BE DONE. TWILLEY STATED SHE FELT VERY THREATENED BY KHALIL & BY WHAT NASH SAID SHE CALLED CHANNEL FOUR KFOR TV & SPOKE WITH BRAD EDWARDS ON 7-3-95. TWILLEY FURNISHED THIS DETECTIVE WITH PHOTOS WHICH SHE TOOK OF THE INSIDE OF THE RESIDENCE SHE RENTED FROM THE SUSPECT. PHOTOS WERE TAKEN OF A FRONT WINDOW, WALLS, CURTAINS & HER VEHICLE.

INTERVIEW WITH JAMES STRICKLAND

THIS DETECTIVE CALLED THE F.B.I. OFFICE & SPOKE WITH AGENT JAMES STRICKLAND. STRICKLAND ADVISED THAT AGENT DAVE SWANSON DID SPEAK TO TWILLEY IN REFERENCE TO KHALIL. STRICKLAND REQUESTED A COPY OF THE CRIME INCIDENT REPORT. THIS DETECTIVE FAXED A COPY TO THE ABOVE AGENT.

INTERVIEW WITH GLEN MOORE

ON 7-6-95 I CONTACTED GLENN MOORE AT HIS PLACE OF EMPLOYMENT. MOORE STATED ON THE MORNING OF 7-3-95 AT APPROX 3:30-4:00 HE HEARD GUN SHOTS. MOORE GOT UP & LOOKED OUT THE WINDOW AND SAW A DARK SKINNED MALE RUNNING FROM THE HOUSE. I ASKED HIM IF IT WAS MR. KHALIL. MOORE STATED I THINK IT WAS HIM, BUT I'M NOT SURE. IT LOOKED LIKE HIM BUT I'M NOT POSITIVE. HE WAS DRIVING THE SAME WHITE NISSAN PICK UP THAT HE DRIVES, BUT

Standard Trailer - Continuation

Reporting Officer: EINHORN JAY   Number: 000183   Date: 07/06/95   Time: 10:05
Typed by: EINHORN   Number: 183   Date: 07/06/95   Time: 10:05
Approving Officer: Number: Date: Time:

```
Standard Continuation Page
```

Reported Date: 07/03/95 Time: 03:52
Code: 21-1278 SS   Crime: WPN UNLAW INT   Case: 95-062979   Page:
Class:

I'M NOT SURE.

INTERVIEW WITH JAMIR KHALIL

ON 7-6-95 I CONTACTED THE LISTED SUSPECT AT HIS PLACE OF BUSINESS. I ADVISED HIM I WAS WORKING A COMPLAINT IN WHICH HE WAS LISTED AS THE SUSPECT. HE AGREED TO MEET WITH ME AT 14:00 HOURS TODAY AT OCPD FOR AN INTERVIEW.

ON 7-6-95 AT 1400 HRS I MET WITH MR. KHALIL AT OCPD. HE WAS ADVISED OF HIS RIGHT VIA MIRANDA. WAIVED HIS RIGHTS AND WAS QUESTIONED. KHALIL WAS ASKED WHERE HE WAS ON THE NIGHT OF 7-3-95 AT 0352. KHALIL STATED HE WAS HOME SLEEPING. I ASKED KHALIL WHERE HIS NISSAN PICK UP TRUCK WAS THAT NIGHT & HE STATED PARKED IN HIS DRIVEWAY & IT STILL WAS THERE WHEN I WOKE UP.

KHALIL STATED THAT HE EMPLOYED SHARON FOR 3-4-YEARS SHE WORKED LEASING HIS RENTAL PROPERTY. KHALIL STATED HE RENTS TO LOW INCOME FAMILIES. KHALIL WAS ASKED IF SHARON WAS FIRED A FEW DAYS AFTER THE BOMBING AT THE MURRAH BUILDING. KHALIL STATED YES. I TOLD HIM SHE WAS FIRED BECAUSE YOU FOUND OUT SHE TALKED TO FEDERAL AGENTS WHEN THEY ASKED ABOUT HIM....KHALIL STATED... "OH NO SIRE' SHE DIDN'T TALK TO THE FBI. I ADVISED HIM THAT I DIDN'T TELL YOU THAT IT WAS THE FBI.

THIS DETECTIVE CONTACTED ASST DA SHERRY TODD AND REVIEWED THE CASE WITH TODD. TODD VIEWED THE PHOTOS AND DETERMINED THAT THERE WAS INSUFFICIENT EVIDENCE TO PROSECUTE THE CASE & DECLINED.

DISPOSITION: DA DECLINED; VICTIM NOTIFIED.

```
============================================================================
                    Standard   Continuation   Page
============================================================================
Reported Date: 07/03/95   Time: 03:52            Case: 95-062979    Page: 2
Code: 21-1278 SS          Crime: WPN UNLAW INT   Class: 150300
```

=========================== PROPERTY ===
Item Number: 0001   Evid/Cust: C   Property Type: X   Cat: F   Article: AMMUNI
Brand: Model: Serial: Group Serial:
Descr: Qty: 1 Value:

=========================== NARRATIVE ==

RELATED CASE NUMBER: 95-062709

BODY OF REPORT:

ON 7-3-95, 3B12 RECEIVED A CALL TO THE LISTED ADDRESS IN REFERENCE TO SHOT'S
FIRED.

UPON ARRIVAL AT THE SCENE, I OBSERVED A BULLET HOLE IN THE VEHICLE PARKED IN
THE DRIVEWAY. THE BULLET HOLE WAS IN THE HOOD AND THE REAR WINDOW OF THE
VEHICLE WAS ALSO SHATTERED. I ALSO OBSERVED A BULLET HOLE IN THE NORTH WINDOW
OF THE RESIDENCE.

I SPOKE WITH THE RESIDENT, VI, WHO ADVISED SHE HEARD THREE-FOUR GUN SHOTS NEAR
HER HOME. VI ADVISED, HER NEIGHBOR TO THE EAST PHONED HER AND ADVISED HE SAW
THE PERSON AROUND HER HOUSE SHOOTING.

I SPOKE WITH THE NEIGHBOR, IP, WHO ADVISED HE HEARD SHOTS AND LOOKED OUT THE
WINDOW AND SAW AN IRANIAN LOOKING MAN RUNNING AWAY FROM VI'S HOUSE. IP SAW
THIS MALE GET INTO A WHITE, EXTENDED BED, TOYOTA PICKUP AND FLEE EASTBOUND FROM
THE RESIDENCE.

VI ADVISED THAT SHE BELIEVES IT IS HER LANDLORD, WHO IS AN IRANIAN MALE. HIS
NAME IS SAMIR KAHLIL HE RESIDES AT 2109 NW. 32. VI ADVISES, THAT THE LANDLORD
HAS NOT SERVED HER EVICTION PAPERS, BUT HE HAS BEEN TRYING TO GET HER TO MOVE.

VI STATES, SHE CANNOT MOVE RIGHT NOW BECAUSE SHE IS NOT FINANCIALLY ABLE AT THE
MOMENT, AND ALSO SHE DOESN'T HAVE ANYWHERE OR ANYONE TO MOVE IN WITH. VI
ADVISES THAT HER LANDLORD IS NOT ACCEPTING ANY RENT MONEY FROM HER.

THIS INCIDENT ALSO RELATED TO CASE #95-62709 BURGLARY II, IN WHICH THE SUSPECT
MAY HAVE ALSO BEEN THE LANDLORD.

END OF REPORT

```
----------------------------------------------------------------------------
              Standard  Trailer  -  Continuation                    [29]
----------------------------------------------------------------------------
Reporting Officer: NASH, TYARA D   Number: 000784   Date: 07/03/95   Time: 03:52
       Typed by: DE6244            Number: DE6244   Date: 07/03/95   Time: 19:41
Approving Officer: EA4352          Number: EA4352   Date: 07/10/95   Time: 15:02
```

LATIN AMERICAN NEWS SYNDICATE®
Box 781464
San Antonio, TX 78278
lans@txdirect.net

Breene, Robert G. Jr. (Curriculum Vitae)

HISTORY

1945-1947: Regular Officer, US Army; fighter pilot, ZI and Far East
1947-1950: Reg ofcr, US Air Force; experimental test pilot (ftrs), Wright Field
1953-1956: Reg ofcr, USAF; theoretical physicist, AFCRL; plt.
1956-1960: Vice President, Transportation Consultants, Inc. [Washington based engineering firm involved in transportation surveys and construction supervision in various Near East, Far East and South American countries.]
1956-1958: Radiation Specialist, Missiles and Spaces Vehicles Department, GE
1960-1980: President, Physical Studies, Inc. [Consulting firm carrying out basic and applied research in theoretical physics.]
1956-1965: Part time teaching various universities, e.g., Univ. Penna., Univ. Nevada.
1969-1971: Professor of Physics, West Virginia University
1971-1977: Owner and operator of 600-head cow-calf operation on 226,000 acres of Nevada desert
1980   : Visiting Scientist, Max Planck Institute, Munich, Germany.
1980-1997: Investigative reporter and writer on Latin American affairs for various periodicals and research organizations.
1996-   : Editor, Latin American News Syndicate

EDUCATION

B.S.   Military Science and Engineering, West Point, 1945
Ph.D.   Mathematical Physics, Ohio State University, 1953
        Air Tactical School, 1947
         Flight Test Performance Course, 1948

PUBLICATIONS

A. Books
The Shift and Shape of Spectral Lines. Pergamon Press. Oxford. 1961
Theories of Spectral Line Shape. Wiley-Interscience. New York. 1981
ORDEAL BY PERJURY: *The Persecution of John Hull, the Destruction of the Contras.* Faustian Press. 1989.
DRUGS AND TERRORISM IN LATIN AMERICA: *The Communist Connection.* Faustian Press. 1990.
Latin American Political Yearbook 1997. Transaction Publishers. Rutgers Univ. 1999.
Ibid 1998, 1999.
THE STRUCTURE OF HISTORY: *A Revision and Extension of Spenglerian Theory.* [To be published]
Wright's Georgia Brigade: First at Gettysburg. [TBP]
THE MIND OF AN ARMY AND AN EMPIRE: *Napoleon at Jena.* [TBP]

B. Articles
1953-1981: Fifty some articles in the scientific literature of six countries.
1981-   : Articles in various periodicals and dailies and in the organs of various research organizations.

LATIN AMERICAN NEWS SYNDICATE®
Box 781464
San Antonio, TX 78278
lans@txdirect.net

Vol.2　　　　Latin American Special Report, 22 Aug 96　　　　No.2

The Bombing of the Murrah Building in Oklahoma City

On 19 April 1995 the Alfred P. Murrah Building in Oklahoma City was substantially damaged by explosive charges. "Who" was responsible for the bombing and "Why" the bombing was carried out are questions which have produced extensive speculation of dubious value.[1] The "How," on the other hand, is worthy of, and appropriate for, specific consideration here.

The US Government is apparently still taking the position that the only demolition charge involved in the operation was the ANFO [ammonium nitrate-fuel oil] vehicle bomb. However, available experimental and theoretical evidence indicates that a vehicle bomb alone could not have done the structural damage suffered by the Murrah Bldg. Since some of the experimental evidence comes from South America, the subject is relevant to LANS objectives.

Experimental Evidence

Two of the structures to be considered as experimental examples are multi-storied and were constructed using reinforced-concrete vertical-strength members. The three buildings to be considered here were demonstrably subjected only to the blast effects of a vehicle bomb located outside their structure.

In all cases, the vehicle bomb wiped the facade off the building but left the vertical-strength members essentially unaffected.

(1) In 1989 Colombian terrorists detonated a vehicle bomb near the entrance to the DAS [National Security Department] headquarters in Bogota, which is housed in a building with which the LANS Editor is familiar. The vehicle was parked next to the curb, the curb separated from the building by a one-meter sidewalk and a short set of stairs for a total separation of two to three meters from curb to facade. Thus, this bomb was much closer to the building than was the Oklahoma bomb. The blast wiped the facade off the building, its vertical-support columns unaffected. Those who have access to *Revista DAS* [Informative Organ of DAS] will find a before-and-after photograph of the building on the cover of issue No.8, Dec 90. [DAS address: Carrera 28 No 17-50, Bogotá, D.E., - Colombia.]

(2) The recent bombing of the Saudi Arabian building housing US Air Force personnel is the second example. The wirephotos clearly show that the damage is the result of a vehicle bomb, the facade again wiped off the building, the vertical strength members essentially unaffected.

(3) AFP [*Agence France Presse*] carried a wirephoto on 31 July 1996 of the vehicle-bombed home of Peruvian Gen Manuel Varela Gamarra in Lima. There were apparently no reinforced-concrete vertical-strength members in this three-story home. Nevertheless, the facade-destroying effects of such a blast were evident in this brick structure.

These three examples suggest that the effects of a vehicle bomb will be, not to demolish the vertical-strength members in a structure such as the Murrah Bldg, but to wipe the facade off the building. The theory supports such a conclusion.

Theoretical Evidence

It is important to realize that an explosive charge, detonated at a distance from its target and, for all practical purposes, suspended above the ground, damages its target ONLY by means of the air pressure in the blast wave created by the detonation. Such a blast is immensely less effective than that of a contact explosive strapped on - or otherwise temporarily attached - or sunk into its target.

Brig. Gen. Benton K. Partin (USAF, Ret) is a lifelong demolitions expert; on 13 July 1995 he released a 23-page report entitled "Bomb Damage Analysis of Alfred P. Murrah Building, Oklahoma City, Oklahoma" which we synopsize.[2] He used the official estimate as to amount (4800 pounds) of explosive in the truck. From this he calculated that the resulting 4-1/2-foot-diameter explosive sphere would yield an over-pressure[3] of about one-half million pounds per square inch (psi) on explosion, this falling off to about 375 psi by the time the blast wave reached the first A-row column WHICH WAS COLLAPSED. [The A-row columns occupied the first row parallel to the building front, the B-row the second.] The yield strength of concrete is some 3,500 psi, so that the vehicle bomb would have had to deliver ten times as much pressure as it did in order to destroy A-3. Further, the nearest A-row column (A-4) WAS NOT COLLAPSED. One B-row column (B-3) was collapsed, and at its location the blast wave was down in strength to some 27 to 38 psi, the wave thus 100 times as weak as would have been required for column destruction. But how was this calculation carried out?

Gen Parton used a simple inverse-cube dependence of the over-pressure on separation from blast center.[4] This relation appears to have been generally supported by experimental testings of overpressure. A simple analysis may be introduced in favor of this relation. In the general case, an infinite series may be written for the overpressure as follows:

$$...+ ar^3 + br^2 + cr + d + e/r + f/r^2 + g/r^3 + ...$$

The letters, a,b,c,..., are constants, the variable being "r," the separation from blast center. Here r^3, for example, represents r-cubed, g/r^3 represents g divided by r-cubed, and so on. This series therefore includes all powers and all inverse powers of the separation from blast center, the constants accompanying each of the terms in the series to be adjusted through experiment so as to precisely portray the overpressure as a function of separation from blast center.

The first point to be made about this series is that the terms in the powers of r - r, r – r^2, etc. - can be eliminated with a simple physical argument. These terms in the series will induce an INCREASE in the overpressure with separation from blast center. The physics of the situation clearly demonstrates that such could only occur if there were additional energy sources - additional detonations - along the path from blast center. These powers of r may therefore be discarded. In the most general case, a constant term, d, appears in the series separating the powers of r from the inverse powers of r, that is, there would be no attenuation with distance. This may, from the boundary conditions of the problem, also be discarded, and only the inverse powers of r remain. Ignoring the inverse r and inverse r^2 terms, if the inverse r^3 term is kept, the higher inverse powers – r^4, etc. - become irrelevant at very short distances from blast center. Which leaves only the inverse r, r^2, and r^3 terms.

The constants e, f, and g might be adjustable so that columns A-3, A-5, A-7, and B-3 could be destroyed as actually occurred. This would be a meaningless exercise, however, since such an equation would be certain to destroy columns A-4 and A-6 - which were not destroyed - and probably others. There is no rational way to destroy the four columns, and only the four columns with this ANFO vehicle bomb although:

The ANFO vehicle bomb might have been utilized as the trigger in conjunction with, say, a pressure-sensitive detonator for contact explosives which were attached to the destroyed vertical support members. Which is not to say that the ANFO explosive did act as a trigger, but it is to say that in this way only could it have been primarily responsible for the damage done to the Murray Bldg.

Gen Partin's examination of photographs of the destroyed columns indicates that there were such contact charges used on these columns. Unfortunately, the surprising haste with which the building was demolished and removed rendered a thorough investigation of such allegations impossible. In keeping with the situation, considerable speculation has revolved around the reasons for the hurried building demolition after the bombing.

---

[1] LANS has received some such information from Latin America, but it has been too nebulous to deserve repetition.

[2] A LANS subscriber sent us the 20/3/96 issue of "Strategic Investment" [Baltimore, MD] wherein (p.3) it was reported that "A classified Pentagon study determines Oklahoma bombing was caused by...five separate bombs." If "bomb" is replaced by "explosive charge," this is what is being said here.

[3] The "over-pressure" is the pressure at a given space point in the blast wave which is "over" the practically negligible ambient air pressure.

[4] By "inverse cube" the following is meant: Take the separation from blast center as "r." For the overpressure at a distance "r," cube "r" and divide it into 1, take its inverse. Thus if the over-pressure is 500,000 at blast center, it is 500,000/(10)(10)(10)=500 at 10 units of length from blast center.

© Copyright 1996 by LANS

ALVIN V. NORBERG
Electrical Engineer

25748 Table Meadow Rd.
Auburn, CA 95602

November 1, 1999
TEL (530) 269-1573
FAX (530) 269-0341

Charles D. Key
The Oklahoma Bombing
Investigation Committee
P.O. Box 75697
Oklahoma City, OK 73147-0697

Subject: Bomb Damage Analysis of
Alfred P. Murrah Federal Building
Oklahoma City, Oklahoma

Dear Mr. Key,

On 1/30/97 I received a report based on data originating from the Department of the Air Force, Wright Laboratory (AFMC), Eglin Air Force Base, Florida. The report is based on information provided in a memo titled "Memorandum for Brigadier General Benton K. Partin, USAF (Ret.), 8908 Captains Row, Alexandria, VA 22308; From WL/MN, 101 West Eglin Blvd., Suite 101, Eglin AFB, IL 32542-6810. Subject: Requested Images of Blast Effects on Conventional Urban Structures. The report bears no wet signature or legible date. The report consists of: cover letter; two pages of photographs of an exemplar test structure; 18-page report; and 32 pages of "Blast Effect Testing - Pressure Mapping Project" data. You have requested my professional opinion which I offer as follows:

I have read and studied the above report and concur with the "conclusions" stated in the report, with no exceptions taken, that the damage to the Murrah Building on April 19, 1995 <u>cannot</u> be ascribed to a <u>single</u> truck bomb containing 4800 lbs of ANFO.

The damage pattern on the exemplar concrete, steel reenforced structure, identified as "ETS", with "before" and "after" photographs, and blast pressure attenuation data verifies that the severe structural damage to the Murrah Building was not caused by a truck bomb outside the building.

The damage pattern on the exemplar structure, as revealed by tests 1, 2, and 3, show that the collapse of the Murrah Federal Building was the result of "mechanically coupled devices" (bombs) placed locally within the structure adjacent to critical columns.

I have a copy of an analysis dated July 30, 1995 prepared by Benton K. Partin, Brigadier General, USAF (Ret.), complete with photograph evidence of the Murrah Building damage and calculated bomb pressure attenuation from the single truck bomb. The Partin analysis, with no exceptions taken, reveals that there were at least four (4) internal explosive devices placed strategically on certain columns that were triggered by "shock wave coupling" to the truck bomb.

The actual tests conducted by the U.S. Air Force, Wright Laboratory, on an exemplar structure with exemplar explosive devices prove conclusively that the Partin report of July 30, 1995 is correct.

Alvin V. Norberg, PE

Qualifications

Alvin V. Norberg holds a BS Degree from University of California, Berkeley, Dec. 1939, and is a currently licensed professional engineer in the State of California. He is the elecrical engineer of record of over 5000 building construction projects and has served as "expert witness" in 150 fire and accident investigations and testified in Superior Court on a number of cases. Mr. Norberg resides at 15748 Table Meadow Rd., Auburn, CA 95602.

UNIVERSITY OF OREGON

20 August 1997

Charles D. Key
State Representative of Oklahoma, Dist.90
Oklahoma City, Oklahoma

Dear Representative Key,

Just received your letter of August 14 which invited me to provide a letter summarizing my credentials, which I gather you feel might help your Oklahoma County Grand Jury procedure in some way. If that is the case, I am glad to help.

I was graduated from Carleton College, Minnesota in 1943 with a BA in Chemistry, then served in the U.S.Army Air Corps as a Communications Tech until 1946. I earned an MS in Physical Science at Stanford University in 1948, and eventually a Doctor of Aeronautical Engineering in 1982 from Nagoya University, Japan. Primarily I worked 30 years with NASA as a Research Scientist and Chief of the Physical Gasdynamics Branch at the Ames Research Laboratory, Moffett Field, California; 7 years as Head of Earth and Astro Sciences at the General Motors Defense Research Laboratories in Santa Barbara, California; and 7 years as President of JAI Associates Inc., Mt.View, California, a small independent company working on problems in gasdynamics for government and private concerns. In addition I was part time Prof. of Physics at San Jose State for 2 years and Prof. of Aeronautics and Astronautics at Stanford for 10 years; also full time one year Visiting Prof. of Mechanical Engineering at MIT and a year each as a Professor at the University of Nagoya, Japan, at the Indian Institute of Science, Bangalore, India, and at the Chung King National University, Tainan, Taiwan. Presently I am about to retire as Visiting Professor of Physics at the University of Oregon, a position I have held since 1989, while also working from my own company, Hansen Research Associates.

The main reason I have supported your Grand Jury inquiry into the Oklahoma City bombing is that I feel certain truth has been deliberately obscured in the first inquiry. Part of my specialty with NASA was on shock waves and detonation waves, and I know how quickly a blast wave attenuates as it travels through air. I am absolutely certain that the explosion in front of the building could not have sheared the columns of the building. Most likely a high explosive like RDX was placed on those columns, perhaps to detonate upon arrival of the blast wave. I do not know General Partin, but his written testimony demonstrates the accuracy of his knowledge in my opinion. I understand that seismograph records exist which confirm the occurrence of multiple explosions.

DEPARTMENT OF PHYSICS

College of Arts and Sciences · 1274 University of Oregon · Eugene OR 97403-1274 · (503) 346-4751 · Fax (503) 346-5861

*An equal opportunity, affirmative action institution committed to cultural diversity
and compliance with the Americans with Disabilities Act*

In addition, I am incensed that the building rubble was removed before all the evidence there could be assessed, a procedure which fairly shrieks out "cover up". My father was for a time an Asst.U.S.District Attorney in Minnesota, and I am indignant that any District Attorney would pervert the Grand Jury process and hide evidence, for whatever reason. I hope that all the perpetrators of the bombing can be brought to justice, but even more--for the sake of our Republic--I hope that all District Attorneys and the U.S. Dept. of Justice might get the message that they cannot get away with such flagrant perversion of justice as appears to have occurred. Therefore, I am enclosing an additional contribution to help your cause.

The above are, of course, my own opinions and do not necessarily reflect the position of the University of Oregon. However, I believe I have the privilege of offering testimony on technical matters as a Professor of Physics.

Sincerely,

C. Frederick Hansen
Visiting Professor of Physics
University of Oregon
541-342-6183

UNIVERSITY OF OREGON

13 February 1998

Charles D. Key
State Representative of Oklahoma, Dist.90
Oklahoma City, Oklahoma

Dear Representative Key,

I have carefully reviewed the following two reports which present technical information relating to assessment of damage to the Murrah Federal Building, Oklahoma City, Oklahoma, on 19 April 1995:

"Bomb Damage Analysis of the Alfred P. Murrah Federal Building, Oklahoma City, Oklahoma", Benton K. Partin, 30 July 1995.

"Memo for Brig.Gen. Benton K. Partin, USAF (ret), re: Blast Effects on Conventional Urban Structures", Dr.Robert Whalen, Eglin Air Force Base, Florida, April 1996.

Based on my knowledge regarding blast waves in air and a somewhat limited knowledge of detonation waves in chemically active solids, I judge both of the above reports to have been prepared by highly competent professionals and that the conclusions reached in them are valid. Before I provide a few additional comments of my own, I will briefly review my experience which pertains to the problem.

I was a research scientist with NACA and NASA from 1950 to 1961 and again from 1967 to 1982. I became Chief of the Fluid Mechanics Branch and later the Physical Gasdynamics Branch at the Ames Research Center of NASA. In that position I supervised the construction and operation of the most powerful research shock tube in the world known as the EAST (Electric Arc Driven Shock Tube) facility. This was used to duplicate conditions similar to gas produced in the stagnation region of space vehicles returning from lunar mission. In this work I attained some international recognition as an expert on exceedingly high temperature air, and a monograph which I prepared for NASA, "Molecular Physics of Equilibrium Gases" NASA SP-3096, 1976, was used at times as a text for graduate courses in astronautics at various universities including Stanford, MIT, and Nagoya University. In addition to studying properties of shock heated air, I was involved in research using explosives to accelerate models to velocities up to 30,000 ft/sec and beyond, in order to measure the aerodynamics and heating of very high speed vehicles in gaseous media. This gave me some understanding of detonation waves in solids and explosives.

DEPARTMENT OF PHYSICS

College of Arts and Sciences · 1274 University of Oregon · Eugene OR 97403-1274 · (503) 346-4751 · Fax (503) 346-5861

An equal opportunity, affirmative action institution committed to cultural diversity and compliance with the Americans with Disabilities Act

In addition to the above, I was Head of Earth and Astro Sciences at the General Motors Defense Research Laboratories in Santa Barbara, California, 1961-1976. I was part time Prof. of Physics at San Jose State, California 1959-1961 and part time Prof. of Aeronautics and Astronautics at Stanford 1972-1982. I was full time Prof. of Mechanical Engineering at MIT 1965-1966; Prof. of Aeronautics at Nagoya University, Japan 1982; Prof. of Chemistry at Indian Institute of Technology, New Delhi, India 1983; Prof. of Aeronautics at Indian Institute of Science, Bangalore, India 1983; and Prof. of Aeronautics at Cheng Kung University, Tainan, Taiwan 1984-1985--teaching graduate courses in high energy shock wave properties. From 1985-1989 I was President of JAI Associates, a private research company developing advanced computer codes for aerodynamics, and since 1990 I have been Prof. of Physics at the University of Oregon where I have continued research on very high temperature gases and published a number of papers on this subject.

Comments about the Benton and Whalen reports follow:

1. I agree with Gen. Parton that blast through air is a very inefficient coupling mechanism against structures. Only by containing or focusing the blast can extensive damage be inflicted on reinforced structures. Large panels, such as walls or ceilings or windows, that are not reinforced can be collapsed by relatively small pressure waves, the order of 10 psi. But T-bar reinforced concrete columns require blast pressures that exceed several thousands of psi.

2. Three dimensional blast pressures in air fall off rapidly. The exact fall off is complex for high energy shocks, depending on reactions such as dissociation and ionization of the air molecules, but a decrease in pressure as the inverse cube of distance from the blast source gives a reasonably good approximation; in fact the measured decrease is usually somewhat greater than this.

3. I do not have direct knowledge that the initial blast produced by ANFO explosion is about 500,000psi, but this seems reasonable since much faster burning TNT explosions produce initial pressures the order of 1,500,000 psi. I can say that unless the ANFO is very tightly packed it will not support detonation wave but will instead produce a lesser blast by very rapid burning similar to gunpowder. Also complete conversion of a sizable mass of explosive requires sophisticated ignition methods. My group was never able to get 100% energy conversion except from very small samples of explosive, which incidentally is the same problem that occurs with nuclear explosion. In the absence of a sophisticated ignition scheme, I would be surprised if 4800 lbs. of ANFO stored in separate barrels resulted in more than about 75% conversion efficiency.

4. One element that may have been overlooked is the pressure increase that occurs when a shock wave is reflected. In ideal air the reflected shock pressure approaches a limit of 8 times the incident pressure. At column B3 which was demolished, a 500,000 psi. initial pressure wave would have reduced to about 30 psi. 57 feet from the explosion (my calculation agrees with Partin's). and

if the reflected wave were 8 times greater, this would still be far short of the 3500 psi or more required to exceed the yield strength of the column. Moreover, at the 3rd floor where column B3 failed, the shock intensity would have been reduced by about the cosine of 23 degrees and an extra 5 feet of spherical attenuation. Everything considered, it is hard to avoid the conclusion that only an explosive detonated right at the column could have sheared it.

You have my permission to use my comments in whatever way is helpful to your investigation. On another matter, Ms. McCauley of your staff asked about an expert on Seismology who could provide reliable interpretation of the earth tremors recorded at the time of the blast. Prof. Gene Humphreys at the University of Oregon Geology Department suggested that you contact Dave Simpson or Greg Van der Vink at IRIS, which is a university consortium on seismology which considers interpretations of pressure waves and reflections in earth. Simpson can be contacted by e-mail (simpson@iris.edu). I hope this may help.

Sincerely,

C. Frederick Hansen
Prof. of Physics

cfh:mjm

Rodger A. Raubach Ph.D
P.O. Box 3042 , Casper , WY. 82602-3042
Phone: (307)-577-5775 ; FAX: (307)-237-2500

28 June 1995

The Honorable Charles Key
State Capitol , Oklahoma

Dear Rep. Key;

Thank you very much for your call this morning. I will attempt to answer the questions that you posed this morning in as simple terms as possible. As to my qualifications , I have a Ph.D. degree in physical chemistry granted in 1972 by the University of Wyoming. I have subsequently involved in either chemical/medical research or supervisory positions in industry since that time.

Physical chemistry is the sub discipline in the field of chemistry that deals with rates of chemical reaction and the heat-energy relations involved in reactions. Evaluation of explosives and their properties falls within the realm of the physical chemist.

You initially asked whether or not I supported BG Partin's position regarding the tragic bomb blast in Oklahoma City which involved much loss of life , and suffering by both the injured and surviving family members. I have no reservations in supporting Gen. Partin , since I would consider him to be an "Expert's Expert" in this field. Gen. Partin's position regarding the use of an ammonium nitrate fertilizer bomb mirrors my views exactly. The possibility of an ammonium nitrate fertilizer bomb , regardless of size , demolishing a reinforced concrete structure at a twenty or thirty foot standoff
not only strains the limits of credibility but exceeds it by a considerable margin. Ammonium nitrate is categorized as a low velocity explosive that finds it's use primarily in the mining industry. Explosives are very useful tools in industry and warfare. The selection of the proper tool for the job at hand is a job for the military ordnance specialist or the mining engineer , as the specific case may require. In the case of the destruction of the Murrah Building in OKC , the alleged "tool" in the guise of an ammonium nitrate bomb was wholly inadequate for the following reasons:

(1) Explosives, in general, possess two properties : power and brisance. Power may generally be regarded as the ability to move or displace matter , as in heaving dirt or rock in either mining , construction , or agriculture. Brisance , on the other hand , refers to the ability of an explosive to shatter , crack , or destroy structures. Brisance , in general , is directly related to the velocity of the shock wave generated by the detonation.
(2) Ammonium nitrate has a detonation velocity that varies with the admixture of diesel fuel , powdered aluminum , and other readily oxidizable chemical species , within the lower limit of

3000 meters / sec. to an upper limit of 4000 meters / sec. Not "fast" enough to shatter concrete and break steel reinforcing rods. An example of an explosive "fast" enough is T.N.T. with a detonation velocity of ca. 7000 meters /sec.
(3) Ammonium nitrate does not completely detonate unless very tightly packed against the target for the charge to affect. Had ammonium nitrate been detonated in plastic barrels , the entire area would have been covered with unexploded prill (the production form of ammonium nitrate).

All in all , the story widely disseminated in the press leaves many questions unanswered , and that since most of the evidence has subsequently destroyed with demolition of the structure , I have very serious misgivings about the "investigation" that is to take place by the federal government. Many of the inconsistencies in the official story point to the possibility of an "inside job" with the possible involvement of agents of the agencies "investigating" the explosion.
Since when can any agency or person investigate itself in a manner that is free of self-conflict? We do not need a whitewash job and coverup of the truth. The American People demand and **DESERVE** to know the truth.

If I can be of any further assistance , please contact me A.S.A.P.

Sincerely,

Rodger Raubach

Rodger A. Raubach Ph.D.

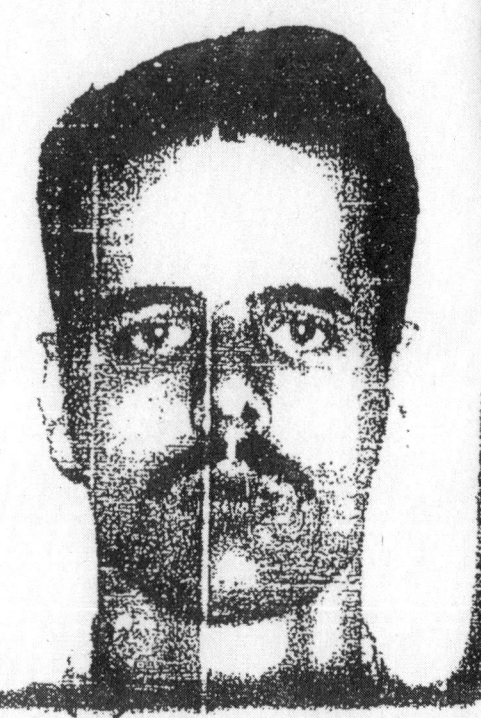

DRIVER LICENSE

CLASS ENDRSE. RESTRICTIONS
D*** **** ***********

LICENSE NO.   DATE OF BIRTH   AUDIT NO.
72631155   051759   225532269

SEX HGT. EYES ISSUED EXPIRES
M   601   GL   082892   05171996

21st BIRTHDAY

C-6275

ANDREAS CARL STRASSDMEIR
7613 THORNGROVE PIKE
KNOXVILLE TN 37914

SIGNATURE

- DO NOT MUTILATE FOLD OR ALTER
- YOU MUST SIGN CARD WITH YOUR USUAL SIGNATURE
- YOUR SIGNATURE ABOVE CERTIFIES THE FINANCIAL RESPONSIBILITY LAW AND VEHICLE FOR WHICH I AM NOT LICENSED

78631155000517

B-DL-1A

U.S. Department of Justice

Federal Bureau of Investigation

Post Office Box 54511
Oklahoma City, OK 73154

In Reply, Please Refer to
File No.

April 25, 1995

PRESS RELEASE

    Attached is an updated composite sketch of the unidentified individual known as "John Doe # 2" who is being sought in connection with the Oklahoma City bombing. The new sketch is based on additional information provided to investigators that indicates he may wear baseball style caps. "John Doe # 2" should be considered armed and dangerous. Anyone with information that may assist in the identification and location of "John Doe # 2" should contact the Oklahoma City bombing toll-free hot line at 1-800-905-1514 or the nearest FBI office.

JOHN DOE #2

My name is Joe Harp. I reside at ███████████████

On the morning of April 19, 1995, sometime after 9:00 a.m., I received a telephone call from the mother of a friend of mine, Mike, in Oklahoma City. She told me that Mike was in the Murrah Building, which had just been bombed, and asked me to go help find him. I left soon after that in a private plane with a friend of mine.

My friend and I arrived in Oklahoma City, rented a car at the airport, and were at the Alfred P. Murrah Building before 11:30. There was still a great deal of confusion in the area and we immediately joined in the search effort, looking specifically for Mike.

I knew right away that the explosive device that had caused the building damage was not an ANFO (ammonium nitrate fuel oil) bomb, for two reasons:

1) There was a strong sulfur smell in the air that was very reminiscent of the gas-enhanced "Daisy cutter" bombs I am familiar with from my tours of duty in Vietnam, as well as other military experience. It was not an ANFO smell.
2) I could see right away from the bomb signature -- the damage to the structure of the building -- that there must have been explosive charges inside the building. The truck bomb could not have done that damage from out on the street.

However, I was most interested at the time to find Mike, so went to work searching the building. While I was up in the building, the police and fire department started evacuating people from the area because of the discovery of additional explosive devices. Most of the rescuers at the ground level and the spectators evacuated the area, but many of us up inside the building did not leave. I observed members of the fire department EOD removing two devices and placing them in the bomb disposal unit. The devices were military olive drab in color, and the size of round five-gallon drums, with black lettering designating the contents as fulminated mercury, a high-grade explosive. I was also close enough to see what looked to me like mercury switches on the devices, which I presumed were for detonation purposes. I have had significant experience with these materials in the military and so readily recognized them.

My friend and I took residue samples from the bomb site and scrapings from another building across the street from the Murrah Building to a laboratory for chemical analysis. That analysis showed that there was fulminated mercury residue, along with other chemicals, in the sample.

I affirm that the above statements are true

Benton K. Partin
Brigadier General USAF (Ret)
8908 Captains Row
Alexandria, VA 22308
P/F 703-780-7652

August 18, 1997
Federal Express

The Honorable Patrick J. Morgan
First Assistant District Attorney
505 County Office Building
Oklahoma City, OK 73102

Dear Mr. Morgan:

Thank you for responding to my request to be subpoenaed to appear before the Oklahoma County Grand Jury to testify about my technical analysis and bomb damage assessment of the Murrah Building.

I am writing in response to your letter to me dated July 28, 1997 in which you requested additional information and to provide the following documents and information.

ATTACHMENT 1 is my Bomb Damage Analysis of Alfred P. Murrah Federal Building, dated July 30, 1995. Copies were provided previously to Mr. Macy and to Mr. Elliott. Copies of this report were individually addressed and hand delivered to all 535 Senators and Congressmen. Additionally, over 500 copies were distributed to major media outlets.

ATTACHMENT 2 is a copy of a letter I hand delivered to Senator Nichols' office before the Murrah Building remains were imploded. Information copies were sent to about 75 Senators and Congressmen. I had previously met with Senator Nichols' assistant, Mr. Lee Morris, to encourage him to arrange for the National Guard or an independent group to do an independent bomb damage assessment because the FBI was reporting information inconsistent with scientific fact. Mr. Morris' failure to take action because of "differences of opinion in Oklahoma" prompted me to prepare the Attachment 1 report.

ATTACHMENT 3 is the Oklahoma City Bombing: Improving Building Performance Through Multi-Hazard Mitigation report prepared jointly by the Federal Emergency Management Agency (FEMA) and the American Society of Civil Engineers (ASCE). Based on the size of the crater (28 ft across and 6.8 ft. deep) the report presumed a truck bomb with the blast equivalence of 4,000 pounds of TNT. Ammonium Nitrate and Fuel Oil (ANFO) was, according to the FBI, the type of explosive used in the truck bomb. ANFO has an equivalence of 0.27 pounds of TNT to 1.0 pound of ANFO (Ref: Explosives Counter-Measures Group - ECMG@crestviewfl.com). The 4,000 pounds of TNT would have an equivalence of 14,800 pounds of ANFO this would be a radically different truck bomb than what McVeigh was alleged to have used. The 4,000 pounds of ANFO alleged to be in McVeigh's truck bomb would have had the equivalence of only 1,080 pounds of TNT.

The FBI Inspector in charge of OK BOMB Task Force, Mr. Danny A. Defenbaugh, came to my home on June 17, 1997, to get answers to questions I may be asked if I were called as a witness. He put his finger on the crater photograph at Attachment 1, Tab 7 and asked "Suppose I told you that that was not the crater?"

There are other photographs that show a smaller crater. Moreover, the crater rim in Attachment 1, Tab 7, is not what one would expect. It appears to have been modified. In my experience gained in the research of runway cratering munitions and other photographs of near surface burst of large bombs over concrete, the soil under the crater rim is usually recessed. Because the FEMA/ASCE analysis totally depends on crater size assumptions, I would think the Grand Jury would want to know what Mr. Defenbaugh knows about the crater.

ATTACHMENT 4 is the Department of Justice, Office of the Inspector General's sworn interview of Agent Dave Williams about his report on the OK BOMB. The best that can be said is that there was no scientific determination of configuration, composition or weight of the explosive in the truck bomb.

ATTACHMENT 5 is Section G from the Department of Justice, Office of the Inspector General's Special Report: The FBI Laboratory: An Investigation into Laboratory Practices and Alleged Misconduct in Explosive-Related and Other Cases. On Page 1, the Inspector General's report concludes that, "Williams repeatedly reached conclusions that incriminated the defendants without a scientific basis and that were not explained in the body of the report." On page 7, the IG report states, "We conclude that Williams' weight estimate was flawed because it was more specific than warranted by the application of the forensic science and because it was based in part on collateral sources unrelated to laboratory or crime scene observations." Also, "Williams assumed that the main charge was ANFO." On page 8, the IG report states "that Williams' conclusions are overstated."

ATTACHMENT 6 is information on a controlled blast damage test against an integrally poured, reinforced concrete building structure at Eglin AFB, Florida. The building has many similarities to the Murrah Building. However, compared to the Murrah Building, it is a much more flimsy structure. The damage shown in Figure 2 was caused by blast from an explosive charge 25 feet away with the equivalence of 830 pounds of TNT. With the conversion factor 0.27, that would be equivalent to 3074 pounds of ANFO. That is 23 percent less than the FBI reported 4000 pounds of ANFO in OK BOMB.

The Attachment 6, Figure 2, bottom floor center saw maximum zero degree face-on pressure, but the upper floor saw moderate side-on pressure at a nominal 45 degrees. The 4000 pounds of ANFO would have produced the same damage at 27.4 feet, *i.e.*, 2.4 feet farther out than the test of 25 feet. However, the Murrah Building shows a more heavily reinforced concrete third floor stripped out 90 feet away with minimum side-on pressures at 90 degrees. From these facts, I conclude that the FBI hypothesized 4000 pound ANFO truck bomb could not in any way have caused all the damage to the Murrah Building.

ATTACHMENT 7 is a forensic exhibit I was asked to do on the bomb, or reported "propane tank", explosion at Waco. The hole at Exhibit A is typical of the kind of brisance damage one gets with height explosives in contact with a reinforced concrete panel. The concrete in the hole turned to dust and was blown away leaving the reinforcement rods relatively undamaged.

ATTACHMENT 8 contains two articles, one from the *New York Times*, dated October 28, 1993, and one from the *Wall Street Journal*, dated August 22, 1995. They both show that the Trade Center bombing in New York was a counter-terrorism sting "messed up." I would think the Grand Jury in Oklahoma County would want to examine all evidence that this could also have happened in Oklahoma City.

ATTACHMENT 9 is a more detailed resume than the one previously provided.

Relevant Facts Derived from the Attachments

1. The weight and composition of OK BOMB was never competently determined (Ref: Attachment 4)

2. The FEMA/ASCE report is about a different bomb than that imputed to those being prosecuted. (Ref: Attachment 3)

3. The reported 4000 pounds of ANFO in the OK BOMB had nowhere near the destructiveness of the 4000 pounds equivalent of TNT used in the FEMA/ASCE analysis. The 4000 pounds of TNT has the equivalence of 14,800 pounds of ANFO, and 4000 pounds of ANFO has the equivalence of only 1080 pounds of TNT. You cannot haul 14,800 pounds of ANFO in a 2 1/2 ton truck and 1080 pounds of TNT would not have done the damage according to the FEMA/ASCE report, Attachment 3, or my reports at Attachments 1 and 2.

4. Either there were supplemental explosive charges inside the Murrah Building or the Ryder truck contained an explosive charge radically different from the alleged 4000 pounds of ANFO. There is strong evidence that demolition charges were in the building irrespective of the size of the truck bomb.

5. Four thousand pounds of Ammonium Nitrate can be boosted to approximately 5000 pounds equivalent of TNT by adding 1 part by volume nitromthane to 3 parts ammonium nitrate. This could be done by grinding the ammonium nitrate to a very fine powder and immediately adding the nitromethane. This would require a far more sophisticated grinding and mixing facility than was ever identified in the Denver trial.

6. The Eglin AFB test results at Attachment 6 provides irrefutable evidence that 4000 pounds of ANFO could not have blown out floors at the 90 foot range as is evident in the Murrah Building.

The impossible single, pristine bullet theory, advanced by then Staff Attorney Arlen Specter (now U.S. Senator) on the Warren Commission, put blinders on the commission's investigations. This led to the specious "one man, one gun" conclusion. Similar blinders were placed on the Denver trial by the judge's exclusion of evidence beyond a "one man, one bomb" scenario. Alternative explanations of the data were labeled conspiracy theories and not allowed. It appears that Judge Burkett has put similar blinders on the Oklahoma County Grand Jury.

The August 1997 issue of *Media Bypass* Magazine states as follows: "Judge Barkett told grand jurors not to accept hearsay, 'only those witnesses who would present facts, which if true, would substantiate an indictable offense and not needlessly delay the courts in their other functions by listening to radical person or facts about which you could do nothing if they were true'." Grand juries are not bound by the same rules as petit juries.

To determine what really happened in Oklahoma City will be a most difficult task for any grand jury and their advisors. However, I would expect many of the witnesses the grand jury will need to subpoena will first have to be identified by hearsay evidence.

The prohibition blinders precluding Representative Charles Key from showing a TV tape containing real-time, on-the-scene witnesses tends to perpetuate the blinders imposed in Denver by Judge Matsch. I would hope that the District Attorney would challenge any judicial restriction that would keep the Grand Jury from identifying all evidence which could lead to indictable suspects. It is one thing to permit all witnesses to testify who want to testify but it is another matter to pursue all avenues necessary to identify and prosecute all of those culpably involved. That will include some who do not want to testify, and some who can only be identified by what may be considered hearsay evidence.

I do appreciate your efforts to explore the full range of relevant incriminating evidence and I do appreciate the magnitude of this effort on behalf of justice for all Americans. If I can provide any technical assistance, do not hesitate to call. If I am subpoenaed to testify before the Oklahoma County Grand Jury it will be my first priority. However, I do have contractual commitments between September 2nd and September 26th. Accordingly, it would be helpful if I were not called during that period.

Sincerely yours,

Benton K. Partin
B/G USAF (Ret)

Attachments:
1. Bomb Damage Analysis of Alfred P. Murrah Federal Building
2. Letter to Senator Nichols
3. FEMA/ASCE Report on <u>The Oklahoma City Bombing</u>

05 November 1999

The Oklahoma Bombing Investigation Committee
P.O. Box 75697
Oklahoma City, OK 73147-0697

Attn: Charles D. Key

Dear Mr. Key:

This letter is in response to your inquiry of 26 Oct 1999. My analysis is based on the pictures published in the news media and some technical reports sent to me by Mr. William Jasper of *The New American* magazine, so it is primarily a qualitative analysis. Part of my 40 or so years experience as an aerospace engineer in the field of structural mechanics and dynamics has been devoted to the topography of failed structural systems and structural components.

Structural elements present different fracture surface topographies depending on three main factors and several subfactors related thereto. The three main factors are (1) loading conditions, (2) type of material out of which structure was built, and (3) geometry of structural system or element. A complete list of the subfactors involved would exceed the scope of this letter, but I shall give a couple of examples to show what I mean.

For instance, a slowly applied load to failure of a structural element made out of a ductile metallic material will result in a different fracture surface pattern from that obtained when the same element is loaded cyclically (repeated load applications) to failure. If that same element is loaded to failure with a high rate loading such as impact, shock, or explosive force, the fracture surface geometry will again be different from the two situations just previously described.

In reference to the previous paragraph, I would suggest that photographs of the fracture surface of that part of the failed exterior columns (and one interior) column) still in the ground, after the rubble was removed, should be studied, if such photographs exist. Explosives generated shock waves in reinforced concrete beams or columns will pulverize the material in that area where the charge was placed in contact with that beam or column. A truck bomb can generate only air shock waves which propagate orders of magnitude more slowly than shock waves in solid materials. A case in point is the structural damage pattern due to the van bomb in the World Trade Center in New York City.

In summary, an engineer who knows the laws of physics and is experienced in fracture mechanics and dynamics of materials can look at a failed part and tell you what kind of loading conditions caused the failure. Given more time, he can probably quantify the loading conditions that would have caused failure (sometimes called forensic analysis).

A number of years ago I received training in the U.S. Army Engineers Corps at Ft. Leonard Wood, MO. Part of that training involved the use of explosives to destroy different types of structures. Based on that training alone, I would say that a 4800 lb ANFO truck bomb is an extremely inefficient way to bring down a reinforced concrete structure. It might blow a hole in the curtain wall closest to the truck, but it would hardly affect the massive supporting columns of the building (which themselves would probably have a cross-sectional area of 50 % reinforcing steel), because air is such a poor coupling media for explosive force. In fact, to be assured of destroying any structure, one would have to place a sufficient amount of explosive charge in <u>intimate contact</u> with the pertinent supporting members.

The damage pattern of any structure will indicate how the loading conditions which caused failure were applied. In the case of the OKC Murrah Building, the failure pattern demonstrated to me that individual charges were placed on each of the failed columns inside the building. I was favorably impressed when I read General Partin's careful analysis as reported in *The New American*, because his quantitative analysis confirmed my qualitative analysis. In addition, the report on the bomb destruction of the reinforced concrete structure at Eglin AFB, which I read in detail, gives further confirmation that additional charges had to be placed at the bases of the supporting columns of the OKC Murrah Building in order to cause the resultant pattern of destruction.

In closing, I would suggest that you contact a company who is in the business of bringing down buildings in populated areas. I saw a video presentation of buildings that were selectively destroyed in urban areas to make way for new structures. Since they have to calculate carefully the amount and placement of charges to destroy a structure without harming adjacent buildings, I would surmise that they would be able to tell you how the OKC Murrah building was brought down, and I conjecture that their conclusions would confirm General Partin's analysis.

Yours sincerely,

Ernest B. Paxson, PhD, PE

Affidavit of Virgil Steele Regarding The Bombing Of The Alfred P. Murrah Federal Building

State of Oklahoma)
) SS:
County of Grady)

I, affiant herein, being of legal age, and having been duly sworn, does hereby state as follows:

1) That my date of birth is January 11th, 1959.

2) That I am a resident of Grady County, State of Oklahoma.

3) That on April 19, 1995, I was employed by Mid-Western Elevator Company.

4) That I have been employed in the elevator trade for eight years.

5) That my duties with Mid-Western Elevator Company included servicing and inspecting elevators at The Federal Court complex, including the Alfred P. Murrah Federal Building.

6) That on the morning of the bombing I was inspecting an elevator at the 2000 Classen Center when the explosion occurred.

7) That after I heard the explosion I immediately went to the parking lot of the 2000 Classen Building to get into my vehicle and drive downtown.

8) That while in the parking lot of the 2000 Classen Building, I looked towards the downtown area and observed a projectile with a trail of smoke behind it streaking through the air in a southeasterly direction from the downtown area.

9) That I arrived at The Murrah Building at approximately 9:07am and entered the building from the south side.

10) That upon entering the building it was my job to access all of the elevators and determine whether or not there were any victims trapped in the elevators.

11) That the elevators in the building had been shut off electrically with no safeties set and no governors set and upon searching all of the elevators in the building, I found no victims trapped in the elevators and began searching through the rubble in an attempt to rescue victims.

12) That while attempting to rescue victims I observed agents from the ATF and the FBI stepping over and going around victims who were partially covered in rubble to pick up files and look at the files.

13) That approximately an hour and a half to two hours after I arrived on the scene, someone ordered everyone to evacuate the building because someone stated that they had found a bomb in the building.

14) That I did not evacuate the building and continued to look for victims in the day care center during the evacuation.

15) That there were law enforcement personnel from the ATF, A law enforcement Bomb Squad and officers from the Oklahoma City Police Department in the building during the evacuation.

16) That approximately twenty five minutes after the building was evacuated, someone announced that the building was clear and the rescue effort was continued.

17) That after the evacuation I observed personnel from a law enforcement bomb squad remove a silver canister from the building and place it in a bomb squad disposal box.

18) That approximately an hour after the first evacuation I was on the mezzanine level on the south side of the building when someone stated that another bomb had been found in the building and the building was evacuated again.

19) That after the second evacuation, and after I went back into the building, I observed a devise being removed from the building by a law enforcement bomb squad.

20) That I assisted in attempting to rescue victims until approximately 5:00pm that day.

21) That during the next two days, April 20th and April 21st., I assisted in getting the passenger and freight elevators in working order.

22) That from either the third or fourth day of the rescue attempt until the building was imploded I was an attendant in a freight elevator and worked 12 hour shifts and was responsible for operating the elevators and assisting in the cleanup process.

23) That while operating the elevator during the cleanup process I assisted agents from the ATF and other agencies in removing weapons from the building.

24) That I have worked in demolition for Thompkins Construction and Midwest Wrecking Company.

25) That I have attended various guns shows and consider myself to be knowledgeable in weapons.

26) That from my knowledge of weapons and explosives, I observed and assisted the ATF in removing AR 15 and M 16 assault rifles, several different varieties of hand guns, hand grenades, boxes that were marked "explosives", C4 plastic explosives and at least 3 anti-tank missles or shoulder/hip-type rocket launchers and thousands of rounds of ammunition.

27) That I observed ATF agents hand carry 3 anti-tank missles into the elevator and these missles were taken to the parking garage of the building.

28) That I observed large amounts of cash being removed from the building.

FURTHER, AFFIANT SAYETH NOT:

Virgil Steele

SUBSCRIBED TO AND SWORN BEFORE ME ON THE 22nd DAY OF June 1998

NOTARY PUBLIC

Jim Grace
Notary Public - Oklahoma
Cleveland County
My Commission Expires Mar 19, 2000

Arlene Blanchard's Press Release
Made Prior To Her Appearence Before The OK County Grand Jury
March 9, 1998
Reprinted with her permission by the Oklahoma Bombing Investigation Committee.

Good morning. My name is Arlene Blanchard. On April 19, 1995, I was a Personnel Sergeant in the OK City Army Recruiting Battalion Headquarters. My desk was on the north wall of the building. I am one of two female soldiers who survived.

I have been subpoenaed to testify before the OK County Grand Jury investigating the bombing. I am thankful to be here and happy to answer their questions and hope to tell them information that may be helpful to their investigation and widen their focus.

Although I have often wanted to go public about some of the things I hope to testify about today, I was prevented from doing so by the Army. Specifically, by my Battalion Commander, Lieutenant Colonel Regis Carr, and a public affairs Colonel from the 5th Army Recruiting Brigade. They gave me a direct order on Saturday, April, 22 1995, that of I talked to the press again without their written permission (which they weren't ever going to give!), that I would be subject to the Uniform Code of Military Justice and a possible Court Martial.

Fortunately, the U. S. Army cannot quash a subpoena by this Grand Jury.

When State Rep. Charles Key and the late Glenn Wilburn began to raising questions about the official government version of the bombing and asking for an independent investigation, my husband and I thought they were off their rockers.

My husband knew Charles Key, and confronted him. Asked to keep an open mind, coupled with what I and other Army Recruiters were telling him, my husband began to believe that Rep. Key was on to something.

With various statements made by the Federal prosecutors, when the victims families and survivors met prior to the Terry Nichols trial, we became even more certain that the information I have needed to be in the hands of the Grand Jury.

My husband arraigned a meeting between me and Rep. Key, along with the two independent investigators assisting their inquiry, a couple of months ago. They interviewed me and my husband for several hours. I assume Rep. Key made known to the Grand Jury my existence and information the last time he went before the Grand Jury for that purpose.

I am eternally grateful to Charles Key and the late Glenn Wilburn who took, and continue to take, unwarranted attacks and smears from both liberals and conservatives, politicians and various federal government agencies who have continually distorted what they are trying to do.

Incidentally, the still-living grandfather of the late Chase (3) and Colton (2) Smith (also the Wilburn's grandsons), Reverend Richard Coss, worked for my husband's father 25 years ago. He saved my husband who was then only an eighth grader from drowning at a job site. It's a small world!

I am also grateful that Robert Macy is our district attorney. Although I don't necessarily agree with his decision to retry McVeigh and Nichols, I am hopeful that his preparation for these trials, along with information gathered by this Grand Jury, will finally ferret out the remaining "unindicted co-conspirators."

Political memories are short, and most people probably don't remember that Bob Macy turned down a very lucrative offer (reportedly over $250,00 per year) to be a lobbyist or general manager for the National Rifle Association several years ago.

Like Mordecai, who in the Old Testament book, told Esther, "who knows but thou art come to the Kingdom for such a time as this..." I truly believe in my heart of hearts that Mr. Macy if, and when, confronted with solid evidence of others involved, or a cover-up of a bungled sting operation by the FBI and/or the ATF, will not knuckle under to their pressure and "will do the right thing."

Dumping the information that I have on the Grand Jury's lap will lift a burden from my shoulders that I have been carrying for the last two years.

Thank you and God bless you for braving this bitter cold day to take my statement.

— Arlene Blanchard, March 9, 1998

Editor's notes:
Arlene Blanchard, and other bombing survivors, are featured in the April 1998 issue of Glamour Magazine.

The following is the transcript of a telephone conversation between a local rescue worker and survivor of the bombing (female voice) and a not-identified man who, for the purpose of this transcript, will be identified as male voice. The actual tape recording will be given to Congressional investigators in the event they choose to investigate the Oklahoma City Bombing.

note: dashes (---) indicate missing or unintelligible words
        periods (...) indicate pauses in speech

<u>Male Voice</u>: ---which would allow McVeigh to get away, and then arrest him later on. I don't think they expected the truck to blow up--- I believed...and I've believed this for a long time...I believe that number two...John Doe #2...was a Federal agent working undercover. **And I believe that he helped McVeigh steal the goods and helped buy the equipment, and I believe that he helped McVeigh make the bomb,** and I believe that his whole task in this whole thing...his only real task was to render the device safe so that the federal agents could pretend to remove it and move in. ---(external noise)---right path. They did not want to move in until he was cleared of the scene so that they wouldn't tip their hands. See what I'm saying? And the odds are pretty good the whole reason behind that is because they were after someone bigger than McVeigh which means they probably think he was linked to somebody in the militia movement or something like that.

So I think what you're saying...you know I understand what you're saying...**but I don't think you see the big picture.** I don't think that, you know, I'd only divulge a look at the big picture if that's the actual scenario. If that's the actual scenario, which I believe it to be, I think there really is no claim that the agent, that was John Doe #2, did not render the bomb safe. Which he very well may have rendered the bomb safe, and then McVeigh may have put in a second fail-safe which he didn't know about. Which is probably what's happened.

Because if they knew the truck was loaded with bombs, and they'd go off, they would have evacuated the building. The only reason they wouldn't have, was if they had prior knowledge that the bombs were rendered safe. Which is probably the situation here.

<u>Female Voice</u>: Uh...Okay.

<u>M:</u> I would bet money on that's, in fact, the way this whole thing came down. Yes, they stood out in front of the building...yes, they followed him directly to the building. Yes, they watched him get out of the building...get out of the truck...Yes, they watched him drive off. That's not...that was their <u>plan.</u> I don't believe they ever planned to apprehend him anywhere near the building. I believe that John doe #2 was a Federal witness. His job was to render the device safe. Therefore, the only thing sitting out in front of that building was a bomb...a truck loaded with a bomb that would not go off. And I think that's the situation. **In fact I know it is.**

<u>F:</u> Okay...s...so why didn't they just come out and explain that to everybody?

<u>M:</u> —**public doesn't have to know that. When it comes to the national security and things like this, the public does not know...the public is not required to know.** First of all, by doing

that, they wouldn've, uh, put their witness, which is the Federal agent John Doe #2, they would have blown his cover, first of all. Which possibly he's involved in something right now that you have no idea about. You know, there very well may have been numerous plots involving numerous buildings. See what I'm saying? ---**you don't have the whole picture.** ---without full knowledge---**and what you do may cost them their lives.** You should be very aware---

F: Okay. Well, that's what I've been trying to be very careful of. I don't want to see anyone else get hurt. At the same time...

M: (interrupts) ---Well, if that guy's cover's been blown, he's dead already.

F: Do you think so?

M: Sure...I'm sure. Once you have gone up to this point, it has gotten out...which I'm sure it has, because there are moles everywhere...the chances are good that he's been terminated already and this whole thing has blown up in their face. I don't believe that, out of an act of negligence, these highly trained professionals would have allowed that man to leave that truck out in front of that building with its live bomb in it.

F: No, no, no. It stood out there for the whole time, from the time it pulled up until that went off.

M: That's what I'm saying. They would not have allowed it. The only reason they allowed that truck to sit there so long, is because in my opinion they were under the impression that that bomb was rendered safe. And I'd say that there was no rush...there was no reason...to evacuate the building. **There was no rush to make an arrest.** The truck was just going to sit out there until they went and towed it off. So I don't think they thought it was an emergency and I think either that John Doe #2 made a mistake in rendering the bomb safe, or McVeigh was smart enough to plant a second fail-safe. **Which most bomb makers do.**

F: Do you think that's why they didn't tell anybody?

M: No...

F: Well---

M: ---exactly...the bomb was safe as far as they knew.

F: Okay. Well, that explains why there was so many of them there so fast.

M: Exactly. They followed him to the building, their agent was in the truck with him when they followed him to the building, everything was under control, as far as they thought. As far as they thought, all they had was the man who built the bomb that was not going to go off, because their agent rendered it safe. And their whole thing was not a problem. Let him drive his truck right in front of his target---(baby crying)---allowed him to drive off.

Once he drives off, he renders the truck safe---(baby crying)---and then we can have the chauffeur arrested on the interstate for bogus charges. Which they did...and this was all planned out 100 percent. I...I...(baby crying) ---I don't believe they allowed that truck---

F: You don't think they intentionally let the bomb go off?

M: No, that's right. I'll never believe that...

F: Well, I mean, that's the only thing about this that I found so hard to believe.

M: They...they thought the bomb was safe. **They thought that their agent, who was in the truck and who helped prepare the bomb,** would set it so it would not go off. Now, whether McVeigh went back to the truck...where the agent did not know...and put a second fail-safe...or the agent made a mistake and did not actually render the bomb safe like he was supposed to...that's what's going on here.

F: Well, see, that's it then...I wanted someone that would be able to tell us for a fact if this was, like, deliberate or not. You know what I'm saying?

M: I'm not going to tell you that. Let me tell you something...I'm sure they had...everything was under surveillance there. So I'm sure they <u>do</u> have audio tapes of them saying, "Let 'em go, let 'em go... Wait...wait...wait...." There was no rush in their mind. In their mind, there was no rush to get that truck away from that building. Because that building...that bomb...was not supposed to go off.

Therefore, everything they did fits...if you think about it. They followed it, they allowed it to drive up there knowing that there was a bomb in the truck. Their idea was to let John Doe #2---(external noise) ---Federal agent and they would be able to use him in further investigations of these bombings...of these groups that are in militia groups. And this was a perfect entry in, because he could have went through there.

After McVeigh was arrested. John Doe #2 would have become a hero to the cause of the militias. And the militias would have taken him in and hid him, which would have made him part of the infrastructure of the militias. **Which is what their goal was for this whole thing...was to bust the militias.** If you take the big picture...and look at the <u>big picture</u>...**there were very few mistakes made on this sting operation. With the exception that John Doe #2, the Federal agent, did not render the bomb safe.** Just think of it this way, [Name deleted]...

F: (interrupts) I've always been a big fan of the United States and that, but then...I've always been...this was the one thing that bothered me.

M: They didn't let this building fall intentionally. Their opinion was that this bomb was rendered safe and this bomb would not go off. And their whole thing on this thing...if you think about it...it makes sense from a tactical standpoint. You would follow the truck to the building. You allow your lead suspect to get away clean. OK? Then, you set up a deal where you take the truck away from the building because it didn't blow up because it's not supposed to. You take John Doe #2...he gets away, which is your Federal agent. John Doe #1, McVeigh, is arrested on a bogus charge and then later proven that he's the one who planted the bomb that did not go off.

F: But you honestly don't think that they really intended...

M: Not at all. Not at all. They would not have. No.

F: Okay. Well, see, that was the only thing. Because, see, I'd heard from very beginning that they intended for the building to blow up.

M: **These are dedicated professionals.** I don't believe that.

F: Oh, well, see, all I've been wanting to hear is just someone to tell me that was an accident.

M: Basically, what happened is, this was a mistake. **Someone screwed up and the only one that screwed...The agents on the scene? They didn't' screw up...they did exactly what their orders were:** Wait...allow the suspect to leave the scene...Once the suspect has left the scene, then render the truck safe, which is already safe. All they have to do is get in give it a hot-wire, and drive it off to a safe location and then open up the back and disarm the bomb. Which was supposedly rendered safe to begin with. Okay?

F: Yeah, okay.

M: And then from there---(baby crying)---they charge in---See, the plan---they allow John Doe #2---This plan was put in motion before the bomb ever went off. Their intent was to allow McVeigh to be arrested later on...John Doe #2 to get away...and then---John Doe #2, the Federal government would have released a sketch or picture. And then, that man would have had to go underground and hide. Where would he hide? He would have hid with the militias. The militias would take him in as a hero. The militias would give him hero status in the militia movement, which would allow him to be privy to information that the government could use later on...

F: Yeah, and also it could keep other people from being blown up, too.

M: That's exactly correct.

F: That makes a lot more sense than anything I've ever heard.

M: I mean, if you think about it at all...and I know how these agents in these types of scenarios---

F: (interrupts) But I hope you understand why, you know, well because someone explained to me what had happened, you know, and I just couldn't help but feel like, you know, that...because I heard from these radical groups that they let the building blow up.

M: No. They did not want that building to blow up. ---I guarantee you this...their whole intent was that that bomb was rendered safe before it was ever parked in front of that---(baby crying)---first available emergency---otherwise, they would have quietly---

F: (interrupts) Got everybody out of the building?

M: Got everybody out of the building, before the bomb ever even pulled up I front of the building. There was no reason for them to do that, because according to their plan, the bomb was safe now. There was no reason to evacuate the building and the panic---because there was a truck loaded with a bomb that was not going to blow up.

F: Yeah, because it was just ammonium nitrate, right? And we have ammonium nitrate all over town.

M: Exactly. And their whole thing was **John Doe #2, who helped him to build this bomb was a Federal witness, a Federal agent. In his job, I'm sure he's a trained explosives expert.** His job was to render the device safe. But something happened and there was a mistake made. Either he did not...either he thought he had rendered it safe and he did not, or he rendered it safe and then later on after it was rendered safe, McVeigh went back to the truck and set a second time. Which is probably what's happened.

F: Okay...

M: See what I'm saying? And John Doe #2...

F: (interrupts) Why didn't you talk to me about this a long time ago?

M: **Well, I didn't know that you'd be able to get this far with it.** ---By going this far with it....Let me explain something to you...**Your actions have consequences.** There are a lot of witnesses, there are a lot of agents right now in the hills that are infiltrating these militia groups--- and...

F: Uh-huh. I will shut up...I will put a stop to it.

M: ---all these people will get killed. **Their blood will be on your hands.** I understand that you want---. If I really thought that the government allowed the building to blow up, I would be with you 100%. But I know---

F: (interrupts) Okay, I give you my word. I will drop it right now. If you believe that, Bob...Okay, if you believe it, then I'll drop it right now.

M: I'll just say that I appreciate your saying that---and I believe that's the truth. ---They were horrified when the bomb went off...really horrified.

F: Yeah, they all looked like they were in shock.

M: ---They figured, as soon as McVeigh got free, as soon as he got...drove off in his car...and I'll tell you another thing they did...---big deal? They did ---his car. You know what they did?

F: What?

M: They stole his license plate off that car. You know why?

F: Why?

M: So they'd have probable cause to stop him on the interstate.

F: Oh, okay.

M: They stole his plate. Why do you think the plate was never found? His plate was stolen from the vehicle and the Federal government stole the plate from the vehicle. So that he would be arrested, John Doe #2 would go free, they would put a sketch out that would make him like "America's Most Wanted." The only place that a man that would be wanted by the government can hide would be to be hid by the militia groups inside their infrastructure.

But once he infiltrates the infrastructure...and he's in...all of a sudden he's a hero. And right now, you know, these groups probably believe that they have John Doe #2 and that they're hiding him from the government and they're doing the patriotic thing---and they believe that the building should have blown up. So they're holding him. Now this man's privy to all kinds of information about future bombings, which we don't even know how many bombs they have stopped because of the agents---

F: Okay...

M: ---how many lives have been saved because that agent's now in the militia? **And, if this comes to light**---(baby crying)---operation---]

F: Okay...okay, let me...I'll tell you what. Let me, let me cancel the meeting for tomorrow, Okay? Let me do it right now, let me do it right now, okay, while I think of it.

M: Is it awkward?

F: No, no, no, no...listen, you're the only one that's sat down and talked to me that made any sense. 'Cause up until now, I...I...I---

M: Does it not make perfect sense?

F: Ye, it does...but let me stop it right now.

M: It makes perfect sense to me.

F: Okay, let me stop it right now.

M: If I was the one who made command decisions on it, that's exactly how I would have handled it.

F: Okay, well let me stop it right now...Okay, bye.
CONVERSATION ENDS

June 29, 1995

STATEMENT BY SAM COHEN

Due to circumstances beyond my control regarding the Uni-Bomber and the conditions at the Los Angeles airport, my flight to Oklahoma City could not be guaranteed. I regret that I will not be able to give this statement in person at the press conference in Oklahoma City Friday, June 30 at 11:00 a.m., instead, I am issuing this written statement:

"I believe that the demolition's charges in the building were placed inside at certain key concrete columns did the primary damage to the Murrah Federal Building. It would have been absolutely impossible and against the laws of nature for a truck full of fertilizer and fuel oil ... no matter how much was used ... to bring the building down. I concur with the opinion that an investigation by the Oklahoma State Legislature is absolutely necessary to get at the truth of what actually caused the tragedy in Oklahoma City."

If you should have further questions or wish to obtain more information from Mr. Cohen, you may do so by contacting him at his home:

Mr. Sam Cohen
13241 Riviera Ranch Road
Los Angles, CA 90049
(310) 454-1804

Biography of:
SAM COHEN

Mr. Cohen is retired after a 40 year career in the nuclear weapons issue. During W W II, he was assigned to the Manhattan Project at Los Almos, New Mexico. After the war, he joined the RAND Corporation as a nuclear weapons analyst. In the course of his work, he developed the technical slant military concept of the Neutron Bomb in 1958 and consulted with the Lose Almos and Livermore Nuclear Weapons Laboratory, U.S. Air Force and Office of the Secretary of Defense.

He has authored numerous articles and books over the years dealing with nuclear issues. Some of them are: "U.S. Strategic Nuclear Weapon Policy" Air University Review, January and February, 1975; "Whither the Neutron Bomb? A Moral Offense of Nuclear Radiation Weapons.", Parameters (U.S. Army), June, 1981; "A New Nuclear Strategy", New York Times Magazine, January 24, 1982 and "Arms Limits from Open Skies to Open Spies", Wall Street Journal, June 29, 1983.

Some of the books Mr. Cohen has authored are: "The Truth About The Neutron Bomb - Cohen, The Author Speaks Out" William Morrow and Company, New York, 1983; "We Can Prevent World War III" Jameson Books, Ottaway, Illinois, 1985; "Checkmate On War" Additions Copernic, Paris, 1980.

STATEMENT OF MELVIN DENNIS BEALL

RE: SUSPECT TIMOTHY McVEIGH AND OTHER UNKNOWN INDIVIDUALS

On Saturday, April 22, 1995, while watching TV reports re the bombing of the Alfred P. Murrah Federal Building in Oklahoma City, which reports were showing suspect Timothy McVeigh and the yellow Mercury auto driven by McVeigh, I realized that I had seen both the vehicle and McVeigh in Oklahoma City prior to the bombing. I immediately began to think back and attempt to establish the time and place where I had seen McVeigh and the yellow Mercury. To the very best of my memory on 4/6/95 at approximately 1:00 P.M., while I was on duty as a Security Guard for OG&E (which is my regular job) at their building located at 321 North Harvey, McVeigh, along with a Spanish appearing (not Indian or Mexican appearing - but Spanish or Latino) male and two white females came into the OG&E building. I was seated at my security desk located in the middle of the lobby of the building and facing towards the revolving doors and entrance to the building which is located on NE corner of said OG&E Building at Dean A. McGee and North Harvey. At approximately 1:00 P.M. I saw a Spanish appearing male (apprx. 25 - 32 years of age) coming through the revolving doors and into the lobby and he was smoking a cigarette. He was accompanied by two white females (18 - 25 yrs. of age) and a white male who I am convinced was Timothy McVeigh. They were all laughing and talking together and seemed perfectly at ease and relaxed.

Due to the fact that the OG&E Building is a "non-smoking" building, I got up from my desk, pointed to the Spanish appearing male and advised him he would have to take the cigarette out of the building. He immediately did so and came immediately back into the building. He and the two females approached me at my desk and he apologized for the cigarette. By this time McVeigh had moved to the east window of the building over by North Harvey, stood there for about 10 seconds, and then went to the north window where he remained until they left. The two females began talking to me and told me they were from Kansas. When I asked them where in Kansas, they told me the name of the town at which point I asked them where the town was located and they stated "south of Manhattan and Junction City, Kansas." I told them I had been to Manhattan to attend softball tournaments with my daughter, and that we had also been to tournaments in Topeka four or five years ago. In making general conversation with them, I also told them that while in the army I had been stationed at Ft. Riley in 1960. At this time the Spanish male stated he had been stationed at Ft. Riley at one time. He was familiar with how Ft. Riley is laid out, because when I mentioned that Ft. Riley is like four mini-posts consisting of Funkston (sp?), Forsythe (sp?) Custer Hill and the Main Post, he agreed. He also stated he was not a native Kansan, but that his home was in Kingman, Arizona. I told him I knew Kingman pretty good, as I had stayed at motels there during the late seventies or early eighties when bringing new Peterbilt trucks from the factory in Newark, California, to Oklahoma City, during the Oil Boom.

At this point in the conversation, one of the white females asked me where the Social Security Office was, and I told her "two blocks north on Harvey, turn east 1/2 block on 5th Street, and the entrance to the Federal Building was right there. The two females and the Spanish male headed toward the door, where they were joined by McVeigh, at which time a conversation took place between the individuals. I could not hear anything of the conversation except at the end one of the females said "it's up that way" and pointed her finger north toward Harvey. They then went out of the front doors and turned around the corner heading west in the 300 block of Dean A. McGee along the north side of the OG&E Building. I then went outside and looked down the street, where I noticed all four individuals get into a yellow Mercury Marquis exactly like the one I saw on TV. The vehicle was a 4-door vehicle. I went back inside to my desk and was looking directly to the north out of the windows when I noticed the yellow Mercury with the four individuals inside heading east on Dean A. McGee. They stopped at the light at Harvey and then turned North on Harvey. I just automatically looked at the tag on the vehicle (this is a sub-conscious habit with me as I was on Oklahoma City Police Force for 21 years). The tag appeared to be maroon in color, such as a Missouri or Arizona tag, but the tag was very dirty and I was unable to see any of the numbers.

I then went over to OG&E tellers Margaret Stotteman, Phone 341-3079, and Marie Dobrowski, Phone 632-3319 - Pager 647-0943, and asked them if they had noticed the guy with the "flat-top" haircut (which I believe to be McVeigh). They both said "yes" they had noticed this guy, along with the others. I made some joking conversation with them about the "flat-top" and that I had that type of haircut when I was in the service.

On 4/23/95 [Sunday] I went to the FBI office at 50 Penn Place at approximately 9 to 9:15 P.M. I went into the parking lot where I met a female FBI employee (name unknown). She advised me to call in with this information the next morning (4/24/95) [Monday]. On 4/24/95 between 8:00 & 9:00 A.M. I called the FBI Command Post at 235-1206; line was busy at all times - could never get through to FBI.

At approximately 10:00 A.M. 4/24/95 two OG&E employees met with me and advised that on 4/19/95 at approximately 11:00 to 11:30 A.M. they were working in the area of 8th & Hudson Street where they had found a small amount of metal and a key tumbler from an automobile lying in the street. They wanted me to go with them to turn this in to the authorities, thinking it might possibly be evidence. I took them to the Command Post Gate at 8th & Harvey and we turned the evidence in to FBI Agent McBride. At this time I advised Agent McBride that I had been trying to contact FBI and that I was down at 321 North Harvey. I informed McBride that I believed that McVeigh had been in our office sometime around the last week of March or 1st week of April, and that I needed to talk to FBI agent about this. Agent McBride stated he would come down to my work place when he got off duty. I informed him that I had talked to an Agent at 50th & Penn FBI office (842-7471) at which time that agent (name unknown) told me that someone would be contacting me. I then left and went back to my office at 321 North Harvey. At approximately 11:00 A.M. I noticed that Major Steve Upchurch (of OKC Police Dept.) was across the street from my office. I went over to where Major Upchurch was and where he had a mobile phone and asked him if he could call the FBI and have an agent come down to talk with me about what I knew about McVeigh and the others being in OKC. Major Upchurch then called and approximately one hour later FBI Agent Tommy Ross and another OSBI Agent (name unknown) came and interviewed me, at which time I informed him regarding the Spanish appearing male, 2 white females and McVeigh being in the OG&E building the last week of March or approximately 4/6/95. I related to him the fact that while these four individuals were in the OG&E Building, they had asked me where the Social Security Office was, and that they had left in a yellow Mercury Marquis. I also gave him information on how to contact the three female employees who were on duty in the same area where I was in the OG&E Building on the date the four individuals came into the building, giving him their names - Margaret Stotteman - Phone 341-3079; Marie Dobrowski - Phone 632-3319, Pager 647-0943, and Holly _____ - Phone 390-1555. He did contact all three of the OG&E female employees and they confirmed what I had related to the agents. MARGARET STOTTMAN

After I had conversed with Margaret Stotteman again about the incident when the individuals were in the lobby and what she remembered about the incident, while sitting at my desk on 4/25/95 *Tuesday* at approximate 1:00 P.M. I remembered again that the two white females had told me they were from Kansas. At approximately 1:40 P.M. I notice that FBI Agent Tommy Ross was walking North on Harvey. I went up to Agent Ross and told him about the girls telling me they were from Kansas, and also told him that the very best I could remember the date was that these indviduals were in the OG&E Building on 4/6/95 at approximately 2:00 P.M.. Later this same day *Tuesday* (4/25/95) while driving home from work, I was again concentrating and prodding my memory about the matter and trying to remember exactly what the two females had said, when I again recalled the entire conversation with the Spanish appearing male and the two females as I set out in the beginning of this report.

While at home later on in the evening of *Tuesday* 4/25/95 I received a call from FBI Agent Gerstein. At this time I learned he was the agent who was to have contacted me when I called at 8:00 A.M. 4/24/ 95. I told Agent Gerstein the whole story and informed him I had talked with Agent Tommy Ross. Agent Gerstein said since I had already talked with Agent Ross, he did not want to duplicate reports. I told him that I needed to talk with Agent Ross again to give him more details of my conversation with the Spanish male and the 2 females in reference to their statements as to where they were from i.e., Ft. Riley, Kingman, Arizona, etc.. He stated he would contact Agent Ross and have him get back in contact with me.

Page Four

On 4/26/94 at approximately 11:15 A.M. - not having been contacted by anyone from the FBI or Agent Ross - I called the U.S. Attorney's Office at 231-5281 and asked to speak to Ted Richardson, Deputy U.S. Attorney, whom I had known when he was with the Oklahoma County District Attorney's office and I was with the Oklahoma City Police Department. The person who answered the phone told me Mr. Richardson was not in. I was advised to call 879-3170 and talk to Hank Gibson who is supposed to be the agent in charge of taking main "tips". On calling 879-3170, I was advised by another agent (name unknown) that Gibson was not in. I then informed this agent of all the above details and he said he would contact FBI Agent Tommy Ross and tell him to contact me.

On 4/27/95 was met by FBI Agent Ron Ware, Special Agent out of St. Louis, Missouri, and another FBI Agent (name unknown) at OG&E 101 North Robinson; was interviewed and gave them the complete information as I have outlined in the above report, at which time they advised me they would report that information to Agent Tommy Ross.

AS OF 6/8/95 I HAVE NOT BEEN CONTACTED BY ANYONE ELSE FROM ANY AGENCY RE THIS MATTER.

SIGNED: *Melvin D. Beall*
Melvin D. Beall
OG&E SECURITY OFFICER
(Retired OKC Police Officer)
Phone: Office 553-3563
8499

Oklahoma Historical Society — Founded May 27, 1893

2100 NORTH LINCOLN BLVD. • OKLAHOMA CITY OK 73105-4997 • (405) 521-2491 • Fax (405) 521-2492

June 8, 2001

V.Z Lawton
814 N.W. 17th
Oklahoma City, OK 73106

Dear Mr. Lawton:

I enjoyed our recent conversation about the history of law enforcement.

For the past 25 years I have studied law enforcement in Oklahoma, the West, and the nation. My Ph.D. dissertation focused on law enforcement in Oklahoma from 1803 to 1976, with an emphasis on the changing nature of jurisdictions, threats to public safety, and the methods for keeping the peace.

One of the consistent themes that runs through all law enforcement agencies is the need for internal review and external oversight. In my opinion, lawmen are given such extraordinary powers that abuse of power is common regardless of the time or place. Throughout history it has been shown that the best law enforcement organizations have strong internal affairs departments to police their own members, and often there is a need for external review and vigilance to control abuse. Most lawmen are dedicated public servants, but there will always be a need for external review and restraint.

I hope these observations will help with your analysis of the Murrah bombing.

Sincerely,

Bob Blackburn

Bob L. Blackburn, Ph.D.

INDEX

Ace, 148,
Adomitis, Dan, 11, 227, 323,
Ahmad, Abraham Abdullah, 290,
Alainger, Lauren Merville, 22,
Albin, Max, 150,
Albrecht, Udo, 285,
All Points Bulletin (APB), 153,
Alley, Judge Wayne, 13, 266-267, 349,
Allison, James, 287,
Amish Inn, 80,
Ammonium Nitrate, 13, 66-74, 84, 134, 139-140, 171, 175,
Anderson, Karen, 86, 89, 92, 93, 94, 336,
ANFO, 7, 10, 42, 65, 96, 175, 183, 239, 247-248, 322, 348,
ANNM, 65, 175, 239, 241,
Arafat, Yassir,
Armstrong, Ken, 324,
Athenian Restaurant, 13, 25,
Austin, Mark E., 282,
Avey, Candy, 168,
Axle, 23-25, 84,
Bai, Yuhua, 106,
Ballew, Dane, 35,
Barrels, 15, 25, 76, 79, 81, 102-104, 138-139
Bates, Darvin, 335,
Beemer, Vicki, 45, 114, 119-121, 123, 160,
Behenna, Vicki, 14,
Bell Taxi, 113,
Bible, Tiffany, 175, 178, 270, 343, 353,
Black Forest, 273,
Blanchard, Arlene, 174, 350,
Blood, Ken, 316,
Blume, Tara, 171,
Bodziak, William, 81-84,
Bomb Squad, 11, 176, 177, 276-278 323,
Boots U-Store It, 87,
Bowers, Rodney, 93,
Boyd, Jim, 171,
Boyd, Shane, 110-111, 152, 155,
Boylan, Jeanne, 8, 156, 161, 309-310, 335,
Bradley, Daina, 167, 281,
Brassier, Tony, 271,
Breene, Robert G, Jr., 189,
Brescia, Michael, 286, 301-303, 337,
Bridges Calling Card, 15, 65, 75-77, 80, 85-87, 100-101, 113-114, 127, 301,
Brisance, 212-213,
Brokaw, Tom, 282,
Brooklyn Delicatessen, 95,
Brooks, Leroy, 166,
Brown pickup truck, 153, 156, 159, 289-291, 293-295,
Brown, John, 93,
Brown, Raymon L., 179-182, 221,
Broyles, Jeffrey H, 272,
Bunting, Todd, 121, 338,
Burdick, Debbie, 341,
Burkett, William R., 4, 6, 13-14, 316, 318, 325
Burmeister, Steven, 32-34, 38, 40-41, 52-53, 55, 57-66, 95, 97, 346, 349,
Burr, Richard, 14-15,
Bush, George W, 25,
Cadigan, James, 97, 99,
Cannistraro, Vince, 265, 333,
Cardie's Corner, 148,
Carille, James, 343,
Carr, Regis, 351,
Carter, Pat, 278,
Cash, J. D, 9, 57, 277, 305, 321, 329,
Cebu, Philippines, 77, 80, 283,
Chambers, Timothy, 79-80,
Chapman, Larry Clinton, 22,
Charles, Roger, 178, 268,
Chowdhury, Mesbah, 86, 90,
Clark, Kay Herrin, 169, 281,
Clear, Taylor Jesse, 290,
Clinton, William J, 25, 171,
Cohen, Sam, 10, 187,
Colbern, Stephen G, 295,
Coniglione, Tom, 178, 327,
Connelly, Sean, 14,
Convenant, Sword & Arm of the Lord (CSA), 8, 298-299, 320,,
Cooper, Renae, 11, 276, 323,
Cornett, Jack, 5, 7, 11,
Coyle, John, 4, 7,
Coyne, Randy, 14-15,

Criss, Claude, 11, 278, 323,
Cruz, Miguel, 149,
D'Albini, David, 113-114,
Daly, Patrick, 23,
Darlak, David, 74-76, 85,
Darlak, Patrick, 74,
DAS Building, 189,
Davidson, Joe Lee, 148, 309,
Davis, Jayna, 328, 355,
Davis, John Jeffrey, 8, 106-108, 110, 156, 342, 352, 354,
Decker, MI, 15-16, 87, 106, 304,
Defenbaugh, Danny, 232, 321,
Dellinger, Larry, 14, 318-319,
Dennis, Robert, 174,
Denny's Restaurant, 341,
Dies, Jan, 93-94,
Donahue Ranch, 73, 86, 96,
Donahue, Timothy, 73, 96, 138,
Dooley, Diane, 173,
Doyle, Stuart, 77,
Dreamland Motel, 6, 104, 106, 113-114, 124, 126, 136, 152, 156, 158, 335-336,
DRMO, 86, 127-131,
Ear Plugs, 55, 57,
Ebel, Daniel, 35,
Edmondson, Drew, 3, 6, 315-316, 318, 325,
Edt, Andy, 22,
Edwards, Charles, 43-46,
Edwards, Patty, 139,
Eglin AFB report, 186,
Elliott, Eldon, 5, 114, 117-121, 123, 137, 154, 159-160,
Elliott, James, 24-25,
Elliott's Body Shop, 5, 45, 82, 114, 121, 137, 154, 159-160 ,
Ellison, Jim, 39,
Elohim City, 8, 264, 286,298-300, 302, 304-305, 320, 337, 339-340,
Emerson, Steve, 290,
Ennis, TX, 14, 79-80, 239,
Eppright, William, III, 51-53,
Espe, Brian, 172,
Evans-Pritchard, Ambrose, 301,
Evidence Recovery Center, 25-26, 30, 51, 294,

Farley, Charles William, 134-135, 163, 352, ,
FEMA, 201, 226, 248, 274, 327, 353,
Ferris, David, 113,
Ferris, Don, 159,
Fingerprints, 20, 45, 57, 87, 105, 123, 163, 336,
Finley- Graham, Angela, 8, 264, 320-321, 340,
Firestone, 105,
Fort Riley, KS, 15, 18, 90, 107, 114, 121, 127, 129-130, 132, 134-137, 155, 163,
Fortier, Lori, 22, 77-78, 100,
Fortier, Michael, 77-78, 99-100, 286, 336,
Foust, Kevin L, 265,
Franey, Luke, 267, 349 ,
Freeh, Louis, 302, 345 ,
Frias, Robert, 187,
Fuel Oil, 65, 73-75, 171,
Furman, Sharri, 87,
Gagan, Cary, 264-265, 286- 288, 339-341,
Gaines, Charles, 267,
Garland, Merrick, 10-11,
Garrett, Toni, 177,
Garza, Mary, 130-131,
Geary Lake, 85, 104, 127, 132-135, 151, 157, 336, 352,
German- Bundesnachrichtendienst (BND), 265, 349 ,
Ghilarducci, Mark, 211,
Gibbons, Henry, 290,
Glessner, Rickey D, 133, 157,
Gobin, Jack, 172,
Goelman, Aitan, 15, 333,
Graham, Danny, 296 ,
Graham, Jane C, 3, 10, 151, 172, 315, 322, 350,
Grassley, Charles E, 344-345,
Gray, Joe, 170,
Great Western Motel, 124, 163, 167, 336, ,
Green, Eric, 147,
Green, Russel Stuart, 333, 275,
Grey, Wade, 77,
Grimsley, William R, 278,
Groves, Calena Flo, 268,
Gulker, Kelly, 134,

Gump, Suzanne, 4, 6, 12-13, 316, 318, 324-326,
Gun shows, 16, 22, 86, 88, 90, 92, 95, 100, 102,
Guthrie, Jim, 173,
Guthrie, Richard L. "Wild Bill," 306,
Hahn, Rick, 4,
Haines, Sean Michael, 297,
Hall, Elenora, 152, 155,
O' Halloran, Phil, 177,
Hamm Rock Quary, 96, 132,
Hammons, Don, 269-270,
Haney, Preston Scott, 296,
Hanger, Charles, 5-6, 47-51, 55, 102, 137,
Hansen, Fredrick C, 10, 188,
Harp, Joe, 178,
Harris, Dan, 136,
Hartzler, Joe, 14-15, 24, 97,
Havens, Joe, 131,
Havens, Mike, 67-70,
Havens, Terry, 130,
Hayes, Jeffrey C, 103,
Heady, Bob, 277, 328,
Heath, Paul, 150,
Heather, Randall, 177, 328,
Heildelberg, Hoppy, 338-339,
Herrington, KS, 14,
Hersley, Jon, 4-8, 14, 68, 337,
Hertig, Michael, 121,
Hester, Dawn, 43,
Hiley, Robin, 62-63,
Hinman & Hammond, 249, 327,
Hinton, Michael, 173,
Hodge, Dale Steven, 21-22,
Hofer, Helmut, 104,
Hoffman, David, 5-6, 121, 317-318, 331,
Holzer, Thomas L, 179-180,
Hood, Connie, 156, 160,
Hood, Donald, 160,
Horiuchi, Lon, 20,
Horton, Brad, 79,
Howe, Carol, 8, 121, 264, 286, 304-305, 321, 337, 339-340,
Howland, Ronald, 3-11,
Hunan Restaurant, 106-107,
Hunt, Kyle, 165,
Hupp, Louis, 57, 105, 336,
Hussian, Al Hussnai, 292,
Imperial Motel, 104,
Istook, Ernest, 269-270, 342,
J & K Bus Depot, 105,
Jacks, Robert, 148, 151, 308-310,
Jacobsen, John M, 5, 317,
Jacquez, Robert, 310,
James, Duane, 9, 321, 272,
James, Suzanne, 335,
Jarriel, Tom, 9, 321,
Jasnowski, Mary, 87, 103,
Jasper, William, 263,
Jaynes, Robert, 135, 155,
Jockney, Bill, 4,
John Doe #2, 7, 21-51, 78, 153-155, 161, 167, 281, 298, 303, 331, 335-336, 338-350,
Johnson, Lindy, 147, 154,
Johnson, Oscar, 9, 272, 320-321,
Johnson, Rodney, 167-168,
Johnson, Rose, 163,
Johnston, Germaine, 169,
Jones, Linda, 40-42, 61-62, 63, 65-66, 103, 213, 226,
Jones, Stephen, 14-15, 21, 284, 330, 336,
Joplin, Arlene, 4,
Joslin, Norma, 11, 277, 323,
Journal Record Building, 230, 281, 331,
Juhl, Linda, 76,
Junction City, KS, 5-6, 8, 10-11, 77, 91, 104-105, 110, 113, 127-130, 136-137,
Kane, John, 86,
Karchefski, Ronald, 89,
Keating, Frank, 171, 178, 325, 328,
Kehoe, Chevie, 296-298,
Kehoe, Cheyne, 296-298,
Kehoe, Kirby, 297,
kelly, Ronald, 26-31, 55,
Kennedy, Weldon, 309, 344, 346,
Kenney, Shawn, 306,
Kerr-Mc Gee Building, 169, 342,
Kessinger, Thomas, 5, 114, 119, 121, 159,
Key to Ryder Truck, 43-45,
Key Charles, 1, 5-6, 13, 43-47, 188, 268, 270,

273, 313, 316-319, 324-326, 355,
Khalil, Samir, 291,
Khobar Towers, 189,
Kindle, Nancy Jean, 157-158, 341,
King, David, 126,
King, Herta, 157,
Kingman, AZ, 16, 18-19, 22, 74-75, 77, 90, 100, 104-105, 138,
Kitchener, Gary, 352,
Kitchener, Kerry L, 132,
KKK, 264, 303, 307, 337,
Klaus, Kyle, 19,
Kling, Robert D., 5, 8, 106, 114-123, 126, 155, 159,
Koalska, Norma Chloe, 22,
Kochendorfer, David L, 269-270, 343, 352,
Kuhen, Michael, 285,
Kuper, Morris, 164,
Kyle, Joe, 18, 86-88, 90, 130,
Land, Gary Allen, 308-309, 151,
Langan, Peter " Commando Pedro," 306,
Las Vegas, NV, 78, 93, 127 138,,
Lauck, Gary, 304 ,
Lawrence, KS,
Lawson, Catina, 147, 168 301, 303, 337,
Lawton, V. Z, 3, 13, 174, 273, 315,
Lee, Daniel, 296,
Leonard, Judy, 163,
Leonard, Terry, 163 ,
Lewis, Gary, 7,
Lewis, Larry, 166,
Lewis, Steve, 305,
License Plate, 7,14, 25-26, 70, 88, 106,
Liedtke, J. Brent, 4,
Linehan, James, 165, 331, 342, ,
Livingstone, Neil, 282,
Lloyd, John, 40, 42, 57- 65,
Lockport, NY, 92,
Logan County Jail, 14,
Long, Leonard, 164,
Lonspaugh, Jerry, 328,
Looney, Paul, 4,
Lucas, Frank, 351 ,
Lyons, Kirk, 285,

Mackey, Larry, 14-15, 49, 84,,
Macy, Robert, 2, 6, 13, 314, 318, 324-325,
Magaw, John, 175, 266, 271,
Mahon, Dennis, 264, 286, 303-305, 336, 256,
Mallette, Katherine E, 271, 342,
Maloney, William, 148, 309,
Manhattan, KS, 76-77, 81, 87-88, 105, 124-126, 129-130, 132, 137,
Manning, Thomas, 105, 131,
Marin, Carolyn, 131 ,
Marshall, Thomas, 42-43,
Martin, Jeffrey, 336,
Martz, Lester, 9, 272, 321,
Matsch, Richard, 11, 13, 16, 267, 323, 346, 351, 355-356, 367 ,
Mauk, Jake, 335,
Mauro, Lou, 296,
McCaleb, Darrel, 131 ,
McCallum, Anthony, 23 ,
McCarthy, Kevin, 307,
McCarvel, Mike, 14, 181, 270, 326 ,
McCauley, Alex, 9, 271, 321 ,
McCraw, Daryl, 22,
McDonald, Peter, 85,
McDonald, William, 131,
McDonald's, 113-114, 121, 128-130, 137, 158-159, 331,
McDowell, Bob, 149,
McGown, Eric, 6, 106, 124-126,
McGown, Kathleen, 136,
McGown, Lea, 6, 106, 112, 126, 136, 152, 156, 162,
McNally, Kevin, 4,
McPherson, KS, 13, 105, 67, 69,
McVeigh, Jennifer, 50-52, 55 305, 336,
Mearns, Geoffrey, 14-15,
Mendeloff, Scott, 14-15, 68,103,
Mercury Marquis, 7-9, 11, 47-55, 106, 124, 136, 152, 165, 166, 169, 336, 342,
Merritt, Jerri, 14 ,
Mid-Kansas Co-Op., 66-73,
Mikita Drill, 97, 100,
Millar, Bruce, 303,
Millar, Joan, 302-303,
Millar, Robert, 8, 298, 300, 302, 304, 320,

Miller, Chuck, 291,
Miller, Dick, 177, 329,
Miller, James, 275, 333-334,
Mini Storage, 80-81, 100,
Mistry, Mr., 124, 160,
Mitchell, Helen, 80,
Mohave Inn, 100,
Moore, Roger, 14, 86-95, 301, 336,
Morgan, Pat, 6, 12, 14, 318, 324, 326,
Moroz, Mike, 165, 281,
Morris, Lee, 182,
Morton, Robert, 102,
Moushey, Bill, 358,
Muellar, William, 37,
Murphy, Mike, 351,
Musich, Stephen, 307,
Myers, Lawrence, 338,
Myllroce, Laurie, 290,
Nakanashi, Debbie, 161, 335,
National Alliance, 308,
Nattier, Louis, 66-67,
Neureiter, Reid, 15,
Nicholas, Jo Lynn, 88,
Nicholas, Kevin, 19, 88, 100, 140, 336,
Nichols, Don, 182,
Nichols, James, 100, 304, 336,
Nichols, Josh, 154, 332,
Nichols, Marife, 130, 283, 336,
Nichols, Nicole, 332,
Nichols, Richard, 23,
Niemczyis, Sylvia, 149,
Nigh, Rob, 15,
Nitromethane, 14, 65, 74-82, 86,
Noble, Terry, 39,
Norman, Jim, 4,
Northern Storage, 137,
Northrup, William, 265, 349,
O'Carroll, Richard, 320,
O'Connell, Robert, 8, 131,
Ogle, Kevin, 177,
OIG, 11, 65, 226, 234-235, 344-345,
Omniplex, 201, 221, 223,
Opperaun, David, 23,
Orenstein, Jamie, 15,
OSBI, 161,
Ostenoski, Barry Lawrence, 94,
Otto, Susan, 4, 11,
Owens, Daniel L, 2, 314,
Paddock, Edward, 23, 25, 43-44,
Padilla, Lana, 78, 86, 94, 127, 138, 332,
Palmer, Anthony, 22,
Parker, Ted, 87-88, 130,
Partin, Benton K, 10, 182-186, 188, 205, 216, 220, 253, 322,
Pauls Valley, OK, 80,
Paulsen, David, 50, 100-102,
Paulsen, Edward, 336,
Paulsen's Military Supply, 50,
Paxson, Ernest B, 189,
Pence, Kenny, 301,
Peterson, Clark, 174,
PETN, 58-63,
Petruskie, Vincent, 300,
Pfaff, Gregory, 95,
Philippines, 86-88, 94, 283,
Powell, Lance, 89,
Powell, Martin Walton "Walt", 88-89,
Powell, Verta "Pudge," 89, 92,
Priddy, Jan, 94,
Primadet, 97, 139-140, 348,
Prosch, Terry, 22,
Puett, Ann, 113,
Q507, 23, 26-42,
Radke, Allen "Bud," 96-97,
Ralko, George, 302,
Ramsey, Cheryl, 15,
Raulbach, Roger, 188,
Reed, J. D, 11, 174, 277, 323,
Regency Towers, 23-25, 165-166, 224, 331,
Reno, Janet, 325,
Reyna, Richard, 93,
Ricks, Bob, 267, 305,
Ridge, Ruby, 348,
Rivers, Joe, 130,
Rivers, Shawn, 80-81,
Roberts, David, 321, 305,
Roberts, Edwin L, 132, 133, 159,
Roberts, Mike, 15,
Rockwood, Anthony, 136-137,
Roe, Russel, 335,

Rosencrans, Jim, 310,
Ross, Ryan, 336,
Rowe, Tina, 288,
Royers, Joe & Mrs., 293,
Rucker, Georgia, 151,
Russel, David L, 338-339,
Ryan, Patrick, 15,
Sachtleben, Donald, 23,
Sargent, James, 132, 151,
Schickendanz, Dave, 9, 271, 321,
Schlender, Rick, 67, 69-73, 73,
Schwecke, Joe, 350,
Scott, Cullen, 97,
Sengel, Randal, 15,
Shapiro, Howard, 334, 345,
Sharp, J.D., 278,
Shaw, Bernard, 310,
Shaw, Bruce, 343,
Showalter, Gary, 67-68,
Siek, Kevin Ray, 133,
Siek, Raymond, 133,
Sinnett, Rick, 161-162,
Skrdla, Fredrick Wade, 163,
Smith, Connie, 148, 301, 337-338,
Smith, Stephen, 128,
Smurfit, 103,
Snell, Richard, 8, 299-300,
Snider, David, 126, 165,
Sostre, Hilda, 6, 158,
Southwestern Bell Telephone Building, 276, 328, 331,
Spivey, Richard, 93-94,
Sprague, Lowell, 23,
State Security Services, 22,
Stedeford, Scott, 307,
Steele, Virgil, 172,
Steinberger, Gary Wayne, 22,
Strassmeir, Andreas, 147-148, 264, 286, 300-303, 337, 356,
Sunset Motel, 86, 90-92,
Talley, Toria, 176,
Terry, Shelby, 90,
Thomas, Joanne, 73, 87,
Thomas, Mark, 307,
Thompson, Deborah, 57,

Thurschwell, Adam, 15,
Tigar, Jane, 15,
Tigar, Michael 14, 34, 330, 332,
Tikuisis, Tony, 139, 333,
Tipton, Glynn, 76-78,
Tire Tracks, 81,
Tire Treads, 81-84,
Tobin, William A, 99, 345,
Tolson, Kimberly, 275, 333-334,
Tongate, Larry, 15,
Torres, Herriam, 288,
Torres, Michele, 288,
Trigen Corporation, 279,
Tritico, Chris, 15,
Truong, Renda, 157,
Tru-Value Hardware, 86-87,
Turner Diaries, 17-21, 52-53, 74, 308,
Twilley, Sharon, 31-32,
Tyree, Lana, 269-270,
Udell, Theodore, 103,
Underhill, Troy, 339,
Vehicle identification number, 24,
Vernon, Robert D, 190,
Viefhaus, James Dodson Jr, 340,
VP Racing Fuels, 76-77, 79, 81, 241,
Waco, TX, 8, 16-19, 22-23, 54-55, 89, 93, 143, 309, 320, 348, 353,
Wallace, George, 4, 173, 316,
Walter Reed Hospital, 274,
Walter, James Lee, 336,
WAR, 264, 303-304, 337,
Ward, Peter, 298,
Ward, Tony, 298,
Watts, Charles, 173,
Weathers, Harvey, 267, 349,
Welch, Mandy, 15,
Wells, Arthur, 105,
Whatney, Chris, 337,
White, Lenard, 136, 157,
White, Sharen, 134,
Whitehurst, Dr. Fredrick, 31-32, 35-38, 42, 64-65, 235, 343-345,
Whitttenburg, Barbara, 154, 309-310,
Wilburn, Glenn, 2, 267, 313,
Wilburn, Kathy, 2, 336,

Wild, Larry, 149,
Wilkerson, Danny, 165-166,
Wilkinson, Beth, 15, 333, 356,
Williams, David, 10, 31, 65, 234-235, 346-348,
Wilson, Alton, 23, 29-31,
Winters, Jay, 297,
Wintory, Richard M, 315-316,
Witt, Gary, 80, 90-92,
Wolf, Frank, 182,
Woodcock, Sid, 233,
Woods, Ed, 47,
Woods, Ron, 15,
World Trade Center, 346,
Wyatt, Bob, 15,
Yount, Randall A, 276, 328-330, 342,
Yousef, Ramzi, 283, 355,